Texas Politics Today

2015–2016 Edition

William Earl Maxwell   San Antonio College

Ernest Crain   San Antonio College

Mark P. Jones   Rice University

Morhea Lynn Davis   El Paso Community College

Christopher Wleizen   The University of Texas at Austin

Elizabeth N. Flores   Del Mar College

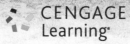

CENGAGE
Learning

Australia • Brazil • Mexico • Singapore • United Kingdom • United States

Lynn B. Mueller Photography/Moment/Getty Images

**Texas Politics Today,
2015–2016 Edition, 16th edition**
**William Earl Maxwell, Ernest Crain,
Mark P. Jones, Morhea Lynn Davis,
Christopher Wleizen, Elizabeth Flores**

Product Manager: Carolyn Merrill

Content Developer: Jennifer Jacobson

Managing Developer: Joanne Dauksewicz

Associate Content Developer: Jessica Wang

Media Developer: Laura Hildebrand

Marketing Manager: Valerie Hartman

Senior Content Project Manager:
    Cathie DiMassa

Art Director: Linda May

Manufacturing Planner: Fola Orekoya

IP Analyst: Alex Ricciardi

IP Project Manager: Sarah Shainwald

Production Service: Integra Software
    Services Pvt. Ltd

Compositor: Integra Software Services
    Pvt. Ltd

Text and Cover Designer: Chris Miller

Cover Image: John B. Mueller Photography/
    Moment/Getty Images

For product information and technology assistance,
contact us at **Cengage Learning
Customer & Sales Support, 1-800-354-9706**

For permission to use material from this text or product,
submit all requests online at **www.cengage.com/permissions**.
Further permissions questions can be emailed to
permissionrequest@cengage.com.

Library of Congress Control Number: 2014955954

Package:
ISBN-13: 978-1-285-85313-0

Text-only student edition:
ISBN-13: 978-1-285-86191-3

Loose-leaf edition:
ISBN-13: 978-1-305-63389-6

Cengage Learning
20 Channel Center Street
Boston, MA 02210
USA

Cengage Learning is a leading provider of customized learning solutions with office locations around the globe, including Singapore, the United Kingdom, Australia, Mexico, Brazil, and Japan. Locate your local office at **www.cengage.com/global**.

Cengage Learning products are represented in Canada by Nelson Education, Ltd.

To learn more about Cengage Learning Solutions, visit **www.cengage.com**.

Purchase any of our products at your local college store or at our preferred online store **www.cengagebrain.com**.

Printed in Canada
Print Number: 01   Print Year: 2014

Brief Contents

Prologue:	Texas's Political Roots	xxii
Chapter 1	Texas Culture and Diversity	1
Chapter 2	Texas in the Federal System	28
Chapter 3	The Texas Constitution in Perspective	55
Chapter 4	Voting and Elections	78
Chapter 5	Political Parties	113
Chapter 6	Interest Groups	138
Chapter 7	The Legislature	164
Chapter 8	The Texas Executive Branch	199
Chapter 9	The Judiciary	232
Chapter 10	Law and Due Process	257
Chapter 11	Local Government	286
Chapter 12	Public Policy in Texas	313

Contents

CHAPTER 1
Texas Culture and Diversity 1

Political Culture, Public Opinion, and Public Policy 2
Ideology 2
Partisanship 3
Public Opinion 3
Public Policy 5

Types of Political Cultures and Texas's Political Regions 5
State Political Cultures 7
  Moralistic Culture 7
  Individualistic Culture 7
  Traditionalistic Culture 7
Political Culture and Political Participation 7
Texas Cultural Regions 8
  East Texas 8
  The Gulf Coast 8
  A Boom Based in Houston 9
  South Texas 10
  Far West Texas 10
  The Texas Border 10
  Immigration and National Security 11
  German Hill Country 12
  West Texas 12
  The Panhandle 12
  North Texas 13
  Central Texas 13

Politics and Cultural Diversity 14
Texans Struggle for Equal Rights 14
  Female Texans 14
  African Texans 15
  Latino Texans 17
  Gay, Lesbian, and Transgendered Texans 19
Cultural Diversity Today 21

Applying What You Have Learned about Texas Political Culture 21
Politicians, Vigilantes, and the Quest for Civil Rights in Texas *by Denise McArthur* 22

CHAPTER 2
Texas in the Federal System 28

What Is Federalism? 29
Unitary Systems 29
Confederal Systems 29
Federal Systems 30

The U.S. Constitution and Federalism 30
Types of Powers in Our Federal System 31
Article I, Section 8 32
McCulloch v. *Maryland* and the Necessary and Proper Clause 32
The Early View: Dual Federalism and the Tenth Amendment 33
The Development of Cooperative Federalism 34
Civil Rights versus States' Rights 35

Texas and the Federal System 37
Coercive Federalism and Texas 38
Federal Grants-in-Aid in Texas 39
Unfunded Mandates 40
The Affordable Care Act: A Challenging Case in Federalism 41
Texas and the U.S. Abortion Debate: From *Roe* to Wendy Davis 45
States as Laboratories: Marijuana Legalization 46
Federalism and Casino Gambling 47

Applying What You Have Learned about Texas in the Federal System 48
The State of Federalism *by Neal Coates* 49

CHAPTER 3
The Texas Constitution in Perspective 55

Texas Constitutions in History 56
Early Texas Constitutions 56
  Republic of Texas Constitution 56
  Constitution of 1845 57
  Constitution of 1861 57

Reconstruction Constitutions and Their Aftermath 57

Constitution of 1866 57

Constitution of 1869 57

The Constitutional Convention of 1875 58

The Texas Constitution Today 60

Bill of Rights and Fundamental Liberty 60

Separation of Powers 62

Legislative Branch 63

Executive Branch 65

Judicial Branch 67

Suffrage 67

Direct Democracy 67

Public Education 69

Local Government 69

Amending and Revising the Texas Constitution 70

Amendment Procedures 70

Constitutional Amendments: 1995–2014 70

Criticisms of the Texas Constitution 71

Attempts to Revise the Texas Constitution 72

Applying What You Have Learned about the Texas Constitution 72

The Texas Constitution and Public School Funding
  by Timothy Hoye 73

CHAPTER 4
Voting and Elections 78

Political Participation 79

The Participation Paradox and Why People Vote 79

Who Votes? 80

The Practice of Voting 81

Voter Turnout in the United States and in Texas 82

Reasons for Low Voter Turnout in Texas 86

Legal Constraints 86

Demographic Factors 88

Political Structure 88

Party Competition 88

Political Culture 88

Types of Elections in Texas 90

Primary Elections 90

Who Must Hold a Primary? 90

Financing Primaries 91

Administering Primaries 91

The Majority Rule 92

Closed Primary 92

Crossover Voting 93

General Elections 93

Special Elections 94

The Conduct and Administration of Elections 94

County-Level Administration 95

Ballot Construction 95

The Politics of Ballot Construction 95

Getting on the Ballot 97

Write-In Candidates 97

The Secret Ballot and the Integrity of Elections 98

Multilingualism 98

Early Voting 100

Counting and Recounting Ballots 100

Electronic Voting 101

Election Campaigns in Texas: Strategies, Resources, and Results 101

The General Election Campaign 102

Mobilizing Groups 102

Choosing Issues 103

The Campaign Trail 103

Timing 103

Money in Election Campaigns 104

Where Does the Money Go? 104

Control over Money in Campaigns 105

Who Gets Elected 107

Applying What You Have Learned about Voting and Elections in Texas 108

Politicians Don't Represent Most Texans *by Ross Ramsey* 109

CHAPTER 5
Political Parties 113

Characteristics of American Political Parties 114

Two-Party System 114

Pragmatism 115

Growing Polarization? 116

Decentralization 116

The Development of the Texas Party System 117

The One-Party Tradition in Texas 117

Ideological Factions in America and Texas 118

Conservatives 118

Liberals 119

Conservatives and Liberals and Texas Democrats 119

The Rise of the Republican Party 120

The Republicans Become Competitive 121

The Era of Republican Dominance 122

Sources of Republican Strengths and Weaknesses 123

Conservatives and Moderates and Texas Republicans 125
Can the Democrats Still Compete? 126
The Organization of Texas Political Parties 126
Temporary-Party Organization 126
Precinct Convention 126
County and Senatorial District Conventions 128
State Conventions 128
Permanent-Party Organization 128
Precinct-Level Organization 129
County-Level Organization 129
State-Level Organization 130
The Functions of Political Parties 130
The Party in the Electorate 130
The Party as Organization 130
The Party in Government 131
Applying What You Have Learned about Texas Political Parties 132
Let's Party *by Malcolm L. Cross* 133

CHAPTER 6
Interest Groups 138

Types of Interest Groups 139
Economic Groups 139
Noneconomic Groups 139
Mixed Groups 140
Interest Groups' Targets and Tactics 140
Lobbying the Legislature 141
Preparing to Lobby 141
Socializing 142
Using Tools of Persuasion 142
Targeting Key Legislators 142
Influencing and the Executive Branch 144
Targeting the Rule-Making Process 144
Targeting the Appointment Process 144
Co-opting State Agencies 145
Targeting the Courts 145
Influencing the Judicial Selection Process 145
Filing Suit in Court 146
Shaping the Political Environment 146
Electioneering 146
Contributing to Campaigns 147
Educating the Public 147
Organizing Public Demonstrations 148

The Balance of Political Power in Texas 148
Texas's Most Powerful Interest Groups 148
Interest Group Alliances and the Dynamics of Power 150
Iron Triangles 150
Issue Networks 151
Political Movements 151
Sizing Up Interest Groups and Their Influence 151
The Positive Role of Interest Groups 152
Representation and Mobilization 152
The Benefits of Pluralism 152
Criticisms and Reforms 153
Elitism and the Culture of Nonparticipation 153
Exploitation of Weak State Institutions 153
The Revolving Door 154
Suspect Interest-Group Practices 155
The Regulation of Lobbying 157
Lobbyist Reports 157
Evaluating Reporting Requirements 157
Applying What You Have Learned about Interest Groups 158
The Tea Party: Civic Activism and Grassroots Change *by Blayne Primozich* 158

CHAPTER 7
The Legislature 164

The Limited Legislature 165
The Legislative Terms and Sessions 165
Legislative Salaries and Compensation 167
Legislative Staff 169
Electing Legislators 169
Party 169
Campaign Funding 170
Demographic Identity 172
Occupation 173
Education 173
Economic Status 173
Geographic Districting 173
Gerrymandering 178
Gerrymandering Techniques 178
Alternatives to Gerrymandering 179
Legislative Organization 180
Powers of the Presiding Officers 180
Lieutenant Governor 180
Speaker of the House 181

The Legislative Committees 182
    Standing Committees 182
    Subcommittees 183
    Joint Committees 183
    Ad-hoc and Select Committees 183
    Conference Committees 183
    Interim Committees 183

The Legislative Process 183
  The Standing Committees 184
    House Committee Membership 184
    Senate Committee Membership 184
  Scheduling 184
    House Calendars Committees 184
    Senate Calendar 185
    Two-Thirds Rule 185
    Senate Floor Action 186
    House Floor Action 186
  Conference Committees 187
  How a Bill Becomes a Law 187

Institutional Tools of Leadership 190
  The Legislative Budget Board 190
  The Legislative Council 190
  The Legislative Audit Committee 191
  The Sunset Advisory Commission 191

Applying What You Have Learned about the Texas Legislature 191
  A Tale of Two Speakers and the Purple Legislation
    of 2013 *by Mark P. Jones* 192

CHAPTER 8
The Texas Executive Branch 199

The Governor's Office: Qualifications, Tenure and Staff 200
  Qualifications and Elections 200
    Ethnicity 200
    Gender 200
    Middle-Aged Businessperson or Attorney 201
    Today a Republican 201
    The Nomination 201
    Well-Funded Campaigns 201
  Tenure, Removal, Succession, and Compensation 201
    Compensation 201
  Staff 202
    Evaluating Appointees 202
    Legislative Liaisons 202
    Budget Preparation 202
    Planning 202

The Governor's Powers of Persuasion 202
  The Governor as Chief Executive 203
    Appointive Powers 204
    Removal Powers 205
    Law Enforcement Powers 205
    Military Powers 205
    Clemency Powers 205
    Judicial Powers 206
  The Governor as Chief of State 206
    International Function 206
    Federal–State Relations 206
  Governor as Party Chief 206
    National Party Leader 207
    Positions on National Issues 207
  Legislative Tools of Persuasion 207
    Message Power 207
    Budget Powers 207
    The Veto 207
    No Pocket Veto 208
    The Item Veto 208
    The Threat of a Veto 208
    Special Sessions 209
    Fact-Finding Commissions 209

The Texas Administration 210
  Elected Executives and the Plural Executive System 210
    Lieutenant Governor 210
    Attorney General 211
    Comptroller of Public Accounts 212
    Commissioner of the General Land Office 212
    Commissioner of Agriculture 213
  Appointed Executives 213
    Secretary of State 213
    Adjutant General 213
    Health and Human Services Commissioner 213
    Insurance Commissioner 214
  Boards and Commissions 214
    Elective Boards 214
    Ex-Officio Boards 215
    Appointed Boards 215
    Advisory Boards 215
  Characteristics of Bureaucracy 216
    Size 216
    Neutrality 216

Privatization 217

Hierarchy 218

Expertise 218

Public Support 218

The Bureaucracy, Politics, and Public Policy 220

Clientele Groups 220

The Agency–Clientele Alliance 220

The Governor 221

Public Policy and the Iron Texas Star 222

How the Coalition Functions 223

The Legislature, the Lieutenant Governor, and the Speaker 223

The Control of Information 224

Administration of the Law 224

Bureaucratic Accountability 224

Accountability to the People 224

Accountability to the Legislature 225

Accountability to the Chief Executive 225

Bureaucratic Responsibility 226

Open Meetings and Open Records 227

Whistleblowers and Ombudspersons 227

Applying What You Have Learned about the Texas Executive Branch 227

Bureaucracy and the Welfare State in Texas *by Alexander Hogan* 228

CHAPTER 9
The Judiciary 232

Legal Cases and Jurisdiction 233

Civil and Criminal Cases 233

Original and Appellate Jurisdiction 234

Court Organization 235

Municipal Courts 235

Justices of the Peace 238

County Courts 238

District Courts 239

Courts of Appeals 240

Court of Criminal Appeals 240

Supreme Court 242

Juries 243

Grand Jury 243

Petit (Trial) Jury 244

Selection of Judges 245

The Politics of Judicial Selection in Texas 247

Voter Knowledge 247

Partisanship 247

Campaign Contributions 247

Ethnic/Racial and Gender Diversity 250

Applying What You Have Learned about Texas Courts 251

Judicial Impartiality and Independence in Texas: Democratic Ideals vs. Electoral Realities *by Sergio Saenz-Rivera* 251

CHAPTER 10
Law and Due Process 257

Civil Law 258

Types of Civil Law 258

Family Law 258

Real Estate Law 259

Probate Law 259

Business Regulations 259

Corporate Law 259

Labor Law 259

Torts 260

Issues in Civil Law 260

Tort Reform 260

Liability Insurance 261

Eminent Domain 262

The Elements of Crime 262

The Crime 262

Felonies 263

Misdemeanors 263

Victimless Crimes 264

The Criminal 264

Failing to Accept Social Values 264

Age 264

Gender 265

Ethnicity 265

Income and Education 265

Urban Life 265

Drug Addiction 266

White-Collar Crime 266

The Victim 266

The Due Process of Law 267

Searches 268

Probable Cause 268

The Exclusionary Rule 268

Arrests 268

Detention 269

  The Right to Remain Silent 269

Pretrial Court Activities 269

  The Charges 270

  The Right to an Attorney 270

  Setting Bail 270

  Examining Trials 271

  Formal Charges 271

  Pretrial Hearings 271

  Plea Bargaining 272

The Trial 272

  Trial by Jury 272

  The Adversary System 273

  The Jury Charge 273

  The Verdict 273

  The Sentence 273

Post-Trial Proceedings 274

  The Appeals Process 274

The Special Case of Juvenile Courts 275

Rehabilitation and Punishment 275

Felony Punishment 275

  Probation 275

  Prison 275

  Parole 276

Misdemeanor Punishment 276

Juvenile Rehabilitation 277

Clemency 277

Evaluating Punishment and Rehabilitation Policies 277

  Punishment and Isolation 277

  Deterrence 279

  Rehabilitation 279

Sizing Up the Death Penalty Debate 279

  The Case for the Death Penalty 279

  The Case against the Death Penalty 279

Applying What You Have Learned about the Due Process of Law 280

A Historic Murder Case: Obstruction of Texas Justice *by Brian Farmer* 280

CHAPTER 11
Local Government 286

Municipalities 287

General-Law and Home-Rule Cities 288

  Direct Democracy at the Municipal Level 288

  The Limits of Home Rule 289

Forms of Municipal Government 289

  Council-Manager System 289

  Mayor-Council System 290

  Commission System 291

Municipal Election Systems 291

  Nonpartisan Elections 291

  Election System Options 292

Revenue Sources and Limitations 293

  Sales Taxes 294

  Property Taxes 294

  Limits on Property Taxes 295

  Rollback Elections 295

  User Fees 296

  Public Debt 296

Municipalities: Issues, Trends, and Controversies 296

  Population Growth and Demographic Change 296

  Economic Development 296

  Government Mandates 296

  Annexation 297

  City Hall and Social Issues 298

Counties 299

Functions of Counties 299

  Structure and Organization of Counties 299

Counties: Issues, Trends, and Controversies 302

  Constitutional Rigidity 302

  Long Ballot 302

  Unit Road System 303

  Spoils System versus Merit System 303

  Consolidation 303

Special-District Governments 304

Reasons for Creating Special District Governments 305

Special Districts: Issues, Trends, and Controversies 306

  Multiplicity of Governments and Lack of Visibility 306

  Cost and Inefficiency 306

Councils of Governments 307

Councils of Governments (COGs) 307

Applying What You Have Learned about Local Government 307

Sales Tax Equitability *by Eric Miller* 308

CHAPTER 12
Public Policy in Texas 313

Revenues 315

Taxation 315

  National Taxes 315

State Taxes 315

Local Taxes 316

The Politics of Taxation 316

The Tax Base: Who Should Pay? 316

Tax Rates: Progressive or Regressive Taxes? 318

Other Revenues 322

Federal Grants-in-Aid 322

Borrowing and Other Revenues 322

State Spending 323

The Appropriations Process 324

The Politics of State Spending 324

Education 324

Elementary and Secondary Schools 325

History 325

Recent Trends 325

Public School Administration 326

The Politics of Public Education 327

Curriculum 327

The Curriculum and the Culture Wars 327

Textbooks 328

Faculties 329

Students 330

Public School Finance 330

School Privatization 332

Higher Education 333

Administration of Colleges and Universities 333

The Politics of Higher Education 334

Faculty Issues 335

Financial Issues 335

Student Accessibility 335

Student Diversity 336

Student Retention 337

Quality 337

Health and Human Services 338

Health Programs 338

Direct Health Services 340

State Health Insurance Programs 340

Private Health Insurance 341

The Uninsured 341

Health-Care Reform 341

Income Support Programs 343

Temporary Assistance to Needy Families 343

Unemployment Insurance 343

The Politics of Welfare and Income Redistribution 344

Defining Welfare 344

Welfare Myths 345

Welfare Realities 345

The Causes of Poverty 346

Transportation 346

Highway Programs 346

The Politics of Transportation 347

Highway Privatization 347

Mass Transit 348

Applying What You Have Learned about Public Policy Issues 348

Spending More to Improve Public Education? Texans Say Yes … and No *by James Henson* 349

Glossary 357

Index 367

 **MindTap™**

1. To get started, navigate to: www.cengagebrain.com **and select "Register a Product".**

A new screen will appear prompting you to add a Course Key. A Course Key is a code given to you by your instructor - this is the first of two codes you will need to access MindTap. Every student in your course section should have the same Course Key.

2. Enter the Course Key and click "Register".

If you are accessing MindTap through your school's Learning Management System such as BlackBoard or Desire2Learn, you may be redirected to use your Course Key/Access Code there. Follow the prompts you are given and feel free to contact support if you need assistance.

3. Confirm your course information above, and proceed to the log in portion below.

If you have a CengageBrain username and password, enter it under "Returning Students" and click "Login". If you are new to the site, register under "New Students" and click "Create a New Account".

4. Now that you are logged in, you can access the course for free by selecting "Start Free Trial" for 20 days, or enter in your Access Code.

Your Access Code is unique to you and acts as payment for MindTap. You may have received it with your book or purchased it separately in the bookstore or at CengageBrain.com. Enter it and click "Register".

NEED HELP?

For CengageBrain Support: Login to Support.Cengage.com. Call **866-994-2427** or access our **24/7 Student Chat!** Or access the **First Day of School PowerPoint Presentation** found at cengagebrain.com.

Letter to Instructor

Dear Texas Government Instructor:

You may be familiar with previous editions of *Texas Politics Today,* as it has served as the standard text for the introductory Texas government course for many years. However, we thoroughly revised this edition to tailor the precise content of the text to focus exclusively on **state learning outcomes** and core objectives. Each chapter learning objective is targeted to help students achieve one or more of these learning outcomes, and we have tightly organized each chapter to help students use higher order thinking to master these objectives. We link each major chapter heading to one of the chapter objectives and recap how the student should achieve those objectives in both the new chapter summaries and review questions.

We have put together a strategy for meeting **core objectives**—each photo, figure, boxed feature, essay, and project-centered Get Active feature prompts students to engage in critical thinking, develop communication skills, evaluate social responsibility, and reflect on their own sense of personal responsibility. Each of these exercises is designated by icons throughout the text:

 Critical Thinking Questions

 Communications Skills Questions

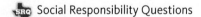 Social Responsibility Questions

 Personal Responsibility Questions

New to This Edition

- Streamlined chapters on the legislature and the executive branches to give the students greater focus.
- A completely reorganized interest groups chapter allows the students to evaluate their role in a democratic system.
- A revised political parties chapter to lead students to evaluate the role of political parties in Texas.
- Each chapter concludes with a specific and fully developed exercise to allow the student to apply the chapter's major theoretical themes to new material presented in an original essay commissioned for this edition. All essays are new, and many feature compelling visuals. Essays include "Politicians, Vigilantes and the Quest for Civil Rights in Texas" by Denese McArthur, Tarrant County Community College District (Chapter 1); "The Texas Constitution and Public School Funding" by Timothy Hoye, Texas Woman's University (Chapter 3); "The Tea Party: Civic Activism and Grassroots Change" by Blayne Primozich, El Paso Community College (Chapter 6); "A Historic Murder Case: Obstruction of Texas Justice" by Brian Farmer, Amarillo College (Chapter 10); and "Spending More to Improve Public Education? Texans Say Yes . . . and No" by James Henson of The University of Texas at Austin (Chapter 12).
- Updated and targeted **Texas Insiders** and **How Does Texas Compare** boxes are visually distinct and provide the reader with an uninterrupted flow through the text.
- Each chapter now ends with a **Get Active** feature that supports purpose-driven activities and introspection to close the gap between theory and practice in the state's political system.
- Pedagogy links to targeted objectives throughout the chapter and delivers students a cohesive learning experience.

MindTap

As an instructor, you will find that MindTap is here to simplify your workload, organize and immediately grade your students' assignments, and allow you to customize your course as you see fit. Through deep-seated integration with your Learning Management System, grades are easily exported and analytics are pulled with just the click of a button. MindTap provides you with a platform to easily add in current events videos and RSS feeds from national or local news sources. Looking to include more currency in the course? Add in our **KnowNow American Government Blog** link for weekly updated news coverage and pedagogy.

We hope these compelling new features will benefit your students as they experience Texas politics today. Please contact us personally to let us know how this text works for you.

Sincerely,

William E. Maxwell: willmaxwell@att.net
Ernest Crain: ernestcrain@hotmail.com
Mark P. Jones: mpjones@rice.edu
Morhea Lynn Davis: salas15@epcc.edu
Christopher Wleizen: wlezien@austin.utexas.edu
Elizabeth N. Flores: eflores@delmar.edu

Follow us on Twitter @TXPolToday

Letter to Our Students

Dear Student:

Americans in general, and perhaps Texans more than most, are apathetic and disillusioned about politics. Government seems so big, so remote, so baffling that many people have a sense of powerlessness. Now you have an opportunity to do something about this. *Texas Politics Today* explores Texas government, its background, the rules of the political game, and the political players who make the most important decisions in Texas. The text plainly explains public policy, why it is made, and who benefits from it. The book shows you how to think about yourself in the political universe, how to explore your own political values and ethics, and how to make a difference.

However, we know that you probably did not enroll in this course to achieve some kind of altruistic or idealistic goal, but to get credit for a course required for your degree plan. And we know that most of you are not political science majors. So we have written this book to be a reader-friendly guide to passing your tests and a hassle-free tool for learning about Texas government and politics.

Here are some tips on how you can exploit student-centered learning aids to help you make the grade:

- Target your focus on the **learning objectives** that open each chapter. Each chapter is organized around them, and your instructor will use them to track your progress in the course. Bulleted **chapter summaries** give you a recap of how the chapter handles these objectives, and **review questions** help you break the larger chapter objectives into manageable themes that you should understand as you prepare for exams.

- Zero in on the **key terms** defined in the margins and listed at the end of each chapter. These are the basic concepts that you need to use to understand Texas politics today.

- Go behind the scenes with the **Texas Insiders** features to see who influences policy making in Texas. These features put a face on the most powerful Texans and help you close the gap between theory and practice in Texas politics.

- Put Texas in perspective with the **How Does Texas Compare?** features. These features invite you to engage in critical thinking and to debate the pros and cons of the distinct political institutions and public policies in force in the fifty states.

- Link to the websites in the **Get Active** features to explore current issues, evaluate data, and draw your own conclusions about the Texas political scene.

- Take advantage of carefully written photo, figure, and table captions that point you to major takeaways from the visuals. These visuals provide you with critical analysis questions to help you get started thinking about Texas politics.

As a student, you will find the benefits of using MindTap with this book are endless. With automatically graded practice quizzes and activities, automatic detailed revision plans on your essay assignments offered through Write Experience, an easily navigated learning path, and an interactive eBook, you will be able to test yourself in and outside of the classroom with ease. The accessibility of current events coupled with interactive media makes the content fun and engaging. On your computer, phone, or tablet, MindTap is there when you need it, giving you easy access to flashcards, quizzes, readings, and assignments.

You are a political animal—human beings are political by their very nature. You and other intelligent, well-meaning Texans may strongly disagree about public policies, and *Texas Politics Today* is your invitation to join the dynamic conversation about politics in the Lone Star State. We hope that this book's fact-based discussion of recent high-profile, and often controversial, issues will engage your interest and that its explanation of the ongoing principles of Texas politics will help you understand the role you can play in the Texas political system.

Sincerely,

William E. Maxwell: willmaxwell@att.net
Ernest Crain: ernestcrain@hotmail.com
Mark P. Jones: mpjones@rice.edu
Morhea Lynn Davis: lsalas15@epcc.edu
Christopher Wleizen: wlezien@austin.utexas.edu
Elizabeth N. Flores: eflores@delmar.edu

Follow us on Twitter
@TXPolToday

Resources for Students and Instructors

Students

Access your Texas Politics Today resources by visiting
www.cengagebrain.com/shop/isbn/9781285853130

If you purchased MindTap or CourseReader access with your book, enter your access code and click "Register." You can also purchase the book's resources here separately through the "Study Tools" tab or access the free companion website through the "Free Materials" tab.

Instructors

Access your Texas Politics Today resources via
www.cengage.com/login

Log in using your Cengage Learning single sign-on user name and password, or create a new instructor account by clicking on "New Faculty User" and following the instructions.

Texas Politics Today—Text Only Edition

ISBN: 9781285861913
This copy of the book does not come bundled with MindTap.

MindTap for *Texas Politics Today*

ISBN for Instant Access Code: 9781305078697 | ISBN for Printed Access Code: 9781285861906
MindTap for Maxwell is a highly personalized, fully online learning experience built upon Cengage Learning content and correlating to a core set of learning outcomes. MindTap guides students through the course curriculum via an innovative Learning Path Navigator where they will complete reading assignments, challenge themselves with focus activities, and engage with interactive quizzes. Through a variety of gradable activities, MindTap provides students with opportunities to check themselves for where they need extra help, as well as allowing faculty to measure and assess student progress. Integration with programs like YouTube, Evernote, and Google Drive allows instructors to add and remove content of their choosing with ease, keeping their course current while tracking local and global events through RSS feeds. The product can be used fully online with its interactive eBook for *Texas Politics Today, 2015–2016 Edition,* or in conjunction with the printed text.

Instructor Companion Website for *Texas Politics Today*— For Instructors Only

ISBN: 9781305078871
This Instructor Companion Website is an all-in-one multimedia online resource for class preparation, presentation, and testing. Accessible through Cengage.com/login with your faculty account, you will find

available for download: book-specific Microsoft® PowerPoint® presentations; a Test Bank compatible with multiple learning management systems; an Instructor Manual; Microsoft® PowerPoint® Image Slides; and a JPEG Image Library.

The Test Bank, offered in Blackboard, Moodle, Desire2Learn, Canvas, and Angel formats, contains Learning Objective–specific multiple-choice and essay questions for each chapter. Import the Test Bank into your LMS to edit and manage questions, and to create tests.

The Instructor's Manual contains chapter-specific learning objectives, an outline, key terms with definitions, and a chapter summary. Additionally, the Instructor's Manual features a critical-thinking question, lecture launching suggestion, and an in-class activity for each learning objective.

The Microsoft® PowerPoint® presentations are ready-to-use, visual outlines of each chapter. These presentations are easily customized for your lectures and offered along with chapter-specific Microsoft® PowerPoint® Image Slides and JPEG Image Libraries. Access the Instructor Companion Website at www.cengage.com/login.

IAC Cognero for *Texas Politics Today*, 2015–2016 Edition— For Instructors Only

ISBN: 9781305081345

Cengage Learning Testing Powered by Cognero is a flexible, online system that allows you to author, edit, and manage test bank content from multiple Cengage Learning solutions, create multiple test versions in an instant, and deliver tests from your LMS, your classroom, or wherever you want. The test bank for *Texas Politics Today* contains Learning Objective–specific multiple-choice and essay questions for each chapter.

Student Companion Website

ISBN: 9781305078895

This free Student Companion Website for *Texas Politics Today*, 2015–2016 Edition, is accessible through cengagebrain.com and allows students access to chapter-specific interactive learning tools including flashcards, glossaries, and more.

CourseReader

CourseReader for *Texas Politics Today*

ISBN for CourseReader 0-30 Instant Access Code: 9781133350279
ISBN for CourseReader 0-30 Printed Access Code: 9781133350286
CourseReader: *Texas Politics Today* allows instructors to create their reader, their way, in just minutes. This affordable, fully customizable online reader provides access to thousands of permissions-cleared readings, articles, primary sources, and audio and video selections from the regularly updated Gale research

library database. This easy-to-use solution allows instructors to search for and select just the material they want for their courses. Each selection opens with a descriptive introduction to provide context and concludes with critical-thinking and multiple-choice questions to reinforce key points. CourseReader is loaded with convenient tools like highlighting, printing, note-taking, and downloadable PDFs and MP3 audio files for each reading. CourseReader is the perfect complement to any Political Science course. It can be bundled with your current textbook, sold alone, or integrated into your learning management system. CourseReader 0-30 allows access to up to 30 selections in the reader. Instructors should contact their Cengage sales representative for details. Students should check with their instructor to see if CourseReader 0-30 is required for their specific course.

Acknowledgments

We are grateful to our families for their patience and encouragement as we have developed the manuscript for this book, and we especially appreciate our students and colleagues who have given us helpful practical advice about how to make the book a more useful tool in teaching and learning Texas politics. We would like to give special thanks to Denese McArthur of Tarrant County Community College, who authored this edition's Instructor's Manual, and Alexander B. Hogan of Lone Star College–CyFair, who authored this edition's Test Bank.

In addition, we thank the essay contributors for this edition.

Chapter 1	**Politicians, Vigilantes and the Quest for Civil Rights in Texas** *by Denese McArthur* Tarrant County Community College District
Chapter 2	**The State of Federalism** *by Neal Coates* Abilene Christian University
Chapter 3	**The Texas Constitution and Public School Funding** *by Timothy Hoye* Texas Woman's University
Chapter 4	**Politicians Don't Represent Most Texans** *by Ross Ramsey* Executive Editor, Texas Tribune
Chapter 5	**LET'S PARTY** *by Malcolm L. Cross* Tarleton State University
Chapter 6	**The Tea Party: Civic Activism and Grassroots Change** *by Blayne Primozich* El Paso Community College
Chapter 7	**A Tale of Two Speakers and The Purple Legislation of 2013** *by Mark P. Jones* Rice University
Chapter 8	**Bureaucracy and the Welfare State in Texas** *by Alexander Hogan*
Chapter 9	**Judicial Impartiality and Independence in Texas: Democratic Ideals vs. Electoral Realities** *by Sergio Saenz-Rivera* El Paso Community College
Chapter 10	**A Historic Murder Case: Obstruction of Texas Justice** *by Brian Farmer* Amarillo College
Chapter 11	**Sales Tax Equitability** *by Eric Miller* Blinn College—Bryan Campus
Chapter 12	**Spending More to Improve Public Education? Texans say Yes . . . and No** *by James Henson* The University of Texas at Austin Co-director of the University of Texas/Texas Tribune Poll

Reviewers

We would also like to thank the instructors who have contributed their valuable feedback through reviews of this text:

Lisa Perez-Nichols, *Austin Community College*
Herman Prager, Ph.D., *Austin Community College*
John Rausch, *West Texas A&M University*
Floyd Holder, *Texas A&M University at Kingsville*
Denese McArthur, *Tarrant County College*
Diane Gibson, *Tarrant County College, Trinity River Campus*
David Smith, *Texas A&M University at Corpus Christie*
Alexander Hogan, *Lone Star College at CyFair*
Mary Barnes-Tilley, *Blinn College–Brenham*

Previous edition reviewers:
Jessika Stokley, *Austin Community College*
John David Rausch, Jr., *West Texas A&M University*
Eric Miller, *Blinn College–Bryan Campus*
Jack Goodyear, *Dallas Baptist University*
Woojin Kang, *Angelo State University*
David Smith, *University of Texas at Dallas*
Sarah Binion, *Austin Community College*
Larry E. Carter, *The University of Texas–Tyler*
Neil Coates, *Abilene Christian College*
Malcolm L. Cross, *Tarleton State University*
Laura De La Cruz, *El Paso Community College*
Kevin T. Davis, *North Central Texas College*
Brian R. Farmer, *Amarillo College*
Frank J. Garrahan, *Austin Community College*
Glen David Garrison, *Collin County Community College–Spring Creek*
Robert Paul Holder, *McLennan Community College*
Timothy Hoye, *Texas Woman's University*
Casey Hubble, *McLennan Community College*

About the Authors

William Earl Maxwell is a professor emeritus at San Antonio College, where he taught courses in United States and Texas Government. San Antonio College is a teaching institution, and Maxwell focused on innovative teaching techniques and improving the learning environment for students. As a part of that effort, Maxwell co-authored *Understanding Texas Politics* in 1975, his first text on Texas government. In the years that followed, he co-authored *Politics in Texas* (1975), *Texas Politics Today* (1978–2015), *The Challenge of Texas Politics: Text with Readings* (1980), and *American Government and Politics Today: Texas Edition* (2006–2012). Maxwell's home town is Lovelady in East Texas. He completed his undergraduate and graduate studies at Sam Houston State University, specializing in comparative government.

Ernest Crain did his graduate work at the University of Texas at Austin, spent 35 years teaching Texas government at San Antonio College, and now lives in Montgomery County, Texas. Crain has co-authored *Understanding Texas Politics, Politics in Texas: An Introduction to Texas Politics, The Challenge of Texas Politics: Text with Readings, American Government and Politics Today: Texas Edition,* and *Texas Politics Today*. His special areas of interest include party competition, comparative state politics, and Texas public policy.

Mark P. Jones is the James A. Baker III Institute for Public Policy's Fellow in Political Science, the Joseph D. Jamail Chair in Latin American Studies, and the Chair of the Department of Political Science at Rice University. His articles have appeared in publications such as the *American Journal of Political Science*, the *Journal of Politics, Legislative Studies Quarterly, Texas Monthly,* and the *Texas Tribune*. Jones is a frequent commentator on Texas politics in the state and national media, and his research on the Texas legislature is widely cited by media outlets and political campaigns. Jones received his B.A. from Tulane University and his Ph.D. from the University of Michigan.

M. Lynn Davis teaches government at El Paso Community College, where she has served as Blackboard Trainer and Mentor, Faculty Senator, and Government Discipline Coordinator. Her community involvement includes being past president of Planned Parenthood Center of El Paso, past board member for the Texas Association of Planned Parenthood Affiliates, and the PPCEP Board Liaison to the Ryan White Administrative Agency. She is a past board member of the Shakespeare on the Rocks Society and the El Paso Commission for Women. She has also participated in campaigns for various candidates. Ms. Davis has published articles on topics ranging from the current political environment to the viability of primaries and caucuses in today's election processes.

Christopher Wlezien is Hogg Professor of Government at the University of Texas at Austin. He previously taught at Oxford University, the University of Houston, and Temple University, after receiving his Ph.D. from the University of Iowa in 1989. Over the years, Wlezien has published widely on elections, public opinion, and public policy, and his books include *Degrees of Democracy, Who Gets Represented?* and *The Timeline of Presidential Elections*. He has founded a journal, served on numerous editorial boards, established different institutes, advised governments and other organizations, held visiting positions at many universities around the world, received various research grants, and won a number of awards for his research and teaching.

Elizabeth N. Flores is professor of political science at Del Mar College. She teaches courses on national government, Texas government and Mexican-American politics, and serves as program coordinator for the Mexican-American Studies Program. Flores earned a master of arts degree in political science at the University of Michigan and a bachelor of arts degree in political science (magna cum laude) at St. Mary's University. Her awards include the 2014 League of United Latin American Citizens (LULAC) Council Educator of the Year Award, the 2013 Del Mar College Dr. Aileen Creighton Award for Teaching Excellence, and a 1998 Excellence Award from the National Institute for Staff and Organizational Development (NISOD).

Prologue: Texas's Political Roots

The English–Scots–Irish culture, as it evolved in its migration through the southern United States, played an essential part in the Texas Revolution. Sam Houston, Davy Crockett, Jim Bowie, and others were of Scotch–Irish descent, and these immigrants from the Scots–English border, by way of Northern Ireland, led the Anglo-American movement west and had a major impact on the development of modern mid-American culture.

The successful end to the Texas Revolution in 1836 attracted more immigrants from the southern United States. Subsequently, the Anglo-Texan population grew dramatically and became the largest Texas ethnic group. As a result, Anglo Texans controlled the politics and economy and Protestantism became the dominant religion.

The Anglo concept of Manifest Destiny was not kind to Latino and Native Texans. Native Americans were killed or driven into the Indian Territory, and many Latino families were forced from their property. Even Latino heroes of the Texas Revolution with names like Navarro, Seguin, de Zavala, and de Leon were not spared in the onslaught.[1]

Politics and Government: The Early Years

The Republic of Texas had no political parties. Political conflict revolved around pro-Houston and anti-Houston policies. Sam Houston, the hero of the battle of San Jacinto, advocated peaceful relations with the eastern Native Americans and U.S. statehood for Texas. The anti-Houston forces, led by Mirabeau B. Lamar, believed that Native-American and Anglo-American cultures could not coexist. Lamar envisioned Texas as a nation extending from the Sabine River to the Pacific.[2]

JOINING THE UNION

Texas voters approved annexation to the United States in 1836, almost immediately after Texas achieved independence from Mexico. However, because owning human property was legal in the republic and would continue to be legal once it became a state, the annexation of Texas would upset the tenuous balance in the U.S. Senate between proslavery and abolitionist senators. This and other political issues, primarily relating to slavery, postponed Texas's annexation until December 29, 1845, when it officially became the 28th state.

Several Texas articles of annexation were unique. Texas retained ownership of its public lands because the U.S. Congress refused to accept their conveyance in exchange for payment of the republic's $10 million debt. Although millions of acres were ultimately given away or sold, those remaining continue to produce hundreds of millions of dollars in state revenue, largely in royalties from the production of oil and natural gas. These royalties and other public land revenue primarily benefit the Permanent University Fund and the Permanent School Fund. The annexation articles also granted Texas the privilege of "creating…new states, of convenient size, not exceeding four in number, in addition to said State of Texas."[3]

---

[1] See David Montejano, *Anglos and Mexicans in the Making of Texas, 1836–1986* (Austin: University of Texas).

[2] The information in this and subsequent sections depends heavily on Seymour V. Connor, *Texas: A History* (New York: Thomas Y. Crowell, 1971); Rupert N. Richardson, *Texas: The Lone Star State*, 3rd ed. (Englewood Cliffs, NJ: Prentice Hall, 1970); T. R. Fehrenbach, *Lone Star: A History of Texas and the Texans* (New York: Collier Books, 1980).

[3] The Annexation of Texas, Joint Resolution of Congress, March 1, 1845, *U.S. Statutes at Large, Vol. 5.*

EARLY STATEHOOD AND SECESSION: 1846–1864

The politics of early statehood soon replicated the conflict over slavery that dominated politics in the United States. Senator Sam Houston, a strong Unionist alarmed by the support for secession in Texas, resigned his seat in the U.S. Senate in 1857 to run for governor. He was defeated because secessionist forces controlled the dominant Democratic Party. He was, however, elected governor two years later.

The election of Abraham Lincoln as president of the United States in 1860 triggered a Texas backlash. A secessionist convention was called and it voted to secede from the Union. Governor Houston used his considerable political skills in a vain attempt to keep Texas in the Union. At first, Houston declared the convention illegal, but the Texas legislature later upheld it as legitimate. Although only about 5 percent of white Texans owned slaves, the electorate ratified the actions of the convention by an overwhelming 76 percent.[4]

Houston continued to fight what he considered Texans' determination to self-destruct. Although he reluctantly accepted the vote to secede, Houston tried to convince secessionist leaders to return to republic status rather than join the newly formed Confederate States of America—a plan that might have spared Texans the tragedy of the Civil War. Texas's secession convention rejected this political maneuver and petitioned for membership in the new Confederacy. Houston refused to accept the actions of the convention, which summarily declared the office of governor vacant and ordered the lieutenant governor to assume the position. Texas was then admitted to the Confederacy.

POST–CIVIL WAR TEXAS: 1865–1885

The defeat of the Confederacy resulted in relative anarchy in Texas until it was occupied by federal troops beginning on June 19, 1865, a date celebrated by African Texans as freedom day.

Texas and other southern states resisted civil rights and equality for freed slaves, resulting in radical Republicans gaining control of the U.S. Congress. Congress enacted punitive legislation prohibiting former Confederate soldiers and officials from voting and holding public office.

Texas government was controlled by the U.S. Army from 1865 through 1869, but the army's rule ended after the new state constitution was adopted in 1869. African-Texan men were granted the right to vote, but it was denied to former Confederate officials and military. In the election to reestablish civilian government, Republican E. J. Davis was elected governor and Republicans dominated the new legislature. Texas was then readmitted to the United States, military occupation ended, and civilian authority assumed control of the state. Unlike either previous or subsequent constitutions, the 1869 Constitution centralized political power in the office of the governor. During the Davis administration, Texas began a statewide public school system and created a state police force.

Republican domination of Texas politics was a new and unwelcome world for most white Texans, and trouble intensified when the legislature increased taxes to pay for Governor Davis's reforms. Because Texas's tax base was dependent on property taxes, eliminating human property from the tax rolls and the decline in value of real property placed severe stress on the public coffers. Consequently, state debt increased dramatically. Former Confederates were enfranchised in 1873, precipitating a strong anti-Republican reaction from the electorate, and Democrat Richard Coke was elected governor in 1875.

Texas officials immediately began to remove the vestiges of radical Republicanism. The legislature authorized a convention to write a new constitution. The convention delegates were mostly Democrats, Anglo Texans, and representatives of agrarian interests. The new constitution decentralized the state government, limited the flexibility of elected officials, and placed public education under local control. It was ratified by the voters in 1876 and an often-amended version is still in use.

Politics and Government: 1886–1945

Many reform measures were enacted and enforced in Texas in the 1880s, especially laws limiting corporate power. Attorney General James S. Hogg vigorously enforced new laws curtailing abuses by insurance companies, railroads, and other corporate interests.

---

[4]See *A Declaration of the Causes Which Impel the State of Texas to Secede from the Federal Union*, http://avalon.law.yale.edu/19th_century/csa_texsec.asp.

GOVERNOR HOGG: 1891–1895

Attorney General James Hogg was an important reformer in Texas politics and developed a reputation as the champion of common people. Railroad interests dominated most western states' governments, prompting Hogg to run for governor with the objective of regulating railroads. Although he faced strong opposition from powerful corporate interests that viewed him as a threat, Hogg won the nomination in the 1890 Democratic State Convention.

A commission to regulate railroads was authorized in the subsequent election. The Railroad Commission was eventually given the power to regulate rubber-tired vehicles used in Texas commerce and the production and transportation of oil and natural gas.

Politics in the early 1900s distinguished Texas as one of the most progressive states in the nation. Texas pioneered the regulation of monopolies, railroads, insurance companies, and child labor. It reformed its prisons and taxes, and in 1905, replaced nominating conventions with direct primaries.

FARMER JIM: 1914–1918

James E. Ferguson entered the Texas political scene in 1914 and was a controversial and powerful force in Texas politics for the next 20 years. Ferguson owned varied business interests and was the president of the Temple State Bank. Although sensitive to the interests of the business community, Ferguson called himself "Farmer Jim" to emphasize his rural background.

The legislature was unusually receptive to Ferguson's programs, which generally restricted the economic and political power of large corporations and tried to protect the common people. It also enacted legislation designed to assist tenant farmers, improve public education and colleges, and reform state courts.

The legislature also established a highway commission to manage state highway construction. Texas's county governments had been given the responsibility of constructing state roads within their jurisdictions. The result was that road quality and consistency varied widely between counties. The agency's authorization to construct and maintain Texas's intrastate roadways standardized the system and facilitated motorcar travel.

Rumors of financial irregularities in Ferguson's administration gained credibility, but his declaring war on The University of Texas would prove fatal. Ferguson vetoed the entire appropriation for the university, apparently because the board of regents refused to remove certain faculty members whom the governor found objectionable. This step alienated politically powerful graduates who demanded that he be removed from office. Farmer Jim was impeached, convicted, removed, and barred from holding public office in Texas.

WORLD WAR I, THE TWENTIES, AND THE RETURN OF FARMER JIM: 1919–1928

Texas saw a boom during World War I. Its favorable climate and the Zimmerman Note, in which Germany allegedly urged Mexico to invade Texas, prompted the national government to station troops in the state. Texas became and continues to be an important training area for the military.

Crime control, education, and the Ku Klux Klan, a white supremacist organization, were the major issues of the period. Progressive measures enacted during this period included free textbooks for public schools and the beginning of the state park system. The 1920 legislature also ratified the Eighteenth Amendment to the U.S. Constitution establishing national Prohibition.

The strongest anti-Klan candidate in 1924 was Miriam A. "Ma" Ferguson, wife of the impeached Farmer Jim. She ran successfully on a platform of "Two Governors for the Price of One," becoming the first female governor of Texas. Detractors alleged that she was only a figurehead and that Farmer Jim was the real governor. Nonetheless, Ma's election indicated that Texas voters had forgiven Farmer Jim for his misbehavior. She was successful in getting legislation passed that prohibited wearing a mask in public, which resulted in the end of the Klan as an effective political force.

National politics became an issue in Texas politics in 1928. Al Smith, the Democratic nominee for president, was a Roman Catholic, a "wet," and a big-city politician. Herbert Hoover, the Republican nominee, was a Protestant, a "dry," and an international humanitarian. Hoover won the electoral votes from Texas—the first Republican ever to do so.

THE GREAT DEPRESSION: 1929–1939

The stock market crashed in 1929 and Texas, along with the entire nation, was economically crushed. Prices dropped, farm products could not be sold, mortgages and taxes went unpaid, jobs evaporated, and businesses and bank accounts were wiped out.

In 1932, Ma Ferguson, using economy in government as her campaign issue, was reelected governor. The 1933 ratification of the Twenty-first Amendment to the U.S. Constitution brought an end to nationwide Prohibition. Prohibition ended in Texas two years later with the adoption of local-option elections, although selling liquor by the drink was still forbidden statewide.

Politics and Government after World War II: 1948–Today

The 1948 senatorial campaign attracted several qualified candidates. The runoff in the Democratic primary pitted former governor Coke Stevenson against U.S. Congressman Lyndon Johnson.

The election was the closest statewide race in Texas history. At first, the election bureau gave the unofficial nomination to Stevenson, but the revised returns favored Johnson. The final official election results gave Johnson the nomination by a plurality of 87 votes. Both candidates charged election fraud.

Box 13 in Jim Wells County, one of several *machine*-controlled counties dominated by political boss George Parr (the Duke of Duval), was particularly important in the new figures. This box revised Johnson's vote upward by 202 votes and Stevenson's upward by only one. Box 13 was also late in reporting, thereby tainting Johnson's victory. About the election, historian T. R. Fehrenbach wrote, "There was probably no injustice involved. Johnson men had not *defrauded* Stevenson, but successfully *outfrauded* him."

THE 1950s AND 1960s: LBJ, THE SHIVERCRATS, AND THE SEEDS FOR A REPUBLICAN TEXAS

Allan Shivers became governor in 1949, and in 1952 the national election captured the interests of Texans. Harry Truman had succeeded to the presidency in 1945 and was reelected in 1948. Conservative Texas Democrats became disillusioned with the New Deal and Fair Deal policies of the Roosevelt–Truman era and wanted change.

Another major concern for Texans was the tidelands issue. With the discovery of oil in the Gulf of Mexico, a jurisdictional conflict arose between the government of the United States and the governments of the coastal states. Texas claimed three leagues (using Spanish units of measure, equal to about 10 miles) as its jurisdictional boundary; the U.S. government claimed Texas had rights to only three miles. At stake were hundreds of millions of dollars in royalty revenue.

Both Governor Shivers and Attorney General Price Daniel, who was campaigning for the U.S. Senate, attacked the Truman administration as being corrupt, soft on communism, eroding the rights of states, and being outright thieves in attempting to steal the tidelands oil from the schoolchildren of Texas. State control of the revenue would direct much of the oil income to the Permanent School Fund and result in a lower tax burden for Texans. The Democratic nominee for president, Adlai Stevenson of Illinois, disagreed with the Texas position.

The Republicans nominated Dwight Eisenhower, a World War II hero who was sympathetic to the Texas position on the tidelands. Eisenhower was born in Texas (but reared in Kansas), and his supporters used the campaign slogan "Texans for a Texan." The presidential campaign solidified a split in the Texas Democratic Party that lasted for 40 years. The conservative faction, led by Shivers and Daniel, advocated splitting the ticket, or voting for Eisenhower for president and Texas Democrats for state offices. Adherents to this maneuver were called Shivercrats. The liberal faction, or Loyalist Democrats of Texas, led by Judge Ralph "Raff" Yarborough, campaigned for a straight Democratic ticket.

Texas voted for Eisenhower, and the tidelands dispute was eventually settled in its favor. Shivers was reelected governor and Daniel won the Senate seat. Shivers, Daniel, and other Democratic candidates for statewide offices were also nominated by the Texas Republican Party. Running as Democrats, these candidates defeated themselves in the general election.

Lyndon B. Johnson, majority leader of the U.S. Senate and one of the most powerful men in Washington, lost his bid for the Democratic presidential nomination to John F. Kennedy in 1960. He then accepted the nomination for vice president. By the grace of the Texas legislature, Johnson was on the general election ballot as both vice-presidential and senatorial nominee. When the Democratic presidential ticket was successful, he was elected to both positions, and a special election was held to fill the vacated Senate seat. In the special election, Republican John Tower was elected and became the first Republican since Reconstruction to serve as a U.S. senator from Texas.

THE 1970s AND 1980s: REPUBLICAN GAINS AND EDUCATION REFORMS

In 1979, William P. Clements became the first Republican governor of Texas since E. J. Davis was defeated in 1874. The election of a Republican governor did not affect legislative–executive relations and had limited impact on public policy because Clements received strong political support from conservative Democrats.

Democratic Attorney General Mark White defeated incumbent governor Bill Clements in 1982. Teachers overwhelmingly supported White, who promised salary increases and expressed support for education. The first comprehensive educational reform since 1949 became law in 1984. House Bill 72 increased teacher salaries, made school district revenue somewhat more equitable, and raised standards for both students and teachers.

In 1986, voter discontent with education reform, a sour economy, and decreased state revenue were enough to return Republican Bill Clements to the governor's office. In 1988, three Republicans were elected to the Texas Supreme Court and one to the Railroad Commission—the first Republicans elected to statewide office (other than governor or U.S. senator) since Reconstruction.

In 1989, the Texas Supreme Court unanimously upheld an Austin district court's ruling in *Edgewood* v. *Kirby*[5] that the state's educational funding system violated the Texas constitutional requirement of "an efficient system" for the "general diffusion of knowledge." After several reform laws were also declared unconstitutional, the legislature enacted a complex law that kept the property tax as the basic source for school funding but required wealthier school districts to share their wealth with poorer districts. Critics called the school finance formula a "Robin Hood" plan.

THE 1990s: TEXAS ELECTS A WOMAN GOVERNOR AND BECOMES A TWO-PARTY STATE

In 1990, Texans elected Ann Richards as their first female governor since Miriam "Ma" Ferguson. Through her appointive powers, she opened the doors of state government to unprecedented numbers of women, Latinos, and African Texans. Dan Morales was elected the first Latino to statewide office in 1990, and Austin voters elected the first openly gay legislator in 1991. Texas elected Kay Bailey Hutchison as its first female U.S. senator in 1992. She joined fellow Republican Phil Gramm as they became the first two Republicans to hold U.S. Senate seats concurrently since 1874.

When the smoke, mud, and sound bites of the 1994 general election settled, Texas had become a two-party state. With the election of Governor George W. Bush, Republicans held the governor's office and both U.S. Senate seats for the first time since Reconstruction. Republicans won a majority in the Texas Senate in 1996, and voters ratified an amendment to the Texas Constitution that allowed them to use their

---

[5]777 S.W.2d 391 (Tex. 1989).

home equity (the current market value of a home minus the outstanding mortgage debt) as collateral for a loan.

The 1998 general election bolstered Republican political dominance as the party won every statewide elective office, positioning Governor George W. Bush as the frontrunner for the Republican nomination for president. Legislators deregulated electric companies, the legal blood-alcohol level for driving drunk was reduced to 0.08 percent, and the state's city annexation law was made more restrictive. Public school teachers received a pay raise but were still paid below the national average. Taxpayer-funded vouchers to pay for children's private school education failed. And Texas adopted a program to provide basic health insurance to some of the state's children who lacked health coverage, although more than 20 percent of Texas children remained uninsured.

THE 2000s: TEXAS BECOMES A REPUBLICAN STATE, CONTROVERSY AND CONFLICT

The 2001 legislature enacted a hate crimes law that strengthened penalties for crimes motivated by a victim's race, religion, color, gender, disability, sexual orientation, age, or national origin. The legislature also criminalized open alcohol containers in most motor vehicles, established partial funding for health insurance for public school employees, and made it easier for poor children to apply for health-care coverage under Medicaid. The legislature also increased subsidies to corporations by agreeing to reimburse school districts that give corporations reduced taxes.

Republicans swept statewide offices and both chambers of the legislature in the 2002 elections, returning Texas to a one-party status. A nonpartisan policy, however, remained in effect in the legislature because the lieutenant governor and speaker appointed Democrats to some committee chair and vice-chair positions.

A projected $10 billion budget deficit created an uncomfortable environment for Republicans. Politically and ideologically opposed to new taxes and state-provided social services, the legislature and the governor chose to reduce funding for most state programs; expenditures for education, health care, children's health insurance, and social services for the needy were sharply reduced.

Meanwhile, attempts to effectively close tax loopholes failed. For example, businesses and professions of all sizes continued to organize as partnerships to avoid the state corporate franchise tax. The legislature placed limits on pain-and-suffering jury awards for injuries caused by physician malpractice and hospital incompetence and made it more difficult to sue the makers of unsafe, defective products.

The legislature's social agenda was ambitious. It outlawed civil unions for same-sex couples and barred recognition of such unions from other states. It imposed a 24-hour waiting period before a woman could have an abortion.

Although the districts for electing U.S. representatives in Texas had been redrawn by a panel of one Democratic and two Republican federal judges following the 2000 Census, Texas Congressman and U.S. House Majority Leader Tom DeLay was unhappy that more Republicans were not elected to Congress. Governor Rick Perry agreed and called a special session to redraw the redrawn districts to increase Republican representation. Democrats argued that the districts had already been established by the courts and that Perry and DeLay only wanted to increase the number of Republican officeholders. The legislature adopted the Republican proposal and the U.S. Supreme Court affirmed that states could redistrict more than once each decade and rejected the argument that the redistricting was either illegal or partisan.

The Texas government in 2007 waged almost continuous battle with itself. Conflict between the house and the speaker, the senate and the lieutenant governor, the senate and the house, and the legislature and the governor marked the session. Legislators did restore eligibility of some needy children for the Children's Health Insurance Program.

The 2009 legislature seemed almost placid after the unprecedented house revolt against Speaker Tom Craddick and election of Joe Straus as new speaker. However, consideration of the contentious voter identification bill caused conflict in the last days of the session and resulted in a parliamentary shutdown. The house adjourned without resolution of a voter identification bill and postponed other important matters to be resolved by a special session. The legislature passed new laws, including limited restrictions on using a cell phone when driving through a school zone and a tax increase on smokeless tobacco.

THE 2010s: CONSERVATIVE POLITICS, POLICIES, AND LITIGATION

In 2010, much of the state's political attention was focused on disputes about Texas's acceptance of federal funds. Texas accepted federal stimulus money to help balance the state's budget but turned down more than $500 million in federal stimulus money for unemployed Texans. The state declined to apply for up to $700 million in federal grant money linked to Race to the Top, a program to improve education quality and results. Then-Governor Perry believed the money would result in a federal takeover of Texas's schools. Texas also became one of seven states to reject the National Governors Association effort to establish national curriculum standards called the common core.

Former Governor Perry failed to get the Republican nomination for president in 2012 but continued to make national news arguing for his agenda of low taxes, minimal business regulation, and opposition to the Affordable Care Act. Using taxpayer money from the Texas Enterprise Fund, he was able to persuade several businesses to relocate to Texas. Among his most notable successes, the governor took credit for persuading Toyota to move its headquarters and high-paying jobs from California and Kentucky to the Dallas–Fort Worth metroplex.

In the past few years, Texas adopted an ambitious conservative political and social agenda. Outnumbered in the legislative and executive branches, liberal and Democratic strategists turned to the courts to battle against these policies. For example, opponents challenged the state's legislative and congressional districts as being gerrymandered to dilute minority votes and to favor Republican candidates. The courts upheld the legislative districting map with only minor changes.

Meanwhile the state legislature adopted strict voter ID laws requiring voters to present specific forms of identification as a condition for voting. Opponents charged that these laws were designed to discourage voting by young, minority, and elderly citizens who were less likely to have these forms of identification. The courts initially upheld Texas's voter ID laws, but legal battles continue.

Although the U.S. Supreme Court struck down provisions of the Voting Rights Act of 1965 that required states, like Texas, that have a history of racial discrimination to get preclearance of new election laws from the U.S. Department of Justice, challengers can still show that particular elections laws are racially discriminatory and, therefore, a violation of the U.S. Constitution. Challenges to new Texas election laws are likely to continue indefinitely.

The Texas legislature also passed regulations that required abortion clinics to meet the hospital-like standards of ambulatory surgical centers. Opponents argued that these regulations compromised a woman's constitutional right to abortions. Despite the well-publicized filibuster by former state senator Wendy Davis, the law was adopted. Court challenges to the law immediately followed. Although the Texas abortion law was initially upheld, court challenges continue.

Travis County District Judge Dietz held the Texas system of school finance unconstitutional. The judge found "that the legislature has failed to meet its constitutional duty to suitably provide for Texas public schools because the school finance system is structured, operated and funded so that it cannot provide a constitutionally adequate education for all Texas schoolchildren." As a result, the legislature and courts will spend much of their time in the near future attempting to reform public school finances.

In yet another legal action, a grand jury indicted a sitting governor—for the first time since James Ferguson was indicted in 1917. Former Governor Perry was indicted for threatening to use his line-item veto to force the resignation of a public official. Perry was charged with two felonies—abuse of office and coercion of a public official.

In the polarized political environment at the time, reaction to the indictment fell largely along partisan lines. Perry and his Republican defenders argued that the state constitution gives the governor power to strike out items of appropriations, and Perry was justified in threatening to cut off state funds to force

Travis County District Attorney Rosemary Lehmberg to resign because she had brought shame to the office with her high-profile DWI arrest.

Perry's mostly Democratic critics argued that, although the constitution clearly gives the governor the line-item veto, it does not give him the power to use it to intimidate public officials and hobble legitimate criminal investigations. Some critics suspected that Perry's veto was payback because the Public Integrity Unit in Lehmberg's office had been investigating alleged improprieties involving the Cancer Prevention Research Institution of Texas and a major Perry donor, and they believed that Perry wanted to use his power to fill a vacancy in the DA's office to put one of his allies in charge of the office.

Despite the legal and political turmoil that permeated the political environment, Republicans continued to dominate state politics after the 2014 elections. Former attorney general Greg Abbott defeated Democrat Wendy Davis to become the first Roman Catholic elected to be governor, and Texas Republicans firmly embraced tea party politics as its most conservative candidates rolled over "establishment" candidates like former lt. governor David Dewhurst and several other traditional Republican politicians. The new lieutenant governor, Dan Patrick, has promised a more partisan conservative agenda as he manages the state senate.

CHAPTER 1

Texas Culture and Diversity

LEARNING OBJECTIVES

LO 1.1 Analyze the relationships among Texas political culture, its politics, and its public policies.

LO 1.2 Differentiate among the various types of state political cultures and the attributes that describe the major Texas regions.

LO 1.3 Analyze Texans' political struggles over equal rights and evaluate their success in Texas politics today and in their impact on the state's political future.

LO 1.4 Apply what you have learned about Texas political culture.

Political culture
The dominant political values and beliefs of a people.

A political culture reflects the political values and beliefs of a people. It explains how people feel about their government—their expectations of what powers it should have over their lives, the services it should provide, and their ability to influence its actions. A political culture is developed by historical experience over generations through agents of socialization such as family, religion, peer group, and education. It is characterized by the level of ethnic, social, and religious diversity it tolerates; by the level of citizen participation it allows; and by citizens' perception of their status within the system.

A people's political behavior is shaped by the culture that nourished it. The Spanish conquest and settlement of Texas provided the first European influence on Texas culture. Some elements of the ranchero culture and the Catholic religion continue to this day and are the enduring Spanish influence on our culture. The immigration of Anglo-Saxon southerners in the early 1800s brought Texas the plantation and slave-owning culture. This culture became dominant following the Texas Revolution. Although it was modified to an extent by the Civil War, it has remained the dominant Texas culture. Ethnic diversification and urbanization are, however, beginning to challenge the dominance of the traditional southern Anglo culture as Texas is becoming a multicultural state.

We will begin by exploring the state's dominant political culture, its ideology, and how each influences public opinion, partisanship, and public policy. Then we will look at other aspects of the state's political culture and examine the subtle variations in the state from one region to another. We will conclude with a discussion of rising minority cultures and their impact on the state's political future.

POLITICAL CULTURE, PUBLIC OPINION, AND PUBLIC POLICY

LO 1.1 Analyze the relationships among Texas political culture, its politics, and its public policies.

Conservative
A political ideology marked by the belief in a limited role for government in taxation, economic regulation, and providing social services; conservatives support traditional values and lifestyles, and are cautious in response to social change.

Texas's political culture is **conservative**. Many Texans share a belief in a limited role for government in taxation, economic regulation, and providing social services; conservatives support traditional values and lifestyles, and are cautious in response to social change. Figure 1.1a shows that in a recent public opinion survey, 48 percent of Texans rate themselves as slightly to extremely conservative, while only 20 percent label themselves as slightly to extremely liberal.

Ideology

The Texas brand of conservatism is skeptical of state government involvement in the economy. Most Texans favor low taxes, modest state services, and few business regulations. Because they support economic individualism and free-market capitalism, Texans generally value profit as a healthy incentive to promote economic investment and individual effort, while they see social class inequality as the inevitable result of free-market capitalism. For them, an individual's quality of life is largely a matter of personal responsibility rather than an issue of public policy.

Some conservatives accept an active role for the government in promoting business. They are willing to support direct government subsidies and special tax breaks for businesses to encourage economic growth. They may also support state spending for infrastructure, such as transportation and education that sustains commercial and manufacturing activity. These conservatives often advocate vigorous state regulation of labor unions.

Social conservatives support energetic government activity to enforce what they view as moral behavior and traditional cultural values. For example, they usually champion vigorous law enforcement, drug control, and immigration enforcement. Social conservatives, who often are Christian fundamentalists, usually advocate the use of state power to restrict gambling, pornography, abortion, and same-sex relationships.

Did You Know? About 44 percent of Texas Christians consider themselves to be "born again."[1]

A distinct minority in Texas, **liberals** believe in positive government action to improve the welfare of individuals; they favor government regulation of the economy, support civil rights, and tolerate social change. Liberals believe state government can be used as a positive tool to benefit the population as a whole. Most Texas liberals accept private enterprise as the state's basic economic system but believe excesses of unregulated capitalism compromise the common good. They endorse state policies to abate pollution, to enforce the rights of workers and consumers, and to protect ethnic and sexual minorities.

Liberals
A political ideology marked by the advocacy of positive government action to improve the welfare of individuals, government regulation of the economy, support for civil rights, and tolerance for social change.

Liberals often believe that a great deal of social inequality results from institutional and economic forces that are often beyond a single individual's control. As a result, they support the use of government power to balance these forces and to promote a better quality of life for middle- and lower-income people. For example, liberals argue that it is fair to tax those with the greatest ability to pay and to provide social services for the community as a whole.

A significant number of Texans have mixed views. On some issues, they take a liberal position, but on others they have a conservative perspective or no opinion at all. Others have moderate views—Figure 1.1a shows that 32 percent of Texans say that they are "in the middle"; that is, their beliefs are between conservative and liberal viewpoints. The "Get Active" features in later chapters will give you the tools to explore Texans' policy differences in greater depth and to engage with various ideological groups in Texas.

Partisanship

Texans' conservative political views are reflected in political party affiliations. Figure 1.1b shows that 48 percent of all Texans self-identify as Republicans. Only 42 percent call themselves Democrats, and 10 percent are independents who refuse to admit a leaning toward either party. Polling and actual election results prove the dominance of the more conservative Republican Party in Texas. We will examine the ideological and policy differences between the two parties in greater depth in Chapter 5.

Public Opinion

Table 1.1 shows that when Texans are asked about their specific policy opinions on state taxes and social policies, they do, indeed, have conservative views. However, that pattern is not as clear regarding state spending. Even during the state budget crisis of 2011, when voters were asked whether they supported spending cuts in various state services to balance the budget, a large majority of Texas voters refused to support cuts in a single major state program. In fact, 53 percent believed Texas spent too little on elementary and secondary education.

---

[1]University of Texas/Texas Tribune, *Texas Statewide Survey*, February 7–17, 2014, at http://s3.amazonaws.com/static.texastribune.org/media/documents/utttpoll-201402-1summary.pdf.

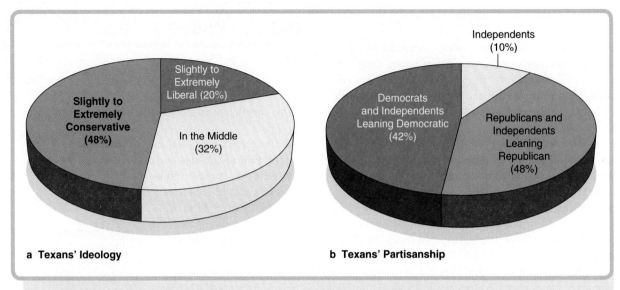

a **Texans' Ideology**   b **Texans' Partisanship**

Figure 1.1
Texans' Ideology and Partisanship

Public opinion polling confirms that the majority of Texans identify themselves as conservative ad that the Republican Party has a 6-point advantage in party identification.

Source: University of Texas/Texas Tribune, *Texas Statewide Survey*, Survey of 1,200 adults conducted February 7–17, 2014, with a margin of error (MOE) +/–2.83 percent, published at http://s3.amazonaws.com/static.texastribune.org/media/documents/utttpoll-201402-1summary.pdf.

 Explain the differences between conservative and liberal ideologies. Why is it difficult for Democrats to win statewide offices?

TABLE 1.1 Public Opinion and Public Policy in Texas

Public Policy Option	Percent Supporting	Percent Opposing
Tax Policies		
Increase the state tax on business.[b]	18	82
Increase the state sales tax rate.[b]	12	88
Implement a state income tax on individuals.[b]	6	94
Spending Policies		
Cut funding for elementary and secondary education.[b]	15	85
Cut funding for higher education.[b]	27	73
Cut funding for children's health program.[b]	10	90
Close one or more adult prisons.[b]	30	70
Cut funding for new highways.[b]	28	72
Social Policies		
Provide a pathway to citizenship for illegal aliens.[a]	39	51*
Use the death penalty for those convicted of violent crime.[a]	74	21*
Always allow abortion as a matter of personal choice.[a]	36	59*

TABLE 1.1 Public Opinion and Public Policy in Texas *(continued)*

Public Policy Option	Percent Supporting	Percent Opposing
Require a sonogram (ultrasound) as a condition for abortion.[c]	62	37*
Legalize possession of marijuana for any purpose.[c]	49	51**
Support a comprehensive immigration overhaul.[c]	51	44*

*Some results may not total 100 percent because "no opinion" responses are not reported here.
**Includes respondents who oppose any form of legalization (23 percent) and those who would legalize it only for medicinal purposes (28 percent).
[a]University of Texas/Texas Tribune, *Texas Statewide Survey,* 800 registered voters, October 19–26, 2011, at http://d2o6nd3dubbyr6.cloudfront.net/media/documents/uttt201110.summary-all.pdf.
[b]University of Texas/Texas Tribune, *Texas Statewide Survey,* 800 registered voters, May 11–18, 2011, at http://d2o6nd3dubbyr6.cloudfront.net/media/documents/uttt-201105-summary-all.pdf.
[c]University of Texas/Texas Tribune, *Texas Statewide Survey,* 1,200 adults, February 7–17, 2014, at http://s3.amazonaws.com/static.texastribune.org/media/documents/utttpoll-201402-fullsummary.pdf#page=3&zoom=auto,0.

Although responses may vary from one survey to the next depending on how questions are phrased, University of Texas/Texas Tribune polls indicate Texans generally have conservative opinions about selected taxing policies and social issues. However, Texans support major state spending programs.

▲ **On which public policy issues would conservatives favor increased state control? On which issues would liberals favor smaller government? Explain how Texans' support for spending and opposition to taxes complicate policy making.**

These survey results come as no surprise because numerous national and state surveys conducted over several decades indicate a paradox in public opinion. Many voters support cutting the size of government but balk when asked about cutting specific programs. They favor spending cuts in the abstract but support spending for most government programs in practice. This paradox creates the potential for decision-making gridlock, and it presents an enormous dilemma for policy makers.

Public Policy

Conservative opinions have been translated into most of Texas's public policies. Texas state taxes are very low compared to other states and, despite the public's ambiguous attitudes about spending, the state has committed far fewer financial resources to public services than most other states. Texas takes in less per capita revenue than all but four states and, per capita, it spends less per person than forty-seven other states.

Texas, however, has not been reluctant to use the power of the state to enforce certain traditional values, to restrict abortions, to prohibit same-sex marriages, and to impose relatively severe penalties on lawbreakers. We will analyze Texas public policy in considerable depth in Chapter 12.

In this photo, you see many of the colorful elements of the state's political culture. In this chapter, you will learn about Texas's dominant political culture, the state's increasing diversity, and how cultural attitudes impact Texas politics today.

Identify the major features of Texas political culture depicted in this photo.

TYPES OF POLITICAL CULTURES AND TEXAS'S POLITICAL REGIONS

LO 1.2 Differentiate among the various types of state political cultures and the attributes that describe the major Texas regions.

We now consider some other approaches to describe the Texas political culture, including Elazar's classical model for classifying state political cultures and a discussion of regional

HOW DOES TEXAS COMPARE?
How Texas Ranks among the 50 States: Public Policy and Quality of Life

Public Policy	Texas's Rank*
Revenue and Spending	
Tax revenue per capita	45th
Tax expenditure per capita	48th
Public Education Spending	
Average public school teacher salary	31st
State and local spending per student	43rd
High school graduation rate	50th
Health Care	
Percentage of population uninsured	1st
Percentage of low-income population covered by Medicaid	48th
Per capita spending on mental health	50th
Public Safety	
Rate of incarceration	4th
Number of executions	1st
Quality of Life	
Percent of adults (over age 25) with a high school diploma	50th
Percentage of uninsured children	2nd
Percent of children living in poverty	7th
Amount of atmospheric carbon dioxide emissions	1st
Amount of toxic emissions released into water	4th
Percentage of population with employer backed insurance	43rd
Home ownership rate	42nd
Percent living below federal poverty level	8th
Teenage birth rate	4th
Inequality between rich and poor	8th

*First is highest and fiftieth is lowest.

Source: The Texas Legislative Study Group, *Texas on the Brink: How Texas Ranks Among the 50 States*, 6th ed., March 2013, at https://leafmedium-live.s3.amazonaws.com/blog/texaslsg/TexasOnTheBrink2013.pdf.

FOR DEBATE

 Texas's various ranks among the 50 states are often used to make a political point or further a political agenda. How would liberals use these rankings? Which of these rankings would conservatives tout with pride?

 Looking only at the public policy matters, explain how these rankings show that Texas public policy is conservative in comparison to other states.

 Looking at quality-of-life issues, explain how liberals would see these rankings as a call to government action. Discuss how conservatives, with their limited-government philosophy of self-reliance, would see these quality-of-life issues as a matter of individual personal responsibility and not within the proper purview of state government action.

cultural differences within the state. We will conclude with a sketch of Texas's rich ethnic and demographic diversity.

State Political Cultures

A number of different approaches have been used to study diversity in nations, regions, states, and communities. One popular approach is that of Daniel J. Elazar, who depicted American political culture as a mix of three distinct subcultures, each prevalent in at least one area of the United States.

Moralistic Culture Elazar used the term *moralistic* to describe a culture whose adherents are concerned with "right and wrong" in politics. **Moralistic culture** views government as a positive force, one that values the individual but functions for the benefit of the general public. Discussion of public issues and voting are not only rights but also opportunities to better the individual and society alike. Furthermore, politicians should not profit from their public service. Moralistic culture is strongest in New England and, although historically a product of Puritan religious values, today it is associated with more secular (nonreligious) attitudes.

Moralistic culture
A political subculture that views government as a positive force; one that values the individual but functions for the benefit of the general public.

Individualistic Culture In contrast, an **individualistic culture** embodies the view that government is practical; its prime objective should be to further private enterprise, but its intervention into people's lives should be strictly limited. Blurring the distinction between economic and political life, individualistic culture sees business and politics as appropriate avenues by which an individual can advance her or his interests. Accordingly, business interests play a very strong role, and running for office is difficult without their support. Conflicts of interest are fairly commonplace, and political corruption may be expected as a natural political activity. The individualistic culture predominates in the commercial centers of the Middle Atlantic states, moving west and south along the Ohio River and its tributaries.

Individualistic culture
A political subculture that views government as a practical institution that should further private enterprise but intervene minimally in people's lives.

Traditionalistic Culture Widespread throughout America, **traditionalistic culture** in Texas derives primarily from the plantation society of the Old South and the patrón system of northern Mexico and South Texas. Government is seen to have an active role but primarily to maintain the dominant social and religious values. Government should also help maintain accepted class distinctions and encourage the beliefs of the dominant religion. Traditionalistic culture views politics as the special preserve of the social and economic elite—as a process of maintaining the existing order. Believing in personal rather than public solutions to problems, it views political participation as a privilege and accepts social pressure and restrictive election laws that limit participation.[2]

Traditionalistic culture
A political subculture that views government as an institution to maintain the dominant social and religious values.

Political Culture and Political Participation

Elazar considered Texas a mix of traditional and individualistic cultures. The traditional overrides the individualistic in East Texas, which was initially settled by immigrants from the Upper Old South and Mexican border areas, where the patrón system dominated early Texas. The individualistic supersedes the traditional throughout the rest of the state. As a result, in Texas, participation in politics is not as highly regarded as in those states with a moralistic culture. Voter turnout in Texas is, in fact, well below the national average. Texans see politics largely as the domain of economic interests, and most tend to ignore the significance of their role in the political process and how it might benefit them.[3]

Did You Know? Voter turnout in Texas is consistently counted among the lowest of the fifty states.

---

[2]Daniel J. Elazar, *American Federalism: A View from the States*, 3rd ed. (New York: Harper & Row, 1984).
[3]Ibid.

Texas Cultural Regions

D. W. Meinig found that the cultural diversity of Texas was more apparent than its homogeneity and that no unified culture has emerged from the various ethnic and cultural groups that settled Texas. He believed that the "typical Texan," like the "average American," does not exist but is an oversimplification of the more distinctive social, economic, and political characteristics of the state's inhabitants.[4]

Both Meinig and Elazar see modern regional political culture as largely determined by migration patterns because people take their culture with them as they move geographically. Meinig believed that Texas had evolved into nine fairly distinct cultural regions. However, whereas political boundaries are distinct, cultural divisions are often blurred and transitional. For example, the East Texas region shares political culture with much of the Upper South, whereas West Texas shares a similar culture with eastern New Mexico, and so forth (Figure 1.2).

The effects of mass media, the mobility of modern Texans statewide and beyond, and immigration from Mexico blur the cultural boundaries within Texas, between its bordering states, and with Mexico. Although limited because they do not take into account these modern-day realities, both Meinig's and Elazar's explanations are useful guides to a general understanding of contemporary Texas culture, attitudes, and beliefs.

East Texas East Texas is a social and cultural extension of the Old South. It is basically rural and biracial. Despite the changes brought about by civil rights legislation, African-American "towns" still exist alongside Anglo-American "towns," as do many segregated social and economic institutions, such as churches, fraternal lodges, and chambers of commerce.

East Texas counties and towns are often dominated by old families, whose wealth is usually based on real estate, banking, construction, and retail merchandising. Cotton—once "king" of agriculture in the region—has been replaced by beef cattle, poultry, and timber. As the result of a general lack of economic opportunity, young East Texans migrate to metropolitan areas, primarily Dallas–Fort Worth and Houston. Seeking tranquility and solitude, retiring urbanites have begun to revitalize some small towns and rural communities that lost population to the metropolitan areas. Fundamentalist Protestantism dominates the region spiritually and permeates its political, social, and cultural activities.

The Gulf Coast Texas was an economic colony before 1900—it sold raw materials to the industrialized North and bought northern manufactured products. However, in 1901, an oil well named Spindletop drilled near Beaumont ushered in the age of Texas oil, and the state's economy began to change. Since the discovery of oil, the Gulf Coast has experienced almost continuous growth, especially during World War II, the Cold War defense buildup, and the various energy booms of the late-twentieth and early-twenty-first centuries.

In addition to being an industrial and petrochemical center, the Gulf Coast is one of the most important shipping centers in the nation. Out-of-state investors, largely from the northeastern states, backed Spindletop, and its success stimulated increased out-of-state investment. Local wealth was also generated and largely reinvested in Texas to promote long-range development. Nevertheless, much of the economy is still supported by the sale of raw materials.

---

[4]Information for this section is adapted from D. W. Meinig, *Imperial Texas: An Interpretive Essay in Cultural Geography* (Austin, TX, and London: University of Texas Press, 1969).

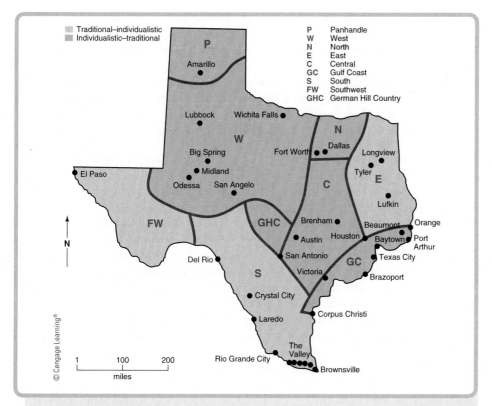

Figure 1.2
Texas Political Culture

Maxwell's original figure is based on Elazar and Meinig concepts.

 In which political cultural area do you reside? Construct your own cultural description of the area in which you live. To make your essay complete, present evidence as to whether the area is predominantly liberal or conservative; Democratic or Republican; urban, suburban, or rural. Present evidence of which industries and ethnic groups predominate. Is your area prosperous? What is the extent of poverty and inequality? Use census data and election returns from the secretary of state's office to support your conclusions.

A Boom Based in Houston   Through boom and bust, the petrochemical industry, which is concentrated on the Gulf Coast, has experienced unprecedented growth, creating a boomtown psychology. Rapid growth fed real estate development and speculation throughout the region. The Houston area especially flourished, and Harris County (Houston) grew to become the third-most-populous county in the United States.

Houston's initial growth after World War II was fueled by a flood of job seekers from East Texas and other rural areas of the state. This influx gave the Gulf Coast the flavor of rural Texas in an urban setting. Houston's social and economic elite were generally composed of second- and third-generation rich whose wealth came from oil, insurance, construction, land development, or banking.

Houston's rural flavor diminished over the years as the U.S. economy changed from an industrial to a service basis. This transformation attracted migrants from the "Frost Belt" (the Great Lakes and Mid-Atlantic states). This migration included both skilled and unskilled workers and added large numbers of well-educated young executives and professionals to the Houston elite pool. Today, the Gulf Coast has become a remarkably vibrant and energetic region, and Houston, the worldwide oil and gas capital, boasts many corporate headquarters.

The Gulf Coast economy also attracts heavy immigration from the Americas, Africa, Europe, and Asia, which gives modern Houston an international culture comparable to Los Angeles or New York. In fact, modern Houston has street signs in Vietnamese, Chinese, and English in areas with large Vietnamese and Chinese populations.

South Texas The earliest area settled by Europeans, South Texas developed a ranchero culture on the basis of livestock production that was similar to the feudal institutions in faraway Spain. The **ranchero culture** is a quasi-feudal system whereby a property's owner, or patrón, gives workers protection and employment in return for their loyalty and service. The rancher or ranchero and workers all live on the *rancho*, or ranch. **Creoles**, who descended from Spanish immigrants, were the economic, social, and political elite, whereas the first Texas cowboys who did the ranch work were Native Americans or **Mestizos** of mixed Spanish and Native-American heritage. Anglo Americans first became culturally important in South Texas when they gained title to much of the real estate in the region following the Texas Revolution of 1836. However, modern South Texas still retains elements of the ranchero culture, including some of its feudal aspects. Large ranches, often owned by one family for several generations, are prevalent; however, wealthy and corporate ranchers and farmers from outside the area are becoming common.

Because of the semitropical South Texas climate, **The Valley** (of the Rio Grande) and the Winter Garden around Crystal City became major producers of vegetable and citrus products. These areas were developed by migrants from the northern United States in the 1920s and continue to be important multi-use agricultural assets. The development of citrus and vegetable enterprises required intensive manual labor, which brought about increased immigration from Mexico. Modern South Texas Latinos can usually trace their U.S. roots to the 1920s or later because many of the original Latino settlers had been driven south of the Rio Grande after the Texas Revolution.

Far West Texas Far West Texas, also known as the "Trans-Pecos region," exhibits elements of two cultures, many of the same **bicultural** characteristics as South Texas. Its large Mexican-American population often maintains strong ties with relatives and friends in Mexico. The Roman Catholic Church strongly influences social and cultural attitudes on both sides of the border.

Far West Texas is a major commercial and social passageway between Mexico and the United States. El Paso, the "capital city" of Far West Texas and the sixth-largest city in Texas, is a military, manufacturing, and commercial center. El Paso's primary commercial partners are Mexico and New Mexico. The economy of the border cities of Far West Texas, like that of South Texas, is closely linked to Mexico and has also benefited from the economic opportunities brought about by NAFTA. The agricultural economy of much of the region depends on sheep, goat, and cattle production, although some irrigated row-crop agriculture is present. Most of the labor on ranches, as well as in manufacturing and commerce, is Latino.

The Texas Border South and Far West Texas comprise the area known as the "Texas Border." A corresponding "Mexico Border" includes parts of the Mexican states of Chihuahua, Coahuila, Nuevo León, and Tamaulipas. It can be argued that the Texas Border and the Mexico Border are two parts of an economic, social, and cultural region with a substantial degree of similarity that sets it off from the rest of the United States and Mexico.

Ranchero culture

A quasi-feudal system whereby a property's owner, or patrón, gives workers protection and employment in return for their loyalty and service. The rancher or ranchero and workers all live on the *rancho*, or ranch.

Creoles

A descendant of European-Spanish (or in some regions, French) immigrants to the Americas.

Mestizos

A person of both Spanish and Native-American lineage.

The Valley

An area along the Texas side of the Rio Grande River known for its production of citrus fruits.

Bicultural

Encompassing two cultures.

The Border region, which is expanding in size both to the north and to the south, has a binational, bicultural, and bilingual subculture in which internationality is commonplace and the people, economies, and societies on both sides constantly interact.[5]

South and Far West Texas are "mingling pots" for the Latino and Anglo-American cultures. Catholic Latinos often retain strong links with Mexico through extended family and friends in Mexico and through Spanish-language newspapers. Many Latinos continue to speak Spanish; in fact, Spanish is also the commercial and social language of choice for many of the region's Anglo Americans. The Texas Border cities are closely tied to the Mexican economy on which their prosperity depends. Although improving economically, these regions remain among the poorest in the United States.

The economy of the Texas Border benefits economically from **maquiladoras**, which are Mexican factories where U.S. corporations employ inexpensive Mexican labor for assembly and piecework. Unfortunately, lax environmental and safety standards result in high levels of air, ground, and water pollution in the general area. In fact, the Rio Grande is now one of America's most ecologically endangered rivers.

The ongoing **North American Free Trade Agreement (NAFTA)**, a treaty that has helped remove trade barriers among Canada, Mexico, and the United States, is an economic stimulus for the Texas Border because it is a conduit for much of the commerce with Mexico.

Immigration and National Security Poverty, military conflicts, crime, political disorder, and suppression of civil liberties in Central America and Mexico have driven hundreds of thousands of immigrants into the border regions of the United States. This flow of immigrants continues but has begun to level off because of the economic downturn, tightened security measures, and fence construction. The Texas Border is a major staging ground for the migration of both legal and illegal immigrants as well as human traffickers into the interior of Texas and the rest of the United States.

The craving of some Americans for illegal, mind-altering, addictive chemicals provides a steady flow of American capital through the Texas Border into Mexico and South America. Basically, the drug traffic is uncontainable as long as its U.S. market exists, but newspapers and other media virtuously trumpet feel-good headlines about "record drug busts" and arrests while the drug trade continues unabated.

This "invisible trade," because of its illegal status, inevitably results in violence as surely as did the failed American experiment prohibiting the sale and consumption of alcoholic beverages from 1919 to 1933. The collateral damage of the drug trade is readily visible and all too common as stories of death and destruction are lead stories for evening news and provide villains and endless plots for movies and television detective programs. Although the worst of the violence is confined to the border areas of Mexico and the United States, the political, economic, lawless, and violent geographic extension of the drug trade is increasingly evident throughout both countries.

Collateral to the drug traffic and its companion violence is a reverse cash flow from Mexico to the United States for weapons purchases. The illegal weapons traffic moves easily obtained weapons, ammunition, and explosives from Texas and other states into Mexico and South America. However, the incoming cash from weapons is far less than the amount of money leaving the United States for drug purchases in Mexico and South America.

When the expenditures by the Mexican, Texas, and U.S. governments for narcotics agents and immigration agents, prison construction and operation, equipment purchases, related

Maquiladoras
Mexican factories where U.S. corporations employ inexpensive Mexican labor for assembly and piecework.

North American Free Trade Agreement (NAFTA)
A treaty among Canada, Mexico, and the United States that has helped remove trade barriers.

---

[5]"Texas Border Region," July 1998, p. 3; Jorge Bustamante, "A Conceptual and Operative Vision of the Population. Problems on the Border," in *Demographic Dynamics on the U.S.–Mexico Border*, eds. John R. Weeks and Roberto Ham Chande (El Paso, TX: Texas Western Press, 1992).

military operations, and increased police employment are combined with the expenses, wages, and bribe money spent by drug, weapon, and human traffickers, the result is increased employment and a significant but unwholesome economic infusion to both sides of the border. Immigration; illegal trafficking in humans, drugs, and weapons; and border security will continue to be major political issues for both Democrats and Republicans in the foreseeable future.

German Hill Country   The Hill Country north and west of San Antonio was settled primarily by immigrants from Germany but also by Czech, Polish, and Norwegian immigrants. Although the immigrants mixed with Anglo Americans, Central European culture and architecture were dominant well into the twentieth century. Skilled artisans were common in the towns; farms were usually moderate in size, self-sufficient, and family owned and operated. Most settlers were Lutheran or Roman Catholic, and these remain the most common religious affiliations for modern residents.

The German Hill Country is still a distinct cultural region. Although its inhabitants have become "Americanized," they still cling to many of their Central European cultural traditions. Primarily a farming and ranching area, the Hill Country is socially and politically conservative and has long been a stronghold of the Texas Republican Party.

Migration into the region, primarily by Anglo Americans and Latinos, is increasing. The most significant encroachment into the Hill Country is residential growth from rapidly expanding urban areas, especially San Antonio and Austin. Resorts, country homes, and retirement villages for well-to-do urbanites from the Gulf Coast and Dallas–Fort Worth area are beginning to transform the cultural distinctiveness of the German Hill Country.

West Texas   The defeat of the Comanches in the 1870s opened West Texas to Anglo-American settlement. Migrating primarily from the southern United States, these settlers passed their social and political attitudes and southern Protestant fundamentalism on to their descendants.

Relatively few African Americans live in modern West Texas, but Latinos have migrated into the region in significant numbers, primarily to the cities and the intensively farmed areas. West Texas is socially and politically conservative, and its religion is Bible Belt fundamentalism. West Texas voters in the past supported conservative Democrats and today favor the Republican Party. Indeed, this is true of most conservative Texans throughout the state.

The southern portion of the area emphasizes sheep, goat, and cattle production. In fact, San Angelo advertises itself as the "Sheep and Wool Capital of the World." Southern West Texas, which is below the Cap Rock Escarpment, is the major oil-producing area of Texas. The cities of Snyder, Midland, and Odessa owe their existence almost entirely to oil and related industries.

Northern West Texas is part of the Great Plains and High Plains and is primarily agricultural, with cotton, grain, and feedlot cattle production predominating. In this part of semiarid West Texas, outstanding agricultural production is due to extensive irrigation from the Ogallala Aquifer. The large amount of water used for irrigation is gradually depleting the Ogallala. This not only affects the current economy of the region through higher costs to farmers but also serves as a warning signal for its economic future.

The Panhandle   Railroads advancing from Kansas City through the Panhandle brought Midwestern farmers into this region, and wheat production was developed largely by migrants from Kansas. Because the commercial and cultural focus of the region was Kansas City, the early Panhandle was basically Midwestern in both character and institutions.

The modern Texas Panhandle shares few cultural attributes with the American Midwest. Its religious, cultural, and social institutions function with little discernible difference from those of northern West Texas. The Panhandle economy is also supported by production of cotton and grains, the cultivation of which depends on extensive irrigation from the Ogallala Aquifer. Feedlots for livestock and livestock production were established because of proximity to the region's grain production but are major economic enterprises in their own right. Effective conservation of the Ogallala Aquifer is critical to the economic future of both northern West Texas and the Panhandle.

North Texas   North Texas is located between East and West Texas and exhibits many characteristics of both regions. Early North Texas benefited from the failure of the French socialist colony of La Réunion, which included many highly trained professionals in medicine, education, music, and science. (La Réunion was located on the south bank of the Trinity River, across from modern downtown Dallas.) The colonists and their descendants helped give North Texas a cultural and commercial distinctiveness. North Texas today is dominated by the Dallas–Fort Worth metropolitan area, often called the **Metroplex**. Dallas is a banking and commercial center of national importance, and Fort Worth is the financial and commercial center of West Texas.

Metroplex
The greater Dallas–Fort Worth metropolitan area.

When railroads came into Texas from the North in the 1870s, Dallas became a rail center, and people and capital from the North stimulated its growth. Fort Worth became a regional capital that looked primarily to West Texas. The Swift and Armour meatpacking companies, which moved plants to Fort Worth in 1901, became the first national firms to establish facilities close to Texas's natural resources. More businesses followed, and North Texas began its evolution from an economic colony to an industrially developed area.

North Texas experienced extraordinary population growth after World War II, with extensive migration from the rural areas of East, West, and Central Texas. The descendants of these migrants, after several generations, are now urbanites and tend to have urban attitudes and behavior. Recent migration from other states, especially from the North, has been significant. Many international corporations have established headquarters in North Texas. Their executive and support staffs contribute to the region's diversity and cosmopolitan environment.

Although North Texas is more economically diverse than most other Texas regions, it relies heavily on banking, insurance, and the defense and aerospace industries. Electronic equipment, computer products, plastics, and food products are also produced in the region.

Central Texas   Central Texas is often called the "core area" of Texas. It is roughly triangular in shape, with its three corners being Houston, Dallas–Fort Worth, and San Antonio. The centerpiece of the region is Austin, one of the fastest-growing metropolitan areas in the nation. Already a center of government and education, the Austin metropolitan area has become the "Silicon Valley" of high-tech industries in Texas. Although the worldwide downturn in the high-tech sector after 2000 dealt a serious blow to the area's economy, high-tech industries still make a major economic contribution.

Austin's rapid growth is a result of significant migration from the northeastern United States and the West Coast, as well as from other regions in Texas. The influx of well-educated persons from outside Texas has added to the already substantial pool of accomplished Austinites, making it the intellectual and governmental capital of the state, as well as the economic center of Central Texas. The cultural and economic traits of all the other Texas regions mingle here, with no single trait being dominant. Although the Central Texas region is a microcosm of Texas culture, the city of Austin itself stands out as an island of liberalism in a predominantly conservative state.

POLITICS AND CULTURAL DIVERSITY

LO 1.3 Analyze Texans' political struggles over equal rights and evaluate their success in Texas politics today and in their impact on the state's political future.

The politics of cultural regions have begun to lose their distinctive identities as Texas has become more metropolitan in outlook and as it became more economically and ethnically diverse. With these changes, a number of groups have begun to aspire toward greater cultural, political, social, and economic equality.

Texans Struggle for Equal Rights

Anglo male Texans initially resided atop the pyramid of status, wealth, and civil rights in organized Texas society. They wrote the rules of the game and used those rules to protect their position against attempts by females, African Americans, and Latinos to share in the fruits of full citizenship. Only after the disenfranchised groups organized and exerted political pressure against their governments did the doors of freedom and equality open enough for them to slip inside.

Texan Minnie Fisher Cunningham was a champion for women's suffrage in the state.

Bettmann/Corbis

Describe legal restrictions on women before the suffrage movement. What explains the opposition to women's right to vote?

Female Texans Women in the Republic of Texas could neither serve on juries nor vote, but unmarried women retained many of the rights that they had enjoyed under Spanish law, which included control over their property. Married women retained some Spanish law benefits because, unlike Anglo-Saxon law, Texas marriage did not join the married couple into one legal person with the husband as the head. Texas married women could own inherited property, share ownership in community property, and make a legal will. However, the husband had control of all the property, both separate and community (including earned income), and an employer could not hire a wife without her husband's consent.[6]

Divorce laws were restrictive on both parties, but a husband could win a divorce for the wife's "amorous or lascivious conduct with other men, even short of adultery," or if she had committed adultery only once. He could not gain a divorce for concealed premarital fornication. On the other hand, a wife could gain a divorce only if "the husband had lived in adultery with another woman." Physical violence was not grounds for divorce unless the wife could prove a "serious danger" that might happen again. In practice, physical abuse was tolerated if the wife behaved "indiscreetly" or had "provoked" her husband. Minority and poor wives had little legal protection from beatings because the woman's "station in life" and "standing in society" were also legal considerations.[7]

Governor Jim Ferguson unwittingly aided the Women's Suffrage movement during the World War I period. Led by Minnie Fisher Cunningham, Texas suffragists organized, spoke out, marched, and lobbied for the right to vote during the Ferguson years but were unable to gain political traction because of Ferguson's opposition. When he became embroiled in political controversy over funding for the University of Texas, women joined in the groundswell of opposition. Suffragists effectively lobbied state legislators "through the back door" and organized rallies advocating Ferguson's impeachment.[8]

---

[6]Elizabeth York Enstam, "Women and the Law," *Handbook of Texas Online*, www.tshaonline.org.
[7]Ibid.
[8]Women of the West Museum, "Western Women's Suffrage—Texas," http://theautry.org/research/women-of-the-west.

Texas women continued to actively participate in the political arena although they lacked the right to vote. They supported William P. Hobby for governor as "The Man Whom Good Women Want." Hobby was considered receptive to women's suffrage. The tactic was ultimately successful and women, with some delays, won the legislative battle and gained the right to vote in the 1918 Texas primary.[9]

Did You Know? Women and Latinos were excluded from Texas juries until 1954.

National suffrage momentum precipitated a proposed constitutional amendment establishing the right of women to vote throughout the United States. Having endured more than five years of "heavy artillery" from Cunningham and the Texas Equal Suffrage Association, legislative opposition crumbled, and Texas became one of the first southern states to ratify the Nineteenth Amendment. Texas women received full voting rights in 1920.[10]

Women were given the right to serve on juries in 1954. Texas's voter ratification of the Equal Rights Amendment in 1972 and the passage of a series of laws titled the Marital Property Act amounted to major steps toward women's equality and heralded the beginning of a more enlightened era in Texas. The Act granted married women equal rights in insurance, banking, real estate, contracts, divorce, child custody, and property rights. This was the first such comprehensive family law in the United States.[11]

Until 1973, abortion in Texas was illegal, as it was in many states. In that year, Texas attorney Sarah Weddington argued a case before the U.S. Supreme Court that still stands at the center of national debate—*Roe* v. *Wade*. The *Roe* decision overturned Texas statutes that criminalized abortions and in doing so established a limited, national right of privacy for women to terminate a pregnancy. *Roe* followed *Griswold* v. *Connecticut*, a 1965 privacy case that overturned a state law criminalizing the use of birth control.[12]

Since that time, the Texas legislature has, once again, imposed new limits on abortions. Texas law now requires that women must undergo a sonogram, have the fetal image described to her, and wait 24 hours before having an abortion. Abortion clinics must meet the standards of hospital surgical centers; abortion doctors must have admitting privileges at hospitals within 30 miles; and women may not have abortions after 20 weeks of pregnancy. Some of these restrictions are being challenged as unconstitutional.

African Texans Africans from other areas of the United States were brought to Texas as slaves and served in that capacity until the end of the Civil War. They first learned of their freedom on June 19, 1865. During Reconstruction, African Texans both voted and served in numerous political positions, but the end of Reconstruction and Anglo-Texan opposition effectively ended African Texans' political participation.

Civil rights were an increasingly elusive concept for racial minorities following Reconstruction. African Texans were legally denied the right to vote in the Democratic **white primary**, the practice of excluding blacks from primary elections in the Texas Democratic Party. Schools and public facilities such as theaters, restaurants, beaches, and hospitals were legally segregated by race. Segregation laws were enforced by official law enforcement agents as well as by Anglo-Texan cultural norms and unofficial organizations using terror tactics. Although segregation laws were not usually directed at Latinos, who were legally white, such laws were effectively enforced against them as well. The white supremacist organization known as the **Ku Klux Klan (KKK)**,

White primary
The practice of excluding African Americans from primary elections in the Texas Democratic Party.

Ku Klux Klan (KKK)
A white supremacist organization.

[9]Ibid.
[10]Ibid.
[11]Enstam, "Women and the Law."
[12]*Roe* v. *Wade*, 410 U.S. 558 (1973); *Griswold* v. *Connecticut*, 381 U.S. 479 (1965); Sarah Weddington, "*Roe* v. *Wade*," *Handbook of Texas Online*, www.tshaonline.org/handbook/online/articles/jrr02.

local law officers, and the Texas Rangers actively participated in violence and intimidation of both Latinos and African Texans to keep them "in their segregated place." Lynching was also used against both groups, often after torture.[13]

The KKK was first organized in the late 1860s to intimidate freed African slaves. A modified, enlarged version was reborn in the 1920s with a somewhat-altered mission. The new Klan saw itself as a patriotic, Christian, fraternal organization for native-born white Protestants. Its members perceived a general moral decline in society, precipitated by "modern" young people, and a basic threat to the Protestant white Christian "race." Klansmen sensed a threat to their values from African Texans, Jews, Catholics, Latinos, German Texans, and other "foreigners." Acting on its paranoia, the 1920s Klan set out to force society to comply with its version of fundamentalist Christian morality. It used intimidation, violence, and torture that included hanging, tarring and feathering, branding, beating, and castration as means of coercion. As many as 80,000 Texans may have joined the "invisible empire" in an effort to make the world more to their liking. Many elected officials—U.S. and state legislators as well as county and city officials—were either avowed Klansmen or friendly neutrals. In fact, the Klan influenced Texas society to such an extent that its power was a major political issue from 1921 through 1925.[14]

In response to this racially charged atmosphere, a number of organizations committed to civil rights were founded or grew larger during the 1920s. These included the National Association for the Advancement of Colored People (NAACP), established in 1909, and the League of United Latin American Citizens (LULAC), which was formed in Corpus Christi in 1929.

When Dr. L. H. Nixon, an African Texan from El Paso, was denied the right to vote in the Democratic primary, the NAACP instituted legal action and the U.S. Supreme Court found in *Nixon* v. *Herndon* (1927) that the Texas White Primary law was unconstitutional. However, the Texas legislature transferred control of the primary from the state to the executive committee of the Texas Democratic Party and the discrimination continued. Dr. Nixon again sought justice in the courts, and in 1931 the U.S. Supreme Court ruled the new scheme was also unconstitutional. Texas Democrats then completely excluded African Texans from party membership. In *Grovey* v. *Townsend* (1935), the U.S. Supreme Court upheld this ploy, and the Texas Democratic primary remained an all-white organization. Although it had suffered a temporary setback in the episode, the NAACP had proven its potential as a viable instrument for African Texans to achieve justice.[15]

The Texas branch of the NAACP remained active during the World War II period and served as a useful vehicle for numerous legal actions to protect African-Texan civil rights. African Texans eventually won the right to participate in the Texas Democratic primary when the U.S. Supreme Court ruled in *Smith* v. *Allwright* (1944) that primaries were a part of the election process and that racial discrimination in the electoral process is unconstitutional. Twenty years later, the first African Texans since Reconstruction were elected to the Texas legislature.

World War II veteran Heman Sweatt applied for admission to The University of Texas Law School, which by Texas law was segregated. State laws requiring segregation were constitutional as long as facilities serving blacks and whites were equal. Because Texas had no law school for African Texans, the legislature hurriedly established a law school for Sweatt and, for his convenience, located it in his hometown of Houston. Although officially established,

---

[13]Texas State Historical Association, *Handbook of Texas Online*, www.tshaonline.org/handbook/online.
[14]Christopher Long, "KU KLUX KLAN," *Handbook of Texas Online*, published by the Texas State Historical Association at www.tshaonline.org/handbook/online/articles/vek02.
[15]*Seymour* v. *Connor, Texas: A History* (New York: Thomas Y. Crowell, 1971), pp. 378–379.

the new law school unfortunately lacked both faculty and a library and, as a result, the NAACP again sued the state. The U.S. Supreme Court ruled that Sweatt's new law school indeed was not equal to The University of Texas Law School and ordered him admitted to that institution. It is worth noting that "separate-but-equal" facilities remained legal after this case because the court did not overturn *Plessy* v. *Ferguson*, which granted the constitutional sanction for legal segregation. Instead, the court simply ruled that the new law school was not equal to The University of Texas.[16] The U. S. Supreme Court did not finally outlaw segregation until the *Brown* v. *Board of Education* decision in 1954.

Heman Sweatt successfully integrated Texas public law schools after the U.S. Supreme Court began to chip away at the "separate-but-equal" doctrine in the landmark case Sweatt v. Painter, *339 U.S. 629 (1950).*

The political and social fallout from the U.S. Supreme Court's *Brown* v. *Board of Education* (1954) public school desegregation decision did not bypass Texas.[17] When the Mansfield school district, just southeast of Fort Worth, was ordered to integrate in 1956, angry whites surrounded the school and prevented the enrollment of three African-Texan children. Governor Allan Shivers declared the demonstration an "orderly protest" and sent the Texas Rangers to support the protestors. Because the Eisenhower administration took no action, the school remained segregated. The Mansfield school desegregation incident "was the first example of failure to enforce a federal court order for the desegregation of a public school." Only in 1965, when facing a loss of federal funding, did the Mansfield ISD desegregate.[18]

 The Fourteenth Amendment to the U.S. Constitution says that no state shall deny any person the equal protection of the law. Why did the Supreme Court hold that state laws requiring racial segregation violate this provision?

Federal District Judge William Wayne Justice in *United States* v. *Texas* (1970) ordered the complete desegregation of all Texas public schools. The decision was one of the most extensive desegregation orders in history and included the process for executing the order in detail. The U.S. Fifth Circuit Court of Appeals largely affirmed Justice's decision but refused to extend its provisions to Latino children.[19]

The 1960s is known for the victories of the national civil rights movement. Texan James Farmer was cofounder of the Congress of Racial Equality (CORE) and, along with Dr. Martin Luther King Jr., Whitney Young, and Roy Wilkins, was one of the "Big Four" African Americans who shaped the civil rights struggle in the 1950s and 1960s. Farmer, who followed the nonviolent principles of Mahatma Gandhi, initiated sit-ins as a means of integrating public facilities and freedom rides as a means of registering African Americans to vote. The first sit-in to protest segregated facilities in Texas was organized with CORE support by students from Wiley and Bishop Colleges. The students occupied the rotunda of the Harrison County courthouse in Marshall.[20]

Did You Know? CORE founder James Farmer was a member of the 1935 national champion debate team at Wiley College that inspired the critically renowned movie *The Great Debaters*, starring Denzel Washington.

Latino Texans Like most African Texans, Latinos were relegated to the lowest-paid jobs as either service workers or farm workers. The Raymondville Peonage cases in 1929 tested for the first time the legality of forcing vagrants or debtors to repay farmers by requiring them to work off debts and fines as labor on private farms.

[16]*Sweatt* v. *Painter*, 339 U.S. 629 (1950); *Plessy* v. *Ferguson*, 163 U.S. 537 (1892).
[17]*Brown* v. *Board of Education of Topeka*, 347 U.S. 483 (1954).
[18]George B. Green, "Mansfield School Desegregation Incident," *Handbook of Texas Online*, published by the Texas State Historical Association at www.tshaonline.org/handbook/online/articles/jcm02.
[19]Frank R. Remerer, "*United States* v. *Texas*" (1970), *Handbook of Texas Online*, accessed November 18, 2011.
[20]For more information, see http://CORE-online.org.

AP Images

Texas Southern University students stage a sit-in at a Houston supermarket lunch counter, 1950.

Why did students risk arrest in protests that focused national attention on segregation? Why do minorities use tactics other than voting to achieve their strategic goals?

The practice violated federal statutes but was commonplace in some Texas counties. The Willacy County sheriff stated in his defense that Mexicans often sought arrest to gain shelter and that "peonage was not an unknown way of life for them." The trials resulted in the arrest and conviction of several public officials and private individuals. The outcome of the trials was unpopular in the agricultural areas and contrary to the generally accepted belief that farmers should have a means of collecting debts from individual laborers.[21]

World War II Latino-Texan veterans, newly returned from fighting to make the world safe for democracy, found discrimination still existed in the homeland. A decorated veteran, Major Hector Garcia, settled in Corpus Christi and became convinced by conditions in the Latino-American community in South Texas that still another battle was yet to be fought—and in his own backyard. Garcia, a medical doctor, found farm laborers enduring inhuman living conditions; deplorable medical conditions in slums; disabled veterans starving, sick, and ignored by the Veterans Administration; and an entrenched unapologetic Anglo-Texan culture continuing public school segregation.

To begin his war, Dr. Garcia needed recruits for his "army." With other World War II veterans, Dr. Garcia organized the American G.I. Forum in a Corpus Christi elementary school classroom in March 1948. This organization spread throughout the United States and played a major role in giving Latino Americans full citizenship and civil respect.[22]

One of the incendiary sparks that ignited Latino Texans to fight for civil rights was Felix Longoria's funeral. Private Longoria was a decorated casualty of World War II whose body was returned to Three Rivers for burial in the "Mexican section" of the cemetery, which was separated from the white section by barbed wire. But an obstacle developed—the funeral home's director refused the Longoria family's request to use the chapel because "whites would not like it." Longoria's widow asked Dr. Hector Garcia for support, but the funeral director also refused his request. Dr. Garcia then sent a flurry of telegrams and letters to Texas congressmen protesting the actions of the director. Senator Lyndon B. Johnson immediately responded and arranged for Private Longoria to be buried at Arlington National Cemetery.[23]

The fight to organize into labor unions was the primary focus for much of the Latino civil activism in the 1960s and 1970s. In rural areas, large landowners controlled the political as well as the economic systems and were united in opposition to labor unions. The United Farm Workers (UFW) led a strike against melon growers and packers in Starr County in the 1960s, demanding a minimum wage and resolution of other grievances. Starr County police officers, the local judiciary, and the Texas Rangers were all accused of brutality as they arrested and prosecuted strikers for minor offenses.

On February 26, 1977, members of the Texas Farm Workers Union (TFWU), strikers, and other supporters began a march to Austin to demand a $1.25 minimum wage and other improvements for farm workers. Press coverage intensified as the marchers slowly made their way north in the summer heat. Politicians, members of the American Federation of Labor–Congress of

---

[21]Alicia A. Garza, "Raymondville Peonage Cases," *Handbook of Texas Online*, published by the Texas State Historical Association at www.tshaonline.org/handbook/online/articles/pqreq.

[22]www.justiceformypeople.org/drhector2.html.

[23]V. Carl Allsup, "Felix Longoria Affair," *Handbook of Texas Online*, published by the Texas State Historical Association at www.tshaonline.org/handbook/online/articles/vef01.

Industrial Organizations (AFL–CIO), and the Texas Council of Churches accompanied the protestors. Governor John Connally, who had refused to meet them in Austin, traveled to New Braunfels with then–House Speaker Ben Barnes and Attorney General Waggoner Carr to intercept the march and inform strikers that their efforts would have no effect. Ignoring the governor, the marchers continued to Austin and held a 6,500-person protest rally at the state capitol. The rally was broken up by Texas Rangers and other law enforcement officers. The Union took legal action against the Rangers for their part in the strike and the protest. The eventual ruling of the U.S. Supreme Court held that the laws the Rangers had been enforcing were in violation of the U.S. Constitution. The Rangers were subsequently reorganized and became a part of the Texas Department of Public Safety.[24]

One of the first successful legal challenges to segregated schools in Texas was *Delgado* v. *Bastrop ISD* (1948). The suit by Gustavo C. (Gus) Garcia charged that Minerva Delgado and other Latino children were denied the same school facilities and educational instruction available to other white races. The battle continued until segregated facilities were eventually prohibited in 1957 by the decision in *Herminca Hernandez et al.* v. *Driscoll Consolidated ISD*.[25]

Important to Latinos and, ultimately, all others facing discrimination was *Hernandez* v. *State of Texas* (1954). Pete Hernandez was convicted of murder in Edna, Jackson County, Texas, by an all-Anglo jury. Latino attorneys Gustavo "Gus" Garcia, Carlos Cadena, John Herrera, and James DeAnda challenged the conviction, arguing that the systematic exclusion of Latinos from jury duty in Texas violated Hernandez's rights to equal protection of the law guaranteed by the Fourteenth Amendment of the U.S. Constitution. Texas courts had historically ruled that Latinos were white, so excluding them from all-Anglo (white) juries could not be legal discrimination. To change the system, the Latino team of lawyers would have to change the interpretation of the U.S. Constitution. The stakes were high. If they failed, Latino discrimination throughout the southwestern United States could legally continue for decades. Garcia argued before the U.S. Supreme Court that Latinos, although white, were "a class apart" and suffered discrimination on the basis of their "class." The U.S. Supreme Court agreed, overturned the Texas courts, and ruled that Latinos were protected by the Constitution from discrimination by other whites. The Hernandez decision established the precedent of Constitutional protection by class throughout the United States and was a forerunner for future decisions prohibiting discrimination by gender, disability, or sexual preference.[26]

Library of Congress Prints and Photographs Division|LC-USZ32-137627|

Gus Garcia, legal advisor for the American G.I. Forum, is shown during a visit to the White House. Garcia was the lead attorney in the U.S. Supreme Court decision Hernandez v. Texas, 347 U.S. 475 (1954).

 Why is it unconstitutional to deny a person the right to serve on a jury because of ethnicity?

Gay, Lesbian, and Transgendered Texans
Discrimination against gay, lesbian, and transgendered Texans has long been considered a God-given right by some Texas heterosexuals. Neither workplace, school, nor church has provided sanctuary from prejudice for gay, lesbian, and transgendered Texans. Furthermore, state law has criminalized certain intimate sexual conduct by two persons of the same gender.

A Harris County sheriff's deputy discovered two men having intimate sexual conduct in a private residence, and the men were arrested and convicted for violating a Texas anti-sodomy statute. Their conviction was appealed and eventually reached the U.S. Supreme court in the case *Lawrence* v. *Texas*. In Justice Kennedy's opinion for the court, he stated that the Texas law violated the due process clause of the Fourteenth Amendment, which does not protect sodomy but does protect personal relationships. The Texas statute intended to control the most intimate of all human activity, sexual behavior, in the most private of places, the home.

[24]See Robert E. Hall, "Pickets, Politics and Power: The Farm Worker Strike in Starr County," *Texas Bar Journal*, Volume 70, number 5, 2007.

[25]V. Carl Allstrop, "*Delgado* v. *Bastrop ISD*," *Handbook of Texas Online*, published by the Texas State Historical Association at www.tshaonline.org/handbook/online/articles/jrd01.

[26]V. Carl Allstrop, "*Hernandez* v. *State of Texas*," 347 U.S. 475 (1954), *Handbook of Texas Online*, published by the Texas State Historical Association.

Citizens of Texas are able to legally have personal relationships without fear of punishment or criminal classification. The decision also invalidated sodomy laws in thirteen other states, thereby protecting same-sex behavior in every state and territory in the United States.[27]

The right to marry is the current frontline of the gay, lesbian, and transgendered battle for equal rights. The Defense of Marriage Act (DOMA) complicated the battle. DOMA defined marriage as a legal union between a man and a woman and further stipulated that the federal government would not recognize same-sex marriages for purposes of benefits such as social security, veterans' benefits, and income tax filings.[28] In 2013, the U.S. Supreme Court decided the case *United States* v. *Windsor* in which it held that federal discrimination against same-sex couples violates the Fourteenth Amendment of the U.S. Constitution, but it did not rule state bans on same-sex marriages unconstitutional.

However, state and federal courts in serveral states used the Supreme Court's reasoning to rule that state laws against same-sex marriage are unconstitutionally discriminatory. It remains to be seen whether higher courts will agree that all state bans on such marriages—including the one in Texas—are unconstitutional.

Texans, by the overwhelming majority of 76 percent, added an amendment to the Texas Constitution in 2005 banning both gay and lesbian marriage and civil unions. The amendment also prohibits hospital visitation rights, community property rights, and survivors' benefits for gay and lesbian couples. The authority to make medical decisions for an incapacitated loved one is also prohibited. The couple also faces discrimination in employment, housing, and public accommodations, and gay or lesbian children often lack protection in the state's schools.

Table 1.2 summarizes Texas practices that the U.S. Supreme Court has ruled violate the U.S. Constitution.

TABLE 1.2 Key U.S. Supreme Court Decisions Protecting Texans' Rights to Equality and Privacy

Unconstitutional Texas Practice	U.S. Constitutional Violation	Landmark Supreme Court Case
Texas laws permitting the Democratic Party to conduct whites-only primaries. Also used in other Southern states.	No state shall deny any person the right to vote on account of race—Fifteenth Amendment.	*Smith* v. *Allwright* (1944)
Texas law requiring racially segregated law schools. Professional schools were segregated throughout the South.	No state shall deny any person the equal protection of the law—Fourteenth Amendment.	*Sweatt* v. *Painter* (1950)
Texas practice of denying Latinos the right to serve on juries.	No state shall deny any person the equal protection of the law—Fourteenth Amendment.	*Hernandez* v. *State of Texas* (1954)
State laws mandating statewide segregation of public schools and most facilities open to the public. Texas was among the 17 mostly Southern states with statewide laws requiring segregation at the time of the decision.	No state shall deny any person the equal protection of the law—Fourteenth Amendment.	*Brown* v. *Board of Education of Topeka* (1954)
Texas law making abortion illegal; 30 states outlawed abortions for any reason in 1973.	No state shall deny liberty without due process of law—Fourteenth Amendment.	*Roe* v. *Wade* (1973)
Texas law making homosexual conduct a crime; 14 mostly Southern states made homosexual conduct a crime at the time of the decision.	No state shall deny liberty without due process of law—Fourteenth Amendment.	*Lawrence* v. *Texas* (2003)

This table shows the important U.S. constitutional decisions that have expanded minority rights in Texas and nationwide.

▲ **How has Texas's Southern conservative political culture resisted social change? Why have ethnic and sexual minorities sought remedy for discrimination in the U.S. Supreme Court, an institution outside the control of state politics?**

---

[27]*Lawrence* v. *Texas* (539 US 558 (2003).
[28]Defense of Marriage Act, enacted September 21, 1996.

Cultural Diversity Today

Demographics are population characteristics, such as age, gender, ethnicity, employment, and income, that social scientists use to describe groups in society, and in Texas these characteristics are rapidly changing. Texas is one of the fastest-growing states in the nation. No longer predominantly rural and agrarian, Texas is becoming more culturally diverse as immigrants from other nations and migrants from other states continue to find it a desirable place to call home. The 2010 Census showed a significant trend toward greater ethnic diversity. Figure 1.3 shows that the growing diversity of Texas's population is projected to continue, and Texans now have the opportunity to continue to build on their already-rich cultural pluralism. Increasing diversity could also have a significant impact on Texas's politics and culture.

Voter participation in Texas is historically low, often ranking toward the bottom among the states in voter turnout. Social scientists argue that this is attributable to political conditioning as well as social and economic reality. Latino participation is low even by Texas standards, but because Latinos are predicted to become the largest plurality in Texas by 2015, there could be significant political impact if this sleeping political giant arises.

Equally important, changes in the ethnic makeup of the state's population will present decision makers with enormous challenges. Figure 1.4 shows that income inequality parallels ethnic divisions in Texas. Poverty rates are higher and overall incomes are lower among African Texans and Latinos. Lower incomes are associated with limited educational opportunity, lack of health insurance, and lower rates of participation in the state's civic life. Poverty drives up the cost of state social services and is a factor that contributes to crime, family breakups, and illegitimate births even as it drives up the cost of social services. How Texas deals with changes in the state's demographics is likely to be the focus of political controversy for years to come.

Demographics
Population characteristics, such as age, gender, ethnicity, employment, and income, that social scientists use to describe groups in society.

APPLYING WHAT YOU HAVE LEARNED ABOUT TEXAS POLITICAL CULTURE

LO 1.4   Apply what you have learned about Texas political culture.

The following essay will give you the opportunity to examine the clash of political cultures that grew out of the civil rights movements and Texas reaction to it. You will see how different political regions in Texas reacted to the struggle for equality. You will see that East Texas, dominated by a traditionalistic subculture inherited from the Old South, resisted much more intensely than

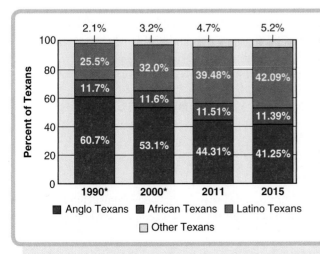

Figure 1.3

Texas Ethnic Populations, Past and Present: 1990–2015

This figure shows the changing demographics of Texans.

Source: Adapted from "Projections of Texas and Counties in Texas by Age, Sex and Race/Ethnicity for 1990, 2000, 2011, and 2015," Texas State Data Center, Office of the State Demographer; and Census Bureau, Census 2000 and 2010.

 What implications do Texans' changing ethnic makeup have for the state's political future?

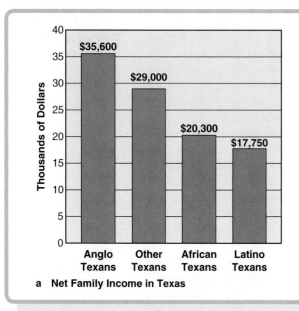

a   **Net Family Income in Texas**

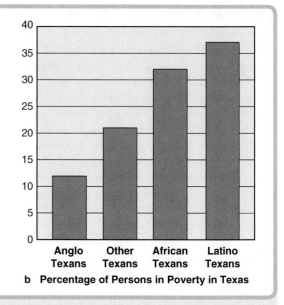

b   **Percentage of Persons in Poverty in Texas**

Figure 1.4
Ethnicity, Income, and Poverty in Texas

Today, inequality among ethnic groups is no longer so much reflected by overt official legal discrimination as by unequal wealth, income, and access to health care.

Source: The Henry J. Kaiser Family Foundation, "State Health Facts Online," www.statehealthfacts.kff.org.

 Why do ethnic minorities earn less that Anglo Texans? How do income inequality and increasing ethnic diversity challenge policy makers in Texas?

other regions of the state that are more influenced by the individualistic subculture. You will see the elements of the traditionalistic subculture that conflicted with the rising influence of minority cultures in Texas in the past, and you can draw parallels with politics in modern Texas.

After you have read the essay, you will be asked a series of questions that will require you to employ critical-thinking skills to apply what you have learned in this chapter to the new information in this essay. Your analysis will require you to make an ethical judgment about the potential conflict between individual freedom and social equality for cultural minorities. You will be asked to reflect on the racial and political motivations of those who today seek to limit the political influence of cultural minorities through gerrymandering and those who seek to limit ballot access to the same groups through strict enforcement of voter identification laws.

Politicians, Vigilantes and the Quest for Civil Rights in Texas

by Denese McArthur
Tarrant County Community College District

Two years after the U.S. Supreme Court declared that public schools must end the practice of segregation,[29] Governor Allan Shivers summoned the Texas Rangers to Mansfield, a town

---

[29]*Brown* v. *Board of Education*, 347 U.S. 483 (1954).

seventeen miles southeast of Fort Worth. Although over 100 other districts in the state had quietly and peacefully desegregated prior to the start of the school year, Mansfield stood its ground, even after a federal court had ordered the town to comply with the law. Three- to four-hundred white men and women stood watch at Mansfield High, defiant against the three black teenagers who were to be the first enrolled in the previously all-white school. In town, businesses closed as a sign of solidarity with those who were protesting desegregation. Citizens blocked the roads into town to prevent the entry of anyone who might support school integration. The three black children were burned in effigy. The arrival of the Texas Rangers ended the crisis, because the Rangers had been sent to ensure that the practice of segregation remained intact. This outcome emboldened other districts in the South to refuse integration as well. The following year (after his re-election was secured) President Eisenhower intervened in another school integration case, when he ordered the National Guard to enforce desegregation in Little Rock, Arkansas.[30]

Texas's traditionalist and individualist political culture has strongly influenced its historical resistance to civil rights movements. From its roots as a Southern, slave-holding state, Texas developed a strong sense of continuity and appreciation of the status quo. The belief that social, political, and economic hierarchies exist because the people at the top are inherently more deserving than those below encouraged an almost unwavering sense of respect for authority and status while at the same time discouraging efforts to increase access to the system for "outsiders." Thus, African Americans, Latino Americans, and other groups have faced many obstacles in their quest for equality. While much of the oppression of Latinos in the state was centered in the South Texas region discrimination against blacks was significantly more prevalent in the eastern part of the state. By the mid-1950s, Mexican-American groups such as the League of United Latin American Citizens (LULAC) and the American G.I. Forum were at the forefront of legal efforts to end discrimination against Hispanics in education and in the electoral system. At the same time, the National Association for the Advancement of Colored People (NAACP) was beginning to achieve success in their attacks on the legal front, as well.

In the immediate aftermath of the *Brown* decision, many southern states struggled to develop an effective response. Their strategies depended largely upon how well prepared each was to resist the high court's decree. Unlike most of the other states of the "old Confederacy,"[31] Texas (along with North Carolina and Tennessee) hesitantly agreed, in principle, to accept the legitimacy of the Supreme Court's ruling. In reality, sentiments varied across Texas; the western areas were much more willing to desegregate while the east remained defiant. Across the south, however, a movement arose to counter the push for civil rights and racial equality under the law. Called "Massive Resistance," this movement was largely responsible for the slow pace of public integration, and also a significant factor in the organized and institutionalized racism that remained prevalent across the region.[32]

Originally developed in Virginia, the rationale behind "massive resistance" was to incorporate multiple simultaneous tactics for countering the federal government's efforts at desegregation and the larger civil rights movement in general. While Texas joined the other southern states in carrying out many of the practices of the massive resistance movement, with half of

[30]George N. Green, "MANSFIELD SCHOOL DESEGREGATION INCIDENT," *Handbook of Texas Online*, www.tshaonline.org/handbook/online/articles/jcm02, accessed March 16, 2014, uploaded on June 15, 2010, published by the Texas State Historical Association.

[31]The term is typically used to refer to Alabama, Arkansas, Florida, Georgia, Louisiana, Mississippi, North Carolina, South Carolina, Tennessee, Texas, and Virginia.

[32]Davison M. Douglas, "The Rhetoric of Moderation: Desegregating the South During the Decade After Brown" (1994). *Faculty Publications,* Paper 116, at http://scholarship.law.wm.edu/facpubs/116.

the state's congressmen signing the Southern Manifesto (a document that harshly criticized the Supreme Court's decision making in the *Brown* case) and with the creation of Citizen's Councils (quasi-official groups that were created to help organize "respectable" whites in the fight against segregation), the most pervasive aspects of Texans' involvement was through physical intimidation. The initial lack of an organized political and legal response across the south led to the development of grassroots movements that sought to maintain the status quo through the spread of violence and fear. Groups like the Ku Klux Klan grew steadily in size and strength, its members emboldened in many places by the inability or unwillingness of local law enforcement to protect the lives and property of minorities. Although violence against minorities was carried out across the state, the majority of the most egregious cases were found in East Texas.

Several scholars have offered theories about why most of Texas remained comparatively moderate. The general consensus is that local political considerations across the South had a strong effect on the attitudes of candidates running for office. The activism of segregationist groups eventually had an impact on electoral campaigns. Under normal circumstances in a two-party system, we can expect candidates to develop positions on issues that mimic to a significant degree those of the likely voters. The extent of the grassroots movement against desegregation and civil rights across the South, therefore, encouraged a large number of candidates to compete to be seen as the most conservative, most anti-integrationist option on the ballot.[33]

By the mid-1960s, resistance to the civil rights movement was waning in many parts of Texas, though it did not completely vanish. After the U.S. Congress passed the Voting Rights Act of 1965, the writing was on the wall for segregationists. Realizing that their ability to prevent racial minorities from voting was severely diminished, new strategies had to be developed. Redistricting (and racial gerrymandering) became a popular tool for diluting the impact of the emerging minority vote.[34] Because it was expected that African Americans and Latinos would vote for candidates that supported the civil rights movement, it was simple to claim that the motivation was political and not racial.[35]

Soon, the federal courts would begin reviewing and ultimately rejecting the redrawn district maps in states that had a history of discrimination. The line between racial and political gerrymandering became even more blurred. For those who wanted to hold on as long as possible to a segregated past, a new strategy and a new vocabulary were adopted. They folded themselves into the conservative movement that was growing across the country and rebranded themselves as proponents of "individual freedom." Taking up this banner has allowed them to continue their struggle against equality for all races, with the claim that since the government cannot "legislate what is in people's hearts" it should not try to force them to behave counter to those beliefs. Reflections of this position can be seen in many of the current debates over discrimination against other groups in today's American society (like those concerning gay marriage, birth control, for example). The Constitution protects our right to our beliefs, but does not protect all actions based on those beliefs, particularly if those actions harm others. It is up to our government and ultimately to us to decide whether this remains a fundamental principle of American society.

---

[33]Similar behaviors can be seen whenever an active voting bloc emerges on the political scene. The modern tea party movement is a good example. The dramatic shakeup of the Republican Party is a direct reflection of the activism of the most politically conservative voters.

[34]George Lewis, *Massive Resistance: The White Response to the Civil Rights Movement* (Oxford University Press, 2006), p. 172.

[35]Several states across America have recently enacted "Voter I.D." laws, which have the effect of limiting access to the polls for those people who have limited resources and transportation access (typically college students, the elderly, and people living in urban areas, all of whom tend to vote for the Democratic Party).

JOIN THE DEBATE

 Does the concept of "individual liberty" necessarily contradict political and social equality for ethnic minorities? Can government prohibit racial discrimination without limiting the freedom of racists to act on their personal beliefs? Explain the similar dilemma that protecting same-sex partnerships and women's rights to abortion and contraception can conflict with some traditional religious beliefs.

 How do we know whether political maneuvers such as gerrymandering and voter ID laws are racially motivated or based solely on political machinations? Can you devise a way to test for this? How do these political efforts reflect a traditionalistic political culture?

CHAPTER SUMMARY

LO 1.1 Analyze the relationships among Texas political culture, its politics, and its public policies. A political culture reflects the political values and beliefs of people. It explains how people feel about their government—their expectations of what powers it should have over their lives and what services it should provide. Texans' predominantly conservative political culture is reflected in voters' Republican affiliation and in the state's conservative public policies. Republicans control state political institutions and have enacted low tax and spending policies and conservative policies on social issues such as gun rights, abortion, same-sex marriage, and capital punishment.

LO 1.2 Differentiate among the various types of state political cultures and the attributes that describe the major Texas regions. Various areas of Texas display varying degrees of traditionalistic, individualistic, and moralistic traditions. In the traditionalistic culture, government is seen as having an active role to maintain dominant social and religious values. Social and religious values are important to the more traditionalistic Texans, who are today focusing on same-sex issues and abortion.

The individualistic culture views government as a practical institution that should further private enterprise, but should intervene minimally in people's lives. Today, individualistic Texans support low taxes and limited business regulation and oppose expansion of the federal government. People from the individualistic culture are less motivated by social and religious issues than traditionalists.

The moralistic political culture is one that views government as a positive force to better the individual and society alike. The moralistic culture encourages active civic involvement and honesty in government. Although it arose out of puritanical religious traditions, the moralistic tradition is largely secular in character today. The moralistic tradition dominates no particular region of Texas, but many recent migrants from Northern states to Texas suburbs and cities exhibit moralistic values in their approach to politics.

Texas can be divided into a series of cultural regions with differing characteristics and traditions: (1) East Texas, (2) the Gulf Coast, (3) South Texas, (4) Far West Texas, (5) the German Hill Country, (6) West Texas, (7) the Panhandle, (8) North Texas, and (9) Central Texas. Each region is characterized by

distinctive historical, ethnic, and economic influences, and each looks to the major cities as their media, cultural, and financial centers.

These regions display varying combinations of moral, traditionalistic, and individualistic cultures. A traditionalistic culture is most evident in the East, South, and Far West Texas regions. Many East Texans' political attitudes descended from the settlers who migrated from the plantation societies of the Old South. The traditionalism in South and Far West Texas may have been inherited from the patròn system that once dominated the Border areas with Mexico. Although many residents of other regions may have traditionalistic values, individualism is prevalent in most of the rest of the state.

LO 1.3 Analyze Texans' political struggles over equal rights and evaluate their success in Texas politics today and in their impact on the state's political future. Texas social conservatism inherited from the Old South traditionalistic culture has resulted in resistance to cultural minorities' demands for social and political equality. In several instances, cultural minorities have succeeded in their struggles for equality by appealing to the federal courts outside of the political control of Texas institutions.

Women were not legally equal to men in early Texas, and their path to equality has been a winding and occasionally hesitant one. Activists finally won the long battle for the right to vote in 1918. It was not until 1972, however, that women won equal rights in real estate, contracts, divorce, child custody, and property rights. The judicial decision in *Roe* v. *Wade* that further clarified the right of women to control their reproductive functions is still at the center of a national controversy.

African Texans' struggle for legal equality reflected similar struggles being simultaneously waged in other Southern states. The battle to vote in the Democratic primary and the right for admission to public accommodations and public schools were settled only by national courts or congressional intervention.

The Latino struggle in Texas was similar to that of African Texans and was resolved only by national action. Several Latino rights organizations were founded in Texas, and the judicial decision in *Hernandez* v. *Texas* (1954) that established the constitutional concept of a "class apart" became important throughout the United States. The right to form labor unions occupied much of the Latino movement in the 1960s and 1970s.

Gays, lesbians, and transgendered Texans are now waging similar battles for legal equality. *Lawrence* v. *Texas* (1973) gained national significance by decriminalizing sexual activity between consenting persons of the same gender.

Projections of population growth and immigration predict a shift in Texas's population away from an Anglo-Texan plurality to a Latino-Texan plurality. Increased political clout can come with increased population, and Latino Texans could begin to challenge the political and economic dominance of Anglo Texans.

Regardless of the political outcome of population shifts, Texas is becoming more culturally diverse and now has an opportunity to build on its already rich cultural pluralism.

LO 1.4   Apply what you have learned about Texas political culture. You applied the concept of Texas traditionalistic culture to the clash of cultures that emerged when ethnic minorities began their struggles for social and political equality. You examined how the traditionalistic subculture is still apparent in today's struggles between social groups. You weighed the balance between personal freedom to discriminate against society's need for fair and equal treatment for its members.

KEY TERMS

bicultural, *p. 10*
conservative, *p. 2*
Creole, *p. 10*
demographics, *p. 21*
individualistic culture, *p. 7*

Ku Klux Klan (KKK), *p. 15*
liberal, *p. 3*
Maquiladora, *p. 11*
mestizo, *p. 10*
Metroplex, *p. 13*

moralistic culture, *p. 7*
North American Free Trade Agreement (NAFTA), *p. 11*
political culture, *p. 2*
ranchero culture, *p. 10*

The Valley, *p. 10*
traditionalistic culture, *p. 7*
white primary, *p. 15*

REVIEW QUESTIONS

LO 1.1 Analyze the relationships among Texas political culture, its politics, and its public policies.

- Describe the policy differences between Texas conservative and liberal ideologies.

- Specifically show how Texans' conservatism is reflected in the state's partisanship, public opinion, and public policies.

LO 1.2 Differentiate among the various types of state political cultures and the attributes that describe the major Texas regions.

- Describe the general cultural characteristics of Texas's regions. Does the description fit your home area?

- Describe *moralistic, traditionalistic*, and *individualistic* cultures. Explain the how the historical development of these regions influenced which of these subcultures came to dominate each region of the state.

- Briefly describe each of the state's major cultural regions. How do they differ historically, economically, and ethnically?

LO 1.3 Analyze Texans' political struggles over equal rights and evaluate their success in Texas politics today and in their impact on the state's political future.

- Describe the major developments in the struggle of Texas women, African Texans, Latinos, gays, lesbians, and transgendered persons to achieve social and political equality. What cultural factors explain the resistance to the social change that their struggles brought about?

- How will Texas's population growth and its changing demographics affect the state's political landscape? What challenges does a more diverse population present for policy makers?

GET ACTIVE

Get involved and learn about your own culture. Talk to grandparents, parents, uncles, and aunts to learn what they know about your culture and family history. Record as much oral history as you can about their personal lives, experiences, and political recollections as well as family myths and traditions. You may find this information priceless as you talk to your own children and grandchildren about their culture.

Research the background and richness of your family culture. Here are a few reliable sources:

- Institute of Texan Cultures: **www.texancultures.com**
- Texas State Library and Archives Commission: **www.tsl.state.tx.us**
- Texas State Historical Association and Center for Studies in Texas History: **www.tshaonline.org**

The *Handbook of Texas Online* is a great source for information on Texas history, culture, and geography. A project of the Texas State Historical Association, it is an encyclopedia of all things Texan at **www.tshaonline.org**. Use it to sketch the historical changes in the status of one or more of the ethnic or gender groups discussed in the civil rights section in this chapter. Then search census data at **www.census.gov** to evaluate their income, education, and quality of life in today's Texas.

Show how Texas has a conservative political culture. Select examples of Texas rankings on public policy and quality-of-life issues to show Texas is conservative. Use *Texas on the Brink,* a report by the liberal-leaning Texas Legislative Study Group that focuses on where the state of Texas stands compared to other states in the United States at **https://leafmedium-live.s3.amazonaws.com/blog/texaslsg/TexasOnTheBrink2013.pdf**.

Broaden your cultural and political experiences. Sample ethnic, religious, and ideological groups that are different from your own to get a perspective on the rich diversity of modern Texas political life at representative websites. Engage conservative political views at the Right Side of Austin website **http://therightsideofaustin.wordpress.com** and liberal political perspectives at the *Texas Observer* website **www.texasobserver.org**. Check out a major Latino organization, the Texas League of United Latin American Citizens at **www.txlulac.org** and a major African Texan site, Texas's National Association of Colored People, at **www.texasnaacp.org**.

Explore gender sites such as the Texas chapter of the National Organization for Women at **www.nowtexas.org**; the Texas Eagle Forum at **www.texaseagle.org**; and a gay, lesbian, bisexual, and transgender group's website at **www.equalitytexas.org**.

 How much respect do you owe people whose political or cultural identity differs from your own? Evaluate use of labels that these groups might find offensive. How does "political correctness" affect your personal behavior?

CHAPTER 2

Texas in the Federal System

LEARNING OBJECTIVES

LO 2.1 Differentiate among unitary, confederal, and federal systems of government.

LO 2.2 Distinguish among the types of powers in our federal system, and explain dual and cooperative federalism within the context of the evolution of federalism in the United States.

LO 2.3 Analyze Texas's relationship with the federal government and the prominent role the state has played in the national debate over coercive federalism.

LO 2.4 Apply what you have learned about Texas in the federal system.

*T*he relationship between the Texas state government and the U.S. federal government has been tense in recent years. The members of the Texas state executive branch, including the governor, lieutenant governor, and attorney general, have increasingly viewed the federal government as encroaching on the state's sovereignty, while the federal government, especially under President Barack Obama, has attempted to enforce new laws, rules, and regulations in the state. From health-care reform to voting rights, to environmental policy, Texas and the federal government have disagreed on the proper role of each in the creation, enactment, and enforcement of public policy. Tension between the federal government and the states is nothing new and has constantly redefined our concepts of federalism. Today's conflicts between the two levels of government may once again change our understanding of the federal system.

We begin by defining federalism and discussing how the concept has evolved over time in the United States. We then turn our attention to Texas and how federalism specifically affects the state's policies, politics, and society.

WHAT IS FEDERALISM?

LO 2.1　Differentiate among unitary, confederal, and federal systems of government.

Governmental systems are often classified into three basic types based on the degree of centralization present in their constitutions—unitary, confederal, and federal. The United States was the first country in the world to employ a federal system of government.

Unitary Systems

An overwhelming majority of the world's countries are governed by a **unitary system**, a system of government in which constitutional authority rests with a national or central government; any regional or local governments are subordinate to the central government. Unitary governments may be democratic like those in France, Japan, and Panama or nondemocratic like those in China, Cuba, and Saudi Arabia. They are all considered to be unitary governments simply because the constitution vests the power to govern the entire nation in a single central government.

Unitary governments frequently choose to create regional and local governments for administrative purposes; these regional and local governments are allowed varying latitude in the design and implementation of public policies across the world's unitary systems. However, in the end, these subnational governments remain creations of the national government and have only those powers the national government chooses to give them—powers that the national government is empowered to take away at its discretion.

Unitary system
A system of government in which constitutional authority rests with a national or central government; any regional or local governments are subordinate to the central government.

Confederal Systems

As a consequence of their negative experience with unitary rule under the British, Americans first adopted a **confederal system** of government following independence, a system that quickly proved to be unworkable. A confederal system of government is one in which member state or regional governments have all authority, and any central government has only the power that state governments choose to delegate to it. This system is also known as a confederation.

Under the Articles of Confederation drafted by the Continental Congress following independence in 1776, all power was placed in the hands of the state governments, and the central government had only the power that the states chose to give it. The best example of a modern-day confederation is the European Union (EU). In 2014 the EU contained 28 independent nation-states stretching from Ireland in the west to Romania in the east, and from Finland in the north to the Mediterranean island-state of Cyprus in the south, with a half-dozen more nations currently on the road to EU membership.

Confederal system
A system of government in which member state or regional governments have all authority, and any central government has only the power that state governments choose to delegate to it.

Federal Systems

The country's failed experiment with a confederal form of government ended with the U.S. Constitutional Convention in 1787. In that year, the Americans meeting in Philadelphia invented an entirely new form of government—a federal system. Federalism represents an attempt to combine the advantages of a unitary government (national unity and uniformity where they are necessary) with the advantages of a confederacy (local control and policy diversity from state to state where possible).

Federal states can be either democratic, as in Germany, Mexico, and the United States, or nondemocratic, as in Ethiopia, Pakistan, and Russia. The concept of federalism has flourished in many places throughout the world, especially in nations that encompass a vast territory and/or possess a large or diverse population. Today, in addition to the United States, federal systems are employed by many of the world's largest (in terms of population and/or territory) democracies, including Argentina, Australia, Brazil, Canada, Germany, India, and Mexico.

Federal system

A system of government in which governmental power is divided and shared between a national or central government and state or regional governments.

A **federal system** of government is one in which governmental power is divided and shared between a national or central government and state or regional governments. Although original definitions of federalism considered only two levels of government, the concept can easily be extended to encompass multiple levels of government. In the United States, governmental power is shared among the national government, state governments, and local governments.

THE U.S. CONSTITUTION AND FEDERALISM

LO 2.2 Distinguish among the types of powers in our federal system, and explain dual and cooperative federalism within the context of the evolution of federalism in the United States.

When the framers of the U.S. Constitution set out to revise the Articles of Confederation in 1787, they opted to give more authority to the central government. One of their critical challenges was the creation of a representative government for a large nation with a diverse population. The Founding Fathers wanted to achieve a balance between parochial interests and broader national concerns. The federal system was the solution to this challenge. James Madison wrote in *Federalist 10:*

> By enlarging too much the number of electors, you render the representatives too little acquainted with all their local circumstances and lesser interests; as by reducing it too much, you render him unduly attached to these, and too little fit to comprehend and pursue great and national objects. The federal Constitution forms a happy combination in this respect; the great and aggregate interests being referred to the national, the local and particular to the State legislatures.[1]

The federal system that James Madison and the other Founding Fathers drafted was designed to create an optimal balance between local and national interests and concerns.

Over the course of our nation's history, the shift in power has been from a form of government where the states reserved many of their powers to one where the federal government has become more dominant. For every action, there is a reaction, and this growing power of the federal government has caused an increased level of activism by citizens who believe the

---

[1]James Madison, *Federalist 10*, November 23, 1787.

pendulum of power in the country has swung too far to the federal government side. These individuals want at the minimum to avoid any further erosion of state autonomy and at the maximum to restore a greater level of power and authority to the fifty state governments. Over the past ten years, perhaps nowhere in the country has this pushback against the federal government been more visible and vocal than in Texas, where many of the state's most powerful and high profile politicians have been actively working to shift power away from the federal government and toward the states.

Types of Powers in Our Federal System

In the U.S. federal system, there are three types of powers—delegated, reserved, and concurrent. **Delegated powers** are those that the constitution gives to the national government. These include those enumerated powers found in Article I, Section 8 of the U.S. Constitution as well as a few other powers that have evolved over time. Note that there are three types of delegated powers—expressed, implied, and inherent. **Expressed powers** are those powers that are clearly listed in in Article I, Section 8 of the U.S. Constitution. **Implied powers** are those delegated powers that are assumed to exist in order for the federal government to perform the functions that are expressly delegated. These powers are granted by the necessary and proper clause in Article I, Section 8 of the U.S. Constitution. **Inherent powers** are those delegated powers that come with an office or position—generally, the executive branch. Although the U.S. Constitution does not clearly specify these powers granted to the executive branch, over time, inherent powers have evolved as powers found to be needed to perform the functions of the executive branch.

A second group of powers in the federal system is known as **reserved powers**. Reserved powers are those powers that belong to the states. The legitimacy of these powers comes from the Tenth Amendment. Finally, there are **concurrent powers**, which are those powers shared by the national government and the states. Examples of these delegated, reserved, and concurrent powers are listed in Table 2.1.

The U.S. Constitution addresses the sharing of power between the state and federal governments in various sections. Article I, Section 8, for instance, lists the enumerated powers "expressly" granted to Congress by the Constitution. Article VI, Section 2 provides the Supremacy Clause, which reads:

> This Constitution, and the Laws of the United States which shall be made in Pursuance thereof; and all Treaties made, or which shall be made, under the Authority of the United States, shall be the supreme Law of the Land; and the Judges in every State shall be bound thereby, any Thing in the Constitution or Laws of any State to the Contrary notwithstanding.[2]

In the event that conflict should arise between federal and state law, the **Supremacy Clause** states that the U.S. Constitution, as well as laws and treaties created in accordance with the U.S. Constitution, supersede state and local laws. That is, when federal law and state law are in conflict, the federal law must be followed. The **Tenth Amendment** to the U.S. Constitution also helps define the balance of power in the federal system. The Tenth Amendment is the section of the U.S. Constitution that reserves powers to the states. It reads as follows: "The powers not delegated to the United States by the Constitution, nor prohibited by it to the States, are reserved to the States respectively, or to the people." Some read the Tenth Amendment as limiting the federal government, shifting greater power to the states. The Fourteenth Amendment also affects the balance of power in the federal system. It was adopted following the Civil War and dramatically improved the protection of civil rights and equality for all Americans.

---

[2]"The Constitution of the United States," Article VI, Section 2.

Delegated powers
Those powers that the constitution gives to the national government. These include those enumerated powers found in Article I, Section 8 of the U.S. Constitution as well as a few other powers that have evolved over time.

Expressed powers
Those powers that are clearly listed in in Article I, Section 8 of the U.S. Constitution.

Implied powers
Those delegated powers that are assumed to exist in order for the federal government to perform the functions that are expressly delegated. These powers are granted by the necessary and proper clause in Article I, Section 8 of the U.S. Constitution.

Inherent powers
Those delegated powers that come with an office or position—generally the executive branch. Although the U.S. Constitution does not clearly specify powers granted to the executive branch, over time, inherent powers have evolved as part of the powers needed to perform the functions of the executive branch.

Reserved powers
Those powers that belong to the states. The legitimacy of these powers comes from the Tenth Amendment.

Concurrent powers
Those powers shared by the national government and the states.

Supremacy Clause
States that the U.S. Constitution, as well as laws and treaties created in accordance with the U.S. Constitution, supersede state and local laws.

Tenth Amendment
Section of the U.S. Constitution that reserves powers to the states. It reads as follows: "The powers not delegated to the United States by the Constitution, nor prohibited by it to the States, are reserved to the States respectively, or to the people."

TABLE 2.1 Examples of Major State and Federal Powers		
Delegated Powers—Federal Government Powers	**Reserved Powers—Exclusive to the States Government**	**Concurrent Powers—Shared by Federal and State Government**
Declare war	Conduct elections	Borrow money
Raise armies	Provide for the public health and safety	Levy taxes
Enter into treaties	Ratify constitutional amendments	Make and enforce the law
Coin money	Establish and provide for local governments	Establish courts
Regulate international and interstate commerce	State police powers	Charter banks

Among these examples of national powers, the powers to provide for the common defense and to regulate commerce have, since the 1930s, been interpreted broadly to allow the national government to expand dramatically.

▲ **Give examples of national government programs that have been justified as a regulation of interstate commerce.**

Article I, Section 8

Conflicts between the national government and states have arisen on a number of occasions, in part because of different understandings of two sections of the U.S. Constitution—Article I, Section 8 (see Table 2.2) and the Tenth Amendment. Article I, Section 8 of the U.S. Constitution enumerates the powers granted to Congress, including the power to regulate interstate commerce. It is this **"commerce clause"** in Article I that was used to justify the Patient Protection and Affordable Care Act (also known as the ACA and "Obamacare") as well as several other broad national government actions.

More important for a discussion of federalism, however, is the last clause on the list, "To make all Laws which shall be necessary and proper for carrying into Execution the foregoing Powers, and all other Powers vested by this Constitution in the Government of the United States, or in any Department or Officer thereof."[3] This is known as the **necessary and proper clause**, or the elastic clause, of the U.S. Constitution, which was given a very expansive meaning early in the nation's history.

Commerce clause

An enumerated power in Article I, Section 8 of the U.S. Constitution that gives Congress the power to regulate commerce.

Necessary and proper clause

The last clause in Article I, Section 8 of the U.S. Constitution; also known as the elastic clause, which was given a very expansive meaning early in the nation's history.

McCulloch v. *Maryland* and the Necessary and Proper Clause

In 1819, the U.S. Supreme Court expanded the power of the U.S. Congress. In *McCulloch* v. *Maryland*, the state of Maryland, in a desire to limit competition with banks chartered by the state of Maryland, attempted to tax the Second Bank of the United States, a bank created by the federal government. The head of the Baltimore Branch of the Second Bank of the United States refused to pay the tax. The state of Maryland argued that the U.S. Constitution did not give the national government the power to create a national bank, and thus the Bank of the United States was unconstitutional. Chief Justice John Marshall argued that, although it was true that the creation of a bank was not an enumerated power under Article I, Section 8, the Supremacy Clause of the Constitution, and the necessary and proper clause, gave Congress authority to create the bank. Justice Marshall wrote, "The Government of the Union, though limited in its powers, is supreme within its sphere of action, and its laws, when made in pursuance of the Constitution, form the supreme law of the land."[4] The Court further concluded that if the end or goal is legitimate, then the act is constitutional. If Congress has the power to regulate commerce, for instance, then Congress can enact legislation that will help it carry out that end.[5] *McCulloch* v. *Maryland* broadly expanded the powers of the federal government.

---

[3]"The Constitution of the United States," Article I, Section 8, Necessary and Proper Clause.
[4]*McCulloch* v. *Maryland*, 17 U.S. 316 (1819).
[5]Ibid.

TABLE 2.2 Powers Granted to Congress under Article I, Section 8

The Congress shall have Power To lay and collect Taxes, Duties, Imposts and Excises, to pay the Debts and provide for the common Defence and general Welfare of the United States; but all Duties, Imposts and Excises shall be uniform throughout the United States;

To borrow money on the credit of the United States;

To regulate Commerce with foreign Nations, and among the several States, and with the Indian Tribes;

To establish an uniform Rule of Naturalization, and uniform Laws on the subject of Bankruptcies throughout the United States;

To coin Money, regulate the Value thereof, and of foreign Coin, and fix the Standard of Weights and Measures;

To provide for the Punishment of counterfeiting the Securities and current Coin of the United States;

To establish Post Offices and Post Roads;

To promote the Progress of Science and useful Arts, by securing for limited Times to Authors and Inventors the exclusive Right to their respective Writings and Discoveries;

To constitute Tribunals inferior to the supreme Court;

To define and punish Piracies and Felonies committed on the high Seas, and Offenses against the Law of Nations;

To declare War, grant Letters of Marque and Reprisal, and make Rules concerning Captures on Land and Water;

To raise and support Armies, but no Appropriation of Money to that Use shall be for a longer Term than two Years;

To provide and maintain a Navy;

To make Rules for the Government and Regulation of the land and naval Forces;

To provide for calling forth the Militia to execute the Laws of the Union, suppress Insurrections and repel Invasions;

To provide for organizing, arming, and disciplining, the Militia, and for governing such Part of them as may be employed in the Service of the United States, reserving to the States respectively, the Appointment of the Officers, and the Authority of training the Militia according to the discipline prescribed by Congress;

To exercise exclusive Legislation in all Cases whatsoever, over such District (not exceeding ten Miles square) as may, by Cession of particular States, and the acceptance of Congress, become the Seat of the Government of the United States, and to exercise like Authority over all Places purchased by the Consent of the Legislature of the State in which the Same shall be, for the Erection of Forts, Magazines, Arsenals, dock-Yards, and other needful Buildings; And

To make all Laws which shall be necessary and proper for carrying into Execution the foregoing Powers, and all other Powers vested by this Constitution in the Government of the United States, or in any Department or Officer thereof.

The meaning of these powers, especially the necessary and proper clause, is subject to legal and political interpretation.

▲ **Give examples of national programs that are the product implied powers.**

The Early View: Dual Federalism and the Tenth Amendment

Even with the broad powers granted to the federal government by *McCulloch* v. *Maryland*, the relationship between the federal government and state governments in its aftermath was one that left clear demarcations between the two levels of government. Scholars have dubbed the type of federalism that existed during the nineteenth century and the early part of the twentieth century as **dual federalism**. The dominant concept of federalism until the 1930s, dual federalism is characterized by four features that indicate demarcations between the states and the federal government.

1. The national government is one of enumerated powers only.
2. The purposes which the national government may constitutionally promote are few.
3. Within their respective spheres the two centers of government are "sovereign" and hence "equal."
4. The relation of the two centers with each other is one of tension rather than collaboration.[6]

Dual federalism

The understanding that the federal government and state governments are both sovereign within their sphere of influence.

---

[6]Edward S. Corwin, "The Passing of Dual Federalism," *Virginia Law Review*, Vol. 36, No. 1. (1950) p. 4.

These four characteristics were postulated by Edward S. Corwin in his 1950 eulogy to the concept of dual federalism.[7] Corwin argued that, "what was once vaunted as a Constitution of Rights, both State and private, has been replaced by a Constitution of Powers."[8] Although this claim may be debated, it was clear that a new understanding of the relationship between federal and state governments was under way.

The Tenth Amendment was the bulwark for dual federalism. It ensured that states like Texas retained those powers that were not given to the federal government. The Tenth Amendment was written to limit the powers of the national government to those stipulated in Article I, Section 8. But, as early as 1789, supporters of the federal system were endeavoring to weaken the Tenth Amendment. In the process of writing the Tenth Amendment, Representative Thomas Tudor Tucker proposed adding the term *expressly* so that the amendment would read, "The powers not *expressly* delegated to the United States."[9] He believed that adding the term would limit the powers of the federal government to those *expressly* stated in the Constitution. James Madison and others argued against the proposal, and it was rejected.

As a result, the Tenth Amendment was left to be interpreted as limiting national powers either a little or a lot. After the replacement of Chief Justice John Marshall with Chief Justice Roger Taney, the Supreme Court began to rein in the national government. When faced with a case that pitted the federal government's power to regulate commerce on the one hand and the states' internal police power on the other, the Supreme Court would side with the states.[10] This would be the dominant concept of federalism until the 1930s.

The Development of Cooperative Federalism

The exclusion of the term *expressly* made it much easier for the national government to expand its powers, but a new set of national and global challenges served as the trigger that contributed to the shift in power from state governments to the federal government. Two world wars, the Great Depression, advances in technology, the civil rights movement, and the Cold War with the Soviet Union contributed to a greater need for centralizing power. Edward Corwin surmises, "The Federal System has shifted base in the direction of a consolidated national power, while within the National Government itself an increased flow of power in the direction of the President has ensued."[11]

Corwin's concept of dual federalism would be replaced by **cooperative federalism**, a relationship where "the National Government and the States are mutually complementary parts of a *single* government mechanism all of whose powers are intended to realize the current purposes of government according to their applicability to the problem in hand."[12] Cooperative federalism used the power of the national government to encourage the states to pursue certain public policy goals. When the states cooperated, they would receive matching funds or additional assistance from the national government. When the states did not cooperate, funds could be withheld from the states.

The development of the concept of cooperative federalism was largely the result of a vast expansion of federal grants-in-aid. The evolution of federal grants to state and local governments has a long and controversial history. Although some grants from the

Cooperative federalism

A relationship where "the National Government and the States are mutually complementary parts of a *single* government mechanism all of whose powers are intended to realize the current purposes of government according to their applicability to the problem in hand."[13]

---

[7]Ibid.
[8]Ibid.
[9]*Annals of Congress, The Debates and Proceedings in the Congress of the United States*, "History of Congress," 42 vols. (Washington, DC: Gales & Seaton), pp. 1834–1856.
[10]See *New York* v. *Miln*, 36 US 11 Pet. 102 (1837).
[11]Corwin, "The Passing of Federalism," p. 2.
[12]Ibid., p. 19.
[13]Ibid.

national government to the states began as early as 1785, the adoption of the federal income tax in 1913 drastically altered the financial relationship between the national and state governments by making possible extensive federal aid to state and local governments.

The Great Depression of the 1930s brought with it a series of financial problems more severe than the state and local governments had previously experienced. Increased demand for state and local services, when revenues were rapidly declining, stimulated a long series of New Deal grant-in-aid programs, ranging from welfare to public health and unemployment insurance.

Most of these early grant-in-aid programs were **categorical grants**. Under such aid programs, Congress appropriates funds for a specific purpose and sets up a formula for their distribution. Certain conditions are attached to these grant programs:

1. The receiving government agrees to match the federal money with its own, at a ratio fixed by law.
2. The receiving government administers the program. For example, federal funds are made available for Medicaid, but it is the state that actually pays client benefits.
3. The receiving government must meet minimum standards set by federal law. For example, states are forbidden to spend federal money in any way that promotes racial segregation. Sometimes additional conditions are attached to categorical grants, such as regional planning and accounting requirements.

Most federal aid, however, now takes the form of **block grants** that specify general purposes such as job training or community development but allow the state or local government to determine precisely how the money should be spent. Conditions may also be established for receipt of block grants, but state and local governments have greater administrative flexibility than with categorical grants. Federal transportation, welfare, and many other grants have been reformed to allow for significant **devolution**, that is, the attempt to enhance the power of state or local governments, especially by replacing relatively restrictive categorical grants-in-aid with more flexible block grants.

Civil Rights versus States' Rights

Heated civil rights battles developed during the nation's transition from dual federalism to cooperative federalism in the middle of the past century. During this period, states, especially southern states, claimed the federal government was encroaching on states' rights, and no public policy area garnered more opposition from the southern states than civil rights issues.

During the period of dual federalism, the U.S. Supreme Court created the **separate-but-equal doctrine** in *Plessy* v. *Ferguson* (1896). The court used a novel interpretation of the Fourteenth Amendment to protect "states' rights" when it held that segregation did not violate the constitutional requirement that no state shall deny any person the equal protection of the laws. It held that state and local governments could pass laws requiring racial segregation because, as long as physical facilities were equal for both races, African Americans were as separate from whites as whites were from African Americans. This interpretation ignored the intent in segregation laws to communicate a sense of social inferiority to African Americans by making it a crime for them to associate with whites. The court also neglected the fact that the "separate" African American facilities were either clearly inferior to those enjoyed by whites or simply nonexistent.

The *Plessy* decision allowed continued discrimination against African Americans, and the decision's impact was felt throughout the South. In its aftermath, states enacted **Jim Crow laws**, which mandated racial segregation in almost every aspect of life.

Categorical grants
Federal aid to state or local governments for specific purposes, granted under restrictive conditions and often requiring matching funds from the receiving government.

Block grants
Federal grants to state or local governments for more general purposes and with fewer restrictions than categorical grants.

Devolution
The attempt to enhance the power of state or local governments, especially by replacing relatively restrictive categorical grants-in-aid with more flexible block grants.

Separate-but-equal doctrine
Doctrine that resulted from the Supreme Court ruling in *Plessy* v. *Ferguson* that legalized segregation.

Jim Crow laws
State and local laws that mandated racial segregation in almost every aspect of life.

After World War II, the separate-but-equal doctrine would slowly be weakened, and Texas contributed to this weakening by providing the setting for the Supreme Court case of *Sweatt* v. *Painter* (see Chapter 1). After graduating from Yates High School in Houston and Wiley College in Marshall, Texas, Heman Marion Sweatt, an African American student, hoped to go to law school in Texas. But at the time, The University of Texas at Austin law school did not admit African Americans. African American students from Texas who wanted to attend law school were told to go to schools out of state. The Supreme Court ruled that, in shifting its responsibilities to other states, the State of Texas was not providing separate accommodations—a requirement under the doctrine of separate but equal.

Sweatt v. *Painter* led to the creation of what are now Texas Southern University (TSU) and TSU's Thurgood Marshall School of Law. Although graduates of the Thurgood Marshall School of Law represent only 3 percent of the membership of the Texas state bar, they currently account for 14 percent of Texas attorneys who are ethnic/racial minorities.[14] But perhaps more significantly, *Sweatt* helped to further weaken the doctrine of separate but equal, paving the way for *Brown* v. *Board of Education* in 1954, which eventually reversed *Plessy* v. *Ferguson*.

Brown v. *Board of Education* would lead to the desegregation of schools (see Chapter 1). The Twenty-fourth Amendment (which outlawed poll taxes), the Civil Rights Act of 1964, the Voting Rights Act of 1965, and many other laws that promoted equality would follow. The white political leadership in southern states generally saw such legislation as an encroachment on their sovereignty—or states' rights.

The Voting Rights Act of 1965, and its extensions in 1970, 1975, 1982, and 2006, required, among other things, that a small number of states obtain approval (referred to as **pre-clearance**) under the law's Section 5 for any election law changes from either the U.S. Department of Justice or the U.S. District Court for the District of Columbia. Initially, six southern states (Alabama, Georgia, Louisiana, Mississippi, South Carolina, and Virginia) were included as well as counties and other local political districts in other states. In 1975, Alaska, Arizona, and Texas were added to this list when the Voting Rights Act (VRA) was expanded to include the protection of linguistic minorities (Asian Americans, Latinos, Native Americans) in addition to racial minorities (African Americans).

Conservatives have long argued that the VRA violated the Tenth Amendment of the U.S. Constitution by singling out a small number of states, one being Texas, along with selected political subdivisions in other states for additional scrutiny and legal requirements under its Section 5. Furthermore, they objected to the formula used to determine which states and jurisdictions were required to seek pre-clearance, because the formula was based on electoral results and legislation from the 1960s and early 1970s, which they claimed did not accurately reflect present-day conditions.

In 2013 the U.S. Supreme Court agreed with Alabama (where Shelby County is located), Texas, and other states in *Shelby County* v. *Holder* that the criteria (located in Section 4 of the VRA) under which states were included in the pre-clearance group were out of

Pre-clearance

Any administrative or legislative change to the rules governing elections in covered states must be submitted for pre-approval to either the U.S. Department of Justice or the U.S. District Court for the District of Columbia.

Did You Know? Texas was not included among the original six states required to seek pre-clearance in 1965 because the VRA's architect, President Lyndon Baines Johnson (LBJ), did not want his home state's reputation tarnished by being placed alongside states so strongly associated with racial discrimination and oppression like Alabama and Mississippi.[15]

[14]*Racial/Ethnic Minority Attorneys: Attorney Statistical Profile (2012–13)*. Austin, Texas: Department of Research and Analysis, State Bar of Texas, 2013.
[15]"Terral Smith Says that 40 Years Ago, U.S. Placed Texas Under Voting Rights Act for Failing to Print Ballots in Spanish," *Austin American-Statesman/PolitiFact Texas*, November 16, 2012, www.politifact.com/texas/statements/2012/nov/16/terral-smith/terral-smith-says-40-years-ago-us-placed-texas-und.

date and needed to be updated in order for Section 5 to be applied. The Supreme Court, however, did not find Section 5 to be unconstitutional, but until Congress develops a new formula for placing states and political subdivisions under the pre-clearance requirements, Section 5 will be inoperative. The 2013 *Shelby* ruling allowed Texas's controversial 2011 Voter ID law, which had been denied pre-clearance in 2012 because it would have a disproportionately negative effect on Hispanic voters, to go into effect in 2013. Texas voters must now present one of seven forms of approved photo-identification in order to cast a ballot in person.

Controversy erupted after the Supreme Court's *Shelby* decision was announced. Some Texans were upset that the decision would allow Texas to implement its voter ID legislation, which a district court had ruled would depress minority voter turnout. The same district court had ruled that the redistricting plans passed by the Republican-controlled Texas legislature in 2011 discriminated against minorities, and opponents of the Shelby decision feared that such practices in the future might go unchallenged. Many Democrats claimed that the passage of these discriminatory laws is evidence that the VRA is still needed in states like Texas. Republicans argued that these laws are not discriminatory; they are simply efforts to prevent voter fraud and engage in entirely legal partisan gerrymandering.

TEXAS AND THE FEDERAL SYSTEM

LO 2.3   Analyze Texas's relationship with the federal government and the prominent role the state has played in the national debate over coercive federalism.

Some Texans interpret support in the state for states' rights (or state sovereignty) as an effort to thwart civil rights for ethnic and racial minorities. However, other Texans see states' rights as reflecting a genuine concern with a growing federal government that they believe has simply become too large and powerful and carried out functions that states could perform better—or that individuals can or should do for themselves. They are especially concerned with the coercive power of the federal government over both state governments and individuals.

So far, we have been looking at the U.S. Constitution and how the national political and legal climates have affected the relative powers of the national and state governments. Now we will look at federalism from a Lone Star State perspective, at how the national government's powers have affected the state, at the role played by the state in our federal system, and at how Texas political leaders have coped with and reacted to the changing nature of U.S. federalism.

Jim Watson/AFP/Getty Images

Former Governor Rick Perry meets President Barack Obama at an airport in August 2010 to present him with a list of grievances against the federal government.

CTQ Why would conservative Texans object to federal policies so strenuously?

Coercive Federalism and Texas

Many Texans would argue that a shift away from cooperative federalism has been under way since the late 1970s. This new form of federalism has been referred to as **coercive federalism**. Coercive federalism is defined as a relationship between the national government and states in which the former directs the states on policies they must undertake. In this shift to coercive federalism, the federal government has centralized more power and has increasingly obstructed the states when they attempt to pursue policies with which the federal government does not agree. As evidence of this shift, the U.S. Advisory Commission on Intergovernmental Relations reported that more than half of all preemption laws—going back to the nation's founding— were enacted between the 1970s and 1980s.[16] Such encroachment on states was not ideologically one-sided. The federalism scholar John Kinkaid writes, "Liberals, lacking revenue for major new programs, and conservatives, lacking public support for major reductions in equity programs, switched from fiscal to regulatory tools."[17] Because neither liberals nor conservatives had the political support to expand or contract programs that promoted equity, lawmakers in Congress and the White House opted to enact new rules.

A classic example of federal encroachment using regulatory mechanisms was the passage of the National Minimum Drinking Age Act of 1984. The law required all states to set their minimum drinking age to at least 21 or run the risk of the federal government reducing their federal highway construction funding by 10 percent (which in 2012 would have represented a cut of $254 million in Texas), a reduction that would have a dramatic adverse impact on the state's infrastructure. As a result of the passage of this legislation, the approximately two-fifths of the nation's states that were not in compliance raised their minimum drinking age to 21, including Texas, where it was increased from 19 to 21.

Anxious about the growth of national government power, some Texas tea party protesters have been sympathetic to secessionist rhetoric.

What drives such antifederalist sentiments?

During former Governor Rick Perry's unsuccessful 2011–2012 presidential bid, he invoked the Tenth Amendment frequently. Perry argued that the federal government has increasingly taken over more activities that were once the purview of state governments. Perry's general philosophy in the area of state sovereignty is nicely summarized in the following position statement made during his last gubernatorial re-election campaign.

States are best positioned to deal with state issues, a fact the founding fathers had in mind when they included the 10th Amendment in the Bill of Rights. Over the years, that right has been clouded by ongoing federal encroachments that are reflected in a recent series of attempts by Washington to seize even more control over numerous Texas programs, including some of the most successful initiatives of their kinds in the country.[18]

Former Governor Perry considers the Affordable Care Act health-care reform legislation of 2010,

---

[16] *Federal Preemption of State and Local Authority* (Washington, DC: Advisory Commission on Intergovernmental Relations, draft report, 1989).

[17] John Kinkaid, "From Cooperative to Coercive Federalism," *Annals of the American Academy of Political and Social Sciences*, Vol. 509, 1990, pp. 139–152.

[18] *Governor's Initiatives* (Austin, TX: Office of the Governor Rick Perry, June 2010, p. 3), http://governor.state. tx.us/initiatives/10th_amendment.

Environmental Protection Agency regulations, cap-and-trade legislation efforts, and VRA enforcement as recent examples of the national government placing undue burdens on Texas.

Supporters of federal efforts see the national government as requiring Texas to do what it has been reluctant to do, such as protecting the environment and public health. For instance, supporters of federal involvement question the Texas Commission on Environmental Quality's (TCEQ) efforts to enforce air and water quality standards. If the state does not meet air quality standards as called for by the federal government, then the state could lose federal funds for transportation projects.

Federal Grants-in-Aid in Texas

Grants from the federal government constitute the second largest source of revenue for the state of Texas after those obtained from the state's assortment of taxes, headed by the sales tax revenue, which is expected to account for 54.6 billion during the 2014–2015 biennium (Texas drafts separate annual budgets every two years rather than every year). Table 2.3 shows the sources of state revenue, the estimated amount, and the percentage of the total represented by the line item for the 2014–2015 biennium. They are listed from the largest amount to the smallest amount. Of the $208.2 billion in state revenue, $73.9 billion is projected to come from the federal government—35.5 percent of the total state revenue.

The percentage of the state's revenue provided by the federal government has grown in recent decades. In 1978, about a quarter of the state's revenue was supplied by the federal government. During the worst of the Great Recession, the percentage of state revenue accounted for by federal funds briefly exceeded 40 percent, reaching a peak of 41 percent in 2011 as a result of the federal government's stimulus efforts, before dropping back to pre-recession levels (35 percent in 2012 and 33 percent in 2013). Figure 2.1 shows the percentage of Texas revenue coming from the federal government between 1978 and 2013. This growth can be explained in large part by the formulas the federal government uses to calculate need in a state. Texas's rapidly expanding population, combined with a comparatively large low-income population, and a rapid rise in the number of senior citizens living in the state, has contributed to this growth.

TABLE 2.3 Texas Revenue by Source for 2014–2015 Biennium

Source	Amount in Billions	Percentage of Total
Tax collections	98.8	47.4
Federal income	73.9	35.5
Licenses, fees, fines, and penalties	16.5	7.9
Lottery proceeds	3.2	1.5
Interest and investment income	2.2	1.0
Land income	2.4	1.1
Settlement of claims	1.1	0.5
Sales of goods and services	0.8	0.4
Other revenue sources	9.5	4.6
Total net revenue	208.2	100

Source: Comptroller of Public Accounts 2014–2015 Certification Revenue Estimate. December 2013, www.texastransparency.org/State_Finance/Budget_Finance/Reports/Certification_Revenue_Estimate/cre1415.

This table shows the sources of all types of Texas state revenues. Note that federal funds account for almost as large a share of those revenues as all state taxes combined.

▲ **How might a reduction in the overall level of federal government spending and consequent drop in the amount of income received by Texas from the federal government affect the provision of government-provided services and state and local tax rates in Texas?**

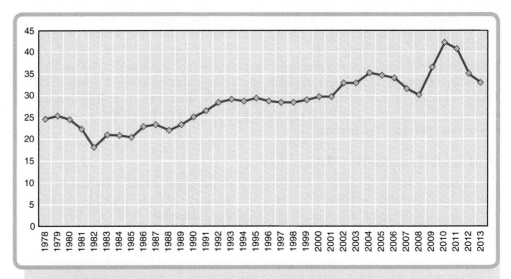

Figure 2.1
Percentage of Texas Revenue Coming from the Federal Government (1978–2013)

This figure shows that Texas, like most states, has become increasingly reliant on federal funding to finance state programs in the areas of education, health, and transportation.

 Is Texas's growing reliance over the past four decades on federal funds to support state government operations a positive or negative development for the state?

Unfunded Mandates

Unfunded mandates

Obligations the federal government imposes on state governments while providing little to no funds to pay for the mandated activities.

Unfunded mandates are obligations the federal government imposes on state governments while providing little to no funds to pay for the mandated activities. Even after the enactment of the Unfunded Mandates Reform Act of 1995 during the administration of President Bill Clinton, the federal government has found ways of getting around the law. Loopholes and exemptions have made it possible for Congress to obligate Texas and other states to implement and pay for certain policies or risk losing federal funds. Former Governor Perry was critical of unfunded mandates, even criticizing President George W. Bush's No Child Left Behind Act for forcing the states to make changes to their educational systems without providing the needed federal funds to actually implement the program.[19] Unfunded mandates allow elected officials to take credit for the passage of legislation while avoiding the hard and generally unpopular work of raising the revenue to fund the program created by the legislation.

The federal government is not the only level of government that adopts legislation containing unfunded mandates. The State of Texas also has created a fair number of unfunded

---

[19]"George W. Bush Defends No Child Left Behind Reform from Attacks by Rick Perry, others," *Houston Chronicle,* January 12, 2012, http://blog.chron.com/txpotomac/2012/01/george-w-bush-defends-no-child-left-behind-reform-from-attacks-by-rick-perry-others.

mandates that require local governments and other public institutions such as community colleges and universities to take certain actions without providing these entities with adequate funds to implement the requirements.

The Texas Association of Counties, which works on behalf of the state's 254 counties, has been critical of the state's unfunded mandates. It reports, "Unfunded mandates impose costs on Texas counties and their taxpayers into the millions of dollars statewide and force counties to increase local property tax rates to pay for edicts from above."[20] The state has mandated that county governments, for example, provide legal counsel for indigent criminal defense and indigent child protective services cases as well as health care for inmates in county jails, but without any appropriations, which means the counties are left footing the bill for these state-mandated services.

In recent legislative sessions, the Texas Association of Counties lobbied for the passage of an amendment to the Texas Constitution prohibiting the state from requiring counties to expend money on a task without either appropriating state revenue to support it or providing reimbursement. None of these reform proposals, however, has been successful, with the counties left waiting until the 2015 legislative session to try again.

On a brighter note in the battle against state-government-created unfunded mandates, during the 2013 legislative session the state's public colleges and universities received some redress in relation to a 2009 unfunded mandate. In that year, the Texas Legislature significantly expanded the 1929 Hazelwood Act. The Hazelwood Act exempted qualified veterans and dependent children of disabled or deceased veterans from paying tuition and fees at Texas public colleges and universities up to a maximum of 150 credit hours.

The 2009 Hazelwood Legacy Act allowed veterans to transfer their credit hours to their dependent children (under the age of 26), which substantially increased the number of students benefiting from this measure. In 2009, prior to the expansion, the cost to schools as a result of the Hazelwood Act was $24.6 million, a cost that increased more than fourfold in 2012 ($110.8 million).[21] Although higher education leaders widely agreed with the spirit of the expansion, they complained that it represented an unfunded mandate, in which the Texas Legislature significantly expanded the number of students attending the schools (for free) without appropriating funds to cover the increased cost the schools would bear as a result of the arrival of these non-revenue-producing students on campus. The legislators were able to claim credit for the legislation without paying the costs associated with financing it. In 2013 the Texas Legislature responded to the complaints of higher education officials and passed legislation that provides approximately $30 million to help colleges and universities partially defray some of the increased cost associated with the Hazelwood Legacy Act.

The Affordable Care Act: A Challenging Case in Federalism

Probably no current controversy better illustrates the competing visions of our federal system than the ongoing debate over national health-care reform. Shortly after the passage of the Patient Protection and Affordable Care Act (ACA, or, as it is often popularly referred to,

---

[20]*Significant Unfunded and Underfunded Mandates on Texas County Governments* (Austin, TX: Texas Association of Counties, 2011).

[21]"Colleges Seek Help on Vets' Waivers," *San Antonio Express-News*, March 4, 2013, www.mysanantonio.com/news/local_news/article/Colleges-seek-help-on-vets-waivers-4325254.php#ixzz2US3VDsmj.

"Obamacare"), former Texas Attorney General Greg Abbott joined twenty-five other state attorneys general in opposing the new health-care law. At issue, among other things, was the law's mandate that individuals purchase health insurance and the requirement that the states expand Medicaid coverage.

The ACA's Medicaid expansion required the states to expand Medicaid coverage to people under 65 (those 65 and older have access to Medicare) earning up to 138 percent of the federal poverty level (FP); the law states 133 percent, but due to a somewhat complicated calculation methodology, the effective threshold under the ACA is 138 percent. In 2014, 138 percent of the federal poverty level for a single person in Texas was $16,105; for a family of four, it was $32,540.[22] Under the legislation signed into law by President Obama in 2010, the federal government would cover the entire cost of this expansion for the first three years before gradually reducing the federal contribution to 90 percent of the cost in 2020 and beyond. States that did not opt in to the Medicaid expansion could face the loss of all of their Medicaid funds. A total of 26 states formally challenged the constitutionality of the Medicaid expansion, 13 filed *amicus* briefs with the Supreme Court in support of the expansion, and in two states the governor and attorney general took opposing sides on this issue.[23]

The limits on what Congress can do are stipulated in Article 1, Section 8 of the U.S. Constitution. Among Congress's powers is the power to regulate commerce. It is this authority that Congress used to justify the ACA. Congress argued that because it has the power to regulate commerce, and the buying of health insurance is a commercial activity, Congress has the power to regulate health-care coverage.

Some disagreed that the ACA regulated commerce and concluded that it infringed on states' rights. Although it is the case that some powers are shared between the states and the federal government, others are exclusive to either one or the other. For example, the power to regulate commerce is granted to Congress. The power to provide for the public health and safety is deemed a power reserved to the state by the Tenth Amendment.

Former Attorney General Abbott argued in his *amicus* brief that the ACA did not regulate commerce, but rather that it created policing authority that is generally the purview of the states.[24] In June 2012, in the case of the *National Federation of Independent Business v. Sebelius*, the U.S. Supreme Court, led by Chief Justice John Roberts, rejected the federal government's claim that the commerce clause allowed Congress to create the individual mandate. But, Roberts argued, the "penalty" that the law required be paid to the Internal Revenue Service (IRS), is in actuality a "tax," which Congress has the power to levy. As a result, the most controversial aspect of the law—the individual mandate—was deemed constitutional.

At the same time, however, the Supreme Court found that the ACA's requirement that the states expand access to Medicaid or suffer the potential penalty of losing all Medicaid funding was excessively coercive and, therefore, unconstitutional. This ruling removed a major pillar of the ACA and has left almost seven million Americans without health insurance in those states that have opted not to expand their Medicaid coverage in line with the ACA.

Nowhere was the impact of this ruling more strongly felt than in Texas. Because Texas has, at least for the time being, opted out of the Medicaid expansion, 1.7 million Texans are not eligible to for health coverage under Medicaid; if Texas had opted in (as was the case in

---

[22] *2014 Poverty Guidelines* (Washington, DC: Office of the Assistant Secretary of Planning and Evaluation, U.S. Department of Health and Human Services, 2013). http://aspe.hhs.gov/poverty/14poverty.cfm.

[23] *A Guide to the Supreme Court's Accordable Care Decision* (Menlo Park, CA: Kaiser Family Foundation, 2012), http://kaiserfamilyfoundation.files.wordpress.com/2013/01/8332.pdf.

[24] "Abbott on the Legal Case Against Health Care," *Texas Monthly: Burkablog*, March 30, 2010.

California, New York, and other states), these Texans would be eligible for health coverage through Medicaid. And, because the ACA provides health-care subsidies only to individuals with incomes more than 138 percent of the FPL, three-fifths of these 1.7 million Texans are ineligible for federal government subsidies to purchase health-care coverage through the federally operated health-care exchange in Texas. As a consequence, more than one million Texans find themselves today in a health-care purgatory known as the "coverage gap"—too wealthy to qualify for Medicaid and too poor to qualify for federal health insurance subsidies.[25]

Former Governor Perry and other Texas opponents of Medicaid expansion argued the state cannot afford to pay 10 percent of the cost of this expansion in 2020 and beyond. They also believe the current Medicaid system is broken and expanding it is "like putting 1,000 more people on the *Titanic* when you knew what was going to happen."[26] Finally, they also highlight that fewer and fewer doctors are accepting Medicaid patients in Texas and question the wisdom of adding 1.7 million patients to a system in which Medicaid patients already find it very difficult to schedule appointments with doctors. A 2012 survey of physicians by the Texas Medical Association (TMA) found that only 32 percent were still accepting all new Medicaid patients, down from 42 percent in 2010.[27] More than two-fifths of Texas physicians (42 percent) were no longer accepting any new Medicaid patients at all in 2012, a proportion that will quite possibly be more than 50 percent in the 2014 TMA survey.

Supporters of Medicaid expansion argue that not expanding adversely affects the health of millions of Texans who lack insurance as a result of the decision to not expand Medicaid. Of course, many of these 1.7 million people when ill or injured will be able to seek care in the state's hospitals, hospitals that will send them bills that most will never be able to pay. But these debts will not be fully absorbed by the hospitals, and in the end the bills will be paid indirectly by homeowners in the form of taxes to their local hospital districts and by Texans with private insurance and Texas employers in the form of higher insurance premiums; instead of by the federal government in the form of additional Medicaid payments. Had Texas expanded Medicaid, it would have seen in 2016 alone an increase in federal expenditures to support the expansion in the amount of $6.6 billion.[28]

The controversy surrounding the ACA is an excellent example of the friction that can arise between the federal government and the states. This friction is generated by differences in opinions revolving around the proper balance of power between the federal and state governments. This balance is in turn determined by a combination of the rules laid out in the Constitution, in statute, and in the interpretation of these rules by our elected officials, especially our appointed federal judges. We can see that Texas has played an active role in the constant redefining of the concept of federalism, a topic we explore in greater detail in the following pages.

---

[25]"A Closer Look at the Impact of State Decisions Not to Expand Medicaid on Coverage for Uninsured Adults," Menlo Park, CA: Kaiser Family Foundation, 2014. http://kff.org/medicaid/fact-sheet/a-closer-look-at-the-impact-of-state-decisions-not-to-expand-medicaid-on-coverage-for-uninsured-adults.

[26] "Health Care Law Is Dividing Republican Governors," *New York Times*, November 21, 2013, www.nytimes.com/2013/11/22/us/politics/health-law-is-dividing-republican-governors.html?hp&_r=0.

[27]*Survey of Texas Physicians 2012: Research Findings* (Austin, Texas: Texas Medical Association, 2013).

[28]John Holahan, Matthew Buettgens, and Stan Dorn, *The Cost of Not Expanding Medicaid* (Menlo Park, CA: Kaiser Family Foundation, 2013), http://kff.org/medicaid/report/the-cost-of-not-expanding-medicaid.

HOW DOES TEXAS COMPARE?
Medicaid Expansion: How Does Texas Compare?

In 2014 Texas was one of 21 primarily Southern and Great Plains states that had firmly decided not to expand their Medicaid coverage under the ACA .[29] In contrast, 26 states and Washington, D.C., had decided to move forward with the expansion. The 3 remaining states were still debating whether or not to expand as the year ended. The 21 states contain close to seven million people who would have been insured if their state had opted-in to the ACA Medicaid expansion.[30] Although Texas is only one of these 21 states, Texans account for almost a quarter of those potential beneficiaries whose state has clearly decided at present not to expand Medicaid under the provisions of the ACA.

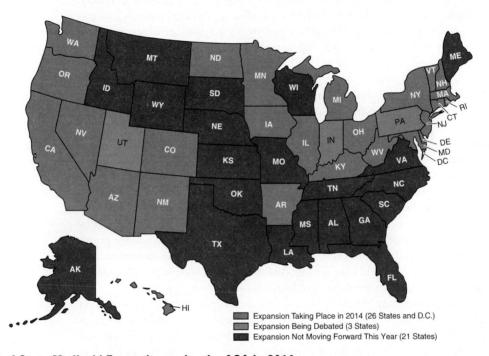

Expansion Taking Place in 2014 (26 States and D.C.)
Expansion Being Debated (3 States)
Expansion Not Moving Forward This Year (21 States)

The Status of State Medicaid Expansion under the ACA in 2014

This figure highlights that Texas is among the minority of U.S. states that at the present time have firmly opted to not partici-pate in the ACA linked expansion of Medicaid.

http://kff.org/health-reform/state-indicator/state-activity-around-expanding-medicaid-under-the-affordable-care-act.

FOR DEBATE

 Is it a problem that some Americans are benefiting from the ACA Medicaid expansion while others are not, due to the differing position of their state's politicians in favor of or against the ACA? Or is this simply an example of how a federal system works in practice, with individual states having a say on which federal policies they embrace and which ones they reject?

 Was former Governor Perry right that Texas could not afford to pay for the Medicaid expansion? Or were support-ers right that Texas should expand Medicaid on both moral and financial grounds?

---

[29] Current Status of State Medicaid Expansion Decisions, 2014. Menlo Park, CA: Kaiser Family Foundation, 2014. http://kff.org/health-reform/slide/current-status-of-the-medicaid-expansion-decision.
[30]Ibid., Holahan et al.

Texas and the U.S. Abortion Debate: From *Roe* to Wendy Davis

The Lone Star State has had a Texas-sized impact on the abortion debate in the United States. From its pivotal role in the 1973 *Roe* v. *Wade* case, which legalized abortion, through the second trimester nationwide to former Texas State Senator Wendy Davis's filibuster against strict anti-abortion legislation in 2013 (and the subsequent federal court challenges to that law), Texas has been at the center of our nation's debate concerning the practice of abortion for more than forty years.

Prior to 1973, every state possessed its own legislation on abortion, with abortion being legal in a relatively small number of states (and even there only during the latter half of the 1960s) such as New York and Washington and illegal in an overwhelming majority of the states, including Texas. In 1973, the U.S. Supreme Court, in *Roe* v. *Wade*, declared Texas's legislation that made abortion illegal (except when the mother's life was in danger) was unconstitutional. This landmark ruling, which was based in large part on the Supreme Court justices' belief that the Texas legislation violated a woman's constitutional right to privacy, effectively made abortion through the second trimester legal throughout the entire country. The suit was filed by pro-choice activists on the behalf of a pregnant Texas woman (Norma McCorvey), who used the pseudonym of Norma Roe, and was filed in Dallas, making the Dallas County District Attorney at the time, Henry Wade, the defendant in the suit.

During the 2013 legislative session, Texas once again vaulted to the national stage as the result of the debate over legislation that would place some of the strictest restrictions in the nation on the practice of abortion. In June 2013, this legislation was scuttled on the final night of the 30-day special session by former State Senator Wendy Davis's 12½-hour filibuster, which brought national attention, including tweets by President Obama and Vice President Joe Biden supporting Davis, to the Texas abortion debate and to Davis. Davis's victory, however, was only temporary; former Governor Perry quickly called a second special legislative session, where with ample time the Republican Party's legislative majorities guaranteed the passage of the bill (HB 2).

Among other things, the new law prohibits abortions after twenty post-fertilization weeks (unless needed to avoid the mother's death or serious physical injury), requires abortion clinic physicians to have admitting privileges at a hospital located within thirty miles of the clinic, places greater restrictions on the use of abortion-inducing drugs, and mandates that all abortion clinics meet the same standards as ambulatory surgical centers (ASC).

When HB 2 passed in July of 2013, Texas had forty abortion clinics located in cities throughout the state, including three cities in South Texas (Corpus Christi, Harlingen, McAllen) and four in West Texas (El Paso, Lubbock, Midland, San Angelo). One year later, in July of 2014, that number had been reduced to twenty-one.[31] When the final mandate that abortion clinics meet ASC standards goes into force on September 1, 2014, unless there is injunctive relief (or additional construction), only seven abortion clinics will be left open in Texas: two in Dallas and Houston and one each in Austin, Fort Worth, and San Antonio.

Opponents of HB 2 argue it was designed to make it much more difficult for women to obtain abortions by significantly reducing the number of clinics in Texas and requiring many women to travel long distances, often at a substantial cost. Proponents of HB 2 counter that the goal of the law is solely to protect women's health. They further state that the reduction in the number of clinics and cities with clinics does not significantly hinder a woman's ability to obtain an abortion in Texas.

---

[31]"Watch Abortion Vanish in Texas (GIF)," *Mother Jones*, July 23, 2014, www.motherjones.com/politics/2014/07/watch-abortion-access-melt-away-texas.

This legislation, in particular the requirements that abortion clinic doctors possess hospital admitting privileges and that abortion clinics meet ASC standards, is currently being challenged in the courts by pro-choice activists, activists who experienced a setback in late March 2014 when the U.S. Court of Appeals for the Fifth Circuit upheld portions of the law related to admitting privileges and abortion-inducing drugs. These multiple challenges are expected by both proponents and opponents of the legislation to eventually reach the U.S. Supreme Court, with the challenge to the admitting privileges requirement expected to reach the justices first.

In its most significant post-*Roe* abortion-related case, in 1992 the U.S. Supreme Court, in what is widely referred to as the *Casey* case, concluded that although states had a right to regulate abortion, they could not use these regulations to place an "undue burden" on a woman's access to abortion. It is very likely that Texas abortion legislation will once again be under scrutiny in the U.S. Supreme Court during 2015, with the nine justices left to determine whether or not Texas legislation places an undue burden on women who seek abortions.

States as Laboratories: Marijuana Legalization

One of the benefits of federalism is the ability for individual states to serve as public policy laboratories, providing insights on how well different policies actually work when taken from theory to practice. Successful policies are likely to be adopted by other states; failures are likely to be shelved or revised significantly by states that were contemplating the adoption of the policy.

On November 5, 2012, voters in Colorado and Washington decided to make an audacious move in the area of drug policy by legalizing the sale of recreational marijuana to those twenty-one years of age and older and regulating and taxing the production and sale of marijuana. In both states, citizens obtained signatures to place the reforms on the ballot, an option that does not exist in Texas, where only the Texas legislature is authorized to put amendments before voters. Retail sales began in early 2014 in Colorado and in the summer of 2014 in Washington. Similar reforms are now being actively considered in Alaska and Oregon, and the Colorado and Washington experiences are likely to have a profound impact on the debate over legalization in those and other states, including Texas.

The Colorado and Washington cases will provide crucial evidence on the economic, legal, and social consequences of marijuana legalization. They will help answer questions that today are mostly a matter of conjecture, such as the impact of legalization and associated taxes and regulation on the market for illegal marijuana, on the use of marijuana by adolescents, on the abuse of marijuana, on the number of people driving under the influence of marijuana, on the number of individuals penalized and incarcerated for possession, and on the amount of tax revenue generated from marijuana sales and production. This information will be used by other states to decide whether or not to proceed with legalization efforts and how to best design legislation if they do move forward.

Although Colorado and Washington are in the vanguard of marijuana legalization efforts, depending on the outcomes of their experiments, they may not be alone for long. In 1996, California became the first state to legalize the medical use of marijuana. Since that time, due in part to the success of the California experiment, twenty-two other states have adopted similar medical marijuana legislation. Texas, however, is not one of those twenty-two states. Many supporters of legalization, though, were heartened by former Governor Rick Perry's statements during 2014 in support of the decriminalization of marijuana use.[32] In contrast to Colorado, where the possession of up to an ounce of marijuana for personal use is now legal, in Texas the possession of a similar quantity of marijuana is a Class B misdemeanor, punishable by up to 180 days in prison and a fine of up to $2,000.

---

[32]"Gov. Rick Perry for Decriminalization of Pot," *San Antonio Express-News*, January 23, 2014, www. mysanantonio.com/news/local/article/Gov-Rick-Perry-for-decriminalization-of-pot-5168667.php.

Federalism and Casino Gambling

Our federal system allows the nation's fifty states to adopt different laws in a wide range of policy areas—legislation that often reflects the distinct preferences and values of the state's residents. As a result, even states that share borders (see Figure 2.2) can have policies that differ noticeably regarding the same activity. One such example can be seen today when crossing the Texas border into Louisiana, Oklahoma, or New Mexico: the presence of casinos clustered along the Texas border, especially in those parts of Oklahoma and Louisiana nearest the heavily populated Texas metro areas of Dallas–Fort Worth (DFW) and Houston. The explanation for this clustering is easy to explain: Although neighboring Louisiana, Oklahoma, and New Mexico have over the past twenty years passed legislation allowing casino gambling to flourish, Texas continues to maintain a ban on casino gambling.

Texas at present has only one small Tribal Class II gaming facility operated by the Kickapoo in Eagle Pass on tribal land under the authority of the federal Indian Gaming Regulatory Act. Class II facilities are restricted to poker, bingo, and bingo-related pull-tab machines designed to look like slot machines. Unlike neighboring Louisiana, New Mexico, and Oklahoma, Class III gambling (generally referred to as casino gambling), principally baccarat, blackjack, craps, roulette, and slot machines, is constitutionally prohibited throughout the Lone Star State.

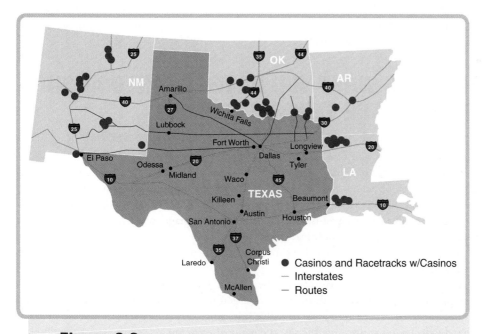

Figure 2.2

Casinos Proximate to the Texas Border in Neighboring States: 2012

The map highlights the large number of Louisiana and Oklahoma casinos clustered on their border with Texas along major interstate highways. These locations allow the casinos to attract gamblers from major population centers in Texas.

Let Texans Decide, http://lettexansdecide.com/facts/gaming-in-neighboring-states.
Casino City, http://us.casinocity.com.

 Should gambling legislation be identical across the entire country or should individual states be allowed to determine the extent to which gambling takes place within their borders?

Proponents of casino gambling in Louisiana, New Mexico, and Oklahoma point to the economic benefits of casinos, ranging from job creation and tourism to tax revenue. In Texas, advocates for casinos highlight the flow of wealth out of Texas to neighboring states, wealth that would mostly remain in Texas if the state would allow casinos to be built. One study (by a pro-casino group) found that vehicles with Texas license plates accounted for approximately 40 percent to 90 percent of the cars in casino parking lots located within 50 miles of the Texas border.[33]

The maintenance of the Texas ban on casino gambling is in large part due to two principal sources of opposition, combined with internal disputes among the pro-gambling forces. The first is opposition based on moral principles, with a significant minority of Texans viewing gambling as a vice and believing it to be morally wrong for the state to sanction casino gambling. A second form of opposition is not morally based, but rather grounded in the concern that the establishment of casino gambling will increase social problems such as child neglect, crime, domestic violence, evictions and home foreclosures, job absenteeism, and poverty stemming from gambling addiction and abuse.

Until now, opponents of casino gambling have retained the upper hand in Texas, in part due to the relatively steep hurdle (a two-thirds vote in each chamber of the Texas Legislature) needed to place the necessary constitutional amendment referendum on the ballot, a referendum opinion polls suggest would pass easily if put before Texas voters.[34] What we can be sure of is that advocates of casino gambling will be back again during the 2015 regular session of the Texas Legislature, hoping to hit the jackpot and pass the constitutional reform legislation that has eluded them for two decades.

APPLYING WHAT YOU HAVE LEARNED ABOUT TEXAS IN THE FEDERAL SYSTEM

LO 2.4 Apply what you have learned about Texas in the federal system.

This essay will show you that, although the academic community has been losing interest in federalism, the tea party movement and states themselves have intensely fought to limit the growth of federal power and revitalize the states. You will then have the opportunity to examine federalism as the central issue of our day. From the ACA (Obamacare), marijuana legalization, budget issues, and same-sex marriage to voting rights, the underlying theme of almost every political issue you can name is federalism—how much power should the national government have and how much power should be left in the hands of the states?

After you have read the essay, you will be asked a series of questions that will require you to employ critical-thinking skills to apply what you have learned in this chapter to the new information in this essay. Your analysis will require you to explain how most modern political issues divide Texans concerning the role the national government and the states should play. You will be asked to reflect on why liberals and conservatives take contradictory positions on the powers of the states depending upon which policy is at stake.

---

[33]*Gaming in Neighboring States* (Austin, TX: Let Texans Decide, 2013), http://lettexansdecide.com/facts/gaming-in-neighboring-states.

[34]"UT/TT Poll: Texans Are Ready to Roll the Dice," *Texas Tribune*, February 23, 2013, www.texastribune.org/2011/02/23/uttt-poll-texans-are-ready-to-roll-the-dice.

THE STATE OF FEDERALISM

by Neal Coates

CHAIR, DEPARTMENT OF POLITICAL SCIENCE
ABILENE CHRISTIAN UNIVERSITY

Your political science teachers can't be that wrong, can they? After all, they are having you read this essay about federalism, a topic long thought to be core to the American governmental system.

But a 2014 survey revealed the startling statistic that only 36.3 percent of 281 undergraduate political science departments across the United States offer a course on American federalism.[35] The surveyed department heads reported that the most important factors in not offering this type of course (they could choose several options) were "A lack of willing faculty" (41 percent), "Low student interest" (37.6 percent), and "Other courses are more important to degree plans" (37.1 percent). And if a federalism course was offered it was mainly as an elective in 87.8 percent of the departments.

Thus, for whatever reasons, two thirds of colleges today are not requiring or even offering courses explaining what many teachers had long thought important—the relationship and shared powers of the American federal and state governments.

The department heads did report, though, they believed 75.5 percent of students were "Somewhat interested" in a federalism type of course ("Very interested" won 7.4 percent, "Not very interested" received 17 percent, and—fortunately—"Not at all interested" garnered 0 percent). Hope is not lost if you believe in the importance of federalism! And even though the survey did not report the results for Texas colleges and universities, a significant number of these still require a course that covers federalism.

At my university, political science majors are required to make at least a "C" in two basic courses dealing with federalism—in national government and in states and the federal system—so the national survey results were surprising. Federalism is all about power—specifically, which "part" of government is responsible for government action or authority. Whether the national or state level of government sets the rules for defense, currency, police power, commerce, and health is a crucial question and was first debated even before the creation of the United States of America. The division of power settled upon was one of separate and, perhaps, equal authority between federal and state governments and was enshrined in the U.S. Constitution and the Tenth Amendment. Regardless, since the 1790s there has been a historical tug of war between the national and state governments regarding the responsibilities of each, and virtually all observers believe today that the growth of the national government has resulted in its taking the lead at the expense of the states.

Will my university stop offering a course on federalism and join what has become the mainstream? Our students go on to graduate school and law school and they find good jobs. But are they out of touch with current trends in education across America, or as some of us suspect, are those students at schools where federalism is not emphasized instead the ones missing out?

History of Federalism in America After the failure of the Articles of Confederation, which had left too much power in the hands of the states, the representatives who assembled in Philadelphia in 1787 to debate a new form of government wanted to create a more balanced system. They certainly did not want to create a unitary system, where

---

[35]Richard L. Cole and John Kincaid, "Unpublished Survey on American Federalism, Intergovernmental Relations, and Multilevel Government," March 12, 2014, www.surveymonkey.com/sr.aspx?sm=taZXx6HU4i2x ZMXNMyB3xMgWj_2bPm6stEny4YkuPxEco_3d.

sovereignty rests only in the national government. Instead they formulated a new system in which authority was divided between national and state levels.

Because the states were pre-existing political entities, and the issues were sharp in their minds, the Framers did not need to define or explain federalism. They specified in the U.S. Constitution that the federal government has certain express powers (enumerated powers), including the right to declare war, levy taxes, and regulate commerce. In addition, the Necessary and Proper Clause provides the federal government implied power to pass any law "necessary and proper" for the execution of its express powers. All other power is reserved to the people or the states via the Tenth Amendment. This quickly became known as dual federalism, or bi-federalism—federal and state governments are co-equals, each sovereign in certain areas that would benefit citizens.[36]

The federal government's power was significantly expanded, though, by the Supreme Court in *McCulloch* v. *Maryland* (1819) and after the Civil War under the broad theory that the states were subject to the final dictates of the national government. These powers were increased for reasons such as the allowance for Native American governments, to regulate businesses and industries that cross state borders, and to protect civil rights. In fact, from 1938 until 1995, the Court never invalidated any federal statute as exceeding the Commerce Clause. Much of this movement came from the 1960's Great Society program—although the Constitution does not give Congress power to regulate social welfare, it is now established that Congress can tax and spend for public housing, nutrition, public assistance, urban development, and education. In short, some observers say that dual federalism no longer exists.[37]

The Tea Party, Senator Ted Cruz, and Mark Levin
The most recent movement of the national government into an area historically regulated by the states is the Patient Protection and Affordable Care Act and its requirement that every American obtain health insurance. The Supreme Court in 2012 upheld "the most significant federalism decision since the New Deal."[38]

Reacting against the explosion in the size of government especially during the past two administrations, since 2009 the fastest growing American political movement has been the tea party, named for the 1773 famous event at Boston Harbor. Its supporters and leaders identify with the Republican Party and call for a balanced budget, reduction of taxes and national debt, and, notably, a return to an earlier balance of federalism. Based on the number of seats won and the speed of the movement's growth, the tea party is probably the most successful political grassroots movement in decades. Their activism in 2010 was mainly the cause of the U.S. House flipping to a 60-seat majority for the Republicans, and they even won five contested Senate races. The 2012 election of Ted Cruz to the U.S, Senate from Texas and the results of the 2014 Texas Primary showed that the tea party, at least in Texas, remains a real force in politics.

One of the main proponents of the tea party view is Mark Levin, lawyer and host of "The Mark Levin Show," heard widely on WBAP 820AM in Dallas. The syndicated radio program ranks fourth to sixth nationally in talk radio—at least 7.75 million persons listen every week.[39] Levin worked in the Reagan Administration and was chief of staff for Attorney General Edwin Meese, and he is fond of saying we now live in a "post-constitutional country."

[36]Thomas Patterson, *We the People: A Concise Introduction to American Politics*, 9th ed., 2011, pp. 67–75.
[37]Ibid., pp. 78–89 and 86–96.
[38]Adam Liptak, "Supreme Court Upholds Health Care Law, 5–4, in Victory for Obama," *New York Times*, June 28, 2012, at www.nytimes.com/2012/06/29/us/supreme-court-lets-health-law-largely-stand.html?pagewanted=all&_r=0).
[39]"Mark Levin," *Talkers Magazine*, March 26, 2014.

In Levin's newest book, *The Liberty Amendments: Restoring the American Republic* (2013),[40] he criticizes the movement away from a limited constitutional republic and toward a view that government should provide for all of society's needs (and the resulting enormous spending by both major political parties). Using original sources such as notes from the Constitutional Convention, as well as the *Federalist Papers*, Levin makes three basic points. He claims the Sixteenth and Seventeenth Amendments unwisely increased the power of the federal government. The Sixteenth Amendment allows the national government to tax incomes giving it the financial resources to vastly expand its reach, and Seventeenth Amendment provided for the popular election of senators, ending a vital check the Framers had created—state legislatures having direct representation in the U.S. Senate. Second, the Supreme Court surrendered up its strict interpretation of the Commerce Clause to President Franklin Roosevelt during the New Deal. Finally, both parties in Congress have fueled a massive increase in power of the executive by granting more and more power to an ever-growing administrative state. In 2011 alone, there were 3,807 new regulations, while the president signed only 81 laws passed by Congress; in 2012, there were $236 billion in new regulatory costs. Cruz, Levin, and the tea party argue loudly that the country is at risk.

Response from the States The Council of State Governments, along with many Republican governors and/or majorities in the legislature, is now pushing back against this federal "overreach." They point out that before 1900 only 29 federal statutes pre-empted state law, but now they exceed 500. In addition, the president and Congress increasingly use rulemaking and laws to impose mandates on states, often with little or no funding. For example, as of 2011 unfunded mandates and regulations cost states as much as $62 billion.[41] The states also complain about more than costs—there is a tradition in America that states are the "laboratory" of democracy, where the most effective innovations in public policy occur. For example, states can enter into interstate compacts on distance learning to bring down higher education costs and learn from each other how to reduce Medicaid costs through program management.

State governments are challenging federal policies in education, health care, environment, energy, and immigration, and often refuse federal grants, file lawsuits, and enact policy at the state level to supplant federal policy. Partly because of the return to gridlock in Washington, D.C., after the 2010 elections, and strapped for funds to balance their budgets, state and local governments are now practicing "bottom-up" activism to create initiatives in areas such as education and high-speed rail.[42]

Conclusion So, what is next for federalism? And will more universities drop courses on this topic? Fortunately, only 3.4 percent of the departments in the 2014 survey reported their decision to not offer such a course was due to "declining relevance of federalism due to nationalization of our governmental system." Instead, it may be the pressure of offering fewer courses to allow students to graduate on time, and the hope that students were instead exposed in high school government class to the powers of the federal and state governments. Regardless, this study of power is too important to ignore. The future of how this country and our 50 states are governed and what policy decisions they make are at stake.

---

[40]Simon & Shuster.

[41]Alaska Senator Gary Stevens and Tennessee Senator Mark Norris, *Capitol Ideas*, "Focus on Federalism: CSG Initiative Aims to Restore 'Laboratories of Democracy,'" The Council of State Governments, Jan./Feb. 2014 at www.csg.org/pubs/capitolideas/2013_july_aug/federalism.aspx.

[42]Shama Gamkhar and Mitchell Pickerill, "The State of American Federalism 2011–2012: A Fend for Yourself and Activist Form of Bottom-Up Federalism," *Publius: The Journal of Federalism*, Vol. 42, Iss. 3, pp. 357–386 at http://publius.oxfordjournals.org/content/42/3/357.full.

JOIN THE DEBATE

 Pick a major issue in modern politics and organize a well-constructed presentation to show the issue has implications for the concept of federalism. To make your essay complete, show how much the national (federal) government and the states are now involved in the policy area you have chosen. Then show why various groups would prefer that the policy area be handled by the states while other groups would prefer that the policy be handled by the national government.

 Should the power of the national government be expanded or should state powers be protected? Can you identify reasons why the national government is inherently better able to handle some issues? Which policies are the states better able to handle than the federal government?

 Explain why some conservative groups would prefer states to handle certain issues like health care or civil rights while they advocate that the national government enforce a nationwide definition of marriage or national enforcement of marijuana laws. Do liberals and conservatives have different views about what states should do?

CHAPTER SUMMARY

LO 2.1   Differentiate among unitary, confederal, and federal systems of government. Federalism is a system of government in which power is constitutionally divided between a national government and state or regional governments. It differs from unitary systems of government, where power is centralized in the hands of the national government, and confederal systems of government, where the national government exercises only those powers delegated to it by the confederation's member-states.

LO 2.2   Distinguish among the types of powers in our federal system, and explain dual and cooperative federalism within the context of the evolution of federalism in the United States. The view of how much power should be granted to each level of government has changed considerably over our nation's history. During the earliest constitutional period, U.S. Supreme Court Chief Justice John Marshall took a broad view of national powers. By the 1830s, a concept of dual federalism developed in which the national government was limited and distinctly separate from the states, but that view changed in the 1930s when the New Deal began to offer extensive grants-in-aid to the states to help finance common national programs—the basis for cooperative federalism. Since the 1970s, some states, especially conservative ones, have come to resent national government mandates and conditions necessary to

receive federal grants—they view today's federal–state relationship as coercive federalism.

LO 2.3   Analyze Texas's relationship with the federal government and the prominent role the state has played in the national debate over coercive federalism. Texas has contributed to shaping this concept of federalism not only by bringing key Supreme Court cases to the debate, but also because the state's current political leadership has actively participated in the debate. Former Governor Perry and the Texas legislature have raised concerns about the impact that the federal government may have on Texas, basing their position for greater state sovereignty on the Tenth Amendment and those other powers reserved to the states in the Constitution. The current debate over health-care reform fits into the broader debate over states' rights that has taken place throughout our country's history.

LO 2.4   Apply what you have learned about Texas in the federal system. Although the academic community may be losing some interest in federalism, in the real world most of the central policy issues of today in one way or another are linked to our federal system of government and the balance of power between the federal government and the states. Where disputes most commonly arise in these different policy arenas is over what the proper of balance between federal and state power should be.

KEY TERMS

block grants, *p. 35*
categorical grants, *p. 35*
coercive federalism, *p. 38*
commerce clause, *p. 32*
concurrent powers, *p. 31*
confederal system, *p. 29*
cooperative federalism, *p. 34*

delegated powers, *p. 31*
devolution, *p. 35*
dual federalism, *p. 33*
expressed powers, *p. 31*
federal system, *p. 30*
implied powers, *p. 31*
inherent powers, *p. 31*

Jim Crow laws, *p. 35*
necessary and proper clause, *p. 32*
pre-clearance, *p. 36*
reserved powers, *p. 31*
separate-but-equal doctrine, *p. 35*

Supremacy Clause, *p. 31*
Tenth Amendment, *p. 31*
unfunded mandates, *p. 40*
unitary system, *p. 29*

REVIEW QUESTIONS

LO 2.1 Differentiate among unitary, confederal, and federal systems of government.

- What distinguishes a federal system of government from both a unitary system of government and a confederal system of government?

- What are the advantages and disadvantages of each type of system of government?

- What would be the pros and cons of replacing our country's current federal system with a unitary system? What would be the pros and cons of replacing it with a confederal system?

LO 2.2 Distinguish among the types of powers in our federal system, and explain dual and cooperative federalism within the context of the evolution of federalism in the United States.

- Explain the difference between delegated and reserved powers and give examples of each. What is the importance of Article I, Section 8 and the Tenth Amendment in the U.S. Constitution? Define and give examples of exclusive and concurrent powers.

- What is the significance of the implied powers clause and of the necessary and proper clause?

- Explain how the national government has used the necessary and proper clause and the Commerce Clause to expand the scope of its power. Explain how the dominant concepts of federalism in the United States have changed as the political and legal climate has changed.

- Describe the differences between the concepts of dual federalism and cooperative federalism. What historical developments led to the expansion of national government power?

- Explore the role the national government has played in the advancement of civil rights, environmental protection, and public health. Should the federal government be allowed to use Section 5 of the VRA to provide extra oversight of changes in Texas election laws?

LO 2.3 Analyze Texas's relationship with the federal government and the prominent role the state has played in the national debate over coercive federalism.

- Explain the concept of coercive federalism.

- How does the current debate over the ACA health-care reform legislation reflect growing tension in the era of coercive federalism between the federal government on one hand and the state governments on the other, particularly in those instances when the federal political leadership and the political leadership in a specific state or group of states do not see eye to eye on a policy issue?

- Evaluate the arguments for states' rights and the argument that has become increasingly common during the current era of coercive federalism that the national government's powers should be limited. Assess the claims that states serve as policy laboratories in a federal system and that federalism allows public policy to best reflect the unique and diverse interests of citizens across the fifty states. What role has Texas played in recent efforts to limit national government power?

GET ACTIVE

Learn more about the debates over federalism. Consider joining the *American Constitution Society for Law and Policy* or the *Federalist Society*. Student membership rates are affordable. You may consider attending meetings and, if possible, presenting student research papers at those meetings. Joining may also give your résumé a little more cachet. Be aware that the *American Constitution Society* is a progressive organization, and the *Federalist Society* is a conservative and libertarian organization. To learn more and join, explore the following:

- Visit the American Constitution Society at **www.acslaw.org** and read more about them. Then click on *Join ACS*. Rates are $10 for students.

- View the Federalist Society at **www.fed-soc.org** and read more about them. Then click on *Membership*. Student rates are $5.

- Watch videos from the American Constitution Society (**www.acslaw.org/news/video**) and the Federalist Society (**https://www.youtube.com/user/TheFederalistSociety**) and follow them on Twitter (@acslaw; @FedSoc). These videos and twitter feeds will provide you with different perspectives on a host of current issues that feature prominently in our country's ongoing debate over the functioning of federalism in the United States.

Find out how federalism affects the right to vote. Discover more about voting rights and electoral transparency in Texas. Check out the liberal-leaning Brennan Center for Justice website (*www.brennancenter.org*) and the conservative-leaning Texas-based True the Vote website (*www.truethevote.org*). And, follow each organization on Twitter (@BrennanCenter; @TrueTheVote)

Explore the social issues facing federalism. Get more information about marijuana legalization efforts nationwide at **www.norml.org**, a website run by advocates of marijuana legalization. Learn more about efforts to permit casino gambling in Texas at the pro-gambling **www.lettexansdecide.com.** Follow them on Twitter (@NORML; @LetTexansDecide) and search for websites of organizations opposing casino gambling and marijuana legalization in the Lone Star State.

 Texans spent close to $3 billion in 2012, gambling in neighboring states. Should Texas legalize casino gambling to keep as many of these gambling dollars in the state as possible and to draw gamblers from beyond the state's borders? Or, are the negative social consequences and moral issues associated with gambling so profound that Texans are best served by the state's not hopping aboard the "casino gambling train"?

CHAPTER 3

The Texas Constitution in Perspective

LEARNING OBJECTIVES

LO 3.1 Explain the origins and evolution of the Texas Constitution, including the Constitutional Convention of 1875.

LO 3.2 Describe the major constitutional structures, functions, and limits of Texas's legislative, executive, and judicial branches.

LO 3.3 Explain the process of amending and revising the Texas Constitution and the reasons that amendments are frequently necessary.

LO 3.4 Apply what you have learned about the Texas Constitution.

*T*he real character of a government is determined less by the provisions of its constitution than by the hearts and minds of its citizens. Government is a process of decision making conditioned by its history, its people, and pressures exerted by citizens, interest groups, and political parties.

Still, our national, state, and local governments would be vastly different were it not for their constitutions. Although the exact meaning of constitutional provisions may be disputed, there is general agreement that constitutions should be respected as the legal basis controlling the fundamentals of government decision making. Constitutions serve as a rationalization for the actions of legislatures, executives, and courts—and of the people themselves. Indeed, the very idea of having a written constitution has become part of the political culture—the basic system of political beliefs in the United States.

Constitutions establish major governing institutions, assign them power, and place both implicit and explicit limits on the power they have assigned. And, because Americans respect constitutions, they promote *legitimacy*, the general public acceptance of government's "right to govern," and also the legality of a government's existence conferred by a constitution.

Legitimacy

General public acceptance of government's "right to govern"; and also, the legality of a government's existence conferred by a constitution.

TEXAS CONSTITUTIONS IN HISTORY

LO 3.1 Explain the origins and evolution of the Texas Constitution, including the Constitutional Convention of 1875.

Like all constitutions, the first Texas constitutions reflected the interests and concerns of the people who wrote and amended them. Many of their elements paralleled those of existing state constitutions; others were at the time unique to the Lone Star State.

Early Texas Constitutions

The constitutions of the Texas Republic and the first state constitutions of Texas were products of the plantation culture of Anglo-Protestant slaveholders. These early constitutions adopted some institutions from Texans' experiences during Spanish and Mexican rule and forthrightly rejected others.

Republic of Texas Constitution
The first Texas Constitution after independence from Mexico was written in 1836 for the Republic of Texas. In reaction to the prominent influence of the Catholic Church during Mexican rule, the largely Protestant Texans wrote a constitution with careful separation of church and state, forbidding clergymen of any faith from holding office. It changed the antislavery policies that had been in force when Texas was part of Mexico by forbidding masters to free their own slaves without the consent of the Republic's congress and denied citizenship to descendants of Africans and Native Americans. Remembering the abuses of the dictatorial Mexican military and political leader Antonio López de Santa Anna, Texans limited the terms of their presidents to three years and prohibited them from being elected to consecutive terms.

The Republic of Texas Constitution did adopt some provisions from Spanish-Mexican law. It created the constitutional figure of a **homestead**, an owner-occupied property protected from forced sale under most circumstances. It also enshrined the concept of **community property**, which signifies that property acquired during marriage is owned equally by both spouses. These elements of Mexican law would later be absorbed into American political culture as other states adopted similar provisions.

Still, the Republic's constitution was mostly a product of the political culture of the Anglo-American southern planters. It incorporated English **common law**, the process under which law is developed based on judicial rulings and customs over time. Common law differs from the Spanish tradition of code law, where legal rulings are made according to what is written in a systematic set of laws.

Homestead

An owner-occupied property protected from forced sale under most circumstances.

Community property

Property acquired during marriage and owned equally by both spouses.

Common law

The process under which law is developed based on judicial rulings and customs over time.

The Texas Constitution also lifted many provisions almost word for word from the U.S. Constitution and from southern states like Tennessee from which many Texas settlers had migrated, including the first president of Texas, Sam Houston, who before coming to Texas had served as Tennessee's governor. Acting in haste because of the fear of attack from the Mexican cavalry, the Republic's constitutional convention wrote a concise document establishing a *unitary* form of government (see Chapter 2), free of many of the detailed restrictions that would later come to limit Texas government.

Constitution of 1845 A new constitution was written in 1845 in preparation for Texas's admission to the United States. It is interesting to note that it required a two-thirds vote in the Texas House of Representatives to establish any corporation and made bank corporations illegal altogether. Although the 1845 Constitution contained many provisions similar to the Republic's constitution, it also introduced features recognizable in today's state constitution. For example, it was almost twice as long as the Republic of Texas's Constitution and restricted the power of the legislature, which was allowed to meet only once every two years. The statehood constitution limited state debt to $100,000 except in cases of war, insurrection, or invasion, and it established the Permanent School Fund. The only amendment to the 1845 Constitution was adopted to limit the power of the governor by providing for the election of some of the officers that governors previously were allowed to appoint. This reform established the use in Texas of a **long ballot**, that is, a ballot that results from the independent election of a large number of executive and judicial officers; giving the chief executive the power to appoint most executive and judicial officers results in a short ballot.

Long ballot
A ballot that results from the independent election of a large number of executive and judicial officers; giving the chief executive the power to appoint most executive and judicial officers results in a short ballot.

Constitution of 1861 The 1861 Constitution was basically the same as that of 1845. The principal exception was that unlike its immediate predecessor, the 1861 Constitution reflected the poignant reality that Texas had become one of the Confederate states at war with the Union—it increased the debt ceiling and prohibited the emancipation of slaves.

Did You Know? The Texas Constitution of 1836 was written during a mere 17 days in Washington, Texas, near the confluence of the Brazos and Navasota rivers, a location memorialized by the Washington-on-the-Brazos State Historic Site.

Reconstruction Constitutions and Their Aftermath

Although earlier constitutions contained a number of elements still found in today's Texas Constitution, it was the aftermath of the Civil War—the political reaction to Reconstruction—that affirmed Texans' fear of government and set the stage for the writing of today's state constitution.

Constitution of 1866 After the Civil War, Texans wrote the 1866 Constitution, which they thought would satisfy the Unionists and permit the readmission of Texas under President Andrew Johnson's mild Reconstruction program. This document nullified secession, abolished slavery, and renounced Confederate war debts. Under its terms, a civilian government was elected and operated for several months despite some interference from the federal government's Freedmen's Bureau.

The 1866 Constitution soon became void after the Radical Republicans in Congress passed the Reconstruction Act of 1867, which required the Confederate states to adopt constitutions that met with the approval of the U.S. Congress. As a result of this act, and operating under congressional authority, the military deposed Texas's civilian elected officials and effectively restored military rule.

Constitution of 1869 With most whites either barred from participating in the election or boycotting it, voters elected members to a constitutional convention in 1868.

Texas State Library and Archives Commission

E. J. Davis remained loyal to the United States, and his service in the Union army was a bitter reminder of Texas's defeat in the Civil War.

SRQ **How did resentment against Governor Davis lead to the writing of the current Texas Constitution?**

The convention produced a document that centralized state power in the hands of the governor, lengthened the chief executive's term to four years, and allowed the governor to appoint all major state officers, including judges. It provided annual legislative sessions, weakened planter-controlled local government, and centralized the public school system. The convention in 1868 reflected little of the fear of centralized government power that was later to become the hallmark of Texas government. The proposed constitution was ratified in 1869.

The 1869 Constitution served as the instrument of government for an era that most Texans and traditional historians would regard as the most corrupt and abusive in the state's history. Under Republican Governor E. J. Davis, large gifts of public funds were made to interests such as railroads; tax rates skyrocketed to fund ambitious and wasteful public programs, with many Texans simply refusing to pay these exorbitant taxes; and the state government accumulated what was for that time a massive public debt. Law and order collapsed, and much of the state's population fell prey to attacks by Native Americans and outlaws. Instead of using the state police and militia to maintain the peace, Governor Davis made them a part of his powerful political machine and a symbol of tyranny. He took control of voter registration, intimidated unsupportive newspapers, and arrested several political opponents. In 1874, his handpicked supreme court used the location of a semicolon in the state constitution as a pretext for invalidating the election of Democrat Richard Coke, with Davis going so far as to wire President Ulysses S. Grant to send federal troops to prevent Democrats from taking power. Grant refused, and Democrats slipped past guards at the capitol and gathered in the legislative chambers to form the new government.

According to legend, Davis, determined not to give up his office, surrounded himself with armed state police in the capitol. Only when a well-armed group of Coke supporters marched toward the capitol singing "The Yellow Rose of Texas" did Davis finally vacate his office. For most Texans, Reconstruction left a bitter memory of a humiliating, corrupt, extravagant, and even tyrannical government.

Revisionist historians argue that Governor Davis was not personally corrupt and that Reconstruction brought progressive policies and built roads, railroads, and schools while protecting the civil and political rights of former slaves. Some see it as a period in which an activist government attempted to play a positive role in people's lives. The period that followed was characterized by a conservative Anglo reaction to these policies.

The Constitutional Convention of 1875 Whichever historical view is more accurate, it is clear that most Texans of the day were determined to strip power away from the state government by writing a new constitution. The Texas Grange, whose members were called Grangers, organized in 1873. Campaigning on a platform of "retrenchment and reform," it managed to elect at least 40 of its members to the constitutional convention of 1875. Like most of the 90 delegates, they were Democrats who were determined to strike at the heart of the big government associated with the Reconstruction era.

To save money, the convention did not publish a journal—reflecting the frugal tone of the final constitution. The convention cut salaries for governing officials, placed strict limits on property taxes, and restricted state borrowing; it also was miserly with the power it granted government officials. It stripped most of the governor's powers, reduced the term of office from four to two years, and required that the attorney general and state judges be elected rather than appointed by the governor.

Nor did the legislature escape the pruning of the convention. Regular legislative sessions were to be held only once every two years. Legislative procedure was detailed in the

Delegates to the constitutional convention of 1875 substantially limited the power of state government.

CTO **What did delegates consider abuses of state power that needed to be prevented in the future?**

constitution, with severe restrictions placed on the kinds of policies the legislature might enact. In fact, a number of public policies were written into the constitution itself.

Local government was strengthened, and counties were given many of the administrative and judicial functions of the state. Although the Grangers had opposed the idea of public education, they were persuaded to permit it with the condition that local governments would establish segregated schools.

The 1875 convention largely reacted to Reconstruction abuses by constraining state power. When the convention ended, some of the money appropriated for its expenses remained unspent. Despite opposition from African Americans, Republicans, most cities, and railroad interests, voters ratified the current state constitution of 1876.

THE TEXAS CONSTITUTION TODAY

LO 3.2 Describe the major constitutional structures, functions, and limits of Texas's legislative, executive, and judicial branches.

Many students begin their examination of state constitutions with some kind of ideal or model constitution in mind. Comparisons with this ideal then leave them with the feeling that if only this or that provision were changed, state government would somehow find its way to honesty, efficiency, and effectiveness. In truth, there is no ideal constitution that would serve well in each of the uniquely diverse 50 U.S. states, nor is it possible to write a state constitution that could permanently meet the dynamically changing needs and concerns of citizens. Further, because a government is much more than its constitution, honest and effective government must be commanded by the political environment—leaders, citizens, parties, interest groups, and so forth; constitutions cannot guarantee it. Scoundrels will be corrupt and unconcerned citizens apathetic under even the best constitution.

However, this pragmatic view of the role of state constitutions should not lead to the conclusion that they are only incidental to good government. A workable constitution is necessary for effective government even if it is not sufficient to guarantee it. Low salaries may discourage independent and high-caliber leaders from seeking office or lead to potential conflicts of interest for public officials who, due to low pay, must simultaneously hold another job. Constitutional restrictions may make it virtually impossible for government to meet the changing needs of its citizens, and institutions may be set up in such a way that they will operate inefficiently and irresponsibly.

The events preceding the adoption of the 1876 Texas Constitution did not provide the background for developing a constitution capable of serving well under the pressures and changes that would take place in the century to follow. The decade of the 1870s was an era of paranoia and reaction, and the constitution it produced was directed more toward solving the problems arising from Reconstruction than toward meeting the challenges of generations to follow—it was literally a reactionary document.

The current Texas Constitution is also an expansive document, approximately 87,000 words in length. It is more than nine times longer than the U.S. Constitution, and ranks second in length among the 50 states, bested only by the gargantuan Alabama Constitution.

Bill of Rights and Fundamental Liberty

Although the Texas Constitution has been the target of much criticism, it contains a Bill of Rights (Article 1) that is often held in high regard because it reflects basic American political culture and contains provisions that are similar to those found in other state charters and the U.S. Constitution.

The Fourteenth Amendment to the U.S. Constitution provides that no state shall deny any person life, liberty, or property without the due process of law. As the U.S. Supreme Court has interpreted this Amendment, it has ruled that states must respect most of the U.S. Bill of Rights because its provisions are essential to "liberty" and "due process." As a result, many individual rights are protected by both the state and federal courts. If the state

TABLE 3.1 BASIC RIGHTS IN THE TEXAS AND U.S. CONSTITUTIONS

Basic Right	Texas Constitution	U.S. Constitution
Religious liberty	Article 1, Sections 4–7	First and Fourteenth Amendments
Freedom of expression	Article 1, Sections 8 and 27	First and Fourteenth Amendments
Right to keep and bear arms	Article 1, Section 23	Second and Fourteenth Amendments
Against quartering troops	Article 1, Section 25	Third Amendment
Against unreasonable search and seizure	Article 1, Section 9	Fourth and Fourteenth Amendments
Right to grand jury indictment for felonies	Article 1, Section 10	Fifth Amendment
Right to just compensation for taking property for public use	Article 1, Section 17	Fifth and Fourteenth Amendments
Right to due process of law	Article 1, Section 19	Fifth and Fourteenth Amendments
Right against double jeopardy	Article 1, Section 14	Fifth and Fourteenth Amendments
Right against forced self-incrimination	Article 1, Section 10	Fifth and Fourteenth Amendments
Right to fair trial by jury	Article 1, Section 10	Sixth and Fourteenth Amendments
Rights against excessive bail or cruel and unusual punishment	Article 1, Sections 11 and 13	Eighth and Fourteenth Amendments

These rights are guaranteed by both the U.S. and Texas Constitutions.

▲ **Explain how states can set higher standards than the national government does for applying these provisions. What rights does the Texas Constitution protect that the U.S. Constitution does not?**

courts fail to protect an individual's rights, that person can also then seek a remedy in the federal courts. Table 3.1 shows important basic rights protected by both the U.S. and Texas Constitutions.

State constitutional guarantees are not redundant, however, because the U.S. Constitution establishes only *minimum* standards for the states. Texas's courts have interpreted some state constitutional provisions to broaden basic rights beyond these minimums. Although the U.S. Supreme Court refused to interpret the Fourteenth Amendment as guaranteeing equal public school funding,[1] Texas's Supreme Court interpreted the efficiency clause of Texas's Constitution (Article 7, Section 1) as requiring greater equity in public schools.[2] By using Texas's constitutional and **statutory law** (law passed by legislatures and written into books of code), Texas courts have struck down polygraph tests for public employees, required workers' compensation for farmworkers, expanded free-speech rights of private employees, and affirmed free-speech rights at privately owned shopping malls.

The Texas Bill of Rights guarantees additional rights not specifically mentioned by the U.S. Constitution. Notably, Texas has adopted an amendment to prohibit discrimination based on sex. A similar guarantee was proposed as the Equal Rights Amendment to the U.S. Constitution, but it was not ratified by the states. The Texas Constitution also guarantees victims' rights and access to public beaches. It forbids imprisonment for debt or committing the mentally ill for an extended period without a jury trial. It also prohibits monopolies and the suspension under any circumstances of the **writ of habeas corpus**, which is a court order requiring that an individual be presented in person and that legal cause be shown for confinement; it may result in release from unlawful detention. Article 16 protects homesteads and prohibits the garnishment of wages except for court-ordered child support.

Statutory law
Law passed by legislatures and written into books of code.

Writ of habeas corpus
A court order requiring that an individual be presented in person and that legal cause be shown for confinement; it may result in release from unlawful detention.

---

[1] *San Antonio Independent School District* v. *Rodriguez,* 411 U.S. 1 (1973).
[2] *Edgewood* v. *Kirby,* 777 S.W. 2d 391 (Tex. 1989).

Although the state constitution forbids same-sex marriages, the Texas Bill of Rights and other provisions guarantee the average citizen a greater variety of protections than most other state constitutions. We will extensively discuss Texans' basic rights in Chapter 10.

Separation of Powers

Separation of powers

The principle behind the concept of a government where power is distributed among at least three different branches—legislative, executive, and judicial.

Like the state bill of rights, Article 2 of the Texas Constitution limits government. To prevent the concentration of power in the hands of any single institution, the national government and all states at the minimum have provided for a **separation of powers** among three branches of government—legislative, executive, and judicial. The function of the legislative branch is to make laws, and it is by law that governments define crime, establish the basis of civil suits, determine what will be taxed and who will pay how much in taxes, and set up government programs and the agencies that administer them. The function of the executive branch is to carry out the law, to arrest criminals, to collect taxes, to provide public services, to hire government employees, and to supervise their day-to-day conduct. The function of the judicial branch is to interpret the law as it applies to individuals and institutions.

checks and balances

The concept that each branch of government is assigned power to limit abuses by the others.

Despite the separation of powers, there is still the potential for any of these three branches to abuse whatever powers they have been given. The Texas Constitution also follows American tradition in subsequent constitutional articles—it sets up a system of **checks and balances**, the concept that each branch of government is assigned power to limit abuses by the others. Table 3.2 illustrates that, under certain circumstances, a function normally assigned to one branch of government can be influenced by another. For example, the veto power that deals with lawmaking (a legislative function) is given to the governor (an executive). Impeachment and conviction, which deal with determining guilt (a judicial function), are given to the legislature. The state senate (a house of the legislature) confirms appointments the governor makes in the executive branch. Although there is a separation of powers, the checks-and-balances system requires that each branch have the opportunity to influence the others. The three branches specialize in separate functions, but there is some sharing of powers as well. In Chapters 7 through 9, you will see how extensively these three branches of government interact.

TABLE 3.2   Texas's Constitutional Checks and Balances

Checks on the Legislature	Checks on the Executive Branch	Checks on the Judicial Branch
• The governor may veto bills passed by the legislature subject to a two-thirds vote to override.	• Texas's House of Representatives may impeach an executive by a majority vote.	• The governor appoints judges to fill vacancies in district and higher courts until the next election.
• The governor may use the line-item veto on appropriations bills.	• Texas's Senate may convict and remove an executive by a two-thirds vote.	• The House may impeach and the Senate may remove state judges.
• The governor may call special legislative sessions and set their agenda.	• The Senate confirms official appointments of the governor by a two-thirds vote.	• The legislature sets judicial salaries.
• The governor may address the legislature and designate emergency legislation that can be considered in the first 30 days of the session.	• The legislature creates nonconstitutional executive agencies, assigns them their powers, and appropriates their funds.	• The legislature establishes many lower courts by statute.
• The courts use *judicial review* to declare legislative acts unconstitutional.	• The courts may declare actions of the governor or state agencies unconstitutional or illegal.	• The legislature may pass new laws if they disagree with court interpretation of existing ones.
		• Two-thirds of the legislature may propose constitutional amendments to overturn court decisions.

This table shows the major checks and balances in the Texas Constitution. In practice, the political environment determines how effectively they limit each branch of government.

▲ **How effective are these checks when, as in Texas today, all three branches of government are controlled by the same political party? Do these checks lead to gridlock when control of the three branches is divided between two parties?**

Legislative Branch

The legislative article (Article 3) is by far the longest in the Texas Constitution. As is the case at the federal level and in every one of the 50 states but Nebraska (which has a unicameral legislature), the Texas Constitution provides for a **bicameral** (consisting of two houses or chambers) legislative body constituted by the 31-member Senate and the 150-member House of Representatives.

The 1876 Constitution raised the number of senators to 31 and representatives to 93, with the provision that the size of the House could increase as the state's population grew, but only up to a maximum of 150 representatives. Following the drafting of the 1876 Constitution and the 1880 census (i.e., in the 18th Legislature of 1883), each senator represented an average of 51,000 people and each representative an average of 17,000. Today, the average number of Texans per representative is ten times greater (168,000) and the comparable number represented by a senator 16 times greater (811,000) than was the case almost 140 years ago, when these limits were put in place (see Figure 3.1). As of the 2010 Census, more people (844,000) lived in the most populous Texas state senate district (SD-3) than lived in the entire state of Texas in 1870 (819,000). In fact, more Texans live in the average Texas senate district than in four states, including North Dakota, which has 47 senators (1 for every 14,000 North Dakotans).

Senators are elected for a four-year term (with one-half of the body elected in one general election and the other half in the next except immediately after redistricting when all senators stand for election at the same time) from single-member districts. Each senator must be at least 26 years old, be a citizen, and have resided in the state for five years and in the district for one year. Representatives are elected for a two-year term with the entire house elected every two years. Each representative must be at least 21 years old, a citizen, and a resident of the state for two years and of the district for one year. Unlike the case in 15 U.S. states, there are no limits placed on the number of terms, consecutive or lifetime, that a Texas legislator can serve. The current dean of the Texas legislature is Representative Tom Craddick of Midland, who first arrived in the House in January 1969.

The Texas Constitution sets the salary of a state legislator at $7,200 per year. This amount can be changed only by voter approval of a recommendation for an increase made by the Texas Ethics Commission. The Ethics Commission has made no such recommendation but has exercised its power to increase the per diem (daily) allowance for legislators, currently $150, while the legislature is in session. This meager salary is noticeably lower than that in other major states with, for instance, California legislators receiving a salary of $90,526 per year and New York legislators earning $79,500.[3] These low salaries result in most Texas legislators holding jobs outside the legislature, jobs that can create a potential conflict between legislators' personal financial interests and their mandate to represent the public's interest.

In Texas, regular legislative sessions are scheduled by the constitution. They are held once every two years and hence are referred to as **biennial regular sessions**. These biennial regular sessions are convened for 140 days between January and May/June of odd-numbered years. This contrasts to the pattern of other major states such as California, Michigan, and New York, where no limits are placed on the length of sessions.

As a result of the relatively short sessions, important legislation may be rushed through the legislative process with insufficient analysis and debate. Other important legislation may never reach the floor or even be discussed in a legislative committee due to time limitations. In fact, the leadership of the Texas Senate and House frequently strategically uses this short time period to block legislation that it does not want to see passed, without paying the political cost of voting against it on the Senate or House floor.

Bicameral

Consisting of two houses or chambers; applied to a legislative body with two parts, such as a senate and a house of representatives (or assembly).

Biennial regular sessions

In Texas, regular legislative sessions are scheduled by the constitution. They are held once every two years and, hence, are referred to as biennial regular sessions.

[3]*2013 Book of the States* (Lexington, Kentucky: Council of State Governments, 2013).

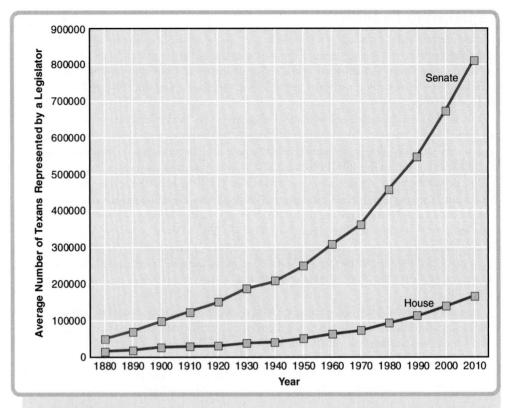

Figure 3.1

The Growth in the Number of Texans Represented by Each State Legislator: 1880–2010

The figure highlights the dramatic increase over the past 130 years in the average number of Texans represented by each state senator and representative following each decennial census.

Note: For each census date, the number of legislators used in calculation is that for the first legislative election held after the census data became available.

United States and Texas Populations: 1850–2012. Austin: Texas State Library and Archives Commission, https://www.tsl.texas.gov/ref/abouttx/census.html.

 The size of the Texas Senate has not increased since the drafting of the 1876 Constitution, although that of the House has remained at its ceiling of 150 since 1922. As a result, each senator now represents an average of more than 800,000, and each representative has about 150,000 constituents. In order to improve the level of two-way communication between these legislators and the people they represent, should the Texas Constitution be amended to increase the number of senators and/or representatives?

Special sessions

A legislative session called by the Texas governor, who also sets its agenda.

Filibuster

An extended discussion by a legislator on the floor with the goal of delaying or blocking a final vote on a bill.

Except to deal with extremely rare instances of impeachment, Texas's legislature may not call itself into **special sessions** or determine the issues to be considered during a special session. Lasting no more than 30 days, the governor convenes special sessions to consider only the legislative matters he or she presents. The governor can call as many special sessions as he or she wishes, providing him or her with a powerful legislative advantage. For example, former State Senator Wendy Davis successfully blocked legislation designed to regulate and limit abortions in Texas on the final day (June 25) of the first special session in 2013 by engaging in a 12½-hour **filibuster**, an extended discussion by a legislator on the floor with the goal of delaying or blocking a final vote on a bill. The following day, however, former Governor Rick Perry called a second special session to begin on July 1, where the same legislation was re-introduced. Given the additional time, it easily passed both the House and the Senate, reaching the latter chamber on July 12, a full 19 days prior to the session's end on July 30.

The Texas Constitution establishes more specific procedural requirements than most other state constitutions. Although the provision is often suspended, the constitution requires that a bill must be read on three separate days unless four-fifths of the legislature votes to set aside the requirement. It stipulates when bills may be introduced and how they will be reported out of committee, signed, and entered in the legislative journal once enacted. It even specifies how the enacting clause will read.

Although most states legally require a balanced budget, Texas's constitutional restriction would appear to be more effective than most. Article 3, Section 49 strictly limits the legislature in authorizing state debt except under rare conditions. The comptroller of public accounts is required to certify that funds are available for each appropriations measure adopted. Although specific constitutional amendments have authorized the sale of bonds for student loans, parks and water development, and prison construction, Texas's per capita state debt remains among the lowest in the nation.

Constitutional detail further constrains the legislature by making policies on subjects that normally would be handled by legislative statute. Much of the length of Article 3 results from its in-depth description of state policies such as the Veterans' Land Program, Texas park and water development funds, student loans, welfare programs, a grain warehouse self-insurance fund, and the municipal donation of outdated firefighting equipment. The constitution establishes the design of the great seal of Texas, authorizes the legislature to pass fence laws, and even explains how the state must purchase stationery! Article 16 authorizes the legislature to regulate cattle brands; Article 11 permits the building of seawalls. By including such statute-like details in the Texas Constitution, its drafters guaranteed that even relatively unimportant decisions that could easily be handled by the legislature can be changed only by constitutional amendment.

Events may outstrip detailed constitutional provisions, leaving **deadwood**, inoperable constitutional provisions that have been either voided by a conflicting U.S. constitutional or statutory law or made irrelevant by changing circumstances and contexts, that voters must approve amendments to remove. The basic distrust of the legislature, however much it may have been deserved in 1876, put a straitjacket on the state's ability to cope with the challenges of the twenty-first century.

Deadwood
Inoperable constitutional provisions that have been either voided by a conflicting U.S. constitutional or statutory law or made irrelevant by changing circumstances and contexts.

Executive Branch

Article 4 establishes the executive branch, with the governor as its head. The governor must be a citizen, at least 30 years of age, and a resident of the state for five years immediately preceding his or her election to a four-year term. The constitution no longer limits the governor's salary, and, according to statute, it is presently $150,000.

Although the constitution provides that the governor shall be the chief executive, it actually establishes a **plural executive**, which is an executive branch where power is divided among several independently elected officials—the governor, lieutenant governor, attorney general, comptroller of public accounts, commissioner of the general land office, and three railroad commissioners—thereby weakening the power of the chief executive, which, in Texas, is the governor. All of these officials are elected for four-year terms with the exception of the railroad commissioners, who are elected for six-year terms on a staggered cycle with one position renewed every two years. There are also provisions for a state board of education to be either elected or appointed. The constitution stipulates that the governor appoint the secretary of state. Texas is one of only seven states lacking a formal cabinet.

Plural executive
An executive branch where power is divided among several independently elected officials, thereby weakening the power of the chief executive, which, in Texas, is the governor.

Texas places no limits of any type on the re-election of the members of its plural executive. In the case of the governor, Texas is one of only 14 states that does not limit their governors' opportunity for re-election in any way. Prior to the 14-year-long governorship of former Governor Perry (December 2000 to January 2015), however, the record for the number of consecutive years served by a Texas governor was only 7½ (Allan Shivers, 1949–1957); the record for the total number of years was 8 (Bill Clements, 1979–1983, 1987–1991). A 1972 constitutional amendment increased the term length for the governor and other non-collegial members of the plural executive to four years.

In the tradition of the constitutional plural executive, the legislature by statute has also established an elected commissioner of agriculture and has exercised its option to make the state board of education elected independently of the governor. The result of electing so many state executive officers is a long ballot that many voters find confusing because it is difficult for them to assign responsibility in a system of diffused power.

Most of the remaining agencies that the legislature has established to administer state programs are run by appointed multimember boards with substantial formal independence from the governor. The governor has **indirect appointive powers** to appoint supervisory boards but not the operational directors for most state agencies. The governor is empowered to name the members of supervisory boards to six-year staggered terms with the approval of two-thirds of the state senate. Each board in turn appoints its agency's director. The governor usually does not appoint the agency administrator directly—the board does. Among the appointments made by the governor with senate approval are those of the members of the boards of regents of the Texas A&M University, Texas State University, and University of Texas systems—appointments that during recent years have led to considerable tension between the University of Texas at Austin and some of the UT System regents appointed by former Governor Perry.

The Texas governor has limited **removal powers** (the authority to fire appointed officials); they extend only to officials he or she has appointed and are subject to the consent of two-thirds of the state senate. The governor may fire his or her own staff and advisors at will, but removal of state officers is more difficult. The governor may fire appointed officers only if two-thirds of the senators agree that there is just cause for removal, making firing almost as difficult as impeachment and conviction. Furthermore, the governor may not remove anyone appointed by a preceding governor. **Directive authority** (the power to issue binding orders to state agencies) is still quite restricted, and **budgetary power** (to recommend to the legislature how much it should appropriate for various executive agencies) is limited by the competing influences of the Legislative Budget Board.

The statutes and the constitution combine to make the governor a relatively weak executive, but the veto power provides the governor with a profound amount of influence over the legislative process. Since 1942, Texas governors have vetoed 1,240 bills, but only once during that entire time period did the Texas legislature muster the necessary two-thirds vote to override a governor's veto. In 1979, a veto by Governor Bill Clements of legislation granting the Comal County Commissioners Court the power to regulate hunting and fishing in the county was narrowly overridden. The Texas legislature, though, often lacks the opportunity to override a veto because major legislation may be adopted during the last days of the session. The Texas Constitution allows the governor ten days (excluding Sundays) to act during the session and 20 days after it adjourns. For legislation passed during the final days of the legislative session, the governor may avoid the threat of an override by simply waiting until the legislature adjourns before vetoing the bill.

Texas is among 44 states that give the governor **line-item veto** power to strike out particular sections of a bill without vetoing the entire bill in the area of appropriations. Several states also allow their governors to item veto matters other than appropriations, but Texas does not, only permitting line-item vetoes of appropriations legislation. The governor of Texas lacks

Indirect appointive powers
Texas governor's authority to appoint supervisory boards but not the operational directors for most state agencies.

Removal powers
The authority to fire appointed officials.

Directive authority
The power to issue binding orders to state agencies.

Budgetary power
The power to recommend to the legislature how much it should appropriate for various executive agencies.

Line-item veto
The power to strike out sections of a bill without vetoing the entire bill.

both the **reduction veto** (the power to reduce amounts in an appropriations bill without striking them out altogether) and the **pocket veto** (the power to kill legislation by simply ignoring it after the end of the legislative session).

Judicial Branch

Just as the constitution limits the power of the chief executive, Article 5 also fragments the judicial branch. Texas is the only state other than Oklahoma that has two courts of final appeal. The highest court for civil matters is the nine-member Texas Supreme Court; the other, for criminal matters, is the nine-member Texas Court of Criminal Appeals. Leaving some flexibility as to number and jurisdiction, the constitution also creates courts of appeals, as well as district, county, and justice of the peace courts. The same article describes the selection of grand and trial juries and such administrative officers as sheriff, county clerk, and county and district attorneys.

The number and variety of courts are confusing to the average citizen, and coordination and supervision are minimal. State courts have also come under attack due to the lack of qualified judges. The constitution specifies only general qualifications for county judges and justices of the peace, who need not be lawyers. There were very likely good reasons for people without legal training to serve as judges during the latter part of the nineteenth century, but today many Texans regard them as an anachronism.

The manner of selecting judges is another factor that affects their qualifications. In Texas, judges are chosen in **partisan elections**, general elections where the candidates are nominated by the political parties and their respective party labels appear on the ballot. Trial judges are elected to serve for four years and appeals court judges for six, but judges often leave office before the end of their last term. The governor has the power to fill most judicial vacancies until the next election—a power that gives the governor considerable influence over the makeup of the courts because, once in office, incumbent judges are commonly returned to office without facing a serious challenge in the next election due to the advantages of incumbency.

Suffrage

A major function of state and local governments in the United States is to determine the character of democracy as they set requirements for **suffrage** (the legal right to vote) and administer elections. Article 6 of the Texas Constitution deals with suffrage requirements. It denies the right to vote to persons under age 18, certain convicted felons, and individuals found mentally incompetent by a court of law. We will extensively discuss the development of Texans' suffrage rights in Chapter 4.

Direct Democracy

Although constitutional restrictions on their qualifications are now as minimal as any in the nation, Texas voters still lack certain opportunities to directly participate in state government. Unlike many states (see "How Does Texas Compare"), the Texas Constitution does not allow **initiatives**, an election method that empowers citizens to place a proposal on the ballot for voter approval. If the measure passes, it becomes law. Neither does the constitution permit **referendums**, elections that permit voters to determine whether an ordinance or statute will go into effect. Finally, there is no vehicle in the Texas Constitution that would allow for **popular recalls**, special elections to remove an official before the end of his or her term, initiated by citizen petition. Initiatives, referendums, and popular recall are available in many other states and even in some Texas cities, but are absent at the state level.

Reduction veto
The power to reduce amounts in an appropriations bill without striking them out altogether; this power is not available to Texas's governor.

Pocket veto
The power to kill legislation by simply ignoring it after the end of the legislative session; this power is not available to Texas's governor.

Did You Know? The annual salary of the Texas lieutenant governor is only $7,200 while that of the governor, attorney general, and comptroller is $150,000?

Partisan elections
General elections where the candidates are nominated by the political parties and their respective party labels appear on the ballot.

Suffrage
The legal right to vote.

Initiatives
An election method that empowers citizens to place a proposal on the ballot for voter approval. If the measure passes, it becomes law (permitted in some Texas cities but not at the state level).

Referendums
An election that permits voters to determine if an ordinance or statute will go into effect (permitted in some Texas cities but not at the state level).

Popular recalls
A special election to remove an official before the end of his or her term, initiated by citizen petition (permitted in some Texas cities but not at the state level).

HOW DOES TEXAS COMPARE?
Methods of Direct Democracy

One-half (25) of the U.S. states allow citizens to play a direct role in either the passage or repeal of legislation and/or the reform the state constitution (see Figure 3.2). Among these states are Colorado and Washington, where citizens in 2012 utilized the provisions in their respective state's constitution to put initiatives on the ballot legalizing the sale and consumption of marijuana for personal use (see Chapter 2).

Citizens are most empowered in those states whose constitutions provide for an initiative process to pass statutes and/or reform the state constitution. In these states proponents of laws or constitutional reforms may submit petitions signed by a minimum number of registered votes, normally equivalent to a percentage of the vote cast in a

recent election. Proposals that meet the signature requirements are placed on the ballot either directly or indirectly (i.e., only if the proposal fails to be passed into law through the standard legislative process). Proposals that receive voter approval become law (statutory initiatives) or part of the state's constitution (constitutional initiatives).

A second form of direct democracy is the popular referendum. If voters object to legislation approved by the state legislature, they may organize a petition to place the objectionable legislation on the ballot. If the petition possesses a sufficient number of valid signatures, the law's implementation is delayed until a referendum can be held. If voters reject the legislation, then the law is voided; if a majority votes in favor, then the legislation goes into effect.

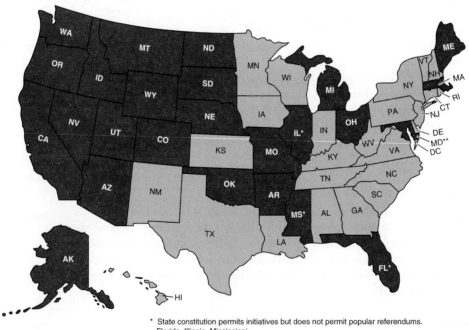

* State constitution permits initiatives but does not permit popular referendums.
Florida, Illinois, Mississippi

** State constitution permits popular referendums but does not permit initiatives.
Maryland

Figure 3.2
States Where the Constitution Allows Citizens to Put Initiatives and Popular Referendums on the Ballot
This figure details the presence of mechanisms of direct democracy in 25 states (in ■) across the United States and highlights that the Texas Constitution does not empower the state's citizens to place any type of legislation on the ballot.

2013 Book of States (Lexington, KY: Council of State Governments, 2013)

Note: Due to the limited thematic range of laws for which it is permitted and substantial ballot access barriers, the popular referendum-only state of New Mexico is not included as a direct democracy state.

FOR DEBATE

 Supporters of initiatives highlight how they can be used to get legislation passed that is supported by a majority of voters but blocked by legislators and/or powerful special interests. Opponents often argue that legislation is too complex to be condensed into a simple yes or no question, that legislators are better able than voters to evaluate the pros and cons of proposed legislation, and that the initiative process benefits special interests and wealthy individuals who can use their monetary advantage to prevail in the popular vote. Should the Texas Constitution be reformed to allow citizens to place proposed legislation or constitutional amendments on the ballot using the initiative process?

 Provide examples of constitutional amendments and laws that you think would be approved by voters if Texas citizens were to be granted the ability to place them on the ballot via the initiative process.

Texas permits voters to decide directly on only three matters: constitutional amendments, the establishment or subsequent modification of a state income tax, and legislative salaries. Texas's political parties often place referendums on their primary ballots, but the results are purely symbolic and are not legally binding.

Public Education

Article 7, Section 1 of the Texas Constitution states that a "general diffusion of knowledge being essential to the preservation of the liberties and rights of the people, it shall be the duty of the Legislature of the State to establish and make suitable provision for the support and maintenance of an efficient system of public free schools." In the seminal case of *Edgewood Independent School District* v. *Kirby* in 1989, the Texas Supreme Court found that the then-existing method of financing the state's public schools violated the Texas Constitution due to dramatic differences in per-student spending levels among the state's school districts. *Edgewood* eventually led to school finance reforms that made funding more equitable across districts, but the case also spawned an ongoing legal debate over the funding of public education in Texas, where judges have served as the arbiters in a continuing series of disputes over what constitutes a suitable and efficient education system.

Local Government

The Texas Constitution subordinates local governments to the state, and it decentralizes government power by assigning many state responsibilities to local governments, especially counties. As a result, the constitution describes a rigid organizational structure for counties in Articles 9 and 16, and voters of the entire state were once required to approve amendments so individual counties could abolish obsolete county offices like hide inspector, superintendent of schools, and weigher. The constitution now authorizes county voters to abolish certain offices, but there is no provision for county home rule. As in state government, the constitution divides and diffuses county powers through a plural executive system.

The legislature has the power to set up structures for city governments and offers municipalities several standard alternative *general-law charters*. Cities with populations of more than 5,000 may adopt *home-rule charters* that may establish any organizational structure or program that does not conflict with state law or the constitution (see Chapter 11).

Generally, the legislature has the power to provide for the establishment of limited-purpose local governments known as *special districts*. Numerous special districts are also established by the constitution itself, and to eliminate one of these requires a constitutional amendment. Many of them have been created to perform functions that general-purpose local governments, such as counties and cities, cannot afford because of constitutional tax and debt limits. Arising out of constitutional restrictions, special districts have multiplied taxing and spending authorities and, except for school districts, operate largely outside of the public's view.

AMENDING AND REVISING THE TEXAS CONSTITUTION

LO 3.3 Explain the process of amending and revising the Texas Constitution and the reasons that amendments are frequently necessary.

Given the level of detail in the Texas Constitution, it is frequently necessary to amend it to reflect changing realities. The large number of constitutional amendments ratified since 1876 suggests that Texans understand the need to amend the constitution, even though they have steadfastly resisted any attempts to systematically revise it.

Amendment Procedures

Proposal of constitutional amendments

In Texas, the proposal of a constitutional amendment must be supported by two-thirds of the total membership of each house of the Texas legislature (at least 21 senators and 100 representatives).

Ratification

Approval by a majority of those persons voting on the amendment in either a general or a special election.

Article 17 of the Texas Constitution provides that the **proposal of constitutional amendments** must be supported by two-thirds of the total membership of each house of the Texas legislature (at least 21 senators and 100 representatives). **Ratification** of constitutional amendments requires approval by a majority of those persons voting on the amendment in either a regular or special election. Because such an extraordinary majority of legislators must agree merely to propose constitutional amendments, a number of them are relatively uncontroversial. Since 1876, voters have approved almost three-quarters of all proposed constitutional amendments, and during the past twenty years the approval rate for amendments has been greater than 90 percent.

Constitutional Amendments: 1995–2014

During every regular legislative session, the Texas legislature votes to send a varying number of constitutional amendments to the voters for ratification. The last regular legislative session where no constitutional amendments were proposed took place more than 50 years ago in 1961. The topics of these amendments range from the minor (e.g., Proposition 2 in 2013, which repealed the constitutional provision for a state medical education board and fund that had ceased to operate and had no funds) to the major (e.g., Proposition 6 in 2013, which created a $2 billion dollar fund to support water-related infrastructure projects).

Between 1995 and 2014, the legislature voted to present a total of 145 proposed constitutional amendments to Texas voters. With two exceptions (in 2002 and 2014 voters ratified single amendments concurrently with the November general election), these amendments were voted on during odd-numbered years, most commonly in November. Primarily as a result of no federal, state, or county elections (with the exception of rare special elections) being on the ballot in November of odd-numbered years (off-years), voter participation in these constitutional amendment elections is extremely low. Between 1995 and 2013, an average of only 7 percent of the state's voting age population cast a ballot in these contests, ranging from a low of 5 percent to a high of 14 percent. This average contrasts with the level in the subsequent general election held the following November (e.g., for the November 2011 election, the subsequent general election was in November 2012). Although still low compared to most states (see Chapter 4), an average of 36 percent of voting age Texans cast ballots on

TABLE 3.3 Amending the Texas Constitution in Off-Year Elections: 1995–2013

Election Year (month)	Number of Amendments Proposed	Number of Amendments Passed	Voter Turnout (percent of Voting Age Population)	Voter Turnout in Subsequent Even Year General Election (percent of Voting Age Population)
2013 (Nov)	9	9	6	24
2011 (Nov)	10	8	4	44
2009 (Nov)	11	11	6	27
2007 (Nov)	16	16	6	46
2007 (May)	1	1	5	46
2005 (Nov)	9	7	14	26
2003 (Sept)	22	22	9	46
2001 (Nov)	19	19	6	29
1999 (Nov)	17	13	7	44
1997 (Nov)	14	12	9	27
1997 (Aug)	1	1	5	27
1995 (Nov)	14	11	6	41
Total/Average %	143	130 (90%)	7%	36%

This table shows that most voters ratify most constitutional amendments that the legislature proposes. Notice how few Texans actually participate in the ratification process compared to those who vote in general elections.

Texas Secretary of State.

 Currently almost all constitutional amendments are voted on during November of odd-numbered years, when voter turnout is substantially lower than in even-numbered Novembers, when federal, state, and county offices are on the ballot. Does the low level of voter turnout in these off-year elections undermine the legitimacy of the constitutional amendment process in Texas? Should the constitution be reformed to require that voting on constitutional amendments only take place in November of even-numbered years?

average in the even-year general elections. This is more than five times greater than the average turnout in the odd-year amendment elections, where virtually all of the constitutional amendments are placed before the state's voters for ratification.

The data in Table 3.3 also highlight the reality that most constitutional amendments presented to voters since 1995 have been approved. Only around one out of every ten amendments failed to be ratified by voters during this period. All eleven and nine amendments on the ballot in 2009 and 2013, respectively, were ratified, but three of the nine amendments placed before voters in 2011 were rejected. Perhaps not coincidentally, all three of the rejected amendments in 2011 were portrayed by opponents as backdoor attempts to increase taxes.

Criticisms of the Texas Constitution

The Texas Constitution is one of the longest, most detailed, and most frequently amended state constitutions in the nation. With approximately 87,000 words, it is the nation's second longest after Alabama's; with 483 amendments, it is the fourth most-amended state constitution because Texans have often responded to emerging challenges by further amending their constitution. The constitution, reformers charge, is poorly organized and confusing to most of the state's citizens.

Although only one state (Vermont) constitution (along with the U.S. Constitution) contains fewer than 10,000 words, few are as restrictive as the Texas Constitution. The continuing need to amend a detailed and restrictive state constitution means that citizens are frequently called on to pass judgment on proposed amendments. Although some of the constitution's defenders maintain that giving Texas voters the opportunity to express themselves on constitutional amendments reaffirms popular control of government, voters display little interest in amendment elections. Faced with trivial, confusing, or technical amendments, turnout in constitutional amendment elections has (with the exception of the single amendments in 2002 and 2014) averaged only 7 percent of the voting age population over the past 20 years.

Attempts to Revise the Texas Constitution

Attempts to substantially revise the constitution have met with successive failures. Ironically, in 1972, Texas voters had to amend the constitution to provide for its revision. Under the provisions of that amendment, the legislature established a constitutional revision commission of 37 members appointed by the governor, lieutenant governor, speaker of the house, attorney general, chief justice of the supreme court, and presiding judge of the court of criminal appeals. The commission made several proposals. Meeting in 1974, the legislature acted as a constitutional convention and agreed to many of these recommendations. However, the convention divided over the issue of a right-to-work provision, and the final document could not muster the two-thirds vote needed to submit the proposal to the electorate.

In the 1975 regular session, the legislature proposed eight constitutional amendments to the voters. Together, the proposed amendments were substantially the same as the proposals the legislature had previously defeated. If they had been adopted, the amendments would have shortened the constitution by 75 percent through reorganization and by eliminating statute-like detail and deadwood. The legislature would have been strengthened by annual sessions, and a salary commission would have set the legislators' salary. Although limited to two terms, the governor would have been designated as the chief planning officer and given removal powers and certain powers of fiscal control. The court system would have been unified and its administrative procedure simplified. Local governments would have operated under broader home-rule provisions, and counties would have been authorized to pass general ordinances and to abolish unneeded offices.

Opponents' chief arguments were against more power for the legislature, greater government costs, and the possibility of an income tax—all of which are serious issues for many Texans. Because the legislature had written the proposals, it was easy for the Texas voter to see such things as annual sessions and flexibility concerning their salaries as a "grab for power" that would substantially increase government expenditures. Despite an emotional campaign, only 15 percent of voting age Texans cast ballots in the election, and they overwhelmingly rejected all of the proposed amendments.

APPLYING WHAT YOU HAVE LEARNED ABOUT THE TEXAS CONSTITUTION

LO 3.4 Apply what you have learned about the Texas Constitution.

As you have learned in this chapter, the Texas Constitution is a detailed document that spells out many public policies. Many other state and national constitutions leave these detailed public policies to ongoing institutions, such as the legislature and the executive branch, to enact and implement. By including details of public policies such as education in the Texas Constitution, the framers have perhaps unintentionally opened the door to extensive court intervention in public school finance.

The following essay will help you close the gap between theory and reality by showing you how constitutional policy regarding education is being implemented in practice. After you have read the essay, you will be asked to apply your critical-thinking skills to new information that the new essay presents.

THE TEXAS CONSTITUTION AND PUBLIC SCHOOL FUNDING

by *Timothy Hoye*

TEXAS WOMAN'S UNIVERSITY

Among the most vexing challenges to policy makers in any state, or in any nation-state, is the provision of a quality education for the children of its citizens. And central to that challenge is the more specific decision on how best to fund that education. Traditionally, in the United States, these challenges have been left to the state and local governments. Also, traditionally, education issues have been addressed in both constitutional and statutory provisions. And this has meant running battles between various legislative majorities and various courts, with particular reference to the state supreme courts. In Texas, among the most contested features of the Texas Constitution is Article VII, which is simply titled "Education." Of primary importance is the language in Section 1 and the meaning of the responsibility it places on the Texas legislature to provide for "the general diffusion of knowledge," a "suitable," and "efficient" system of public free schools."[4] The high drama here really begins with the case of *Edgewood Independent School District* v. *Kirby* in 1989, also known as *Edgewood I.* But some background is required.

San Antonio v. *Rodriguez* (1973)

Constitutional challenges to the property tax based scheme of funding K-12 public education in Texas began in the federal courts, in 1968, when concerned parents in several school districts in the San Antonio area brought a case to the U.S. District Court, Western District, in San Antonio, Texas, arguing that the various districts, and the state of Texas, were in violation of the equal protection clause of the Fourteenth Amendment to the United States Constitution. The essential argument was that education is a fundamental right and that a property or wealth based system of funding created a discriminatory "suspect classification" and, therefore, is in violation of the equal protection guarantee in the Fourteenth Amendment. Though successful in the lower federal court, plaintiffs failed to convince the United States Supreme Court. Writing for the court on March 21, 1973, Justice Lewis Powell, in a 5–4 decision, and despite acknowledging a "dual system," and the contrasts between Edgewood ISD spending per pupil and spending per pupil in Alamo Heights, and drawing on precedent cases in Illinois, North Carolina, California, and Washington, wrote that "we find neither the suspect classification nor the fundamental interest analysis persuasive."[5]

The effect of this ruling was to send the issue back to the state of Texas: "the ultimate solutions must come from the lawmakers and from the democratic pressures of those who elect them." Justice Potter Stewart wrote a concurring opinion. Justices William Brennan, Byron White, and Thurgood Marshall wrote dissenting opinions with Justice William O. Douglass concurring with Justice Marshall. Justice Marshall's dissent was especially critical of the majority: "… the majority's holding can only be seen as a retreat from our historic commitment to equality of educational opportunity and as unsupportable acquiescence in a system which deprives children in their earliest years of their chance to reach their full potential as citizens."[6] Writing on the twenty-fifth anniversary of the ruling, Douglas S. Reed noted that in the interim much had been done at the state level: "Relying on arguments rooted in both state equal protection provisions and in language in state education clauses, litigators have pursued these claims to state supreme courts in 36 states."[7] The Texas case came out of the Edgewood ISD and went before the Texas Supreme Court in 1989. It would be back five more times through 2006.

---

[4] *The Constitution of the State of Texas*, Article VII, Section 1.
[5] *San Antonio Independent School District* v. *Rodriguez*, 411 U.S. 1 (1973).
[6] Ibid.
[7] Douglas S. Reed, "Twenty-Five Years After Rodriguez: School Finance Litigation and the Impact of the New Judicial Federalism," *Law and Society Review* 32, no. 1 (1998), 175–220.

Edgewood v. *Kirby,* **Six Times** The new strategy for plaintiffs in Texas was to argue that the funding system in Texas was in violation of Article VII of the Texas Constitution, which guarantees an "efficient system of public free schools." The case was first brought by the Mexican American Legal Defense and Education Fund in 1984 on behalf of the Edgewood District against the Commissioner of Education at that time, who was Dr. William N. Kirby. The case went to trial in 1987 in state district court in Travis County. In June, the court ruled on behalf of the plaintiffs that the state's method of public school funding was in violation of the "efficiency" clause above noted and also on grounds that it did not provide for "equal protection."[8] A state appellate court, however, overruled the lower court ruling primarily that the question of "efficiency" was a "political" question for the state legislature to determine. This set the basis for the *Edgewood* appeal to the Texas Supreme Court. Justice Oscar Mauzy wrote the opinion for a unanimous Supreme Court. Among facts cited in the opinion are that the richest districts in Texas have "over $14,000,000 of property wealth per student, while the poorest has approximately $20,000," a disparity that reflects a "700 to 1 ratio." Additionally, the "average property wealth in the 100 wealthiest districts is more than twenty times greater than the average property wealth in the 100 poorest districts." Using the same districts compared in the *Rodriguez* case, the court also noted that "Edgewood ISD has $38,854 in property wealth per student" while Alamo Heights ISD, "in the same county," has "$570,109." Based on these and similar facts the court ruled that property poor districts "are trapped in a cycle of poverty from which there is no opportunity to free themselves." With modifications, focusing mostly on the efficiency clause in Article VII of the Texas Constitution, but also noting the failure to provide for a "general diffusion of knowledge"[9] the Supreme Court affirmed the original District Court decision. Despite "good faith efforts" the Texas Legislature had failed to reform an inefficient system: "A band-aid will not suffice; the system itself must be changed."[10] The court set a legislative deadline to address the inefficiencies of May 1, 1990. Former Governor Bill Clements called a Special Session of the Legislature for November 14, 1989. This would be the first of four consecutive sessions in attempts to meet the court's directives. All efforts, however, failed to satisfy plaintiffs in the original suit and so the state was back in the Travis County District Court and, eventually, in the State Supreme Court five more times in what came to be known as Edgewood II, III, IV, V, and VI.

In Edgewood II, in 1991, the Supreme Court recommended "consolidation" of "school districts" and "tax bases," a recommendation accepted by the Texas Legislature in regular session in the spring of 1991. The legislature created 188 County Education Districts (CEDs) in a complex scheme to satisfy the court. In Edgewood III, however, in 1992, referring to several provisions not previously central to the case, the court invalidated the new CEDs. In May 1993, the legislature tried again and in Edgewood IV the Supreme Court, for the first time, upheld their actions. Edgewood V (2001–2003) and Edgewood VI (2003–2006) represented challenges by wealthy districts dissatisfied with what has come to be known as the Robin Hood Plan for funding schools in Texas, where poorer districts rob from the richer. In dismissing numerous challenges by a variety of groups and interests, the court, in Edgewood VI, concluded that though conditions showed "an impending constitutional violation" there was "not an existing one."[11]

---

[8]Billy D. Walker and John D. Thompson, "Special Report: The Texas Supreme Court and *Edgewood ISD* v. *Kirby,*" *Journal of Education Finance* 15 (Winter 1990), 414–428.

[9]*Constitution of the State of Texas,* Article VII, Section 1.

[10]*Edgewood Independent School District* v. *Kirby,* 777 S.W. 2d 391 (TX 1989).

[11]Albert H. Kauffman, "The Texas School Finance Litigation Saga: Great Progress, Then Near Death by a Thousand Cuts," *St Mary's Law Journal,* 40 (January 2009), 511–579.

The West Orange-Cove Case In 2005, and in the words of Justice Nathan Hecht who wrote the opinion for the court in the West Orange-Cove case, the Texas Supreme Court was "once again" asked "to determine whether the funding of Texas public schools violates the Texas Constitution." Numerous districts brought suit, once again in the name of the two provisions in Article VII regarding "diffusion of knowledge" and efficiency, but a new contention was argued. Article VIII, Section 1-e of the Constitution of the State of Texas provides that no state "ad valorem tax shall be levied upon any property within this state." Many of the districts claimed that under pressures from the state, local districts were compelled to tax local property at the maximum rate, thus in effect leaving them "without meaningful discretion." Without such discretion, the state was in effect levying a state property tax in violation of the Constitution. Regarding the Article VII questions the court, in a long and detailed summary, continued to uphold its earlier ruling: "... the possibility of improvement does not render the present system unsuitable for adequately and efficiently providing a public education." But on the question of whether the state had, through controlling the process, in effect enacted a state property tax in violation of Article VIII, the court ruled differently: "We agree with the district court that it does."[12] The court set a June 1, 2006, deadline for the legislature to remedy the system. Former Governor Rick Perry called a special session for April and the legislature addressed the concerns of the court by passing tax reform legislation, the primary purpose being to reduce local property tax rates.

Moving Forward In 2014, Judge John Dietz, of the same District Court in Travis County where the Edgewood cases originated, ruled, once again, that the Texas system of funding public education violates the Texas Constitution, on multiple levels. The state is appealing and the case is headed, also once again, to the Texas Supreme Court. What all of these cases illustrate is that constitutions are subject to interpretation both by legislators who make policy in issue areas like education, and by judges who make rulings in cases and controversies which come before their courts. In a state like Texas, where property value disparities are indeed great, questions regarding taxation, fairness, and the meaning of constitutional phrases like the "general diffusion of knowledge" and "efficient system" will continue into the distant future.

JOIN THE DEBATE

 Given what you know about the framers of the Texas constitution, do you think that they would have expected the state courts to play a large role in the finance of state public schools?

 Evaluate the ethics of public school finance. Does the state have the responsibility to ensure that students have access to equally funded public schools? Or should parents who live in wealthier districts and pay higher school taxes be able to offer their children the privilege of attending better local schools?

Many political pundits argue that the courts should simply read constitutions the way they are written. Using the constitutional provisions discussed in this article as examples, write an essay to explain clearly whether or not this is possible in actual practice. Who should be responsible for determining whether the schools provide a "general diffusion of knowledge" though an "efficient system" as required by the state constitution?

---

[12]*West Orange-Cove Consolidated Independent School District* v. *Neeley*, 176 S.W. 3d 746 (2005).

CHAPTER SUMMARY

LO 3.1   Explain the origins and evolution of the Texas Constitution, including the Constitutional Convention of 1875. The first Texas Constitution combined elements drawn from the U.S. Constitution and the constitutions of the states from which the Anglo settlers had migrated with unique elements based on the state's former status as a Spanish colony and Mexican state. The current constitution was written in the period following Reconstruction. Most Anglo Texans viewed the Reconstruction state government as abusive and tyrannical. In 1875, a state constitutional convention reacted to the Reconstruction regime by limiting state government in almost every imaginable way.

LO 3.2   Describe the major constitutional structures, functions, and limits of Texas's legislative, executive, and judicial branches. The Texas Constitution includes a bill of rights that is more expansive than those in most state constitutions. It follows the national pattern by establishing a separation of powers between legislative, executive, and judicial branches and establishes a system of checks and balances that allows each branch to check or limit the powers of the others.

In addition to the limits that are common to the U.S. Constitution and all state constitutions, the Texas constitution also strictly limits the legislature with short, infrequent sessions, low salaries, and statute-like details that the legislature cannot change without amending the constitution. The governor is limited in his or her role as chief executive because Texas has a plural executive system that includes many independently elected executives over whom the governor has no control. Texas has divided power between two final courts of appeals and judges are elected in partisan elections.

LO 3.3   Explain the process of amending and revising the Texas Constitution and the reasons that amendments are frequently necessary. Constitutional amendments are proposed by two-thirds of each chamber of the state legislature and must be ratified by a majority of voters before going into effect. The Texas Constitution has been amended more than most, but efforts to systematically revise the state constitution have failed.

The constitution's critics argue that a constitution should establish essential governing principles and structures, but some state constitutions, like that of Texas, also go beyond those essentials to establish many details of routine government and, as a consequence, require frequent amendment to reflect new realities.

LO 3.4   Apply what you have learned about the Texas Constitution. You learned that the state constitution established standards by which Texas public schools should be judged, a constitutional detail that set off a torrent of lawsuits against the Texas system of pubic school finance. You considered how the constitution is applied in practice and whether the courts should be allowed to decide important issues like education policy. You weighed the ethics of public policies that confine Texas students to unequal public schools funding.

KEY TERMS

bicameral, *p. 63*
biennial regular sessions, *p. 63*
budgetary power, *p. 66*
checks and balances, *p. 62*
common law, *p. 56*
community property, *p. 56*
deadwood, *p. 65*
directive authority, *p. 66*

filibuster, *p. 64*
homestead, *p. 56*
indirect appointive
    powers, *p. 66*
initiative, *p. 67*
long ballot, *p. 57*
legitimacy, *p. 56*
line-item veto, *p. 66*

long ballot, *p. 57*
partisan elections, *p. 67*
plural executive, *p. 65*
pocket veto, *p. 67*
popular recall, *p. 67*
proposal of constitutional
    amendments, *p. 70*
ratification, *p. 70*

reduction veto, *p. 67*
referendum, *p. 67*
removal powers, *p. 66*
separation of powers, *p. 62*
special session, *p. 64*
statutory law, *p. 61*
suffrage, *p. 67*
writ of habeas corpus, *p. 61*

REVIEW QUESTIONS

LO 3.1 Explain the origins and evolution of the Texas Constitution, including the Constitutional Convention of 1875.

• How did Texas's origins as a Spanish colonial possession and a Mexican state influence the drafting of the state's first constitutions?

• Evaluate the evolution of the state's constitutions from independence through the 1875 Constitutional Convention.

• What are the historical reasons for the restrictive nature of the Texas Constitution? What benefits did the state constitution's writers hope to achieve by limiting state government?

LO 3.2 Describe the major constitutional structures, functions, and limits of Texas's legislative, executive, and judicial branches.

- How does the Texas Constitution differ from the constitutions of other states and the U.S. Constitution?

- Describe the constitutional organization of each of the three branches of Texas government.

- Discuss the major constitutional provisions that restrain each branch of state government. What are the consequences of these restraints?

LO 3.3 Explain the process of amending and revising the Texas Constitution and the reasons that amendments are frequently necessary.

- How is the state's constitution amended?

- Why does Texas amend its constitution so frequently?

- How vibrant is voter participation in the constitutional amendment ratification process?

- What are the strengths and weaknesses of the Texas Constitution? Should the Texas Constitution be substantially revised? Why or why not?

GET ACTIVE

Explore different views of constitutional rights and liberties.

Conservative Groups

- The National Rifle Association at **www.nra.org (Twitter: @nra)** supports the right to keep and bear arms.

- Students for Concealed Carry on Campus at **http://concealedcampus.org (@concealedcampus)** fights to repeal restrictions on carrying firearms on college campuses.

- Texas Right to Life at **www.texasrighttolife.org (@TXRightToLife)** is a pro-life group.

- Texans for Fiscal Responsibility at **www.empowertexans.com (@EmpowerTexans)** is a prominent conservative activist organization in the state.

- Texas Public Policy Foundation at **www.texaspolicy.com (@TPPF)** is a leading conservative Texas think tank.

Liberal Groups

- The Brady Campaign at **www.bradycampaign.org (@bradybuzz)** advocates for gun control.

- NARAL Pro-Choice Texas at **www.prochoicetexas.org (@naraltx)** supports abortion rights.

- Texas Coalition to Abolish the Death Penalty at **www.tcadp .org (@TCADPdotORG)** fights capital punishment.

- The American Civil Liberties Union of Texas at **www .aclutx.org (@ACLUTx)** advocates for the protection of civil liberties.

- The Center for Public Policy Priorities at **forabettertexas. org (@CPPP_TX)** is a leading liberal Texas think tank.

Sample the Texas Constitution. The complete text of the Texas Constitution is at **www.constitution.legis .state.tx.us**. In the index, click on *Article 3, "Legislative Department."* Click on *Section 29* and notice that even the enacting clause for legislation is included in the constitution. Click on *Article 16, Section 6* and notice the level of detail. Read the deadwood provision in Article 9, Section 14. Contrast the legislative and executive articles (Articles 3 and 4) of Texas's Constitution with those of Illinois (Articles 4 and 5) at **www.ilga.gov/commission/ lrb/conmain.htm**.

Evaluate how well Texas limits borrowing. Article 3, Section 59 of Texas's Constitution severely limits state debt. Research how effective these restrictions have been by comparing per capita debt among the 50 states at **http:// taxfoundation.org/blog/monday-map-state-debt-capita**. **Play a role in the continual rewriting of the state's fundamental law.** Vote in Texas elections to ratify or reject state constitutional amendments (the next election most likely will be held in November 2015). Note that proposals are sometimes detailed and confusing, and beware of biased special-interest group television and Internet ads describing them. Good amendment summaries and analyses written by the nonpartisan Texas Legislative Council can be found at **www.tlc.state.tx.us**.

Read constitutional amendments that have been proposed by the Texas Legislature, their legislative history, and the level of popular support for them at **www.tlc .state.tx.us/pubsconamend/constamend1876.pdf**.

 Are the proposed constitutional amendments that Texans voted on too complex for the average voter to decide? Should you and other voters be called upon to make these sorts of decisions or should you leave these matters to the legislature?

CHAPTER 4

Voting and Elections

LEARNING OBJECTIVES

LO 4.1 Explain why voter turnout is low in Texas.

LO 4.2 Describe the types of Texas elections.

LO 4.3 Understand how elections are administered in Texas.

LO 4.4 Identify the factors that advantage (or disadvantage) candidates in Texas elections.

LO 4.5 Apply what you have learned about voting and elections in Texas.

One of the distinguishing features of Texas politics is the number and variety of elections held in the state. Texas elects a large number of officials to do different things at different levels of government. See for yourself: Go to your county website and locate a sample ballot. To find your county's URL, go to **www.state.tx.us**. On this home page, under "Living," click on "Texas Cities and Counties," and then open the "County Directory."

Once you have located your county website, find a sample ballot. Ballots are usually stored on the county clerk's section of the site. You may be able to click on a link marked "Elections" or "County Clerk," although a site's structure is sometimes not so straightforward. In some instances, you may find that your county simply does not post a sample ballot. You might mention this in an email to the county clerk. Perhaps the clerk's office will send you one.

If your county website does not have a sample ballot, try another county's, such as Bexar, Dallas, Denton, El Paso, Harris, Jefferson, or Travis, all of which include a full sample ballot before primary and general elections. Examine the ballot from top to bottom, keeping in mind that it may take some time. Indeed, in some areas, people may be asked to vote for more than 100 different offices, from governor to railroad commissioner, from state representative to city council members, from state judges to county judges, justices of the peace, and constables. There are other offices as well, and often a constitutional amendment or two is included.

Learn about current elections at **www.localvoter.com**. Here you will find information about candidates and issues in your community, learn how to get involved, and get links to other resources.

Fact-check Texas politicians' claims at **www.politifact.com/texas**.

Democracy makes demands on its citizens, in terms of both time and money. A sacrifice of time is required if voters are to inform themselves of the qualifications of the large number of candidates who compete in the spring for nomination in the party primaries. Then, in November, roughly 4,200 of these party nominees ask the voters to elect them in the general election to numerous local, state, and national offices.

POLITICAL PARTICIPATION

LO 4.1　Explain why voter turnout is low in Texas.

Voting in elections is the most basic and common form of political participation. Many people take part in other ways, such as discussing political issues with friends and co-workers, writing letters to local representatives or to newspaper editors, distributing campaign literature or contributing money to a campaign, or placing bumper stickers on cars. Some people are members of interest groups, whether neighborhood or trade associations, serve on political party committees, or act as delegates to conventions. Yet others participate in demonstrations or sit-ins, such as the flurry of tea party protests.

The Participation Paradox and Why People Vote

Elections, of course, are the defining characteristic of representative democracies. It is through our votes that we hold elected officials accountable. After all, votes are what matter to politicians, at least those interested in winning and holding office. If we vote—and reward and punish elected officials for what they do while in office—politicians have an incentive to do what we want. If we do not vote, elected officials are largely free to do what they want. Clearly, voting is important in a representative democracy.

The problem is that a single individual's vote is rarely decisive because few elections are decided by a single vote. This may leave you wondering: Why do people vote? Among political

Voters sometimes wait in long lines to cast their ballots. In this chapter, you will explore who votes in which elections and how campaigns affect their votes.

Participation paradox

The fact that citizens vote even though a single vote rarely decides an election.

scientists, this is known as the **participation paradox**. The point of this paradox is not to suggest that people should not vote but rather to highlight that they vote for other reasons.

Who Votes?

Over the years, political scientists have learned quite a lot about why people go to the polls. It is now clear that a relatively small number of demographic and political variables are especially important.[1] The most important demographic variables are education, income, and age. The more education a person has, the more likely the person is to vote. The same is true for income, even "controlling for" education; that is, among people with the same level of education, the more income a person has the more likely he or she is to vote. Age also matters. As people grow older, they are more likely to vote, at least until they become very old. Why do these factors matter? The answer is straightforward: People who are educated, have high incomes, and are older are more likely to care about and pay attention to politics. Thus, they are more likely to vote.

In addition to demographic factors, certain political factors influence the likelihood of voting, especially one's expressed interest in politics and intensity of identification with political parties. The more a person is interested in politics, the more likely the person is to vote. The effect is fairly obvious but nevertheless quite important. Consider that a person who does not have a lot of education or income is still very likely to vote if he or she has a strong interest in politics.

Identification with either of the major political parties also makes a person more likely to vote. This pattern reflects

Did You Know? Although voting is the most common form of political participation, a much smaller number of Americans participate in other ways. In 2012, surveys indicate that 16 percent wore a button or displayed a bumper sticker, 13 percent donated money to a political party or campaign, 6 percent attended a political meeting or rally, and 4 percent worked for a political party or candidate.[2]

---

[1]Raymond E. Wolfinger and Steven Rosenstone, *Who Votes?* (New Haven, CT: Yale University Press, 1980). Also see Sydney Verba and Norman H. Nie, *Participation in America* (New York: Harper & Row, 1972).

[2]American National Election Studies, University of Michigan, www.electionstudies.org. Note that these numbers may overstate the actual levels of participation because they are difficult to verify, and we know that survey respondents tend to exaggerate turnout. Also note that the level of the self-reported participation was lower in 2012 than in 2008.

the fact that strong partisan identifiers, on average, care a lot more about who wins than people who do not identify with the parties. It also reflects the mobilization of identifiers by the political parties—that is, the more one identifies with a party, the more likely it is that the person will be contacted by the party and its candidates during election campaigns.

In one sense, deciding to vote is much like deciding to attend a sporting event, for example, a professional baseball game. We do not go to a game to affect the outcome. We go for other reasons, because we like baseball and care about it. The same is true for voting; education, income, age, interest, and party identification are important indicators of our desire to participate.

Of course, other factors are also important for explaining electoral participation, but the small set of demographic and political variables tells us quite a lot. With this information, we can pretty much determine whether a person will or will not vote in a particular election. We also can account for most of the differences in turnout among different groups, such as African Americans, Asian Americans, Latinos, and whites. This issue is picked up later in the chapter.

The Practice of Voting

The legal qualifications for voting in Texas are surprisingly few and simple. Anyone who is (1) a citizen of the United States, (2) at least 18 years of age, and (3) a resident of the state is eligible to register and vote in Texas. The only citizens prohibited from voting are those who have been declared "mentally incompetent" in formal court proceedings and those currently serving a sentence, parole, or probation for a felony conviction.

Establishing residence for voting is no longer a matter of living at a place for a specified time. Residence is defined primarily in terms of intent; that is, people's homes are where they intend them to be. No delay in qualifying to vote is permitted under U.S. Supreme Court rulings except for a short period of time in which the application is processed and the registrant's name is entered on the rolls. In accordance with the Court's ruling, that delay in Texas is fixed at 30 days.

Meeting these qualifications does not mean that a person can simply walk into the voting booth on election day. In order to vote, a person must be registered. As a result of the Voting Rights Acts of 1965 and 1970, a number of U.S. Supreme Court rulings, and congressional action, the registration procedure is almost as simple as voting itself. (This was not always true—see the Legal Constraints section.)

A person may register in person or by mail at any time of the year up to 30 days before an election. Since the passage of federal "motor voter" legislation, a person can also register when obtaining or renewing a driver's license; indeed, every person renewing a driver's license is asked whether he or she wants to register to vote. The secretary of state makes postage-free registration applications available at any county clerk's office and at various other public offices. Spouses, parents, or offspring also can register the applicant, provided that they are qualified voters.

Once they register, voters are automatically sent renewals at their address of record by January 1 in even-numbered years, but these renewals cannot be forwarded to new addresses. Thus, voters are permanently registered unless their nonforwardable certificate is returned by mail to the voter registrar.

Names on returned certificates are stricken from the eligible voters list and placed on a strike list. The strike list is attached to the list of voters for each precinct; for three months, the previously registered voters whose names are on the strike list can vote in their old precincts if they have filled out a new voter registration card for the new residence. They can vote, however, only for those offices that both residences have in common. Thus, the person who has moved can vote on at least a portion of both the first and runoff primary ballots.

Coroners' reports, lists of felony convictions, and adjudications of mental incompetence are also used to purge the list of eligible voters. Anyone can purchase the computer-generated voter list for each county in the state. Political parties and candidates make extensive use of voter lists when trying to identify likely voters during election campaigns.

The present Texas registration system is as open and modern as that of any other state that requires advanced registration. A number of states, including Maine, Minnesota, and Wisconsin, do permit election-day registration, and North Dakota has no registration at all. There, one just walks in, shows identification, and votes.[3]

Once registered, voting in Texas is fairly easy. Texas was one of the first states to institute early voting, which allows people to vote at a number of different sites before election day. Indeed, many people who are unable to vote on election day can vote in advance by mail. Consider also that, in counties with a 5 percent or greater language minority, Texas requires that all ballots and election materials be printed in other languages in addition to English.

Recent decisions have halted the trend of making voting easier in Texas. Most notably, the legislature enacted a voter identification (ID) requirement in 2011. This law requires voters to show one of five forms of identification when they go to vote: a driver's license, military ID, a passport, a concealed handgun license, or a voter ID card that the state provides for free. There are arguments in favor of having a voter ID requirement and also arguments against it, though most observers expect it to dampen turnout, particularly among minorities. (It thus is more likely to hurt Democratic candidates.) In March 2012, the U.S. Department of Justice raised an objection to the law (and a similar one in South Carolina), which puts the policy on hold. The U.S. District Court for the District of Columbia agreed with the objection and struck down the law in 2012, just prior to the November general election in that year. The U.S. Supreme Court invalidated that decision in 2013, and voter IDs were required in the November 2013 election.

Voter Turnout in the United States and in Texas

Voter turnout

The proportion of eligible Americans who actually vote.

Making registration and voting easier was expected to result in increased **voter turnout**—the proportion of eligible Americans who actually vote. Such has not been the case; indeed, the reverse has been true. Since 1960, turnout has actually declined. This is not to suggest that the actual number of voters has diminished. In fact, the number has steadily increased, from 70.6 million votes for president in 1964 to an estimated 129 million votes in 2012—an increase of 83 percent. However, the number of voting-age Americans increased from 114.1 million to 241 million during the same period—an increase of more than 100 percent. Thus, the **voting-age population (VAP)**, the total number of persons in the United States who are 18 years of age or older, has grown at a much faster rate than the actual voting population.[4]

Voting-age population (VAP)

The total number of persons in the United States who are 18 years of age or older.

Figure 4.1 shows voter turnout in presidential elections from 1932 to 2012. Voter turnout peaked in 1960 and has not reached that all-time high since. In 2012, turnout among the

---

[3]*Do* note that some Republican-controlled legislatures have tried to repeal election-day registration and were successful in Montana and Maine, although voters in the latter overturned the decision in a referendum. Efforts to repeal it still are under way in Wisconsin. In Democrat-controlled Connecticut, conversely, there are moves to institute election-day registration.

[4]The VAP is an imperfect measure of the voting-eligible population (VEP) because it includes people who cannot vote (noncitizens and felons) and excludes people who can (eligible citizens living overseas). Because the number of noncitizens and felons is large and the sum of these far exceeds the number of overseas eligibles, the VAP exaggerates the actual VEP. In 2012, for example, the difference was substantial (approximately 19 million people). The VAP measure will therefore understate rates of participation. Unfortunately, reliable measures of VEP over long stretches of time are not readily available, particularly at the state level, which is why VAP is used here. For more information on measuring turnout, see the United States Elections Project at http://elections.gmu.edu.

VAP was 53.6 percent.[5] There are two main reasons for the decrease in voter turnout in the United States after the 1960s. The first reason can be traced to the Twenty-sixth Amendment, which lowered the voting age from 21 to 18 in 1972. The amendment was passed at the height of the Vietnam War, with proponents arguing that a person who could be drafted and sent off to war should be able to vote. By extending the vote to 18- to 20-year-old citizens, the amendment expanded the eligible voting population. As we have already seen, however, these young people are less likely to vote than are older persons—since they were given the right to vote, citizens in the 18- to 20-year-old age group have rarely posted turnout rates as high as 40 percent, even in presidential elections. Thus, adding the age group to the lists of eligible voters in 1972 slightly reduced the overall turnout rate. Second, identification with the two major political parties dropped substantially after the 1960s, and more than one-third of all Americans now consider themselves *independents*—that is, unattached to either of the parties.[6] (The proportion is greater for younger voters.) As noted earlier, these voters are less likely to vote than are partisans.[7]

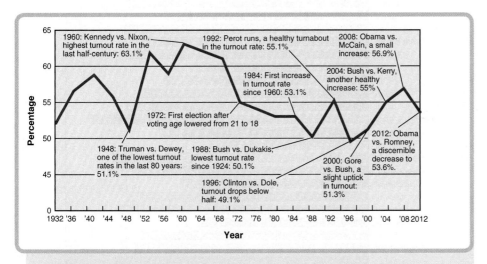

Figure 4.1

How Many People Vote in the United States? Presidential Election Turnout, 1932–2012

Here we see that turnout declined in the early 1970s but has not changed much during the last 30 years. A little more than 50 percent of the voting-age population now vote in presidential elections.

 Describe the groups that are most likely to vote. Does one party or the other benefit more when there is a high turnout of voters?

---

[5]When the VEP is used (see footnote 4), the estimated turnout in 2012 was 58.2 percent, almost 5 points greater than estimated with the VAP.

[6]See Paul R. Abramson and John H. Aldrich, "The Decline of Electoral Participation in American," *American Political Science Review* 76 (June 1982), pp. 502–521.

[7]Some scholars attribute part of the decline in turnout to the increasing tendency toward divided government at the national level, where the president is from one political party and the majority in Congress is from the other. The argument is that divided government makes it more difficult for voters to assign responsibility for policy decisions and that, as a result, voters cannot easily reward or punish specific elected officials at the polls. See Mark N. Franklin and Wolfgang P. Hirczy De Mino, "Separated Powers, Divided Government, and Turnout in U.S. Presidential Elections," *American Journal of Political Science Review* 42 (January 1998), pp. 316–326.

Turnout in American general elections is significantly lower than that in other industrialized democracies of the world. Figure 4.2 shows that in most comparable nations, voter turnout is approximately 20 percent higher than in the United States. Interestingly, American political attitudes seem more conducive to voting than those in countries with far higher turnouts. Low voter turnout in the United States is caused by other factors, including institutional structures (primarily the strength of political parties) and the fact that we require voters to register—in some nations, citizens are automatically registered to vote when they meet age requirements.[8]

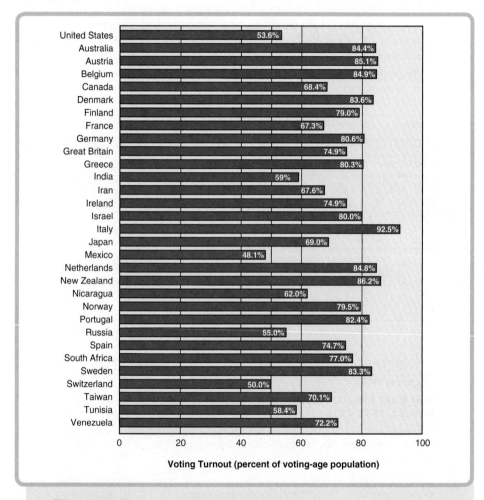

Figure 4.2
Voter Turnout from around the World

The United States is most similar to India, Russia, and Tunisia.

Source: International Institute for Democracy and Electoral Assistance, *www.idea.int.*

 Why is turnout so far below what we observe in other established, industrialized democracies?

---

[8]G. Bingham Powell Jr., "American Voter Turnout in Comparative Perspective," *American Political Science Review* 80 (March 1986), pp. 17, 23. Switzerland, the only country studied where turnout is lower than in the United States, was not included in this computation.

HOW DOES TEXAS COMPARE?
Voter Turnout in the State and Nation

Table 4.1 shows that voter turnout in Texas (as in most of the South) has remained fairly stable at levels far below the national average. In the presidential elections of 2012, for example, Texas turnout was 41.7 percent, about 12 percent below the rest of the nation. That year, Texas had the second lowest turnout rate of any state in the nation, just above Hawaii.

In midterm elections, Texas's turnout has bounced around a lot from election to election but is consistently lower than in most other states (see Table 4.2). The turnout rate typically has been between 20 and 30 percent, while Louisiana has often vied with Texas for the dubious honor of the lowest turnout in the nation.[9] In 2014, voter participation was only 23.9 percent, lower than any

other state. The very low turnout in midterm elections heightens the impact of the most politically active people in Texas, who consistently turn out to vote. (Recall our earlier discussion of "who votes.")

FOR DEBATE

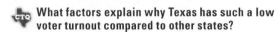
What factors explain why Texas has such a low voter turnout compared to other states?

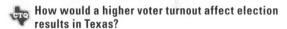
How would a higher voter turnout affect election results in Texas?

Should the government take steps to encourage more people to vote? Why or why not?

TABLE 4.1 Percentage of the Voting-Age Population Casting Ballots in Presidential General Elections, 1972–2012

	1972	1976	1980	1984	1988	1992	1996	2000	2004	2008	2012
United States	55.5	53.3	52.6	53.1	50.1	55.2	49.1	51.3	55.4	56.9	53.6
Texas	45.3	46.2	44.9	47.2	45.5	49.1	41.3	43.1	45.5	45.6	41.7
Difference (Texas vs. United States)	10.2	7.1	7.7	5.9	4.7	6.1	7.8	8.2	9.9	11.3	11.9
Rank of Texas among the 50 states	43rd	44th	44th	45th	46th	46th	48th	48th	49th	49th	49th

Sources: Lester Milbrath, "Participation in the American States," in Herbert Jacob and Kenneth N. Vines (eds.), *Politics in the American States*, 2nd ed. (Boston: Little, Brown, 1971), pp. 38–39; *Statistical Abstract of the United States, 1976, 1979, 1983, 1986, 1989, and 1993* (Washington, DC: U.S. Government Printing Office); Federal Election Commission, "Voter Registration and Turnout," www.fec.gov; United States Elections Project, http://elections.gmu.edu/Turnout_2004G.html, http://elections.gmu.edu/Turnout_2008G.html. For 2012, turnout estimates are based on data from the Texas Secretary of State and VAP numbers are from the United States Elections Project.

TABLE 4.2 Percentage of the Voting-Age Population Casting Ballots in Nonpresidential General Elections, 1974–2014

	1974	1978	1982	1986	1990	1994	1998	2002	2006	2010	2014
United States	36.1	35.3	38.0	33.4	33.1	36.0	36.4	36.2	37.1	37.8	33.9
Texas	18.4	24.1	26.2	25.5	26.8	31.3	26.1	28.8	25.8	26.7	23.9
Difference (Texas vs. United States)	17.7	11.2	11.8	7.9	6.3	4.7	10.3	7.4	11.3	11.1	10.0
Rank of Texas among the 50 states	49th	46th	48th	45th	42nd	45th	47th	49th	50th	50th	50th

Sources: *Statistical Abstract of the United States, 1976, 1979, 1983, 1989*, and *1996* (Washington, DC: U.S. Government Printing Office); Federal Election Commission, "Voter Registration and Turnout," www.fec.gov; United States Elections Project, http://elections.gmu.edu/Turnout_2002G.html; http://elections.gmu.edu/Turnout_2006G.html; http://elections.gmu.edu/Turnout_2010G.html; preliminary 2014 data from http://www.electproject.org/2014g.

[9]In Louisiana, the state and local contests are decided before the general election, so the motivation for voting is low. Louisiana's "blanket primary" ballot lists all candidates from all parties. If no one receives a majority of the votes in a given race, the top two vote recipients compete in a runoff primary, irrespective of political party affiliation, and the winner of the primary is elected.

When former State Senator Wendy Davis ran against former Attorney General Greg Abbott for the governorship in the 2014 election, approximately 24 percent of the voting-age population turned out to vote.

 Why do so few voters turn out in nonpresidential elections in Texas? Would a larger number of Texans cast their ballots for governor if the election were held at the same time as the presidential election?

Reasons for Low Voter Turnout in Texas

Most Texans probably think that Texas is in the mainstream of American society. Why, then, is there such a difference between Texas and other urbanized and industrialized states in its political behavior? Why does Texas compare more closely with states of the Deep South in voter turnout? The answer may lie in its laws, socioeconomic characteristics, political structure, party competition, and political culture.

Legal Constraints Traditionally, scholars interested in the variation in turnout across the American states have focused on laws regulating registration and voting. Clearly, the most important of these laws were the restrictions on who may vote, such as the poll tax, property ownership requirements, or the outright exclusion of African Americans and women.

Although these restrictions disappeared some time ago, other barriers to registration and voting persisted, and some remain in effect today.[10] One can ask: Does a state promote political participation by setting the minimum necessary limitations and making it as convenient as possible for the citizen to vote? Or, does a state repeatedly place barriers on the way to the polls, making the act of voting physically, financially, and psychologically as difficult as the local sense of propriety will allow? There is no doubt into which category Texas once fell—the application has been uneven, but historically Texas was among the most restrictive states in its voting laws.

However, nearly all of these restrictions have been changed by amendments to the U.S. Constitution, state and national laws, rulings by the U.S. Department of Justice, and judicial decisions. Even a cursory examination of these restrictions and the conditions under which

---

[10]See Glenn Mitchell II and Christopher Wlezien, "The Impact of Legal Constraints on Voter Registration, Turnout, and the Composition of the American Electorate," *Political Behavior* 17 (June 1995), pp. 179–202.

they were removed makes one appreciate the extent to which Texas's elections were at one time closed. Consider these changes in Texas voting policies:

1. *Poll tax.* The payment of a poll tax as a prerequisite for voting was adopted in 1902. The cost was $1.75 ($1.50 plus $0.25 optional for the county) and represented more than a typical day's wages for some time. Many poor Texans were kept from voting. When the Twenty-fourth Amendment was ratified in 1964, it voided the poll tax in national elections. Texas and only one other state kept it for state elections until it was held unconstitutional in 1966 (*United States* v. *Texas*, 384 U.S. 155).

2. *Women's suffrage.* An attempt was made to end the denial of the ballot to women in 1917, but the effort failed by four votes in the Texas legislature. Women were allowed to vote in the primaries of 1918, but not until ratification of the Nineteenth Amendment in 1920 did full suffrage come to women in Texas.

3. *White primary.* African Americans were barred from participating when the first party primary was held in 1906. When movement toward increased participation seemed likely, Texas made several moves to avoid U.S. Supreme Court rulings allowing African Americans to vote. Not until 1944 were the legislature's efforts to deny African Americans access to the primaries finally overturned (*Smith* v. *Allwright*, 321 U.S. 649).

4. *Military vote.* Until 1931, members of the National Guard were not permitted to vote. Members of the military began to enjoy the full rights of suffrage in Texas in 1965, when the U.S. Supreme Court voided the Texas constitutional exclusion (*Carrington* v. *Rash*, 380 U.S. 89).

5. *Long residence requirement.* The Texas residence requirement of one year in the state and six months in the county was modified slightly by the legislature to allow new residents to vote in the presidential part of the ballot, but not until a 1972 ruling of the U.S. Supreme Court were such requirements abolished (*Dunn* v. *Blumstein*, 405 U.S. 330).

6. *Property ownership as a requirement for voting in bond elections.* Texas held to this requirement until the U.S. Supreme Court made property ownership unnecessary for revenue bond elections in 1969 (*Kramer* v. *Union Free District No. 15*, 395 U.S. 621), and for tax elections in 1969 (*Cipriano* v. *City of Houma*, 395 U.S. 701), and in 1975 (*Hill* v. *Stone*, 421 U.S. 289).

7. *Annual registration.* Even after the poll tax was voided, Texas continued to require voters to register every year until annual registration was prohibited by the federal courts in 1971 (*Beare* v. *Smith*, 321 F. Supp. 1100).

8. *Early registration.* Texas voters were required to meet registration requirements by January 31, earlier than the cutoff date for candidates' filings and more than nine months before the general election. This restriction was voided in 1971 (*Beare* v. *Smith*, 321 F. Supp. 1100).

9. *Jury duty.* Texas law provided that the names of prospective jurors must be drawn from the voting rolls. Some Texans did not like to serve on juries, and not registering to vote ensured against a jury summons. (Counties now use driver's licenses for jury lists.)

Texas used almost every technique available except the literacy test and the grandfather clause[11] to deny the vote or to make it expensive in terms of time, money, and aggravation. This is not the case today. Most barriers to voting in Texas have been removed and, as was mentioned previously, the legislature has instituted a number of provisions that make voting easier than in most states. As noted earlier, some new barriers have been added, most notably, the voter ID law that went into effect for the November 2013, election. Although the law surely has not helped turnout, it is unclear how much it has hurt. Putting aside voter ID, the

---

[11]The grandfather clause gave white citizens who were disenfranchised by poll tax or literacy requirements the right to vote if they had been eligible to vote before the passage of the restricting legislation. These laws were found unconstitutional by the U.S. Supreme Court in *Guinn* v. *United States*, 238 U.S. 347 (1915).

laws in Texas mostly explain why turnout was low in the past and why, with the relaxing of restrictions, it has increased somewhat since 1960. The laws do not help us understand why turnout in Texas has remained low in recent years. For this, we need to look elsewhere.

Demographic Factors Texas is known as the land of the "big rich" cattle barons and oil tycoons. What is not so well known is that Texas is also the land of the "big poor" and that more than 4 million persons—more than in any other state—live in poverty here. Although nationally the proportion of people living below the poverty level in 2010 was 15.3 percent, in Texas the proportion was 17.9 percent. For African-American and Latino Texans, almost 25 percent have incomes below this level. Of the more than 4 million individuals in Texas living in poverty, more than one-third are children. Understandably, formal educational achievement is also low. Of Texans older than 25 years of age, one in four has not graduated from high school. Among African Americans, the ratio is just less than one of three, and among Latinos, it is almost one of two.[12]

Given that income and education are such important determinants of electoral participation, low voter turnout is exactly what we should expect in Texas. Because income and education levels are particularly low among African Americans and, especially, Latinos, turnout is particularly low for these groups. Voting by Texas minorities is on the rise, however, and this has led to much greater representation of both groups in elected offices, as we will see. These trends should continue as income and education levels among minorities increase.

Political Structure Another deterrent to voting in Texas is the length of the ballot and the number of elections. Texas uses a long ballot that provides for the popular election of numerous public officers (who some people believe should be appointed). In an urban county, the ballot may call for the voter to choose from as many as 150 to 200 candidates vying for 50 or more offices. The frequency of referendums on constitutional amendments contributes to the length of the ballot in Texas. Voters are also asked to go to the polls for various municipal, school board, bond, and special-district elections. Government is far more fragmented in Texas than in other states, and the election of so many minor officials may be confusing and more frustrating for voters.

Party Competition The competitiveness of elections is important to voters. The closer the race, the greater the interest, attention, and participation during the campaign and on election day itself. The problem for Texas and other Southern states is that general elections between the two parties are not competitive, and this has been true for a long time even when the party in power changed. In the past, Texas was a one-party Democratic state, and this held until the 1990s. Since that time, the Republicans have dominated statewide races. With rare exceptions, then, the races between candidates of the two parties in November elections in Texas have not been competitive. This dampens voter interest and turnout.

Political Culture Insights into voter participation levels have been derived from the concept of political culture, which, as defined in Chapter 1, describes the set of political values and beliefs that are dominant in a society. Borrowed from social anthropologists, this concept has been found to be applicable to all political systems, from those of developing countries to modern industrial democracies. It has been especially useful in the study of American politics, where federalism has emphasized the diversity among regions, states, and communities—a diversity that cries out for some approach that can effectively explain it.

---

[12]U.S Census Bureau, www.census.gov/prod/2011pubs/acsbr10-01.pdf and www.census.gov/hhes/www/poverty/data/threshld/thresh10.xls. The definition of *poverty* depends on the size and composition of the family. For a family of four (two adults and two children), the threshold in 2010 was an annual income of $22,314 or less.

As we saw in Chapter 1, the American political culture is actually a mix of three subcultures, each prevalent in at least one area of the United States.[13] The *moralistic culture* is a product of the Puritan era and is strongest in New England. The *traditionalistic culture* comes to us via the plantation society of the Deep South. The *individualistic culture* was born in the commercial centers of Middle Atlantic states, moving west and south along the Ohio River and its tributaries. It is the mix as well as the isolation of these cultures that gives American politics its flavor.

Important to students of electoral politics is that "the degree of political participation (i.e., voter turnout and suffrage regulations) is the most consistent indicator of political culture."[14] The moralistic culture perceives the discussion of public issues and voting as not only a right but also an opportunity that is beneficial to the citizen and society alike. In contrast, the traditionalistic culture views politics as the special preserve of the social and economic elite and a process of maintaining the existing order. Highly personal, it views political participation as a privilege and uses social pressure as well as restrictive election laws to limit voting. The individualistic culture blurs the distinction between economic and political life. Here, business and politics are both viewed as appropriate avenues by which an individual can advance his or her interests, and conflicts of interest are fairly common. In this culture, business interests can play a very strong role, and running for office is difficult without their support.

Low voter turnout in Texas may be due in part to the state's political culture, which is a mix of the traditionalistic and the individualistic. The traditionalistic aspect is especially characteristic of East Texas, settled primarily by immigrants from the Deep South in the years prior to the Civil War. The individualistic aspect predominates throughout the rest of the state. As a result, participation in politics is not as highly regarded as it is in other states, particularly those with a moralistic culture, and politics in Texas is largely the domain of business interests. People may be less likely to vote in Texas because they do not value political participation itself and because they tend to think that they play only a little role in politics.

Signing petitions and attending rallies are important forms of political participation. Although people are less likely to vote in the United States and especially in Texas, by comparison with people in other countries, they are more likely to take part in other ways.

CTQ Identify forms of participation other than voting. Which forms of participation have the greatest impact in Texas politics?

[13]Daniel J. Elazar, *American Federalism: A View from the States*, 3rd ed. (New York: Harper & Row, 1984).
[14]David C. Saffel, *State Politics* (Reading, MA: Addison-Wesley, 1984), p. 8.

TYPES OF ELECTIONS IN TEXAS

LO 4.2 Describe the types of Texas elections.

Winning an office is typically a two-stage process. First, the candidate must win the Democratic or Republican Party nomination in the primary election. Second, the candidate must win the general election against the other party's nominee. It is possible for a candidate to get on the general-election ballot without winning a primary election (as will be discussed shortly), but this is rare. As in most other states, elections in Texas are dominated by the Democratic and Republican parties.

Primary Elections

Three successive devices for selecting political party nominees have been used in the history of this country, each perceived as a cure for the ills of a previously corrupt, inefficient, or inadequate system. The first was the caucus, consisting of the elected political party members serving in the legislature. The "insider" politics of the caucus room motivated the reformers of the Jacksonian era to throw out "King Caucus" and to institute the party convention system by 1828. In this system, ordinary party members select delegates to a party convention, and these delegates then nominate the party's candidates for office and write a party platform. The convention system was hailed as a surefire method of ending party nominations by the legislative bosses. By 1890, the backroom politics of the convention halls again moved reformers to action, and the result was the direct primary, adopted by most states between 1890 and 1920. Texas's first direct primary was held in 1906, under the Terrell Election Law passed in 1903. The **direct primary** enables party members to participate directly in the selection of a candidate to represent them in the general election.

Direct primary

A method of selecting party nominees in which party members participate directly in the selection of a candidate to represent them in the general election.

Traditionally regarded as private activities, primaries were at one time largely beyond the concern of legislatures and courts. Costs of party activities, including primaries, were covered by donations and by assessing each candidate who sought a party's nomination. Judges attempted to avoid suits between warring factions of the parties as much as they did those involving church squabbles over the division of church property. This was the basis on which the U.S. Supreme Court upheld in 1935 the Texas Democratic Party convention's decision barring African Americans from participating in the party primary.[15] Because political party activities were increasingly circumscribed by law, the Court reversed itself in 1944 and recognized the primary as an integral part of the election process.[16]

It argued that in a one-party state, which Texas was at the time, the party primary may be the only election in which any meaningful choice is possible. Because the Democratic Party seldom had any real opposition in the general election, winning the nomination was, for all practical purposes, winning the office. The party balance in Texas has changed quite a lot in recent years, however. The Republicans have overtaken the Democrats and now hold every statewide elected office.

Who Must Hold a Primary? Any party receiving 20 percent of the gubernatorial vote must hold a primary, and all other parties must use the convention system.[17] New parties must meet additional requirements if their nominees are to be on the general-election ballot. In addition to holding a convention, these parties must file with the secretary of state a list of supporters equal to 1 percent of the total vote for governor in the last general election.

---

[15]*Grovey* v. *Townsend*, 295 U.S. 45 (1935).

[16]*Smith* v. *Allwright*, 321 U.S. 649 (1944).

[17]The La Raza Unida Party challenged this limitation. The Justice Department and federal courts sustained the challenge but only as it applied to La Raza Unida, which was permitted to conduct a primary in 1978. Otherwise, the law stands as written.

The list may consist of the names of those who participated in the party's convention, a nominating petition, or a combination of the two. Persons named as supporters must be registered voters who have not participated in the activities (primaries or conventions) of either of the two major parties. Each page (although not each name) on the nominating petition must be notarized. Such a requirement is, as intended, difficult to meet and therefore inhibits the creation of new political parties.[18]

Financing Primaries Party primaries are funded partly by modest candidate filing fees, but most of the primaries' costs come from the state treasury. The parties' state and county executive committees initially make the expenditures, but the secretary of state reimburses each committee for the difference between the filing fees collected and the actual cost of the primary. To get on the party primary ballot, a candidate needs only to file an application with the state or county party chair and pay the prescribed fee. The categories of fees, applicable also for special elections, are summarized in Table 4.3.

So that no person is forced to bear an unreasonable expense when running for political office, the legislature provided that a petition may be submitted as an alternative to the filing fee. Such petition must bear the names of at least 5,000 voters for candidates seeking nomination to statewide office. For district and lesser offices, the petition must bear the signatures of voters equal to 2 percent of the vote for the party's candidate for governor in the last election, up to a maximum of 500 required signatures.

Administering Primaries In the county primaries, the chair and county executive committee of each party receive applications and filing fees and hold drawings to determine the order of names on the ballot for both party and government offices. They then certify the ballot, choose an election judge for each voting precinct (usually the precinct chair), select the voting devices (paper ballots, voting machines, or punch cards), and arrange

TABLE 4.3	Fees for Listing on the Party Primary Ballot in Texas, Selected Offices
Office	**Fee**
U.S. Senator	$5,000
U.S. Representative	$3,125
Texas Statewide Officers	$3,750
State Senator	$1,250
State Representative	$750
County Commissioner	$750–$1,250
District Judge	$1,500–$2,500
Justice of the Peace, Constable	$375–$1,000
County Surveyor	$75

 How much do filing fees limit candidates' access to the state ballot? Should election laws attempt to discourage frivolous candidates?

---

[18]The necessity of notarizing the pages increases the difficulty. The application of technical aspects of the law and adverse interpretations are but a part of the harassment that minor parties and independents have traditionally encountered in their quest for a place on the ballot. For example, in 1976, the secretary of state interpreted the law as requiring that each signature must be notarized. The next year, the legislature specified that a notary need sign only each part of the petition. See Richard H. Kraemer, Ernest Crain, and William Earl Maxwell, *Understanding Texas Politics* (St. Paul, MN: West, 1975), pp. 155–157.

for polling places and printing. After the primary, the county chair and executive committee canvass the votes and certify the results of their respective state executive committees.

In the state primary, the state party chair and the state executive committee of each political party receive applications of candidates for state offices, conduct drawings to determine the order of names, certify the ballot to the county-level officials, and canvass the election returns after the primary.

The Majority Rule

The Majority Rule   In Texas, as in other southern states (except for Tennessee and Virginia) that were once predominantly Democratic, nominations are by a majority (50% plus 1) of the popular vote. If no candidate receives a majority of votes cast for a particular office in the first primary, a **runoff primary** is required in which the two candidates receiving the greatest number of votes are pitted against each other. Outside the South, where the balance between the two major parties has traditionally been more equal, only a plurality of the votes (more votes than for anyone else) is required, and consequently no runoff is necessary. The election rule used may influence the number of candidates that run in primaries, as there is more reason to enter the race where the majority rule is used. That is, one does not need to expect to win the first primary, but just finish in the top two and get to the runoff.

Primary elections in Texas are held on the first Tuesday in March of even-numbered years. The runoff primary is scheduled for the fourth Tuesday in May or more than two months after the initial party primary election. Although there are earlier presidential primaries, no other state schedules primaries to nominate candidates for state offices so far in advance of the general election in November.

Turnout in Texas primaries is much lower than in general elections. Take 2014 for example: Despite a competitive gubernatorial nomination contests, particularly in the Republican primary, only 2 million Texans voted, approximately 10 percent of the more than 19 million people who were 18 years of age or older. The people who do vote in primary elections are hardly representative of the population—they tend to be better educated, more affluent, and more ideologically extreme.

Closed Primary

Closed Primary   Party primaries are defined as either *open* or *closed*. These terms relate to whether or not participation is limited to party members. Because the purpose of a primary is to choose the party's nominee, it may seem logical to exclude anyone who is not a party member. However, not every state recognizes the strength of that logic. Texas and fifteen other states have an **open primary** in which voters decide at the polls (on election day) in which primary they will participate. Of course, a person is forbidden to vote in more than one primary on election day, and once she has voted in the first primary cannot switch parties and participate in the runoff election or convention of any other party. In contrast, the typical **closed primary** requires that a person specify a party preference when registering to vote. The party's name is then stamped on the registration card at the time of issuance. Each voter may change a party affiliation at any time up to thirty days (usually) before participating in a primary or a convention. Voters are limited, however, to the activities of the party they have formally declared as their preference. If the individual registers as an independent (no party preference), that person is excluded from the primaries and conventions of *all* parties. Twenty states have closed primaries.

Some states have a semiclosed (or semiopen) system, in which independents are allowed to vote in either primary. Five other states have a mixed system, where one party has an open and the other a closed (or semiclosed) primary. Another three states use a top-two primary, in which candidates from different parties compete in a single primary and the top two vote-getters proceed to the general election. Primary elections clearly differ quite a lot across states, but those differences have little bearing on the general election. Whether voters participate in a party primary or not, they are completely free to vote for any party candidate, the Democrat, the Republican, or another candidate in the general election in November.

Runoff primary
A second primary election that pits the two top vote-getters from the first primary, where the winner in that primary did not receive a majority. The runoff primary is used in states such as Texas that have a majority election rule in party primaries.

Open primary
A type of party primary where a voter can choose on election day in which primary they will participate.

Closed primary
A type of primary where a voter is required to specify a party preference when registering to vote.

Crossover Voting   The opportunity always exists in Texas for members of one political party to invade the other party's primary. This is called **crossover voting**. It is designed to increase the chances that the nominee from the other party will be someone whose philosophy is like that of the invader's own party. For example, Democrats might cross over to vote for the more moderate candidate in the Republican primary, or Republicans might cross over into the Democratic primary to support the candidate who is least objectionable from their viewpoint.

Crossover voting
When members of one political party vote in the other party's primary to influence the nominee that is selected.

General Elections

The purpose of party primaries is to nominate the party's candidates from the competing intra-party factions. General elections, in contrast, are held to allow the voters to choose the people who will actually serve in national, state, and county offices from among the competing political party nominees and write-in candidates. General elections differ from primaries in at least two other important ways. First, since general elections are the official public elections to determine who will take office, they are administered completely by public (as opposed to party) officials of state and county governments.[19] Second, unlike Texas's primaries, in which a majority (50% plus 1) of the vote is required, the general election is decided by a **plurality vote**, whereby the winning candidate needs to receive only the largest number of the votes cast for all the candidates for that office. This may discourage third-party candidates from running, that is, by comparison with primary elections in Texas, where the majority rule is used, as discussed earlier.

Plurality vote
An election rule in which the candidate with the most votes wins regardless of whether it is a majority.

General elections in Texas are held every other year on the same day as national elections—the first Tuesday after the first Monday in November of even-numbered years. In years divisible by four, we elect the president, vice president, all U.S. representatives, and one-third of the U.S. senators. In Texas, we elect all 150 members of the state house during these years and roughly half (15 or 16) of the 31 senators. We also elect some board and court positions at the state level as well as about half of the county positions. However, most major state executive positions (governor, lieutenant governor, attorney general, and so forth) are not filled until the midterm national election, when the U.S. representatives and one-third of U.S. senators (but not the president) again face the voters. All state representatives and half of the senators also are elected in these years. Some board members, judges, and county officers are, too.

Holding simultaneous national and state elections has important political ramifications. During the administration of Andrew Jackson, parties first began to tie the states and the national government together politically. A strong presidential candidate and an effective candidate for state office can benefit significantly by cooperating and campaigning under the party label. This usually works best, of course, if the candidates are in substantial agreement with respect to political philosophy and the issues.

In Texas, which is more politically conservative than the average American state, fundamental agreement is often lacking. This has been especially true for Democratic candidates. Popular Democrats in the state often disassociate themselves from the more liberal presidential nominees of the party. As Democratic candidate for governor, Bill White played down his connections to national Democrat Bill Clinton and rarely mentioned Democratic President Barack Obama.

When the Texas Constitution was amended in 1972 to extend the terms (from two years to four years) for the governor and other major administrative officials, the elections for these offices were set for November of midterm election years. This change had two main effects. First, although candidates are also running for Congress in midterm elections, separation of presidential and state campaigns insulates public officials from the ebb and flow of presidential politics and allows them to further disassociate themselves from the national political parties. Elections for statewide office now largely reflect Texas issues and interests. Second,

---

[19]County officials help administer general elections on behalf of the state.

the separation reduces voting in statewide elections and makes the outcomes much more predictable. As was shown earlier, turnout in midterm elections is much lower than in presidential election years, when many people are lured to the polls by the importance of the office and the visibility of the campaign. The independent and the marginal voters are active, and election results for congressional and state-level offices are less predictable. In midterm election years, however, the less-informed and the less-predictable voters are more likely to stay home, and the contest is largely confined to political party regulars. Most incumbent state politicians prefer to cast their lot with this more limited and predictable midterm electorate.

Special Elections

As the name implies, special elections are designed to meet special or emergency needs, such as ratification of constitutional amendments or filling vacant offices. Special elections are held to fill vacancies only in legislative bodies that have general (rather than limited) lawmaking power. Typical legislative bodies with general power are the U.S. Senate and U.S. House of Representatives, state legislatures, and city councils in home-rule cities. (All other vacancies, including judgeships and county commissioners, are filled by appointment.) Runoffs are held when necessary. The elections provide for the filling of a vacancy only until the end of the regular term or until the next general election, whichever comes first.

Because special elections are not partisan, the process of getting on the ballot is relatively easy and does not involve a primary.[20] All that is required is the filing of the application form in a timely and appropriate manner and the payment of the designated filing fee. Unlike in general elections, the winner of a special election must receive a majority of the votes. Thus, a runoff special election may be necessary when no candidate wins outright the first time around. The runoff requirements have been enacted in piecemeal fashion—an illustration of how public policy is often enacted only for political advantage. Those in control of the legislature can and do change the rules of the game to benefit those who share their political views.

Before 1957, all special elections required only a plurality vote, but when candidates identified as "liberals" began to win elections under the plurality requirement, the legislature acted quickly to require a majority. During the special election in 1957, the liberal candidate, Ralph Yarborough, appeared likely to win, so the Texas House (then controlled by conservative Democrats) quickly passed a bill requiring a runoff in any election to fill a vacated U.S. Senate seat. However, a few liberal legislators were able to delay the bill in the state senate until after the election, in which Yarborough led the field of 23 candidates. Because he received only 38 percent of the popular vote, it is possible that Yarborough would have lost in a runoff. Sixteen days later, the senate passed the bill, and it was signed into law by the governor—too late to affect Yarborough's election. Once in office, Senator Yarborough was able to capitalize on his incumbency and served for thirteen years.

THE CONDUCT AND ADMINISTRATION OF ELECTIONS

LO 4.3 Understand how elections are administered in Texas.

Texas's secretary of state is the state's chief elections officer and interprets legislation and issues guidelines. The secretary of state has the responsibility of disbursing funds to the state and county executive committees to pay for the primary elections and is the keeper of election records, both party and governmental. The secretary of state also receives certificates of nomination from parties that have conducted primaries and conventions and uses these

---

[20]The nonpartisan nature relates only to the fact that the party label does not appear on the ballot and certification by the party is not necessary. Special elections are, in fact, often partisan because regular party supporters work for "their" candidates.

certificates to prepare the ballot for statewide offices. Along with the governor and a gubernatorial appointee, the secretary of state sits on the three-member board that canvasses election returns for state and district offices.

County-Level Administration

Except for the preparation of the statewide portion of the ballot, county-level officials actually conduct general elections. Counties may choose from three options for the administration of general elections. The first option is to maintain the decentralized system that the counties have used for decades. Under this system, the major portion of responsibility rests with the county clerk. By the time the clerk receives the state portion of the ballot from the secretary of state, he or she will have constructed the county- and precinct-level portion by having received applications and certified the candidates' names. The board of elections (consisting of the county judge, sheriff, clerk, and chair of the two major parties' executive committees) arranges for polling places and for printing ballots. The county tax assessor–collector processes all voter applications and updates the voting rolls. The county commissioners' court draws precinct voting lines, appoints election judges, selects voting devices, canvasses votes, and authorizes payment of all election expenses from the county treasury.

The two other options available are designed to promote efficiency. One is for the county commissioners' court to transfer the voter registration function from the tax assessor–collector's office to that of the county clerk, thus removing the assessor–collector from the electoral process. The other option represents more extensive reform. It calls for all election-related duties of both the assessor–collector and the county clerk to be transferred to a county election administrator. This officer is appointed for a term of two years by the County Elections Commission, which, in those counties that choose the election administrator option, replaces the board of elections. (Membership is the same, except that in the use of the commission, the county clerk serves instead of the sheriff.)

Ballot Construction

Like so many other features of an election system, ballot construction reflects both practical and political considerations. Two basic types of general-election ballots are available—the party-column ballot and the office-block ballot. On the **party-column ballot**, the names of all the candidates of each party are listed in parallel columns under the party label. This type traditionally has been used in Texas. The ballot itemizes the offices as prescribed by law in descending order of importance, and the candidates are listed in each row. Beside each name is a box (on paper ballots) or a lever (on voting machines) that the voter must mark or pull if the voter wishes to vote a split ticket. **Split-ticket voting** is selecting candidates from one party for some offices and candidates from the other party for other offices. At the top of each column is the party's name and a box or lever. To vote a straight-party ticket, the voter need only mark the box or pull the lever for the party of his or her choice. **Straight-ticket voting** is selecting all of the candidates of one particular party.

On the **office-block ballot**, the names of the parties' candidates are randomly listed under each office. To vote a straight-party ticket, the voter must pick that party's candidates in each of the blocks. Several states use the office-block ballot, which is also called the "Massachusetts ballot" because it originated there. Minor parties in Texas and independent voters advocate the use of this ballot type because it makes straight-ticket voting for the major parties more difficult.

The Politics of Ballot Construction Understandably, supporters of the major Texas political parties strongly support the use of the party-column ballot. It enables lesser-known candidates to ride on the coattails of the party label or a popular candidate running for major office. There may also be an extra payoff in the use of this type of ballot when a party is listed in the first column. The parties are slated from left to right on the

Party-column ballot

A type of ballot used in a general election where all of the candidates from each party are listed in parallel columns under the party label.

Split-ticket voting

A voter selecting candidates from one party for some offices and candidates from the other party for other offices.

Straight-ticket voting

Selecting all of the candidates of one particular party.

Office-block ballot

A type of ballot used in a general election where the names of the parties' candidates are randomly listed in under each office.

ballot according to the proportion of votes that each party's candidate for governor received in the most recent gubernatorial election. Thus, the majority party (Republicans) benefits by occupying the coveted first column on the ballot. Democrats usually come second; next come third-party candidates and candidates of parties that were not on the ballot in the last election; and last come the independents.

Most Texas counties have moved away from a strict party-column ballot. Partly because of the adoption of electronic voting machines (discussed later in this chapter), ballots in these counties combine features of both the office-block and party-column designs (Figure 4.3).

SAMPLE BALLOT
BOLETA DE MUESTRA
BEXAR COUNTY
(CONDADO DE BEXAR)
Joint General, Amendment, Special
and Bond Election
(Elección Conjunto General, Enmienda A La
Constitución, Especial y Elección De Bonos)
Tuesday, November 4, 2014
Martes, 4 de Noviembre de 2014

"Vote for the candidate of your choice in each race by darkening in the oval provided to the left of the name of that candidate. You may cast a straight party vote (that is, cast a vote for all the nominees of one party) by darkening in the oval provided to the left of the name of that party. If you cast a straight party vote for all the nominees of one party and also cast a vote for an opponent of one of that party's nominees, your vote for the opponent will be counted as well as your vote for all the other nominees of the party for which the straight party vote was cast. You may vote for a write-in candidate by writing in the name of the candidate on the line provided and darkening in the oval provided to the left of the line. Use a #2 pencil." *(Vote por el candidato de su preferencia en cada carrera llenando completamente el espacio ovalado a la izquierda del nombre de ese candidato. Usted podrá votar por todos los candidatos de un solo partido político (es decir, votar por todos los candidatos nombrados del mismo partido político) llenando completamente el espacio ovalado a la izquierda del nombre de dicho partido político. Si usted vota por un solo partido político ("straight-ticket") y también vota por el contrincante de uno de los candidatos de dicho partido político, se computara su voto por el contrincante tanto como su voto por todos los demás candidatos del partido político de su preferencia. Usted podrá votar inserción escrita escribiendo el nombre del candidato en la linea provista y llenando completamente el espacio ovalado a la izquierda de la linea. Solamente use un lápiz de #2.)*

General Election (Elección General)

Straight Party (Partido Completo)
☐ Republican Party (REP)
(Partido Republicano) (REP)
☐ Democratic Party (DEM)
(Partido Demócrata) (DEM)
☐ Libertarian Party (LIB)
(Partido Libertario) (LIB)
☐ Green Party (GRN)
(Partido Verde) (GRN)

FEDERAL *(FEDERAL)*

United States Senator
(Senador de los Estados Unidos)
☐ John Cornyn (REP)
☐ David M. Alameel (DEM)
☐ Rebecca Paddock (LIB)
☐ Emily "Spicybrown" Sanchez (GRN)
☐ _____ write in

United States Representative, District 20
(Representante de los Estados Unidos, Distrito Núm. 20)
☐ Joaquin Castro (DEM)
☐ Jeffrey C. Blunt (LIB)

United States Representative, District 21
(Representante de los Estados Unidos, Distrito Núm. 21)
☐ Lamar Smith (REP)
☐ Ryan Shields (LIB)
☐ Antonio Diaz (GRN)

United States Representative, District 23
(Representante de los Estados Unidos, Distrito Núm. 23)
☐ Will Hurd (REP)
☐ Pete P. Gallego (DEM)
☐ Ruben Corvalan (LIB)

United States Representative, District 28
(Representante de los Estados Unidos, Distrito Núm. 28)
☐ Henry Cuellar (DEM)
☐ Will Aikens (LIB)
☐ Michael D. Cary (GRN)

United States Representative, District 35
(Representante de los Estados Unidos, Distrito Núm. 35)
☐ Susan Narvaiz (REP)
☐ Lloyd Doggett (DEM)
☐ Cory W. Bruner (LIB)
☐ kat swift (GRN)

STATE *(ESTADO)*

Governor (Gobernador)
☐ Greg Abbott (REP)
☐ Wendy R. Davis (DEM)
☐ Kathie Glass (LIB)
☐ Brandon Parmer (GRN)
☐ _____ write in

Lieutenant Governor (Gobernador Teniente)
☐ Dan Patrick (REP)
☐ Leticia Van de Putte (DEM)
☐ Robert D. Butler (LIB)
☐ Chandrakantha Courtney (GRN)

Attorney General (Procurador General)
☐ Ken Paxton (REP)
☐ Sam Houston (DEM)
☐ Jamie Balagia (LIB)
☐ Jamar Osborne (GRN)

Comptroller of Public Accounts
(Contralor de Cuentas Publicas)
☐ Glenn Hegar (REP)
☐ Mike Collier (DEM)
☐ Ben Sanders (LIB)
☐ Deb Shafto (GRN)

Commissioner of the General Land Office
(Comisionado de la Oficina General de Tierras)
☐ George P. Bush (REP)
☐ John Cook (DEM)
☐ Justin Knight (LIB)
☐ Valerie Alessi (GRN)

Commissioner of Agriculture
(Comisionado de Agricultura)
☐ Sid Miller (REP)
☐ Jim Hogan (DEM)
☐ David (Rocky) Palmquist (LIB)
☐ Kenneth Kendrick (GRN)

Railroad Commissioner
(Comisionado de Ferrocarriles)
☐ Ryan Sitton (REP)
☐ Steve Brown (DEM)
☐ Mark A. Miller (LIB)
☐ Martina Salinas (GRN)

Chief Justice, Supreme Court
(Juez Presidente, Corte Suprema)
☐ Nathan Hecht (REP)
☐ William Moody (DEM)
☐ Tom Oxford (LIB)

Justice, Supreme Court, Place 6 Unexpired Term
(Juez, Corte Suprema, Lugar Núm. 6 Duración Restante del Cargo)
☐ Jeff Brown (REP)
☐ Lawrence Edward Meyers (DEM)
☐ Mark Ash (LIB)

Justice, Supreme Court, Place 7
(Juez, Corte Suprema, Lugar Núm. 7)
☐ Jeff Boyd (REP)
☐ Gina Benavides (DEM)
☐ Don Fulton (LIB)
☐ Charles E. Waterbury (GRN)

Justice, Supreme Court, Place 8
(Juez, Corte Suprema, Lugar Núm. 8)
☐ Phil Johnson (REP)
☐ RS Roberto Koelsch (LIB)
☐ Jim Chisolm (GRN)

Judge, Court of Criminal Appeals, Place 3
(Juez, Corte de Apelaciones Criminales, Lugar Núm. 3)
☐ Bert Richardson (REP)
☐ John Granberg (DEM)
☐ Mark W. Bennett (LIB)

Judge, Court of Criminal Appeals, Place 4
(Juez, Corte de Apelaciones Criminales, Lugar Núm. 4)
☐ Kevin Patrick Yeary (REP)
☐ Quanah Parker (LIB)
☐ Judith Sanders-Castro (GRN)

Judge, Court of Criminal Appeals, Place 9
(Juez, Corte de Apelaciones Criminales, Lugar Núm. 9)
☐ David Newell (REP)
☐ William Bryan Strange, III (LIB)
☐ George Joseph Altgelt (GRN)

Member, State Board of Education, District 3
(Miembro de la Junt a Estatal de Educación, Publica, Distrito Núm. 3)
☐ Dave Mundy (REP)
☐ Marisa B. Perez (DEM)
☐ Josh Morales (LIB)

State Senator, District 25
(Senador Estatal, Distrito Núm. 25)
☐ Donna Campbell (REP)
☐ Daniel Boone (DEM)
☐ Brandin P. Lea (LIB)

Figure 4.3
A Typical Texas Ballot from Bexar County

Recall from the text that Republican candidates were listed first in 2014 because their candidate (former Governor Rick Perry) received the most votes in the previous gubernatorial election. Notice that voters are able to vote for all of the candidates of a single party—that is, vote a straight ticket—by making a single mark on the ballot. It is in midterm elections, like this one in 2014, that state executives are elected.

 Why would party leaders prefer such a ballot arrangement?

As with the office-block ballot, candidates are listed underneath each office. As with the party-column ballot, however, one can vote a straight-party ticket with a single mark; that is, before turning to specific offices, voters are first given the option to vote a straight ticket. Republican candidates are consistently listed first; Democrats come next, followed by other candidates.

Getting on the Ballot For a name to be placed on the general-election ballot, the candidate must be either a party nominee or an independent. For any party that received at least 5 percent of the vote for any statewide office in the previous general election, the full slate of candidates is placed on the ballot automatically. Thus, the Democratic and Republican parties have no problem submitting candidate names, and certification by the appropriate party officials for primary or convention winners is routine.

Minor parties have a more difficult time. For instance, in 2010 the Green Party again broke the 5 percent barrier and, along with the Libertarians, earned a place on the 2012 ballot—any other minor parties must petition for a ballot position. Independent candidates for president have the most difficult challenge because they must present a petition signed by 1 percent of the total state vote for president in the last election. In 1992, Ross Perot's supporters presented 54,275 signatures, which qualified him to appear on the ballot.

For all other offices except president, the total vote for governor is the basis for determining the required number of signatures for both independents and third-party candidates. For statewide office, signatures equaling 1 percent of the total gubernatorial vote are needed; for multicounty district offices, 3 percent; and for all other district and local offices, 5 percent. Although the number of signatures is relatively small for some offices (a maximum of 500 at the local level), the process of gaining access to the ballot by petition is difficult.[21]

Did You Know? Getting off a ballot can be as difficult as getting on. Take the case of Tom DeLay, the former member of the U.S. House of Representatives. After he resigned from Congress in June 2006, the Republican Party tried to have him replaced on the general-election ballot. U.S. District Judge Sam Sparks ruled that he must remain on the ballot, and the Fifth Circuit Court of Appeals upheld the decision.

Write-In Candidates Write-in candidates are not listed on the ballot—voters must write them on the ballot. These candidates often are individuals who have entered and lost in a party primary. A different type of write-in candidacy developed in 1976 when Charles W. Barrow, Chief Justice of the Fourth Court of Civil Appeals in San Antonio, was thought to be virtually unopposed for the Democratic nomination for associate justice of the Texas Supreme Court. The legal establishment was stunned when Don Yarbrough, a young Houston attorney involved in a number of legal entanglements, upset Barrow in the quest for the Democratic nomination. Apparently, the voters had confused the young attorney's name with former gubernatorial candidate Don Yarborough. No one had filed in the Republican primary.

Embarrassed, the legal establishment sought to have the primary winner disqualified from the ballot. Failing that, they mounted a write-in campaign supported strongly by the leaders of both political parties. Playing the name game themselves, they chose as their candidate District Judge Sam Houston Jones. The write-in campaign failed miserably. Don Yarbrough's victory was short-lived, however. Under threat of removal by the legislature, he resigned after serving approximately six months. He was replaced through gubernatorial appointment by Judge Charles W. Barrow, his opponent in the Democratic primary.

Write-in candidates have had an easier time as a result of a law subsequently passed by the legislature, though it still is not easy. A candidate must file a declaration of

---

[21]Signers must be registered voters and cannot have participated in the selection of a nominee for that office in another party's primary.

candidacy with the secretary of state 70 days before election day. With the declaration the candidate must include either the filing fee or a nominating petition with the required number of signatures. The names of write-in candidates must be posted at the election site, possibly in the election booth. A candidate not properly registered cannot win, regardless of the votes he or she receives. Even when registered, write-in candidates are seldom successful.

The Secret Ballot and the Integrity of Elections
The essence of the right to vote is generally viewed as the right to cast a ballot in secret, have the election conducted fairly, and have the ballots counted correctly. The **Australian ballot**, adopted by Texas in 1892, allowed people to vote in secret. It includes names of the candidates of all political parties on a single ballot printed at the public's expense and available only at the voting place.[22] Given a reasonably private area in which to mark the ballot, the voter was offered a secret ballot for the first time.

Australian ballot
A ballot printed by the government (as opposed to the political parties) that allows people to vote in secret.

Although there are legal remedies such as the issuance of injunctions and the threat of criminal penalties, Texas has looked primarily to "political" remedies in its effort to protect the integrity of the electoral process. Minor parties have reason to be concerned that irregularities in elections administered by members of the majority party may not be observed or, if observed, may not be reported. Even in the absence of wrongdoing, the testimony of the correctness of an election by individuals with opposing interests helps ensure public faith in the process.

Traditional practice has been that in general and special elections, the county board of elections routinely appoints as election judges the precinct chair of the political party whose members constitute a majority on the elections board. Each election judge is required to select at least one election clerk from a list submitted by the county chair of each political party. Moreover, law now recognizes the status of poll watchers, and both primary candidates and county chairs are authorized to appoint them.

Candidates can ask for a recount of the ballots. The candidate who requests a recount must put up a deposit—$60 per precinct where paper ballots were used and $100 per precinct using electronic voting—and is liable for the entire cost unless he or she wins or ties in the recount. In a large county, a recount can be quite costly. Consider Dallas County, which has almost 700 precincts. Despite this drawback, the current practice marks a real improvement over the days when often ineffective judicial remedies were the only recourse.

Multilingualism
Ballots in most Texas counties are in English. In more than 100 counties, the ballot is in both English and Spanish. In 2002, the U.S. Department of Justice ordered Harris County, which includes Houston, to provide ballots (and voting material) in Vietnamese as well (Figure 4.4). It is the only county in Texas to be included in the order and the only county outside California to do so. In 2012, Harris County added Chinese language to the ballot. In some parts of the country, other languages are required, including Eskimo, Filipino, Japanese, and Korean. In Los Angeles County alone, ballots are printed in seven different languages. This all is due to the Voting Rights Act of 1965 and its subsequent amendment in 1992. According to Section 203 of the act, a political subdivision (typically, a county) must provide language assistance to voters if significant numbers of voting-age citizens are members of a single-language minority group and do not speak or understand English "well enough to participate in the electoral process." Specifically, the legal requirement is triggered when more than 5 percent of voting-age citizens or 10,000 of these citizens meet the criteria. The 2010 Census shows that more than 80,000 people living in Harris County identify themselves as Vietnamese, and the U.S. Department of Justice determined that at least 10,000 of them are old enough to vote but

---

[22]Optional at first, the Australian ballot was made mandatory in 1903.

SAMPLE BALLOT   LÁ PHIẾU MẪU
Harris County – November 6, 2012 – General and Special Elections
Quận Harris – 6 tháng Mười Một, 2012 – Các Cuộc Tổng Tuyển Cử và Bầu Cử Đặc Biệt

Straight Party
Bỏ phiếu cho các ứng cử viên của cùng một đảng

☐ Republican Party
Đảng Cộng Hòa

☐ Democratic Party
Đảng Dân Chủ

☐ Libertarian Party
Đảng Tự Do

☐ Green Party
Đảng Xanh

President and Vice President
Tổng Thống và Phó Tổng Thống

☐ Mitt Romney / Paul Ryan
Republican Party *Đảng Cộng Hòa*

☐ Barack Obama / Joe Biden
Democratic Party *Đảng Dân Chủ*

☐ Gary Johnson / Jim Gray
Libertarian Party *Đảng Tự Do*

☐ Jill Stein / Cheri Honkala
Green Party *Đảng Xanh*

☐ Write-in
Bầu chọn ứng cử viên không có tên trong lá phiếu

United States Senator
Thượng Nghị Sĩ Hoa Kỳ

☐ Ted Cruz
Republican Party *Đảng Cộng Hòa*

☐ Paul Sadler
Democratic Party *Đảng Dân Chủ*

☐ John Jay Myers
Libertarian Party *Đảng Tự Do*

☐ David B. Collins
Green Party *Đảng Xanh*

United States Representative, District 2
Dân Biểu Hoa Kỳ Khu vực số 2

☐ Ted Poe
Republican Party *Đảng Cộng Hòa*

☐ Jim Dougherty
Democratic Party *Đảng Dân Chủ*

☐ Kenneth Duncan
Libertarian Party *Đảng Tự Do*

☐ Mark A. Roberts
Green Party *Đảng Xanh*

United States Representative, District 7
Dân Biểu Hoa Kỳ Khu vực số 7

☐ John Culberson
Republican Party *Đảng Cộng Hòa*

☐ James Cargas
Democratic Party *Đảng Dân Chủ*

☐ Drew Parks
Libertarian Party *Đảng Tự Do*

☐ Lance Findley
Green Party *Đảng Xanh*

United States Representative, District 8
Dân Biểu Hoa Kỳ Khu vực số 8

☐ Kevin Brady
Republican Party *Đảng Cộng Hòa*

☐ Neil Burns
Democratic Party *Đảng Dân Chủ*

☐ Roy Hall
Libertarian Party *Đảng Tự Do*

United States Representative, District 9
Dân Biểu Hoa Kỳ, Khu vực số 9

☐ Steve Mueller
Republican Party *Đảng Cộng Hòa*

☐ Al Green
Democratic Party *Đảng Dân Chủ*

☐ John Wieder
Libertarian Party *Đảng Tự Do*

☐ Vanessa Foster
Green Party *Đảng Xanh*

United States Representative, District 10
Dân Biểu Hoa Kỳ, Khu vực số 10

☐ Michael McCaul
Republican Party *Đảng Cộng Hòa*

☐ Tawana W. Cadien
Democratic Party *Đảng Dân Chủ*

☐ Richard Priest
Libertarian Party *Đảng Tự Do*

United States Representative, District 18
Dân Biểu Hoa Kỳ Khu vực số 18

☐ Sean Seibert
Republican Party *Đảng Cộng Hòa*

☐ Sheila Jackson Lee
Democratic Party *Đảng Dân Chủ*

☐ Christopher Barber
Libertarian Party *Đảng Tự Do*

United States Representative, District 22
Dân Biểu Hoa Kỳ, Khu vực số 22

☐ Pete Olson
Republican Party *Đảng Cộng Hòa*

☐ Kesha Rogers
Democratic Party *Đảng Dân Chủ*

☐ Steve Susman
Libertarian Party *Đảng Tự Do*

☐ Don Cook
Green Party *Đảng Xanh*

United States Representative, District 29
Dân Biểu Hoa Kỳ, Khu vực số 29

☐ Gene Green
Democratic Party *Đảng Dân Chủ*

☐ James Stanczak
Libertarian Party *Đảng Tự Do*

☐ Maria Selva
Green Party *Đảng Xanh*

United States Representative, District 36
Dân Biểu Hoa Kỳ, Khu vực số 36

☐ Steve Stockman
Republican Party *Đảng Cộng Hòa*

☐ Max Martin
Democratic Party *Đảng Dân Chủ*

☐ Michael K. Cole
Libertarian Party *Đảng Tự Do*

Railroad Commissioner
Ủy Viên Ngành Hỏa Xa

☐ Christi Craddick
Republican Party *Đảng Cộng Hòa*

☐ Dale Henry
Democratic Party *Đảng Dân Chủ*

☐ Vivekananda (Vik) Wall
Libertarian Party *Đảng Tự Do*

☐ Chris Kennedy
Green Party *Đảng Xanh*

Railroad Commissioner, Unexpired Term
Ủy Viên Ngành Hỏa Xa, Nhiệm Kỳ Vô Thời Hạn

☐ Barry Smitherman
Republican Party *Đảng Cộng Hòa*

☐ Jaime O. Perez
Libertarian Party *Đảng Tự Do*

☐ Josh Wendel
Green Party *Đảng Xanh*

Justice, Supreme Court, Place 2
Chánh Án, Tối Cao Pháp Viện, Vị Trí số 2

☐ Don Willett
Republican Party *Đảng Cộng Hòa*

☐ RS Roberto Koelsch
Libertarian Party *Đảng Tự Do*

Justice, Supreme Court, Place 4
Chánh Án, Tối Cao Pháp Viện, Vị Trí số 4

☐ John Devine
Republican Party *Đảng Cộng Hòa*

☐ Tom Oxford
Libertarian Party *Đảng Tự Do*

☐ Charles E. Waterbury
Green Party *Đảng Xanh*

Justice, Supreme Court, Place 6
Chánh Án, Tối Cao Pháp Viện, Vị Trí số 6

☐ Nathan Hecht
Republican Party *Đảng Cộng Hòa*

☐ Michele Petty
Democratic Party *Đảng Dân Chủ*

☐ Mark Ash
Libertarian Party *Đảng Tự Do*

☐ Jim Chisholm
Green Party *Đảng Xanh*

Presiding Judge, Court of Criminal Appeals
Chánh Án Chủ Tọa, Tòa Kháng Án Hình Sự

☐ Sharon Keller
Republican Party *Đảng Cộng Hòa*

☐ Keith Hampton
Democratic Party *Đảng Dân Chủ*

☐ Lance Stott
Libertarian Party *Đảng Tự Do*

Judge, Court of Criminal Appeals, Place 7
Chánh Án, Tòa Kháng Án Hình Sự, Vị Trí số 7

☐ Barbara Parker Hervey
Republican Party *Đảng Cộng Hòa*

☐ Mark W. Bennett
Libertarian Party *Đảng Tự Do*

Judge, Court of Criminal Appeals, Place 8
Chánh Án, Tòa Kháng Án Hình Sự, Vị Trí số 8

☐ Elsa Alcala
Republican Party *Đảng Cộng Hòa*

☐ William Bryan Strange, III
Libertarian Party *Đảng Tự Do*

Member, State Board of Education, District 4
Hội Viên, Hội Đồng Quản Trị Giáo Dục Tiểu Bang, Khu Vực số 4

☐ Dorothy Olmos
Republican Party *Đảng Cộng Hòa*

☐ Lawrence Allen, Jr.
Democratic Party *Đảng Dân Chủ*

Figure 4.4
An English–Vietnamese Ballot Used in Harris County for the 2012 General Election

This ballot offers the straight-party option and then the candidates for the separate offices, consistently listing the Republicans first, then the Democrats, followed by other candidates.

Source: Harris County Clerk's Office.

 What are the arguments for and against bilingual ballots such as the one shown here? Should government facilitate voting? Think of other ways to make it easier for people to vote.

are not sufficiently proficient in English, thereby triggering the requirement. Given the levels of immigration into the United States, the number of ballot languages is almost certain to increase.

Early Voting All Texas voters can now vote before election day.[23] Some voters can vote by mail, specifically those who plan to be away from the county on election day, those who are sick or disabled, anyone who is 65 years or older, and people who are in jail but are otherwise eligible to vote. The rest of us can only vote early in person. Generally, **early voting** begins the seventeenth day before election day and ends the fourth day before election day. In addition to traditional election-day voting sites, such as schools and fire stations, there are several other more familiar places to vote early, including grocery and convenience stores. This innovation has clearly made voting easier in Texas, and people are using it. In the 2010 midterm election, more than 53 percent of the votes were cast before election day, and in 2012, early votes were 63 percent of the total. Although people are voting earlier, they are not voting in greater numbers, as we noted earlier in the chapter. The growing tendency toward early voting may still have important implications for when and how politicians campaign.

Counting and Recounting Ballots

We take for granted that when we vote, our votes count. As we learned in Florida in the 2000 presidential election, this is not true. The first machine count of ballots in Florida showed George W. Bush with a 1,725-vote lead. In a mandatory machine recount of the same ballots, the same machines cut his lead to 327. We were also told that some 2 to 3 percent of the ballots were not counted at all. How could this happen? What does this mean? The answer is simple: Machines make mistakes. Some ballots are not counted. Some may even be counted for the wrong candidate. This shocked most Americans.

Experts have known for a long time that vote counting contains a good amount of error. By most accounts, the error rate averages 1 to 2 percent, although it can be higher depending on the ballot and the machines themselves. The error rate is largest for punch-card ballots, which traditionally have been used in big cities in Texas and other states. To vote, one inserts the ballot into a slot in the voting booth and then uses a stylus to punch holes corresponding to candidates' names that are printed on separate lists, usually in the form of a booklet. There are two sources of error associated with these ballots. First, some voters do not fully punch out the pieces of paper from the perforated holes. That is, these pieces of paper, which are called **chad**, remain attached to the ballot. Second, even where the chad are completely detached, machines do not read each and every ballot. This is of importance to voters. It is typically of little consequence for election outcomes, however. Counting errors tend to cancel out, meaning that no candidate gains a much greater number of votes. Thus, the errors are important only when elections are very close, within a half percentage point, which is not very common. When it does happen, the losing candidate can request a recount.

Texas has fairly specific laws about recounts. A candidate can request a recount if he or she loses by less than 10 percent. This is a fairly generous rule compared to other states. The candidate who requests the recount does have to pay for it, however, which means that most candidates do not request a recount unless the margin is much closer, say, one percentage point or less. As for the recount itself, the Texas Election Code states that "only one method may be used in the recount" and "a manual recount shall be conducted in preference to an electronic recount." The procedures are fairly detailed. What may be most interesting is the set

---

Early voting

The practice of voting before election day at traditional voting locations, such as schools, and other locations, such as grocery and convenience stores.

Chad

The small pieces of paper produced when voting with punch-card ballots.

---

[23]For a nice description of early voting and a preliminary assessment of its effects, see Robert M. Stein and Patricia A. Garcia-Monet, "Voting Early But Not Often," *Social Science Quarterly* 78 (December 1997), pp. 657–671. For a more recent review and assessment, see Paul Gronke, Eva Galanes-Rosenbaum, and Peter A. Miller, "Early Voting and Turnout," *PS: Political Science and Politics* 40 (December 2007), pp. 639–645.

of rules for how chad should be interpreted. Indeed, canvassing authorities are allowed to determine whether "an indentation on the chad from the stylus or other object is present" and whether "the chad reflects by other means a clearly ascertainable intent of the voter to vote."[24] This leaves a lot of room for discretion on the part of canvassing authorities in the various Texas counties.

Electronic Voting

Partly in response to the events in Florida—and the seeming potential for similar problems in Texas—a number of counties introduced **electronic voting** in the 2002 midterm elections to allow voting by using touch screens. Instead of punching holes in ballots or filling in bubbles on

Tom carter/Alamy

Voters cast their votes electronically by touching screens.

Does electronic voting solve the problems with paper ballots? How can we tell?

scannable sheets, most voters today cast ballots by touching screens. The technology is similar to what is used in automated teller machines (ATMs) and electronic-ticket check-ins at many airports and promises an exact count of votes. It is now used for voting throughout much of Texas and the United States. As with the introduction of any new technology, problems have occurred.[25]

Electronic voting
Voting by using touch screens.

ELECTION CAMPAIGNS IN TEXAS: STRATEGIES, RESOURCES, AND RESULTS

LO 4.4 Identify the factors that advantage (or disadvantage) candidates in Texas elections.

The ultimate aim of party activity is to nominate candidates in the party primary or convention and get them elected in the general election. The campaign for the parties' nomination is often more critical in one-party areas of the state—Democrats in South Texas and in some large urban areas and Republicans in many rural and suburban areas. For local and district offices in these areas, the key electoral decision is made in the primaries because the dominant parties' nominee is almost certain to win the general election. In statewide elections, the crucial electoral decision is often made in the Republican primary where the party's nominee is chosen. The Republican candidate then has a relatively clear path to winning office.

Candidates seeking their parties' nomination in a primary pursue a different sort of campaign strategy than they do when they later run in the general election. The primary

---

[24]Texas Code 127.130. Also see Carlos Guerra, "Texas Is Far Friendlier to *All* Our Chad," *San Antonio Express-News*, November 25, 2000, p. B–1.

[25]Rachel Konrad, "Reports of Electronic Voting Trouble Top 1,000," *USA Today*, November 4, 2004.

electorate is usually much smaller and made up of more-committed partisans. As a result, primary candidates are likely to strike a more ideological or even strident approach that appeals to activists. Once they have won their primaries, candidates will often moderate their views to win over swing voters and independents in the general election. For little-known candidates, money and the endorsement of party elites are more crucial in the primary than in the general election. Little-known candidates can frequently count on the party label to sweep them into office in general elections.

The General Election Campaign

To a large extent, general election outcomes are predictable. Despite all the media attention paid to the conventions, the debates, the advertising, and everything else involved in election campaigns, certain things powerfully structure the vote in national and state elections.[26] In state elections, two factors dominate: party identification and incumbency.

First, where more people in a state identify with one political party than with the other, the candidates of the preferred party have an advantage in general elections. For instance, when most Texans identified with the Democratic Party, Democratic candidates dominated elected offices throughout the state. As Texans have become more Republican in their identification, Republican candidates have done very well; indeed, as was mentioned earlier, Republicans now hold every statewide elected office. Identification with the political parties varies a lot within Texas, however, and this has implications for state legislative elections. In some parts of the state, particularly in the big cities, more people identify with the Democratic Party, and Democratic candidates typically represent those areas in the state house and senate (see Chapter 7). Thus, party identification in the state and in districts themselves tells us a lot about which candidates win general elections.

Second, incumbent candidates—those already in office who are up for reelection—are more likely to win in general elections. This is particularly true in state legislative elections, where the districts are fairly homogeneous and the campaigns are not very visible, but incumbency is also important in elections for statewide office. Incumbents have a number of advantages over challengers, the most important of which is that they have won in the past. To become an incumbent, a candidate has to beat an incumbent or else win in an open-seat election, which usually involves a contest among a number of strong candidates. By definition, therefore, incumbents are good candidates. In addition, incumbents have the advantage of office. They are in a position to do things for their constituents and thus increase their support among voters.

Although party identification and incumbency are important in Texas elections, they are not the whole story. What they really tell us is the degree to which candidates are advantaged or disadvantaged as they embark on their campaigns. Other factors ultimately matter on election day.[27]

Mobilizing Groups Groups play an important role in elections for any office. A fundamental part of campaigns is getting out the vote among groups that strongly support the candidate. To a large extent, candidates focus on groups aligned with the

---

[26]Most of the research has focused on presidential elections. See Robert S. Erikson and Christopher Wlezien, *The Timeline of Presidential Elections: How Campaigns Do (and Don't) Matter* (Chicago: University of Chicago Press, 2012). Some research has also been done on state gubernatorial and legislative elections. See, for example, Mark E. Tompkins, "The Electoral Fortunes of Gubernatorial Incumbents," *Journal of Politics* 46 (May 1984), pp. 520–543; Ronald E. Weber, Harvey J. Tucker, and Paul Brace, "Vanishing Marginals in State Legislative Elections," *Legislative Studies Quarterly* 16 (February 1991), pp. 29–47.

[27]For a detailed analysis of election campaigns in Texas in a single election year, see Richard Murray, "The 1996 Elections in Texas," in Kent L. Tedin, Donald S. Lutz, and Edward P. Fuchs (eds.), *Perspectives on American and Texas Politics*, 5th ed. (Dubuque, IA: Kendall/Hunt, 1998), pp. 247–286.

political parties.[28] At the state level, business interests and teachers are particularly important. Republican candidates tend to focus their efforts on the former and Democratic candidates on the latter. Candidates also mobilize other groups, including African Americans and Latinos. Traditionally, Democratic candidates emphasized these minority groups, though Governor Bush broke somewhat with this tradition and focused substantial attention on the Latino community in Texas. Mobilizing groups does not necessarily involve taking strong public stands on their behalf, especially those that are less mainstream. The mobilization of such groups is typically conducted very quietly, often through targeted mailings and phone calls.

Choosing Issues Issues are important in any campaign. In campaigns for state offices, taxes, education, immigration, and religious issues are salient, and abortion matters a lot too. Just as they target social groups, candidates focus on issues that reflect their party affiliations, but they avoid unpopular positions like higher taxes or budget cuts for education or law enforcement. Where candidates do differ is in their emphasis on particular issues and their policy proposals. These choices depend heavily on carefully crafted opinion polls. Through polls, candidates attempt to identify the issues that the public considers to be important and then craft policy positions to address those issues. The process is ongoing, and candidates pay close attention to changes in opinion and, perhaps most important, to the public's response to the candidates' own positions. Public opinion polling is fundamental in modern election campaigns in America, and campaign messages are often presented in advance to focus groups—test groups of selected citizens—to help campaign strategists tailor their messages in a way that will appeal to particular audiences.

The Campaign Trail Deciding where and how to campaign are critical elements in campaign strategy. Candidates spend countless hours "on the stump," traveling around the state or district to speak before diverse groups. In a state as large as Texas, candidates for statewide office must pick and choose areas so as to maximize their exposure. Unfortunately for rural voters, this means that candidates spend most of their time in urban and suburban areas where they can get the attention of a large audience through the local media.

Nowadays, no candidate gets elected by stumping alone. The most direct route to the voters is through the mass media. There are 20 media markets in Texas. These include approximately 200 television and cable stations and more than 500 radio stations. In addition, 79 daily newspapers and many more weekly newspapers are dispersed throughout the state's 254 counties.[29] Candidates hire public relations firms and media consultants, and advertising plays a big role. These days, a successful campaign often relies on **negative campaigning**, in which candidates attack opponents' issue positions or character. As one campaign consultant said, "Campaigns are about definition. Either you define yourself and your opponent or [the other candidates do]. . . . Victory goes to the aggressor."[30] Although often considered an unfortunate development in American politics, it is important to keep in mind that negative campaigning can serve to provide voters with information about the candidates and their issue positions.

Negative campaigning

A strategy used in election campaigns in which candidates attack opponents' issue positions or character.

Timing The timing of the campaign effort can be very important. Unlike presidential elections, campaigns for state offices, including the governorship, begin fairly late in the

[28]For an analysis of how membership in various demographic groups influences voting behavior, see Robert S. Erikson, Thomas B. Lancaster, and David W. Romero, "Group Components of the Presidential Vote, 1952–1984," *Journal of Politics* 50 (May 1988), pp. 337–346. For an analysis of how identification with various social groups influences voting behavior, see Christopher Wlezien and Arthur H. Miller, "Social Groups and Political Judgments," *Social Science Quarterly* 78 (December 1997), pp. 625–640.

[29]*Gale Directory of Publications and Broadcast Media*, 148th ed. (Detroit, MI: Gale Research, 2012).

[30]Quoted in Dave McNeely, "Campaign Strategists Preparing Spin Systems," *Austin American-Statesman*, October 21, 1993, p. A11.

election cycle. Indeed, it is common to hear little from gubernatorial candidates until after Labor Day and from candidates for the legislature not until a month before the election.

Candidates often reserve a large proportion of their campaign advertising budget for a last-minute media "blitz." However, early voting may affect this strategy somewhat. Recall that in 2012, approximately 63 percent of the votes in Texas were cast early, during the weeks leading up to the election, which means that the final campaign blitz came too late to have any effect on more than half of all voters. Consequently, candidates in the future may be less likely to concentrate their efforts so tightly on the final days of the campaign.

Money in Election Campaigns

Election campaigns are expensive, which means that candidates need to raise a lot of money to be competitive. Indeed, the amount of money a candidate raises can be a deciding factor in the campaign. Just how much a candidate needs depends on the level of the campaign and the competitiveness of the race. High-level campaigns for statewide office are usually multimillion-dollar affairs.

In recent years, the race for governor has become especially expensive. In 2006, the four candidates vying spent a much smaller amount, about $46 million in total, with former Governor Perry leading the way at $23 million. In 2010, former Governor Perry spent $40 million to Bill White's $25 million and won yet again. Spending in the 2014 race for governor has not been finally tallied, but it is expected to far exceed previous amounts.

Although lower-level races in Texas are not usually million-dollar affairs, they can be expensive as well. This is certainly true if a contested office is an open seat, where the incumbent is not running for reelection, or if an incumbent is from a marginal district—one in which the incumbent won office with less than 55 percent of the vote. It is not unusual for a candidate in a competitive race for the state house to spend between $100,000 and $200,000.

Where does this money come from? Candidates often try to solicit small individual contributions through direct-mail campaigns. However, to raise the millions required for a high-level state race, they must solicit "big money" from wealthy friends or business and professional interests that have a stake in the outcome of the campaign; see some examples in the Texas Insiders feature. Another source of big money is loans—candidates often borrow heavily from banks, wealthy friends, or even themselves.[31]

Political action committees (PACs)

Organizations that raise and then contribute money to political candidates.

Banks, corporations, law firms, and professional associations, such as those representing doctors, real estate agents, or teachers, organize and register their **political action committees (PACs)** with the secretary of state's office. PACs serve as the vehicle through which interest groups collect money and then contribute it to political candidates.

Where Does the Money Go?

In today's election campaigns, there are many ways to spend money. Newspaper ads, billboards, radio messages, bumper stickers, yard signs, and phone banks are all staples in traditional campaigns. Candidates for statewide and urban races must rely on media advertising, particularly television, to get the maximum exposure they need in the three- or four-month campaign period. Campaigns are becoming professionalized, with candidates likely to hire consulting firms to manage their campaigns. Consultants contract with public opinion pollsters, arrange advertising, and organize direct-mail campaigns that can target certain areas of the state.

Did You Know? A small sampling of the PACs include AQUAPAC (set up by the Water Quality Association), BEEF-PAC (Texas Cattle Feeders Association), SIX-PAC (National Beer Wholesalers Association), WAFFLEPAC (Waffle House, Inc.), and WHATAPAC (Whataburger Corporation of Texas).[32]

---

[31]For a comprehensive treatment of money in election campaigns, see Frank J. Sorauf, *Inside Campaign Finance: Myths and Realities* (New Haven, CT: Yale University Press, 1992).

[32]Federal Election Commission, www.fec.gov.

We can get some idea about spending in campaigns from what candidates pay for advertising and political consultants in Harris County, which includes Houston:[33]

★ A 30-second TV "spot" costs about $1,500 for a daytime ad, $2,000 to $5,000 for an ad during the evening news, and $5,000 to $20,000 during prime time (8:00 P.M. to 11:00 P.M.), depending on the show's popularity rating; for some popular programs such as CSI, the cost can be as much as $25,000.

★ Prime time for most radio broadcasting is "drive time" (5:00 A.M. to 10 A.M. and 3:00 P.M. to 8:00 P.M.), when most people are driving to or from work. Drive-time rates range from $250 to $2,000 per 60-second spot.

★ Billboards can run from $600 to $15,000 a month, depending on the location (billboards on busy highways are the most expensive).

★ Newspaper ads cost around $250 per column inch ($300 to $500 on Sunday). In 2008, a half-page ad in the *Houston Chronicle* run on the day before the election cost about $15,000. Advertising rates for election campaigns are actually higher than standard rates because political advertisers do not qualify for the discounts that regular advertisers receive.

★ Hiring a professional polling organization to conduct a poll in Harris County costs $15,000 to $30,000.

★ Hiring a political consulting firm to manage a campaign in Harris County runs up to $50,000 plus a percentage of media buys. (Technically, the percentage is paid by the television and radio stations.) Most firms also get a bonus ranging from $5,000 to $25,000 if the candidate wins.

Clearly, money is important in election campaigns. Although the candidate who spends the most money does not always win, a certain amount of money is necessary for a candidate to be competitive. Speaking with his tongue partly in his cheek, one prominent politician noted, in regard to high-level statewide races in Texas, that, even if "you don't have to raise $10 million, you have to raise $8 million."[34]

Control over Money in Campaigns Prompted by the increasing use of television in campaigns and the increasing amount of money needed to buy it, the federal government and most state governments passed laws regulating the use of money in the early 1970s. The Federal Elections Campaign Act of 1972 established regulations that apply only to federal elections: president, vice president, and members of Congress. It provided for public financing of presidential campaigns with tax dollars, limited the amount of money that individuals and PACs could contribute to campaigns, and required disclosure of campaign donations. In 1976, the Supreme Court declared that it was unconstitutional to set spending limits for campaigns that were not publicly funded; this means there are no spending limits for congressional races.[35] The same is true for Texas state elections.

Not surprisingly, expenditures in election campaigns continue to increase. The Federal Election Commission reported that $211.8 million was spent in the 1976 election of the president and members of Congress, with $122.8 million spent in the presidential race alone. Of the $60.9 million spent in the elections of the 435 House members, more money was spent on behalf of the candidates in Texas ($4.5 million) than on those of any other state except California.[36] Such expenditure levels (only $140,000 per seat) appear modest by today's

[33]Nancy Sims of Pierpont Communications, with offices in Austin and Houston, graciously provided this information.

[34]"The Senate Can Wait," interview with Jim Hightower, *Texas Observer*, January 27, 1989, p. 6.

[35]*Buckley* v. *Valeo*, 424 U.S. 1 (1976).

[36]*Congressional Quarterly Almanac, 1977* (Washington, DC: CQ Press, 1977), p. 35A; *Congressional Quarterly Weekly Report*, March 5, 1989, p. 478. Since 1976, the federal government has actually expanded the role of money in elections.

Profiles of Texas Campaign Megadonors

Table 4.4 shows the ten largest campaign donors in Texas campaigns during 2012. It illustrates who contributes, how much they contribute, and in which kinds of public policy decisions they have an interest. Altogether the top 150 contributors spent a total of $107 million contributing to Texas political campaigns.

Thinking about the role of elites in Texas politics. Because of the enormous amounts of money spent by just a few campaign contributors, some critics have been worried that large contributions buy outsized political influence for their donors. Most observers agree that campaign contributions open doors, giving contributors access to public officials to argue the case for their interests; some critics argue that candidates' reliance on large campaign contributions corrupts state politics and skews public policy toward the interests of wealthier individuals and groups.

Others argue that the influence of large contributions is balanced by other influences, such as small contributions, public opinion, and alert media. They defend the donors' right to give money to candidates who share their viewpoints as a form of expression essential to a free society.

 Explain how Texas campaign finance regulations are designed to hold public officials and campaign contributors accountable by shining the light of publicity on them. Think of other ways to limit potential corrupting influences that do not interfere with freedom of expression.

Sources: Texas Ethics Commission data compiled by Texans for Public Justice, *Texas Top Contributors*, June 10, 2013 at http://info.tpj.org/reports/Top%20Donors%202013.pdf; Alexander Duzak and Dave Levinthal, *Donor Profile: Harold Simmons*, Center for Public Integrity, March 17, 2013, at www.publicintegrity.org/2012/04/26/8460/donor-profile-harold-simmons; Matt Stiles, "Executive Profile: Harold Simmons." *Bloomberg Businessweek* at http://investing.businessweek.com/research/stocks/people/person.asp?personId=311732&ticker=VHI.

TABLE 4.4 Profiles of Texas Campaign Megadonors

Donor	Total Contributions	Donor's Special Interest
Texans for Lawsuit Reform PAC	$7,046,424	Limiting lawsuits against businesses and professionals
Bob and Doylene Perry* (Perry Homes)	$6,961,500	Protecting homebuilders against liability; opposing business regulation
Texas Association of Realtors PAC	$4,272,231	Real estate industry; property rights
Harold Simmons** (Contran Corporation; Waste Control Specialists; Vahi, Inc.)	$3,444,850	Protecting chemical plants against regulation; limiting lawsuits
Mostyn Law Firm	$2,915,334	Protecting plaintiffs' right to sue insurance companies and other businesses
Texans for Insurance Reform	$2,530,211	Protecting plaintiffs' right to sue insurance companies and other businesses
Texas Medical Association PAC	$2,188,077	Protecting the medical profession against lawsuits; public health
Steven and Amber Mostyn	$1,588,672	Protecting plaintiffs' right to sue insurance companies and other businesses
Energy Future Holdings	$1,497,585	Protecting coal-fired utilities against regulation
AT&T, Inc. PAC	$1,487,585	Favorable regulation and low taxes on the communications industry

*Bob Perry, now deceased, was not related to former Governor Rick Perry.
**Deceased December 28, 2013.

standards. By 2012, the average was nearly $1.6 million per U.S. House seat and substantially larger for U.S. Senate elections—at least $15 million. The level of campaign spending is likely to continue to rise.

Later amendments to the Federal Elections Campaign Act made it legal for national political parties to raise and spend unlimited amounts of **soft money**, funds spent by political parties on behalf of political candidates. Party funds could be used to help candidates in a variety of ways, especially through voter registration and get-out-the-vote drives. The U.S. Supreme Court further opened up spending in 1985 by deciding that **independent expenditures** could not be limited.[37] As a result, individuals and organizations could spend as much as they want to promote a candidate as long as they were not working or communicating directly with the candidate's campaign organization. The 2002 Campaign Reform Act limited independent expenditures by corporations and labor unions, but this was overturned by the Supreme Court in its 2010 decision in *Citizens United* v. *Federal Election Commission*.[38] This may have implications for state and local races that have bans on corporate spending, including Texas. The 2002 Act also deprived the parties of their soft money resources, but activists simply set up nonparty organizations to collect and disperse such funds. Understandably, it has been difficult to effectively control money in election campaigns.

FEC regulations apply only to candidates for national office. For candidates running for state offices, the most important provisions of Texas law regarding money in campaigns are as follows:

★ Candidates may not raise or spend money until an official campaign treasurer is appointed.
★ Candidates and PACs may not accept cash contributions for more than an aggregate of $100, but checks in unlimited amounts are permitted.
★ Direct contributions from corporations and labor unions are prohibited, though this may change in the wake of the recent Supreme Court decision, *Citizens United* v. *Federal Elections Commission,* 558 U.S. 50 (2010).
★ Candidates and treasurers of campaign committees are required to file sworn statements listing all contributions and expenditures for a designated reporting period to the Texas secretary of state's office.
★ Both criminal and civil penalties are imposed on anyone who violates the law's provisions.
★ Primary enforcement of campaign regulations is the responsibility of the Texas Ethics Commission.

Although these provisions may sound imposing, the fact is that raising and spending money on Texas campaigns still is pretty much wide open. For example, corporations and labor unions may not give directly to a candidate, but they may give via their PACs. Note also that there are no limits on the amount a candidate may spend. Probably the most important effect of the campaign finance law in Texas comes from the requirement of disclosure. How much money a candidate raises, who makes contributions, and how campaign funds are spent are matters of public record. This information may be newsworthy to reporters or other individuals motivated to inform the public.

Who Gets Elected

It is useful to think of elected offices in Texas as a pyramid. At the bottom of the pyramid are the most local of offices; at the top is the governor. Moving from bottom to top, the importance of the office increases and the number of officeholders decreases. It thus gets

Soft money

Money spent by political parties on behalf of political candidates, especially for the purposes of increasing voter registration and turnout.

Independent expenditures

Money individuals and organizations spend to promote a candidate without working or communicating directly with the candidate's campaign organization.

---

[37]Federal Election Commission, www.fec.gov.
[38]*Citizens United* v. *Federal Election Commission*, 558 U.S. 50 (2010).

more and more difficult for politicians to ascend the pyramid, and only the most effective politicians rise to the top. This tells us a lot about candidates and elections in Texas and elsewhere.

In local elections, the pool of candidates is diverse in many ways, including educational background, income, and profession. As we move up the pyramid, however, candidates become much more homogeneous. For statewide office, the typical candidate is middle or upper class, from an urban area, and has strong ties to business and professional interests in the state. Most elected state officers in Texas, including the governor, lieutenant governor, and attorney general, must be acceptable to the state's major financial and corporate interests and to its top law firms. These interests help statewide candidates raise the large amounts of money that are critical to a successful race.

Successful candidates for statewide office in Texas have traditionally been white Protestant males. Prior to 1986, when Raul Gonzalez was elected to the state supreme court, no Latino or African American had been elected to statewide office, though these two ethnic groups combined represent one-half of the state's population. The only female governor until that time was Miriam A. "Ma" Ferguson, who in the 1920s served as surrogate for her husband, Jim. In 1982, Ann Richards was elected state treasurer, becoming the second woman ever to be elected to statewide office in Texas.

Women and minorities have made substantial gains in statewide offices. Ann Richards became the first woman elected governor in her own right in 1990. Kay Bailey Hutchison captured the state treasurer's office and in 1993 won a special election to become the first woman from Texas elected to the U.S. Senate. Dan Morales was the first Latino to win a state executive office when he captured the attorney general's office. More history was made when Morris Overstreet of Amarillo won a seat on the Texas Court of Criminal Appeals and became the first African American elected to a statewide office.

Women and ethnic groups are starting to make inroads in other elected offices in Texas. In the 83rd Legislature (2013–2014), 31 women were elected to the 150-member house and 6 to the 31-member senate. Women have also held the post of mayor in five of the state's largest cities: Houston, Dallas, San Antonio, El Paso, and Austin. Latinos hold 40 seats in the state legislature, and African Americans occupy 20. Among the state's 36 U.S. congressional representatives, there are 3 women, 6 Latinos, and 4 African Americans. Clearly, Texas politics has changed a lot over time. The changes have reflected the changing composition of Texas, though with a noticeable lag.

APPLYING WHAT YOU HAVE LEARNED ABOUT VOTING AND ELECTIONS IN TEXAS

LO 4.5 Apply what you have learned about voting and elections in Texas.

In this chapter, you have learned about the factors that affect the number of voters who turn out to vote in various elections, including primaries and general elections. You have learned about the legal, demographic, cultural, and social factors that determine who actually votes. You have learned that, in practice, Texas has a lower percentage of residents casting ballots than do most other states. The following essay will give you the opportunity to put this low voter turnout into perspective and evaluate the implications of low voter turnout for the quality of democracy in Texas.

After you have read the essay, you will be asked a series of questions that will require you to employ critical-thinking skills to apply what you have learned in this chapter to the new information in this essay. You will be required to analyze and evaluate the quality of representation in the Texas democracy and the role of elections in the state's political system.

Finally, you will be asked to think about who bears the responsibility to make certain that the system reflects the needs and values of its citizens.

POLITICIANS DON'T REPRESENT MOST TEXANS

by Ross Ramsey

EXECUTIVE EDITOR, *TEXAS TRIBUNE*

It's very easy for Texas politicians to represent the people who elect them without necessarily representing the people of the state. The extent of the difference depends on whether the people who vote accurately reflect the views of those who don't. The latter group is much bigger than the former.

The math is simple, and the numbers are readily available from a couple of state agencies, the Texas Legislative Council and the Texas Secretary of State. In 2012, Texas had 26.1 million residents, a voting age population of 18.3 million, a citizen voting age population of 15.6 million, and 13.6 million registered voters. Just under 8 million people voted in that year's November general election; 1.4 million voted in the Republican primary, and another 600,000 or so voted in the Democratic primary.

The influence of a small number of voters is compounded by the dominance of the Republican Party in Texas elections since 1994, which marked the start of an unbroken 20-year (and counting) winning streak by the GOP's candidates in statewide executive and judicial elections. With the support of fewer than 800,000 Republican primary voters—well over the 50 percent needed to win the primary in 2012—a Texas Republican is able to assume statewide office representing more than 26 million people.

In congressional and legislative elections, the number of people who vote in primaries is critical. Only a handful of those districts are competitive in November elections, thanks to the strength of political redistricting efforts designed to carve the state into distinctly Republican and Democratic territories. That protects the interests of the parties—and often, their incumbents—while taking most of those decisions out of the hands of general election voters, who greatly outnumber their counterparts in the party primaries.

Texas is divided into 36 congressional districts, only one of which—CD-23, which stretches from El Paso to San Antonio along the Texas–Mexico border—is generally considered to be competitive in general elections. Of the rest, 11 were designed to elect Democrats to Congress and 24 were drawn to elect Republicans. As the numbers indicate, the maps were initially drawn by a Legislature with a Republican supermajority.

In the same way, the 31-member Texas state Senate was elected from districts drawn to favor 11 Democrats and 20 Republicans. As with the congressional map, one of those Republican seats remained competitive in general elections. The rest of the incumbents were vulnerable in their own primaries, but not in November's general elections.

The smallest legislative districts are those drawn for the 150 House districts; likewise, most were set up to elect Democrats or Republicans and only a handful were left to swing from one party to the other in general elections.

Voters from the majority party in each district (or, in top elections, the whole state) get their say in primary elections and, more often than not, watch their candidates coast to victory in November.

The numbers can change over time. Lawmakers are required to revisit the political maps after every decade's national census. In the years that follow, voting patterns can change—sometimes dramatically—depending on demographic shifts, local issues and voter participation.

Having control of the state legislature at the beginning of the decade, when it is time to draw new maps, is a powerful advantage that allows a party to institutionalize its position, at least for a while. For example, strong national Republican victories in 2010—an election marked by the tea party's rocketing popularity—were mirrored in Texas. What had been a relatively even partisan balance in the state legislature was instantly replaced by a Republican supermajority, with devastating timing for Texas Democrats. Instead of a chance to win back some of their seats in 2012, they were forced to compete on a new playing field that was drawn to their disadvantage by 2010's winners.

In 2008, the Democratic nomination for president was still in question when the Texas primaries began. Voters got an unusual treat, since those decisions are more often made in early primary states and Texas voters are left with little to do other than ratify those choices. The competition between Barack Obama and Hillary Clinton dramatically increased turnout in the Democratic primary that year, to 16 percent of the voting age population from 5 percent four years earlier. The Republicans also saw their turnout increase to 8 percent of the voting age population in 2008 from 4 percent in 2004.

That 2008 election produced the evenly balanced legislature that was upended in 2010. Voter turnout tells part of the story. Republicans kept coming to the polls after 2008, holding at about 8 percent of the voting age population in their primaries in 2010 and 2012. The Democrats, meanwhile, dropped to about 4 percent of the voting age population in their primaries in those two years. More than 2 million Texans who voted in the 2008 Democratic primary stayed home in 2010 and in 2012, a number sufficient to swamp Republican turnout in either year and possibly a pool of partisans large enough to turn November elections, too (it is also possible that many of them voted in general elections but not in primaries in those years).

Texas was one of the fastest-growing states in the U.S. during the first decade of the 21st century, and most of that growth was attributable to increases in minority populations. In particular, the state's Hispanic population accounted for two-thirds of the overall increase.

Those numbers caught the attention of partisans on both sides. Democrats in Texas hope that increases in a population that has traditionally favored Democratic candidates could break the Republican hold on the state. Republicans fear the same thing, but also maintain that Hispanics are more in tune with their conservative ideological and cultural positions than with those of the Democrats.

That demographic shift might eventually change Texas politics, but campaign plans based on a dramatic transformation of the electorate continue to fall short. The changes in the state's overall population are not matched, so far, by changes in the state's electorate. In the population, Anglos no longer constitute a majority; in the electorate, they do. Hispanics in Texas are not yet voting in proportion to their population numbers, and it won't be clear until they do start voting whether new Hispanic voters are as reliably Democratic as established Hispanic voters.

In the meantime, campaigns on both sides concentrate on voters they can reasonably expect to participate, based on past performance. Once elected, officeholders make changes to election law and election maps that solidify their positions (or, at the least, that do not weaken them)—also based on the past performance of voters.

In other words, they answer to the people who elect them, and if they do that faithfully, they generally remain in power. When voter turnout is as low as it has been in Texas in modern times, that can mean that politicians and officeholders—always responsive to voters' interests and tendencies—find themselves responding to the most active and partisan Texans.

Texans who do not vote might wonder why state policies sometimes seem out of the mainstream. The answer is simple: Elected officials are more responsive to the people who vote than to its non-participants.

JOIN THE DEBATE

 Organize a presentation or essay that explains which factors lead to the low levels of voter turnout in Texas compared to other states. To be complete, your work should explain legal constraints as well as demographic, political, and cultural factors that contribute to low voter turnout.

 Explain why Texas elections do not reflect the wishes of all Texans. How does this fact affect the quality of representation in Texas politics?

 Many Texans are simply not qualified to vote for various reasons, but many simply choose not to participate. Should the choice of whether or not to vote be entirely a matter of personal responsibility, or does the political system have a responsibility to adopt policies to encourage participation in order to make election results reflect the needs and values of as many citizens as possible? Explain.

CHAPTER SUMMARY

LO 4.1   Explain why voter turnout is low in Texas. Before you can vote in Texas, you must first register. Once registered, voting in Texas is easy, though the recent passage of voter identification requirements may make things harder for some people, particularly minorities.

National turnout has fluctuated between 50 and 55 percent in presidential elections and hovered around 40 percent in midterm elections, much lower rates than we find in most other advanced democracies. Voter turnout in Texas is usually about 10 percent below the national average.

Low voter turnout in Texas may be due in part to the state's socioeconomic characteristics. A comparatively large percentage of Texans live below the poverty level and many have not graduated from high school; these people are not very likely to vote. The large numbers of ethnic minorities and lack of party competition also account for low turnout in the state.

LO 4.2   Describe the types of Texas elections. In Texas, as in most American states, winning elected office usually requires candidates to win both a primary and general election. Party primaries are used to select the parties' nominees, and in Texas candidates must win the primary by a majority vote or face a runoff primary between the two highest vote-getters.

The election that officially determines who will take office is the general election in which all party nominees and independent candidates face off against each other. Whichever candidate gets the most votes, the plurality, wins. Except for some municipal elections, the candidate does not need a majority to be victorious.

LO 4.3   Understand how elections are administered in Texas. Getting on the ballot in Texas general elections is difficult. The easiest way is to win the Democratic or Republican primaries, and that is not easy. Third-party and independent candidates also find it difficult to get on the ballot.

Ballot design is an important factor in elections. Texas traditionally has used the party-column ballot, in which the names of all the candidates of each party are listed in parallel columns. The main alternative is the office-block ballot, in which the names of candidates are listed underneath each office. Many Texas counties have now adopted electronic voting systems, which combine features of the two designs.

Another innovation has been the adoption of an early voting option, which allows voting before election day at a variety of locations. In 2012, almost two-thirds of all votes in Texas were cast early. This has fairly obvious implications for the timing and effects of election campaigns.

LO 4.4   Identify the factors that advantage (or disadvantage) candidates in Texas elections. In Texas, as in other states, voters' choices on election day are driven to a large extent by party affiliation, and Republican candidates usually win statewide office. Democrats, though, have large pockets of supporters in some areas, particularly the big cities—Austin, Dallas, Houston, and San Antonio—as well as the Rio Grande Valley.

Aside from the partisan balance, incumbency is also important and candidates need to be able to campaign effectively by mobilizing groups and choosing attractive issue positions. Candidates must raise an increasing amount of funding to be competitive.

LO 4.5   Apply what you have learned about voting and elections in Texas. You learned various reasons for the low voter turnout in Texas and you explored some of the implications of low voter turnout for the quality of democracy in the state. You considered the ethical issue of whether voting is purely a matter of personal responsibility or whether the political system has a stake in making certain that elections reflect the basic values and needs of its citizens.

KEY TERMS

australian ballot, *p. 98*
chad, *p. 100*
closed primary, *p. 92*
crossover voting, *p. 93*
direct primary, *p. 90*
early voting, *p. 100*

electronic voting, *p. 101*
independent
   expenditures, *p. 107*
negative campaigning, *p. 103*
office-block ballot, *p. 95*
open primary, *p. 92*

participation paradox, *p. 80*
party-column ballot, *p. 95*
plurality vote, *p. 93*
political action committees
   (PACs), *p. 104*
runoff primary, *p. 92*

soft money, *p. 107*
split-ticket voting, *p. 95*
straight-ticket voting, *p. 95*
voter turnout, *p. 82*
voting-age population
   (VAP), *p. 82*

REVIEW QUESTIONS

LO 4.1 Explain why voter turnout is low in Texas.

- What explains why some people are more likely to vote than others?

- Why does the number of elections in Texas lead to lower turnout?

- How does Republican dominance of statewide office impact turnout in Texas?

LO 4.2 Describe the types of Texas elections.

- What is the majority vote rule, and why do we use it in Texas primaries?

- What is the plurality vote rule, where is it used, and what difference does it make in elections?

LO 4.3 Understand how elections are administered in Texas.

- Why is it hard for candidates to get on the ballot in Texas?

- Ballot design seems a technical issue but is seriously contested by parties and candidates. Why?

LO 4.4 Identify the factors that advantage (or disadvantage) candidates in Texas elections.

- Why are some candidates more likely than others to win elections in Texas? Do candidates have much control over the things that matter?

- Have the efforts of elected officials in the United States and Texas to control money in election campaigns been effective?

- What explains the growing diversity of elected officials in Texas? Is it likely to continue? Why or why not?

GET ACTIVE

- **Become politically active.** Register to vote at the Texas Secretary of State's website: **www.sos.state.tx.us/elections/voter/reqvr.shtml**. Act out, join the movement, start a street team, and register to vote at the Rock the Vote website: **www.rockthevote.com/home.html**.

- **Choose your candidates on the issues.** Project Vote Smart provides information about candidates at **http://votesmart.org**. There you can search by zip code to find the elections—federal, state, and local—in which you can vote. The site shows the candidates' positions and has a feature to help you pick the right candidate based on your positions and how important you think each is. You might be surprised by how well it works. Vote Smart also lets you see which interest groups support which candidates.

- **See where candidates get their money.** Money is important in election campaigns and may tell you something about candidates, too. You can follow contributions in

Texas elections at the National Institute on Money in State Politics' excellent searchable website at **www.followthemoney.org/index.phtml**.

- **Keep up with elected officials.** You can follow the "roll call" votes of Texas legislators at Texas Legislature Online at **www.capitol.state.tx.us/Home.aspx**. The Texas Tribune provides good, politically neutral coverage of the legislative votes and gubernatorial proposals and vetoes, and it can be found online at **www.texastribune.org**.

 In deciding how you will cast your vote, should you consider candidates' actual positions on public policy, or is it enough for you to cast your vote based on advertising-based images and personalities? How important is your assessment of a candidate's character?

CHAPTER 5

Political Parties

LEARNING OBJECTIVES

LO 5.1 Identify the characteristics of American political parties.

LO 5.2 Understand the evolution of the party system in Texas.

LO 5.3 Evaluate the importance of party organization.

LO 5.4 Assess the functions of political parties in American and Texas politics.

LO 5.5 Apply what you have learned about Texas political parties.

RODGER MALLISON/MCT/Landov

Here you see some of the excitement that party politics generates at the 2014 Republican state convention. In this chapter, you will learn why parties generate such excitement, how they are organized, and the important role they play in the Texas political system.

*T*he Founders created our complicated system of federal government and provided for the election of a president and Congress. However, the U.S. Constitution makes no mention of political parties. Indeed, the Founders held negative attitudes toward parties. George Washington warned of the "baneful effects of the spirit of party" in his farewell address. James Madison, in Federalist Paper 10, criticized parties or "factions" as divisive but admitted that they were inevitable. Madison and others thought that parties would encourage conflict and undermine consensus on public policy. Yet despite their condemnation of parties, these early American politicians engaged in partisan politics and initiated a competitive two-party system.

Parties, then, are apparently something we should live neither with nor without. They have been with us from the start of this country and will be with us for the foreseeable future, influencing our government and public policy. It is important, therefore, to gain an understanding of what they are all about.

What is a political party? This question conjures up various stereotypes: smoke-filled rooms of the past where party leaders or bosses make important behind-the-scenes decisions; activists or regulars who give time, money, and enthusiastic support to their candidates; or voters who proudly identify themselves as Democrats or Republicans. Essentially, though, a political party is simply a broad-based coalition of people whose primary purpose is to win elections. Gaining control of government through popular elections is the most important goal for political parties, and most of the activities parties pursue are directed toward this purpose. Parties recruit and nominate their members for public office. They form coalitions of different groups and interests to build majorities so that they can elect their candidates.

Political parties are vital to democracy in that they provide a link between the people and the government. Parties make it possible for the ordinary citizen and voter to participate in the political system; they provide the means for organizing support for particular candidates. In organizing this support, parties unify various groups and interests and mobilize them behind the candidate who supports their preferred positions.

CHARACTERISTICS OF AMERICAN POLITICAL PARTIES

LO 5.1   Identify the characteristics of American political parties.

The American political party system has three distinct characteristics not always found in parties elsewhere in the world: (1) two-party system, (2) pragmatism, and (3) decentralization.

Two-party system

A political system characterized by two dominant parties competing for political offices. In such systems, minor or third parties have little chance of winning.

Two-Party System

In Texas and the other U.S. states, political competition is usually between the two major parties—the Democrats and the Republicans. Such a system is called a **two-party system** because only two dominant parties compete for political office and minor or third parties have little chance of winning.

The two-party system partly results from our electoral system, which relies on single-member districts—election districts in which one candidate is elected to a legislative body. If only one representative can be elected in a district, voters tend to cast their ballots for the major-party candidates that have the best chance of winning and not "waste" their vote on a third party destined to lose. That a plurality voting rule is employed in general elections, which was noted in Chapter 4, only reinforces two parties because there is no electoral reason to run as a third-party candidate or support one unless the party actually can win. By contrast, under a majority voting rule, which is used in Texas primary elections, there may be a benefit to finishing second because it can lead to a runoff election between the top-two candidates if the plurality winner in the first election does not a get a majority of the votes.[1]

In addition to the electoral system, laws put in place by the Democratic and Republican parties make it hard for third parties to form. As mentioned in the chapter on voting and elections, third parties such as the Libertarian Party or Green Party must receive at least 5 percent of the vote in the previous election to gain automatic ballot status in Texas. Failure to gain this vote share means that third parties can get on the ballot only by launching petition drives that gather the signatures of registered voters who did not vote in either party's primary. Independent candidates must also meet this standard. For example, in the 2006 gubernatorial election, independent candidates Carole Keeton Strayhorn and Kinky Friedman were required to collect 45,000 signatures from eligible voters who had not voted in the March 7 primary to compete in the November election against then-governor Rick Perry. The Democratic and Republican candidates just had to win their primaries.

Despite the electoral system and election laws, there have been third parties in the United States and Texas. Most have come and gone, partly because of the difficulties of competing but also because of the major parties' efforts to absorb third parties by adopting their issues. One notable example is the Populist Party of the 1890s, which was absorbed by the Democratic Party. Only rarely have new parties survived, and they have thrived only at the expense of one of the two preexisting parties. The one American case occurred during the 1850s, when the Republican Party emerged after the collapse of the Whigs. Since that time there have been numerous attempts to form and develop third parties, and yet the Democratic and Republican parties remain and the challenges they face are slight.

Pragmatism

Pragmatism in politics means that ideas should be judged on the basis of their practical results rather than on the purity of their principles.[2] In other words, a pragmatist is interested in what works. American parties are sometimes willing to compromise principles to appeal successfully to a majority of voters and gain public office. They willingly bargain with most organized groups and take stands that appeal to a large number of interests to build a winning coalition in a two-party system. American parties thus are much less programmatic than those in many Western European countries that have multi-party systems in which parties are more likely to be committed to a particular ideology and their supporters are committed to programmatic goals.

Pragmatism often means taking clear-cut positions only on those issues on which virtually all of the public agrees, what political scientists often refer to as **valence issues**. Leading examples are peace and prosperity, which feature prominently in American elections, especially the

Pragmatism
The philosophy that ideas should be judged on the basis of their practical results rather than on the purity of their principles.

Valence issues
Issues on which virtually all of the public agree, for instance, such as peace and prosperity.

---

[1]There is even more incentive in other countries, many of which use proportional representation, where parties gain seats in proportion to their share of the vote. The principle that single-member districts and plurality elections encourage two parties is known as "Duverger's Law," so-named after the French sociologist Maurice Duverger, who identified the pattern back in the 1960s. Do note that it is not really a law, but a tendency, as there are plenty of examples that contrast with what Duverger would have predicted based on the electoral system.
[2]Marjorie Randon Hershey, *Party Politics in America*, 14th ed. (New York: Longman, 2011), p. 289.

economy. This may have been made most clear by former President Bill Clinton's political strategist James Carville, who famously focused Clinton's successful 1992 campaign on the phrase "It's the Economy, Stupid." Economic growth is something on which the public agrees, after all, and in 1992 people mostly thought that things under sitting President George H. W. Bush were not going well. By contrast, taking clear stands on controversial issues may alienate potential members of the party's electoral coalition. Political parties and their candidates, including those in Texas, thus prefer to deemphasize **position issues** on which the public is divided and instead focus on valence issues. They also may stress leadership potential and statesmanship as well as family life and personality.

Position issues
Issues on which the public is divided.

Growing Polarization?

Although the broad electoral coalitions that comprise American parties make it difficult for them to achieve ideological consistency, it would be a mistake to assume that parties in America do not differ from one another. Indeed, most observers think that American parties have become more programmatic and more polarized in recent years.[3] To succeed, they must satisfy their traditional supporters: voters, public opinion leaders, interest groups, and campaign contributors. The candidates are not blank slates but have their own beliefs, prejudices, biases, and opinions. In most elections, broad ideological differences are apparent. Voters who participated in the presidential election of 2012 could easily differentiate between the conservative orientation of Mitt Romney and the more liberal philosophy of his opponent, Barack Obama. Such philosophical differences also were evident between the parties' candidates for Texas state offices in the 2014 election.

Decentralization

At first glance, American party organizations may appear to be neatly ordered and hierarchical, with power flowing from the national to state to local parties. In reality, however, American parties are not nearly so hierarchical. They reflect the American federal system, with its **decentralization** of power to the state and local levels of government. Political party organizations operate at the precinct, or neighborhood, level; the local government level (city, county, or district); the state level (especially in elections for governor); and the national level (especially in elections for president).

Decentralization
Exercise of power at the state and local levels of government in addition to the national level.

Figure 5.1 illustrates the nature of power in American political parties. State and local party organizations are semi-independent actors who exercise considerable discretion on most party matters. The practices that state and local parties follow, the candidates they recruit, the campaign money they raise, the innovations they introduce, the organized interests to which they respond, the campaign strategies they create, and most importantly, the policy orientations of the candidates who run under their label are all influenced by local and state political cultures, leaders, traditions, and interests.[4]

Although the American party system is quite decentralized, Figure 5.1 also illustrates how power has shifted to the national party organizations in recent years. Both the Democratic and Republican national parties have become stronger and more involved in state and local party activities through various service functions. By using new campaign technologies—computer-based mailing lists, direct-mail solicitations, and the Internet—the national parties have raised hundreds of millions of dollars. Accordingly, the national party organizations have assumed a greater role by providing unprecedented levels of assistance to state parties and candidates. This assistance includes a variety of services—candidate recruitment,

---

[3]For an overview of the literature, see Barbara Sinclair, *Party Wars: Polarization and the Politics of National Policy-Making* (Norman: University of Oklahoma Press, 2006).

[4]Norman J. Ornstein, Andrew Kohut, and Larry McCarthy, *The People, the Press, and Politics: The Times Mirror Study of the American Electorate* (Washington, DC: Times Mirror Center for the People and the Press, 1988).

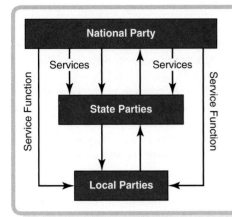

Figure 5.1

The Decentralized Nature of American Political Parties and the Importance of the National Party's Service Function

The diagram shows the semi-independent relationship that exists among national, state, and local party organizations and the increasingly important services and funds provided by the national party organization.

 As national party organizations grow stronger, how much influence should they have over state and local parties and candidates? Should the latter pay close attention to the positions of the national party platform? Should voters hold state and local candidates accountable for the performance of national leaders?

research, public opinion polling, computer networking, production of radio and television commercials, direct mailing, consultation on redistricting issues, and the transfer of millions of dollars' worth of campaign funding. Not surprisingly, as national parties provide more money and services to state and local parties, they exercise more influence over state and local organizations, issues, and candidates.[5]

THE DEVELOPMENT OF THE TEXAS PARTY SYSTEM

LO 5.2 Understand the evolution of the party system in Texas.

Although for most of its existence the United States has had a two-party system, many states and localities—including Texas—have been dominated by just one party at various times in history. Texas formerly was a one-party Democratic state but is no longer. To understand political parties in Texas, it is necessary to examine the historical predominance of the Democratic Party, the emergence of two-party competition in the state, and the reality of Republican Party domination at present.

The One-Party Tradition in Texas

Under the Republic of Texas, there was little party activity. Political divisions were usually oriented around support of, or opposition to, Sam Houston, a leading founder of the Republic. After Texas became a state, however, the Democratic Party dominated Texas politics until the 1990s. This legacy of dominance was firmly established by the Civil War and the era of Reconstruction, when Yankee troops, under the direction of a Republican Congress, occupied the South. From the time that the Republican and former Union soldier Edmund J. Davis's single term as governor ended in 1873 until the surprising victory of the Republican gubernatorial candidate Bill Clements in 1978, the Democrats exercised almost complete control over Texas politics.

The Democratic Party was at times challenged by the emergence of more liberal third parties. The most serious of these challenges came in the late nineteenth century with the Populist revolt. The Populist Party grew out of the dissatisfaction of small farmers who demanded government regulation of rates charged by banks and railroads. These farmers—joined by

---

[5]Margaret Randon Hershey, *Party Politics in America*, 14th ed. (New York: HarperCollins, 2011), pp. 71–74.

sharecroppers, laborers, and African Americans—mounted a serious election bid in 1896 by taking 44.3 percent of the vote for governor. Eventually, however, the Democratic Party defused the threat of the Populists by co-opting many of the issues of the new party. The Democrats also effectively disenfranchised African Americans and poor whites in 1902 with the passage of the poll tax.

Two events in the early twentieth century solidified the position of the Democrats in Texas politics. The first was the institution of party primary "reforms" in 1906. For the first time, voters could choose the party's nominees by a direct vote in the party primary. Hence, the Democratic primary became the substitute for the two-party contest: the general election. In the absence of Republican competition, the Democratic primary was the only game in town, and it provided a competitive arena for political differences within the state.

The second event to help the Democrats was the Depression. Although the Republican presidential candidate, Herbert Hoover, carried Texas in 1928, Republicans were closely associated with the Great Depression of the 1930s. The cumulative effect of this association, the Civil War, and Reconstruction ensured Democratic dominance in state government until the early 1990s.

Ideological Factions in America and Texas

Although members of a political party may be similar in their views, factions or divisions within the party inevitably develop. These conflicts may involve a variety of personalities and issues, but the most important basis for division is ideology.

To understand the ideological basis for factionalism in political parties in Texas, it is necessary to define the terms *conservative* and *liberal*—a difficult task because the meanings change with time and may mean different things to different people.

Conservatives Conservatives believe that individuals should be left alone to compete in a free market unfettered by government control; they prefer that government regulation of the economy be kept to a minimum. They extol the virtues of individualism, independence, and personal initiative. However, conservatives often support government involvement and funding to promote business. They favor construction of highways, tax incentives for investment, and other government aids to business. The theory is that these aids will encourage economic development and hence prosperity for the whole society (the so-called trickle-down theory). On the other hand, conservatives are likely to oppose government programs that involve large-scale redistribution of wealth such as welfare, health-care aid, or unemployment compensation.

Some conservatives view change suspiciously; they tend to favor the status quo—things as they are now and as they have been. They emphasize traditional values associated with the family and close communities, and they often favor government action to preserve what they see as the proper moral values of society. Because conservatives hold a more skeptical view of human nature than liberals do, they are more likely to be tougher on perceived threats to personal safety and the public order as well as to traditional and religious values. For example, conservatives are more likely to favor stiffer penalties for criminals, including capital punishment. Conservatives may combine support for the free market with support for traditional values, or they may adopt only one of these views.

One particular form of conservatism is libertarianism. In recent years, the Libertarian Party has become an active, if not always influential, force in Texas politics. The Libertarian Party has a hands-off philosophy of government that appeals to many Texas conservatives. The party's general philosophy is one of individual liberty and personal responsibility. Applying their doctrine to the issues, Libertarians would oppose Social Security, campaign finance reform, gun control, and many foreign policies. They consider programs like Social

Security to be "state-provided welfare" and believe that regulating campaigns promotes too much government involvement. They also oppose U.S. intervention in world affairs. The Libertarian Party faces the same hurdles as other third parties: poor financing, a lack of media coverage, and in some states, getting access to the ballot.

Liberals   Liberals believe that it is often necessary for government to regulate the economy and to promote greater social equality. They point to great concentrations of wealth and power that have threatened to control government, destroy economic competition, and weaken individual freedom. Government power, they believe, should be used to protect the disadvantaged and to promote equality. Consequently, liberals are generally supportive of the social welfare programs that conservatives oppose. Liberals champion wage and hour laws, the right to form unions, unemployment and health insurance, subsidized housing, and improved educational opportunities. They are also more likely to favor progressive taxes, such as federal income taxes, which increase as incomes increase.

Liberals possess a more optimistic view of human nature than conservatives. They believe that individuals are essentially rational and, therefore, that change will ultimately bring improvement in the human condition. Liberals want government to protect the civil rights and liberties of individuals and are critical of interference with any exercise of the constitutional rights of free speech, press, religion, assembly, association, and privacy. They are often suspicious of conservatives' attempts to "legislate morality" because of the potential for interference with individual rights.

Conservatives and Liberals and Texas Democrats

For many years, factions within the Texas Democratic Party resembled a two-party system, and the election to select the Democratic Party's nominees—the primary—was the most important election in Texas. Until the 1990s, conservative Democrats were much more successful than their liberal counterparts in these primaries, in part because Republican voters, facing no significant primary race of their own, regularly crossed over and supported conservative Democratic candidates. (Recall the discussion of crossover voting in Chapter 4.) Voters in the general elections, facing a choice between a conservative Democrat and a conservative Republican, usually went with the traditional party—the Democrats. These Republican crossover votes enabled conservative Democrats, with few exceptions, to control the party and state government until the late 1970s.

Conservative Democrats in Texas provided a very good example of the semi-independent relationship of national, state, and local party organizations

AP Images/Houston Chronicle, Eric Kayne

Dan Patrick (right) defeated incumbent Lieutenant Governor David Dewhurst (left) in the 2014 Republican primary. Patrick's campaign characterized Dewhurst as the "establishment" candidate and won with the support of the party's ideological conservatives.

CTQ   **Explain why winning the high-stakes Republican primaries is so critical in Texas, where the Republican nominee can expect to win the general election.**

> **Did You Know?** In 1952, conservative Democratic Governor Allan Shivers was nominated by both the Democratic and Republican parties for the same office.

illustrated in Figure 5.1. Texas conservatives traditionally voted Democratic in state and local races but often refused to support the national Democratic candidates for president. Indeed, the development of the conservative Democratic faction in Texas was an outgrowth of conservative dissatisfaction with many New Deal proposals of Franklin D. Roosevelt in the 1930s and Fair Deal proposals of Harry Truman in the 1940s. Conservative Democrats in Texas continued their cool relationship with the national party as many of them supported Republican presidential candidates: Dwight Eisenhower in 1952 and 1956, Richard Nixon in 1968 and 1972, and Ronald Reagan in 1980 and 1984.

Several factors accounted for the historical success of conservative Democrats, but the most important were the power and resources of the conservative constituency. Conservatives have traditionally made up the state's power elite, representing such interests as the oil, gas, and sulfur industries; other large corporations; bigger farms and ranches (agribusiness); owners and publishers of many of the state's major daily newspapers; and veterans. In other words, the most affluent people in the state are able and willing to contribute their considerable resources to the campaigns of like-minded politicians. These segments of the population are also the most likely to turn out and vote in elections. This was a significant advantage to conservative Democrats competing in the party primary, in which turnout in the past has been particularly low.

Liberals in the Texas Democratic Party have consisted of groups who have supported the national party ticket and its presidents. These groups include the following:

★ Organized labor, in particular the American Federation of Labor–Congress of Industrial Organizations (AFL-CIO)
★ African-American groups, such as the National Association for the Advancement of Colored People (NAACP)
★ Latino groups, such as the American G.I. Forum, League of Latin American Citizens (LULAC), Mexican American Democrats (MAD), and Mexican American Legal Defense and Educational Fund (MALDEF)
★ Various professionals, teachers, and intellectuals
★ Small farmers and ranchers, sometimes belonging to the Texas Farmers Union
★ Environmental groups, such as the Sierra Club
★ Abortion rights groups, such as the Texas Abortion Rights Action League
★ Trial lawyers—that is, lawyers who represent plaintiffs in civil suits and defendants in criminal cases

The success of liberal Democratic politicians in Texas was infrequent and rarely persisted for more than a few years. In recent years, liberal Texas Democrats have had more success in capturing their party's nomination, largely because conservatives are voting in the Republican primary. Lately, liberal or moderate Democrats have been routinely nominated for all the statewide races. There is irony for the liberal Democrats in Texas: Although they have gained control of the Democratic Party as conservatives have defected from their ranks, these very defections have left the Democrats in the minority and made the Republicans dominant in Texas.

The Rise of the Republican Party

Before the presidential election of November 1988, only three contemporary Republicans had won statewide races in Texas: Senator John Tower (1961–1985), Governor Bill Clements (1979–1983 and 1987–1991), and Senator Phil Gramm (1985–2003). Why had the Republican Party failed to compete in Texas in the past? The most important reason is the bitter memory left by Texas's experience in the Civil War and during Reconstruction. The Republican administration of Governor E. J. Davis under the Texas Constitution of 1869 was considered the most corrupt and abusive period of Texas history. Only in the past few decades has the Republican Party been able to shake its image as the party of Reconstruction.

The Republicans Become Competitive The revival of the Republican Party was foreshadowed in the 1950s by the development of the so-called presidential Republicans (people who vote Republican for national office but Democratic for state and local office). As discussed just above, conservative Democrats objected to the obvious policy differences of the state and national Democratic parties and often voted for Republican presidential candidates.

The first major step in the rejuvenation of the Republican Party in Texas came in 1961, when John Tower, a Republican, was elected to the U.S. Senate. Tower won a special nonpartisan election held when Lyndon Johnson gave up his Senate seat to assume the vice presidency. Tower initially won with the help of many liberal Democrats and was reelected until he retired in 1984. His seat was retained by the Republicans with the election to the Senate of former Representative Phil Gramm over his liberal Democratic opponent Lloyd Doggett in 1984. In November 2002, John Cornyn, a Republican and the state's former attorney general, was elected to replace Gramm.

In November 1978, the Republicans achieved their most stunning breakthrough when Bill Clements defeated John Hill in the race for governor. After losing the governor's seat to moderate-conservative Mark White in 1982, Republicans regained their momentum in 1986, when Clements turned the tables on White and recaptured the governorship. Developments in the 1990s and early 2000s transformed Texas into "Republican country." With the election in 1992 of U.S. Senator Kay Bailey Hutchison, Republicans held both U.S. Senate seats for the first time since Reconstruction. In 1994, Republican George W. Bush defeated incumbent Democratic Governor Ann Richards.

By far the most impressive gains for the GOP came in the November 1998 elections, when incumbent Governor George W. Bush led a sweep of Republicans to victory in every statewide election. For the first time in living memory, no Democrats occupied any statewide executive or judicial office. Republicans have continued to maintain their monopoly on statewide offices. In 2004, after a successful effort at congressional redistricting, the GOP captured a majority in Texas's congressional delegation.

The Republican Party is now dominant in lower-level offices in much of the state, where Democrats were once most firmly entrenched. In 1974, the GOP held only 53 offices at the county level; they now hold a majority in county courthouses representing two-thirds of the state's population. The GOP gained a majority of seats in the state senate in 1996 and has controlled the house of representatives since 2002. Table 5.1 shows the dramatic increases by Republicans in the Texas legislature and the Texas delegation to the U.S. House of Representatives.

TABLE 5.1 Changes in the Number of Republican and Democratic Officeholders in Texas

Body	1973		2013	
	Democrats	Republicans	Democrats	Republicans
Texas House of Representatives	132	17	55	95
Texas Senate	28	3	12	19
U.S. House of Representatives	20	4	12	24
U.S. Senate	1	1	0	2

▲ **What explains the Republican dominance of the Texas political scene today? To what extent will demographic changes affect the future success of the party?**

The Era of Republican Dominance

The Republican Party continues its dominance in Texas state politics. Most observers now agree that Texas has experienced a **party realignment**, the transition from one dominant party system to another. After more than a century of Democratic Party domination after the Civil War, the pendulum has swung to the Republican Party. Realignment involves more than just casting a vote for a Republican Party candidate; it refers to a shift in the attachment to political parties, which is called **partisan identification**. Evidence that Texas is becoming a Republican-dominated state comes from public opinion polls that show that many more Texans are identifying with the Republican Party than in the past. As Table 5.2 indicates, in 1952, an overwhelming percentage of Texans who identified with a political party were Democrats; indeed only 6 percent considered themselves Republicans by comparison with 66 percent for the Democrats. (The remaining 28 percent considered themselves "independents.")

In 2002, exactly 50 years later, polls showed that identification among Texans with the Republican Party exceeded that for the Democratic Party. From Table 5.2, we also can see that the total percentage of partisans decreased during the period, which suggests a period of **dealignment**, when increasing numbers of voters choose not to identify with either of the two parties and consider themselves to be independents. This is not surprising in transition from the one-party Democratic control to Republican dominance, as many Republican-voting Democrats do not completely switch parties, and consider themselves independents, at least for a while.

The partisan balance evened out between 2002 and 2008, when President Obama won his first presidential election, though the split at the time is deceiving, as a significantly larger portion of independents "leaned" toward the Republican Party. (These leaners tend to vote very much like partisans on election day.) By 2014, the Republicans had regained their lead even among partisan identifiers. Including the independents leaners, they held a decided 49–42 advantage. The partisan balance has changed dramatically in Texas, though it didn't happen overnight.

To a large extent the rise of the Republicans reflected the "sorting" of voters' identification to match their conservative ideological orientations.[6] This takes time, as partisan identification in the electorate changes slowly. Political scientists have shown that people's dispositions toward the parties begin to develop at an early age, and that our parents are particularly influential.[7] As these dispositions are reinforced, say, by interactions with friends and neighbors, identifications harden and become resistant to change. This does not mean that they do not

Party realignment
The transition from one dominant party system to another.

Partisan identification
A person's attachment to one political party or the other.

Dealignment
When increasing numbers of voters choose not to identify with either of the two parties and consider themselves to be independents.

TABLE 5.2 Percentage of Voters Indicating a Major Party Identification

Year	Democrats	Republicans	Total
1952	66	6	72
1972	57	14	71
1990	34	30	64
2002	25	37	62
2008	35	36	71
2014	31	38	69

Sources: Polls conducted by Belden and Associates (1952 and 1972), Harte-Hanks Communications (1990), American National Election Studies (2002), and The University of Texas at Austin, *Austin/Texas Tribune* polls (2008 and 2014).

[6]For a general analysis of partisan sorting, see Matthew Levendusky's *The Partisan Sort: How Liberals Became Democrats and Conservatives Became Republicans* (Chicago: University of Chicago Press, 2009).
[7]Angus Campbell, Philip E. Converse, Warrant E. Miller, and Donald E. Stokes, *The American Voter* (New York: Wiley, 1960).

change, of course. Part of the big gains for the Republicans in Texas reflected a shift among conservative middle- and upper-class white Democrats. After years of voting Republican in presidential elections but identifying as Democrats, they began thinking of themselves as Republicans.

What stimulated the change was the behavior of the parties and their candidates. Of special importance was the liberal shift in policies under Democratic presidents during the 1960s. Most notable was the expansion of civil rights, because it seems to have led many white voters to defect to the Republican Party (and many black voters to align with the Democratic Party).[8] Ironically, the main proponent of these policies was Texas's own President Lyndon B. Johnson (1963–1968). He pushed through a lot of other liberal legislation during the period, and there is reason to think that it also influenced voters' perceptions and alignments with the parties. From Table 5.2, it is clear that even these effects were not felt immediately in Texas, as the Democratic lead over the Republicans remained a sizable 43 percent even in 1972.

The performance of Republican presidents also mattered. The election of Ronald Reagan may have been of particular consequence. His victory over the unpopular Democrat Jimmy Carter in 1980 began a 12-year run of Republican control of the White House. Under Reagan the economy boomed; his approval ratings did, too; and the Cold War came to an end. During this short time, the Republicans virtually closed the massive gap on the Democrats in Texas. The election of George W. Bush to the presidency in 2000 and then again in 2004 helped solidify the Republican realignment in Texas, as he had been a very popular governor and president in the state.

Party switching by native Texans is only part of the story of realignment. Another factor involves the newcomers to the state, who came in large numbers during the 1970s and 1980s. These migrants to Texas were less Democratic in their affiliations and this helped break down traditional partisan patterns. Perhaps the most important newcomers of all have been the newcomers from within Texas, that is, the offspring of Texas residents. As Texans switched affiliations and newcomers from other states further diluted the Democratic advantage, young people reflected their parents' more balanced partisanship. Moreover, the short-term forces that swayed their parents tended to have an even greater impact on them, both as children and as young adults going off to vote for the first or second time.

Sources of Republican Strengths and Weaknesses Republican voting strength in Texas has been concentrated in several clusters of counties (see Figure 5.2):

★ Houston suburbs
★ Fort Worth area
★ Midland–Odessa area
★ Northern Panhandle
★ East Texas rural counties
★ Hill Country–Edwards Plateau area

Republican Party support is weaker in the following areas:

★ South Central Texas
★ Central cities of Austin, Dallas, Houston, and San Antonio
★ Southwest Texas

Research on the American public shows that the Republican Party appeals more to white voters, those who attend church regularly, businesspeople, and families with higher incomes.

---

[8]For more on the role of race in the development of partisan identification in the United States, see Edward Carmines and James Stimson's *Issue Evolution: Race and the Transformation of American Politics* (Princeton: Princeton University Press, 1989).

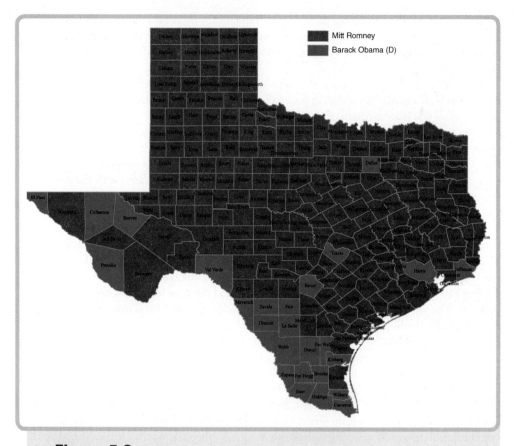

Figure 5.2
Results of the 2012 Presidential Election

The map shows the only 26 counties won by Barack Obama. Note that Obama carried more populous counties like Bexar, Dallas, Harris, and Travis, and Mitt Romney carried the smaller counties outside of South and Southwest Texas.

Source: Office of the Texas Secretary of State.

 What does this mean for the future of the Democratic Party in Texas? Speculate on the strategy Republicans may use to maintain their electoral dominance.

Not all people in these categories identify with and vote for Republicans; they are more likely to, however. Not surprisingly, Republican support is strongest in suburban communities and rural and small towns, and this is true around the country. Texas also has a fairly large number of active and retired military officers, who tend to be Republicans.

The party has benefited from the economic growth and prosperity that occurred in Texas from the end of World War II to the early 1980s. During this period, newcomers from more Republican parts of the country were lured to the state by a sympathetic business climate or by the promise of jobs. These transplanted Texans joined more prosperous native Texans to provide a political climate more conducive to Republican Party politics.

 Did You Know? In the 1890s, the journalist O. Henry wrote, "We only had two or three laws [in Texas], such as against murder before witnesses, and being caught stealing horses, and voting the Republican ticket."

Conservatives and Moderates and Texas Republicans

As the Republican Party becomes dominant in Texas politics, it is experiencing some of the factional differences that characterized the Democratic Party in Texas for years. For example, a bloc of conservative Christians, sometimes referred to as **evangelical** or **fundamentalist Christians**, have increasingly dominated the Texas Republican Party. This group is concerned with such issues as family, religion, and community morals, and it has been effective in influencing the **party platform**, which contains the party's formal issue positions or "planks." Associated with a broad spectrum of Protestant Christianity that emphasizes salvation and traditional values, evangelical voters are likely to support culturally conservative politics.

Since 1994, the Republican state party chair and a majority of the members of its state executive committee have been conservative Christians. This dominance of leadership positions has given the conservative Christians a degree of control of the party machinery that continues today.

The control of the state's Republican Party by the conservative, or right, wing is opposed by the more moderate, or centrist, wing. Many of these moderates fear that the radicalism of the right will interfere with the party's ability to win elections. Many moderates represent business interests and are more concerned with keeping taxes low and limiting the government's interference in business decision making than with moral issues.

Another group that has grown in influence within the Republican Party is the **tea party**, a faction or group of very conservative Republicans generally resistant to compromise of its principles (see the end-of-chapter essay for Chapter 6). This is a conservative movement that began at the grassroots level. It is strongly opposed to the national debt and generally favors lower government spending and involvement in citizens' lives, much like the Libertarian Party. The movement began in response to President Obama's health-care initiative and has expanded greatly over the years.

Although tea party members deny a formal association with either political party, they have worked mostly within the Republican Party and have been responsible for the nomination of numerous conservative candidates around the country. These candidates have not always fared well in general elections, sometimes proving to be too extreme or inexperienced, as in the 2010 U.S. Senate elections in Delaware and Nevada and the 2012 Senate election in Indiana. In Texas, tea party candidates have done fairly well, perhaps most notably Senator Ted Cruz and Lt. Governor Dan Patrick.

In general, the Republican Party has failed to generate much support among the state's minority voters. African-American identification with the GOP consistently hovers around 5 percent. They have had greater success among Hispanics, and this was especially true while George W. Bush was governor and president, although the Democrats still retained an advantage even during that period of relative Republican success. The growing influence of the tea party has not helped in recent years.

evangelical (fundamentalist) Christians
A bloc of conservative Christians who are concerned with such issues as family, religion, abortion, gay rights, and community morals, and often support the Republican Party.

party platform
The formal issue positions of a political party; specific elements are often referred to as *planks* in the party's platform.

AP Images/Tony Gutierrez

Republican candidates like Governor Greg Abbott have been able to appeal to Texans' conservatism by emphasizing religious themes such as opposition to abortion, same-sex relationships, and contraception.

 Write a well-composed essay or form a team to create a well-illustrated presentation identifying the differences between Democrats and Republicans on major social and economic issues. You should be able to easily identify at least a dozen differences. To be complete, your project should offer perspective about the issues on which Democrats and Republicans differ. Explain how these differences reflect modern conservatism and liberalism. How do policy differences affect the electoral coalitions that determine a party's success?

Tea party
A faction or groups of very conservative Republicans generally resistant to compromise of its principles.

Tipping
A phenomenon that occurs when a demographic group grows large enough to change the political balance in the electorate.

Swing voters
Voters who are not bound by party identification and who support candidates of different parties in different election years.

Can the Democrats Still Compete? Some observers believe that Texas will emerge as a competitive two-party state. They note that Democrats still have considerable resources in many local governments, especially in some central cities and South and Southwest Texas.

Democratic strategists are also encouraged by the state's growing population of ethnic minorities, particularly Latinos. These voters tend to support Democratic candidates. Ethnic minorities now make up a majority of the state's population. The growing number of Latinos could cause the phenomenon of **tipping**—that is, growing numbers of a demographically significant group cause significant changes in the electorate. One limiting factor is the low voter turnout rates among Hispanics, but if energy and commitment to politics continue, a significant Democratic resurgence could occur.

Republican Party strategists argue that Hispanic voters might be induced to support the GOP. The latter feels it is more in tune with Latino voters' identification with conservative social positions such as abortion and family values. Democrats, on the other hand, still believe that Latinos will be attracted to the party for its traditional support for social welfare programs and civil rights. Some observers have suggested that a substantial number of Latino voters are persuadable and that they are potentially **swing voters**, voters who are not bound by party identification and who support candidates of different parties in different election years. The Democratic Party cannot afford to take this portion of the electorate for granted, and the GOP cannot assume that Latino party identification will trend its way, particularly given the growing conservatism of the party. How it will play out remains to be seen. For now, consider the polling data, which show that Hispanics in Texas are slightly less supportive of the Democratic Party than Hispanics in other states, although they still are much more likely to support the Democrats than the Republicans.

THE ORGANIZATION OF TEXAS POLITICAL PARTIES

LO 5.3 Evaluate the importance of party organization.

To better understand how political parties are organized in Texas, we can divide the party machinery into two parts: the temporary, consisting of a series of conventions at various levels that happen in each election year, and the permanent, consisting of people elected to leadership positions in the party and who continue in those positions between elections (see Figure 5.3).

Temporary-Party Organization

Consisting of precinct, county or district, and state conventions, the temporary party organizations select delegates to higher conventions that ultimately write party rules, approve the state party platforms, and select the permanent party structures that manage party affairs between conventions.

Precinct convention
A gathering of citizens within a precinct—where people vote—who voted in the party's primary.

Precinct Convention The voting precinct is the starting point of party activity because it is the scene of the **precinct convention**, a gathering of the faithful that is open to all who voted earlier in the day in that party's primary. It is also the key to getting involved in politics. (See the Get Active feature.) Usually on the first Tuesday in March in even-numbered years, both the Democratic and Republican parties in Texas hold conventions in almost all the voting precincts in the state. The ticket of admission is usually a voter registration card stamped to indicate that one has voted in the party's primary earlier in the day. The agenda of the precinct convention includes adoption of resolutions to be passed on to the county or senatorial district convention and selection of delegates to the county or senatorial district convention.

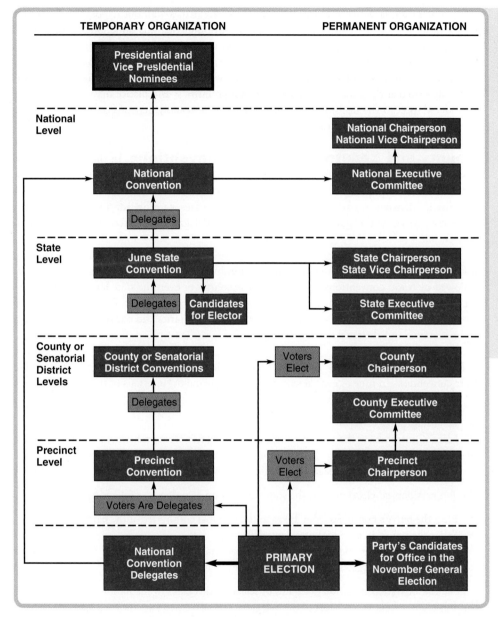

TEMPORARY ORGANIZATION   **PERMANENT ORGANIZATION**

Figure 5.3
Texas Political Party Organization

The chart shows the three levels of state party organization in Texas and the ties of the state organization to the national party organization.

CTQ Describe how voters are involved in both the temporary and permanent state organizations. How does the process of selecting delegates ensure that many of the delegates who attend the national convention have been "grassroots" supporters of the party?

Although eligibility for participation in this grassroots level of democracy is open to all who vote in the first primary election, attendance is minimal—usually only 2 percent to 3 percent of those who vote. This low attendance makes it possible for a small, determined minority of the electorate to assume control of the precinct convention and dominate its affairs.

A precinct convention normally starts with the signing in of those present and certifying that they voted in the party's primary. In presidential years, those signing in also indicate their preference for a presidential candidate; in nonpresidential years, other designations may be used, such as "conservative caucus" or "moderate-progressive caucus." The preferences are used to evaluate the relative strength of support for each candidate or caucus. The factions with the largest numbers present dominate the selection of delegates to the county convention.

If contending factions in a precinct are evenly divided, a walkout is possible if one side or the other loses a key vote and claims that a grave injustice was done. Such a group will conduct its own convention, called a "rump convention," going through the same procedures; then both precinct groups will appeal to a credentials committee appointed by the county executive committee. The credentials committee will decide which set of rival delegates is officially seated at the county convention. Although fairness and justice may occasionally be considered, prevail the decision on which group to seat usually depends on which faction is in the majority on the credentials committee.

County and Senatorial District Conventions In the weeks after the primary and the precinct conventions, county and state senatorial district conventions are held. In the most populous counties, the county convention has given way to state senatorial district conventions within those counties. Delegates vote on adoption of resolutions to be considered at the state convention and select delegates and alternates to attend that convention.

As with the precinct convention, liberal or conservative factions or those representing different presidential candidates will seek to dominate the selection of delegates. Walkouts followed by rump conventions may occur at the county or even the state level. In Texas, bitter intra-party conflict has historically characterized the Democratic Party more than the Republican Party, but that has changed as Republican primaries and conventions have grown in importance and the tea party has emerged.

State Conventions Both the Democratic and Republican parties in Texas hold state conventions in June of even-numbered years. The major functions of these biennial state conventions are to do the following:

★ Elect state party officers.
★ Elect 62 members to the state executive committee, two from each senatorial district.
★ Adopt a party platform (see Table 5.3 for examples of recent Texas party platform planks).
★ Certify to the secretary of state the candidates nominated by the party in its March primary.

If it is a presidential election year, the state convention also does the following:

★ Elect the party's nominees from Texas to the national committee of the party.
★ Select the state's 38 potential presidential electors.
★ Elect some delegates to the party's national nominating convention, held in July or August (the number of delegates selected is determined by national party rules).

The role of state convention delegates in selecting delegates to the national convention has diminished in recent years. Most of the delegates for both parties are now selected on the basis of the party's presidential preference primary. A **presidential preference primary** allows voters in the party primary to vote directly on the party's presidential nominee.

Presidential preference primary
A primary election that allows voters in the party to vote directly for candidates seeking their party's presidential nomination.

Political parties in Texas select delegates to the national nominating convention using both the primary and the caucus system. In a process nicknamed the "Texas Two-Step," those who participate in the primary are then eligible to attend the party caucuses later that evening after the polls close. Texas Democrats choose delegates based on votes in both the primaries and caucuses. In contrast, Republicans select delegates to their national party conventions in the primaries alone; they use caucuses only to select delegates to the state party convention.

Permanent-Party Organization

The permanent structure of the party machinery consists of people selected to lead the party organization and provide continuity between election campaigns.

TABLE 5.3 Excerpts from the 2012 Texas Democratic and Republic Party Platforms

Texas Democrats	Texas Republicans
Believe a democratic government exists to help us achieve as a community, state, and nation what we cannot achieve as individuals, and that it must serve all citizens	Believe in personal responsibility and accountability; a free-enterprise society unencumbered by government; self-sufficient families, founded on the traditional marriage of a natural man and a natural woman
Believe government should "provide multi-language instruction, beginning in elementary school, to make all students fluent in English and at least one other language…"	Support "American English as the official language of Texas" and "encourage non-English-speaking students to transition to English within three years"
Enact a constitutional amendment to prevent extending the sales tax to food and medicine and oppose efforts to impose a national sales tax	Support a national sales tax collected by the states once the IRS is abolished and the Sixteenth Amendment to the U.S. Constitution is repealed
Support abortion by trusting "the women of Texas to make personal and responsible decisions about when and whether to bear children…rather than having these personal decisions made by politicians"	Oppose abortion because "all innocent human life must be respected and safeguarded from fertilization to natural death; therefore, the unborn child has a fundamental individual right to life…"
Would abolish the death penalty in Texas and replace it with the punishment of life imprisonment without parole	Believe that "properly applied capital punishment is legitimate, is an effective deterrent, and should be swift and unencumbered"
Believe "the state should establish a 100% equitable school finance system with sufficient state revenue to allow every district to offer an exemplary program"	Oppose "teaching of Higher Order Thinking Skills (values clarification), critical thinking skills and similar programs" that "have the purpose of challenging the students' fixed beliefs…. We support reducing taxpayer funding to all levels of education institutions."
Support "a path for children of undocumented parents, who were brought here as minors, to earn legal status and future citizenship by going to college or serving in the military"	Support limiting citizenship by birth "to those born to a citizen of the United States with no exceptions"
Believe "the minimum wage must be raised, enforced, and applied meaningfully across-the-board…"	Believe "the Minimum Wage Law should be repealed"

Source: Texas Democratic Party, www.txdemocrats.org, and Republican Party of Texas, www.texasgop.org. Complete 2014 state party platforms can now be found at www.txdemocrats.org/pdf/2014-Platform.pdf and www.texasgop.org/wp-content/uploads/2014/06/2014-Platform-Final.pdf.

Precinct-Level Organization At the lowest, or grassroots, level of the party structure is the precinct chair, who is chosen by the precinct's voters in the primary for a two-year term. Often the position is uncontested, and in some precincts, the person can be elected by write-in vote. The chair serves as party organizer in the precinct, contacting known and potential party members. The chair may help organize party activities in the neighborhood, such as voter registration drives. The precinct chair is also responsible for arranging and presiding over the precinct convention and serving as a member of the county executive committee.

County-Level Organization A much more active and important role is that of the county chair. The voters choose who will hold this office for a two-year term in the party primary. The chair presides over the county executive committee, which is composed of all precinct chairs. With the later concurrence of the county commissioners' court, the county chair determines where the voting places will be for the primary and appoints all primary election judges. Accepting candidates for places on the primary ballot, the printing of paper ballots, and the renting of voting machines are also the chair's responsibilities. Finally, the chair, along with the county executive committee, must certify the names of official nominees of the party to the secretary of state's office.

The county executive committee has three major functions: assembling the temporary roll of delegates to the county convention, canvassing the returns from the primary for local offices, and helping the county chair prepare the primary ballot, accept filing fees, and conduct a drawing to determine the order of candidates' names on the primary ballot. This is an important consideration if "blind voting" may be a problem (in that ill-informed voters may opt for the first name they come across on the ballot).

State-Level Organization Delegates to the state convention choose the state chair—the titular head of the party—at the state convention for a two-year term. The duties of the chair are to preside over the state executive committee's meetings, call the state convention to order, handle the requests of statewide candidates on the ballot, and certify the election runoff primary winners to the state convention.

The sixty-four-member state executive committee has a chair and a vice chair of the opposite sex. In addition, the Democratic and Republican state convention delegates choose one man and one woman from each of the thirty-one state senate districts. Unlike Republicans, the Democrats also include several members from various special caucuses on their state executive committee. The main legal duties of the state executive committee are to determine the site of the next state convention—sometimes a crucial factor in determining whose loyal supporters can attend because the party does not pay delegates' expenses, canvass statewide primary returns, and certify the nomination of party candidates.

The state executive committee also has some political duties, including producing and disseminating press releases and other publicity, encouraging organizational work in precincts and counties, raising money, and coordinating special projects. The state committee may work closely with the national party. These political chores are so numerous that the executive committees of both parties now employ full-time executive directors and staff assistants.

THE FUNCTIONS OF POLITICAL PARTIES

LO 5.4   Assess the functions of political parties in American and Texas politics.

Political parties developed and survived because they perform important functions. In his tripartite conceptualization of parties, V. O. Key identified three main "faces": the party in the electorate, the party as organization, and the party in government.[9]

The Party in the Electorate

The party in the electorate refers to the identification of citizens with the parties, which we already have discussed in a good amount of detail in this chapter. The point here is that parties in effect exist out in the public. The nature and degree of this party attachment is important. As discussed, it influences what voters do but it also influences how they view the political world. These views, in turn, influence what the party organization and in government do.

The Party as Organization

The party as organization is the formal structure of the party itself, which we have discussed in detail as well. This is what first comes to mind for most people when they think about what a political party is—the precinct, district and state (and national) conventions parties run in election years, and the officers at the various levels who actually set up and run party activities, including the primaries themselves.

---

[9]V. O. Key, *Political Parties and Pressure Groups*, 3rd ed. (New York: Crowell, 1952).

Party organizations do more than this, however. They actively recruit candidates for office and, though they do not control how voters decide, they can try to influence who wins the primary election. Party organizations also work to help the primary winners win in the general election. This involves raising money, providing services (campaign organization and advice), and getting out the vote on election day. The latter includes interactions with the party in the electorate by telephone and even door-to-door canvassing. The more organized the party, the more effective it becomes in getting out the vote for its candidates.

In addition to mobilizing partisans, party organizations also reflect and communicate their opinions. This happens partly via the primaries and conventions the parties administer, as these allow the party in the electorate to determine who wins the primary—and thus represents the party in the general election—and to shape the party's platform of positions. There are other less formal channels of communication in party organizations that enhance the representation of the party in the electorate. Of course, members of the party organizations and the party in government have their own preferences.

The Party in Government

The party in government consists of the elected officials in government and what they do while there. This is something we haven't addressed much at all in this chapter, although future chapters will. For now, consider that the party in government in Texas includes the governor and other statewide officials and also the members of the Texas legislature. Co-partisans work together in ways that can impact how government institutions work and the policy outputs that they produce. Elected officials of the same party have similar preferences on many issues, and they have an interest in pushing forward their positions.

The parties in government also serve other functions. They are the parties' most visible faces. Elected officials are on the political front lines, so to speak, driving the policy agenda and the policy-making process. They are at the center of political advocacy and debate. Not surprisingly, they occupy the attention of the mass media. The parties' leading politicians use the media to frame the political debate for voters, especially their partisans. The goal, of course, is to communicate their positions to the public and mobilize support. In the process, the parties in government help voters make sense of the issues, if only imperfectly. By providing a basic understanding of the parties' positions on the issues of the day allows voters to make a more informed choice between the parties on election day. This is critical to representative democracy.

HOW DOES TEXAS COMPARE?
Party Control of Government in the Fifty States

Research in political science has shown that states with higher levels of party competition for control of government have higher levels of voter turnout and also tend to spend more on social programs. Although there is some competition between the two parties in all states, some states are much more competitive than others. The Party Control map (Figure 5.4) provides one indication. The map indicates states in which the Democratic or Republican parties control both the executive and legislative branches of government, in the customary blue and red, respectively, and states where control is divided, depicted in purple. (Nebraska, shown in white, has a nonpartisan legislature and so it is not possible to code party control of both branches.) Keep in mind that the map shows party control in the states and does not necessarily match familiar electoral college maps for presidential elections

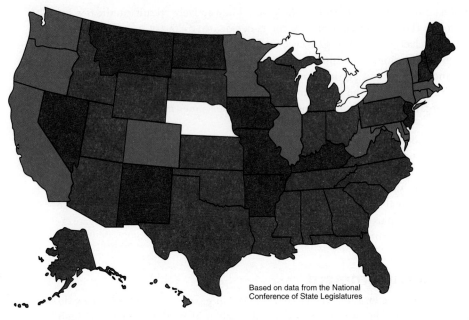

Based on data from the National
Conference of State Legislatures

Figure 5.4
Party Control in the Fifty States: How Texas Compares

The map illustrates party control of government in the American states.

Source: National Council of State Legislatures. The figure depicts whether Republicans control both the executive and legislative branches (red), Democrats control both (blue), or control is divided (purple).

FOR DEBATE

 How would party competition make a state's political system more responsive to residents' needs and preferences?

 Why would there be differences between party control of state government and the state party vote in presidential elections?

 Based on demographic changes in Texas, is the state likely to become more or less competitive in the future?

APPLYING WHAT YOU HAVE LEARNED ABOUT TEXAS POLITICAL PARTIES

LO 5.5 Apply what you have learned about Texas political parties.

This chapter has, thus far, given you the big-picture view of Texas parties. Now, the following essay will show you how a grassroots party activist can gain hands-on political experience, accumulate influence, and move up the party structure. You will learn how practicing party politics can help you express your own personal values even as you fulfill your social responsibility as a good citizen. You will also learn that political activity is an excellent opportunity to socialize, and it is simply great fun. From the time of Aristotle, philosophers have concluded that humans are political animals, that politics is part of our self-identity, and that it is in our nature to enjoy political endeavor.

After you have read the essay, you will be asked a series of questions that will require you to employ critical-thinking skills to apply what you have learned in this chapter to the new information in this essay. You will need to apply your understanding of party hierarchies to understand the author's political activities. Your analysis will require you to identify how political activity can enrich your personal, social, and emotional life, and you will need to reflect on how democracy depends on citizens' willingness to express themselves.

Let's Party

by Malcolm L. Cross
TARLETON STATE UNIVERSITY

Reading about party politics is a great way to start your quest for more knowledge of the political process, but no book or article can ever fully capture the nuances and complexities of modern politics in Texas. To supplement what you learn from reading and attending class, there's no substitute for hands-on experience working for the party of your choice.

When I joined the Social Sciences Department of Tarleton State University in 1987, among the courses I was assigned to teach were the upper-level course in elections and political parties, and the Texas government survey course. I had taken courses in political parties as both an undergraduate and graduate student, and even though I was a transplanted New Englander, I was able to read extensively about Texas politics. Yet I wanted to offer my students more than just book learning. I also wanted to introduce them to the practical side of politics in Texas. I decided that one way to do that was to work for my party, learn what I could as a volunteer activist, and share what I learned with my students.

I took my first step in the fall of 1988, during the presidential campaign season, when I simply walked into the local Republican Party headquarters and offered my services. I was immediately recruited to spend my Saturday afternoons keeping the headquarters open and giving out literature, bumper stickers, and yard signs to anyone who came in to request them. I was on my way.

As somewhat of an oddity—a conservative Republican college professor in a rather liberal Democratic profession, and in a county with few Republicans of any sort at that time—I quickly came to the attention of the chairman of the Erath County Republican Party. In the spring of 1990 he appointed me chair of my election precinct and a member of the county party executive committee. I also attended my first precinct convention, which consisted of me and one other Republican who lived in my precinct and had voted in the Republican primary. We met in a local diner and promptly elected ourselves delegates to the county convention, which in turn sent me to the state convention in Fort Worth, presided over by George W. Bush.

As I continued to serve on the local executive committee, I was requested to take on additional tasks for the county and state party organizations. In 1992, a new county party chair appointed me treasurer—a post I held until 2013. I received contributions, paid bills, planned the budget and administered the finances for party primaries, and filed the necessary reports with the Texas Ethics Commission and the Secretary of State.

I helped plan our county conventions. On several different occasions I served as the chairman of our platform committee, soliciting proposals from local activists, presenting them to the county convention delegates to be debated and voted on, and fashioning our platform for publication. I also frequently chaired the nominations committee which selected, subject to the county convention's approval, our delegations to the state conventions, most of which I've attended myself as either a delegate or an alternate, and once even as delegation chair.

At three successive state conventions—in 1994, 1996, and 1998—I served on the state party Rules Committee, helping review and, when felt necessary, recommend revision to state party by-laws, subject to the convention's approval. As a delegate I also participated in the election of party officials, including the state party chair and vice-chair, and members to the State Republican Executive Committee and the Republican National Committee. In presidential election years, I further helped select candidates for membership in the Electoral College.

My work has not been confined to party organizational activities. When Republican officeholders and candidates came to Stephenville, I was frequently one of the local party officials assigned to meet, greet, and escort them about town. I thereby got to meet Senators Kay Bailey Hutchinson and Phil Gramm, and Rick Perry when he was running for Lieutenant Governor. I especially enjoyed meeting George W. Bush in 1994, when he first ran for governor. I had been appointed to his Stephenville Educational Advisory Committee. When he came to town he had breakfast with us at a restaurant in a local motel and spoke with us about his plans for public education in Texas. Outside in the lobby I could see other educators, including Tarleton officials, who had not been invited to eat with us but who were milling about waiting to see him anyway.

In Texas and other states, Republican and Democratic candidates for office are usually nominated in party primaries, and the party organizations have little formal role to play in the process. But we can recruit and endorse candidates for office, sponsor debates, and provide small amounts of seed money for local candidates whom we choose to support.

In rare instances, when a vacancy occurs in office and it is impractical to hold a primary to select a candidate to fill it, the executive committee can actually nominate its own candidate. Recently, the long-time district court judge—a Democrat with an impeccable record of integrity, ability, and achievement—announced his retirement. The local district attorney, a Republican, announced his intention to seek the judgeship, and a local attorney who served on both the city council and the party executive committee announced his desire to become district attorney should the post be vacated. Former Governor Perry agreed to appoint them to the offices they sought if the executive committee promised to make them our nominees in the next election. We promptly agreed to do so.

My service with the Erath County Republican Party has therefore led me to share in many experiences and thereby learn more about politics than textbooks can cover. But my experiences are by no means unique. Many thousands of other volunteers, Democratic and Republican alike, share them too, as you can yourself, especially if you keep in mind the following lessons I've learned in my twenty-five years of service to the Republican Party.

First, relatively few Americans participate in the political process. A small majority of eligible Americans vote in presidential elections. No other political activity—voting for down-ballot offices, contributing money to campaigns, whatever—attracts as much interest. This doesn't mean that Americans are bad citizens; it simply means that most have interests other than politics, so those who choose to become involved in the political process will frequently find little competition in their quest for roles to play. This is true even in Erath County today, which the Republicans now dominate, but where volunteers are still frequently lacking. Therefore, it's easy to get started. Simply go to your party headquarters, or contact a local party official, and you'll be welcomed with open arms. Party leaders are always looking for volunteers to work for the party itself, or for candidates the party is supporting. In just a few short weeks I went from being a precinct convention delegate, to a county convention delegate, to a state convention delegate largely because there were more positions at each level than there were people to hold them.

Second, it's frequently easy to advance to greater responsibilities—or learning experiences—within a short period of time. People are constantly entering and leaving the political process, meaning that one who remains involved for at least two election cycles will begin to appear knowledgeable, experienced, and trustworthy. In just six years I went from being a party headquarters staffer to serving on a statewide party committee. Others have advanced even more swiftly than I did.

Third, while most party work takes little time, even during elections, a few positions—election judge or party treasurer, for example—can take up more time and therefore be relatively unattractive. But if one wants to serve in such a capacity, one will learn even more about the nuts and bolts of party politics. And getting to serve will not be difficult, given the absence of competition for such positions.

Finally, while party work is a great way to learn the practical side of politics, it's also a great way to advance the interests of America as you define them, while enriching your own life as well. In my quarter century of party work, I've never met a volunteer, either Democrat or Republican, who had anything less than America's best interests at heart, regardless of his or her position on abortion, gay rights, the death penalty, alternative energy sources, public education, law and order, or taxes, just to name a few of the many issues which parties and their candidates must address. In your quest for knowledge of the political process you'll join other patriots in a quest for what's best for America, and with the knowledge, insight, and experience you acquire and put to use, you'll become both a better scholar and a better citizen of a better nation.

JOIN THE DEBATE

 Describe ways that political activity can enrich your personal, social, and emotional life. How can political activity express your personal identity and sense of higher purpose? How much respect do you owe to those whose political identity is different from your own?

 How does a democracy depend on the willingness of citizens to actively participate in the decision-making process?

 Identify the party offices that the author has held and describe how those positions are filled. Why does the author say that it is fairly easy to achieve positions of influence within political parties?

CHAPTER SUMMARY

LO 5.1   Identify the characteristics of American political parties. There are three fundamental characteristics of political parties in the United States: (1) the two-party system, (2) pragmatism, and (3) decentralization.

We have two major parties in the United States and Texas partly because of the elec-toral system—specifically, single-member districts and plurality elections—that make it hard for third parties to succeed. Election laws put in place by the parties make it hard for third parties to emerge in the first place.

Parties in the United States and Texas traditionally have been pragmatic, focused on performance more than policy positions. This is largely the result of there being two parties, which makes it necessary to build majority coalitions to compete and to appeal to voters who are moderate and focused on performance. Recently, however, parties in the United States and Texas have become more programmatic, and Democrats and Republicans have become easier to distinguish.

Parties in the United States and Texas are decentralized, with much of the control of the nominating process (the primary) and party machinery in the hands of state and lo-cal leaders and voters.

LO 5.2   Understand the evolution of the party system in Texas. For much of its history, Texas was a one-party

Democratic state. Until recently, one-party dominance meant that the election to select the Democratic Party's nominees—the Democratic primary—was the most important election in Texas. Moderate and conservative factions within the Democratic Party became the key political players.

After years of domination by the Democratic Party, Texas began to experience a strong two-party competition in the 1980s and the Republicans had become the dominant party in Texas in the 1990s. By the turn of the century, political realignment was fairly complete. By 2002, the GOP controlled the governor's office, all other statewide offices, and both chambers of the state legislature; in 2004, Republicans captured a majority in the state's congressional delegation. The Republicans will no doubt remain dominant in the near future; what happens in the long run is less clear.

LO 5.3   Evaluate the importance of party organization. Political parties consist of permanent organizations that manage operations in between elections and the temporary structures that arise only in election years. The latter are most visible to voters—the primary elections that select candidates as well as the precinct, district, and state (and national) conventions that produce party platforms and guide ongoing operations.

LO 5.4 **Assess the functions of political parties in American and Texas politics.** Despite the hostility of the founders to political parties, they have become an important part of American political life. Parties perform critical functions in a democracy. They nominate and elect their candidates to public office, educate and mobilize voters, and run the government at the different levels (local, state, or national).

LO 5.5 **Apply what you have learned about Texas political parties.** You learned from a party activist how party activity can enrich your social life and sense of personal identity. You found how easily individuals can gain influence within their party and how such party activities can offer individuals a sense of higher purpose. You learned that the quality of democracy in Texas depends on the willingness of activists to participate in the civic life of the state.

KEY TERMS

dealignment, *p. 122*
decentralization, *p. 116*
evangelical (fundamentalist) christians, *p. 125*
partisan identification, *p. 122*

party platform, *p. 125*
party realignment, *p. 122*
position issues, *p. 116*
pragmatism, *p. 115*

precinct convention, *p. 126*
presidential preference primary, *p. 128*
swing voters, *p. 126*

tea party, *p. 125*
tipping, *p. 126*
two-party system, *p. 114*
valence issues, *p. 115*

REVIEW QUESTIONS

LO 5.1 Identify the characteristics of American political parties.

* Explain why there are two major parties in the United States and Texas.

* Why have parties in the United States and Texas traditionally been so pragmatic?

LO 5.2 Understand the evolution of the party system in Texas.

* Define *realignment* and discuss to what extent it has occurred in Texas politics.

* Discuss the reasons for and describe the events that led to the rise of the Republican Party in Texas.

* Is Texas becoming a one-party Republican state? Or is there reason to expect increased competition between the parties in the future? Why or why not?

LO 5.3 Evaluate the importance of party organization.

* What are party platforms and how do political parties in Texas produce them?

LO 5.4 Assess the functions of political parties in American and Texas politics.

* Differentiate between the party in the electorate, the party as organization, and the party in government.

* How do parties help represent the public in government? Are parties always good agents of the public? Why or why not?

GET ACTIVE

Team up with a political party. If you already identify with one, this is easy; if you don't, choose a party. To help you find your way, the state party organizations can be found at the following sites: **www.txdemocrats.org** and **www.texasgop.org**. On-campus organizations include the Young Democrats (**www.texasyds.com**) and Young Republicans (**texasyoungrepublicans.com**).

　Help select your party's nominee. Register and vote in the party's primary election. To vote in the primary, you must be registered at least thirty days in advance. In Texas, you simply decide which party you prefer and vote to select that party's nominee. The only real restriction is that you must choose one party or the other. Go to

your party's precinct convention or caucus. If you vote in your party's primary, you are eligible to attend your party's precinct convention (or caucus, as it is referred to in presidential election years). The convention begins a few minutes after the polls close and is usually in the same location as the primary. Attendance is often sparse, which means you have a good chance of being heard and even being elected as a delegate.

　Attend your party's county- or district-level convention. Delegates selected at the precinct level go on to attend their party's county or district convention. Delegates to these conventions pass resolutions and elect candidates to the state convention, which is held every two years in June. If you are selected as a delegate to the state convention, you have become a serious party activist.

Determine whether you are a liberal or conservative. Sample some liberal and conservative websites to determine whether you are a liberal or conservative. Link up with the liberal *Texas Observer* at **www .texasobserver.org**; plug into **www.offthekuff.com** and **www.texaskaos.com**; nose around Brains and Eggs at **brainsandeggs.blogspot.com**. For the conservative viewpoint, sound out The Conservative Review at **www .texasconservativereview.com/index.html**; tune into the Red State website at **www.redstate.com**; and look into the Texas Insider at **www.texasinsider.org**.

 If you are going to be politically active, why is it important to know who shares your viewpoints? Why is it important to understand the viewpoints of people who differ with you?

CHAPTER 6

Interest Groups

John B. Mueller Photography/Moment/Getty Images

LEARNING OBJECTIVES

LO 6.1 Define *interest groups* and identify their major types.

LO 6.2 Describe how interest groups influence public policies in Texas.

LO 6.3 Analyze the political balance of power among interest groups in Texas.

LO 6.4 Evaluate the role of interest groups in Texas politics and policy formulation.

LO 6.5 Apply what you have learned about interest groups.

*C*itizens may act alone to influence government, and millions do. But when citizens join together in a voluntary organization that strives to influence public policy, they act as an **interest group**, sometimes known as a pressure group. Interest groups often play a high-stakes political game that determines who gets what from state government and who pays for it. As Congresswoman Barbara Jordan famously said, "Government is too important to be a spectator sport."

Interest groups compete with each other as they struggle to benefit from the state's $200.4 billion[1] budget. Such groups often depend on government outlays, and they solicit policy makers for a piece of government spending. Road construction companies ask the governor to support increased spending on infrastructure projects. Schoolteachers pressure the legislature for minimal cuts to public education. Patient advocates ask lawmakers to expand Medicaid spending. Many interest groups press the government to spend more, but usually advocate for less taxation—especially on their own members.

Business and professional groups plead for state regulations friendly to their interests. Because Texas's $1.5 trillion state economy affects a huge part of the national market, out-of-state producers wanting to sell in Texas modify their goods and services to comply with Texas regulations. Texas regulations ripple out to other states, and they can determine what entire industries produce and how they produce it.

For some interest groups, their fundamental values or their very way of life is at stake in public policy making. Some racial and ethnic groups seek government protection for their civil and political rights; other groups endeavor to limit social change brought about by immigration. Certain faith-based groups try to use government to support their religious values by banning abortion, contraception, or same-sex marriage while gun-rights groups urge passage of laws to expand the right to carry weapons. Environmentalist groups fight for government restrictions on pollution; some agricultural groups promote state policies that support traditional rural life.

So many groups, perhaps thousands of them, have their interests at play in the political game that we cannot describe every group and its goals individually. Instead, you should understand the broad types of interest groups that pursue influence in Texas government.

Interest group

A voluntary organization that strives to influence public policy; sometimes known as a *pressure group.*

TYPES OF INTEREST GROUPS

LO 6.1 Define *interest groups* and identify their major types.

Interest groups can be classified in a multitude of ways, but the simplest is to categorize them according to their primary purpose—economic, noneconomic, or both. Table 6.1 gives some examples of Texas interest groups in all three categories.

Economic Groups

Economic interests operating at the state level are business and professional groups, education, agriculture, and labor—these groups seek financial advantages for their members. Business and agriculture are always interested in keeping their taxes low, securing subsidies, avoiding regulation, and receiving government contracts to increase profits. Professional groups want to limit entry into their professions to reduce competition; public education groups fight against school privatization and for increased salaries and benefits for teachers. Labor unions seek generous workers' compensation, better workplace safety regulations, and laws to make it easier for workers to organize unions.

Noneconomic Groups

Noneconomic groups seek the betterment of society as a whole or the reform of the political, social, or economic systems in ways that do not directly affect their members' pocketbooks. Groups like environmentalists and civil liberties activists maintain that the beneficiaries of

---

[1]Legislative Budget Board, *General Appropriations Act for 2014–15* at www.lbb.state.tx.us/Documents/GAA/General_Appropriations_Act_2014-15.pdf.

TABLE 6.1 Interest Group Classifications and Selected Examples

Classification	Sector	Examples
Economic	Agriculture	Texas Farm Bureau
	Business	Texan Association of Business and Chambers of Commerce
	Labor	Texas AFL-CIO; American Federation of State and County Municipal Employees
	Occupations and professions	Texas Association of Realtors; Texas Trial Lawyers Association; Texas Medical Association
Noneconomic	Patriotic	American Legion
	Public interest	Texas Common Cause; Texans for Public Justice
	Religious	Texas Christian Life Commission
	Environmentalists	The Sierra Club; Natural Resources Defense Council
	Personal liberties advocates	The National Rifle Association; the American Civil Liberties Union of Texas
Mixed	Education	Texas State Teachers' Association
	Race and gender	League of United Latin American Citizens; National Association for the Advancement of Colored People; Women's Health and Family Planning Association of Texas; Equality Texas

This table shows the types of interest groups and examples of each.

▲ **Conduct an Internet search to go to these groups' websites, find out which public policies these groups advocate, and then use their policy agendas to show the difference between economic and noneconomic interest groups.**

their programs are the members of society—things like personal freedoms or clean air and water that cannot be directly measured entirely by self-interest. Political reform groups, such as Common Cause or Texans for Public Justice, think of themselves as "public interest" groups because they believe that they are literally acting on behalf of the public. Many individuals who join noneconomic interest groups are motivated by personal values and intense passion like members of the Texas Right to Life movement, who have strong beliefs about conception and when life begins.

Mixed Groups

Many groups do not fit neatly into the economic or noneconomic classification because they pursue social goals that also have clear economic effects. Groups fighting discrimination on the basis of age, disability, ethnicity, gender, or sexual orientation argue that such practices are not only a form of social injustice but also an economic problem that affects wages and promotions in the workplace. Groups pursuing both social equality and economic goals are classified as mixed or hybrid organizations. Few, if any, demands on the political system affect all classes of citizens equally. Any public policy comes with both costs and benefits; some will gain while others bear an economic burden from almost any government decision.

INTEREST GROUPS' TARGETS AND TACTICS

LO 6.2 Describe how interest groups influence public policies in Texas.

Interest groups are collections of citizens with shared interests that pursue public policy goals on behalf of their members. Their interests are narrower than those of political parties. Unlike political parties, they do not nominate candidates for office and may work with officials of both parties to secure their goals. Although interest groups sometimes endorse and support candidates for office, their primary purpose is to influence government policy makers.

Interest groups use a variety of tools to influence state decision makers, and they adapt their tactics to target specific officials. They make face-to-face appeals to legislative and executive officials, and they file suit in the courts. Interest groups use electioneering and public relations to sway elected officials by affecting public opinion.

Lobbying the Legislature

Interest groups' most straightforward tool for influencing public officials is contacting them directly to advocate for a particular public policy—a practice known as **lobbying**. Some interest groups hire individual freelance lobbyists or large lobbying firms to advocate for them on a single issue, while other interest groups employ full-time lobbyists to work exclusively for them as "hired guns." Whether lobbyists work for a single client or have a massive client list to serve, they use a variety of strategies to influence different branches of government. We will go inside lobbying operations to explore some of their most effective techniques to win legislators over to their positions, then we will show how they are also able to bring executives and bureaucrats around to their views on public policy.

Tina Phan/MCT/Newscom

Pro-life and pro-choice interest groups rally in Texas Capitol dome as state Senator Wendy Davis filibusters a bill limiting abortions. Interest groups use techniques such as these to influence public policy in the state.

CTQ **Evaluate public demonstrations as a technique to influence public opinion and policy.**

Lobbying
Directly contacting public officials to advocate for a public policy.

Did You Know? In 2013, Texas special interests hired 1,663 lobbyists and spent at least $155 million to influence state policies.[2]

Preparing to Lobby Before a legislative session begins, a lobbyist must have successfully completed several tasks: (1) learn who is predisposed to support the cause, who is on the other side, and which members can be swayed, (2) memorize the faces of the members, their non-legislative occupation, the counties they represent, and a little about their family, (3) establish rapport through contact with the members of the legislature, (4) get to know the staffs of legislators because through them the member can be influenced, and (5) know the legislative issues, including the arguments of opponents.

Lobbyists must plan a strategy for approaching legislators. How does a lobbyist approach a member of the legislature or the leadership? How do they get in the door, and what do they say once they get in? How much influence does a legislator's staff have on the member's decisions? Is it necessary to see all 181 members of the legislature, the lieutenant governor, and the governor?

Because a session has only 140 days, interest groups' best lobbyists know that lobbying should begin before the legislative session officially begins. The 18-month period between regular sessions provides lobbyists with ample time to work on relationships, learn what proposals have a chance of passing, draft legislative proposals, and line up sponsors to introduce bills in the house and senate at the beginning of the next session.

---

[2]Texans for Public Justice, "Texas Top Lobbyists: Special Interests Paid Lobbyists up to $328 Million in 2013 Session," http://info.tpj.org/reports/Top%20Lobbyists%202013.pdf.

Socializing　Personality can be a valuable asset to a successful lobbyist. Anyone who directly contacts public officials to influence their behavior should be extroverted and enjoy socializing because the lobbyist's first job is to become known and trusted by legislators and any executive officials who have jurisdiction over the interest he or she represents.

Lobbyists organize social functions with legislators to allow them to interact in comfortable settings. A lobbyist may invite legislators to lunch or to a party to begin building a personal relationship of mutual trust. Attending an occasional social event with legislators, however, is not in itself enough to win their trust. Most successful lobbyists spend years cultivating long-standing relationships with decision makers.

Using Tools of Persuasion　Socializing does not obligate legislators to support lobbyists' proposals, but it does open the door for lobbyists to gain access to legislators, which at least gives them the chance to make their case. Once in the door, lobbyists find their most effective tool is providing information useful to a legislator—the facts are often persuasive. But to maintain a relationship, the lobbyist must build the legislator's trust, which means providing sound, accurate information about the legislation the lobbyist is supporting or opposing. This includes "off-the-record" admission of the pluses and minuses of the legislation. Honesty is, in fact, the best policy for a lobbyist when dealing with a public official.

Lobbyists find that framing the issues in terms of the public interest affects how legislators react, and they try to define their positions before their opponents have a chance to cast them in a negative light. For example, groups supporting Texas's new voter ID law (described in Chapter 4) convinced legislators that it was essential to the public interest to protect the integrity of the election process. Voter ID opponents had argued that cases of voter impersonation were virtually unknown and that support for passing the law was in reality a political effort to suppress voting among young people and minorities who are less likely to have government-sanctioned identity cards.

Lobbyists appeal to legislators' emotions and to their ideologies or basic philosophies of government. Lobbyists may gently remind legislators of their interest group's support in past election campaigns or delicately imply the potential for future support. Although lobbyists may not legally offer legislators financial support in exchange for their vote on a bill, it is often simply understood that groups use their resources to help elect legislative candidates who support their interests. Our Texas Insiders feature puts a face on one of the most successful lobby operations in Texas; HillCo has numerous clients and primarily represents business interests.

AP Images/Harry Cabluck

This image shows businesspeople lobbying outside the state department of transportation. Lobbying is when agents of interest groups make direct face-to-face contact with public officials in an effort to affect public policy.

CTQ **What are the tools of persuasion that lobbyists use to convince government officials to adopt the policies they support? What makes them effective?**

Targeting Key Legislators　Not all members of the legislature are equal, and lobbyists target those with the greatest impact on bills critical to the lobbyist's agenda. Establishing rapport and obtaining feedback from the very powerful presiding officers—the speaker of the house and lieutenant governor—is especially useful. No endorsement is more important to an interest group than that of the presiding officers. If an endorsement for the group's legislative proposal is not forthcoming, the lobbyist must persuade the presiding officers at least to remain neutral in the legislative struggle.

Texas Insiders

Hillco: Texas's Premier Lobbying Outfit and Its Influence in Texas

In some years, lobbyists registered with the Texas Ethics Commission outnumber legislators nine to one. Many lobbyists represent only one or two clients, but a few of them conduct sufficient lobby business to qualify as true Texas insiders. Among them is the powerful HillCo.

Founded by Neal "Buddy" Jones and Bill Miller, HillCo has been involved in almost every big legislative fight in the last 15 years. When Bob Perry and Charles C. Butt saw their business interests threatened, they hired HillCo to block the "sanctuary cities" bill in the legislature. One of the most popular and gregarious figures in the Capitol, HillCo partner Bill Miller helped manage Tom Craddick's races for the speakership in the House of Representatives and later helped finance former Lieutenant Governor David Dewhurst's expensive, but ill-fated, campaign for the U.S. Senate in 2012. Altogether, HillCo's political action committee donated $990,465 to various candidates during the two years before the 2012 elections.

Among its notable clients, HillCo partners have represented the following:

- Alcoa
- AT&T
- Continental Airlines
- Farmers Insurance
- General Motors
- H-E-B Grocery
- Koch Industries
- Microsoft
- Perry Homes

- Pharmaceutical Research and Manufacturers of America (known as "big PhRMA")
- Pfizer
- Wyeth Pharmaceuticals

As its website boasts, "HillCo has earned a reputation as the premier government affairs consulting firm, providing unparalleled advocacy. We partner with our clients to identify their specific governmental and business goals, and develop and implement targeted, fully integrated strategies. Our relationships are broad, deep and strong, enabling us to prevail in even the most challenging political environments." HillCo's website lists its services as lobbying, policy analysis, regulatory consulting, communications, public and media relations, procurement, advisory boards, and grassroots organization.

 Thinking about the role of elites in Texas politics Write a carefully constructed essay to describe the techniques that lobby firms such as HillCo use to convince legislators and other policy makers to support their clients' positions. To make your essay thorough, be sure to include each of the services listed on the HillCo website and explain how lobbyists' personal relationships, developed through years of contacts with policy makers, affect the decision-making process.

Sources: Texans for Public Justice, Texas Top 150 Contributors at http://info.tpj.org/reports/Top%20Donors%202013.pdf; HillCo company website at www.hillcopartners.com/about; Nate Blakeslee, Paul Burka, and Patricia Kilday Hart, "Power Company: Who Are the Most Influential People Determining the Fate of Texas—and What Do They Want?" *Texas Monthly*, Volume 32, number 2, February 2011, p. 165.

Getting the endorsement of the chair of each committee through which the legislation must pass before it can go to the floor for a vote is an advantage second only to that of winning the support of the presiding officers. Most of the "experts" who testify at legislative committee hearings represent interest groups; lobbyists know that committee hearings are an ideal forum in which to make their case to key legislators.

Did You Know? Lobbyists outnumber legislators more nine to one.[3]

[3]Ibid.

Influencing and the Executive Branch

Interest groups try to influence the Texas legislature because it creates, finances, and defines government programs, but they also target the executive branch, where enormous sums of money, privilege, and prestige are also at stake. The governor affects policy by appointing officers to head state agencies, and state agencies themselves wield a great deal of power as they award contracts and develop regulations.

Targeting the Rule-Making Process The legislature gives the executive branch and its administrative agencies responsibility for **implementation**, or carrying out broad public policies, enforcing state laws, providing public services, and managing day-to-day government activities. The legislature gives executive agencies a great deal of flexibility as to how to enforce the law; they have administrative **discretion**, which is wide latitude to make decisions within the broad requirements set out in the law. The legislative branch authorizes administrative agencies to establish detailed rules or regulations that determine how the law shall be applied to actual situations.

Agencies publish proposed rules for public comment in the *Texas Register*, the official publication of the state that gives the public notice of proposed actions and adopted policies of executive branch agencies. All citizens have the right to comment in the rule-making process, but only those aware of and interested in a proposed rule participate. Ordinary citizens do not subscribe to the *Texas Register* but corporations, labor unions, law firms, and interest groups do. Organized interest groups have a real stake in shaping these regulations that control how they do business and directly affect their profits. Hence, they know when to send their lobbyists and paid experts to give testimony at public hearings, and they are able to mobilize their members to call or write agencies about proposed rules.

Agency administrators actively seek input about the impact of their rules and policies from the groups they regulate. The Texas Department of Insurance needs to know how its proposed rules will affect the insurance industry; the Texas Railroad Commission will want to know how new fracking rules will affect the drilling industry's use of hydraulic fracturing to extract oil and gas, and the Texas Real Estate Commission consults with the Texas Association of Realtors before adopting new licensing requirements.

Targeting the Appointment Process Lobbyists are actively involved in the appointment process, and they are often able to convince the governor to select agency heads who are friendly to their interests. Most state agencies are headed by boards and commissions recruited from the industry, profession, or group they regulate—they share the same interests. In fact, Texas law requires that many regulatory boards must include members of the business or profession that they regulate. For example, twelve of the nineteen-member Texas Medical Board must be physicians.

Upon retirement from government service, many agency officers go to work for the very industries that they once regulated. Critics doubt that administrative officers can regulate their own business or profession and, at the same time. serve the public interest, especially when they intend to return to the same profession. At least one observer has concluded that "the state's business and political elites are hopelessly intertwined."[5]

Margin glossary

Implementation

Administrative agencies carrying out broad public policies, enforcing state laws, providing public services, and managing day-to-day government activities.

Discretion

Wide latitude to make decisions within the broad requirements set out in the law.

Texas Register

The official publication of the state that gives the public notice of proposed actions and adopted policies of executive branch agencies.

Did You Know? William White is chairman of the State Finance Commission, the agency that regulates payday loans. He is vice president of Cash America and a major campaign contributor.[4]

---

[4]Wayne Slater, "Greg Abbott Goes to Bat for Campaign Contributor Targeted by Wendy Davis as Anti-Consumer," *Dallas Morning News*, January 2, 2014, at http://trailblazersblog.dallasnews.com/2014/01/greg-abbott-goes-to-bat-for-campaign-contributor-targeted-by-wendy-davis.html.

[5]"The Future Is Texas," *The Economist*, December 19, 2002, p. 29.

Co-opting State Agencies Such a close working relationship develops between interest groups and state agencies that agencies often view the interest groups that they regulate as their clients; such interest groups are often called **clientele groups**. These are the groups most affected by a government agency's regulations and programs, and they frequently form close alliances with the agency based on mutual support and accommodation.

Lobbyists for clientele groups often defend "their" state agency as well as its funding and legal powers. This blurring of the line between the state agencies and a special interest is called **co-optation** when such a close alliance develops between state regulatory agencies and their clientele group that the regulated have, in effect, become the regulators. The interest group has captured such complete control of their regulatory agency that they are essentially self-regulated.

The Texas Commission on Environmental Quality (TCEQ) provides an example of a clientele group's influence on a state agency. When the TCEQ ruled that Texas billionaire Harold Simmons could not import radioactive waste from other states, he did it anyway. His company, Waste Control Specialists, planned to bury the waste at its waste dump near Andrews, Texas. This site sits in close proximity to two water tables, including sections of the Ogallala Aquifer—an important source of water for the High Plains region of the United States. The Texas Commission on Environmental Quality warned that "groundwater is likely to intrude into the proposed disposal units and contact the waste from either or both of two water tables near the proposed facility."[6]

After permission to bring in the waste was initially rejected, the company put its lobbyists to work. The team included the former executive director of TCEQ, Jeff Saitas. The company lobbied TCEQ's executive director, Glenn Shankle, who overruled the technical team and gave Waste Control Specialists permission for the site. A few months later, Glenn Shankle himself left TCEQ to become a lobbyist for Waste Control Specialists.

Targeting the Courts

Lobbying is one extremely important interest-group tool, but interest groups employ a wide variety other tactics to influence government policy making as well. For example, interest groups do not directly lobby judges, but they actively campaign for judicial candidates who share their viewpoints; they prevail upon the governor to fill court vacancies with friendly judicial appointees, and they file suit in court to win legal rulings that benefit their interests.

Influencing the Judicial Selection Process Texas is one of a handful of states that elect their trial and appeals court judges in partisan elections (see Chapter 9). Candidates must first win the party's nomination in the primary and then prevail in the general election. Voters who elect judges do not usually have a clear understanding of the law or how it should be applied; instead, they depend on party labels and political campaigns to give them voting cues.

Business groups and law firms, many of them having legal business before the courts, contribute large amounts to judicial campaigns. In 2012, candidates for the just three positions on Texas Supreme Court raised $3.2 million.[7] Even Texas Supreme Court judges not up for election that year received almost $300,000 in campaign contributions that year.

Critics argue that large contributions from pro-business interest groups and corporate law firms have influenced judicial decisions, shifting legal precedent in favor of corporations and

Clientele groups
The groups most affected by a government agency's regulations and programs; frequently these interest groups form close alliances with the agency based on mutual support and accommodation.

Co-optation
Such a close alliance develops between state regulatory agencies and their clientele group that the regulated have, in effect, become the regulators; the interest group has captured such complete control of their regulatory agency that they are essentially self-regulated.

---

[6]TCEQ Interoffice Memo to Susan Jablonski, Director, Radioactive Materials Division from TCEQ RML Team, regarding groundwater intrusion into proposed LLRW facility, August 14, 2007, http://texasnuclearsafety.org/downloads/TCEQ_interoffice_memo_81407.pdf.

[7]National Institute for Money in State Politics at www.followthemoney.org/database/StateGlance/state_candidates.phtml?s=TX&y=2012&f=J.

putting procedural hurdles in the way of consumers and workers who might sue them.[8] Even the U.S. Supreme court recognizes that very large contributions to judicial candidates creates a risk that judges will be biased in deciding cases in which megadonors are involved.[9]

Between elections, judges frequently resign or retire, and the governor is charged with filling the resulting vacancy until the next election. Because such temporary judicial appointees usually run for and subsequently win election to full terms, interest groups set up massive lobbying efforts to persuade the governor to appoint judges favorable to their interests. Many Texas judges were first recruited in this way by interest groups that have much to gain or loose from court rulings.

Filing Suit in Court Major corporations, insurance companies, and powerful professional groups employ attorneys on their staffs or have law firms on retainer to defend their interests when workers and consumers sue them. Influential interests also bring lawsuits to challenge government policies that harm their interests. They may win court rulings that declare hostile legislation is unconstitutional or that inconvenient executive decisions are illegal. Courts might interpret a law or administrative rule in such a way that it works to a group's advantage.

In the past, smaller and less powerful organizations turned to the courts as a last resort after they had lost policy battles in the legislative or executive branches. In recent years, however, changes in the state's political climate, passage of lawsuit reforms, and decisions by the state supreme court have made Texas courts less responsive to groups representing environmentalists, consumers, and ethnic minorities. Some of these groups now simply view filing lawsuits in state courts as a tactic to attract public attention and media coverage of their cause.

Some of these groups have, instead, turned to the federal courts to enforce environmental and consumer protection policies. Chapters 1 and 4 show that various groups have won federal court decisions that protect voting rights and civil rights. The Mexican American Legal Defense and Education Fund and allied minority interest groups recently won a federal court ruling requiring adjustments to discriminatory legislative and congressional districts.[10]

Shaping the Political Environment

Besides working to influence state policy makers directly, interest groups strive to shape the political environment in which policy decisions are made. Interest groups are most effective when they have the support of the public as well as industry and community leaders, and they engage in political campaigns and other public relations efforts to create a political climate favorable to their agendas.

Electioneering Interest groups use their resources to support candidates disposed toward their interests. They endorse and recommend that their members vote for the candidate most aligned with their values; the organizations' newsletters and websites carry messages of support for their chosen candidates. Endorsements from organizations with a large and committed following, like the National Rifle Association or Texas Right to Life, have the greatest impact. Teachers' organizations, organized labor, and tea party activists sometimes help their favorite candidates by providing campaign workers who go door to door, operate phone banks, and hand out literature and yard signs.

---

[8]Billy Corriher, "Big Business Taking over State Supreme Courts: How Campaign Contributions to Judges Tip the Scales against Individuals," Center for American Progress, August 13, 2012 at www.americanprogress.org/issues/civil-liberties/report/2012/08/13/11974/big-business-taking-over-state-supreme-courts; Texans for Public Justice, "Courtroom Contributions Stain Supreme Court Campaigns: October 2008," http://info.tpj.org/reports/courtroomcontributions/index.html.

[9]*Caperton* v. *A.T. Massey* 129 U.S. 2264 (2009).

[10]*Perez* v. *Perry*, 835 F. Supp. 2d. 209 (2011).

Officeholders are responsive to interest groups' potential voting power, the value of their potential endorsements, and the number of their members who may volunteer in the next election campaign. As a result, interest groups are most influential when they represent members on what political strategists call "voting issues," that is, single issues such as opposition to gun control or abortion, about which members feel so passionately as to be decisive for voters in determining how they will cast their ballots. Other groups may represent members who may favor gun control or consumer protection, but voters rarely decide how to vote based on these issues alone.

Contributing to Campaigns Interest groups may also be influential because they provide money—a key resource in campaigns. Executives of banks, insurance companies, the petrochemical industry, and utility companies make large individual contributions and also contribute through political action committees (PACs are discussed in Chapter 4). Professional groups such as physicians, trial lawyers, real estate agents, and teachers also form PACs that aggregate contributions into large memorable sums, which they funnel to their favorite candidates.

Most campaign contributions for the state legislature and the statewide offices come from large donors. These campaign contributors give large amounts because the state legislature, the governor, the Railroad Commission, and other elected officials make decisions that affect these donors' economic well-being. Donors contribute to gain **access** to public officials, meaning their lobbyists are able to "get in the door" to sit down and talk to them about their needs. Substantial contributions seem to create an obligation on the part of an elected official to listen when a contributor calls. Ordinary citizens find access more difficult.

Access
The ability to "get in the door" to sit down and talk to public officials. Campaign contributions are often used to gain access.

Money in politics is the hot topic of the day because the startling amount of money candidates raise and spend in campaigns for elective office at all levels has skyrocketed. Legislative candidates raised $117.1 million in the 2012 election cycle. The 380 candidates vying for a seat in the Texas House raised $73.9 million and 74 candidates for the Texas Senate raised $43.2 million. Nineteen candidates who ran for governor raised $102.3 million in 2010[11] and totals are expected to be considerably higher when 2014 contributions are finally tallied. Even when candidates face little or no opposition, they often raise large amounts of money; the most powerful legislators are able to put together huge campaign war chests because megadonors want clout with the legislative leadership.

Did You Know? The average candidate for the Texas legislature spent more than $257,000 in 2012 to win an office that pays $7,200 a year!

Educating the Public Interest groups shape the political climate by providing the general public with messages designed to build a positive image and to promote their viewpoints. Well-funded interest groups employ the services of public relations firms to promote policy agendas even as they build their reputations for honesty, good citizenship, and concern for the well-being of the customers and good citizenship.

Interest groups may use their organizations' magazines, annual stockholder reports, and press releases to newspapers as vehicles for building their own reputation and educating the public about the wisdom of policy proposals their organizations support. They may purchase print, broadcast, and Internet advertising to shape and mobilize public opinion, and many interest groups now sponsor local "grassroots" organizations and political blogs that share their policy views.

---

[11]National Institute on Money in State Politics, *Follow the Money Database* www.followthemoney.org/database/state_overview.phtml?s=TX&y=2012 and www.followthemoney.org/database/state_overview.phtml?s=TX&y=2010.

AP Images/Deborah Cannon

State employees such as these teachers become an economic interest group when they demonstrate in support of their job benefits.

What is the goal of organizing public demonstrations? What precautions must interest groups take if they are to use public protests as an effective tactic?

Astroturf lobbying

Special-interest groups orchestrating demonstrations to give the impression of widespread and spontaneous public support.

Did You Know? A single corporation— AT&T—reported spending more money on lobbying than all unions combined.

Organizing Public Demonstrations Some interest groups organize marches and demonstrations to generate publicity for their cause. Press coverage is all but guaranteed because demonstrations create a sort of "theater" that is especially suited for television news and Internet video sites like YouTube. When the legislature is in session, demonstrations are plentiful. Public school teachers, immigrants' rights groups, tea party members, and countless others rally in Austin to express their opinion on a whole host of bills.

Using this kind of tactic is a challenge to interest groups that must enlist enough members to be impressive and, at the same time, keep control of the demonstration. Violating the law, forging signatures on letters sent to lawmakers, blocking traffic, damaging property, and using obscenities do not win support from fellow citizens or public officials. Although some groups have used these tactics, most have found that civil and sincere protests are more effective.

Interest groups have a clear advantage if they are well-organized at the grassroots level and if they can mobilize large numbers of supporters to contact officials. Some special-interest groups have used their financial advantages to orchestrate demonstrations to give the impression of widespread and spontaneous public support for their positions—**astroturf lobbying**. Such public demonstrations have been dubbed astroturf lobbying after the artificial grass used in many football stadiums.

THE BALANCE OF POLITICAL POWER IN TEXAS

LO 6.3 Analyze the political balance of power among interest groups in Texas.

Business and professional groups continue to be the most powerful interests in the state, and they are frequently aligned with the majority Republican Party. Generally speaking, the most successful noneconomic interest groups are socially conservative groups with agendas that are consistent with business interests. Environmentalist groups, organized labor, civil rights organizations, and groups advocating for the poor often support policies at odds with business and usually ally themselves with Democrats. Such groups have little impact on Texas policy.

Texas's Most Powerful Interest Groups

One way of gauging which groups swing the greatest weight in state government is by looking at the amount of money they spend to lobby state officials. Table 6.2 shows that the energy and natural resources business accounted for 19 percent (or up to $63 million) of all lobbying contracts as compiled from official reports in 2013. The health, finance, and communications industries were also among the biggest spenders on lobbying.[12] The top five individual businesses spending the most on lobbying were energy and utility companies including AT&T, Energy Future Holdings, American Electric Power, Oncor Electric Delivery Company, and CenterPoint Energy. Obviously, such companies have an intense interest in state utility regulation.

---

[12]Texans for Public Justice, "Texas Top Lobbyists: Special Interests Paid Lobbyists up to $328 Million in 2013 Session," http://info.tpj.org/reports/Top%20Lobbyists%202013.pdf.

TABLE 6.2 The Biggest Spenders on Lobbyists in Texas

Interest Group Type	Minimum Value of Lobbying Contracts*	Maximum Value of Lobbying Contracts*	Percent of Total Lobbying Contract Value
Energy, Natural Resources, and Waste	$31,407,000	$62,516,987	19%
Ideological/Single Issue	$19,235,000	$47,049,984	14%
Health	$21,725,000	$46,474,988	14%
Miscellaneous Business	$19,440,000	$40,759,990	12%
Communications	$10,430,000	$21,014,996	6%
Finance	$8,360,000	$17,999,996	5%
Lawyers and Lobbyists	$9,275,000	$16,284,997	5%
Construction	$5,617,000	$12,166,997	4%
Transportation	$5,370,000	$12,134,997	4%
Insurance	$6,055,000	$11,964,998	4%
Computers and Electronics	$5,070,000	$10,999,997	3%
Real Estate	$4,380,000	$9,869,997	3%
Agriculture	$3,340,000	$7,204,998	2%
Other	$2,730,000	$5,859,998	2%
Labor	$2,690,000	$5,574,999	2%
Unknown	$160,000	$160,000	–
TOTAL	**$155,284,000**	**$328,278,919**	**100%**

*Texas Government Code, Section 305.005, does not require lobbyists to report exact compensation—the value of each contract is reported within specific ranges or brackets.

Table 6.2 shows which interests spent the most on lobbying. By late May2013, 1,663 Texas lobbyists reported that 2,820 clients took out 8,172 paid lobby contracts worth a grand total of from $155 million to $328 million.

Source: Texans for Public Justice, "Texas Top Lobbyists: Special Interests Paid Lobbyists up to $328 Million in 2013 Session," http://info.tpj.org/reports/Top%20 Lobbyists%202013.pdf.

▲ **Search out the policy goals of these big spenders. How many of them represent consumers, workers, or environmentalists?**

Many smaller interests join together into **umbrella organizations**, in which industries, wholesalers, producers, retailers, and professionals form associations to promote common policy goals by making campaign contributions and hiring lobbyists to represent their interests. For example, the Texas Medical Association, the Texas Trial Lawyers Association, the Texas Oil and Gas Association, the Texas Association of Realtors, and the Texas Cable Association have reported spending more than $3.6 million lobbying on behalf of their members during the 2013 legislative session.[13] Texans for Education Reform representing private education companies reported spending more than $600,000 successfully lobbying the Texas legislature to expand charter schools, which are publicly funded but operated by private organizations.[14]

The Texas Association of Business, Texans for Lawsuit Reform, Texas Medical Association, Texas Realtors' Association, and the Texas Oil and Gas Association have been traditionally regarded as being among the most powerful organizations because they have the money to

Umbrella organizations

Associations formed by smaller interests joining together to promote common policy goals by making campaign contributions and hiring lobbyists to represent their interests.

---

[13]Texans for Public Justice, *Texas Top Lobbyists: Top Lobby Clients During the 2013 Session* at http://info.tpj.org/reports/Top%20Lobbyists%202013.pdf.
[14]Ibid.

maintain permanent headquarters in Austin and employ clerical and research staffs as well as lobbyists to make their prominence known. Such special interests have full-time staff, multiple lobbyists, and the ability to disburse sizable campaign contributions. They often achieve more than resource-poor groups, but other factors also tend to affect which interest groups win the influence game.

Most registered lobbyists represent business, but business is a huge category, encompassing both the powerful and the weak. Not everyone in business shares the same viewpoint. Independent and small businesses frequently seek policy outcomes opposed by larger enterprises. Internet businesses differ with brick-and-mortar retailers about whether Internet purchases should be subject to sales tax. Trucking interests are often at odds with railroad freight businesses; petroleum companies have a different perspective from solar companies. Business should not be thought of as monolithic. Powerful business groups may win more than they lose, but they do not own the government and are not guaranteed success.

Media exposure, public opinion, and the competing power of rival interest groups can also have their effect on state policies, especially on policies of sweeping public significance. More far-reaching public policy decisions involve more participants, and the general public is more likely to take an interest. Public officials become quite sensitive to public opinion when voters take an active interest in policy decisions—they must get reelected, after all. No amount of interest-group influence or campaign contributions can cause public officials to sacrifice their political futures to one group's special needs. The scope of a public policy determines who will control the decision-making process and shape the dynamics of power.

Interest Group Alliances and the Dynamics of Power

On issues that are narrow in scope, a single group may find itself unopposed. In the legislature, the interest group must persuade only a few key people, such as legislative committee chairs and presiding officers, to win a floor vote. Administrative agency decisions are even more likely to be controlled by a few interest groups because their decisions usually have a concentrated impact on a single occupation or business sector. For example, real estate brokers are very directly affected by the Real Estate Board's licensing requirements and are acutely active in trying to influence board decisions; the public is affected by the standards the board sets, but few are interested enough to become involved in the process.

Iron Triangles   On such narrow issues, alliances among interest groups, legislators, and bureaucrats can develop such a long-standing relationship held together by mutual self-interest that they act as a subsystem in the legislative and administrative decision-making process.[15] Called **iron triangles**, these alliances operate largely outside public view because they dominate a narrow range of routine decisions that are of marginal interest to the general public but are of critical importance to the interest groups and bureaucrats involved. The clientele group uses its resources, size, lobbying skills, and access to state officials to determine policy outcomes.

Iron triangles
Long-standing alliances among interest groups, legislators, and bureaucrats held together by mutual self-interest that act as subsystems in the legislative and administrative decision-making process.

For example, the oil interests have formed a close association with the Texas Railroad Commission, whose members their campaign contributions help elect. The agriculture industry forms a similar symbiotic relationship with the commissioner of agriculture and agriculture committees in the state legislature. Highway contractors form an alliance with the Texas Department of Transportation and interested legislators; privately owned utility companies work closely with the Public Utilities Commission. We will illustrate these alliances more extensively in Chapter 8 as we discuss the state's bureaucracy.

---

[15]Ernest Griffin, *The Impasse of Democracy* (New York: Harrison-Hilton Books, 1939), p. 182.

Issue Networks Iron triangles may dominate policies of a narrow scope, but broader public policy questions like taxes, education, campaign finance reform, health care, environmental protection, gun control, and abortion have the potential to activate wider ranging coalitions. Alliances among interest groups, career bureaucrats, academic researchers, think tanks, political bloggers, editors, neighborhood leaders, radio talk show hosts, and other community activists may form **issue networks**. These issue-network alliances are dynamic—different activists and interest groups organize around different public issues.[16] Such broad issue networks were activated in 2013 when the legislature established strict abortion clinic regulations that had the effect of limiting the availability of abortions. In fact, state Senator Wendy Davis had a national audience as she filibustered the new abortion restrictions.

Political Movements Issue networks have the potential to blossom into a larger **political movement**, a mass alliance of like-minded groups and individuals seeking broad changes in the direction of government policies. When the web of opinion leaders in issue networks taps into a large set of issues important to the masses of people, they may develop a large following with a fairly stable membership. One example is the tea party, which is not a party at all, but a successful political movement.

Beginning among a relatively small network of activists opposing the federal bailouts of the financial industry, the tea party movement gained strength with the passage of the stimulus bill (The American Recovery and Reinvestment Act of 2009) and finally evolved into a full-fledged antigovernment movement by the time health-care reform was passed (Affordable Care Act of 2010). A small alliance of interested groups had transformed into a mass national political movement. In Texas, the movement's support led to a strong Republican showing in the last three Texas elections, resulting in overwhelming Republican majorities in the Texas legislature and the adoption of policies popular with tea party and business groups.

Issue networks
Dynamic alliances among a wide range of individuals and groups activated by broad public policy questions.

Political movement
A mass alliance of like-minded groups and individuals seeking broad changes in the direction of government policies.

SIZING UP INTEREST GROUPS AND THEIR INFLUENCE

LO 6.4 Evaluate the role of interest groups in Texas politics and policy formulation.

Interest groups are formed by people who are exercising their fundamental constitutional rights in a free society. Both the national and Texas constitutions protect freedom of expression and freedom of association, and they specifically guarantee citizens the right to assemble to petition their government "for redress of grievances." The Texas Constitution (Article 1, Section 27) says that "citizens shall have the right…to…apply to those invested with the powers of government for redress of grievances or other purposes, by petition, address or remonstrance."

The First Amendment to the U.S. Constitution says, "Congress shall make no law…abridging the freedom of speech, or of the press; or the right of the people peaceably to assemble, and to petition government for redress of grievances." These constitutional provisions guarantee citizens the right to join together in political parties and interest groups. The rights to form political organizations, along with the right to vote, are essential to the very existence of a democracy.

---

[16]Hugh Heclo, "Issue Networks and the Executive Establishment," in *The New American Political System*, ed. Anthony King (Washington, DC: American Enterprise Institute, 1978), pp. 87–124.

The Positive Role of Interest Groups

Supporters believe that interest groups provide an essential linkage between members and public officials that makes it possible for the political system to function in a free society. They also believe that our pluralistic society, our governing structures, and our open society protect us from domination by a single narrow elite.

Representation and Mobilization

Interest groups provide members a vehicle to present their values and views in ways that elections cannot. Texas elections are held once every two years, but many interest groups operate continuously and offer their members the opportunity to influence day-to-day decision making. At best, elections offer voters the chance to set the general direction of government as they choose one candidate or party over the other, while interest groups develop specialized tactics to give members the chance to affect the details of policy making. Elections are held in geographical districts and statewide, but interest groups represent people according to their specialized occupational, cultural, and professional groupings, allowing them to articulate their members' unique perspectives on public policies.

Democracy calls for politically attentive and active citizens, but many voters are minimally informed, and they cast their ballots based on broad impressions created during political campaigns. Interest groups draw the most interested and informed citizens into the political processes, educate their members about issues, and mobilize them to participate in ways that advance their own interests. Interest groups report on the activities of government officials and sometimes keep vote tallies to report to their members on how legislators voted on key issues.

Interest groups inform and educate public officials; they provide policy makers valuable information both as they lobby individual government officials and as they testify before legislative committees. Because state law makes it a crime to knowingly share false information with state lawmakers,[17] most special-interest groups are careful to provide truthful, albeit often one-sided, information. Decision makers need to know how a proposed policy will affect various segments of society and how the affected groups feel about it. Interest groups enthusiastically provide this information to public officials free of cost to taxpayers.

Pluralist theory
The view that, in a free society, public policy should be made by a multitude of competing interest groups, ensuring that policies will not benefit a single elite at the expense of the many.

The Benefits of Pluralism

Those who subscribe to the **pluralist theory** take the view that, in a free society, public policy should be made by a multitude of competing interest groups, assuring that policies will not benefit a single elite at the expense of the many. Agricultural, energy, legal, banking, medical, religious, racial, ethnic, and educational interest groups are just a few organized interests in Texas, and all compete with one another for the attention and favor of decision makers. Matters involving large amounts of money or important changes in existing policy invite crowds. In such situations, for anything to happen, some compromise among competing interests must occur, resulting in a mix of values incorporated into the policy decision.

Interest groups' defenders argue that the structure of government is designed to make it hard for any group to dominate the state. The structure of government is characterized by

★ the separation of powers,
★ checks and balances,
★ elected officials responsible to different constituencies at the ballot box at different times,
★ appointed officials with fixed terms, and
★ career bureaucrats.

These structures make the political system difficult for any one interest to capture. The house and senate and the governor must agree to create law. The implementation of law is placed in the hands of elected and appointed executive officers and the unelected bureaucrats below them.

---

[17]Texas Government Code, 305.021.

The media, especially in the computer age, give citizens access to information never before possible and offer a political tool that invites inputs from underrepresented, new voices who otherwise lack the financial and other resources to have a serious impact on policy making. Furthermore, interest groups are limited because they operate in an environment where the general public is critical, if not cynical, of the political process.

Criticisms and Reforms

Critics are not so optimistic about the role of interest groups in the Texas political system. They believe that interest groups are very selective in mobilizing and informing citizens and that the resources of political influence are concentrated in the hands of a very few individuals. They believe that narrow interests are able to commandeer the machinery of government for their own self-interest, and in the process they employ tactics that taint the integrity of the political system itself.

Elitism and the Culture of Nonparticipation

Many Texans come from a traditionalistic political culture (see Chapter 1) that discourages political participation and defers to the power of governing elites. Many Texans are not members of any interest groups at all, and many of those who have joined groups are passive, inattentive members, who leave the leadership role to a few activists.

Wealth, political contacts, access to information, and well-managed lobby operations are controlled by a few powerful interest groups that often use these resources to dominate the political process. For example, Texas has no patients' rights association that has political power comparable to that of the Texas Medical Association; organized labor's power in Texas is trivial compared to that of employers' organizations like the Texas Association of Business. Consumer organizations do not rival the influence of numerous organizations of manufacturers and retailers in the state.

Some critics believe an **elitist theory** of interest groups describes Texas politics; they take the view that that the state is ruled by a small number of participants who exercise power to further their own self-interest. They contend that insurance companies, oil and gas companies, and certain utilities usually have their way with the state because they are able to pour enormous resources into campaign contributions or lobbying. They believe the average citizen cannot compete; highly organized and active groups can threaten the well-being of the unorganized majority.

Elitist theory

The view that the state is ruled by a small number of participants who exercise power to further their own self-interest.

Exploitation of Weak State Institutions

Skeptical of government, Texans have tried to limit and divide the power of state institutions. As a result, interest groups have been able to capitalize on numerous structural weaknesses, and they have been able to take advantage of numerous points of access to assert their influence.

For example, the state legislature meets in regular session only once every other year. Legislators cannot possibly keep up with what is happening in state government while they are not in session. They come to Austin in January of odd-numbered years, depending on full-time professional lobbyists to fill them in.

Texas legislators have limited staffs or other sources of independent information, and they must go to lobbyists for the facts. Interest groups are often the behind-the-scenes source of many bills legislators introduce. As an example, the conservative business think tank the American Legislative Exchange Council (ALEC) wrote the language for Texas voter ID law and has been active in developing gun-rights legislation. Lawmakers rely on interest groups like ALEC to write the bills they then claim as their own.

Executive agencies often lack independent data sources and, in effect, outsource a great deal of information gathering to the interests they regulate. The Texas Department of Insurance depends on the insurance industry to provide claims information necessary to write regulations and set rates. The Public Utilities Commission, the Texas Railroad Commission, the Texas Commission on Environmental Quality, and many other agencies heavily rely on data reported by the industries they regulate.

Reformers advocate strengthening legislative and executive institutions by providing them adequate resources and professional full-time staffs. Ideally, professional staffs should be competent, well-paid state employees hired based on merit and having sufficient job security to protect them against political interference. Reformers believe that only such professional staffs can provide decision makers with enough balanced and objective information to enable them to make policy in the public interest.

Besides limited staffing, low pay is also an institutional weakness that can be exploited. Paid below the poverty level, legislators must depend on outside sources of income to earn a living, making them vulnerable to the temptations of special-interest groups. Many lawmakers are attorneys who, as sitting legislators, have been known to represent special interests before state agencies and courts. Many work for clients who have interests in pending legislation, and no law requires legislators to recuse themselves even when they stand to benefit personally from legislation under consideration.

State representative Gary Elkins, himself a payday lender, took the floor to make a personal plea against saddling his industry with consumer protection legislation.[18] Senators Wendy Davis and Royce West have been paid for legal work for independent school districts that had interests before the legislature. Senator John Corona as CEO of the largest homeowners association management company in America, authored a major bill affecting homeowners associations.[19] Reformers argue for stricter ethics laws to prohibit apparent conflicts of interest such as these.

The Revolving Door

Revolving door
The interchange of employees between government agencies and the private businesses with which they have dealings.

The Revolving Door The public interest may be compromised by the interchange of employees between government agencies and the private businesses with which they have dealings—a peculiar practice referred to as the **revolving door**. For example, as ambitious legislators and executive officials retire and move on to other occupations, many become lobbyists for the very interest groups they once regulated. To be certain, few people would be better suited to serve as lobbyists than ex-lawmakers. Former legislators are intricately familiar with the legislative process, many are policy experts, and they often have friendships with lawmakers who are still in office. Interest groups also seek to hire retiring state agency officials as lobbyists because of their familiarity with the policy-making process, their policy expertise, and their connections inside state government.

Conflict of interest
A situation in which public officers stand to benefit personally from their official decisions.

The revolving door may create opportunities for retiring public officials, but it also creates the potential for **conflict of interest**, a situation in which public officers stand to benefit personally from their official decisions. Lawmakers and bureaucrats, planning their next career move, might be tempted make decisions that will benefit prospective employers.

For example, state representative Jamie Capelo co-authored a bill that capped medical liability lawsuits, and shortly after leaving office he became a lobbyist for the interest groups that benefited from his bill. After Texas Commission on Environmental Quality executive director Glenn Shankle overruled the agency's technical team and gave Waste Control Specialists permission to dump radioactive waste near Andrews, Texas, he became a lobbyist for the company. It is fairly common for interest groups to hire public officials as lobbyists after they have made policy decisions in their favor.

---

[18]Emily Ramshaw, "Legislators Can Carry Bills That Benefit Them," *Texas Tribune*, January 27, 2013, at www .texastribune.org/2013/01/27/personal-professional-lives-can-guide-lawmaking.

[19]Jay Root, "Abbott Proposes Far-Reaching Ethics Reform," *Texas Tribune*, November 14, 2013, at www .texastribune.org/2013/11/14/abbott-proposes-far-reaching-ethics-reform.

Critics wonder how many unscrupulous officials are using public service as a training school or as a steppingstone to a more lucrative career as a lobbyist. "People rightfully wonder when did they stop being a lawmaker and when did they start to become a special interest lobbyist," states Andrew Wheat.[20] Reformers advocate banning public officials from becoming lobbyists for at least a time after their retirement in order to reduce the potential for conflict of interest.

> **Did You Know?** Ex-legislative aid Andrea McWilliams and former legislator Stan Schlueter were the two highest paid lobbyists during the 2013 Texas legislative session, each having lobbying contracts worth between $2 million and $4 million.

Although 31 other states have some ban on legislators becoming lobbyists immediately after leaving office, Texas has no such restrictions.[21] The federal government and a number of states also require "cooling off" periods before bureaucrats leaving the executive branch can become lobbyists, but Texas does not.

Suspect Interest-Group Practices

Do campaign contributions buy sponsorship of bills and special favors? The public and the press think it does. Public officials and lobbyists say that it does not.[22] Anecdotal evidence that contributions buy public policy is mixed, but enough cases have been identified to leave the casual observer with the perception that conflicts of interest do arise. Former Governor Rick Perry, the speaker of the house, and members of both the Texas Senate and House have arranged for special benefits for their campaign contributors or clients.[23] It is common for the governor's campaign contributors to be appointed to public office, to be granted government contracts, or to benefit from executive decisions.

An example of such a case was brought to national attention during a Republican presidential debate in Tampa, Florida, when presidential candidate Michele Bachmann blasted fellow candidate Rick Perry for mandating a vaccine for cervical cancer for girls. The controversy began February 2, 2007, when former Governor Rick Perry issued an executive order to vaccinate preteen school girls against the sexually transmitted human papilloma virus, which causes cervical cancer in women. Expecting opposition from conservative groups that believe such a vaccine would give young girls tacit consent to have sex, Perry circumvented the Texas legislature by issuing an executive order.

The press discovered that Perry's chief of staff Diedre Delisi and other members of the governor's team had met for an "HPV Vaccine for Children Briefing" on the very same day that Merck and Company's political action committee contributed $5,000 to the Perry campaign.[24] Merck, the only manufacturer of the HPV vaccine

Rep. Sylvester Turner, center, is approached by lobbyists outside the Texas House of Representatives chamber.

What is the evidence that campaign contributions influence public policy making?

---

[20]Grissom, Brandi, "Ex-Lawmaker's Lobbying Looks Bad, Group Says," *El Paso Times*, May 21, 2009.

[21]National Conference on State Legislatures, *"Revolving Door" Prohibitions Against Legislators Lobbying State Government After They Leave Office*, December 2012, at www.ncsl.org/legislatures-elections/ethicshome/50-state-table-revolving-door-prohibitions.aspx.

[22]James Gibbons, "Officials Come and Go; the Lobby Rules," *Houston Chronicle*, January 27, 2003.

[23]Matt Stiles and Brian Thevenot, " Perry's Appointed Regents are Big Donors," *The Texas Tribune*, August 24, 2010, www.texastribune.org/texas-state-agencies/governors-office/perrys-appointed-regents-are-big-donors; Texans for Public Justice, "How Politicians Got Fat on a Risky Weight-Loss Stimulant," October 21, 2002, http://info.tpj.org/Lobby_Watch/ephedra.html; "Revolving-Door Lobbyist Adopts So-Craddick Method," November 22, 2002, http://info.tpj.org/Lobby_Watch/caprock.html; "Companies Paid Craddick a Big Income While Claiming His 1999 Energy Tax Cut," December 17, 2002, http://info.tpj.org/page_view.jsp?pageid=236&pf=1; Brandon Formby and Gromer Jeffers Jr., "Questions Raised About Rep. Linda Harper-Brown's Use of a Mercedes," *The Dallas Morning News*, June 18, 2010.

[24]Liz Austin Peterson, "Perry's Staff Discussed Vaccine on Day Merck Donated to Campaign," *Associated Press*, February 22, 2007.

Gardasil, happened to have employed as one of its chief lobbyists Mike Toomey, Rick Perry's former chief of staff and close confidant. The Texas legislature quickly passed a bill rescinding Perry's executive order.

Although the governor's office claims that the connection between the campaign contribution and the meeting held by his chief of staff was merely a coincidence, candidate Michele Bachmann reminded Americans, "We cannot forget that in the midst of this executive order, there was a big drug company that made millions of dollars because of this mandate."[25] Critics contend that the coincidence, at the very least, sheds light on the conflicts of interest that can occur when elected officials raise campaign contributions from special-interest groups that stand to benefit directly from those same officials' decisions.

Another practice that seems to be more than merely coincidental is the biennial ritual in Austin after each election when special-interest groups hold fund-raising events to honor selected legislators. State law forbids giving and accepting campaign contributions 30 days before the start of a legislative session and throughout the session, causing a rush of fund-raising activity in the five weeks after election day. Because these lobbyist fund-raising parties occur after the election, not before, they are not simply an effort to help elect candidates who support their group's cause—they have already been elected. The reason, as one lobbyist said, is to "pay the price of admission" or to obtain good access to legislators. These so-called **late-train contributions** are commonly given to the winning candidates in the executive branch as well. Losers are rarely the beneficiaries of such largess.

Late-train contributions

Campaign funds given to the winning candidate after the election up to 30 days before the legislature comes into session. Such contributions are designed to curry favor with winning candidates.

HOW DOES TEXAS COMPARE?
Corruption Risk among the 50 States

Using several broad measures to evaluate how well state regulations and procedures guard against the potential for corruption, the Center for Public Integrity found that Texas ranks 27th among the 50 states on its *Corruption Risk Report Card.* In the report assembled by The Center for Public Integrity, Public Radio International, and Global Integrity, Texas received a D+ for its performance on 14 different measures of risk for corruption. Although Texas receives good marks for internal audits, state pension fund management, and procurement, it receives failing marks for public access, executive accountability, state civil service management, the state insurance commission, and redistricting. It receives a D− for political financing and a D+ for legislative accountability.

In 1991, Texans voted in favor of creating the Texas Ethics Commission, which should have contributed to minimizing the risk of political corruption. The Texas

Texas Corruption Risk Report Card Categories and Grades			
Public Access to Information	F	Political Financing	D−
Executive Accountability	F	Legislative Accountability	D+
Judicial Accountability	C	State Budget Process	C
State Civil Service Management	F	Procurement	B−
Internal Auditing	A	Lobbying Disclosure	C−
State Pension Management	B−	Ethics Enforcement Agencies	C+
State Insurance Commission	F	Redistricting	F

Sources: The Center for Public Integrity, Public Radio International, and Global Integrity, 2011. *State Integrity Investigation: Keeping Government Honest,* www.stateintegrity. org/your_state; Caitlin Ginley, "Grading the Nation: How Accountable Is Your State?" *Center for Public Integrity,* March 19, 2012, www.iwatchnews.org/2012/03/19/8423/ grading-nation-how-accountable-your-state; Kelley Shannon, "Texas: The story Behind the Score," Center for Public Integrity, *State Integrity Investigation: Keeping Government Honest,* www.stateintegrity.org/Texas_story_subpage.

Ethics Commission, however, has been limited in what it can actually do. Its enforcement functions have mostly been limited to minor cases of failing to submit campaign contribution reports on time. Caitlin Ginley of the

---

[25]Michele Bachmann, CNN–Tea Party Republican Debate in Tampa, Florida, September 12, 2011. Transcripts available at www.nytimes.com/2011/09/13/us/politics/cnn-tea-party-republican-debate-in-tampa-fla. html?pagewanted=all.

Center for Public Integrity reports, "The Texas Ethics Commission is composed of members appointed by the governor and legislature, which not only presents an inherent conflict but often leads to gridlock. Commissioners are typically split along party lines, but in order to pursue an investigation, at least six of the eight commissioners must agree." The structure of the commission severely limits its ability to regulate ethical violations.

FOR DEBATE

 From what you have read, how would you reform campaign finance disclosure requirements and lobby reporting laws to encourage civic responsibility among interest groups? What are some practical ways to limit potential conflicts of interest among policy makers without violating freedom of speech for interest groups?

The Regulation of Lobbying

Fearing the influence of powerful organizations behind the scenes, reformers supported the creation of the Texas Ethics Commission with the power to enforce lobby and campaign finance reporting laws. Reformers believed that reporting requirements respect basic rights to freedom of expression while requiring that lobbyists' efforts be made public. The rationale for these laws is that the public should at least know who backs which policies and who stands to gain from them.

Lobbyist Reports Lobbyists for private interest groups, with few exceptions, must file reports with the Ethics Commission if they are paid $1,000 salary per calendar year or if they spend more than $500 per quarter to communicate directly with any members of the legislative or executive branch to influence legislation or administrative action. Lobbyists must report:

★ their actual clients,
★ the general areas of their policy concerns,
★ the range within which their compensation falls,
★ their expenditures for advertisements, mass mailings, and other communications designed to support or oppose legislation or administrative actions, and
★ their expenditures on members of the state legislature in excess of $50 a day on food, drink, transportation, lodging, or gifts, which must be reported by name, date, place, and purpose.[26]

Campaign contributions are reported as we described in Chapter 4, but they are not classified as lobbying expenses.

Evaluating Reporting Requirements Critics of the lobby reporting law maintain that some provisions leave the public ill-informed because lobbyists' compensation and expenditures are reported in broad categories rather than in specific amounts. In 2013, according to reports, AT&T, paid 108 lobbyists between $3 million and $8 million, but the public is left to guess the exact amount.[27]

Reporting which policy a lobbyist seeks to influence similarly requires only checking the appropriate box on a form. For example, AT&T lobbyists may report contacting public officials about "communications." Reformers charge that these requirements provide very little information that the public can use. To be meaningful, lobby reports would need to list the specific bill numbers on which lobbyists worked or the agency rule-making hearings at which they testified.

---

[26]Texas Ethics Commission Rules, "Chapter 34: Regulation of Lobbyists," www.ethics.state.tx.us/legal/ch34.html#subB.
[27]Texans for Public Justice, "Texas' Top Lobbyists: Special Interests Paid Lobbyists up to $328 Million in 2013 Session," at http://info.tpj.org/reports/Top%20Lobbyists%202013.pdf.

Although critics fault the Texas Ethics Commission for not vigorously enforcing reporting requirements except in high-profile cases, it serves as a comprehensive repository of campaign financial statements, lists of registered lobbyists, campaign contributions, and campaign expenditures. One critic admitted the Texas Ethics Commission is "a pretty darn good library" even if "it's not a good cop."[28]

The members of the Texas legislature are provided a list of registered lobbyists and their clients by February 1 of each legislative session, and the public may obtain copies of registration and activity reports from the Ethics Commission website. By tabulating and publicizing these reports, organizations like Texans for Public Justice, the National Institute on Money in State Politics, and the Center for Public Integrity promote transparency in government and help keep the public informed about interest-group influence in Texas.

APPLYING WHAT YOU HAVE LEARNED ABOUT INTEREST GROUPS

LO 6.5   Apply what you have learned about interest groups.

The following essay will give you the opportunity to examine one of Texas's most important political groups and to identify the major characteristics of interest groups among various tea party organizations. Because tea party groups have attracted such a mass following of like-minded individuals seeking broad changes in the direction of government policies, they can be thought of as a political movement. Many commentators have even come to think of tea party groups as a faction within the Republican Party, although many actual tea party sympathizers prefer to describe themselves as loose associations of independent-minded citizens who are not affiliated with any party.

After you have read the essay, you will be asked a series of questions that will require you to employ critical-thinking skills to apply what you have learned in this chapter to the new information in this essay. Your analysis will require you to identify important elements of interest groups, their policy goals, their strategies, and the targets of their political activities. You will be asked to reflect on the role of political interest groups in the Texas political system.

The Tea Party: Civic Activism and Grassroots Change

by Blayne Primozich
El Paso Community College

The tea party has been difficult to define, and in many cases, it represents different things depending on where you look. According to a 2013 Pew Research Center poll, as many as 41 percent of tea party supporters see themselves as part of the Republican Party, although most see themselves as a separate movement.[29] In truth, the tea party represents a political movement that brought together supporters from the Republican Party, activists from

---

[28]Kelley Shannon quoting Craig McDonald, Executive Director of Texans for Public Justice, in "Texas: The Story Behind the Score," *State Integrity Investigation*, www.stateintegrity.org/texas_story_subpage.
[29]"Tea Party's Image Turns More Negative: Ted Cruz's Popularity Soars Among Tea Party Republicans," *Pew Research Center for the People & the Press*, October 16, 2013, www.people-press.org/2013/10/16/tea-partys-image-turns-more-negative.

independent local tea party groups, and traditional conservative organizations, such as Americans for Prosperity, Americans for Tax Reform, the Cato Institute, and the Family Research Council. Critics argue that the movement was astroturfed, essentially created and funded by national-level conservative strategists and donors. National tea party organizations like FreedomWorks and the Tea Party Express generated protests across the country in 2009 and 2010, trying to give the impression of mass grassroots appeal, sometimes busing in their supporters to attend local town hall meetings. Events such as the 2009 tax day protest at the Alamo were all diligently promoted and covered by FOX News, which even sent host Glenn Beck to San Antonio.

Tea party activists insist it is a true local grassroots movement based on civic activism. FreedomWorks chair Dick Armey points to Saul Alinsky's *Rules for Radicals* as the model upon which the tea party is based.[30] Alinsky created the Industrial Areas Foundation in Chicago, launching generations of community organizers, of which President Obama is one. In Texas, Ernesto Cortez followed this model to create the Communities Organized for Public Service program in San Antonio and helped organize residents of border communities from Brownsville to El Paso, mobilizing new voters and engaging residents with their local governments. From this viewpoint, the tea party is a collection of thousands of locally organized activists who often join efforts with each other or one or more of such state and national umbrella organizations like FreedomWorks, Tea Party Express, Tea Party Nation, and the Tea Party Patriots.

The Tea Party Message Unifying national and local tea party organizations are the principles of fiscal responsibility, constitutionally limited federal government, and free market economics. The goals are to reduce federal spending, eliminate federal debt, end federal mandates on the states, and remove most federal regulations on business. These principles are long established among small government and economic conservatives dating back to Republican Arizona Senator Barry Goldwater and President Ronald Reagan in the 1970s and 1980s.

To keep tea party groups focused on message, the tea party networks host a variety of educational and training programs. The National Center for Constitutional Studies and Hillsdale College offer constitution courses presented from the framer's viewpoint. The Texas Patriots PAC offered a children's vacation constitution school. New Revolutions Now offers a church accountability film series, stressing religion as the foundation for our individual rights and the constitution. FreedomWorks and the Tea Party Patriots provide training kits, videos, and response teams to help local organizations conduct protests, arrange for public speakers, and host candidate forums.

State and local tea parties go beyond the core issues, including discussions as varied as the groups themselves, and reminding us that no one speaks for all tea parties. From 2012 to 2014, The Conservative Texas PAC hosted faith and family days, the last one featuring [former] Governor Rick Perry. Tea Party Nation supported Second Amendment rights. New Revolution Now opposed abortion. Texas Patriots PAC promoted the new high school core curriculum and STAARS testing. The Kingwood Tea Party opposed a bond for the Lone Star Community College. Other popular topics included voter ID laws, immigration, and opposition to toll roads.

---

[30]Dick Armey and Matt Kibbe, *Give Us Liberty: A Tea Party Manifesto* (New York: William Morrow, 2010). For a thorough look at the tea party's grassroots elements, see Theda Skocpol and Vanessa Williams, *The Tea Party and the Remaking of Republican Conservatism* (New York: Oxford University Press, Inc., 2012).

No Squishy Republicans Tea parties want their members to hold elected officials accountable and vote only for candidates who reflect their values. Contact lists for elected officials are commonly found on their websites, as are representatives' voting records and legislative scorecards. The Grassroots Texans Network distributed a 2014 voter guide ranking members of the Texas House according to votes on 16 issues. Accordingly, a true tea party conservative would have voted against banning anonymous campaign donations, opposed use of the state's rainy day fund, prevented state officials from enforcing federal firearms laws, and voted against Medicaid expansion. The Young Conservatives of Texas published similar rankings of the 83rd Texas Legislature, providing a separate RINOs (Republicans in name only) list of those who scored below 55 out of 100 points. In contrast, no Democrat scored above 41. The RINOs, sometimes called squishy Republicans, are attacked for not having solid conservative voting records and frequently become targets for tea party-backed candidates.

Electioneering As many as 40 percent of Republican voters identify with the tea party, and while tea party supporters vote overwhelmingly Republican, many claim to be political independents, favoring conservative ideological allegiance over party loyalties. On average, they are much more educated than other Republican voters, show higher levels of political interest and knowledge, and are much more likely to vote, especially in primary elections.[31] Such dedicated voters have had a big impact on Texas elections, especially considering that in 2010, Texas ranked last in the nation in voter turnout.

Ted Cruz's victory over [former] Lieutenant Governor David Dewhurst in the 2010 U.S. Senate race showed how backing by tea party groups could propel a little-known candidate into the spotlight. Ted Cruz gained financial support and advertising from tea party-backed political action committees like Conservative Texans PAC (CTxPAC) and the Texas Patriots PAC, giving him a victory in the Republican primaries. In 2012, CTxPAC put out a list of ten vulnerable (squishy) Republicans and boasted beating two of them in the primaries, propelling Donna Campbell and Matt Krause into the Texas legislature.

Conservative Texas PAC organized a 2014 Texas tour of tea party candidate forums, joining hundreds of other tea party candidate forums and debates for local and state offices in cities across Texas. To reach wider audiences, videos of many of these debates were posted on tea party websites or on YouTube. At the local level, armies of volunteers go door to door to mobilize voters and build support for tea party candidates. The NE Tarrant Tea Party is one of the most active, organizing block-walks for candidates each month. Most groups use their websites, Facebook, Meet-Up, or other social media to coordinate efforts.

Endorsements, however, have been a controversial topic among tea parties. Some candidates advertise themselves as tea party candidates or refer to themselves as "tea party approved," sometimes even running against each other in the primaries, but unlike a political party, there is no official organization nominating tea party candidates. Instead, organizations like the Texas Patriots PAC and the Central Texas Constitution Alliance will provide lists of endorsements. Others, like the NE Tarrant Tea Party, put out lists of candidates the group's leadership likes, although these lists often do not match. Still others, most notably the Dallas Tea Party, refuse to put out any endorsements, arguing it is every voter's right and responsibility to decide how to vote.

---

[31]Pew Research Center, "Tea Party's Image Turns More Negative: Ted Cruz's Popularity Soars Among Tea Party Republicans" at www.people-press.org/2013/10/16/tea-partys-image-turns-more-negative.

The Legislative Agenda Electoral victories have led to growth in the Texas legislature's Tea Party Caucus, founded by then-Senator Dan Patrick, whose members work to uphold the Texas Conservative Coalition's "Pledge With Texas," promising to cut taxes, balance the budget, limit federal intrusion, improve election integrity, and secure the border. An earlier sign of tea party influence was [former] Governor Rick Perry's 2009 support of HCR 50 and S.C.R. 14, the legislature's joint resolutions on Texas sovereignty under the Tenth Amendment. Following the argument that Texans know best how to govern Texas, Perry's administration filed lawsuits against the federal Environmental Protection Agency, arguing that federal air quality restrictions infringed upon the Texas Commission on Environmental Quality's powers.

The Texas Conservative Coalition's review of the 83rd legislative session heralded numerous tea party victories, including new school standardized testing rules, a revamping of the high school curriculum, dropping the Algebra II requirement for students, bills targeting human trafficking, new fines for businesses hiring illegal immigrants, new felony charges for individuals who forge identification documents, and budget reductions.[32] On top of that, the legislature refused to expand Medicaid coverage under the federal Affordable Care Act. Goals for upcoming legislative sessions include reducing transportation spending without new bond debt or the use of toll roads and opposition to in-state tuition for children of families who illegally entered the country.

Texas tea parties have joined a national "Article V" effort, hoping the Texas legislature will join other states in petitioning for a convention to amend the U.S. Constitution. Proposals include repeal of the Sixteenth and Seventeenth Amendments, removing the income tax and direct election of senators, respectively. Other amendments would mandate balanced budgets, create term limits for members of Congress and the Supreme Court, and repeal most of the Fourteenth Amendment, targeting the definition of citizenship and the equal protection clause. Supporters contend this would restore the framers' view of republican government.

Two Views of Democracy One contradiction is overlooked within the tea party movement. On the one hand, there is an appeal to popular democracy: local activists mobilize supporters to keep elected officials true to the people's demands. On the other hand, there are frequent references to restoring a republican form of government envisioned by the framers, using representatives to filter the people's demands. This is evidenced by actions to end the direct election of senators. Interestingly, Texas high school textbooks have replaced democracy with the term republic.

Two quotes taken from tea party websites illustrate this point. The Texas Tea Party Republican Women website states that "(t)he danger to America is not Barack Obama, but a citizenry capable of entrusting a man like him with the presidency," and it will be hard to "restore the common sense and good judgment to a depraved electorate willing to have such a man as their president."[33] In contrast, an April 1, 2011, entry to the Dallas Tea Party blog explained that the group no longer could stay neutral by refusing to issue endorsements, especially given the gravity of the 2012 elections. The election was too important to leave in the hands of the voters. Of course, the entry ended with "April Fools!"[34]

---

[32]"Accomplishments: 83rd Legislature Summary" *Texas Conservative Coalition*, July 29, 2013, www.txcc.org/files/83rd%20Legislature%20Accomplishments_2.pdf.

[33]"Join TTPRW," *Texas Tea Party Republican Women*, March 11, 2014, http://texasteapartyrw.com/Join_TTPRW.html.

[34]"Dallas Tea Party Issues Endorsement for President of the United States. Update: April Fool's," *Dallas Tea Party*, March 31,2011, http://dallasteaparty.org/page/15.

JOIN THE DEBATE

 Engage in some self-reflection and identify those issues on which you agree or disagree with the tea party movement. If you were going to become a local or state activist and organize a group, what would be the goals of your organization?

 The tea party movement has used a variety of strategies to seek changes in government policies. Identify those strategies and describe how they are similar to other interest groups and how they differ. Explain why tea party groups and other groups with sweeping political goals would choose electioneering and grassroots strategies rather than lobbying as a way to influence government policies. How do interest groups' goals determine their strategies and targets?

 What is your vision of democracy? Evaluate the role that interest groups play in democracy. How do interest group activities benefit the operations of a democratic system? How do they endanger it?

CHAPTER SUMMARY

LO 6.1 Define *interest groups* and identify their major types. Interest groups are organizations of private citizens exercising their constitutional right to organize in an attempt to influence public policy. Economic interest groups seek to influence public policies that affect their pocketbooks, while noneconomic interest groups strive to realize their religious, political, or personal values. Some groups, like civil rights groups, work for the ideal of equality and financial self-interest as well.

LO 6.2 Describe how interest groups influence public policies in Texas. Interest groups adjust their strategies to maximize their potential influence on each major type of policy maker in Texas government. Their major tactics include the craft of lobbying, making campaign contributions, organizing public relations campaigns, and filing suit in the courts.

Interest groups have refined lobbying to a fine craft as they try to sway members of the legislative and executive branches to their policy positions. Like salespersons for their groups' ideas, lobbyists socialize with decision makers to build personal relationships, making them receptive to emotional appeals, to ideological appeals, and to persuasive information. Lobbyists conduct research and draft proposed bills for the legislative branch even as they monitor and shape the rule-making process in the executive branch.

Interest groups have also developed electioneering and public relations into a fine art. Campaign contributions give lobbyists access to elected officeholders, and organizing public demonstrations, letter-writing campaigns, and advertizing campaigns can help create a political environment that makes public officials receptive to interest groups' appeals.

LO 6.3 Analyze the political balance of power among interest groups in Texas. Business interest groups such as the Texas Association of Business, the energy and natural resources industries, utilities, and health-related businesses are dominant

in Texas. Socially conservative groups closely aligned with the state's Republicans have considerable influence as well.

Iron triangles dominate narrow public policy decisions, but, once in a while, public policy battles over broad issues like taxation, abortion, education, or the environment involve broader interest-group alliances as more interest groups and individuals become active on a wider political battlefield.

LO 6.4 Evaluate the role of interest groups in Texas politics and policy formulation. The constitutions of the United States and Texas promote political expression and the right to organize to petition public officials. These rights recognize that representatives can represent their constituents' wishes only when citizens are able to communicate their policy positions effectively.

Interest groups play a positive role in the political system as they mobilize citizens and present their policy viewpoints to public officials. In a diverse, pluralistic state like Texas, no single group is able to dominate completely in a state that has divided and dispersed its institutional powers.

Critics charge that too few Texans have joined any interest groups, and, because effective use of interest-group tools requires money, the most powerful interest groups are those that represent narrow elites. Interest groups create conflicts of interest by opening the revolving door, tempting officials with campaign contributions, and exploiting weak state institutions.

Public interest groups and the media publicize reports on interest-group activity, but lobby reports to the Texas Ethics Commission do not reveal the specific policies on which lobbyists work or the implied understandings that come with campaign contributions.

LO 6.5 Apply what you have learned about interest groups. You looked at tea party groups as a practical example of interest groups in Texas. You examined their policy goals, strategies, and tactics, and evaluated the role of interest groups in the Texas political system.

KEY TERMS

access, *p. 147*
astroturf lobbying, *p. 148*
clientele groups, *p. 145*
conflict of interest, *p. 154*
co-optation, *p. 145*

discretion, *p. 144*
elitist theory, *p. 153*
implementation, *p. 144*
interest group, *p. 139*
iron triangles, *p. 150*

issue networks, *p. 151*
late-train contributions, *p. 156*
lobbying, *p. 141*
pluralist theory, *p. 152*

political movement, *p. 151*
revolving door, *p. 154*
Texas Register, *p. 144*
umbrella organization, *p. 149*

REVIEW QUESTIONS

LO 6.1 Define *interest groups* and identify their major types.

- What are interest groups? What do they do?

- What are the major types of interest groups? Identify an interest group in each subcategory.

LO 6.2 Describe how interest groups influence public policies in Texas.

- How do interest groups use different approaches to influence each of the three branches of government?

- Do campaign contributions affect public policy making in Texas? How?

- What is lobbying? What does a lobbyist do? What techniques do lobbyists use to influence state officials?

LO 6.3 Analyze the political balance of power among interest groups in Texas.

- Which interests are the most powerful in Texas? Why?

- How does the scope of a proposed policy affect the number of interests that attempt to bring their influence to bear in the decision-making process?

LO 6.4 Evaluate the role of interest groups in Texas politics and policy formulation.

- How is interest-group formation a constitutional right? What positive services do they perform for the politicalsystem?

- What are the criticisms of interest groups? Define *conflicts of interest*. Describe regulations that would minimize them.

- Describe the differences between elitist and pluralist theories. Which theory best describes Texas politics? Why?

GET ACTIVE

- **Find out who is lobbying state government.** Go to the Texas Ethics Commission's website at **www.ethics.state .tx.us** to discover which people, corporations, labor unions, and nonprofit organizations are lobbying Texas state government. Use this site to sample interest-group reports about lobbying and campaign contributions.

- **Learn how to lobby** at the Texas State Teachers Association website at **www.tsta.org/issues-action**. Click on "Guide to Lobbying" under Take Action at the State Level!

- **Find out who spent the most money lobbying** Texas decision makers at **http://info.tpj.org/reports/Top%20 Lobbyists%202013.pdf**.

  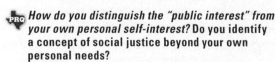 *Identify the state or local interest group related to your career*, professional ambitions, or personal interests. Search at least one of each of the following types of organizations: A major corporation, a labor union, a professional

organization, a nonprofit organization, and a public interest group. From the groups' websites, make a list of the public policy issues each is promoting and write a paragraph explaining why the groups take these positions. Briefly describe the organizations' dues, membership, and type and frequency of any publications.

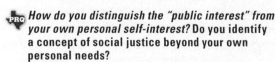 *How do you distinguish the "public interest" from your own personal self-interest?* Do you identify a concept of social justice beyond your own personal needs?

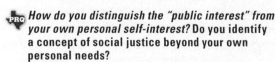 *Create a list of at least ten potential conflicts of interest* using the analyses from *Texas Tribune*'s ethics explorer at *www.texastribune. org/bidness/explore*. Explain why each of your examples represents an ethical conflict.

CHAPTER 7

The Legislature

John B. Mueller Photography/Moment/Getty Images

LEARNING OBJECTIVES

LO 7.1 Describe the limits on the Texas legislature and evaluate the concept of the "citizen legislature."

LO 7.2 Analyze the selection of Texas legislators, their qualifications, elections, and the impact of redistricting.

LO 7.3 Analyze the organization of the Texas legislature, including the powers of the presiding officers and the committee structure.

LO 7.4 Analyze the legislative process and how a bill becomes a law.

LO 7.5 Describe the legislature's institutional tools of leadership.

LO 7.6 Apply what you have learned about the Texas legislature.

*T*he legislative branch is responsible for making law. It is through law that the state makes public policy and basically determines what the state agencies will do. The legislative function is to determine what is a crime, to establish the basis for a civil suit, to establish what services the state will provide, and to provide the funding to carry out the state's priorities.

In Texas, the legislature is bicameral—it consists of two houses, the 31-member Texas Senate and the 150-member Texas House of Representatives. On most matters, the two houses share equal powers and both of them must agree on a proposed bill for it to become law. The senate does have the special power to confirm or approve the governor's appointments of state officers. By establishing a bicameral legislature, framers of the Texas Constitution followed the pattern set for the national Congress and used in every state other than Nebraska, which has a unicameral, or one-house, legislature.

The chief argument for the use of bicameral legislative bodies is that one house can serve as a check on the other so that legislation will not be passed hastily without adequate reflection, and both chambers must consider every bill before it becomes a law. Bicameralism can also slow the lawmaking process down, or can keep laws from passing through one chamber while passing in the other.

Texas has a "citizen legislature," with members who do not hold a full-time professionally paid position. The Texas legislature is a highly centralized institution dominated by its presiding officers—the lieutenant governor in the Texas Senate and the speaker in the Texas House of Representatives, who use standing committees and a variety of other committees to control the lawmaking process in the state.

The Texas House and Senate meet in separate wings of the Capitol building in Austin.

What are the advantages and disadvantages of a bicameral (two-house) legislature?

THE LIMITED LEGISLATURE

LO 7.1 Describe the limits on the Texas legislature and evaluate the concept of the "citizen legislature."

The Texas legislature has often been referred to as a "citizen legislature," which meets for only 140 days every other year and receives only a small income for the work they do. It has been said that the Texas legislature is "full-time only part of the time." The limited sessions, heavy workloads, low salaries, and limited staffing keep the legislature in this "citizen" status. The "informal" qualifications to become a Texas legislator far outweigh the formal requirements. On the surface, it would seem that to become a senator or representative in the state would be relatively easy; however, the informal qualities that a prospective legislator must possess usually determine their ability to be elected to the state legislature. These qualities include party affiliation, demographic identity, occupation, educational level, and economic status.

The Legislative Terms and Sessions

Texas senators are elected for four-year staggered terms and representatives for two-year terms. That means that the entire house and half the senate are elected every two years. All senators are elected in the first election following redistricting (every ten years). At the beginning of the session, the senators draw lots to determine which senators will serve a two-year term. One-half of the senators must run for reelection again in two years, whereas the other half of the senators will not face another reelection campaign for four years. All senators will then serve four-year terms until the next general election.

Although Texas senators tend to serve longer than their representative counterparts, low salaries, short sessions, heavy workloads, and inadequate staff and clerical assistance all diminish the Texas legislators' effectiveness. Texas legislators do not have limits on the number of terms they may serve, but legally mandated restrictions on the number of times that a politician can be reelected to an office or the number of years that a person may hold a particular office, or **term limits**, are quite popular. It reflects an increasing frustration with government, especially the legislative branch, which seems to be more responsive to organized special interests than the residents and businesses located within the home district of the elected official. A legislator's **constituency**, or those residents of the state that are directly affected by a legislator's lawmaking choices, may also feel alienated by the influence of special interests.

Most supporters of term limits assume that electing new legislators could and should disrupt long-established working relationships between legislators and interest groups. A downside to term limits, however, would be that the new legislators would be immediate "lame ducks," or without power, with their ability to run for reelection limited, making them even more vulnerable to influence from expert lobbyists and career bureaucrats.

Contributing to the "citizen" status of the legislature is when and how long its sessions are held. The Texas legislature begins its session on the second Tuesday in January in odd-numbered years for a one hundred forty–day period. Forty-five states have annual legislative sessions; Texas is the only state legislature in the ten most populous states to meet on a biennial schedule. The limited *biennial sessions* tend to work against professional and deliberative legislative practice and ultimately may work against the public interest. Texas legislators cannot possibly acquaint themselves in only one hundred forty days with the immense volume of proposed legislation presented to them, which usually amounts to thousands of proposed bills and resolutions. And, because most of the legislative work must be performed during the regular session, time becomes critical; most pieces of legislation are never considered.

Aside from passing new law and representing their constituents, legislators must adopt the state budget, which will be used for the next two years. They may also propose amendments, initiating changes to the state's very frequently amended constitution. The legislature exercises **bureaucratic oversight**, reviewing state bureaucratic agencies and closing them down (called "sunsetting") if they are no longer viable for the state. They are also responsible for disciplining themselves in legislative redress if a member needs to be censored or removed from office. This is a rare occurrence but can happen if the infraction is severe enough to damage the effectiveness of the chamber or of the elected person.

When work cannot be accomplished or a bill favorable to the governor did not pass during a regular session, a 30-day **special session**, which can be called only by the governor, may take place after a regular session. Special sessions, by their very nature of interrupting the normal schedules of the "citizen legislators" lives, and costing an estimated $1.2 million every time one is called, are not very popular with either the legislators or by the general public. The governor sets the agenda for the special session; however, it does not stop the legislators from introducing new bills during the short, thirty-day session. Once the item, or items, on the agenda have been decided upon, or the 30 days come to a close, the session is complete. If the desired outcome was not reached during the session, some governors, like former Governor Rick Perry in 2013, have called two sequential sessions to begin the very next day, the last one adjourning on August 5, 2013.

Term limits
Legally mandated restrictions on the number of times that a politician can be reelected to an office or the number of years that a person may hold a particular office.

Constituency
Those residents of the state who are directly affected by the lawmaking choices of a particular elected official; usually residents and businesses in the home district of the elected official.

Bureaucratic oversight
The legislative function of reviewing state bureaucratic agencies and closing them down (called "sunsetting") if they are no longer viable for the state.

Special session
A 30-day session of the legislature that can only be called by the governor, which takes place after a regular session to complete work or to consider the agenda set by the governor.

Although the governor is empowered to call special sessions, the house and senate can call an "impeachment session" for the sole purpose of deciding the impeachment and removal of state officers from their position. Texas has impeached and removed one governor from office—Jim Ferguson. After impeachment in the house, the senate may remove an official by a two-thirds vote

In 1993, the house adopted new rules to deal with the end-of-session legislative crunch. During the last seventeen days, the house may consider only bills that originated in the senate or that received previous house approval. The new rules also gave house members 24 hours to study major legislation before floor action. These reforms diminished the volume of last-minute legislation and gave legislators time to become better acquainted with bills.

A **resolution** is a formal recognition by the state legislature to provide support or non-support of events, people or law changes in the state, or a way for the legislative body to make an agreement to support or not support upcoming changes in federal law or laws adopted by other states. Resolutions by legislators to congratulate a distinguished constituent, a winning sports team, or a scout troop for some success or other are common. Legislators usually pay little attention to this legislation, but it is important to the honorees. Each house may pass its own resolutions or the entire legislature may pass joint resolutions. Demonstrating the lack of legislative scrutiny, one such resolution was passed unanimously by the Texas House on April Fools' Day 1971—a congratulatory recognition of Albert De Salvo for his "noted activities and unconventional techniques involving population control and applied psychology." The house later withdrew this recognition when it discovered that De Salvo was in fact the "Boston Strangler," an infamous serial murderer.

Resolution
A formal recognition by the state legislature to provide support or non-support of events, people or law changes, or a way for the legislative body to make an agreement to support or not support upcoming changes in federal law or laws adopted by other states.

Legislative Salaries and Compensation

Legislators receive an annual salary of $7,200 plus $150 **per diem**, an amount paid for each day a legislator is working, during both regular and special sessions and during the interim when committees meet. They also have a travel allowance on a reimbursement basis when the legislature is in session. The Texas Ethics Commission is constitutionally empowered to establish the per diem allowance, which is increased regularly, but voters must approve any salary increase. Texas lawmakers are among the worst paid large-state legislators in the country and have not received a salary increase since 1975, but they have found ways to offset their living expenses through very lax rules governing how a legislator earns money while in elected office.

Per diem
The amount paid each day that a legislator is working, both in regular and special sessions, and when committees meet during the interim between sessions.

Legislators who are lawyers can accept **retainer fees** from a variety of clients, which may also include those who do business with state agencies or may have lawsuits against state agencies. Lawyers and non-lawyers alike can receive **consulting fees** from business clients and can act for their clients based on information that they gain from lobbyists and other information that they gain from their own specialized knowledge of pending legislation, thereby helping clients benefit from legislation currently active in the legislature.

Some reformers believe that legislators' pay should be increased to a professional-level salary and their income from sources outside their government paycheck strictly limited. In the current system, the potential for conflict between the public interest and the interests of lawmakers' private businesses or their employers can be construed to be unethical for an unbiased lawmaker to have access to. And, although higher pay would not guarantee honest legislators, it would enable the conscientious ones to perform their legislative duties without turning to sources of outside income that compromise their ability to represent the constituents who elected them.

Retainer fees
Fees charged by lawyer–legislators for services to clients, including those who have business with state agencies or may have lawsuits against state agencies.

Consulting fees
Fees charged by legislators who may contract with business clients to consult on matters pending in the legislature, thereby helping clients to benefit from legislation currently active in the legislature.

HOW DOES TEXAS COMPARE?
Limits on Legislative Terms, Salaries, and Sessions

Terms Like thirty-four other states, Texas does not limit the number of terms legislators may serve. Voters are left to decide whether to retain experienced incumbents or replace them with fresh legislators.

Salaries Figure 7.1 shows that the Texas Constitution is much more restrictive than most states with respect to legislative salaries and sessions. Although New Hampshire pays its legislators only $200, no other populous state sets legislative pay as low as Texas. Most larger states pay their legislators in the salary range of middle-class employees, and many allow legislators to set their own salary by statute.

Sessions Most states provide annual regular legislative sessions and fourteen states place no limit on their length. Texas is among only five states with biennial legislative sessions. Unlike most legislatures, the Texas legislature may not call itself into special session or determine agendas. Low salaries and limited sessions make it difficult for the Texas legislature to function as a professional institution and may make members more dependent on interest groups for income and research on public policy. Recent research indicates that more-professional legislatures—those with higher salaries, longer sessions, and better staffs—are significantly more responsive to public opinion and enact policies that are more congruent with public preferences.[1]

FOR DEBATE

 Should Texas limit the number of terms legislators serve? Or, would term limits also restrict legislators' experience and, therefore, make them more vulnerable to the influence of lobbyists?

 Should Texas consider increasing legislative salaries and the length of their sessions? Or would doing this give legislators too much power?

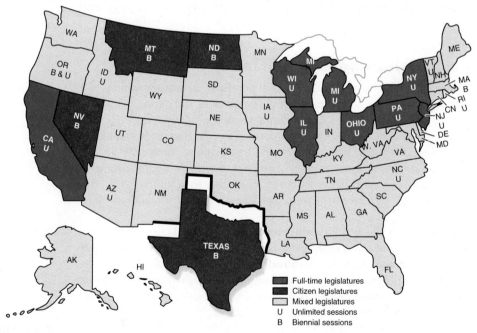

Figure 7.1
Full-Time and "Citizen" Legislature

Note that most large states have full-time legislatures with unlimited annual sessions and yearly salaries over $40,000. In contrast, Texas is among the states that have a "citizen" legislature with limited, biennial sessions and salaries set below $10,000. Many state legislatures have elements of both types.

Based on data from *The Book of the States, 2013* (Lexington, KY: Council of State Governments, 2014), Tables 3.2 and 3.9.

---

[1]Jeffrey R. Lax and Justin H. Phillips, "The Democratic Deficit," Unpublished paper, Midwestern Political Science Association meeting, 2010.

Legislative Staff

The legislature provides only minimal funds for hiring competent staff. Monthly staff allotments are $13,250 for house members and $38,000 for senators; they are also reimbursed for other "reasonable and necessary" office expenses.[2] Texas spends less than 0.3 percent of total state expenditures on legislative staff salaries, services, and other office accommodations for legislators.

Usually, senators and representatives maintain their staff in Austin as well as staff in their home districts. These allotments must pay for staff, equipment, and supplies for both offices as well as rent and utilities for their home district office. House members have about three or four staff people; in the senate, the average staff size is slightly more than seven. Some senators have as many as fourteen staff members, while others have as few as four.

Powerful special interests and administrative agencies have a distinct advantage when it comes to staffing. The need for research data, advice, expertise, and other services gained from interest groups and administrative agencies makes legislators dependent on these groups for staff, information, and advice.[3]

To counteract the dominance of the special interests' informational influence, both legislative houses have established nonpartisan institutions to provide information to legislators. Created by a former house speaker, the House Research Organization provides bill analyses, floor reports, issue focus reports, and interim news to legislators and the public.[4]

The Senate Research Center provides research and bill analysis to the Texas Senate and the lieutenant governor's office. The center's staff also attend meetings and conferences of other governmental entities and report to the senators on their content. This kind of help to the legislative staff relieves the dependence on special interests and administrative agencies.

ELECTING LEGISLATORS

LO 7.2   Analyze the selection of Texas legislators, their qualifications, elections, and the impact of redistricting.

Certain legal, or formal, qualifications must be met before anyone can serve in the state legislature. However, the "informal" qualifications usually limit who will run for the legislature.

To be a Texas state senator, an individual must be a U.S. citizen, a qualified voter, at least twenty-six years of age, and have lived in the state for the previous five years and in the district for one year prior to election. Qualifications for house membership are even more easily met. A candidate must be a U.S. citizen, a qualified voter of the state, at least twenty-one years of age, and have lived in Texas for the two previous years and in the district for one year prior to being elected.

The most important requirements for holding legislative office in Texas are not the legal limitations but the informal ones. Party affiliation, demographic identification, occupation, education, and economic criteria usually not only determine who is elected to the state legislature but also to offices at all levels of government—national, state, county, city, and special district.

Party Party affiliation in Texas often determines whether a candidate will win an election or not. Until the 1990s, the Democratic Party was the dominant party in Texas. However, since then, the resurgence of the Republican Party has made Texas a strongly Republican

[2]Brandi Grissom, "Campaign Accounts Help Legislators Pay Staff, *The Texas Tribune*, April 18, 2013 at www.texastribune.org/2013/04/18/campaign-funds-prop-lawmakers-capitol-operations.
[3]Ibid.
[4]The public can access much of the House Research Organization data by visiting its website, www.hro.house.state.tx.us; the Senate Research Center can be found atwww.senate.state.tx.us/SRC/Index.htm.

Figure 7.2

Partisanship in the Texas House of Representatives, 2003 to the Present

This figure shows the percentage Republican house members since 2003.

CRQ Why is it important which party controls the legislature? Give examples of differences between the parties on districting, setting the legislative agenda, and making public policy.

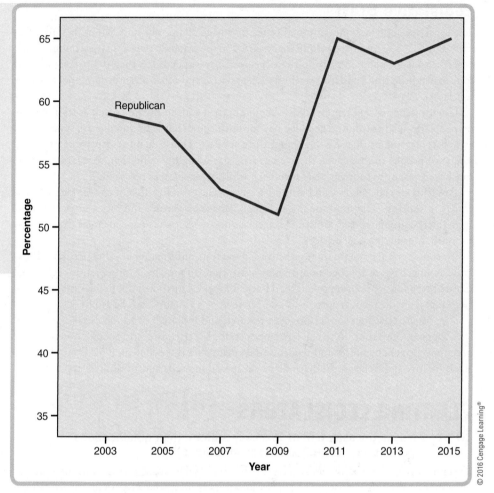

© 2016 Cengage Learning®

state. By the end of 2004, Republicans had established dominance over all three branches of state government, with two Republican U.S. senators and a Republican majority in the U.S. House of Representatives. Figure 7.2 shows that it is increasingly advantageous to be a Republican candidate in Texas electoral politics.

Campaign Funding A primary qualification for winning legislative office is access to money. Many competent, motivated citizens who want to serve are excluded because they are unable to raise the money necessary to finance an adequate campaign. Thus, the voters' pool of potential candidates is initially reduced by the economic special interests that make most campaign contributions. Securing office space, printing campaign literature, buying postage stamps, building a campaign organization, and purchasing advertisements are all among the necessary ingredients for a successful campaign.

In 2012, the National Institute on Money in State Politics found that the 380 candidates who ran for the Texas House raised an average of $194,605 for their campaigns. The 74 Texas Senate candidates raised an average of $583,130 for their campaigns.[5] Candidates raised more than $117 million for their campaigns in the house and senate races.[6] The amount of money

---

[5]National Institute on Money in State Politics, "Texas 2012 Candidates," www.followthemoney.org/database.
[6]Ibid.

Campaign Contributors in Texas Legislative Elections: Following the Money

Table 7.1a shows the total amount of campaign contributions raised by all Texas legislative candidates in 2012 and the average amount they raised. Along with candidates' incumbency and their party affiliation, campaign funding is an outstanding predictor of general election victory—the legislative candidates who outspent their opponents won 92 percent of the time.

Tables 7b and 7c show the largest campaign contributors in all candidates' campaigns for the Texas Senate and Texas House of Representatives. In some instances, organizations themselves did not donate; rather, their money came from the organizations' PACs, their individual members, employees, or owners.

Thinking about the role of elites in Texas politics Large contributors pursue several strategies: In closely contested races, some contributors may be trying to help elect candidates who best represent their interests and viewpoints. In other instances, their pattern of giving does not seem to be directed at affecting election outcomes but, instead, seems to represent an attempt to influence the legislative process itself. For example, contributors may target their giving to incumbents in safe districts, especially those who hold powerful legislative offices such as committee chairs and the speaker; even those who are unopposed for reelection often have huge campaign accounts. Occasionally, a single contributor will give to both candidates in the same closely contested race. Contributors

TABLE 7.1a Campaign Contributions to Candidates for the Texas Legislature

Office	Total	Number of Candidates	Average
Senate	$43,151,597	74	$583,130
House	$73,949,992	380	$194,605

TABLE 7.1b Top Five Campaign Contributors in Texas Senate Races

Contributor	Total	Percentage of Total	Sector
Texans for Lawsuit Reform	$3,881,988	9.00%	General business
Texans for Insurance Reform	$1,062,085	2.46%	Ideology/single issue
Perry, Bob J.*	$1,024,500	2.37%	Construction
Texans for Joan Huffman	$772,038	1.79%	Candidate contributions
Texans for Insurance Reform PAC	$631,831	1.46%	Ideology/single issue

TABLE 7.1c Top Five Campaign Contributors in Texas House Races

Contributor	Total	Percentage of Total	Sector
Texans for Lawsuit Reform	$3,166,060	4.28%	General business
Perry, Bob J.*	$1,527,000	2.06%	Construction
Associated Republicans of Texas	$984,950	1.33%	Ideology/single issue
Texas Association of Realtors	$890,220	1.20%	Finance, insurance, and real estate
Texans for Insurance Reform	$671,065	0.91%	Ideology/single issue

*Bob Perry, now deceased, was unrelated to former Governor Rick Perry.

Source: National Institute on Money in State Politics at www.followthemoney.org/database. The institute's searchable database relies on Texas Ethics Commission reports.

frequently give money to the winner after election day—so-called "late train" contributions.

Whatever their motivations, large donors usually have considerable success with their legislative agendas. In Chapter 10, we will discuss the stunning legislative successes of Texans for Lawsuit Reform, the largest funder of house and senate campaigns.

 What indicates when a campaign contribution might be intended to influence a legislator's vote?

 How can voters, small contributors, and less well-organized groups balance the political influence of large contributors?

needed to win an election is growing and increasingly becoming out of reach for many would-be candidates. Our Texas Insiders feature puts a face on the organizations and individuals who dominate the funding of legislative campaigns.

Demographic Identity The state of Texas has one of the most diverse populations in the United States. It is one of the few states with a majority-minority population, meaning that the majority of the population is a member of a minority group.[7] Currently, 45 percent of the population is non-Hispanic white, 38 percent is Hispanic, 12 percent is African American, 4 percent is Asian American, and the remaining 1 percent is of some other racial or ethnic group.[8] The Texas legislature, although diverse in its makeup, does not fully reach the descriptive representation of its member's districts. **Descriptive representation** is the idea that elected bodies should accurately represent not only constituents' political views but also the ethnic and social characteristics that affect their political perspectives. The following statistics show that there is some diversity in the legislature; however, Anglo-American males are still heavily represented in both the Texas Senate and House of Representatives.

In the 83rd Legislative Session (2013), 22 percent of Texas House members were Latino, 12 percent were African American, and 2 percent (or 3 representatives) were Asian American. Women, who account for slightly more than one-half of the state's population, accounted for 21 percent of the representatives in the Texas House.

The Texas Senate, by contrast, was 23 percent Latino, 6 percent African American, and 19 percent female. Although the non-Hispanic white population accounts for 45 percent of the state's population, 71 percent of the senators are non-Hispanic white.

The Latino population in Texas has grown significantly and discrimination in voting has been reduced since the passage of the Voting Rights Act of 1965. As a result, the number of Latinos in the Texas House and Senate has also increased. Most Latino legislators are Democrats, but the number of Latino Republicans is growing.

The percentage of African Americans in the Texas legislature also improved since the Voting Rights Act of 1965. The African-American population in Texas has remained at about 12 percent for the last several decades, and the proportion of house seats held by African Americans now approximates their proportion of the total population. On the other hand, the percentage of African Americans in the senate remains at 6 percent, well below their percentage in the population as a whole. Although most African-American lawmakers are Democrats, a few African Americans have been elected as Republicans.

Asian Americans account for a little more than 4 percent of the state's population.[9] Nevertheless, three Asian-American members of the Texas House served in the 83rd Legislative Session—Dallas Republican Angie Chen Button, and Houston Democrats Hubert Vo and Gene Wu.

Descriptive representation

The idea that elected bodies should accurately represent not only constituents' political views but also the ethnic and social characteristics that affect their political perspectives.

---

[7]Robert Bernstein, "Texas Becomes Nation's Newest 'Majority-Minority' State, Census Bureau Announces," *US Census Bureau News*, 11, August 2005.
[8]U.S. Census Bureau, *State and County QuickFacts*, http://quickfacts.census.gov/qfd/states/48000.html.
[9]Ibid.

Women are far more underrepresented than major ethnic groups in the Texas legislature. Although slightly more than one-half of the state's population is female, in 2013–2014, only 21 percent of house members and 19 percent of Texas senators were women.

Occupation Descriptive representation is far less apparent in the occupation of most Texas legislators. In the Texas 83rd legislature, those who identify as business owners or executives, 57, slightly outnumber lawyers, 56. Together, they accounted for more than 60 percent of the legislators. Real estate, consulting, ranching, and medical fields accounted for the majority of professions after lawyers and business owners.[10] Occupations can, and do, limit whether or not someone can serve in the Texas legislature, as independence is an important factor for serving for 140 days every other year, as well as attending to constituents and other state business in the off-year.

Education Texas has one of the best educated legislative bodies in the United States, which means that it is unlikely that Texas legislators will ever achieve educational descriptive representation with the general population of the state. Although only 26 percent of Texans age 25 years old and older hold college degrees, nationally, the Texas legislature ranks fifth in the percentage of lawmakers with a college degree. According to the *Chronicle of Higher Education,* less than 74 percent of lawmakers in the nation hold college degrees; more than 86 percent of Texas lawmakers hold a baccalaureate degree or higher. Forty-eight percent have earned degrees beyond a baccalaureate degree. Only 4 percent of Texas lawmakers have not attended college.

Texas ranks first in the percentage of lawmakers who are lawyers, with 30.4 percent of Texas lawmakers holding law degrees.[11] As an informal qualification to become a legislator in the state, educational attainment seems to resonate with voters as being a very important aspect to being electable.

Economic Status Lawmakers in the state Texas are required to report their sources of income, real estate assets, and stocks. However, when it comes to reporting the actual financial worth of the lawmakers' income and stock values, the reporting requirements are less precise; income is reported in ranges, the highest range being $25,000 and above and stock ownership reported in ranges from greater than $500 to $10,000 and above being the highest.[12] Given these parameters, it is difficult to determine the actual net worth of Texas legislators but enough of them are independently wealthy enough to allow the "citizen legislature" to operate on meager public salaries. However, both the wealthy legislators and those that are less well off solicit retainerships and consulting fees, which allow special interests to leverage legislators' financial dependency to press for favorable legislation.[13]

Geographic Districting

Each legislator is elected from a **single-member district**, with the state representative districts being quite a bit smaller than the senate districts. Single-member districts are represented by one representative and should be equal in population. After the ten-year census has

Single-member district

Districts that are represented by one representative that should be equal in population.

---

[10]Ryan Murphy et al., "The Makeup of the Lege, from Education to Employment," *The Texas Tribune,* January 11, 2013, at www.texastribune.org.

[11]*Chronicle of Higher Education*, "How Educated Are State Legislators?" http://chronicle.com/article/Degrees-of-Leadership-/127797.

[12]National Conference of State Legislators, "Personal Financial Disclosure for Legislators: Income Requirements," updated January 2013 at www.ncsl.org/research/ethics/financial-disclosure-legislators-income.aspx#TX.

[13]Ibid.

been completed, redistricting must be done to reflect the population changes in the state and to equalize the population in each district.

After the 2010 census, the average population of an electoral district for the Texas House of Representatives was 171,165; house members now represent 32,000 more people than they did a decade earlier. Texas senators represent approximately 828,216 residents, an estimated 156,000 more people than they did in 2000. The law requires that legislative districts can deviate plus or minus 5 percent from the mean, but not much more.

Geographic districting uses census data to divide the population into approximately equal population districts for every elected position. Historically, malapportioned district lines were drawn based solely on geographic equality but not population equality.

However, in the 1960s, U.S. Supreme Court decisions in several court cases, including *Reynolds* v. *Sims,* made **malapportionment**, the unequal distribution of population during the districting process that would make one district substantially larger or smaller than another, illegal. In this court case, the Supreme Court ruled, "Simply stated, an individual's right to vote for state legislators is unconstitutionally impaired when its weight is in a substantial fashion diluted when compared with votes of citizens living in other parts of the State."[14] Known as "one person, one vote," this decision mandated **reapportionment**, the redistricting or redrawing district lines after every census to reflect the population changes over the previous decade. It also required that district lines for both houses in state legislatures be drawn to represent equal population districts.

Figures 7.3 and 7.4 show how the Texas Senate and House of Representative district lines are currently drawn. The state legislature is responsible for drawing their district lines. But Texas lawmakers have sometimes found it impossible to agree on districts, in which case the state constitution provides for the function to be performed by the Legislative Redistricting Board. The board is **ex officio**, which means that its members hold other offices or positions automatically because they also hold some other office. It is made up of the lieutenant governor, the speaker of the house, the attorney general, the comptroller, and the commissioner of the General Land Office. In practice, rarely has this board been able to check the disagreement between lawmakers, so the courts have been involved in the state's redistricting processes since the 1990s.

After the 2010 elections, Republicans controlled both the house and senate with large majorities and were easily able to agree on district maps that were favorable to the Republican Party, as reflected in Figures 7.3, 7.4, and 7.5. The chief problem for the Republicans was the requirement that district maps had to meet voting rights requirements.

Because Texas has a history of discrimination, it was one of nine states that were once covered under the federal Voting Rights Act (1965) provision that required those states to receive preclearance from the U. S. Judiciary Department for their newly drawn districts. Those states had two options: They could expedite the approval process by asking the U.S. Justice Department for approval, or they could go through the U.S. District Court for the District of Columbia.

Before the redrawn lines were submitted to the Department of Justice for the Voting Rights Act–mandated evaluation, groups representing minority groups sued the state, charging that new district boundaries ignored the growth in the Latino and other minority populations. Latino groups and Republicans were able to come to an agreement on the Texas Senate maps, but the Texas House and U.S. congressional district maps were not settled in time for the regularly scheduled Texas primary date. Both the federal courts and the Justice Department agreed that the Republican-drawn maps violated the Voting Rights Act. As a result, the federal district courts in San Antonio drew interim district boundaries. Figure 7.5 shows how the U.S. congressional districts are currently drawn in Texas.

Malapportionment
The process of the unequal distribution of population during the districting process that would make one district substantially larger or smaller than another.

Reapportionment
The redistricting or redrawing district lines after every census to reflect the population changes over the previous decade.

Ex officio board members
Persons who hold a position automatically because they also hold some other office.

[14]*Reynolds* v. *Sims*, 377 U.S. 533 (1964).

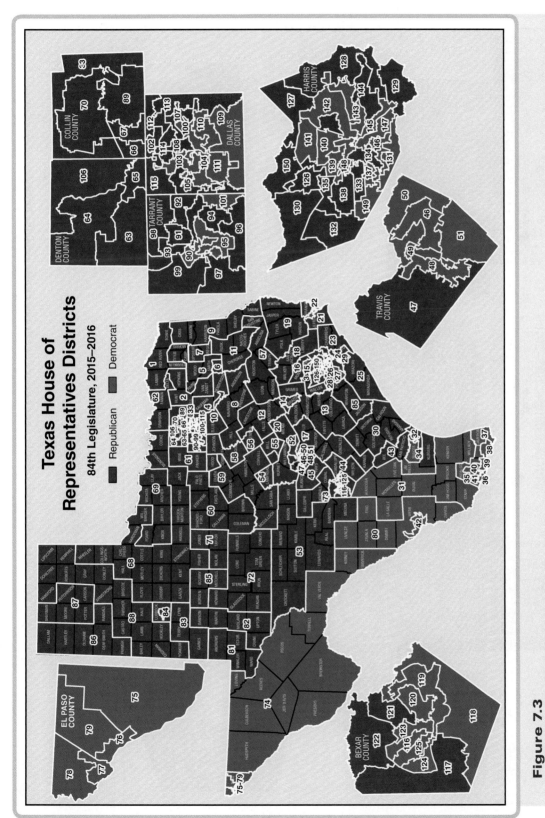

Figure 7.3
Texas House of Representatives Districts, 84th Legislature, 2015–2016

Texas Legislative Council, Plan H309.

How likely is it that Democratic members of the house of representatives, or their constituencies, will have an impact on the lawmaking process in Texas during the next several legislative sessions?

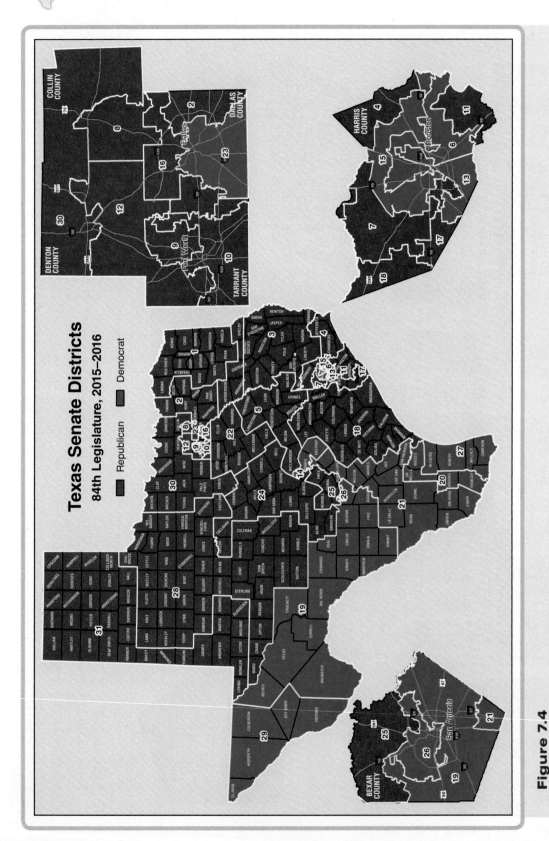

Texas Senate Districts
84th Legislature, 2015–2016

■ Republican
■ Democrat

Figure 7.4
Texas Senate Districts, 84th Legislature, 2015–2016

Texas Legislative Council, Plan S172.

 What districting practices were used to create the senate districts and how will it affect senate lawmaking ability?

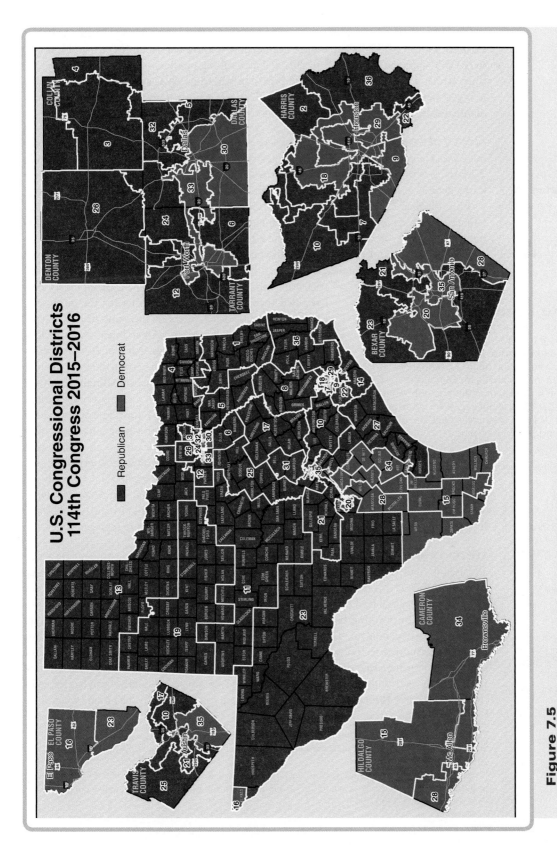

U.S. Congressional Districts
114th Congress 2015–2016

Republican

Democrat

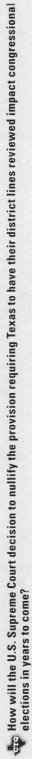

Figure 7.5
U.S. Congressional Districts, 114th Congress, 2015-2016

Texas Legislative Council, Plan C235.

How will the U.S. Supreme Court decision to nullify the provision requiring Texas to have their district lines reviewed impact congressional elections in years to come?

The Democrats and Latino groups, including the League of United Latin American Citizens (LULAC), did not agree with the lines drawn by the San Antonio court and appealed to the U.S. Supreme Court early in 2012.[15] The resulting opinion, in mid-2013, was that the court struck down the four-decade-old provision requiring Texas and the other eight states to report their district lines before they go into effect, making it possible for the Republican-dominated legislature to keep the San Antonio courts' maps.[16]

Gerrymandering   The way districts are drawn at any level of government determines, to a large extent, the political, ideological, and ethnic makeup of the legislative body. With redistricting, political careers may be made or broken, public policy determined for at least a decade, and the power of ethnic or political minorities neutralized. **Gerrymandering**, which is the practice of drawing district lines in such a way as to give candidates from a certain party, ethnic group, or faction an advantage, decreases or increases the political power of specific groups of voters and has a powerful effect on politics and public policy.

Partisan gerrymandering allows for district lines to be drawn so that individuals who tend to vote for the same political party can be drawn into the same district or several districts where that party is a majority. The U.S. Supreme Court has ruled that partisan gerrymandering for the purpose of keeping party-identified voters in the same district is constitutional under the Fourteenth Amendment. Another look at Figures 7.3, 7.4, and 7.5 shows that the 2012 redistricting plans relied heavily on partisan gerrymandering, thereby allowing the Republican voting bloc to maintain control of both the Texas legislature and the U.S. Congress delegation.

Racial gerrymandering—that is, drawing district lines to limit racial minority participation in voting—has been ruled unconstitutional under the same clause of the Fourteenth Amendment, first in the court case *Shaw v. Reno* (1993)[17] and in a subsequent case, *Miller v. Johnson* (1995).[18] Not only did both of these cases rule that racial gerrymandering is unconstitutional, but *Miller v. Johnson* also went so far as to say that some district lines were so obvious as to be "irregular and bizarre in shape that they could not be understood to be anything other than to segregate voters."[19]

Gerrymandering Techniques   Three basic gerrymander techniques are generally used to draw district lines. Diffusion, or **cracking**, of a population involves dividing up geographical areas that have a larger population of one party so that their voting power in any one district is negligible. This will usually affect the minority party in the state. This allows the overall majority-voting bloc to maintain control of areas that would normally vote for a minority party candidate. To get a better idea of how cracking a population works, study Figures 7.6. Another technique of gerrymandering involves concentrating, or **packing**, the same party into the same district so as to ensure that the party can influence one election rather than several. This technique can also affect how many representatives can be elected by the minority party throughout the state. The majority party uses this technique when there

---

Gerrymandering

The practice of drawing district lines in such a way as to give candidates from a certain party, ethnic group, or faction an advantage

Did You Know? Drawing district lines for partisan political advantage got the name *gerrymandering* in 1812, when the Massachusetts legislature and Governor Elbridge Gerry, wishing to preserve a Federalist majority, redrew a district in such a convoluted shape that a political cartoonist portrayed it as a salamander and dubbed it the "Gerrymander." The shapes of several current Texas congressional districts exceed the oddity of those originally gerrymandered districts in Massachusetts.

Cracking

A gerrymandering technique in which concentrated political party voters in one geographical area are split into several districts so that their voting power in any one district is negligible.

Packing

Gerrymandering technique in which members of a party are concentrated into one district, thereby ensuring that the group will influence only one election rather than several.

---

[15]*The Huffington Post*, Chris Tomlinson and Paul J. Weber, "Texas Redistricting Maps 2012: Candidates Study New Setup," February 29, 2012, www.huffingtonpost.com/2012/02/29/texas-redistricting-maps-2012_n_1310569.html.

[16]*Amarillo Globe News*, Enrique Rangel, "Ruling Likely Ends State Redistricting Battles," June 25, 2013, http://amarillo.com/news/local-news/2013-06-25/supreme-court-ruling-should-end-texas-redistricting-fight.

[17]*Shaw v. Reno*, 509 US 630 (1993).

[18]*Miller v. Johnson*, 515 US 900 (1995).

[19]Ibid.

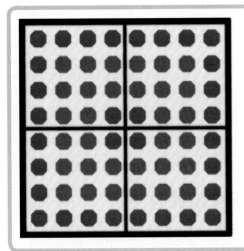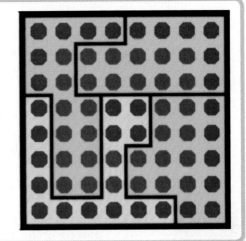

© 2016 Cengage Learning®

Figure 7.6
A Schematic to Illustrate the Process of Gerrymandering

The schematic on the left shows an example with the blue dots representing a number of people in one party and the red dots representing the same number of persons in the other in four equally competitive districts. The figure on the right shows how the same population can be gerrymandered to guarantee a three-to-one advantage in representation for the blue voters. You could try your hand at drawing districts with a three-to-one advantage for the reds.

 Explain the types of gerrymandering strategies.

may be so many votes by the minority party that, if left in non-gerrymandered districts, they could affect the outcome of elections in several districts. See Figure 7.6 to discover how the packing technique might benefit a majority party.

A third form of gerrymandering is a practice called **pairing**. Pairing is a redistricting technique that combines two or more incumbent legislators' residences and parts of their political bases into the same elective district. At election, the voters are then given the choice of the two already elected legislators but only allowed to vote for one, thereby ensuring that one will be defeated. The idea behind this type of redistricting is to create a district that will ensure that one incumbent will win over the other—usually for the majority party's incumbent to be able to represent the new district. By cracking or packing the remaining parts of the paired district into neighboring districts, the majority party can control a larger share of the legislative body.

Pairing

Placing two incumbent officeholders and parts of their political bases in the same elective district through redistricting.

Alternatives to Gerrymandering
During the heat of the redistricting controversy in the winter of 2012, Texans were asked what they felt were the state's most pressing problems. Although the expected issues of the economy, unemployment, and border security were at the top of the list, surprisingly, 5 percent of Texans polled pointed to legislative redistricting as one of the state's most important problems.[20] It ranked in seventh place, ahead of gas prices and water supply.[21] A sizable number of Texans—42 percent—supported the creation of an independent redistricting commission to redraw legislative district lines. Twenty-nine percent of Republicans, 43 percent of independents, and 70 percent of Democrats

---

[20]University of Texas/Texas Tribune Poll, February 2012, http://texaspolitics.laits.utexas.edu/11_5_0.html.
[21]Ibid.

supported the creation of an independent, nonpartisan redistricting commission to reduce political considerations in the drawing of legislative district boundaries.

This support for creating a redistricting commission can be explained in part by the lack of fairness that Democrats and members of minority groups see in the process. As word of the new district boundaries trickled out, it was the current Democratic **incumbents**, or currently elected officials, and many of their Hispanic and African-American constituents who believed that the new district boundaries could lead to a loss of political representation. Support for a redistricting commission may also be favored by those who feel that legislative redistricting efforts lead to less competitive races. When district lines are drawn to make sure a member from one party is elected over the other, viable electoral opposition is greatly diminished.

Incumbents
The currently elected official.

Bob Daemmrich/Alamy

Lt. Governor Dan Patrick defeated incumbent David Dewhurst in the 2014 Republican primary and was elected to an office with power that rivals or exceeds that of the governor.

 Write a carefully constructed essay that explains both the lieutenant governor's executive and legislative powers. Specifically, describe how the lieutenant governor is able to control the Texas Senate. Why do you suppose the senate has written rules that give so much power to its presiding officer when most other states make their lieutenant governor a mere figurehead, like the vice president in the U.S. Senate?

LEGISLATIVE ORGANIZATION

LO 7.3   Analyze the organization of the Texas legislature, including the powers of the presiding officers and the committee structure.

The Texas legislature is bicameral, with a house of representatives and a senate. The presiding officer of the house of representatives is the speaker of the house and the lieutenant governor acts as president of the senate. The legislature is organized by using a committee system, whereby senators and representatives serve on committees of differing subject matter in their respective chambers. Committees are also used as a means for both senators and representatives to work together for specific purposes. The legislature also has at its disposal several boards, councils, and commissions that provide leadership and advice to both the house and the senate.

Powers of the Presiding Officers

The two most powerful individuals in the Texas legislature are the lieutenant governor and the speaker of the house. The rules of each house, formal and informal, give the presiding officers the procedural power to appoint most committee members and committee chairpersons, assign bills to committees, schedule legislation for floor action, recognize members on the floor for amendments and points of order, interpret the procedural rules when conflict arises, and appoint the chairpersons and members of joint and conference committees. Furthermore, statutes grant the presiding officers nonprocedural, institutional power to appoint the members and serve as joint chairs of the Legislative Budget Board and Legislative Council and determine the members of the Legislative Audit Committee and the Sunset Advisory Commission.

Lieutenant Governor The presiding officer in the Texas Senate is the lieutenant governor, who serves as the president of the senate. The position is not an elected office, however; the lieutenant governor is in the unique position of being a member of both the legislative branch and the executive branch. The lieutenant governor is elected independently from the governor in a statewide, partisan election but could succeed the governor in the event of the governor's death or resignation. If the lieutenant governor's office becomes vacant through death, disability, or resignation, the senate elects one of its members to serve as lieutenant governor until the next regular election.

The Texas Constitution allows for the senate to write its own rules for each legislative session, which provides the basis for the lieutenant governor's powers. Under the rules, the powers granted to the lieutenant governor include extensive legislative, organizational, procedural, administrative, and planning authority. These rules are established at the beginning of each session and determine how business will be conducted throughout the 140-day legislative session. This role is also responsible for the staffing of the lieutenant governor's office and the maintenance of the Capitol Building. The position has a four-year term and receives $7,200 a year in compensation.

As president of the senate, the lieutenant governor can break tie votes on bills; the senate rules allow for the entire 31-member senate to convene as a committee of the whole as need be, which allows the lieutenant governor to debate and vote on any bill while the senate is designated as a committee. The lieutenant governor is also required to sign all bills and joint resolutions that are passed by the legislature.

Speaker of the House

The presiding officer of the 150-member house of representatives is the speaker of the house. The speaker of the house is an elected representative and has a two-year term; the salary for the position is $7,200 a year. The speaker is chosen from among the membership of the representatives, and is usually a member of the majority party of the house. Currently, the majority party is Republican; the current speaker is a Republican representative, Joe Straus–R, from San Antonio, Texas.

During the session, the speaker maintains order during floor debate, recognizes legislators who wish to speak on the house floor, and decides on procedural matters as the need arises. The constitution also requires the speaker to sign all bills and joint resolutions passed by the legislature. Unlike the lieutenant governor, as a member of the house of representatives, the speaker may debate on bills and is allowed to vote on all bills and resolutions that pass through the house. The other duties and responsibilities of the speaker are determined by the House Rules of Procedure, which are adopted by a majority vote of the members at the beginning of each regular session of the legislature. The rules give the speaker the authority to appoint the membership of each standing committee, to designate the chairperson and vice chair for each committee, and to refer all proposed legislation to the appropriate committee. The speaker also appoints members to conference and joint committees, creates select committees, and authorizes committees to conduct business during the interim when the legislature is not in session.

What is unique about the speaker position is that it is an elected office, albeit only within the house of representatives, but an elected position nonetheless. As such, there are candidates who want to be elected to the position and so must campaign for it. Candidates may raise and spend money for the campaign, but there are specific rules that must be followed.

Funds raised and spent for a campaign to become speaker are part of the public record. Candidates for speaker are required to file a complete statement of loans, campaign contributions, and expenditures with the secretary of state. No corporation, labor union, or organization may contribute, and individual contributions are limited to $100. All expenditures greater than $10 must be reported. There are no limitations on which individuals can contribute, so many non-representatives, including persons who are employed by interest groups and others who are interested in having favorable legislation pass through the house, contribute to the favorite candidate for speaker.

AP Images/Harry Cabluck

A bipartisan coalition in the Texas House of Representatives first elected Joe Straus in 2009, but his moderate image created political problems among more conservative Republicans and threatened his leadership.

CTQ **How is the speaker's bargaining position affected by the need to win a majority of fellow representatives to get re-elected?**

The Legislative Committees

Because of the volume of legislative proposals offered each session, legislators cannot possibly become familiar with all bills and resolutions—not even all the major ones. The legislature is organized into committees for the division of labor necessary to ensure that every member participates in the debate and discussion on proposed legislation. Committees are often referred to as "**little legislatures,**" which refers to the amount of work and decision-making power of the particular committees. Legislative committees are organized by subject matter and function. Once a committee makes a ruling on a piece of proposed legislation, it is highly likely that the respective chamber will follow whatever decisions the committee makes. Committees are involved in the legislative process from the introduction of the bill to floor debate to negotiation to resolve differences before final passage. The various types of committees include standing committees, subcommittees, joint committees, ad-hoc committees, select committees, conference committees, and interim committees.

Standing Committees   The most common committees within the legislature are **standing committees**. Standing committees are the permanent committees that function throughout the legislative session. There are two types, substantive and procedural, which do much of the legislative work in both chambers of the Texas legislature and are part of the permanent structure of the legislature. Their main function is to consider bills after they are introduced. They hold hearings and debates; they can **mark up**, or rewrite, bills or change bills by adding or deleting portions of them before they are considered for passage. They may also allow bills to be **pigeonholed** (to set aside or not take any action on a bill for the entire legislative session; most bills are pigeonholed) for lack of support from other members or lack of time. Procedural committees, like the House Calendars committee, for example, regulate the flow of legislation by monitoring where a bill is in the legislative process. Other procedures include passing resolutions and holding hearings to conduct investigations on numerous subjects. Substantive committees consider proposed legislation like taxation, education, and agriculture and fill the function of bureaucratic oversight.

Standing committees are made up of a chairperson and vice chairperson, both of whom are appointed by the presiding officers or achieve their positions through the seniority system in the legislature. The presiding officers of the respective chambers appoint the remaining committee members. Most senators and representatives serve on numerous committees; in fact, attending committee meetings takes up most of the legislator's time during the one hundred forty–day session.

Because several thousand bills are introduced into the Texas legislature each session, a division of labor is necessary. Every bill introduced during the legislative session is referred to a standing committee, which conducts public hearings where witnesses—both for and against—may be heard, debates held, and bills marked up. Because standing committees do the basic legislative work, the general membership relies heavily on them for guidance in deciding how to vote on a bill being considered on the floor.

Little legislatures
Another way of referring to committees—refers to the amount of work and decision-making power of the committees.

Standing committees
Permanent committees that function throughout the legislative session. There are two types: substantive and procedural.

Mark up
Rewriting or changing a bill by adding or deleting portions of it before it is considered for passage.

Pigeonhole
To set a bill aside and not take any action on it throughout the entire legislative session; most bills are pigeonholed.

AP Images/Harry Cabluck

Standing committees do much of the legislative work of ignoring or pigeonholing bills lacking significant support, gathering information in public hearings, and rewriting, or marking up, legislation to make essential political compromises that make a bill's passage possible.

CTQ **Explain how the presiding officers influence the work of standing committees.**

Subcommittees Many of the standing committees have been further divided into **subcommittees**, which specialize in particular categories of legislation. The subcommittees are usually the first to become familiar with a bill. Made up of a smaller number of standing committee members, subcommittees hold initial hearings, mark up legislation, and then report their work to the whole standing committee.

Joint Committees **Joint committee** membership is made up of both senators and representatives. Sometimes referred to as *boards,* these committees can be either temporary or permanent and usually serve a specific function, like the Legislative Budget Board (LBB) or the Legislative Education Board (LEB). The presiding officers appoint the membership of these committees and the chair and vice chair are usually the speaker and lieutenant governor, or are appointed by them. The purpose of a joint committee is to help create legislation that will be considered by both chambers, making the passage of the bill easier and faster in the short session.

Ad-Hoc and Select Committees Ad-hoc and select committees are temporary committees that are created for one specific purpose and are usually used in an advisory capacity. **Ad-hoc committees** are designed to address one specific issue in the legislative process. Its function is temporary and is disbanded when the function is complete. As with other committees, it is made up of senators or representatives, or both, and the leadership of both houses appoints the members. **Select committees** are also temporary committees, usually created for an advisory purpose. Membership of a select committee may include members from one or both chambers, but can also include citizens whose interests coincide with the purpose of the committee. Both of these types of committees are used to study specific problems and make recommendations to the legislature.

Conference Committees Because bills passed by both houses must reach the governor in single form, the **conference committee** is the ad-hoc committee that is used to resolve differences between the house and senate versions of the same legislation. It also creates compromises and reworks bills that have differing language after passing both houses. The membership of a conference committee is made up of senators and representatives who "confer" on the bill, and a separate conference committee is created for every piece of legislation that passes both houses. Once the issues of the bill under consideration have been resolved, the committee disbands. It is interesting to note that if the issues needed to create a unified bill cannot be resolved in the conference committee, a bill is not likely to go back to the floor for a final vote nor is it likely to reach the governor for his signature.

Interim Committees Committees that meet between legislative sessions are called **interim committees**, which play a crucial role in the Texas legislature and help to sustain the biennial legislative cycle. During the 18 to 20 months that the legislature is not in session, the state is faced with new challenges and needs, so members who are assigned to these committees are directed to consider proposed legislation for the next session or to address new issues that may be facing the state. Also, most of the preliminary work on larger, sometimes controversial, bills is done in the interim, which allows the membership to spend less time on those bills during the legislative session. What the interim committees decide on the issues they consider is key to whether those issues ever get to the legislature during the regular session.

THE LEGISLATIVE PROCESS

LO 7.4 Analyze the legislative process and how a bill becomes a law.

We will now look at how these legislative structures actually work to pass a bill. Keep in mind as we go through the step-by-step process that a bill can originate in either the house or the senate, and before it can be sent to the governor it must be passed in identical form by both houses.

Subcommittees
Subdivisions of standing committees that consider specialized areas and categories of proposed legislation.

Joint committee
Committee that includes both senators and representatives.

Ad-hoc committee
A committee designed to address one specific issue in the legislative process. Its function is temporary and is disbanded when the function is complete.

Select committee
Temporary committees that are created for one specific purpose and are usually in an advisory capacity.

Conference committee
An ad-hoc committee that meets to resolve differences between senate and house versions of the same legislation; each piece of legislation has its own conference committee.

Interim committee
Committee that meets between legislative sessions.

Although only members of the legislature may introduce a bill or propose a law, most bills originate outside the legislature as ideas of interest groups or the executive branch. Once a bill is introduced, the presiding officer of the house where the bill was introduced refers it to one of the standing committees.

The Standing Committees

Standing committees do much of the legislative work in both chambers of the Texas legislature. The presiding officers' power to appoint their members and chairs gives the speaker and lieutenant governor considerable influence over their work and, therefore, considerable influence over policy decisions.

House Committee Membership
The speaker appoints the total membership as well as the chair and vice chair of all house procedural committees such as calendars, rules, ethics, and redistricting committees.

The speaker also appoints the total membership as well as the chair and vice chair of the most powerful substantive twenty-seven-member Appropriations Committee and the chairs of the five subcommittees into which the Appropriations Committee is divided. The Appropriations Committee strongly influences all state spending and has important budget and oversight functions as well. Other important substantive house committees are the powerful Ways and Means and State Affairs Committees. For the committee membership on these and other substantive committees, a limited seniority system in the house determines up to one-half of a committee's membership; the speaker appoints the other half.

Senate Committee Membership
The lieutenant governor officially appoints all members and the chairs of all senate committees. In practice, an informal seniority system allows senators to choose their preferred committee until one-third of the committee's positions are filled. This ensures that senior senators will serve on some of the more powerful committees such as the Finance, Jurisprudence, and State Affairs committees. The chairs of the standing committees, at their discretion, may appoint subcommittees from the committee membership.

Scheduling

The committee structure of the legislature is integral to the consideration of bills. The leaders of both houses decide upon the senate and house of representatives committee membership. They also decide which committee will be given the responsibility of initially considering, changing, and voting on a bill before it reaches the floor of the respective house. Once it gets out of committee, a bill must be placed on a calendar so that it can be debated and voted on by the legislative body and eventually reach a conference committee for final consideration and change.

House Calendars Committees
The house of representatives has two Calendars committees that handle the schedules of all bills that come out of their standing committees: the House Committee on Calendars and the House Committee on Local and Consent Calendars. These two committees place a bill on any one of the house calendars:

★ Emergency Calendar
★ Major State Calendar
★ Constitutional Amendments Calendar
★ General State Calendar
★ Local and Consent Calendar
★ Resolutions Calendar
★ Congratulatory and Memorial Resolutions Calendar

The calendar schedule includes the time for floor debate and for when the vote on the bill will occur. The membership must cast their vote for a bill during the time allotted for the bill vote, so special attention must be paid to the calendars. Resolutions and bills that pertain to local governments or that can be readily consented to by the membership are placed on special schedules and are usually disposed of promptly with little debate on the house floor. The process is not so automatic for major or controversial legislation; when or whether the legislation will be scheduled on a calendar is a decision largely determined by the speaker and the House Calendars Committee chair. If the bill is important or urgent, it may be scheduled on the Emergency Calendar or Major State Calendar with debate and a preliminary vote scheduled early in the session.

Senate Calendar Officially the senate has a calendar system that advances bills systematically. A senate rule requires that bills be placed on the calendar and then considered on the senate floor in the same chronological order in which they were reported from the committees. In practice, bills are taken off the calendar for senate floor consideration by a **suspension of the rule**, or setting aside of the rule of chronologically ordering bills so that other bills can be considered. This requires a two-thirds majority vote of the senate. The process goes something like this: The first bill placed on the senate calendar each session is called a **blocking bill**, which is usually a bill that will never be considered by the full senate. The blocking bill is never taken up on the senate floor; its only purpose is to stop floor consideration of any other bills except by the two-thirds vote to suspend the rule requiring chronological consideration of bills.

Two-Thirds Rule This time-honored practice affects the senate's entire legislative process because it allows just eleven senators to block a bill. The irony is that although only a simple majority is necessary for final passage of a bill in the senate, a two-thirds majority vote is necessary to get the bill to the floor for consideration by the entire senate. The senate can let a bill die without having a floor vote for or against—it just fails to reach the floor from never being voted off the calendar.

Realizing that eleven senators were prepared to block passage of a bill to establish a new voter ID requirement during the 2011 session, the lieutenant governor and a majority of senators adopted a rule to specifically exempt the two-thirds requirement for the bill requiring voters to show state-issued picture identification before voting. The voter identification bill (SB 14) was taken off the calendar, voted on, and passed in the senate by a simple majority vote. This was done over the strong objections of opponents who believed the ID requirement would disparately impact the elderly and minorities in voting because those populations are less likely to have a state-issued photo identification card.

Floor action refers to action by the entire house or the entire senate to debate, amend, and vote on legislation. To take official action, each house requires a **quorum** of two-thirds of its membership to be present. On several occasions, a determined minority opposed to a scheduled action has used quorum-busting tactics by deliberately absenting themselves to deny their chamber the quorum necessary to proceed on any legislation.

During floor action, the Texas Constitution requires that bills must be "read on three consecutive days in each house." The purpose of the requirement was to ensure that laws would not be passed without adequate opportunity for debate and understanding. Bills are read once upon being introduced and prior to being assigned to a committee by the presiding officer. In practice, though, the entire bill is seldom read at this time. Instead, a caption or a brief summary is read to acquaint

Suspension of the rule
The setting aside of the rule of chronologically ordering bills so that other bills can be considered.

Blocking bill
The first bill placed on the senate calendar in each session, which is usually a bill that will never be considered by the full senate.

Floor action
Refers to action by the entire house or the entire senate to debate, amend, and vote on legislation.

Quorum
To take official action, both houses require two-thirds of the total membership to be present.

Did You Know? In 1979, Lt. Governor Hobby ordered the Texas Rangers to find twelve senators, dubbed the "Killer Bees," who were hiding out. They were able to successfully deny the senate a quorum to pass a split primary bill. During the 2003 gerrymandering battle, house Democrats, known as the "Killer D's," fled to Oklahoma to escape the reach of the Texas Rangers; senate Democrats, known as the "Texas Eleven," later took up the cause and fled to New Mexico for 46 days. Both groups were able to control the actions of their respective houses by not allowing a quorum.

legislators with the subject of the bill. The bill is read the second time before floor debate in each house, and if an entire bill is to be read, it is usually on this second reading. The third reading occurs at least one day after initial floor passage.

The constitution allows bills that are "cases of imperative public necessity" as so stated in the bill to be read for the third time on the same day as floor passage, as long as four-fifths of the membership agrees. All bills now routinely contain this provision and usually pass the third reading immediately following floor passage. A simple majority is required for final passage on the third reading, but amendments to any bill must have a two-thirds majority.

Senate Floor Action In the Texas Senate, all floor action is presided over by the lieutenant governor. Because most bills that come up for vote in the senate are voted off of the calendar by two-thirds vote, it usually means that the bill has already been considered and very little debate is needed. Only rarely does a senator opposing a bill resort to a **filibuster**— a prolonged debate by a senator to delay passing of a bill—on the senate floor. Senators may use a filibuster either to attract public attention to a bill that is sure to pass without the filibuster or to delay legislation in the closing days of the session. In fact, just the *threat* of a filibuster may be enough to compel a bill's supporters to change the content of the bill to reach a compromise with the dissatisfied senator. If a filibuster does occur, it means it was impossible to reach a compromise, usually because a sufficient number of senators strongly favor the bill and refuse to be intimidated by the threat of a filibuster. Democratic Senator Wendy Davis from Fort Worth used the filibuster to protest the billions of dollars in spending cuts to public education that resulted from the 82nd Legislative Session. The filibuster is credited with forcing former Governor Rick Perry to call a special session to address education spending.

Filibuster
A prolonged debate by a senator to delay passing of a bill.

The entire 31-member senate may act as a committee called a **Committee of the Whole**, which helps to speed up the process for bills to be considered or voted on. The lieutenant governor appoints a senator to preside over the 31-member committee and only a simple majority rather than the usual two-thirds is necessary to consider legislation. The lieutenant governor may debate and vote on all questions, but otherwise the senate rules are observed. No journal is kept of the proceedings.

Committee of the Whole
The entire 31-member senate acting as a committee.

Usually after a modest amount of debate, the Texas Senate takes a vote without the benefit of an electronic scoreboard. Senators vote by holding up a single finger for a "yes" vote and two fingers for a "no" vote. A clerk records the vote, and only a simple majority is necessary for passage.

House Floor Action The speaker of the house presides over all floor action. The **floor leaders** are the legislators who are responsible for getting legislation passed or defeated. They stand at the front of the chamber, answer questions, and lead debate on the bill; their job is to negotiate, bargain, and compromise to either pass or defeat a bill. Microphones located in the house chamber are available to lawmakers who wish to speak or ask questions. Each representative is allotted ten minutes to speak; few of them utilize this limited privilege because most representatives have decided how they are going to vote on bills before they reach the floor.

Floor leaders
The legislators who are responsible for getting legislation passed or defeated.

Floor action usually follows a routine, but it can become quite dramatic and debate can become intense when major legislation is brought up for a vote. Representatives opposing legislation may bring up points of order requiring rulings by the speaker. A **point of order** is

Point of order
A formal objection that rules of procedure are not being followed on the house floor.

a representative's formal objection that the rules of procedure are not being followed on the house floor. If the speaker sustains the point of order late in the session, there may not be time to correct the error, and the bill dies. In 1997, one legislator raised points of order that killed some 80 bills at the end of the session.

Late in the session, opponents may attempt to delay action on a bill in an effort to run out the clock on the session. Unlike state senators, representatives do not have the privilege of unlimited debate, but they have developed other strategies to stop legislative action on a bill that they do not want to come up for a vote. For example, knowing that a bill they oppose is scheduled to come up for debate, opponents may engage in **chubbing**, which slows down the whole legislative process. Chubbing includes debating earlier bills for the maximum allotted time, asking the bill's sponsor trivial questions, and proposing so many amendments and raising so many points of order that the house does not get around to the bill to which they ultimately object. The ultimate goal being that the session ends before the bill that is not wanted can reach the floor for a vote.

To vote, house members insert ID cards that allow them to push buttons to record an "aye," "no," or "present" vote on a large electronic scoreboard. The vote each representative makes is visible by means of green, red, and white bulbs next to each legislator's name. Until recently, lawmakers decided many bills by **voice vote** only, that is, to cast an oral vote that is not recorded in the official record. Casting oral votes did not provide constituents with a way to know how lawmakers voted on bills because their votes were not recorded. A state constitutional amendment passed in November 2007 ended this practice by requiring **recorded votes** on final bill passage, which requires that votes, and the names of those who cast the vote, be entered into the official record of each house.

Conference Committees

A unique by-product of bicameralism is the need to resolve differences in similar bills passed by the two houses. A temporary or ad-hoc committee known as a conference committee is appointed for each bill to resolve these differences.

In Texas, conference committees consist of five members from each house, appointed by their respective presiding officer. The conference committee may strengthen, weaken, or not reach a compromise on a bill. The compromise proposal must receive a favorable vote of a majority of the committee members from each house to be reported out of the committee and back to the floor.

After a bill has been reported from the conference committee, it may not be amended by either house but must be accepted or rejected as it is written or sent back to the conference committee for further work. In practice, due to the volume of legislation that must be considered in the limited time available, the Texas legislature tends to accept the conference committee compromise between the house and senate versions of a bill, which is then delivered by a **conference committee report** to each house.

How a Bill Becomes a Law

Bills may be introduced in either house or, to speed the process, in both houses at the same time. Bills are either appropriations, which are bills that fund projects and the budget of the state, or they are procedural, which are bills that change or create law; bills can also

Chubbing
Includes debating earlier bills for the maximum allotted time, asking the bill's sponsor trivial questions, and proposing so many amendments and raising so many points of order that the house does not get around to the bill to which they ultimately object.

Voice vote
To cast an oral vote that is not recorded in the official record.

Recorded votes
On final bill passage, votes and the names of those who cast the vote are recorded in each house's journal.

AP Images/Harry Cabluck

Representative Jim Keffer urges an "aye" vote on the floor of the Texas House of Representatives. The electronic tote board in the background is used to tally votes. Floor debate rarely determines how legislators will vote on a major bill; they usually decide how they will vote long before the bill reaches the floor.

What political factors affect legislators' decisions to support or oppose legislation?

Figure 7.7

How a Bill Becomes a Law

This diagram takes a bill step by step through the legislature from introduction in the Texas Senate to signing by the governor. Bills may also originate in the Texas House and it follows similar steps to passage.

 As a bill works its way through the legislative process, what factors determine whether a bill becomes a law?

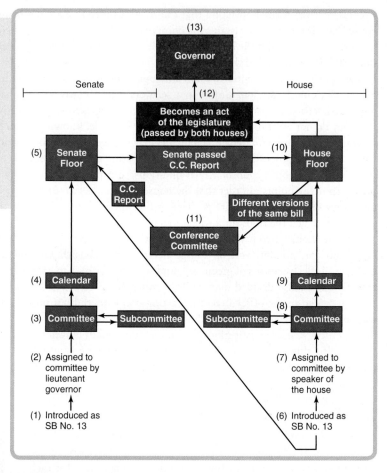

 Did You Know? Legislators sometimes allow other legislators to vote for them although the process is illegal. Sometimes, it even appears that ghosts can come back and vote on bills. On August 7, 1991, three votes were cast on Representative Larry Evans's (D–Houston) electronic voting machine after his death!

Conference committee report

A compromise between the house and senate versions of a bill reached by a conference committee and then delivered to each house.

be a combination of both. How a bill becomes a law is discussed next; the numbers in Figure 7.7 correspond to the numbers in the discussion.

1. ***Introduction to the Texas Senate***. Only a senator may introduce a bill in the senate, and only a representative may do so in the house. The introduction consists of a simple reading of the title or synopsis of the bill so that it can be entered into the record; this is considered the first reading of the bill. Upon introduction, the bill is assigned a number, for example, Senate Bill 13 (SB 13). The first bill introduced in the house of representatives would be styled as HB 1.

2. ***Assignment to a committee***. The lieutenant governor assigns bills to committees in the senate. Bills are usually assigned to committees that have the same or similar subject matter as the committee, but that may not be the case when the lieutenant governor wants a different outcome on bills than what the sponsor intended. Proponents (those senators for a bill) would want the bill to be placed with a committee that would send a favorable report to the floor; opponents would want the bill to not reach the floor for a vote.

3. ***Senate committee action***. As noted earlier, committees are often called "little legislatures" because of the power they have over bills. In both the committee and the subcommittee, the supporters and the opponents (witnesses) of the bill may be allowed to testify. Witnesses may be lobbyists, concerned citizens, or bureaucrats who may be affected by the bill. The subcommittee then marks up the bill (makes changes) and sends it to the committee, where

it may be further marked up. Some senate committees do not have subcommittees; in that case, the entire committee initially hears testimony and marks up the bill. The committee may then report on the bill favorably or unfavorably or may refuse to report on it at all.

4. *Senate calendar*. As described earlier, the senate has only one calendar of bills that lists the bills in the order they come out of committee. The senate calendar is rarely followed. In the usual procedure, a senator makes a motion to suspend the regular calendar order and consider a proposed bill out of sequence. The lieutenant governor must recognize the senator who will make the motion and if two-thirds of the senators agree to the motion, the bill is ready for action on the senate floor.

5. *Senate floor*. The president of the senate (the lieutenant governor) has the power to recognize senators who wish to speak, to vote in the event of a tie, and to interpret rules and points of order. At this time, the bill's sponsor will read the bill in its entirety in the senate chamber.

6. *Introduction to the house*. After the senate passes a bill, the bill is sent to the house of representatives. A procedure similar to that in the senate is followed there.

7. *Assignment to a committee*. It is the responsibility of the speaker of the house to assign each bill to a committee. Bills are usually assigned to committees with similar subject matter; how and when the committee can get to the bill will decide whether it reaches the floor or not.

8. *House committee action*. After committee assignment, the bill is assigned to a subcommittee, which may want to hold public hearings and have witnesses testify. The subcommittee and then the committee may amend, totally rewrite, pigeonhole, or report favorably or unfavorably on a bill.

9. *House calendars*. A bill that is either reported favorably by the committee or receives a favorable minority report by the required number of committee members is placed on one of the house calendars by one of the committees on calendars. This establishes the approximate order in which the whole house will consider the legislation.

10. *House floor*. The speaker of the house has the power to recognize representatives on the house floor and also to interpret the rules and points of order. The representative who sponsored the bill reads the bill in its entirety before debate or voting begins. The size of the house necessitates that debate be more limited than in the senate—usually 10 minutes for each member. Bills may be amended, tabled (prohibits a vote on the bill), have a negative vote, or sent back to committee. "Yes" votes of only a simple majority of members present and voting are necessary for a bill to be passed.

11. *Conference committee*. If the house of representatives makes changes in the senate-passed version of a bill, a conference committee is necessary to resolve the differences between the two houses. Each bill must have its own conference committee and report.

12. *Final passage*. The bill is sent first to the chamber where it originated and then to the other chamber for final approval. The final reading of a bill in both chambers happens at this time. Both the lieutenant governor and the speaker of the house must sign the passed version of the bill before it goes to the governor.

13. *The governor*. The governor has several options concerning an act arriving on his or her desk. First, the governor may sign it into law. Second, the governor may choose not to sign, in which case it becomes law in 10 days if the legislature is in session or in 20 days if the legislature is not in session. Third, the governor may choose to veto the act, but the veto can be overridden by a two-thirds vote in each house. The governor must either accept or veto the complete act if it does not contain provisions for appropriating funds. In appropriations acts, the governor may strike out an item of appropriation, but the governor does not have a reduction veto to reduce spending for an item. Also, the governor may not veto riders on appropriations bills that do not authorize state spending.

The governor often uses the veto late in the legislative session, or within 30 days after the session has ended, without fear of the legislature's overriding it because a veto cannot be overridden in a subsequent session. If the governor signs a bill, it will become law in 90 days—sooner if it has adequate funds for implementation or the legislature has designated it as emergency legislation. If the act requires the expenditure of funds that have not already been designated for it, the comptroller of public accounts must certify that adequate revenue is available for its implementation. If revenue is lacking, the act goes back to the legislature, where either adequate funds are provided or a four-fifths majority in each house must approve it. If neither option is successful, the new law cannot be implemented.

INSTITUTIONAL TOOLS OF LEADERSHIP

LO 7.5   Describe the legislature's institutional tools of leadership.

The Texas State legislative process using the committee structure provides the necessary institutional tools of leadership to pass law and create an extensive state budget that must be in effect for the two-year cycle of the legislature. Included in this are several permanent standing joint boards and commissions that allow for the continuity of work that must be completed during a session. The Legislative Budget Board, the Legislative Council, the Legislative Audit Committee, and Sunset Advisory Commission provide advice and recommendations to the legislature.

The Legislative Budget Board

Legislative Budget Board (LBB)

A ten-member board responsible for creating the state's initial budget and providing planning, analysis, and impact of the budgeting process.

Most states, the U.S. government, and most countries have only one budget. Texas has two. Each agency in state government presents its budget requests to both the governor's office and the powerful **Legislative Budget Board (LBB)**. The LBB provides the governor and the legislature with a draft of the appropriations (budget) bill. The LBB has broad authority for strategic, long-range planning, bill analyses, and policy-impact analyses of education, criminal justice, and financial policies.

The LBB also provides policy recommendations for legislative appropriations; they complete fiscal analyses for proposed legislation, and conduct evaluations and reviews to improve the efficiency and performance of state and local operations.[22]

The LBB consists of 10 members, including the lieutenant governor and the speaker, who serve as joint chairs. The remainder of the board is composed of the chairs of the Senate Finance Committee and the House Ways and Means and Appropriations committees, who serve as automatic members, and two house members and three senate members appointed by their respective presiding officer. The LBB operates continuously, even when the legislature is not in session, under the management of an administrative director appointed by the board.

LBB staff assists the Senate and House Appropriations committees and their chairs, and the LBB serve as an oversight committee on how expenditures are managed by the state executive agencies and departments.

The Legislative Council

Legislative Council

Provides research support, information, and bill-drafting assistance to legislators.

Another institutional tool of leadership is the 14-member **Legislative Council**, which provides research support, information and bill-drafting assistance to legislators. It is made up of six senators, the chair of the House Administration Committee, five other representatives, and the lieutenant governor and speaker, who serve as joint chairs. The lieutenant governor appoints the senate members, and the speaker appoints the house members. With the exception of the speaker and lieutenant governor, the terms of the appointees end with the beginning of each regular legislative session. The presiding officers govern the council during the regular session.

---

[22]www.lbb.state.tx.us.

The Legislative Council, its director, and staff function as a source of information and support to the legislature, state agencies, and other governmental institutions. The council staff is organized into administrative functions and four divisions: document production, information systems, legal, and research. It provides research, computing, and printing support for legislators and helps them draft legislative proposals. The council staff plays a key role in the redistricting process.[23]

The Legislative Audit Committee

The **Legislative Audit Committee** appoints and supervises the state auditor who, with the consent of the senate, heads the State Auditor's Office. The six-member Legislative Audit Committee is composed of the lieutenant governor, the chair of the Senate Finance Committee, one senator chosen by the lieutenant governor, the house speaker, and the chairs of the house Appropriations Committee and Ways and Means Committee.

The authority of the office of the state auditor is both broad and deep. Under the direction of the committee, state agencies and departments, including colleges and universities, as well as any entity receiving funds from the state, can be audited. The auditor's office may conduct financial, compliance, efficiency, effectiveness, and special audits as well.

Legislative Audit Committee
Appoints and supervises the state auditor who, with the consent of the senate, heads the State Auditor's Office.

The Sunset Advisory Commission

The Texas Sunset Act (1977) was enacted in response to the perception of the public that federal and state government spending was escalating beyond control. As a result, Texas created the twelve-member **Sunset Advisory Commission** to enforce the act.

The lieutenant governor appoints five senators and one public member, and the speaker appoints five representatives and one public member to the commission. Public members are appointed for two-year terms and legislators for four-year staggered terms. The presiding officers appoint the commission chair. The chair position alternates between senate and house members. The commission employs a director and a staff that conducts the reviews and presents their findings to the commission.

The commission reevaluates the need for more than 130 statutory state agencies on a twelve-year cycle to determine the need for their continuance. When agencies are created, their particular "sunset" date is included in its charter. Because they are automatically terminated, the Sunset Advisory Commission can recommend keeping, abolishing, reorganizing, or giving a new scope and authority to an agency. About 20 to 30 agencies undergo the sunset review process every biennium.

In the Sunset Advisory Commission's more than 35-year history, the commission has abolished or restructured more than 79 state agencies, including 37 that were completely abolished. The Sunset Advisory Commission estimates that it has saved the state of Texas approximately $945.6 million during its existence.[24]

Sunset Advisory Commission
Recommends keeping, abolishing, reorganizing, or giving a new scope and authority to an agency.

APPLYING WHAT YOU HAVE LEARNED ABOUT THE TEXAS LEGISLATURE

LO 7.6 Apply what you have learned about the Texas legislature.

In the following essay, you will learn how to score the winners and losers in the legislative process, and you will see how the winners have been able to use the rules to shape the final outcomes in the legislative process. You will see that house speakers have been able to use their

[23]www.tlc.state.tx.us.
[24]www.sunset.texas.gov.

powers as presiding officers to tailor their legislative agendas to benefit the coalitions that elected them. In the past, Speaker Craddick wielded these powers to produce solid partisan conservative victories, but Speaker Straus led more moderate, bipartisan coalitions to victory during the 2013 session.

Meanwhile, in the state senate, the lieutenant governor has also asserted a moderating influence, and the minority Democrats have been able to use the two-thirds rule to thwart the majority from passing most ideological legislation. As a result, the Texas Senate has, like the Texas House, produced rather moderate, bipartisan results. Despite some high-profile wins for conservatives on controversial legislation like abortion regulation, the final outcome for the 2013 legislative session could be characterized as purple, a blending of the red, conventionally used to designate Republicans, and the blue, used to represent Democrats.

After you have read the following essay, you will be asked a series of questions that will require you to employ critical-thinking skills to apply what you have learned in this chapter to the new information in this essay. Your analysis will require you to identify critical elements in the legislative process and to evaluate the concentration of power in the Texas legislature.

A Tale of Two Speakers and the Purple Legislation of 2013

by Mark P. Jones
RICE UNIVERSITY

In Texas, the lieutenant governor and speaker of the House exercise considerable control over the legislative process. As presiding officer of the Senate and House, respectively, each names all committee and subcommittee chairs, decides to which committees bills are assigned, and through his appointed chairs and other committee members indirectly determines which bills make it to the floor for a final passage vote (FPV) and which do not. A FPV is the last vote, also referred to as a third reading, on a bill prior to its passage to either the other chamber or the governor's desk.

The lieutenant governor and speaker and their respective leadership teams commonly employ negative agenda control to keep bills opposed by the majority of the members of their governing coalition from reaching the floor (negative agenda control). At the same time, these leaders also orchestrate the crafting of legislation in such a way that the final version that reaches the floor for a FPV is preferred by a majority of their coalition's members (positive agenda control).

A Tale of Two First-Term Speakers: Tom Craddick and Joe Straus
Since 2003 Republicans have continuously held a majority of the seats in the Texas House and the speaker has been a Republican: Tom Craddick of Midland (2003–2009) and Joe Straus of San Antonio (2009–). In spite of the constants of a Republican speaker and legislative majority, the ideological and partisan center of gravity in the House under these two speakers was quite distinct, especially in their inaugural sessions as speaker.

Figure 7.8 shows how the two Republican speakers utilized their similar agenda powers to pursue dissimilar policy agendas. In 2002 Republicans won a majority of the seats in the Texas House for the first time since Reconstruction. Craddick, who had labored for over thirty years to realize his dream of a GOP House majority, was elected speaker with the near universal support of his fellow Republicans in 2003. The 2003 House under Craddick was a very partisan institution, with Republicans uniformly possessing FPV win rates that were greater than those of Democrats, something revealed by the 2003 graph where the red bars rise noticeably higher than the blue bars, underscoring that Democrats were on

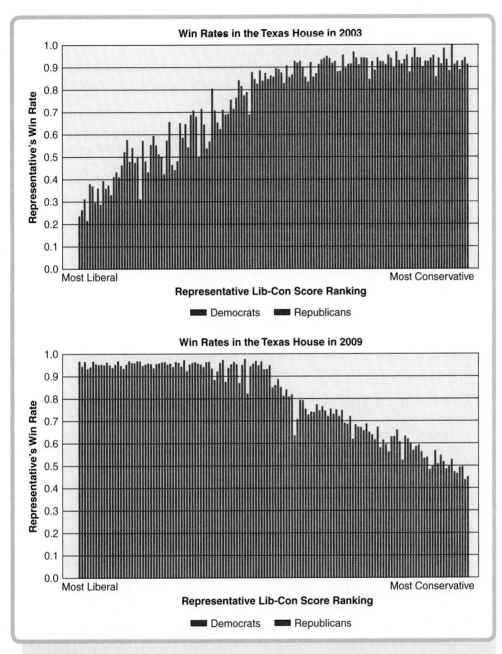

Figure 7.8
Party and Ideology of Winners under Two House Speakers

This figure shows that conservatives were on the winning side much more frequently under Speaker Craddick in 2003 than under Speaker Straus in 2009. These graphs highlight the disparate majority coalitions of Speakers Craddick and Straus during their first term as speaker. In the graphs the members of the Texas House are arrayed along the X-axis from left (most liberal) to right (most conservative) based on their Liberal-Conservative Score, which is constructed from an analysis of the roll call votes cast by the representatives during the legislative period. For these same legislators the Y-axis contains the proportion of non-lopsided FPV votes where the legislator cast a vote and was on the winning side. The vertical bars highlight each representative's FPV win rate, with Democrats denoted by blue bars and Republicans by red.

the losing side of significantly more FPVs than Republicans. Furthermore, the Craddick agenda was especially unpopular among the most liberal Democrats (located at the far left of the graph) who possessed the House's lowest win rates. In 2003, there were no profound differences in win rates among Republicans based on their location along the right side of the ideological spectrum, with GOP representatives in the moderate, centrist and conservative (far right of the graph) wings of the party on the winning side of FPVs in roughly similar proportions.

In 2009, Straus ousted Craddick from the speakership with the backing of a small number of moderate Republicans and an overwhelming majority of Democrats. It would appear that to obtain this critical Democratic support, Straus ceded some of his agenda control powers, especially negative agenda control, to the Democratic House leadership. The Democratic leadership's ability to keep legislation off the agenda that was rejected by a majority of House Democrats reveals how in many respects Democrats were partners with Straus in running the 2009 House, either explicitly or implicitly backing virtually all legislation passed. This reality is highlighted in the graph for 2009, where even the Democrat with the lowest win rate still had a higher win rate than all but a half dozen Republicans, with the most conservative Republicans faring especially poorly (see the low red bars on the far right of the graph).

Both Craddick and Straus utilized the speaker's powers of agenda control to achieve a desired outcome. In the case of Craddick it was to pass legislation that was firmly in line with the preferences of the Republican majority while in the case of Straus it was to pass legislation that corresponded to the preferences of the members of Straus's coalition of moderate conservative Republicans and Democrats.

The Purple Legislation of the 2013 Session
In 2012, Texas reaffirmed its status as the reddest of the nation's most populous states, with Mitt Romney winning 57 percent of the vote to President Barack Obama's 41 percent. Simultaneously, Republicans garnered 19 of 31 seats in the state Senate and 95 of 150 of the seats in the state House. While the November election results were unequivocally red, the legislation passed during the 2013 legislative sessions was nonetheless decidedly purple in content.

In the Capitol's west wing, House Democrats once again maintained a tacit alliance with the GOP's moderate/centrist conservative bloc led by Speaker Straus, albeit one where the Democrats enjoyed noticeably less influence than in 2009. This alliance allowed a relatively cohesive and disciplined Democratic delegation to block the passage of a considerable amount of legislation opposed by its members. In a similar vein, the moderate conservative Republicans prevented the passage of almost all legislation they opposed either on policy grounds or because they believed it would damage the Texas GOP brand and undermine their goal of maintaining the party's majority status in the Lone Star State. Finally, this informal alliance pushed through bills that addressed several, though certainly not all, of these legislators' most pressing policy concerns in areas ranging from public education to water infrastructure.

In the Capitol's east wing, by remaining relatively united and taking advantage of the Senate's two-thirds rule during the regular session (the rule was not in force during the special sessions), Democrats were able to block most legislation they opposed. Under the two-thirds rule, even bills backed by all Republicans still needed the support of at least two Democrats to pass. Like their House counterparts, Senate Democrats in many instances worked with moderate conservative and centrist conservative Republicans to pass legislation over the objection of the most conservative GOP senators.

The two graphs in Figures 7.9 detail the informal alliance that existed during the regular session between Democrats and the moderate conservative and, to a somewhat lesser extent,

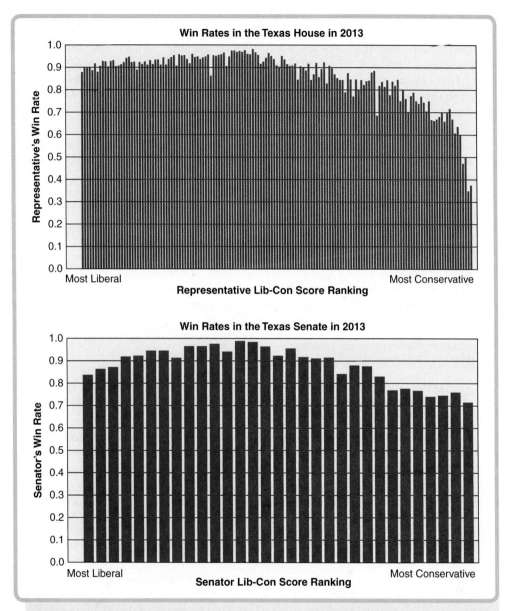

Figure 7.9

Party and Ideology of Winners in the 2013 Legislative Session

This figure shows that the legislature's moderate and liberal members were on the winning side more often than its most conservative members during the 2013 session. The figure shows representatives and senators arranged along the X-axis from most liberal to most conservative based on their Liberal-Conservative Score, and the Y-axis shows the proportion of FPVs where the legislator voted and was on the winning side.

centrist conservative wings of the Republican Party. This alliance produced predominantly purple legislation that was frequently opposed by the House and Senate's more conservative Republicans.

As a result of this alliance, the legislators most likely to find themselves on the outside looking in were the most conservative Republicans. In the Senate, six Democrats and four

Republicans, including the GOP's three least conservative senators, had FPV win rates above 94 percent. The FPV win rates of the eight most conservative Republican senators were substantially lower than those of these ten pivotal senators, and lower than those of every Democrat.

In the House, more than half of the Republicans possessed a FPV win rate below the lowest win rate registered by a Democrat. Included in this group were more than four-fifths of those Republicans with a Liberal-Conservative Score to the right of the party's ideological median.

The combination of the two-thirds rule in the Senate and a tacit alliance between moderate/centrist conservative Republicans and Democrats in both chambers resulted in legislation emerging from the Texas Legislature in 2013 that was less red in tint than one would have expected from a cursory review of the 2012 election results and the legislature's partisan composition. This purple reality has caused considerable consternation among many of the most conservative Republican advocacy groups in Texas that have lobbied for a relaxation of the two-thirds rule and Straus's removal as speaker. It is possible the former wish will be granted in 2015, with the two-thirds rule replaced by a three-fifths rule, in which case Democrats would be powerless to block legislation with unanimous GOP support if, as is expected, there are at least 19 Republican senators. In contrast, it is extremely unlikely that these organizations will be successful in removing the increasingly powerful Straus who, at least for the time being, is safely ensconced in the speakership.

JOIN THE DEBATE

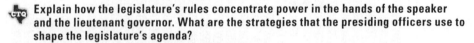
Explain how the legislature's rules concentrate power in the hands of the speaker and the lieutenant governor. What are the strategies that the presiding officers use to shape the legislature's agenda?

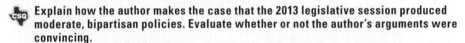
Explain how the author makes the case that the 2013 legislative session produced moderate, bipartisan policies. Evaluate whether or not the author's arguments were convincing.

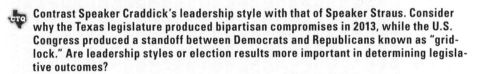
Contrast Speaker Craddick's leadership style with that of Speaker Straus. Consider why the Texas legislature produced bipartisan compromises in 2013, while the U.S. Congress produced a standoff between Democrats and Republicans known as "gridlock." Are leadership styles or election results more important in determining legislative outcomes?

CHAPTER SUMMARY

LO 7.1 **Describe the limits on the Texas legislature and evaluate the concept of the "citizen legislature."** Since the time the Texas Constitution was written, citizens have mistrusted institutions of government, including the state legislature. As a result, Texans have limited their state legislature to meeting only once every two years in regular sessions and not allowed the legislature to call itself into special session. Regular sessions are limited to only 140 days and special sessions can last no more than 30 days. Legislative salaries are among the lowest in the nation and legislative staffs are so restricted that legislators have become dependent on outside interests for both income and information.

LO 7.2 **Analyze the selection of Texas legislators, their qualifications, elections, and the impact of redistricting.** Texas representatives must be at least 21-year-old citizens who have lived in the state for two years and senators must be at least 26-year-old citizens with five years of state residence. These legal requirements obscure the fact that most legislators are, in fact, business or legal professional men and do not reflect the population demographics as a whole.

Politically, most are conservative Republicans with access to major campaign contributors. Districting has a significant impact on the kinds of people who are actually elected to the Texas legislature. As in most states, Texas legislators have gerrymandered districts to give the majority party a significant advantage. A few states have given the process of redistricting after each census to a nonpartisan commission, and many Texans would favor this alternative.

LO 7.3   Analyze the organization of the Texas legislature, including the powers of the presiding officers and the committee structure. The Texas two-chamber legislature is presided over by the lieutenant governor in the senate and the speaker in the house of representatives. The Texas legislature meets in odd-numbered years for 140 days, and has 31 senators and 150 representatives. Legislative action is based on the committee system. Committees initially review legislation, gather information though committee hearings, and mark up bills to meet the wishes of the committees' majority. Committees serve as tools of the speaker and lieutenant governor who decide which committees will consider a bill; they also appoint the chairs and most members of the committees. The presiding officers control floor debate and are able to use their appointive, jurisdictional, and other procedural powers to control the legislative process.

LO 7.4   Analyze the legislative process and how a bill becomes a law. Any legislator may propose a piece of legislation but the idea for much legislation originates with interest groups or the executive branch. Once introduced in the house or senate, the bill is sent to a standing committee for initial review. Before the bill can become law, it must be scheduled for floor debate where the house and senate use differing means to place legislation on the floor for a vote—the senate uses a two-thirds rule and the house uses the calendars. A bill must be passed by a majority vote before it is sent to the other house, where it follows similar steps through committee, scheduling, floor debate, and final vote. The presiding officers appoint a conference committee to resolve differences between the house and senate versions. Bills are sent to the governor and can be signed or vetoed.

LO 7.5   Describe the legislature's institutional tools of leadership. The presiding officers appoint important boards and commissions that help them to lead the legislature. These include the boards and commissions that manage the budgeting function of state government (the Legislative Budget Board), the auditing function (the Legislative Audit Committee), policy research (the Legislative Council) and "sunsetting," or reorganizing state agencies (the Sunset Advisory Commission).

LO 7.6   Apply what you have learned about the Texas legislature. You used your critical-thinking skills to look at the voting patterns in past sessions to see if presiding officers are able to affect the legislature's agenda. You learned that the speaker and lieutenant governor had a moderating influence in the last legislative session, but that Speaker Craddick used his powers to enact a more partisan agenda. You evaluated the importance of personal leadership style of the presiding officers and learned that their approach has a considerable influence on legislative decisions.

KEY TERMS

ad-hoc and select committees, *p. 183*
blocking bill, *p. 185*
bureaucratic oversight, *p. 166*
chubbing, *p. 187*
Committee of the Whole, *p. 186*
conference committee, *p. 183*
conference committee report, *p. 188*
constituency, *p. 166*
consulting fees, *p. 167*
cracking, *p. 178*

descriptive representation, *p. 172*
ex officio board members, *p. 174*
filibuster, *p. 186*
floor action, *p. 185*
floor leaders, *p. 186*
gerrymandering, *p. 178*
incumbent, *p. 180*
interim committee, *p. 183*
joint committee, *p. 183*
legislative audit committee, *p. 191*

legislative budget board (LBB), *p. 190*
legislative council, *p. 190*
little legislatures, *p. 182*
malapportionment, *p. 174*
mark up, *p. 182*
packing, *p. 178*
pairing, *p. 179*
per diem, *p. 167*
pigeonhole, *p. 182*
point of order, *p. 186*
quorum, *p. 185*
reapportionment, *p. 174*

recorded votes, *p. 187*
resolution, *p. 167*
retainer fees, *p. 167*
single-member districts, *p. 173*
special session, *p. 166*
standing committees, *p. 182*
subcommittees, *p. 183*
sunset advisory commission, *p. 191*
suspension of the rule, *p. 185*
term limits, *p. 166*
voice vote, *p. 187*

REVIEW QUESTIONS

LO 7.1 Describe the limits on the Texas legislature and evaluate the concept of the "citizen legislature."

- What is legislative amateurism, and how does it affect the legislative process?

- Explain how low salaries, short biennial sessions, and limited staff are designed to control the legislature's power. Explain how such limits increase the influence of interest groups.

LO 7.2 Analyze the selection of Texas legislators, their qualifications, elections, and the impact of redistricting.

- What are the formal and informal qualifications for holding office in the Texas legislature?

- What are the demographic and political factors that affect who becomes a member of the legislature?

- What are geographic single-member districts? Explain the process of gerrymandering.

LO 7.3 Analyze the organization of the Texas legislature, including the powers of the presiding officers and the committee structure.

- List the powers of the speaker and lieutenant governor. Explain how each of their powers is used to control the legislative process.

- How are the legislature's presiding officers selected? What are the limits on their power?

- Describe the types of legislative committees and explain their function in the legislative process.

LO 7.4 Analyze the legislative process and how a bill becomes a law.

- Describe step by step how a bill is introduced, referred to committee, marked up and reported by committee, scheduled for floor debate, debated, and voted upon in the Texas House. Then, take a bill through with same steps in the Texas Senate. Finally, explain how a compromise is reached on the house and senate versions.

- Show how the presiding officers are able to influence the legislative process at each step in the previous question.

- Explain the role of the governor in the legislative process.

LO 7.5 Describe the legislature's institutional tools of leadership.

- Explain the powers of the Legislative Budget Board, the Legislative Council, the Sunset Advisory Commission, and the Legislative Audit Committee.

- Explain the role of the speaker and lieutenant governor in selecting these institutions of leadership. Explain why state agencies are beholden to each of these.

GET ACTIVE

- **Adopt a bill of your own on a topic in which you have an interest**. (Or visit the website of an organization that you support or admire and choose a bill that they support.) Find out which interest groups favored or opposed your bill. Why did they take the positions they took? Did your bill pass, or did it not make it out of the legislature? Where did it stop? What action did the governor take on the bill?

- Start the exercise at Texas Legislature Online at **www .capitol .state.tx.us** and click on "Legislation." You will also find help at the Legislative Reference Library website at **www.lrl.state.tx.us**. Information about the governor's role and other topics can be found at **www.governor.state .tx.us**.

- **Become a legislative intern for the Texas legislature.** Internship opportunities are listed at **http://laits.utexas. edu/internconnect/listing**. Senator Rodney Ellis offers such internships at **www.rodneyellis.com/tlip**. Senator Gregory Luna's Legislative Scholar Fellows Program at **http://tshrc.org/luna-scholars-fellows-program** also provides internship opportunities. You can check with your own college or university. Many have their own legislative internship programs. Call your representative in the Texas House or Texas Senate for additional internship opportunities. For a listing of Texas House members, check **www .house.state.tx.us**; for a listing of Texas Senate members, check **www.senate.state.tx.us**.

- **Find out how interest groups rate your legislators.** Interest groups rate legislators' votes on major public policy issues. Pick interest groups that share your policy views and see how they rate Texas legislators. Vote Smart at **https:// votesmart.org/interest-groups/TX/#.Uz3vUKJkJiw** is a comprehensive site that links to such interest groups as business, environmental organizations, civil rights organizations, right-to-life groups, and gun rights groups. Interest groups provide a vital public service by keeping track of major legislative issues of which many ordinary citizens are not aware.

- **PRQ** How can you use various interest-group ratings of legislators' votes to help you determine how you will cast your ballot on election day?

CHAPTER 8

The Texas Executive Branch

LEARNING OBJECTIVES

LO 8.1 Describe the governor's office and the characteristics of the typical Texas governor.

LO 8.2 Analyze both the governor's powers of persuasion and the limits on them.

LO 8.3 Analyze the structure and characteristics of the Texas bureaucracy.

LO 8.4 Analyze the political relationships among executive agencies, the public, interest groups, and elected officials.

LO 8.5 Evaluate strategies for holding state agencies accountable.

LO 8.6 Apply what you have learned about the state's executive branch.

*A*lthough the Texas Constitution designates the governor as chief executive, the executive branch is splintered into various offices and agencies that are often beyond the governor's effective control. The division of Texas executive power is largely based on the Jacksonian democratic theory that most major officeholders should be elected. The legislature has recently strengthened the governor's administrative influence over several agencies, but powerful special interest groups, bureaucrats, the legislative leadership, and the general public generally prefer a decentralized government and a weak chief executive. As a result, the Texas administrative structure will continue to be a hodgepodge of administratively independent entities, with no single official formally responsible for either policy initiation or implementation.

The lack of administrative authority does not mean the governor's office lacks the potential for meaningful political power. An astute, politically savvy governor can exert significant influence on both legislative and administrative policy by asserting legislative powers, by managing media access, by using party influence, and by appointing strategic allies to boards, commissions, and the judiciary.

Long tenure and solid interest group support are also important factors in a governor's influence. A long-serving governor with the support of powerful interest groups can wield significant influence over enactment and implementation of public policy in Texas. To be effective, a governor must have appointed most members of administrative boards and commissions, convinced legislators that he or she will punish errant behavior, and won the support of the political and financial power of special interests.

THE GOVERNOR'S OFFICE: QUALIFICATIONS, TENURE, AND STAFF

LO 8.1 Describe the governor's office and the characteristics of the typical Texas governor.

To become governor, a candidate must meet formal or legal qualifications as well as informal requirements that are imposed by the state's political culture.

In 2014, Texans elected Republican Greg Abbott as the state's governor.

CTQ Identify the tools Abbott can employ to become an effective governor.

Qualifications and Elections

As is usual with elective offices, the legal requirements for becoming governor are minimal: One must be 30 years of age, an American citizen, and a citizen of Texas for five years before running for election. Whereas the formal qualifications for governor are easily met, the informal criteria are more selective.

Ethnicity Since the Texas Revolution, all governors have been non-Hispanic whites, whom Texans often refer to as Anglos, and all except former Governor Abbott have been Protestants, usually Methodist or Baptist. Governor Abbott was the first Roman Catholic to be elected to the office.

Gender Historically, most governors have been males. The only female governor of Texas before Ann Richards (1991–1995) was Miriam A. Ferguson, who served for two nonconsecutive terms (1925–1927 and 1933–1935). She ran on the slogan "Two Governors for the Price of One" and did not really represent a deviation from male dominance in Texas politics, for it was clear that her husband, former Governor James E. Ferguson, exercised the power of the office. In reality, former Governor Richards was the first truly independent woman to serve as the governing Texas chief executive.

Middle-Aged Businessperson or Attorney The typical governor will usually be successful in business or law; in fact, more than one-half of the governors who have served since 1900 have been lawyers. The governor will probably be between 40 and 60 years of age, have a record of elective public service in state government or some other source of name recognition, and be a participant in service, social, and occupational organizations.

Today a Republican Texas was a solidly Democratic state following the Civil War. The solid support began to deteriorate in the 1950s and Texas became a two-party state in the 1990 election. Competitive party politics proved uncomfortable for Texans and in only 14 years Texas completed the cycle and became one-party Republican.

The Nomination The Democratic gubernatorial primary is usually a match among one or more moderates and moderate-to-liberal candidates. Democratic candidates must forge a slippery coalition of business leaders, ethnic minorities, unions, intellectuals, teachers, conservationists, and consumer advocates in order to win their party's nomination.

The Republican primary is a joust between business-oriented moderately conservative candidates and more purist conservatives, with the more conservative candidate often winning. Republican gubernatorial candidates usually have the campaign funds to outspend their Democratic opponents, thereby purchasing the all-important political image and name recognition.

Well-Funded Campaigns Money is a critical factor in any serious campaign for Texas governor. Although the candidate who spends the most does not always win the office, a hefty bankroll is necessary for serious consideration. Challengers will usually spend more than incumbents to buy name recognition. Paul Taylor, executive director of the Alliance for Better Campaigns, commented that "the legacy is a political culture in which we auction off the right to free speech 30 seconds at a time to the highest political bidder."[1]

Tenure, Removal, Succession, and Compensation

As in 47 other states, Texas governors serve a four-year term. Unlike most states, however, there is no limit on the number of terms that a governor may serve. The governor may be removed from office only by impeachment by the house of representatives and conviction by the senate. **Impeachment** is bringing formal charges against a public official; it is the legislative equivalent of indictment for improper conduct in office, and requires only a simple majority of the vote. Conviction by the senate removes the official from office and requires a two-thirds majority.

If the governor is impeached and convicted, dies, or resigns, the lieutenant governor becomes governor and the Texas Senate then elects one of its members to serve as the acting lieutenant governor until the next election.

Impeachment
Bringing formal charges against a public official; the legislative equivalent of indictment for improper conduct in office.

Compensation The governor's salary is set by the legislature. At present, it is $150,000 yearly and stands in marked contrast to the low salaries paid to legislators. Although the governor's salary is among the highest in the nation, several other Texas state officials earn more.

In addition to the governor's mansion, there is an expense account to keep it maintained and staffed. The governor also has a professional staff and security detail with offices in the capitol building and in the governor's mansion. An adequate staff is important because the modern chief executive depends heavily on staff to carry out the duties of office.

[1]Colleen McCain Nelson, *The Dallas Morning News*, November 7, 2002.

Staff

The governor's increasing involvement in legislative affairs and the public's growing demands have intensified pressure on the executive's time and resources. The Texas governor, like all executives in modern government, depends on others for advice, information, and assistance when making decisions. A good staff is a key ingredient for successful service as chief executive.

Evaluating Appointees Among the most important concerns of the governor's staff are political appointments. Each year, the governor makes several hundred appointments to various boards, commissions, and executive agencies. The executive also fills newly created judicial offices and those vacated because of death or resignation. Staff evaluation of potential appointees is necessary because the governor may not personally know many of the individuals under consideration.

Legislative Liaisons Legislative assistants provide liaison between the office of the governor and the legislature. Their job is to stay in contact with key legislators, committee chairs, and the legislative leadership. These assistants are, in practice, the governor's lobbyists. They keep legislators informed and attempt to persuade them to support the governor's position on legislation. Often the success of the governor's legislative program rests on the staff's abilities and political expertise.

Budget Preparation Some administrative assistants head executive offices that compile and write budget recommendations and manage and coordinate activities within the governor's office. Staff members also exercise administrative control over the governor's schedule of ceremonial and official duties.

Planning The governor is the official planning officer for the state, although coordination and participation by affected state agencies are voluntary. The planning divisions also help coordinate local and regional planning between the councils of governments in an effort to bring the work of these jurisdictions into harmony with state goals. In addition, national and state funds are available through the governor's office to local units of government for comprehensive planning (master planning).

The governor's staff is primarily responsible for assisting with the everyday duties of the office but can also play a critical role in attempts to persuade legislators, administrators, local governments, and political leaders to follow the governor's leadership.

THE GOVERNOR'S POWERS OF PERSUASION

LO 8.2   Analyze both the governor's powers of persuasion and the limits on them.

Informal (extralegal) powers

Powers that are not stated in rules, law, or a constitution but are usually derived from formal or legal powers.

Formal (legal) powers

Powers that are stated in the law or the constitution.

The governor's ability to influence the making and executing of government policy depends on his or her bargaining skills, persuasiveness, and ability to broker effectively between competing interests—the tools of persuasion. The **informal, or extralegal powers** of the office are not stated in rules, law, or the constitution but are largely derived from the **formal, or legal powers** that are stated in the law or the constitution. They are as important as the legal powers, and the governor's ability to use informal power can determine his effectiveness. Compared to governors of other states (especially other populous, industrialized states), the governor of Texas has weak formal administrative powers. However, some Texas governors have been able to exert substantial influence on policy formulation and even on policy execution when the formal and informal powers are enhanced by a fortunate blending of other conditions, such as a strong personality, political expertise, prestige, a knack for public relations and political drama, good relations with the press, supporters with political and economic strength, a favorable political climate, and simple good luck.

The Governor as Chief Executive

The Texas Constitution charges the governor, as the chief executive, with broad responsibilities. However, it systematically denies the governor the power to meet these responsibilities through direct executive action. In fact, four other important elective executive offices—lieutenant governor, comptroller of public accounts, attorney general, and commissioner of the General Land Office—are established in the same section of the constitution and are legally independent of the governor, thus undermining the governor's executive authority.

Other provisions in the constitution further fragment executive power. For example, the constitution establishes the elective Railroad Commission of Texas and, although the State Board of Education can be either elected or appointed, it too is elected.

Moreover, the Texas legislature, by statute, has systematically assumed executive functions such as budgeting and auditing. It has also created the Department of Agriculture and a multitude of boards and commissions to administer state laws that are independent of direct control of the governor. Although members of these commissions are usually appointed by the governor, their terms are staggered, and it may be several years before the governor's appointees constitute a majority of a board or commission. Boards and commissions perform such functions as hiring and firing agency directors and establishing general agency policies. Figure 8.1 shows the fragmented nature of the executive branch.

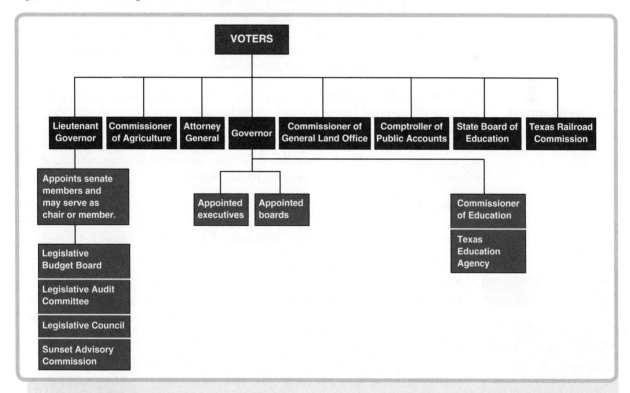

Figure 8.1
Texas's Elected Officials

A combination of political culture and Texas's Constitution has created one of the most structurally fragmented state governments in the nation and limited the governor's formal administrative bargaining powers.

 Organize a carefully constructed presentation or essay showing how the state executive branch could be streamlined. To be complete, you would need to explain why there would be resistance to centralizing power in a unified executive branch responsible to the governor. Explain the arguments for and against electing so many state administrators.

Appointive Powers   An effective governor will use the power of appointment to the maximum. Probably the most important appointments that the governor makes are to the independent boards and commissions. The members of these boards establish general administrative and regulatory policy for state agencies or institutions and choose the top administrators to carry out these policies.

The governor's ability to affect board policy through appointments is not immediate, however, as the boards are usually appointed for fixed, six-year staggered terms. Because only one-third of these positions become vacant every two years, the governor will only have appointed a majority of most boards in the second half of his or her term. Figure 8.2 shows how the board and commission system adds a layer in the organizational structure that limits voters' and the governor's ability to control most state agencies.

Interest-Group Concerns   Interest groups in Texas are vitally concerned with seeing that the "right kinds" of appointees are selected to serve on these boards and commissions. Industry interest groups are particularly eager to have an industry advocate (often an ex-lobbyist or industry executive) appointed to the board that oversees and sets policy for "their" agency. Appointment of a consumer advocate could disorient the close relationship that usually exists between an industry and its agency.

There may also be competing interest groups within one industry that may bargain individually with the governor for an appointee who is favorable to their particular viewpoint. Thus, an appointment to important boards often results in intense lobbying by special interest groups, which conversely gives the governor opportunities to develop support for policies and to help secure funds for future political campaigns.

The Influence of the Senate   Senators may also influence appointments from their districts as a result of **senatorial courtesy**, which is a tradition allowing a senator to reject the governor's appointment of a political enemy from the senator's district. Senators will usually refuse to vote for confirmation if a colleague announces that an appointee from his or her district is "personally obnoxious." Other senators show their courtesy to the disgruntled senator by refusing to confirm the appointment of his political enemy.

Senatorial courtesy
The tradition of allowing a senator to reject the governor's appointment of a political enemy from the senator's district.

Bureaucratic Concerns   Administrators want the governor to appoint sympathetic commissioners who share their goals. Making appointments that are friendly to administrator interests can strengthen a governor's influence with these administrators.

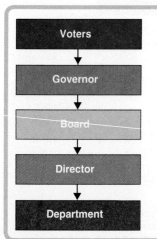

Figure 8.2
The Board and Commission System

This figure shows that voters have very indirect influence on state agencies. Voters elect a governor, who then appoints a multimember board, who then appoints a director to control daily agency operations. In the past, the weak link has been the appointed board whose terms expire in fixed intervals and whom the governor cannot fire or command. Former Governor Perry, however, was in office long enough to fill all state boards with loyal allies who implemented his political priorities.

CTQ How does the board and commission system reflect Texans' traditional fear of executive power?

Removal Powers Although the governor possesses broad appointive power to boards and commissions, the powers of removal are limited. He or she may remove members of the executive office and a few minor administrators. The governor may also remove, for cause and with the consent of two-thirds of the senate, his or her own appointments to boards and commissions. If the governor decides that an elected official is administering a law so as to violate its spirit, there is no official way to force a revision of such administrative interpretation or procedures. In general, the governor cannot issue directives or orders to state agencies or remove executive officials who do not abide by his or her wishes. Only by focusing public attention on the agency and garnering public support can the governor force an administrator to change positions or resign.

Law Enforcement Powers The governor has little law enforcement power. Following Texas tradition, the state's law enforcement power is decentralized at both the state and local levels.

At the state level, the Texas Rangers and the Highway Patrol are responsible for law enforcement. Both agencies are under the direction of the director of public safety, who is chosen by the Public Safety Commission. The three members of the Public Safety Commission are appointed by the governor for six-year staggered terms.

At the local level, police functions are under the jurisdiction of county sheriffs and constables (who are elected) and city chiefs of police (who are appointed by city officials). Criminal acts are prosecuted either by elected district or county attorneys or by appointed city attorneys.

The judiciary, which tries and sentences criminals, is elective (except for municipal judges, who are appointed by city officials).

Military Powers The governor is commander-in-chief of the state militia, which consists of the Texas National Guard and the Texas State Guard. The governor appoints (and can remove) an adjutant general who exercises administrative control over both units.

The Texas State Guard was established during World War II and serves as a backup organization in the event that the National Guard is called to active duty by the president. It cannot be called into active duty by the federal government, and its members receive no pay unless mobilized by the governor.

The governor may declare an area under martial law (usually after a riot or a natural disaster) and send units of the militia to keep the peace and protect public property. The governor may also employ the militia, according to Article 4, Section 7, of the Texas Constitution "to execute the laws of the state, to suppress insurrection, and to repel invasions." The Texas National Guard has both army and air force components and is financed by the U.S. government. It is required to meet federal standards and may be called to active duty by the president. In the event the Texas National Guard is nationalized, command passes from the governor to the president.

Clemency Powers The 1876 Texas Constitution granted the governor virtually unlimited power to pardon, parole, and grant reprieves to convicted criminals; these are known as **clemency powers**. Several governors were very generous with these powers, resulting in a 1936 constitutional amendment that established the Board of Pardons and Paroles. Many of the powers that had been held by the governor were transferred to the board, which grants, revokes, and determines the conditions for parole and makes clemency recommendations to the governor. However, the governor appoints the board's members and can grant less clemency than recommended by the board but not more. Nor can the governor any longer interfere in the parole process by blocking early releases from prison. The governor can postpone executions, but only for 30 days.

Clemency powers
The governor's powers to pardon, parole, and grant reprieves to convicted criminals.

Judicial Powers The governor can also exert influence on the state's judiciary. It is common for judges to retire or resign prior to the end of their terms. The governor is empowered to fill these vacancies until the next general election. The result is that the governor is able to repay political supporters with judicial appointments, and the appointees enjoy the advantage of incumbency in the general election.

The Governor as Chief of State

The governor, as the first citizen of Texas, serves as a symbol of Texas as surely as the bluebonnet or the Alamo. A significant part of the governor's job is related to the pomp and ceremony of the office. These ceremonial duties include throwing out the first baseball of the season, greeting Boy Scout troops at the state capitol, visiting disaster areas, and riding in parades for peanut festivals, county fairs, or cow-chip-throwing contests.

This ceremonial role is important because it can contribute indirectly to the governor's leadership effectiveness through increased popularity and prestige. The governor also broadens the image as first citizen to that of the first family of Texas whenever possible; voters identify with the governor's family, and so the governor's spouse is often included in the visual enactment of the office—particularly if the spouse is attractive and articulate.

International Function The governor performs ceremonial duties and represents the state at meetings with foreign officials and other governors. She or he also serves as a member of (or appoints representatives to) numerous multistate organizations and conferences that work to coordinate relations between Texas and other state governments. These conferences deal with oil, civil defense, nuclear energy, and other important matters. It is also the governor's responsibility to ask other states to extradite fugitives from Texas law and to grant or refuse like requests from other states.

Federal–State Relations In order to facilitate the governor's job of coordinating the activities of state agencies and local governments with the national grant-in-aid programs, the Texas government has established an office in the nation's capital, the Office of State–Federal Relations (OSFR). The governor appoints (and may remove) the director of this office, who serves as a representative from Texas to the federal bureaucracy. "Our person in Washington" tries to keep current on the numerous federal aid programs and grants that might be available to either state agencies or local governments. The director also serves as spokesperson for state agencies and local governments when their ideas and points of view differ from those held by the federal government.

The governor may request federal aid when the state has suffered a disaster, a drought, or an economic calamity. As chief of state, the governor often flies over or visits a disaster area to make a personal assessment of the damage—and also to show the victims that the governor is concerned for their welfare. Then, as a "voice of the people," the governor may make a highly publicized request for federal aid to the area.

Governor as Party Chief

Although there are varying degrees of competition from other elected officials and from political activists, the governor usually maintains the leadership of his or her party by controlling the membership of its executive committee. Although formally elected at the party's state convention, the chair and a majority of the executive committee are typically selected by the governor.

Party control is a useful channel of influence for a governor, and it permits what is often considered one of the most effective tools of persuasion of the governor's office: rewarding supporters with political patronage. Influential party members who support the governor's party choices and proposals and contribute to his or her election may influence the several hundred appointments that the governor makes each year.

National Party Leader The Texas governor can also be a leader in national politics if so inclined. Unless the Texas governor experiences serious public relations problems, any candidate from the governor's party who seeks the nomination for president would want the support of the governor of the nation's second most populous state. Texas's number of electoral votes also makes the governor an attractive candidate for president or vice president. A governor's support for a winning presidential candidate provides influence over the political patronage that flows from Washington into the state. Of course, patronage to the state can be dramatically increased if the Texas governor becomes president.

Positions on National Issues National politics also affords the governor an opportunity to build a firm, clear image for the people back home. The governor can take positions on political issues that do not involve the Texas government and over which, as governor, he or she has no control but with which people can easily identify, for example, such issues as foreign aid or national defense. Issues of state government are often hazy and indistinct because of the complexities of the issues or inadequate reporting by the media. The electorate can more easily make political identifications through more high-profile national issues.

Legislative Tools of Persuasion

Ironically, the most influential bargaining tools that the Texas governor has are legislative. How these tools are used largely determines the governor's effectiveness.

Message Power As a constitutional requirement, the governor must deliver a state-of-the-state message at the beginning of each legislative session. This message includes the outline for the governor's legislative program. Throughout the session, the governor may also submit messages calling for action on individual items of legislation. The receptiveness of the legislature to the various messages is influenced by the governor's popularity, the amount of favorable public opinion generated for the proposals, and the governor's political expertise.

The state constitution gives the governor the **message power** to deliver the state-of-the-state message and special messages to the legislature. This formal power of the governor is enhanced by the visibility of the office. Through the judicious use of the mass media (an informal power), the governor can focus public attention on a bill when it might otherwise be buried in the legislative maze. He or she must not overuse the mass media, however, for too many attempts to urge legislative action can result in public apathy for all gubernatorial appeals. An effective governor "goes to the people" only for the legislation considered vital to the interest of the state or to the governor's political and financial supporters.

Message power
The constitutional power to deliver the state-of-the-state message and special messages to the legislature.

Budget Powers The governor is designated as the chief budget officer of the state. Every other year, the various agencies and institutions submit their appropriation requests to the governor's staff and to the staff of the Legislative Budget Board. Working from these estimates, the governor and staff prepare a budget that is determined by both the state's estimated income and the estimated cost of program proposals. When completed, the budget is submitted to the legislature. However, the governor's proposals are usually not as influential as those prepared by the Legislative Budget Board.

The Veto One of the governor's most powerful formal legislative tools is the **veto**, a power that allows the governor to stop a bill from becoming law. After a bill has passed both houses of the legislature in identical form, it is sent to the governor. If signed, the bill becomes law; if vetoed, the bill is sent back to the legislature with a message stating the reasons for

Veto
A power that allows the governor to stop a bill from becoming law.

opposition. The legislature has the constitutional power to override the governor's veto by a two-thirds vote, but in practice vetoes are usually final.

Because legislative sessions in Texas are short, the vast majority of important bills are passed and sent to the governor in the final days of the session. The governor need take no action on the legislation for ten days when the legislature is in session (20 days when it is not in session), so he can often wait until the legislature has adjourned and thereby ensure that a veto will not be overridden. In fact, it is so difficult to override a veto that it has happened only once since World War II. Thus the veto gives the Texas governor a strong bargaining position with legislators.

No Pocket Veto
The Texas governor lacks the pocket veto that is available to many other chief executives, including the president of the United States. The pocket veto provides that if the executive chooses to ignore legislation passed at the end of a session, it dies without ever taking effect. By contrast, if the Texas governor neither signs nor vetoes a bill, it becomes law. By not signing a bill and allowing it to become law, the governor may register a protest against the bill or some of its provisions.

The Item Veto
The most important single piece of legislation enacted in a legislative session is the appropriations bill. If it should be vetoed in its entirety, funds for the operation of the government would be cut off, and a special session would be necessary. Thus Texas, like most other states, permits the governor an item veto, which allows the governor to veto funds for specific items or projects without killing the entire bill.

If used to its fullest potential, the item veto is a very effective negative legislative tool. Money is necessary to administer laws; therefore, by vetoing an item or a category of items, the governor can in effect kill programs or whole classes of programs. The governor cannot, however, reduce the appropriation for a budgetary item, as some governors may. Because the appropriations bill is usually passed at the end of the session, the item veto is virtually absolute.

The Threat of a Veto
A veto threat is an informal power that enhances the governor's bargaining power with legislators, enabling the governor to shape the content of legislation while it is still in the legislature. By threatening a veto while a bill is still being considered by the legislature, the governor is often able to persuade legislators to reshape the bill to meet the governor's wishes.

Both the veto and the item veto are negative tools that simply kill bills or programs; they do not let the governor shape legislation. However, by threatening to use these formal powers, the governor can often persuade the legislative supporters of a bill to change its content or face the probability of a veto. In this way, a compromise can often be negotiated. Although the veto itself is negative, the threat of veto can be used to positively affect the content of bills during the legislative process.

The threat of veto can also be used to consolidate lobby support for the governor's legislative proposals. Lobbyists may offer to support the governor's position on legislation if the governor will agree not to veto a particular bill that is considered vital to the interests of their employers. The governor can thus bargain with both supporters and opponents of legislation in order to gain political allies.

The governor can also use this powerful informal tool of persuasion to influence bureaucrats. Bureaucrats are very active in the legislative process, often seeking increased funding for favorite programs and projects or seeking authorization to administer new programs. Because of this, the governor may be able to influence the administration of existing programs by threatening to withhold funds or veto bills actively supported by an agency. The agency's legislative liaison personnel (its lobbyists) may also be encouraged to support the governor's legislative program in exchange for support (or neutrality) with respect to agency-supported bills.

Special Sessions The constitution gives the governor exclusive power to call the legislature into special session and to determine the legislative subjects to be considered by the session. The legislature may, however, consider any non-legislative subject, such as confirmation of appointments, resolutions, impeachment, and constitutional amendments, even if the governor does not include it in the call. Special sessions are limited to a 30-day duration, but the governor may call them as often as he or she wants.

Often when coalitions of legislators and lobbyists request a special session so that a "critical issue" can be brought before the legislature, other coalitions of legislators and interests oppose consideration of the issue and, therefore, oppose calling the special session. Because there is seldom any legislation that does not hurt some and help others, the governor has an opportunity to use the special session as a valuable bargaining tool. The governor may or may not call a special session on the basis of some concession or support to be delivered in the future. The supporters and opponents of legislation may also have to bargain with the governor over the inclusion or exclusion of specific policy proposals for the special session. Of course, this position may not be open to negotiation if the governor has strong feelings about the proposal and is determined to call (or not to call) a special session. If the governor does think that an issue is critical, the attention of the entire state can be focused on the proposal during the special session much more effectively than during the regular session.

Fact-Finding Commissions Governors also appoint so-called "blue-ribbon commissions" consisting of influential citizens, politicians, and members of concerned special interest groups. Commissions can serve either as trial balloons to measure public acceptance of the proposal or as a means to inform and increase public and interest-group support. Blue-ribbon commissions are also commonly used to delay the actual consideration of a political hot potato until it has cooled. Politicians know that the attention span of the public is short and that other personally important issues, such as jobs, families, and favorite soap operas or sports teams, easily distract people. Once the public becomes distracted, meaningful action may become unnecessary.

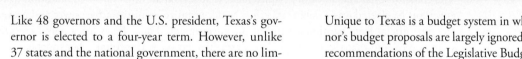

HOW DOES TEXAS COMPARE
The Governor's Power

- Like 48 governors and the U.S. president, Texas's governor is elected to a four-year term. However, unlike 37 states and the national government, there are no limits on the number of terms that can be served.
- The Texas governor's institutional powers are somewhat weaker than the typical state governor. The Texas governor has especially weak administrative powers because he or she shares this power with other elected executives in a plural executive system. And, unlike most governors, the Texas governor does not have a cabinet to coordinate programs, to supervise agencies, and to advise the governor.
- The Texas governor appoints supervisory boards and commissions but directly appoints only a few agency directors. The governor's power to appoint, remove, and direct agency heads is more limited than in most states.

Unique to Texas is a budget system in which the governor's budget proposals are largely ignored in favor of the recommendations of the Legislative Budget Board.

- As in most states, the Texas governor has such legislative powers as the power to call special sessions and to line-item veto spending bills. And, of course, the governor can wield considerable political power, but to do so requires the Texas governor to develop leadership power through informal personal relationships, manipulation of publicity, and vigorous bargaining among special interests.
- The Texas governor's office ranks below the average of other state governors. In fact, the Texas governor's overall institutional power ranking is 35th among the 50 states. By comparison, Massachusetts' governor ranks 1st and Vermont's ranks 50th.

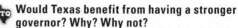
THE TEXAS ADMINISTRATION

LO 8.3   Analyze the structure and characteristics of the Texas bureaucracy.

Bureaucracy

The part of the executive branch that actually administers government policies and programs.

The Texas administration or **bureaucracy** is the part of the executive branch that actually administers government policies and programs. The bureaucracy is usually made up of non-elected employees who administer government policies and programs.

The various divisions of the executive branch can be grouped according to whether the top official in that bureaucracy is a single elected administrator, an appointed executive, or a multimember board or commission that may be appointed, elected, or ex officio.

The most distinctive characteristic of the Texas administration is that no one is really in charge of the administrative apparatus. As in many other states, the administration of laws in Texas is fragmented into several elective and numerous appointive positions. Although the principle of hierarchy exists within each department, the formal organization of the Texas bureaucracy follows the basic administrative principle of hierarchy only as far as the elected administrator or an appointed board. There is no single official in the Texas government who bears ultimate responsibility for the actions of the Texas bureaucracy. And there is no single official who can coordinate either planning or program implementation among the many agencies, commissions, and departments. The Texas bureaucracy can be visualized as almost 200 separate entities, each following its own path of endeavor, often oblivious to the goals and ambitions of other (often companion) agencies.

Elected Executives and the Plural Executive System

The constitutional and statutory requirement that several administrators (in addition to the governor) be elected was a deliberate effort to decentralize administrative power and prevent any one official from gaining control of the government. Thus, Texas has a *plural executive* system, meaning that the governor shares executive power with several other independently elected executives and boards. These elected officials are directly responsible to the people rather than to the governor. The fact that few Texans can name the individuals in these offices, much less judge their competence or honesty, tends to contradict the democratic theory of the popular election of administrators.

Lieutenant Governor Although technically part of the executive branch, the source of executive powers for the office of lieutenant governor comes from the legislative branch. The lieutenant governor, as president of the senate, is an ex-officio chair of the Legislative Budget Board, the Legislative Council, and the Legislative Audit Board and, if he or she desires, can exercise considerable personal influence on the Sunset Advisory Commission and the Legislative Criminal Justice Board. These legislative boards and commissions are not part of the bureaucracy, but they conduct continuing studies of administrative policies and make recommendations to the legislature.

Attorney General The attorney general is elected for a four-year term, with no limit on the number of terms that may be served. Holding one of the four most powerful offices in Texas government, the attorney general is the lawyer for all officials, boards, and agencies in state government. The office is authorized to employ more than 4,150 persons, many of them lawyers. The legal functions of the office include assisting in child support enforcement, antitrust actions, Medicaid fraud investigation, crime victim compensation, consumer protection, and other civil actions concerning insurance, banking, and securities. A broad spectrum of the state's business—oil and gas, law enforcement, environmental protection, highways, transportation, and charitable trusts, to name only a few—is included under the overall jurisdiction of the attorney general.

The attorney general performs two major functions for the state. One is to give an **attorney general's opinion**, which is an interpretation of the constitution, statutory laws, or administrative rules. As the state's chief lawyer, the attorney general advises his or her client. In the absence of a prior judicial interpretation, the attorney general has the power to interpret law or to give an opinion that a law or practice does or does not violate other laws or the Texas or U.S. constitutions. Although these advisory opinions are technically not legally binding, they carry great weight in the Texas government. If an official ignores the opinions, the attorney general will not defend the action in court.

The attorney general's opinion is an interpretation of the constitution, statutory laws, or administrative laws. Government officials may request opinions, and although they are not legally binding, government officials usually follow them.

The attorney general's opinion is usually requested only after the legal staff of another agency or official has been unable to reach a decision. The requests usually concern difficult questions, and several staff attorneys general consider each question. Only agencies and officials may request these opinions, and then only for official business.

A legislator may request an attorney general's opinion during the legislative session (sometimes merely to delay and thus help kill the legislation). The vagueness of laws and, particularly, the ambiguity of the Texas Constitution require the attorney general to give numerous opinions.

The second major function of the attorney general is to represent the state and its government in both civil and criminal litigation. This includes conflicts with the national government, such as the tidelands dispute in the 1950s; the defense of Texas's poll tax, abortion, segregation, and obscenity laws; and challenges to state legislative districts, judicial at-large elections, and affirmative action programs. The attorney general also represents Texas in legal conflicts with the governments of other states, as with Louisiana and Oklahoma over the exact boundary between the two states. The attorney general initiates suits against corporations for antitrust violations or consumer protection. However, the attorney general's criminal power is relatively narrow because the primary responsibility for criminal prosecution in Texas lies with the locally elected district and county attorneys.

AP Images/Harry Cabluck

Attorney General Ken Paxton was first elected in 2014.

CTQ **Which are the attorney general's most important powers? Why?**

The attorney general's opinion
The attorney general's interpretation of the constitution, statutory laws, or administrative rules.

Did You Know? Many state elected executives use their contacts and access to publicity as resources to run for higher office. Former Attorney General Greg Abbott was elected governor in 2014.

Comptroller of Public Accounts Glenn Hegar is the state's chief tax collector and financial officer.

CTQ **What is the comptroller's most important constitutional duty? Explain how Texas enforces its balanced budget requirement.**

AP Images/Harry Cabluck

Part of the importance of the office is that it is viewed as a steppingstone to the governor's chair, even though only 5 of the 22 governors since 1900 have served as attorney general. Political as well as legal considerations must therefore be taken into account. When opinions are handed down and litigation is conducted, the ambitious attorney general must not sever connections to campaign funds and political support if he or she hopes for higher office.

Comptroller of Public Accounts The comptroller is elected for a term of four years, with no limit on the number of terms that may be served. The functions of the comptroller's office encompass either directly or indirectly almost all financial activities of state government. The comptroller is the chief tax collector and the chief pre-audit accounting officer in the Texas government. The comptroller manages state deposits and investments and pays warrants on state accounts.

The comptroller's most important constitutional duty is to certify the state's approximate biennial revenue. The constitution requires a balanced budget, and the state legislature may not appropriate more funds than are anticipated as income for any two-year period. The comptroller also certifies the financial condition of the state at the close of each fiscal year. Any surplus funds can give the governor and legislature fiscal flexibility for tax cuts or increased appropriations without increasing taxes.

Commissioner of the General Land Office The commissioner of the General Land Office is elected for a term of four years. The office has more than 600 employees. Principal duties of the commissioner are managing and collecting rentals and leases for state-owned lands; awarding oil, gas, sulfur, and other hard-mineral leases for exploration and production on state lands; and leasing mineral interests in the state's riverbeds and tidelands, including bays, inlets, and the marginal sea areas.

As is the case with many officials, the land commissioner serves ex officio on several boards and chairs the important Veterans Land and the School Land boards, whose programs are administered by the General Land Office. (Ex-officio members hold their positions because they hold some other elective or appointed office.) The Veterans Land Board was established by a grateful state after World War II. The board loans money to veterans for land purchases and home purchases or improvements.

The School Land Board oversees approximately 20 million acres of public land and mineral rights properties, of which 4 million are submerged tidelands along the Gulf Coast. The lease and mineral income from these public lands varies with the production and price of oil and gas, but revenues from the leases, rents, and royalties from the public lands (recently about $500 million per year) are dedicated to the Permanent School Fund. Interest and dividend income from this fund are used to assist the state's public schools.

Commissioner of Agriculture

The commissioner of agriculture is elected for four years to oversee the Texas Department of Agriculture, which has more than 500 employees and is responsible for the administration of all laws as well as research, educational, and regulatory activities relating to agriculture. The duties of the department range from checking the accuracy of scales in meat markets and gas pumps at service stations to determining labeling procedures for pesticides and promoting Texas agricultural products in national and world markets. The commissioner also administers the Texas Agricultural Finance Authority, which provides grants and low-interest loans to businesses that produce, process, market, and export Texas agricultural products.

Like the U.S. Department of Agriculture, the Texas Department of Agriculture is also charged with administering laws for both consumer and labor protection. This is a classic example of an agency with two contradictory constituencies and often conflicting interests being given the function of protecting each interest from the other. The likelihood of a conflict of interest between these potentially incompatible groups is inescapable, especially if the department begins to protect consumers to the perceived disadvantage of the more powerful agricultural economic interests.

Pool/Getty Images

Land Commissioner George Prescott Bush manages Texas public lands and beaches.

CTQ Why are low-level executive offices considered steppingstones to higher office? What resources could George Prescott Bush bring to a campaign?

Appointed Executives

Besides the executives that voters directly elect, several executives are appointed by the governor. In many states, the governor appoints the heads of most state agencies, but in Texas only a few agency heads answer directly to the governor. These include the secretary of state, the adjutant general, the insurance commissioner, and the health and human services commissioner.

Secretary of State

Appointed by the governor, with confirmation by the senate, the secretary of state serves at the pleasure of the governor. The secretary is keeper of the Seal of the State and also serves as chief election officer for Texas, administers Texas's election laws, maintains voter registration records, and receives election results. The secretary of state's office also serves as a repository for official, business, and commercial records filed with the office.

The secretary publishes government rules and regulations and commissions notaries public. By executive orders, former Governor Rick Perry also directed the secretary of state to serve as his liaison for Texas border and Mexican affairs, and to represent him and the state at international and diplomatic events.

Adjutant General

Also appointed by the governor with the consent of the senate for a two-year term, the adjutant general is the state's top-ranking military officer and exercises administrative jurisdiction over the Texas National Guard and Texas State Guard. It is one of the few state agencies under the direct administrative control of the governor.

Health and Human Services Commissioner

The executive director of the Health and Human Services Commission is appointed by the governor with the advice and consent of the senate. The commissioner heads the Consolidated Texas Health and Human Services System, an umbrella agency or super-agency that oversees and manages four major health and welfare departments.

The director of the commission is also granted extensive administrative and policy-making authority over the departments. The power within the commission clearly rests with the director, who reports directly to the governor. The powers of the governor's office were significantly increased by the 78th Legislature, moving in the direction of a cabinet-type administrative format.

Insurance Commissioner The commissioner of the Texas Department of Insurance is directly appointed by the governor for a two-year fixed term, subject to senate confirmation. The department monitors and regulates the Texas insurance industry. It provides consumer information, monitors corporate solvency, prosecutes violators of insurance law, licenses agents and investigates complaints against them, develops statistics for rate determination, and regulates specific insurance lines such as property, liability, and life.

Boards and Commissions

About 200 elected, appointed, or ex-officio boards and commissions supervise state agencies. Their members may be salaried or serve only for expenses. There are also considerable differences in their political power. Generally speaking, the most important boards are those concerned with chartering or regulating the business, industrial, and financial powers within the state. Power is also measured by the number of people affected by the board's decisions or the size of its agency's appropriations.

These measures are general, however, because a relatively minor licensing board such as the Real Estate Board could be the most important agency in state government to a real estate broker whose license is about to be revoked.

Elective Boards Elective boards include the Texas Railroad Commission and the Texas State Board of Education.

Texas Railroad Commission One of the most important state regulatory boards in the United States is the Railroad Commission, a constitutionally authorized elective board whose three members serve for overlapping six-year terms. The governor fills vacancies on the board, and these appointees serve until the first election, at which time they may win election to the board in their own right.

The board is politically partisan and its members must first win their party's nomination before being elected. The chair position is rotated so that each member becomes the chair during the last two years of his or her term. This forces any candidate who is challenging an incumbent commissioner to run against the chair of the commission.

The Railroad Commission was established in 1891 during the administration of Governor Jim Hogg as a populist reform to protect Texas citizens from unfair railroad practices. Its powers were soon expanded to regulate intrastate wheeled carriers and in 1917 the oil and gas pipelines were added—soon to be followed by the authority to regulate oil well drilling and production.

The regulatory authority to regulate railroads and motor vehicles was gradually stripped away and in 1994 the Texas legislature transferred the commission's remaining motor and rail carrier responsibilities to the departments of Transportation and Public Safety.

The commission's current duties are only concerned with the regulation of gas utilities, oil and gas pipelines, oil and gas drilling, and pumping activities. It is also responsible for regulation of waste disposal by the oil and gas industry and the protection of both surface and subsurface water supplies from oil- or gas-related residues.

Texas State Board of Education The State Board of Education (SBOE) is elected to serve as the policy-making body for the Texas Education Agency (TEA), and the governor appoints the commissioner of education to serve as its chief executive. The TEA oversees and regulates the Texas public school system below the college level and administers national and state education law and SBOE rules and regulations. The SBOE is elected in partisan elections for four-year staggered terms from fifteen single-member districts.

The SBOE establishes policy, implements policy established by law, and oversees the TEA. The board also recommends three nominees for commissioner of education, who is appointed by the governor, with the senate's consent, to a four-year term.

Texas has historically had a decentralized school system in which most educational and administrative policy was established by local school boards. Recently, however, the legislature, the courts, and the TEA began mandating a more uniform educational policy. The TEA writes regulations for and compels local compliance with legislative and judicial mandates and reforms, dispenses state funds, serves as a conduit for some funds from the national government to the local schools, and selects the textbooks to be purchased at state expense for use by local districts.

Ex-Officio Boards Numerous boards have memberships that are completely or partly ex officio, that is, boards whose members are automatically assigned due to their holding some other position. There are two basic reasons for creating such boards. One is that when travel to Austin was expensive and time-consuming, it seemed logical to establish a board with its members already in Austin. Another reason is that subject-matter expertise on the part of the ex-officio members is assumed.

The Texas Bond Review Board is an example of an ex-officio board. It has four ex-officio members—the governor, lieutenant governor, speaker, and comptroller of public accounts. It reviews and approves all bonds and other long-term debt of state agencies and universities. It also engages in various other functions pertaining to state and local long-term debt.

A number of agency boards have some ex-officio members. The Texas Appraiser Licensing and Certification Board (nine members, one ex officio) and the Texas Racing Commission (nine members, two ex officio) are examples of such boards.

Appointed Boards Appointed boards vary greatly in terms of importance, administrative power, and salary. The members of these boards, who are usually unsalaried, set the policies for their agencies and appoint their own chief administrators. The governor, with the consent of the senate, usually appoints board members, but there are many mixed boards whose members are appointed by the governor or by some other official or have partly ex-officio membership. Because of the usual practice of appointing members to staggered terms, six years may lapse before a governor can appoint a complete board.

One example of an appointed board that has become quite powerful in recent years is the Texas Commission on Environmental Quality (TCEQ). It operates under three commissioners who are appointed by the governor for six-year overlapping terms. The commissioners appoint a director who oversees its approximately three thousand employees. The TCEQ is the primary environmental regulator for the state, overseeing cleanups, permitting industrial plants, and writing rules to govern most aspects of the Texas environment.

Also among the most important and powerful appointed boards are the Board of Transportation, the Health and Human Services Commission, the Board of Criminal Justice, and the Higher Education Coordinating Board. In fact, most state agencies are headed by appointed boards and commissions such as these.

Advisory Boards There are also advisory committees and boards that do not make official government decisions but study special issues or make recommendations to operating agencies. Texas has hundreds of advisory boards with their total membership in the thousands.

Board appointees are often representatives of groups that have an economic interest in the rules and policies of the board. Appointments may be either a reward for political support or an attempt to balance competing interest groups whose economic well-being is affected by board rules and policies.

Characteristics of Bureaucracy

Although bureaucracy is often thought of as being exclusive to government, it is also common to corporations, universities, churches, and foundations. Bureaucracies develop wherever human beings organize themselves to systematically accomplish goals and in the process lose some of their flexibility and efficiency. This discussion concentrates on government bureaucracies, especially those in Texas government.

Size The complexities of twenty-first-century society, together with increased demands of government at all levels, have resulted in a dramatic increase in the number of people employed by public administrations, and large numbers of employees mean large bureaucracies. Much of the harshest current criticism of government bureaucracy comes either from those who have simply lost confidence in our federal system or from propagandists in economic, political, and religious special interest groups who, for their own reasons, attack public employees as a means of discrediting specific government programs.

Various public officials, from time to time, attempt to systematically streamline both national and state bureaucracies and to make them more efficient and receptive to the wishes of policy makers. These attempts may or may not have positive results, but their level of success varies widely and is based largely on the expectations, perceptions, and political ideology of the reviewer.

Attacking "the bureaucracy" remains an effective political strategy. It is unfair, however, to compare only the bureaucracies of the state governments. Each state has its own organizational system, and great variations may relate to whether a specific service is provided by the state or by one of its political subdivisions. A reduction in public bureaucracy almost invariably results in either reducing services, government contracting with private firms, or requiring the administration of specific services or programs by lower governments.

Since the 1980s, there has been an increase in privatization as governments have turned to the private sector for services ranging from police to garbage collecting. Texas has privatized some of its prisons, state jails, and highways. It has also experimented with using private companies to determine eligibility for social service programs and some have advocated using publicly funded vouchers to subsidize private school attendance.

The national government has also increasingly mandated policies and regulations but has left the burden for funding and implementation to state and local governments, often forcing them to increase taxes or decrease services (or both). The state of Texas has also shifted much responsibility for public services to local governments through unfunded mandates.

The largest number of government employees work for local governments; the U.S. government actually hires fewer civilian employees than either state or local governments. The fact that it is the largest single government, however, results in its being criticized as excessive "big government."

Neutrality Administration of the laws in a "neutral" fashion—the separation of politics and administration—has long been an aim of reformists in American government. Ideally, elected public officials should establish and define a program's priorities, goals, or services. Administrators should then administer the law the "best way" and equally to all, rich or poor, black or white, powerful or weak, male or female.

The national government took the lead in bureaucratic reform when it established a strong **civil service (or merit) system**, an employment system using competitive examinations or objective measures of qualifications for hiring and promoting employees. The employee spoils system—government employment and promotion based on political support—was replaced by a merit system.

Many other states also adopted a merit system of public employment. However, Texas never implemented systematic statewide civil service reform; it still depends on a spoils or patronage system of public employment. Elected officials in Texas appoint major campaign supporters to top-level positions.

Texas attempted a different way to depoliticize the state bureaucracy by establishing the independent board and commission system, which tries to insulate the bureaucracy from the legislature and the governor, who are elected and hence political by definition. Both agency policy and administrative oversight are the responsibility of boards, usually appointed by the governor with approval by the senate. Their terms are fixed, usually for six years, and are staggered so that it takes two years or more before a new governor can appoint a majority.

Board members cannot be removed until the expiration of their terms unless they have been appointed by the sitting governor, and then only with the concurrence of two-thirds of the senate. However, the governor may "encourage" board members to resign by publicly criticizing the board members or the board's policies. The board appoints a chief executive officer to manage the department and see to the administration of public policy. Administrative power is thus "removed from politics" and excludes the governor from direct executive control over the state bureaucracy. This system also placates the basic Texas fear of power concentrated in the chief executive.

Local governments in Texas have attempted to accomplish similar goals by nonpartisan elections for city officials and special district boards. Many cities have also adopted the council–manager form of government in which an unelected "professional" manager supervises city departments and in school districts a "professional" superintendent administers the public schools.

With these safeguards, reformers believed that administrators could and would treat everyone equally and fairly, simply carrying out the policies of the elected officials. However, the theory of executive neutrality is naive, for public administration cannot be separated from politics—it is politics!

Privatization Conservative, pro-business citizens often support **privatization**, the hiring of private contractors to perform government services and perform government functions. They argue that contracting with private businesses to provide traditional public services both increases efficiency and reduces the size and power of government. Private enterprise is inherently more effective than the public sector, and current agencies lack the forces of the profit motive and competition that energize the private marketplace.

Skeptics of privatization argue that private businesses are profiteering at the public expense because they are likely to "cut corners" on services to improve their "bottom line." Opponents also contend that private businesses are not accountable to the public because their internal operations are not as well publicized as government activities.

Opponents suspect that political contacts and campaign contributions "grease the wheels" for contractors and that a new kind of spoils system is developing. Unlike the historic **spoils system** in which elected officials hired campaign workers as public employees, today's new spoils system is based on the practice of **contract spoils**, or **contract patronage**, in which politicians award contracts to their political supporters and contributors in the business

Civil service (or merit) system
An employment system using competitive examinations or objective measures of qualifications for hiring and promoting employees.

Privatization
The hiring of private contractors to perform government services and perform government functions.

Spoils system
A system in which elected officials hire campaign workers as public employees.

Contract spoils *or* contract patronage
A practice in which politicians award contracts to their political supporters and contributors in the business community.

community. Although the contract patronage system is not new, critics believe that it has become a major political reason for support of the privatization movement. Critics have dubbed this practice "crony capitalism."

Hierarchies

Structures in which several employees report to a higher administrator who reports to higher authorities until eventually all report to the single individual with ultimate authority over the entire organization.

Hierarchy All bureaucracies are formally characterized as **hierarchies**, structures in which several employees report to a higher administrator who reports to higher authorities until eventually all report to the single individual with ultimate authority. Theoretically, formal authority and directives flow down through the chain of command to lower levels, and information filters up through channels to the top from lower-level employees in the field. A framework of rigid rules and regulations formally assigns authority to various levels and defines the relationship between those individual bureaucrats who are of near-equal rank.

A model hierarchy is similar to the military chain of command for the U.S. Army. The president as the commander-in-chief is at the top and outranks the secretary of defense, who outranks the secretary of the army, who outranks all the generals, who in turn outrank all the colonels, and so on, down to the new private E-1 who is out-ranked by everybody. Actually, a hierarchy seldom functions according to its organizational chart. Usually, it can be influenced at all levels by legislators, the chief executive, interest groups, and other bureaucrats regardless of the formal lines of authority.

Although individual units within the Texas government are hierarchically organized, the state's bureaucracy is not because final authority is not centralized in a single executive. As shown in Figure 8.3, hierarchy is evident within Texas Department of Transportation, but there are no direct lines of authority and communication from the governor to the department.

Ironically, the governor is elected by the people to be the chief executive but has little direct authority over most administrators. However the governor's authority to appoint the members of most boards and commissions, together with close personal ties to powerful special interest groups, makes her or him an important player in shaping the direction of independent agencies.

Expertise Individual bureaucrats should have an understanding of their jobs and the effects of their decisions on others. Students of administration have concluded that this can be accomplished by defining the duties of the job and the limit of its authority. Thus, individual bureaucrats, through training and experience in specific job classifications, become experts in specialized areas of administration. Ideally the result will be a more knowledgeable and efficient administration. Expertise is also a major source of bureaucratic power.

A kind of power inherent in any professional bureaucracy stems from administrators' ability to shape public policy because of their knowledge of a given subject. Policy-making officials such as the legislature and governor are seldom as informed in policy-making areas as administrative personnel, who often built a career in a single area of government activity. Policy-making officials, whether appointed or elected, may find themselves forced to rely on government employees for advice regarding both content and procedure. Often seen by the public as only administrators, they are often important players in its conception, promotion, and enactment of public policy.

Public Support Good public relations with the electorate are usually beneficial for any agency, both in its appropriations requests and in its battles with other agencies over areas of jurisdiction. Favorable propaganda combined with myth and literature has created broadly based public support for such agencies as the Texas Department of Criminal Justice, the Texas Rangers, and to some extent the Texas Highway Patrol.

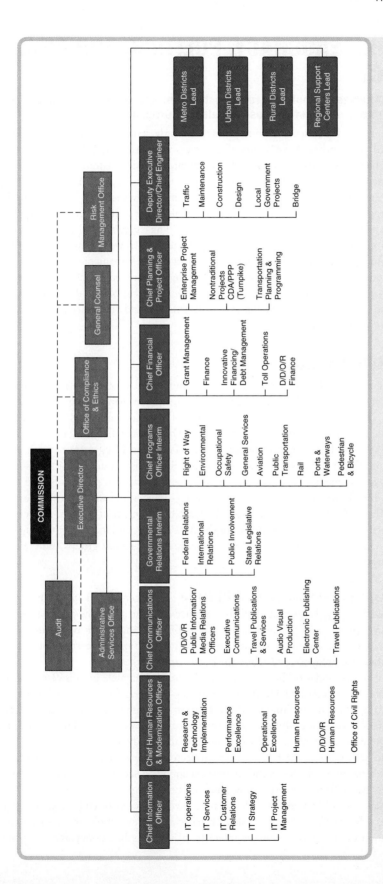

Figure 8.3
Texas Department of Transportation Organizational Structure

The organizational plan for the Texas Department of Transportation illustrates the apparent hierarchy in state agencies.

Texas Department of Transportation.

Keeping in mind that the governor appoints only the supervisory board of the Texas Department of Transportation, how can the governor control the day-to-day operations of this agency? In your answer, remember that the governor is also chief executive of almost 200 state agencies with similar structures, each jealously guarding their bureaucratic turf.

THE BUREAUCRACY, POLITICS, AND PUBLIC POLICY

LO 8.4 Analyze the political relationships among executive agencies, the public, interest groups, and elected officials.

Each attempt to depoliticize the bureaucracy has only resulted in one kind of politics being substituted for another. Most political observers agree that the Texas bureaucracy influences public policy in its conception, development, and administration, and cannot, in fact, be separated from politics. Administration is "in politics" because it operates in a political environment and must find political support from somewhere if it is to accomplish goals, gain appropriations, or even survive. The result of strong political support for an agency is increased size, jurisdiction, influence, and prestige. The less successful agency may experience reduced appropriations, static or reduced employment, narrowed administrative jurisdiction, and possibly extinction. Where, then, does a unit of the bureaucracy look for the political support so necessary for its bureaucratic well-being? It may look to clientele interest groups, the legislature, the chief executive, and the public. Political power also comes from factors within the bureaucracy, such as control of information and flexibility in the interpretation and administration of laws.

Clientele Groups

The most natural allies for an agency are its constituent or clientele interest groups—the groups that are directly affected by agency programs. The agency reciprocates by protecting its clients within the administration. Examples of close-knit alliances at the national level are defense contractors and the Department of Defense, agribusiness and the Department of Agriculture, and drug manufacturers and the Food and Drug Administration. In Texas, some of the closer bedfellows are the Texas Good Roads and Transportation Association and the Texas Department of Transportation; oil and gas producers, processors, and distributors and the Texas Railroad Commission; the banking industry and the Department of Banking; and the Texas Medical Association and the State Department of Health. Agitation by such groups often leads to the establishment of the state agency, and its power and importance are usually directly related to the power and influence of its clientele groups and the intensity of their support.

The Agency–Clientele Alliance The agency and its clientele groups are often allied from the beginning, and this alliance continues to grow and mature as mutual convenience, power, and prosperity increase. Economic and political ties are cemented by mutual self-interest. Agencies and clients share information, have common attitudes and goals, exchange employees, and lobby the legislature together.

Mutual accommodation becomes accepted, and the clientele groups often speak of "our agency" and spend considerable time and money lobbying for it. The agency reciprocates by protecting its clients within the administration. Because neither the bureaucracy nor the special interests are single entities, there is competition between special interests and agencies for appropriations, so both seek allies in the legislative branch.

Ties do not evaporate with retirement or electoral defeat, and many former administrators and legislators work for special interests as lobbyists, consultants, and employees. State employees know from the beginning that, in time, employment may be available from deep-pocketed special interests. This creates a revolving door of employees of special interest groups who move back and forth from special interest employment to public service. This rotation of employees helps the interests influence public policy and is a practice that casts a shadow of doubt over the policy-making process. In this environment, legislators, administrators, and regulators often become promoters of the industry. Unfortunately, this "sleaze factor" negatively affects public perception of all public servants and prompts cynicism toward government.

The Governor

The need of administrative agencies for the governor's support depends on the extent of the governor's formal and informal powers and how successful the agency has been in finding other powerful political allies. See the Texas Insiders feature.

Texas Insiders

Mike Toomey and the Revolving Door: Lobbying and Serving the Governor

After serving in the Texas legislature in the 1980s, Toomey became a lobbyist and established himself as a force to be reckoned with. Then, moving seamlessly between his lobbyist and government roles, Toomey became then-Governor Bill Clements' chief of staff, where he exercised enough behind-the-scenes influence to be labeled "Governor Toomey" by fellow political operatives. Afterward, Toomey once again left government to become a key figure in "The Lobby," a group of influential fixers in Texas government, where he earned a seat in the gallery of the Texas House of Representatives known ironically as "the owners' box."

Toomey developed a mutually beneficial relationship with former Governor Rick Perry. Both as a lobbyist and as Rick Perry's chief of staff between 2002 and 2004, Toomey capitalized on his long-term friendship with Perry to effectively represent his clients, while Perry benefited from Toomey's skillful fund-raising and adept political strategies. Many of the former governor's greatest political success and failures bear Toomey's fingerprint.

Toomey helped hand over the Texas House of Representatives to the Republicans in the 2002 election by raising enormous sums from the Texas Association of Business and his clients like AT&T and Aetna. He persuaded many of his lobbying clients to contribute to Perry's political campaigns for governor and the presidency. Toomey lobbied the legislature to pass the governor's signature bill to limit damage awards that plaintiffs could receive in court.

Toomey's association with Perry did not always turn out well for the governor. Opponents used the fact that Toomey's clients had gotten $2 billion

Mike Toomey has become the ultimate political insider, fixer, lobbyist, campaign fund-raiser, and chief of staff for two governors. Along with Bill Messer, he is currently a partner in The Texas Lobby Group, one of the most powerful lobby firms in Texas.

AP Images/Harry Cabluck

in state government contracts to tarnish Perry's presidential campaign, charging him with running a "pay to play" operation. As a lobbyist for Merck pharmaceuticals, which manufactures a vaccine against sexually transmitted human papillomavirus, Toomey persuaded Perry to issue an executive order requiring sixth-grade schoolgirls to be vaccinated against HPV, a cause of cervical cancer. The mandate outraged Christian fundamentalists and anti-government conservatives, and it was reversed by the Texas legislature.

Thinking about elites in Texas politics

The governor's office is relatively weak, both legally and constitutionally. To be effective, a governor must depend on the support of powerful political operatives like Mike Toomey.

 How can political alliances enhance the power of the governor? What risks do they present?

Sources: Nate Blakeslee, Paul Burka, and Patricia Kilday Hart, "Power Company: Who Are the Most Influential People Determining the Fate of Texas—and What Do They Want?" *Texas Monthly*, Volume 32, number 2, February 2011, p. 164; Jay Root, "Pro-Rick Perry PAC Raised $5.5 Million," *The Texas Tribune*, January 31, 2012, at www.texastribune.org/texas-politics/2012-presidential-election/pro-perry-pac-raised-55-million.

Even when an executive has extensive administrative powers (as the U.S. president does), most agencies have considerable independence. In Texas, where the executive is decentralized and the governor has few direct administrative powers, administrative autonomy is increased. Agencies still need the support of the governor, however, as the governor can influence the legislature when it considers appropriations bills and other matters important to the agency. The governor's item veto can also seriously affect an agency's funding.

The governor's cooperation is also essential because of his or her appointive power to policy-making boards and commissions. Because an agency's interests are usually similar to those of its constituency, both want the governor to appoint board members who will advance their mutual political goals.

Moreover, the governor's support gives the agency greater bargaining power with legislators and interest groups. Although the Texas governor has few direct administrative powers, she or he can influence and shape agency programs and success through veto power and appointments to policy-making boards and commissions.

Public Policy and the Iron Texas Star

The explanation of how public policy is made and implemented is a complex endeavor. Teachers and writers often use models as a means of simplification to explain the process. A model is a simplification of reality in order to explain reality. One such model, the "Iron Texas Star," is depicted in Figure 8.4. This model attempts to explain the relationships between the political actors in Texas government that make public policy happen. It depicts a coalition among political actors that includes interest groups, the lieutenant governor, the speaker, standing committees, the governor, administrators, and boards and commissions.

Texas has weak legislative committees when compared with their counterparts in the U.S. Congress. This is attributable to the hands-on authority of the lieutenant governor and the

Figure 8.4
The Iron Texas Star Model

This model illustrates the relationship among interest groups, the governor, state agencies, and the presiding officers of the state legislature.

 What are the bargaining chips that each of the entities at the five points of the Iron Texas Star bring to the table when engaging in the formulation of Texas public policy?

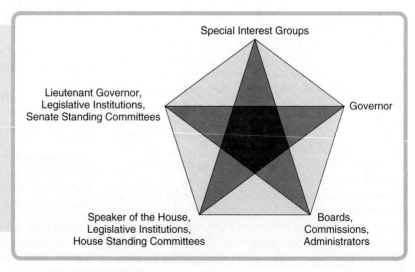

speaker of the Texas House of Representatives, who select most of the members and all of the chairs of the standing committees, conference committees, and legislative boards and com missions. Their exercise of this power includes them as two points of the iron star coalition that formulates and implements public policy in Texas. The elected administrators, boards, and commissions are another point. The governor is also a point as a result of the item veto power and the power to appoint members of state policy-making boards and commissions. The virtual absence of a civil service for Texas government employees makes them more vulnerable to influence by the appointed boards. Finally, economic interest groups make up the final and most important point. They provide the mortar that builds and holds together this five-pointed coalition of administrators, legislators, presiding officers, the governor, and clientele interests.

How the Coalition Functions All economic interests want favorable policies that they gain by acquiring "friends" in the state government. Some industries, such as insurance and oil and gas, have little need for direct appropriations and basically want only to be free of government interference. This class of interests may, however, want to use the powers of government for favorable regulations and protection from consumers and competitors. Other interests, such as the Texas State Teachers Association and the Texas Good Roads and Transportation Association, literally survive on government appropriations.

The basic goal of special interests is to accumulate "friends" among political operatives in the policy-making and regulatory areas of government. It is equally critical for political operatives to acquire friends among economically powerful individuals and special interest groups. The members of the coalition also support the friends of their friends at the other points of the iron star and thereby develop a mutual support group from which all can benefit.

Legislators, administrators, the governor, and the presiding officers rely to varying degrees on the support of their interest-group friends for campaign contributions, supplemental income, political advancement, financial advice and opportunity, and after-office employment and retirement income.

As time passes and members of the coalition become more interdependent, each looks to the other for support. Legislators bargain for the interest of the coalition in the legislature. Administrators issue favorable regulations and administrative policies that support their special interest friends. The presiding officers shepherd the proposals of their friends through the legislative process and also place the friends of economic special interests on powerful legislative committees and legislative boards and commissions. Also, the governor appoints friends and friends of friends to various administrative boards and commissions that make policy affecting these same friends. Other government officials may also broker with political operatives for decisions favorable to their friends and to the friends of their friends inside the iron star coalition. Altogether, it is a system of mutual accommodation.

The Legislature, the Lieutenant Governor, and the Speaker

Bureaucratic power is increased by the support of powerful legislators because an agency is dependent on legislative allies for laws that expand its powers, increase its jurisdiction, appropriate funds for its operation, and protect it from enemies and competitors.

Although committee chairs are important in the Texas legislature, the short session and the power of the presiding officers limit their influence. For this reason, an agency seeks the support of the lieutenant governor and the speaker of the house, as well as members of the finance and appropriations committees, the Legislative Budget Board, and the Legislative Council.

The importance of legislative support explains the intense lobbying surrounding the choice of legislators to leadership positions and continues as legislators are appointed to powerful committees. If the interest group and its agency are unable to get allies appointed or elected to positions of influence in the legislature, they are forced to try to gain support after the legislators are chosen—a more difficult endeavor.

The Control of Information

Because the bureaucracy is the branch of government that works most directly with constituent interest groups and the general public, administrative agencies gather the information used by these groups or the general public to determine what laws are needed or wanted. Information of this nature is valuable to legislators as well as to elected or appointed administrators but may be available only at the discretion of top government administrators. In other words, these administrators may dispense or interpret information in a way that benefits their agency or constituent interests during the enactment of public policy.

Administration of the Law

Administrative law
The rules and regulations written by administrators to implement public policy.

Just as judges use judicial review to interpret the meaning of the law and to write case law for its implementation, bureaucrats use what might be termed "administrative review," and the rules and regulations they write to implement public policy is called **administrative law**. Administrative law defines the meaning of the law and determines its effect on both special interests and the public. A small number of laws undergo judicial review, whereas all laws undergo administrative review.

Decisions by administrator to enforce speed limits either leniently or strictly, pure food regulation, chemical and pesticide use, or underage smoking alters the spirit of the law and affects its impact on citizens.

Although the law may remain on the books indefinitely, its effect is diminished with lax or selective enforcement. In this way, administrators establish public policies that not only affect the lives of the general public but can also modify the decisions of the state's elected policy makers. Although administrative decisions can be overturned by the courts and statutory law can be rewritten by legislatures, administrative review is the first and often the last determination of the meaning of a law and how rigidly it will be enforced.

BUREAUCRATIC ACCOUNTABILITY

LO 8.5   Evaluate strategies for holding state agencies accountable.

Throughout the history of the United States, people have tried to hold government responsible for its policies. The rise of the bureaucratic state is the most recent challenge to responsible government. The size and political power of modern bureaucracy make the problem of administrative accountability ever more difficult. Various organizational arrangements and legal restrictions have been used in attempts to make the bureaucracy accountable to the citizenry, or at least to someone who the citizens can hold responsible.

Accountability to the People

Elective accountability
Electing executive officers to make the bureaucracy directly accountable to the people through the democratic process.

The simplest approach is electing executive officers to make the bureaucracy directly accountable to the people through the democratic process—the theory of **elective accountability**. In Texas, this goal was to be accomplished through the election of administrative officials including the governor, lieutenant governor, attorney general, comptroller of public accounts, commissioner of the General Land Office, and the commissioners of Agriculture, the Railroad Commission, and the State Board of Education. The reasoning was that the public, if given an opportunity, would keep a close watch on elected administrators and refuse to reelect those who were incompetent or dishonest. Administrators would therefore be sensitive to the wishes of the voters and would administer the law in the interest of the general public.

Several problems have developed with the application of this idea. The most obvious is the difficulty of determining the will of the people or even of determining the public interest. Texas is a mixture of many divergent groups with many often incompatible public interests—to please one group frequently means displeasing another.

A further problem is the relative invisibility of elected executives. The list of elected executives is so long that very few voters are even aware of the names of many officeholders, much less their administrative competence. Common everyday ineptitude, inefficiency, corruption, or incompetence goes unnoticed by the public and an apathetic press. Administrators, once elected, are usually returned to office until they die, retire, anger powerful client special interests, or commit an act so flagrant that the voters finally "throw the rascals out." Although elective accountability for local offices may be practical in rural areas, accountability to the general public in an urban setting is an ineffective method of either influencing administrative behavior or enforcing accountability.

Accountability to the Legislature Some advocates of administrative reform argue that the bureaucracy should be accountable to the legislature because many view it as the branch of government "closest" to the people. Because it is elected to protect constituent interests and because legislators establish policies, many argue that these elected representatives should determine if public policies are being administered according to legislative intent.

This principle has been implemented in Texas by establishing legislative committees and various auditing, budgeting, and oversight boards. For example, the Texas legislature established the Sunset Advisory Commission to make recommendations as to the alteration, termination, or continuation of many of the state's state boards, commissions, and agencies. Agencies and their operations are reviewed periodically, usually in 12-year cycles, and cease to exist without specific legislative action to renew them. Functions may also be expanded, diminished, or reassigned to other agencies. Even when agencies are renewed, the Sunset Commission continues to evaluate their compliance with legislative directives. The state auditor also appraises management changes recommended by the commission. It is reasoned that periodic legislative evaluation, together with agency self-evaluation, should result in better, more efficient administration.

However, the principle of accountability to the legislature is questionable. The ability of any government to separate policy formulation from its administration is difficult, and the assumption that the legislature best represents the people is arguable. Legislators' judgments may be compromised by financial conflicts of interest, campaign contributions from special interest groups, and political ambition. Legislative accountability may serve the interests of the individual legislators and special interests but not the general public.

Another problem is the invisibility of the committee hearings and the decision-making processes in the legislature; the public is just not aware of many policy decisions made in its name by the legislature.

Finally, because the Texas legislature is seldom in session, permanent legislative institutions such as the Legislative Budget Board and the Legislative Council are given the task of overseeing the administration. These institutions lack the visibility necessary for effective operation in the public interest. Accordingly, a major question of responsible government is who is watching the watchers.

Accountability to the Chief Executive

Some reformers advocate a Texas administration patterned after the **cabinet system** of the federal government, where the chief executive has the power to appoint and remove top administrators. This would entail a reorganization and consolidation of the executive branch

Cabinet system
A system that allows the chief executive to appoint and remove top administrators.

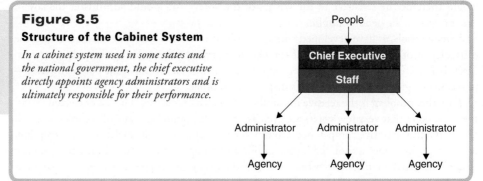

Figure 8.5
Structure of the Cabinet System

In a cabinet system used in some states and the national government, the chief executive directly appoints agency administrators and is ultimately responsible for their performance.

into larger subject-matter departments, with the governor being given power to appoint and remove top administrators and to control the budget. Administrative authority would be concentrated at the top as shown in Figure 8.5. (Advocates argue that this is only proper, as the governor usually receives the blame for administrative blunders anyway.) Furthermore, a governor who had these powers could hold the appointed bureaucrats accountable for their actions.

Theoretically, several benefits could result from accountability to the governor. The office is visible to the general public, so the problem of who watches the watchers would be solved. There would be no question regarding final responsibility for any corruption or incompetence in the administration. Administrative control could be simplified, resulting in coordinated planning and policy implementation. Waste and duplication could be reduced.

Consolidation and reorganization of the Texas administration is, without a doubt, necessary for an orderly, modern executive branch. Analysis of the national government demonstrates that although no person can control the dozens of agencies, their chiefs, and the thousands of government employees who work in these agencies, one means by which the president can influence the bureaucracy is through the executive office. If Texas reorganized public administration along the lines of the federal model, the governor would need a similar executive office. This executive staff, although relatively invisible to the public, would nevertheless be accountable to the governor.

This chain of accountability—administrative agency to appointed executive to staff to governor to the people—is weakened by the close ties usually found among administrators, constituent interest groups, and legislators. Interest groups would continue to influence administrative appointments and removals in "their agencies" just as they now influence appointments to the boards and commissions under the current system. Even under a cabinet system, the governor would have problems imposing accountability on agencies that have allies among powerful interest groups and legislators.

Bureaucratic Responsibility

To whom is the Texas administrator really accountable? The answer is, in all probability, to the interest groups that benefit from the programs administered by the agencies. Politics works on the basic principles of mutual accommodation between allies, conflict between opponents, coalition building, and compromise. Agency officials are often obligated to administer the law and make policy decisions in ways that are favorable to the goals and aspirations of their political allies among private economic interests. Appointees to boards and administrative positions are usually chosen from the industry concerned, and the policy decisions they make tend to benefit the most influential operatives in the industry. In turn, when government employees leave government service, many find jobs in the industry where their expertise lies. Thus, because the success of their agency, their government career, and possible after-government employment often depend on their actions while in the bureaucracy, it is understandable that many administrators feel more directly accountable to the economic powers they affect than to the public at large.

Open Meetings and Open Records

How then, can the Texas administration be made more accountable to the public? There is no single answer. One possibility could be more openness. A basic concept of democratic government is that policy made in the name of the public should be made in full view of the public. Texas has made progresses in this area. **Open-meetings laws** require that meetings of government bodies at all levels of government be open to the general public except when personnel, land acquisition, or litigation matters are being discussed. The laws further prohibit unannounced sessions and splitting up to avoid a quorum, and they require that public notice be posted for both open and closed sessions. However, these laws are continuously being tested by policy makers, who feel more comfortable operating in secret.

Openness is further encouraged by the state's **open-records laws**, which require records kept by the government to be open to the public for only the expense involved in assembling and reproducing them.

Whistleblowers and Ombudspersons

Another source of openness is **whistle-blowers**—government employees who expose bureaucratic excesses, blunders, corruption, or favoritism. These employees could be commended and protected from retribution, but too often they are instead exiled to the bureaucratic equivalent of Siberia or fired for their efforts. To its credit, Texas's whistle-blowers law prohibits governments from acting against employees who report law violations. But enforcement is difficult and time-consuming, and whistle-blowers often suffer.

The appointment of ombudspersons at every level of government would give each individual increased access to the bureaucracy regarding real or imagined administrative injustices. In this way, administrative error, injustice, or oversight could be rectified, allowing individual citizens to have a more positive attitude toward government. Any lack of public accountability by Texas administrators cannot wholly be blamed on poor structural organization or the lack of consumer- or citizen-oriented agencies. No amount of reorganization and no number of consumer agencies can overcome the willingness of an apathetic or indifferent public to accept bureaucratic errors, inefficiency, excesses, favoritism, or corruption.

An **ombudsperson** is an official who takes, investigates, and mediates complaints about government bureaucrats or policy. The office originated in Sweden in 1819 and is currently used by some state and local governments in the United States. As governor, Ann Richards established an ombudsperson in her office in 1991.

Open-meetings laws
Laws requiring that meetings of government bodies at all levels of government be open to the general public with some exceptions.

Open-records laws
Laws that require most records kept by government to be open to the public.

Whistle-blowers
Government employees who expose bureaucratic excesses, blunders, corruption, or favoritism.

Ombudsperson
An official who takes, investigates, and mediates complaints about government bureaucrats or policy.

APPLYING WHAT YOU HAVE LEARNED ABOUT THE TEXAS EXECUTIVE BRANCH

LO 8.6 Apply what you have learned about the state's executive branch.

As you have learned in this chapter, the function of the executive branch is to implement public policies, to put them into effect, and basically to do what government does. The following essay will help you close the gap between theory and reality by giving you a practical example of the role that "bureaucrats" play in carrying out some of the state's human service policies. The essay is based on an interview with a real-life bureaucrat named Wanda Mullen, a retired Medicaid liaison for the Texas Health and Human Services Commission.

After you have read the essay, you will be asked to apply your critical-thinking skills to new information that the new essay presents. Specifically, you will be asked to identify state agency employees' administrative activities and evaluate the importance of their role in the state's social service program. Then you will be asked to explore state social service programs and engage in some self-reflection as you evaluate society's responsibility in providing these services to the state's needy.

Bureaucracy and the Welfare State in Texas

by Alexander Hogan

LONE STAR COLLEGE

Imagine, for a moment, that you are a single parent with two children living in San Antonio. You have not completed a college degree and find that the rising cost of living in the city forces you to take on a second low-wage job to make ends meet. Living without health insurance and without the necessary amount of money to pay all of your competing expenses, you are often forced to decide between basic necessities like food, transportation, and utilities.

Your situation would not be unlike that of 17.9 percent of the population of Texas according to the 2010 U.S. Census.[2] Despite major Texas cities like Houston, Austin, and Dallas being heralded for their strong economic performance while the rest of the nation faced the brunt of the great recession, child poverty has grown rapidly in the shadows of Texas success. From 2000 until 2011 the number of children in poverty grew by 47 percent. This number brought the overall total of Texas children in poverty to 27 percent and placed Texas among the nine worst states in the country for child poverty.[3]

Poverty can put children at risk for a number of problems including poor health care, malnourishment, abuse, and exploitation. Poverty can further impact a child's performance in school and often may be a factor in their decision to drop out of high school. The state of Texas, like most states, has programs to help meet the basic needs of children in poverty.

TANF (Temporary Assistance for Needy Families) is a federal program administered through state government agencies. The Texas Health and Human Services Commission (THHSC) processes applications for TANF and the money is given to the family via The Lone Star Card, an electronic debit card that families may use to purchase food. While adults may receive TANF for anywhere between 12 and 36 months, children are not limited to a set number of months. Benefits for children range from $95 a month for one child to as much as $433 for eight children.

THHSC caseworkers face daunting caseloads and limited staff. In order to meet the urgent and time-sensitive needs of the many Texas children caught in poverty, caseworkers have developed procedures to screen and process requests. Online applications are screened for emergency eligibility by support staff, who then pass the most urgent cases on to caseworkers. In attempt to ensure that children are not left without access to medical care, Medicaid cases are processed with minimal income verifications. Processed, like TANF, within twenty-four hours, caseworkers have access to numerous special online verification sites created to help caseworkers accelerate the disbursement of aid.

While all of these procedures are designed to prioritize the needs of children, the regulations for their adult caregivers can still have a significant impact on a child's benefits. Households drawing TANF aid are required to comply with the Personal Responsibility Agreement (PRA). This agreement requires that caretaker applicants promise to cooperate

---

[2]U.S. Census Bureau, *American Community Survey Briefs*, October 2011, at www.census.gov/prod/2011pubs/acsbr10-01.pdf.
[3]Corrie MacLaggan, "Report: Child Poverty Increases in Texas," *The Texas Tribune*, December 3, 2013, at www.texastribune.org/2013/12/03/report-texas-child-poverty-increases.

with child support requirements, have their children immunized, and ensure their attendance at school. They also agree not to abuse drugs and alcohol or quit their job. In some cases, caretakers may even be required to attend parenting classes. Caregiver applicants are also required to participate in the Texas Choices program. This program, run by the Texas Workforce Commission, offers participants a variety of services—including career counseling and GED programs—designed to reintegrate the adults in the household into the Texas workforce.

Non-compliance with the Choices program is reported by the Texas Workforce Commission to THHSC. This results in a sanction, stopping TANF benefits for the entire household until the non-compliance sanction has been cleared from their file. Regardless of how quickly the caretaker returns to compliance, a 40-day wait period is imposed before benefits are disbursed again.

TANF sanctioned caretakers who need Medicaid to help them pay for a new pregnancy often will try to apply for Medicaid. These caretakers quickly discover that their sanction carries over to Medicaid and the head of household must clear the non-compliance before they can be considered eligible for the benefits to assist in the pregnancy.

Not all children at risk in Texas fall within the benefit scope of the Medicaid program. Roughly half of all Texas households are one emergency away from financial insecurity. The Corporation for Enterprise Development ranks Texas 37th of the fifty states for citizens' financial security.[4] The study suggests that many middle class households in Texas lack the cash on hand to weather a job loss or major health crisis. Though growing up in a financially insecure family, children in these households often are ineligible for Medicaid benefits because the parents earn too much.

THHSC caseworkers refer these families to the CHIP program. CHIP is a health insurance program for the children of families who make too much money to qualify for Medicaid. The program covers not only doctor's office visits and lab tests but also prescriptions as well as dental and vision care.

Despite having programs in place, a number of measures suggest that Texas, when compared with other states, is not keeping up with the depth or scope of the problems facing children in poverty. Perhaps more perplexing is the fact that despite such high rates of poverty in Texas, only 1.9 percent of Texans use welfare to help meet their family's needs. As Texas continues to grow, policy makers and citizens alike will have to seek new and creative ways to ensure children in poverty have access to the opportunity to become a successful part of the state's future.

JOIN THE DEBATE

 From this essay, identify the administrative rules that state agency employees such as caseworkers must enforce as they carry out Texas human service policies. How can state employees' effectiveness affect the delivery of state services?

 Develop a presentation to evaluate the fairness of the rules that Health and Human Services Commission employees must enforce. Visit the TANF website for the Texas Health and Human Services Commission, and examine the maximum benefits available. In a group, create a food budget for a family on TANF. Are the benefits adequate to meet the monthly costs of meals in your community?

 Explore the website of advocacy groups like Children at Risk (childrenatrisk.org), and consider what steps they believe must be taken to help children in Texas. Evaluate the merits of these proposals. Why do Texans use welfare in such low numbers? Should child poverty be a concern of government, or should this be a private responsibility?

---

[4]Corporation for Enterprise Development, Assets and Opportunity Scoreboard, "Treading Water in the Deep End," January 2014, http://assetsandopportunity.org/scorecard/about/main_findings.

CHAPTER SUMMARY

LO 8.1 Describe the governor's office and the characteristics of the typical Texas governor. Texas governors have been white, predominantly male Protestants with surnames from the British Isles. Modern Texas governors are conservative Republicans. Elected for four-year terms, they are usually middle-aged with careers in either business or law and have close connections to state and national moneyed interests.

LO 8.2 Analyze both the governor's powers of persuasion and the limits on them. The governor has relatively strong legislative prerogatives, among which are the veto and the item veto. Although shared with other legislative power bases, his legislative authority together with an astute use of informal powers enables the governor to exert influence on the direction and operation of the legislature and consequently affect public policy.

As chief executive the governor makes hundreds of appointments to boards and commissions in the administration but without meaningful removal or direct administrative powers. Although they are elected to a legally weak office, politically savvy governors can craft a politically formidable position by weaving their legislative, executive, and party powers into a cloth held together by their supporters and lobbyists from special interests.

LO 8.3 Analyze the structure and characteristics of the Texas bureaucracy. Texas has a plural executive system in which several state executives are elected independently of the governor. Most state agencies are actually headed by multimember boards and commissions that the governor appoints, but is unable to control. Board members serve fixed overlapping terms, which limits the governor's powers to control the agencies. With a few exceptions, the board, rather than the governor, appoints the actual chief operating officer, and the governor has limited powers to issue orders to state agencies or to remove state officers.

As a result, unlike most bureaucracies, Texas bureaucracy is decentralized with no single hierarchy and no single officeholder in charge. Instead, the state bureaucracy is an amalgamation of hierarchies, each headed by elected or appointed officers or boards. Aside from hierarchy, the traditional model describes bureaucracies as being characterized by size, expertise, and neutrality. Reformists have pursued the goals of a public administration that is free of bias in applying the law and neutral in politics, but efforts such as the civil service reform creation of independent governing boards have simply substituted one kind of politics for another.

LO 8.4 Analyze the political relationships among executive agencies, the public, interest groups, and elected officials. Clientele interest groups form close alliances with state agencies that administer the government programs that benefit them. Elected officials such as the governor and legislative leaders depend on the political support and expertise provided by these groups. As a result, public policy is often made by a relatively closed network illustrated by the Texas Iron Star.

LO 8.5 Evaluate strategies for holding state agencies accountable. Attempts to hold agency officials accountable have taken several forms, including elective accountability, accountability to the legislature or chief executive, and the use of publicity to check agency abuses. Critics charge that none of these strategies have worked effectively.

LO 8.6 Apply what you have learned about the state's executive branch. You looked at the Health and Human Services Commission as an example of what the bureaucracy does in practice. You looked at the kinds of rules and regulations that bureaucrats must enforce and evaluated society's responsibility in providing social services to the needy.

KEY TERMS

administrative law, *p. 224*
attorney general's opinion, *p. 211*
bureaucracy, *p. 210*
cabinet system, *p. 225*
civil service (or merit) system, *p. 217*

clemency powers, *p. 205*
contract spoils or contract patronage, *p. 217*
elective accountability, *p. 224*
formal (legal) powers, *p. 202*
hierarchies, *p. 218*

impeachment, *p. 201*
informal (extralegal) powers, *p. 202*
message power, *p. 207*
ombudsperson, *p. 227*
open-meetings laws, *p. 227*

open-records law, *p. 227*
privatization, *p. 217*
senatorial courtesy, *p. 204*
spoils system, *p. 217*
veto, *p. 207*
whistle-blowers, *p. 227*

REVIEW QUESTIONS

LO 8.1 Describe the governor's office and the characteristics of the typical Texas governor.

- Describe the politics and demographics of the typical Texas governor.
- Describe the Texas governor's term and salary, and describe methods for removal of the Texas governor.

- Explain the functions of the governor's staff. Why is a competent staff important for a successful administration?

LO 8.2 Analyze both the governor's powers of persuasion and the limits on them.

- Describe the governor's legislative tools of persuasion.

- Describe the executive tools of persuasion. What are the weaknesses in the governor's executive powers? How can the governor adapt to these limits by asserting political influence?

LO 8.3 Analyze the structure and characteristics of the Texas bureaucracy.

- Become familiar with Texas's elected executives and elected boards. To whom are they responsible?

- How does the use of appointed boards affect the governor's ability to serve as the "chief executive" of Texas?

- Define and explain the characteristics of Texas bureaucracy.

- Describe the classical model of bureaucracy and explain how the Texas executive branch differs from other bureaucratic organizations.

- Explain how Texas's historical background and the current Texans' viewpoint of government impacted the current administrative structure.

LO 8.4 Analyze the political relationships among executive agencies, the public, interest groups, and elected officials.

- Discuss the importance of the Texas bureaucracy in policy formation, development, and implementation.

- Describe the Iron Texas Star model.

LO 8.5 Evaluate strategies for holding state agencies accountable.

- Discuss the various methods used to hold the bureaucracy accountable to the people.

- Which methods are used in Texas government? Which are most effective?

- How do open-records and open-meetings laws affect bureaucratic behavior? Why are these laws important?

GET ACTIVE

- **Explore the organization of the governor's office** at **http://governor.state.tx.us/organization** and the appointment process at **http://governor.state.tx.us/appointments**. Find out how you can benefit from the activities of the other elected state officers: the attorney general at **www.texasattorneygeneral.gov;** the comptroller of public accounts at **www.cpa.state.tx.us;** the commissioner of the General Land Office at **www.glo.texas.gov;** and the commissioner of the Texas Department of Agriculture at **www.texasagriculture.gov**.

- **Follow the money.** Investigate the interest groups and individuals that have contributed to the governor's political campaign and those of other elected executives in Texas at the National Institute on Money in State Politics at **www.followthemoney.org**. Trace the links among Governor Abbott, lobbyists, campaign contributors, and the governor's appointments to office with Texans for Public Justice at **www.tpj.org**.

 Use state agencies to become an intelligent consumer. Contact the Consumer Protection Division of the Office of the Attorney General to learn about your rights and how to exercise them at www.texasattorneygeneral.gov/consumer. Before you buy a new vehicle, contact the Texas Department of Motor Vehicles, which maintains "lemon law" records and processes warranty complaints at https://txdmv.gov/motorists/consumer-protection/lemon-law. Find out how to demand your rights as a consumer from state agencies at Texas Watch www.texaswatch.org/consumer-tips. Follow state actions on consumer interests with the Texas Public Interest Research Group at www.texpirg.org.

 Take advantage of available state services. Shop for lower utility bills at www.powertochoose.org. Get help paying for college at the Texas Higher Education Coordinating Board website at www.collegefortexans.com. Financial help for injured crime victims is available from the Crime Victims Compensation Fund at www.texasattorneygeneral.gov/victims/about_comp.shtml. Get tips on buying insurance at www.tdi.texas.gov/consumer/index.html.

CHAPTER 9

The Judiciary

LEARNING OBJECTIVES

LO 9.1 Describe the differences between criminal and civil cases and between original and appellate jurisdiction.

LO 9.2 Explain how the courts are organized in Texas and identify the jurisdiction of each major court.

LO 9.3 Understand the role of grand juries and trial juries and analyze the responsibilities of citizens in the Texas legal system.

LO 9.4 Compare and evaluate the most common methods of judicial selection in the United States and in Texas.

LO 9.5 Apply what you have learned about the Texas Judiciary.

*A*merican society has increasingly turned to the judiciary to find answers to personal, economic, social, and political problems. Courts are often asked to determine our rights, and important legal questions touch almost every aspect of our lives. For example, what level of privacy should we expect in our cars, workplaces, and homes? What treatment should people of different ethnic, racial, gender, sexual orientation, or age groups expect? In a divorce proceeding, with which parent should the children live? Should an accused person go to jail, and if so, for how long? Should a woman be allowed to terminate her pregnancy? Should a patient be allowed to refuse potentially lifesaving treatment? These are among the thousands of questions asked and answered daily by courts in the United States.

In the past few decades, Texas courts have heard important or controversial cases involving topics such as flag burning, the death penalty, school desegregation, school finance, sexual orientation, the welfare of children in a polygamist sect, and one of the largest civil cases in history, in which Texaco was found liable to Pennzoil for more than $10.8 billion in 1985 (that's $23.1 billion in 2014 dollars).

In this chapter, our focus will be the Texas judicial system and general attributes of American legal procedure and process. What will quickly become clear is the sheer size and complexity of the Texas court system. Furthermore, courts are undeniably important because they affect our lives. This is due to the subject matter they consider, which determines our legal rights and often shapes public policy. What should also become clear is that various controversies surround the selection of Texas judges and the politics connected to these courts.

Stockbyte/Getty Images

An attorney addresses a jury in a civil case.

Why have civil suits become so common in Texas?

LEGAL CASES AND JURISDICTION

LO 9.1 Describe the differences between criminal and civil cases and between original and appellate jurisdiction.

Legal cases can be classified into two broad categories: civil and criminal, based on their subject matter. Jurisdiction within the court system is determined by whether the case is being tried for the first time or if a prior court decision is being reviewed on appeal.

Civil and Criminal Cases

In the American legal system, cases are generally classified as either civil or criminal. Table 9.1 shows the most important differences between these two types of cases. A **civil case** concerns private rights and remedies and usually involves private parties or organizations (*Garcia* v. *Smith*), although the government may on occasion be a party to a civil case. A personal injury suit, a divorce case, a child custody dispute, a breach-of-contract case, a challenge to utility rates, and a dispute over water rights are all examples of civil suits.

A **criminal case** involves a violation of penal law that is prosecuted by the state. If convicted, the lawbreaker may be punished by a fine, imprisonment, or both. The action is by the state against the accused (*State of Texas* v. *Smith*). Typical examples of criminal actions range from murder and rape to speeding and jaywalking.

One of the most important differences between civil and criminal cases is the **burden of proof** (the duty and degree to which a party in a court case must prove its position). In civil

Civil case
Concerns private rights and remedies and usually involves private parties or organizations (*Garcia* v. *Smith*), although the government may on occasion be a party to a civil case.

Criminal case
Involves a violation of penal law that is prosecuted by the state.

Burden of proof
The duty and degree to which a party in a court case must prove its position.

TABLE 9.1 Major Differences between Civil and Criminal Cases

Civil Cases	Criminal Cases
Deal primarily with individual or property rights and involve the concept of responsibility but not guilt.	Deal with public concepts of proper behavior and morality as defined in penal law. A plea of guilty or not guilty is entered.
Plaintiff, or petitioner, who brings suit is often a private party, as is the defendant or respondent.	Case is initiated by a government prosecutor on behalf of the public.
Dispute is usually set out in a petition.	Specific charges of wrongdoing are spelled out in a grand jury indictment or a writ of information.
A somewhat more relaxed procedure is used to balance or weigh the evidence; the side with the preponderance of the evidence wins the suit.	Strict rules of procedure are used to evaluate evidence. The standard of proof is guilt beyond a reasonable doubt.
Final court remedy is relief from or compensation for the violation of legal rights.	Determination of guilt results in punishment.

Note: Civil and criminal cases involve very different concepts of law based on different court procedures, who brings the case, and the consequences that result from court decisions in each type of case.

▲ Why should criminal cases require a higher standard of proof than civil cases?

Preponderance of the evidence

Whichever party has more evidence or proof on its side should win the case, no matter how slight the differential is.

Beyond a reasonable doubt

The standard used to determine the guilt or innocence of a person criminally charged. To prove a defendant guilty, the state must provide sufficient evidence of guilt so that jurors have no doubt that might cause a reasonable person to question whether the accused was guilty.

Original jurisdiction

The power to try a case being heard for the first time.

Appellate jurisdiction

The power vested in an appellate court to review and revise the judicial action of an inferior court.

Brief

A written argument prepared by the counsel arguing a case in court that summarizes the facts of the case, the pertinent laws, and the application of those laws to the facts supporting the counsel's position.

cases, the standard used is a **preponderance of the evidence**, meaning that whichever party has more evidence or proof on its side should win the case, no matter how slight the differential is. However, in a criminal case, the burden of proof falls heavily on the government or prosecution. The prosecution must prove that the defendant is guilty **beyond a reasonable doubt**, the standard used to determine the guilt or innocence of a person criminally charged. To prove a defendant guilty, the state must provide sufficient evidence of guilt so that jurors have no doubt that might cause a reasonable person to question whether the accused was guilty.

Sometimes an action may have both civil and criminal overtones. Suppose that in the course of an armed robbery, the perpetrator shoots a clerk at a convenience store. The state could prosecute the suspect for aggravated robbery and assault (criminal action), and the clerk could sue the robber for compensation for medical expenses, lost earning power, and other damages (civil action). This dual nature is not unusual.

Original and Appellate Jurisdiction

Original jurisdiction is the power to try a case being heard for the first time. It involves following legal rules of procedure in hearing witnesses, viewing material evidence, and examining other evidence (such as documentary evidence) to determine guilt in criminal cases or responsibility in civil cases. The judge oversees procedure, but evaluating evidence is the jury's job (unless the right to a jury trial has been waived, in which case the judge weighs the evidence). The verdict or judgment is determined and the remedy set. A trial involves the determination of fact and the application of law.

Appellate jurisdiction refers to the power vested in an appellate court to review and revise the judicial action of an inferior court. Such appeals do not involve a new trial but rather a review of the law as it was applied in the original trial. Many appeals are decided by review of the record (transcript) of the case and the respective lawyers' **brief** (a written argument prepared by the counsel arguing a case in court that summarizes the facts of the case, the pertinent laws, and the application of those laws to the facts supporting the counsel's position). Sometimes, lawyers may appear and present oral arguments. Appellate proceedings are based on law (legal process), not fact (no witnesses, material or documentary evidence). A reversal does not necessarily mean that the individual who was convicted is innocent, only that the legal process was improper. Consequently, that person may be tried again, and questions of **double jeopardy** (a second prosecution for the same offense after acquittal in the first trial) are not involved because the individual waives the right against double jeopardy by appealing the case.

Double jeopardy

A second prosecution for the same offense after acquittal in the first trial.

COURT ORGANIZATION

LO 9.2   Explain how the courts are organized in Texas and identify the jurisdiction of each major court.

Figure 9.1 shows the organizational structure of the Texas court system and the various types and levels of courts in the system. It is important to note that some courts within this rather large and complicated system have overlapping jurisdiction.

Did You Know? Former Texas Supreme Court Chief Justice Tom Phillips summarized the problem of Texas court organization when he said "We simply have too many courts."

Municipal Courts

The state authorizes incorporated cities and towns to establish municipal courts, and city charters or municipal ordinances provide for their status and organization. Legally, municipal courts have exclusive jurisdiction to try violations of city ordinances. They also handle minor violations of state law—class C misdemeanors for which punishment is a fine of $500 or less and does not include a jail sentence. (Justice of the peace courts have overlapping jurisdiction to handle such minor violations.) Most municipal court cases in Texas involve traffic and parking violations.[1]

The legislature has authorized the city governments to determine whether their municipal courts are *courts of record*. Normally, they are not. However, when they are so designated, records from such courts are the basis of appeal to the appropriate county court. Otherwise, where records are not kept, defendants may demand a completely new trial in overworked county courts, where most such cases are simply dismissed. Where it is available, drivers frequently use this procedure to avoid traffic convictions and higher auto insurance rates. In a case, Latin for "anew," a *de novo* trial is conducted in a higher court (as opposed to an appeal). In *de novo* cases, higher courts completely retry cases. On appeal, higher courts simply review the law as decided by the lower courts.

De novo

Latin for "anew"; a *de novo* trial is a new trial conducted in a higher court (as opposed to an appeal). In *de novo* cases, higher courts completely retry cases. On appeal, higher courts simply review the law as decided by the lower courts.

People who favor the court-of-record concept often point to the large amount of revenue lost because trials *de novo* usually result in dismissal. Opponents of the concept argue that municipal courts are too often operated as a means of raising revenue rather than for achieving justice. The fact that municipal courts collected $682 million in 2013 lends some support to the latter argument.[2]

Judges of the municipal courts meet whatever qualifications are set by the city charter or ordinances (see Figure 9.2). Some cities require specific legal training or experience. Other charters say very little about qualifications. Judges may serve for one year or indefinitely. Most are appointed for two-year terms but serve at the pleasure of the governing bodies that have selected them. Furthermore, these judges' salaries are paid entirely by their respective cities and vary widely. Where statutes authorize them, some cities have established more than one municipal court or more than one judge for each court. In view of the volume of cases pending before these courts, the need for a number of judges is obvious.

---

[1]Office of Court Administration, Texas Judicial Council, *Annual Statistical Report for the Texas Judiciary: Fiscal Year 2013*, Austin: Texas, 2013.
[2]Ibid.

Figure 9.1

Court Structure of Texas

This court organizational chart arranges Texas courts from those that handle the least serious cases (bottom) to the highest appeals courts (top). As you read the text, look for ways to simplify and professionalize the state's court structure.

Office of Court Administration, Texas Judicial Council, *Annual Statistical Report for the Texas Judiciary: Fiscal Year 2013*, Austin, Texas, 2013.

How can Texas voters intelligently choose between candidates for so many judicial positions? How could the court structure be simplified?

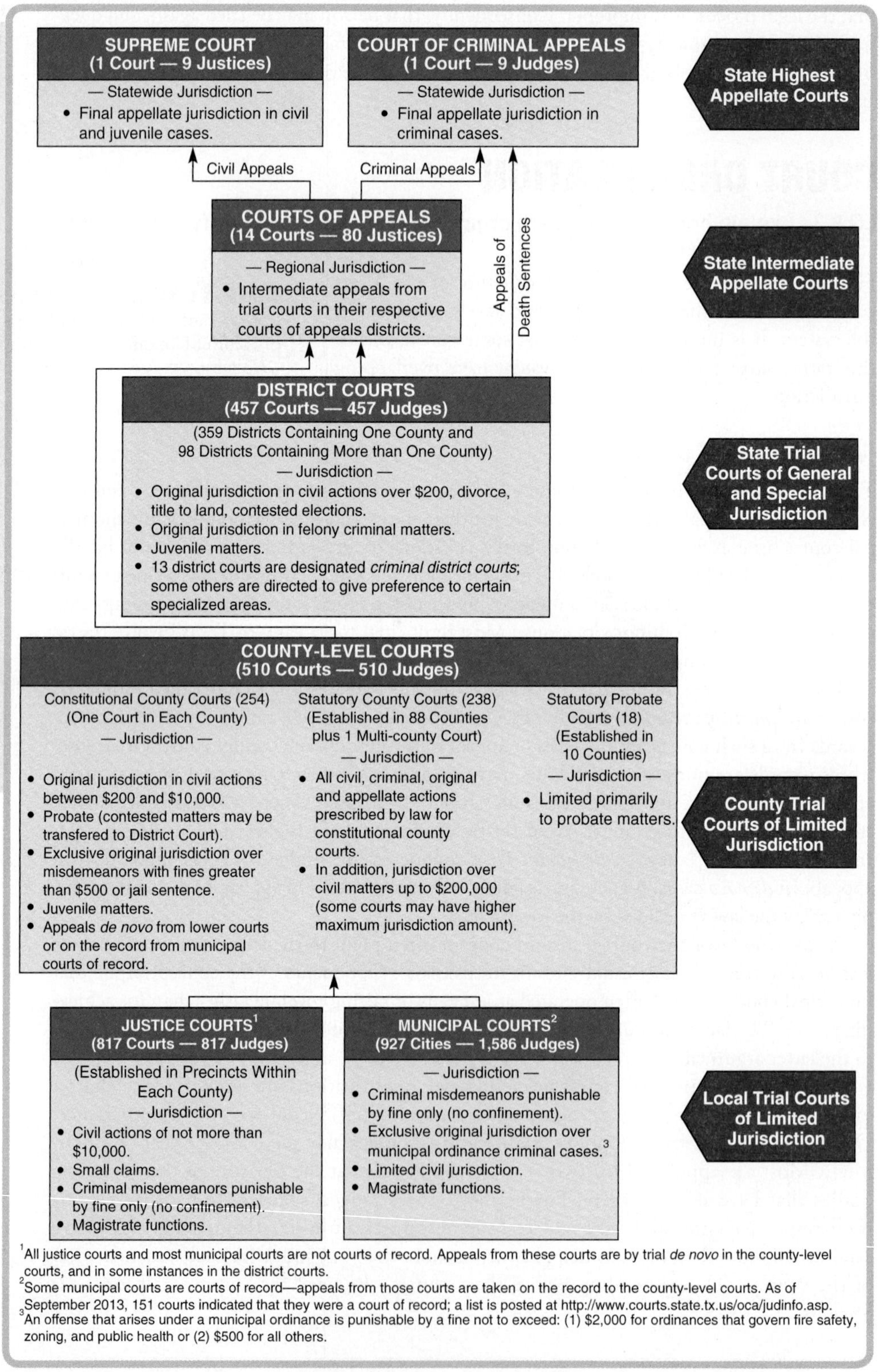

SUPREME COURT
(1 Court — 9 Justices)
— Statewide Jurisdiction —
- Final appellate jurisdiction in civil and juvenile cases.

COURT OF CRIMINAL APPEALS
(1 Court — 9 Judges)
— Statewide Jurisdiction —
- Final appellate jurisdiction in criminal cases.

State Highest Appellate Courts

Civil Appeals | Criminal Appeals

COURTS OF APPEALS
(14 Courts — 80 Justices)
— Regional Jurisdiction —
- Intermediate appeals from trial courts in their respective courts of appeals districts.

Appeals of Death Sentences

State Intermediate Appellate Courts

DISTRICT COURTS
(457 Courts — 457 Judges)
(359 Districts Containing One County and 98 Districts Containing More than One County)
— Jurisdiction —
- Original jurisdiction in civil actions over $200, divorce, title to land, contested elections.
- Original jurisdiction in felony criminal matters.
- Juvenile matters.
- 13 district courts are designated *criminal district courts*; some others are directed to give preference to certain specialized areas.

State Trial Courts of General and Special Jurisdiction

COUNTY-LEVEL COURTS
(510 Courts — 510 Judges)

Constitutional County Courts (254)
(One Court in Each County)
— Jurisdiction —

- Original jurisdiction in civil actions between $200 and $10,000.
- Probate (contested matters may be transferred to District Court).
- Exclusive original jurisdiction over misdemeanors with fines greater than $500 or jail sentence.
- Juvenile matters.
- Appeals *de novo* from lower courts or on the record from municipal courts of record.

Statutory County Courts (238)
(Established in 88 Counties plus 1 Multi-county Court)
— Jurisdiction —

- All civil, criminal, original and appellate actions prescribed by law for constitutional county courts.
- In addition, jurisdiction over civil matters up to $200,000 (some courts may have higher maximum jurisdiction amount).

Statutory Probate Courts (18)
(Established in 10 Counties)
— Jurisdiction —

- Limited primarily to probate matters.

County Trial Courts of Limited Jurisdiction

JUSTICE COURTS[1]
(817 Courts — 817 Judges)
(Established in Precincts Within Each County)
— Jurisdiction —
- Civil actions of not more than $10,000.
- Small claims.
- Criminal misdemeanors punishable by fine only (no confinement).
- Magistrate functions.

MUNICIPAL COURTS[2]
(927 Cities — 1,586 Judges)
— Jurisdiction —
- Criminal misdemeanors punishable by fine only (no confinement).
- Exclusive original jurisdiction over municipal ordinance criminal cases.[3]
- Limited civil jurisdiction.
- Magistrate functions.

Local Trial Courts of Limited Jurisdiction

[1] All justice courts and most municipal courts are not courts of record. Appeals from these courts are by trial *de novo* in the county-level courts, and in some instances in the district courts.
[2] Some municipal courts are courts of record—appeals from those courts are taken on the record to the county-level courts. As of September 2013, 151 courts indicated that they were a court of record; a list is posted at http://www.courts.state.tx.us/oca/judinfo.asp.
[3] An offense that arises under a municipal ordinance is punishable by a fine not to exceed: (1) $2,000 for ordinances that govern fire safety, zoning, and public health or (2) $500 for all others.

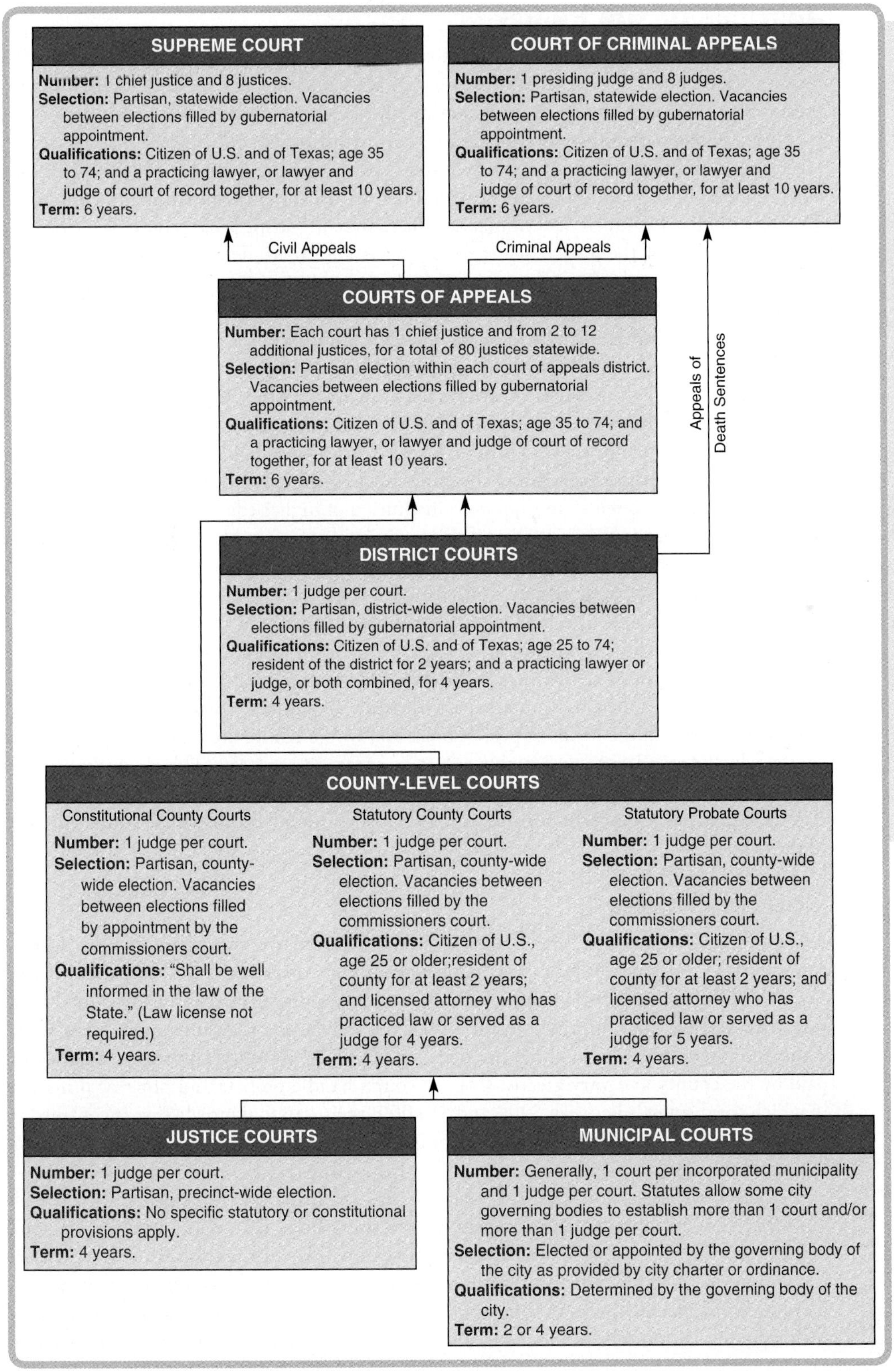

SUPREME COURT
Number: 1 chief justice and 8 justices.
Selection: Partisan, statewide election. Vacancies between elections filled by gubernatorial appointment.
Qualifications: Citizen of U.S. and of Texas; age 35 to 74; and a practicing lawyer, or lawyer and judge of court of record together, for at least 10 years.
Term: 6 years.

COURT OF CRIMINAL APPEALS
Number: 1 presiding judge and 8 judges.
Selection: Partisan, statewide election. Vacancies between elections filled by gubernatorial appointment.
Qualifications: Citizen of U.S. and of Texas; age 35 to 74; and a practicing lawyer, or lawyer and judge of court of record together, for at least 10 years.
Term: 6 years.

Civil Appeals   Criminal Appeals

COURTS OF APPEALS
Number: Each court has 1 chief justice and from 2 to 12 additional justices, for a total of 80 justices statewide.
Selection: Partisan election within each court of appeals district. Vacancies between elections filled by gubernatorial appointment.
Qualifications: Citizen of U.S. and of Texas; age 35 to 74; and a practicing lawyer, or lawyer and judge of court of record together, for at least 10 years.
Term: 6 years.

Appeals of Death Sentences

DISTRICT COURTS
Number: 1 judge per court.
Selection: Partisan, district-wide election. Vacancies between elections filled by gubernatorial appointment.
Qualifications: Citizen of U.S. and of Texas; age 25 to 74; resident of the district for 2 years; and a practicing lawyer or judge, or both combined, for 4 years.
Term: 4 years.

COUNTY-LEVEL COURTS

Constitutional County Courts
Number: 1 judge per court.
Selection: Partisan, county-wide election. Vacancies between elections filled by appointment by the commissioners court.
Qualifications: "Shall be well informed in the law of the State." (Law license not required.)
Term: 4 years.

Statutory County Courts
Number: 1 judge per court.
Selection: Partisan, county-wide election. Vacancies between elections filled by the commissioners court.
Qualifications: Citizen of U.S., age 25 or older; resident of county for at least 2 years; and licensed attorney who has practiced law or served as a judge for 4 years.
Term: 4 years.

Statutory Probate Courts
Number: 1 judge per court.
Selection: Partisan, county-wide election. Vacancies between elections filled by the commissioners court.
Qualifications: Citizen of U.S., age 25 or older; resident of county for at least 2 years; and licensed attorney who has practiced law or served as a judge for 5 years.
Term: 4 years.

JUSTICE COURTS
Number: 1 judge per court.
Selection: Partisan, precinct-wide election.
Qualifications: No specific statutory or constitutional provisions apply.
Term: 4 years.

MUNICIPAL COURTS
Number: Generally, 1 court per incorporated municipality and 1 judge per court. Statutes allow some city governing bodies to establish more than 1 court and/or more than 1 judge per court.
Selection: Elected or appointed by the governing body of the city as provided by city charter or ordinance.
Qualifications: Determined by the governing body of the city.
Term: 2 or 4 years.

Figure 9.2
Judicial Qualifications and Selection in Texas
This figure provides the minimum qualifications to become a judge and the method by which judges are selected for the different Texas courts from those that handle the least serious cases (bottom) to the highest appeals courts (top).

Office of Court Administration, Texas Judicial Council, *Annual Statistical Report for the Texas Judiciary: Fiscal Year 2013*, Austin: Texas, 2013.

SRQ What are the qualifications required to serve as a municipal court judge in the cities near where you live?

Justices of the Peace

The *justice of the peace* courts in Texas are authorized by the Texas Constitution, which requires that county commissioners establish at least one and not more than eight justice precincts per county (the area from which the justice of the peace is elected for each four-year term). County commissioners determine how many justices of the peace shall be elected (determined by the population) and where their courts shall sit. Changes are made continuously, making it difficult to pin down the number of justices of the peace at any given time. The Texas Judicial Council determined that there were 817 justices of the peace in 2013.[3]

The functions of the justice of the peace courts are varied. They have jurisdiction over criminal cases where the fine is less than $500. Original jurisdiction in civil matters extends to cases where the dispute involves less than $10,000. They may issue warrants for search and arrest, serve *ex officio* as notaries public, conduct preliminary hearings, perform marriages, serve as coroners in counties having no medical examiner, and serve as small claims courts. Most cases filed in justice courts are criminal and involve traffic violations.[4]

No specific statutory or constitutional provisions require that a justice of the peace be a lawyer. A justice of the peace who is not a licensed attorney is required by statute to take an 80-hour course in the performance of the duties of the office, plus a 20-hour course each year thereafter at an accredited state-supported institution of higher education. Serious questions have arisen as to the constitutionality of this provision because it adds a qualification for the office not specified in the constitution. Also, justice of the peace salaries vary a great deal from county to county and possibly from justice to justice within the same county.

Thus, despite changes affecting the qualifications, salaries, and responsibilities of justices of the peace, they still do not inspire confidence in many people. Defenders traditionally refer to the justice courts as the "people's courts" and maintain that elimination of the justice courts would remove the close contact many treasure. To eliminate them, it is argued, would put judicial power in the hands of professionals and would ignore the amateur status of these courts, which depend to a considerable extent on common-sense law. This is consistent with the widely held view that government is best when it is closest to the people. Critics counter that incompetence, caprice, and/or bias are not justified simply because these courts are close to the people.

County Courts

Each of the 254 counties in Texas has a *county court* presided over by the county judge (sometimes referred to, respectively, as the *constitutional county court* and the *constitutional county judge*). The Texas Constitution requires that the county judge be elected by voters for a four-year term and be "well informed in the law of the state"—a rather ambiguous stipulation. Thus, the constitution does not require that a county judge possess a law degree. Salaries are paid by the county and vary greatly. County courts handle probate and other civil matters in which the dispute is between $200 and $10,000; their criminal jurisdiction is confined to serious misdemeanors for which punishment is a fine greater than $500 or a jail sentence not to exceed one year.

Because the constitutional county judge also has administrative responsibilities as presiding officer of the commissioners' court (the governing body for Texas counties and not a judicial entity at all), he or she may have little time to handle judicial matters. The legislature has responded to this by establishing county courts-at-law in certain counties to act as auxiliary or supplemental courts in some, but not all, of Texas's counties. The qualifications of the judges of the statutory county courts-at-law vary according to the statute that established

---

[3]Ibid.
[4]Ibid.

each particular court. In addition to residence in the county, a court-at-law judge usually must have four years of experience as a practicing attorney or judge.

Various state laws determine whether these courts have either civil or criminal jurisdiction or a combination of both. Their civil jurisdiction involves cases less than $100,000. Their criminal jurisdiction includes misdemeanors that are more serious than those tried by the justice of the peace and municipal courts or misdemeanors that include a jail sentence or a fine in excess of $500. More than three-fifths of cases disposed in county-level courts are criminal, with cases involving drugs, theft, and driving while intoxicated or under the influence of drugs being the most common. Civil cases include probate matters and suits to collect debt.

Administration of justice is very uneven in Texas county courts. Although many of the judges are competent and run their courts in an orderly manner, others regard their courts and official jurisdictions as personal fiefdoms, paying little attention to the finer points of law or accepted procedures. Opportunities for arbitrary action are compounded if the county judge is performing as a judicial officer as well as the chief administrative officer of the county.

District Courts

District courts are often described as the *chief trial courts* of the state, and as a group, these courts are called the *general trial courts*. Currently, there are 457 district courts, all of which function as single-judge courts. Each judge, elected for a four-year term by voters in their districts, must be at least 25 years of age, a resident of the district for two years, a citizen of the United States, and a licensed practicing lawyer or judge for a combined four years. Texas pays $140,000 of the salary of each district judge, and although each county may supplement the salary, the maximum most district judges may receive in total compensation is $158,000.

District courts possess jurisdiction in felony cases, which comprise approximately one-third of their caseload.[5] Civil cases in which the matter of controversy exceeds $200 may also be tried in district courts, and such cases constitute the greatest share of their workload (see Figure 9.3). In addition, juvenile cases are usually tried in district courts. Although most district courts exercise both criminal and civil jurisdiction, there is a tendency in metropolitan areas for the multiple district courts to specialize in criminal, civil, or family law matters.

The caseload for these courts is so heavy that **plea bargaining**, negotiations between the prosecution and the defense to obtain a lighter sentence or other benefits in exchange for a guilty plea (commonly to a less serious crime) by the accused, is often used to dispose of criminal cases. This process saves the state a tremendous amount of time and cost. For example, it is often estimated that between 90 and 95 percent of criminal cases are disposed of in this way.[6] If plea bargaining was not used in many urban areas, court delays would be increased by months if not years. Although efficient, this practice raises many issues concerning equity and justice because it often encourages innocent people to plead guilty and allows guilty people to escape with less punishment than provided for by the law.

Likewise, many civil lawsuits are resolved by negotiated settlements between the parties. At times this may be an appropriate and just recourse, but in many of the state's most populous counties, there is such a backlog of cases before the courts that it can take years for a matter to be heard and settled. As a result, litigants often choose to settle their case out of court for reasons other than justice.

Plea bargaining

Negotiations between the prosecution and the defense to obtain a lighter sentence or other benefits in exchange for a guilty plea (commonly to a less serious crime) by the accused.

[5]Ibid.

[6]LindseyDevers, *Plea and Charge Bargaining: Research Summary*, Arlington, VA: Bureau of Justice Assistance, U.S. Department of Justice, 2011.

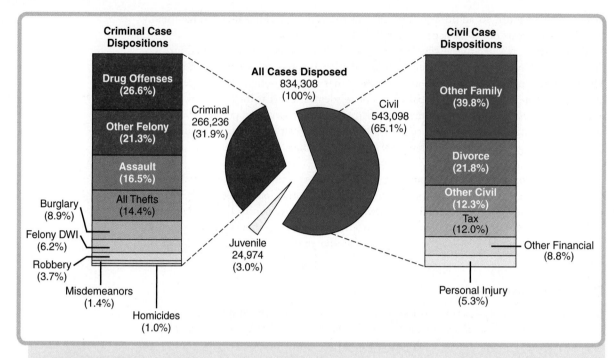

Figure 9.3

District Courts: Categories of Cases Disposed, Year Ending August 31, 2013

The pie chart and bar graphs show the kind of serious legal matters that district courts decide. Explain how many of these district court cases are settled by negotiated agreements between the parties.

Office of Court Administration, Texas Judicial Council, *Annual Statistical Report for the Texas Judiciary: Fiscal Year 2013*, Austin, Texas: 2013.

CTQ What are the benefits and problems resulting from legal negotiations such as plea bargaining?

Courts of Appeals

Fourteen *courts of appeals* hear immediate appeals in both civil and criminal cases from district and county courts in their area. Actually, only a small percentage of trial court cases are appealed; for example, in 2013, the courts of appeals disposed of 11,498 cases, and the appeals courts reversed the decision of the trial court in only 6 percent of those cases.[7]

The state pays each court of appeals chief justice $156,500 and each associate justice $154,000, salaries that the counties may supplement (up to a maximum of $9,000) at their discretion. Appeals judges are elected from their districts for six-year terms (see Figure 9.4) and must be at least 35 years of age, with a minimum of ten years of experience as a lawyer or judge.

Court of Criminal Appeals

Texas has a dual system of courts of last resort. The Texas Supreme Court is the highest state appellate court in civil matters, and the Texas Court of Criminal Appeals is the highest state appellate court in criminal matters. Among the 49 other states, only Oklahoma has a similar system.

---

[7]Office of Court Administration.

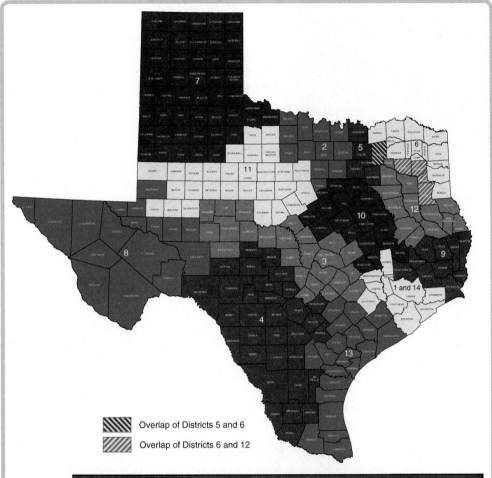

Overlap of Districts 5 and 6

Overlap of Districts 6 and 12

Court No.	Location	Number of Judges
1	Houston	9
2	Fort Worth	7
3	Austin	6
4	San Antonio	7
5	Dallas	13
6	Texarkana	3
7	Amarillo	4
8	El Paso	3
9	Beaumont	4
10	Waco	3
11	Eastland	3
12	Tyler	3
13	Corpus Christi	6
14	Houston	9

Figure 9.4
Appeals Court Districts (Map with Table)

Fourteen courts of appeals serve the geographical areas shown on this map. These courts handle both criminal and civil appeals from district courts in their area.

Office of Court Administration, Texas Judicial Council, *Annual Statistical Report for the Texas Judiciary: Fiscal Year 2013*, Austin, Texas, 2013.

 How does appellate jurisdiction differ from original jurisdiction?

Courtesy of the Texas Court of Criminal Appeals

The Texas Court of Criminal Appeals is the final court for criminal appeals in Texas and automatically reviews death penalty cases.

 How likely is it that a conviction will be reversed on appeal?

Did You Know? All executions in Texas take place at the state's 165-year-old Huntsville Unit, commonly referred to as the "Walls Unit" because of its large red brick walls.

Although most criminal cases decided by the fourteen courts of appeals do not advance further, some are heard by the court of criminal appeals, which consists of a presiding judge and eight other judges. Criminal court judges are elected statewide in partisan elections for six-year overlapping terms. They must be at least 35 years of age and be lawyers or judges with ten years of experience. The presiding judge of the court of criminal appeals receives a salary of $170,500; other judges receive $168,000.

The court of criminal appeals has exclusive jurisdiction over automatic appeals in death penalty cases. Since the U.S. Supreme Court restored the use of capital punishment in 1976, Texas has executed far more people than any other state.

As of October 1, 2014, the state had executed 517 people since 1982, when the death penalty was reinstated in Texas.[8] Since 2000, an average of 22 people has been executed each year, with 16 executions taking place in 2013.[9] Death penalty cases have led to a number of headline-generating stories, including controversies regarding the use of lethal injection, the execution of persons who were juveniles at the time of their crime, foreign nationals denied access to consular assistance, and those who might have been innocent of the crime for which they were sentenced to death.

Supreme Court

The Texas Supreme Court is the final court of appeals in civil and juvenile cases. Original jurisdiction of the court extends to the issuance of writs and the conduct of proceedings for the involuntary retirement or removal of judges. All other cases are in appellate jurisdiction. The court also has the power to establish rules for the administration of justice—rules of civil practice and procedure for courts having civil jurisdiction. In addition, it makes rules governing licensing of members of the state bar.

The supreme court consists of one chief justice and eight associate justices—all elected statewide. As is the case for the criminal court of appeals, three of the nine supreme court justices are elected every two years for six-year terms. Texas Supreme Court justices must be at least 35 years of age, a citizen of the United States, a resident of Texas, and a lawyer or judge of a court of record for at least ten years. The salary of the chief justice is $170,500, and the salary of associate justices is $168,000.

The Texas Supreme Court spends much of its time deciding which petitions for review will be granted because not all appeals are heard. Generally, it takes only cases it views as presenting the most significant legal issues. It should also be noted that the Supreme Court at times plays a policy-making role in the state. For example, in 1989, the court unanimously

[8]*Execution Database*, Death Penalty Information Center, Washington, D.C., October 2014. http://www.deathpenaltyinfo.org/views-executions
[9]Ibid.

declared, in *Edgewood* v. *Kirby* (777 S.W.2d 391), that the wide disparities between rich and poor school districts were unacceptable and ordered changes in the financing of Texas's public schools.

JURIES

LO 9.3   Understand the role of grand juries and trial juries and analyze the responsibilities of citizens in the Texas legal system.

Juries are an important and controversial aspect of the American judicial system. Some people argue that juries are beneficial because they allow for community input and the use of common sense in the legal system. Others claim that they often do not fairly represent the community and that their reasons for their decisions are often inappropriate or suspect. What is certain is that although millions of Americans serve on juries every year, the frequency of their use is declining, and the overwhelming number of cases in our legal system are not decided by them.[10]

Courtesy of the Texas Court of Criminal Appeals

The Texas Supreme Court is the final court of appeals only in civil cases. Such cases can have a broad impact on society, and they generate much attention from interest groups when they affect business regulation or corporate liability.

 Why would corporations and plaintiffs' attorneys have an interest in making contributions to the campaigns of candidates to the Texas Supreme Court?

Grand Jury

When a person is accused of a crime, the matter is likely to be taken to a **grand jury**, which in Texas consists of twelve people who sit in pretrial proceedings to determine whether sufficient evidence exists to try an individual and therefore return an indictment. (Some states do not have grand juries, but in those that do, the size ranges from five to twenty-three members.) An alternative to a grand jury indictment is the **information**, a written accusation made by the prosecutor against a party charged with a minor crime. Filed by the prosecutor with the appropriate court, the information must be based on an investigation by the prosecutor after receiving a complaint and a sworn affidavit that a crime has been committed.

The grand jury does not determine the guilt or innocence of the accused but rather whether there is sufficient evidence to bring the accused to trial. If the evidence is determined to be sufficient, the accused is indicted. An **indictment**, a formal written accusation issued by a grand jury against a party charged with a crime when it has determined that there is sufficient evidence to bring the accused to trial, is sometimes referred to as a **true bill**, an indictment returned by a grand jury, and the vote of at least nine of the twelve grand jurors is needed to indict. If an indictment is not returned, the conclusion of the grand jury is a **no bill**, which is a grand jury's refusal to return an indictment filed by the prosecutor.

At times, a grand jury may return indictments simply because the district attorney asks for them. In fact, grand juries return true bills in approximately 95 percent of the cases brought before them.[11] This high indictment rate is attributable at least in part to the fact

Grand jury
In Texas, consists of twelve people who sit in pretrial proceedings to determine whether sufficient evidence exists to try an individual and therefore return an indictment.

Information
A written accusation made by the prosecutor against a party charged with a minor crime; it is an alternative to an indictment and does not involve a grand jury.

Indictment
A formal written accusation issued by a grand jury against a party charged with a crime when it has determined that there is sufficient evidence to bring the accused to trial.

---

[10]G. AlanTarr, *Judicial Process & Judicial Policymaking*, 5th ed. (Boston: Wadsworth Publishing, 2009), p. 139.
[11]Henry J. Abraham, *The Judicial Process*, 7th ed. (NY: Oxford University Press, 1998), p. 119.

True bill

An indictment returned by a grand jury.

No bill

A grand jury's refusal to return an indictment filed by the prosecutor.

that the accused cannot have an attorney in the room during questioning. Some grand juries, known as *runaway* grand juries, may consider matters independently of the district attorney's recommendation. In general, prosecutors do not like a grand jury to be so assertive and are likely to refer only routine matters to it. To bypass it, the prosecutor may refer cases to a second grand jury meeting simultaneously or postpone action for another, more favorable, grand jury.

The process of selecting the grand jury has also come under criticism in recent years. Because it can be chosen by a grand jury commission (of three to five members) appointed by the district judge, the grand jury panel might not be truly representative of the county's citizenry. A total of 15 to 20 people are nominated by the commission, and 12 are selected to become the grand jury for the term of the court. In some counties, grand juries are chosen through random selection by computer.

The district attorney may determine whether or not a person indicted for a crime will be prosecuted. Some district attorneys will prosecute only if the odds are high that a conviction can be secured. This improves their statistical record, which can be presented to the voters when reelection time comes around. Other prosecutors may take most indicted persons to trial, even if the chances for conviction are low, but this may prove politically costly and can make the prosecutor appear ineffective.

Petit jury

A jury for a civil or criminal trial.

Petit (Trial) Jury

A jury for a criminal or civil trial is known as a **petit jury**. Trial by jury in criminal cases is a right guaranteed by the Texas Constitution and the Sixth Amendment of the U.S. Constitution. Even if the accused waives the right to trial by jury, expecting to be tried by the judge, the state may demand a jury trial in felony cases. Although not required by the U.S. Constitution, in Texas, the parties to a civil case generally decide whether a jury trial will be held. If a jury is to be used in a civil case in district court, the party requesting it pays a nominal fee to see that a jury panel is called. After the panel is summoned, the per diem for each juror is paid from public funds, which can entail considerable expense to the public if a trial becomes lengthy. County courts have six-person juries, whereas twelve people are on juries at the district court level.

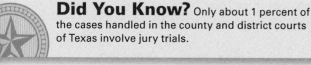

Did You Know? Only about 1 percent of the cases handled in the county and district courts of Texas involve jury trials.

A *venire*, or jury panel, is randomly selected from among those individuals who have registered to vote, hold a Texas driver's license, or hold a Texas identification card. Jurors must be literate citizens at least 18 years of age, qualified to vote, and not indicted or convicted for a theft or felony. Exemptions for jury service are now severely restricted. Persons older than 70 years of age, high school and college students, the primary (noncompensated) caretaker for an invalid, and anyone with legal custody of a child twelve years old or younger whose service would leave the child without adequate supervision are automatically exempt from jury service but may serve if they desire. Other excuses from jury service are at the discretion of the judge. Jurors in Texas must be paid at least $6 a day but not more than $50 a day. At its discretion a county can provide other compensation ranging from transportation reimbursement to free meals. Texas employers are not required to provide paid leave to employees serving as jurors.

Challenge for cause

A request to a judge that a certain prospective juror not be allowed to serve on the jury for a specific reason, such as bias or knowledge of the case.

In cases that receive a great deal of publicity, a special venire may consist of several hundred persons. Jury selection may last days or weeks, sometimes even longer than the trial itself. If either side believes that a prospective juror has a preconceived opinion about guilt or innocence, the prosecutor or defense attorneys may bring a **challenge for cause**, which is a request to a judge that a certain prospective juror not be allowed to serve on the jury for a specific reason, such as bias or knowledge of the case. Challenges for cause extend to any factor that might convince a judge that the juror could not render a fair and impartial decision. No limits are placed on the number of challenges for cause, but the judge decides whether to grant each specific challenge.

Statutes also allow challenges of jurors without cause. A challenge made to a prospective juror without being required to give a reason for removal is known as a **peremptory challenge**; no reason needs to be provided to remove a juror. The possibility exists, therefore, that nothing other than intuition can cause an attorney in a case to ask that a juror be dismissed. The only limitations to this type of challenge occur when the judge believes that prospective jurors are being eliminated solely because of their ethnicity, race or sex. Although peremptory challenges provide lawyers with a great deal of freedom in deciding to remove jurors, each side is given only a limited number of these challenges in each case.

Many lawyers maintain that jury selection is more significant than the actual argument of a case. Some firms hire jury and trial consulting firms to assist in the selection process. Psychological profiles of ideal jurors may be used to try to avoid jurors who might be unfavorable to a client and to identify those who might be supportive. For example, the prosecution would quite possibly want a grandparent or parent of young children on a jury dealing with child molestation, while the defense would wish to avoid such a juror. Many trial law firms and prosecutors also maintain a file on jurors from completed cases to help them select or avoid prospective jurors based on past behavior.

Whereas some states allow non-unanimous jury verdicts in both criminal and civil matters, juries in criminal cases in Texas must agree unanimously (this is not required in civil cases). Even if only one juror disagrees, the result is a **hung jury**, which is a jury that is unable to agree on a verdict after a suitable period of deliberation; the result is a mistrial. In this event, the prosecutor must decide whether to try the case again with a different jury or drop the matter. Because no verdict was reached with a hung jury, the accused person is not put in double jeopardy by a second trial. Usually, in the event of a second hung jury, the prosecution will drop the case.

SELECTION OF JUDGES

LO 9.4 Compare and evaluate the most common methods of judicial selection in the United States and in Texas.

States use several methods to select judges (see How Does Texas Compare?). In fact, some states use different methods for different types of courts. One popular variant is often called the **merit plan** or **Missouri plan**, a method of selecting judges on the basis of the merit or quality of the candidates and not on political considerations. Under this system, the governor fills court vacancies from a list of nominees submitted by a judicial commission, and these appointees later face retention elections. A relatively large number of states elect judges; in some states, the elections are partisan (candidates are officially affiliated with a political party), while in the others they are nonpartisan. Some states also provide for the appointment of judges by governors and a few allow the legislature to make the selections. With the exception of municipal court judges, Texas elects all of its judges in partisan elections.

Reformers developed the merit plan in an attempt to make the selection of judges less political. This method supposedly bases judicial selection on the merit or quality of the candidates as opposed to political considerations. For example, under a merit plan, the governor might fill court vacancies from a list of several nominees submitted by a judicial commission chaired by a judge and composed of both lawyers and laypersons. Appointed judges would hold their posts for at least a one-year probationary period, until the next election. Their names would then be put on a retention ballot, which simply asks whether a judge should be retained. It is a "yes" or "no" vote for the candidate with no other competition. Historically,

Peremptory challenge

A challenge made to a prospective juror without being required to give a reason for removal; the number of such challenges allotted to the prosecution and defense is limited.

Hung jury

A jury that is unable to agree on a verdict after a suitable period of deliberation; the result is a mistrial.

Merit plan or Missouri plan

A method of selecting judges on the basis of the merit or quality of the candidates and not on political considerations. Under this system, the governor fills court vacancies from a list of nominees submitted by a judicial commission, and these appointees later face retention elections.

more than 90 percent of such votes result in the candidate's election (or reelection). It is important to note that scholars have overwhelmingly found that this process is no less political than other selection methods and that there is no clear evidence that this process produces different or more meritorious judges.[12]

HOW DOES TEXAS COMPARE?
Selecting Judges

States use different methods to choose their judges, including those who serve on their supreme court. Figure 9.5 shows that 12 states allow their governor or legislature to appoint the supreme court justices. More commonly, states use elections to select their judges. There are three general types of judicial elections. Texas (along with seven other states) holds partisan elections, whereas 14 other states do not include partisan designations on the ballot (i.e., their elections are nonpartisan). The most popular method of selection (used in 16 states) is the merit, or Missouri, plan that claims to be less political and combines an initial appointment with retention elections.

FOR DEBATE

 What are the advantages and disadvantages of selecting judges through partisan elections? Do these advantages and disadvantages differ depending on the position, for instance, that of supreme court justice, district court judge, or justice of the peace?

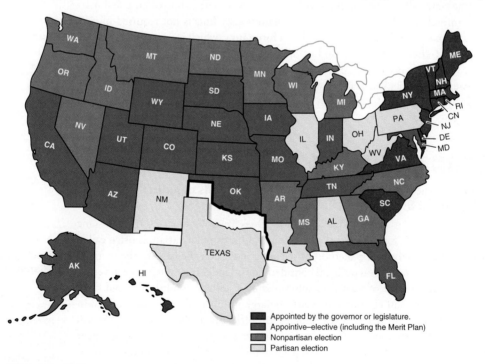

Appointed by the governor or legislature.
Appointive–elective (including the Merit Plan)
Nonpartisan election
Partisan election

Figure 9.5
State-by-State Selection of Supreme Court Justices

2013 Book of States, Lexington, KY: Council of State Governments, 2013.

[12]Henry Glick and Craig Emmert, "Selection Systems and Judicial Characteristics: The Recruitment of State Supreme Court Judges," *Judicature, 70* (1986), pp. 228–235; Roy Schotland, "New Challenges to States' Judicial Selection," *Georgetown Law Journal, 95* (2007), pp. 1077–1105.

The Politics of Judicial Selection in Texas

The system of judicial selection in Texas and practices related to it have been under attack. We shall examine why the courts and judges of Texas are criticized, and in doing so, gain a clearer understanding of the political nature of the court system.

Voter Knowledge Because Texas elects judges, a natural question arises: How knowledgeable are voters in these judicial elections? In other words, are voters cognizant of the candidates and their records in office? Research on the U.S. Supreme Court has repeatedly shown that the vast majority of the public know little about its rulings and actions.[13] Therefore, if most Americans know very little about the U.S. Supreme Court—the court that receives the most media attention in this country—how much do voters know about state and local courts? In a given election, Texas voters are regularly asked to cast a ballot to choose judges for the supreme court, the court of criminal appeals, a court of appeals, district courts, county courts, and for a justice of the peace. For instance, in 2014 many voters in Harris County were charged with the task of electing more than 70 different judges. Both systematic research and abundant anecdotal evidence indicate that most voters in Texas are unaware of candidates' qualifications or experience.

Partisanship Because they know so little about individual candidates, in general elections voters rely heavily on a candidate's partisan affiliation as a cue to determine how to vote. In other words, a voter who has no knowledge of the views or backgrounds of the candidates on the ballot may cast their vote based on the party label (Republican Party, Democratic Party, Libertarian Party, Green Party) next to the candidate's name on the ballot (or simply cast a straight ticket vote for all of a party's candidates). In Texas, this is a very common approach for making selections in judicial elections.

Republican candidates have dominated recent elections for the state's highest courts, occupying all nine positions on the supreme court, eight of nine spots on the court of criminal appeals, and 66 of the 80 judgeships across the state's fourteen courts of appeals (see Table 9.2). Eleven of the fourteen courts of appeals have Republican majorities while only three (based in Corpus Christi, El Paso, and San Antonio) have Democratic majorities. The lone Democrat on the court of criminal appeals, Lawrence "Larry" Meyers, was elected as a Republican (most recently in 2010) but switched his party affiliation from Republican to Democrat in 2013 in order to run for a place on the supreme court on the Democratic Party ticket in the 2014 election.

It has been argued that because judges, especially at the appellate level, make significant policy decisions, it is reasonable for voters to select judges on the basis of political party affiliation.[14] Party affiliation may provide accurate information concerning the general ideology and thus the decision-making pattern of judges. However, even if this is true, voting based solely on a judicial candidate's political party can lead to controversial results.[15]

Campaign Contributions Because voters often look for simple voting cues (such as name familiarity or party identification), candidates often want to spend as much money as possible to make their name or candidacy well known. In recent years, spending in judicial races has increased dramatically. Candidates need to win two elections—their

[13]James L. Gibson and Gregory A. Caldeira, "Knowing the Supreme Court? A Reconsideration of Public Ignorance of the High Court," *Journal of Politics, 71*(2), 2009, pp. 429–441.

[14]Philip L. Du Bois, *Judicial Elections and the Quest for Accountability*, Austin, Texas: University of Texas Press, 1980.

[15]Kiah Collier, "Embattled Judge Pratt Resigns, Suspends Campaign," *Houston Chronicle*, March 28, 2014; Kiah Collier, "Little Recourse in Pratt Case Stirs Reform Calls," *Houston Chronicle*, May 5, 2014.

TABLE 9.2 The Partisanship of Texas Judges, 2014: Supreme Court, Court of Criminal Appeals, and Courts of Appeals				
Court	**Appellate District (see Figure 9.4)**	**Total Number of Judges**	**Republicans**	**Democrats**
Supreme Court		9	9	0
Court of Criminal Appeals		9	8	1*
Courts of Appeals	Total	80	66	14
	First	9	8	1
	Second	7	7	0
	Third	6	6	0
	Fourth	7	3	4
	Fifth	13	13	0
	Sixth	3	2	1
	Seventh	4	4	0
	Eighth	3	0	3
	Ninth	4	4	0
	Tenth	3	3	0
	Eleventh	3	3	0
	Twelfth	3	3	0
	Thirteenth	6	1	5
	Fourteenth	9	9	0

*Lawrence Meyers was elected as a Republican but later switched parties.

Source: Texas State Directory, 2014 (April).

▲ **Does the partisan balance on these courts accurately reflect the partisan balance among Texas voters?**

BirchTree/Alamy

Judicial campaigns in Texas are partisan and expensive affairs.

Daemmrich Photography, Inc.

How much does justice depend on party affiliation and the influence of large campaign contributions?

party's nomination and the general election. In modern politics, this can be an expensive endeavor, and for more than a decade, Republican candidates have dominated the race for campaign contributions.

In addition to questions concerning fairness or the advantages of incumbency surrounding campaign finances, many critics have also asked whether justice is for sale in Texas. More directly, individuals or organizations often appear before judges to whose election campaigns they have contributed. In 2008, Texas Supreme Court incumbents running for reelection received half their support from lawyers, law firms, and lobbyists.[16] The Texas Insiders feature puts a face on major contributors to the Texas Supreme Court candidates.

In 2009, the U.S. Supreme Court weighed in on the question of judicial bias where litigants significantly

[16]Texans for Public Justice, *Interested Parties: Who Bankrolled Texas' High-Court Justices in 2008?* Austin, Texas, 2009.

influenced the election of judges hearing their cases. In *Caperton* v. *A. T. Massey Coal Co., Inc.*, the U.S. Supreme Court held that the chairman of A. T. Massey Coal had created such a question by donating $3 million to help finance the successful election of a new justice to the Supreme Court of Appeals of West Virginia. The possible conflict of interest arose because A. T. Massey Coal Company had a $50 million civil suit appeal pending before the court at the time; it was later decided in their favor by a 3-to-2 vote with the new justice voting with the majority. A 5-to-4 U.S. Supreme Court majority reversed and remanded the case holding "there is a serious risk of actual bias . . . when a person with a personal stake in a particular case had a significant and disproportionate influence in placing the judge on the case."[17]

Part of this debate of possible impropriety involves the battle between plaintiffs' attorneys and defense attorneys in civil cases. Texas has traditionally been a conservative, pro-business state. This perspective was usually reflected in the decisions of the judiciary, which often favored big business and professional groups (such as the medical profession). Plaintiffs' lawyers and their related interest groups have made a concerted effort in the past few decades to make the judiciary more open to consumer suits, often filed against businesses, doctors, and their insurance companies. The plaintiffs' lawyers poured millions of dollars into the campaign accounts of candidates they believed would align more favorably with their perspective. Defense and business attorneys and tort reform advocates such as Texans for Lawsuit Reform (TLR) responded with millions of dollars of their own contributions. These lawyers, from both vantage points, then often appear before the very judges to whom they have given these large sums of money.

Campaign Contributors in Texas Supreme Court Elections: Following the Money

Lawyers are, by far, the single largest group of contributors in judicial campaigns for both trial and appellate courts, including the Texas Supreme Court. Table 9.3a shows the total contributions raised by the winning and losing candidates for the Texas Supreme Court in 2012. As usual, Republicans won all three positions; no Democrat has been elected to the Texas Supreme Court since 1994. Table 9.3b shows the largest contributors to Texas Supreme Court campaigns in 2012.

Thinking about the role of elites in Texas politics The list of top contributors to Texas Supreme Court candidates includes the preeminent corporate defense law firms in the state, those representing insurance companies and other businesses that are often sued. Among the top contributors is Texans for Lawsuit Reform, a business-sponsored

TABLE 9.3a Campaign Contributions to Candidates for the Texas Supreme Court		
Candidates	**Winners' Total Contributions**	**Losers' Total Contributions**
Places 2, 4, and 6*	$2,539,836	$981,910

*Serving six-year overlapping terms, only three of the nine Supreme Court justices are usually elected in each general election held every two years. The "place" simply refers to the particular seat for which a candidate is running, but all of the state's voters may cast one vote for each of the three seats being contested.

Source: National Institute on Money in State Politics at http://www.followthemoney.org/database. The institute's searchable database relies on Texas Ethics Commission reports. The Judicial Campaign Fairness Act limits individual contributions and forbids corporate contributions. These totals represent contributions from affiliated individuals and political action committees.

---

[17]*Caperton* v. *A. T. Massey Coal Co., Inc.*, 556 U.S. (2009).

TABLE 9.3b Top Ten Contributors in Texas Supreme Court Races

Contributor	Total	Percent of Total	Sector
Texans for Lawsuit Reform	$110.961	3.15%	General business
Vinson & Elkins	$86,500	2.46%	Lawyers and lobbyists
Fulbright & Jaworski	$55,651	1.58%	Lawyers and lobbyists
Andrews Kurth LLP	$50,000	1.42%	Lawyers and lobbyists
Texans for Family Values	$49,141	1.40%	Ideology/single issue
Haynes & Boone	$46,565	1.32%	Lawyers and lobbyists
Jackson Walker LLP	$45,000	1.28%	Lawyers and lobbyists
USAA	$45,000	1.28%	Finance, insurance, and real estate
Good Government Fund	$36,000	1.02%	Oil and gas
Bracewell & Guiliani	$36,000	1.02%	Lawyers and lobbyists

Source: National Institute on Money in State Politics at http://www.followthemoney.org/database. The institute's searchable database relies on Texas Ethics Commission reports. The Judicial Campaign Fairness Act limits individual contributions and forbids corporate contributions. These totals represent contributions from affiliated individuals and political action committees.

group that seeks to limit the ability to bring liability suits (see our Texas Insiders feature in Chapter 10). These interests are closely allied with the Republican Party.

Important plaintiffs' attorneys and their umbrella organization, the Texas Trial Lawyers Association, are missing from this list of top contributors. Plaintiffs' lawyers primarily represent injured workers, patients, consumers, and the insured in liability suits against corporations, insurance companies,

and medical providers. These attorneys, including notables like Steve Mostyn, are mostly aligned with the Democratic Party.

 Is there a conflict of interest when law firms represent clients before a judge that their contributions helped elect? Should judges recuse themselves or abstain from cases that affect their largest campaign contributors? In your answer, consider whether any single contributor's share of a judge's campaign treasury is sufficient to create a genuine conflict of interest.

Clearly, the current system is quite political, and many people oppose it for a number of distinct reasons. This has led to repeated attempts to reform the way Texas selects its judges or change what is permissible in campaign fund-raising. Proposals for change have come from many sources, including chief justices of the state supreme court and a committee formed by a lieutenant governor. However, with such divergent interests involved and no clear alternative acceptable to all groups, very little judicial reform has occurred.

Ethnic/Racial and Gender Diversity

A major criticism of the current partisan election system involves one of its outcomes: limited ethnic/racial and gender diversity on the bench. Table 9.4 details the ethnic/racial and gender profile of the state's judges across the judicial spectrum, from the supreme court to the justice of peace and municipal courts. Although Anglos account for less than half (46 percent) of the state's overall population, 78 percent of the state's judges are Anglos. In contrast, only 16 percent of the state's judges are Hispanic, ranging from a low of 11 percent (i.e., one judge) on the state's two highest courts to 17 percent on its lowest courts. Even fewer African Americans hold judicial office from the top to bottom of the Texas judiciary, accounting for a mere 4 percent of all Texas judges.

Women's representation in judicial posts varies considerably across the different court levels. A majority of the court of criminal appeals justices are women, and women are close to

TABLE 9.4 The Ethnic/Racial and Gender Composition of Judges Serving on the Texas Courts: 2013

Court	Anglo	Hispanic	African American	Asian American	Men	Women
Supreme court	78%	11%	11%	0%	78%	22%
Court of criminal appeals	89%	11%	0%	0%	44%	56%
Court of appeals	84%	15%	1%	0%	57%	43%
District courts	77%	16%	5%	1%	70%	30%
County-level courts	84%	14%	2%	1%	80%	20%
Justice of peace and municipal courts	77%	17%	5%	1%	64%	36%
All courts	78%	16%	4%	1%	67%	33%

Source: Office of Court Administration, Texas Judicial Council, *Annual Statistical Report for the Texas Judiciary: Fiscal Year 2013*, Austin, Texas, 2013.

▲ Hispanics, African Americans, and Asian Americans make up 38, 12, and 4 percent of the state's population, respectively, yet account for only 16, 4, and 1 percent of the state's justices. Does this stark underrepresentation of ethnic and racial minorities on the bench undermine the legitimacy of the state's judicial system?

parity (43 percent) in the state's fourteen courts of appeals. However, the lower courts are more male dominated, with women's representation at a nadir on the county-level courts, where only one in five justices is female. Overall, one-third of all Texas judges are women.

APPLYING WHAT YOU HAVE LEARNED ABOUT TEXAS COURTS

LO 9.5 Apply what you have learned about the Texas Judiciary

The following essay challenges you to think about the gap between ideals and reality in the Texas judicial system. You will be asked to consider some of the implicit assumptions that reformists make about what constitutes ethical behavior among judges. You will explore how judges' motivations affect their independence and impartiality and whether judicial selection methods might affect court decisions.

After you have read the essay, you will be presented with several questions that will require you to apply what you have learned in this chapter to new material. Your analysis will require you to engage in self-reflection about the meaning of ethical behavior and apply those concepts to the real-world operation of the judicial system. You also will be asked to identify the elements in the Texas judicial selection process that compromise the independence and impartiality of the state's courts.

Judicial Impartiality and Independence in Texas: Democratic Ideals vs. Electoral Realities

by Sergio Saenz-Rivera

EL PASO COMMUNITY COLLEGE

Introduction This article contrasts the democratic ideals of judicial impartiality and independence with the reality of judicial selection and decision making in Texas. Students can decide whether a different selection method would make Texas's judges fit these democratic ideals.

The Ideals of Impartiality and Independence

Some of the most idealized aspects about democratic governments are the degree of judicial impartiality and the independence with which the judges make decisions.[18] Impartiality is the idea that judges should make decisions neutrally, considering the facts without favoring one individual, group, ideology, or political party over another. The idea of impartiality in America is complex because of a widespread belief that impartial decisions can only be made if judges seek guidance in the Constitution and in the Founding Fathers' "original intent."[19] Under this assumption, judges who follow the Constitution will not promote a personal, contemporary, or partisan political agenda.[20] The other ideal, judicial independence, can be understood as the degree to which the courts' decisions are insulated from other political actors or interests. These can include popular opinion, private interests, political parties, or other branches of government, especially the executive branch. In an ideal democracy, judges should be free from pressure in order to objectively serve the public good.[21]

Are the ideals of impartiality and independence present in Texas? All of the judges in Texas, except for municipal and administrative judges, are elected in a partisan election. In other words, just like any other politicians, judges have to campaign, raise funds, make promises to donors, promote a party agenda, and win the popular vote. It is argued that by receiving campaign money, elected judges could be, at the very least, suspect of upholding a partisan political agenda. In the worst-case scenario, judges could be found guilty of having their decisions openly compromised by campaign money.[22] The question of impartiality and independence is further complicated when the governor of Texas fills a vacancy in the courts. In Texas, the governor alone appoints a successor who will have to eventually win a popular election to continue on the bench.

The implicit assumption behind reforming the judicial selection process is that an alternative system of judicial selection other than partisan elections or gubernatorial appointment would help Texas to more closely reflect the democratic ideals of independence and impartiality.[23] Another implicit assumption is that judicial decision making and, by extension, judges' opinions could be modified by diminishing campaign money in the judicial selection process. Lastly, it is assumed that by removing the powers of gubernatorial appointments, the courts would become independent from the governor's views. But what is the evidence in favor these assumptions? Are independence and impartiality simply dependent on the selection method for judges?

The Evidence

Since the 1980s, when general elections in Texas became more competitive, even Texas Supreme Court justices have called for a selection reform.[24] The general

[18]Aharon Barak. 2006. *The Judge in a Democracy*. Princeton: Princeton University Press, 101–103.
[19]For the classic "originalist" approach to judicial decision making, see Raoul Berger. 1977. *Government by the Judiciary*. Cambridge, MA: Harvard University Press; and for adherence to precedence, see, e.g., Richard Dworkin. 1988. *Taking Rights Seriously*, Cambridge, MA: Harvard University Press.
[20]For a sophisticated understanding of these concepts, read Jeffrey Segal and Harold Spaeth. 2002. *The Supreme Court: The Attitudinal Model Revisited*. Cambridge: Cambridge University Press.
[21]The classic statement about separation of powers is by Charles-Louis de Secondat Baron de Montesquieu, *The Spirit of the Laws [1748]*. See also Mira Gur-Arie and Russell Wheeler. 2001. "Judicial Independence in the United States: Current Issues and Relevant Background Information," Federal Judicial Center in http://www.fjc.gov/public/pdf.nsf/lookup/judindep.pdf/$file/judindep.pdf (accessed January 29, 2014).
[22]Texans for Public Justice. 1988. "Payola Justice: How Texas Supreme Court Justices Raise Money from Court Litigants." http://www.tpj.org/reports/payola/intro.html.Ibid (accessed January 31, 2014).
[23]See, for instance, Skaggs, Adam, Maria da Silva, Linda Casey, and Charles Hall. 2011. "The New Politics of Judicial Elections 2009–2010." 2011. Washington, DC: Brennan Center for Justice at NYU in http://www.brennancenter.org/publication/new-politics-judicial-elections-2009-10.
[24]See Anthony Champagne and Kyle Cheek. 2002. "The Cycle of Judicial Elections: Texas as a Case Study." *Fordham Urban Law Journal,29*(3), 907–940.

claim has been that adopting an alternative method of selection would stop judges from being politicians and force them to become more neutral arbiters. There are actually very few studies on the direct impact of campaign money on judicial decision making, but the data and the circumstantial evidence of those in favor of reform are strong.[25] For example, one report argues that in 1997–1998, 60 percent of cases chosen for review by the Texas Supreme Court had to do with matters involving campaign donors.[26] The ideal court would attract cases that affect other people, not just the judges' wealthy donors. Another recent study found that money negatively affects impartial judicial decisions in Texas but not in places where there are other methods of selection.[27]

Individual court cases also corroborate the reformists' views. One well-known case from 1983, *Manges* v. *Guerra*, concerned a family in South Texas that brought suit against oil tycoon Clinton Manges. Manges was given the responsibility of leasing the family's lands for oil extraction. Instead of leasing the lands to a third party and bringing higher revenues to the family, Manges leased the land to himself at a bargain price. The lower courts decided in favor of the family, but, after many twists and turns, the case reached the Texas Supreme Court. It turned out that one justice had received $100,000 in campaign money from Manges. Another had been in an unrelated lawsuit against Manges, and yet another judge had received campaign money from Manges' attorney. In the end, those three judges recused from the case and "with those recusals, the vote was 4–3 for Manges and for reversal of the lower court."[28] This and other cases have led to a movement to reform the judge's selection process in the state.

Not all judges are openly motivated by campaign money, as the reformists contend; they can also be motivated by personal beliefs. For instance, when questioned about the influence of campaign contributions on his judicial opinions, Raul Gonzalez, a former Texas Supreme Court justice known for his conservative stance, said: "I can tell you unequivocally there was no hint of any improper behavior with regards to the voting on the merits of a case as a result of contributions or political support."[29] However, when questioned about the impact of his religious beliefs on his decisions, he said: "to deny that your faith [...] has any influence is a lie."[30] If these words are true and culture is a motivator, then an election system alone would not do much about preventing judges from being partial, whether or not those agendas coincide with that of a political party.

There are other authors who are more cynical about the ideals of impartiality and independence. For instance, some have argued that expecting judges to be completely neutral stems from historical American judicial myths. In reality, the judges will continue to do whatever their beliefs and interests tells them to.[31] Another author is skeptical about changing the election method. He concludes that: "According to data: [...] elections do not produce inferior or less diverse judges."[32] Actually, judges do not work in a vacuum and there

---

[25]Chris W. Bonneau and Damon M. Cann. "The Effect of Campaign Contributions on Judicial Decision-making," in http://papers.ssrn.com/sol3/papers.cfm?abstract_id=1337668 (accessed January 14, 2014). Also, Victor Flango and Craig Ducat. 1979. "What Difference Does the Method of Judicial Selection Make?" *Justice System Journal*, 5, 25–44.

[26]Texas for Public Justice. Ibid.

[27]Bonneau and Cann. Ibid., p. 20.

[28]Champagne and Cheek. Ibid., pp. 912–915

[29]Robert Gilbreath and D. Todd Smith. 1998. "An Interview with Former Justice Raul A. Gonzalez," Austin: *The Appellate Advocate, 17*(1), 27.

[30]Ibid., p. 29.

[31]Seagal and Spaeth. Ibid., pp. 26, 60–66.

[32]Chris W. Bonneau. 2012."A Survey of Empirical Evidence Concerning Judicial Elections," State Courts White Paper, The Federalist Society, in,http://www.fed-soc.org/publications/detail/a-survey-of-empirical-evidence-concerning-judicial-elections (accessed February 13, 2014).

are mechanisms that prevent undesirable behavior.[33] For example, there is an impeachment process and a Texas Commission on Judicial Conduct. More importantly, voters can vote a partial judge out.

The pressure for reform sometimes comes from the U.S. Supreme Court, which recently stated that "there is a serious risk of actual bias" when a contributor has a personal stake in a case.[34] In Texas, many justices, lawyers, and organizations are in favor of judicial selection reform at the state level.[35] In addition, many Texan voters agree that there is an improper relationship between campaign money and judicial impartiality, but few are willing to let go of their right to appoint judges via vote.[36] The ultimate fate of reform lies in the hands of the 181 members of the Texas legislature.

JOIN THE DEBATE

 Do you believe that judges in Texas can be impartial if they receive campaign money?

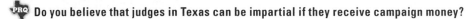 Are personal values and beliefs more important than money in explaining judicial decisions in Texas?

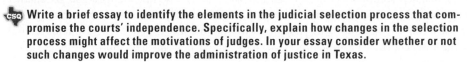 Write a brief essay to identify the elements in the judicial selection process that compromise the courts' independence. Specifically, explain how changes in the selection process might affect the motivations of judges. In your essay consider whether or not such changes would improve the administration of justice in Texas.

---

[33]Ibid.
[34]*Caperton* v. *A. T. Massey*. 2009. 556 U.S.
[35]Ibid.
[36]Champagne and Cheek. *Caperton* v. Ibid., 939.

CHAPTER SUMMARY

LO 9.1 **Describe the differences between criminal and civil cases and between original and appellate jurisdiction.** Cases in the legal system can be classified in two ways. *Civil cases* deal primarily with individual or property rights. *Criminal cases* deal with violations of penal law. There are two types of jurisdiction. *Original jurisdiction* is the basic power to try a case for the first time. Courts with original jurisdiction are called *trial courts* and they determine the facts such as guilt in criminal cases or responsibility in civil cases. Trial courts also apply the law to the facts in each case. *Appellate jurisdiction* is the ability to review the decisions of a lower court by determining if the trial judge properly applied the law.

LO 9.2 **Explain how the courts are organized in Texas and identify the jurisdiction of each major court.** Among the trial courts, municipal- and county-level courts handle minor civil or criminal cases. District courts handle all serious civil and criminal cases. Appeals from district and county courts go to one of the courts of appeal. The court of

last resort for criminal cases is the Texas Court of Criminal Appeals while the Texas Supreme Court makes final decisions in most civil cases.

The organization of the Texas court system is often viewed as too big and complicated. Lines of jurisdiction sometimes overlap. Judicial salaries and the qualifications needed to serve as a judge vary widely across the different levels of the Texas judicial system. Critics have urged reorganization of the courts along more simplified lines for decades.

LO 9.3 **Understand the role of grand juries and trial juries and analyze the responsibilities of citizens in the Texas legal system.** Juries are an important aspect of the American judicial system. The judicial system has two primary types of juries. A *grand jury* issues indictments that indicate whether sufficient evidence exists to bring the accused to trial in criminal cases. A *petit jury* is selected at random to determine the facts in a criminal or civil trial—the jury determines guilt in a criminal case and responsibility in a civil case.

LO 9.4 **Compare and evaluate the most common methods of judicial selection in the United States and in Texas.** Various states use different methods for selecting judges. A few states empower the governor or legislature to appoint their judges, while others allow voters to elect their judges. In many states, the judges are elected by voters sometimes in non-partisan elections and sometimes in partisan elections as in Texas. The goal of electing judges is to give voters democratic control over the judiciary. Many states attempt to combine the advantages of appointment and election by allowing the governor to appoint a judge for a short probationary period after which voters are allowed to decide whether or not to retain the judge. Regardless of the method, judicial selection is highly politicized because courts make life-altering decisions and often shape public policy.

LO 9.5 **Apply what you have learned about the Texas Judiciary.** You explored the gap between ideals and reality in the Texas court system and identified factors that might compromise the independence of Texas judges. You engaged in self-reflection about the meaning of ethical behavior and applied those concepts to the real-world operation of the judicial system in which judges must sometimes decide cases that involve some of their largest campaign donors. You considered whether changing methods of judicial selection might have an effect on how judges make their decisions and administer justice.

KEY TERMS

appellate jurisdiction, *p. 234*
beyond a reasonable doubt, *p. 234*
brief, *p. 234*
burden of proof, *p. 233*
civil case, *p. 233*

challenge for cause, *p. 244*
criminal case, *p. 233*
de novo, *p. 235*
double jeopardy, *p. 235*
grand jury, *p. 243*
hung jury, *p. 245*

indictment, *p. 243*
information, *p. 243*
merit plan or Missouri plan, *p. 245*
no bill, *p. 243*
original jurisdiction, *p. 234*

peremptory challenge, *p. 245*
petit jury, *p. 244*
plea bargaining, *p. 239*
preponderance of the evidence, *p. 234*
true bill, *p. 243*

REVIEW QUESTIONS

LO 9.1 Describe the differences between criminal and civil cases and between original and appellate jurisdiction.

- What are the characteristics that distinguish criminal and civil cases? What is the nature of the parties involved in both types of cases? What are the requisite standards of proof regarding evidence?

- What is the difference between original and appellate jurisdiction? What types of issues and evidence are considered in each?

LO 9.2 Explain how the courts are organized in Texas and identify the jurisdiction of each major court.

- What types of jurisdiction do the different Texas courts have?

- What basic elements of a case determine where the case is heard?

- How do the qualifications of judges vary from court to court?

LO 9.3 Understand the role of grand juries and trial juries and analyze the responsibilities of citizens in the Texas legal system.

- Compare and contrast grand juries and petit juries.

- How are jurors selected to serve on panels?

- What is the function of each type of jury?

LO 9.4 Compare and evaluate the most common methods of judicial selection in the United States and in Texas.

- What are some of the methods employed for selecting judges in the United States?

- How are judges chosen in Texas? How is the process of judicial selection a political one?

- What are some criticisms of the manner in which the state's judges are chosen?

GET ACTIVE

- **Team up with groups that represent your views on the courts.** Groups that advocate using the courts to protect consumers, workers, and patients include the Texas Trial Lawyers Association at **www.ttla.com** (Twitter: @TTLA_). Or work with business-supported groups to fight non-meritorious lawsuits and excessive damage claims with Texans for Lawsuit Reform at **www.tortreform.com** (@lawsuitreform).

- **Find out who the municipal court judges are in your community.** These are judges who hear cases involving traffic tickets or violations of municipal ordinances. Go to **www.courts.state.tx.us** and click on the link to the Judicial Directory located at the top of the page.

- **Support independent courts** at **www.justiceatstake.org** (@JusticeStake). Fight for the independence, ethics, and unbiased selection of judges with the American Judicature Society at **www.ajs.org** (@AJS_org).

- **Find out how various groups rate judicial candidates.** For example, the Texas Bar Association rates candidates for judges at **www.texasbar.com/pollresults**. The Texas League of Women Voters provides valuable information about judicial candidates in their Texas Voters Guide at **www.lwvtexas.org**.

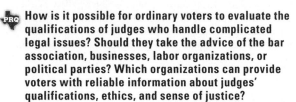 How is it possible for ordinary voters to evaluate the qualifications of judges who handle complicated legal issues? Should they take the advice of the bar association, businesses, labor organizations, or political parties? Which organizations can provide voters with reliable information about judges' qualifications, ethics, and sense of justice?

CHAPTER 10

Law and Due Process

João E. Mueller Photography/Moment/Getty Images

LEARNING OBJECTIVES

LO 10.1 Analyze civil law and the policy issues related to it.

LO 10.2 Analyze the elements and causes of crime.

LO 10.3 Analyze the concepts of due process.

LO 10.4 Evaluate punishment and rehabilitation policies.

LO 10.5 Apply what you have learned about the due process of law.

As you learned in Chapter 9, there are substantial differences between criminal and civil law. Civil law deals largely with private rights and individual relationships, obligations, and responsibilities. Criminal law is concerned with public morality—concepts of right and wrong as defined by government.

*Hence, criminal cases are prosecuted by public officials (usually county or district attorneys) in the name of the public. Civil suits are brought by a **plaintiff**, who is usually a private person or institution, although agents of government occasionally initiate civil suits when seeking to enforce antitrust laws, abate public nuisances, or pursue other noncriminal matters.*

*Perhaps the most important distinction between civil and criminal law is the way each deals with court findings. In criminal law, the aim is punishment, but in civil law, the **remedy** or the means used to redress an injury, is relief from ongoing injury or compensation for past damages. For example, criminal law might punish a thief, but the civil law remedy for the unlawful seizure of property might be the return of the property to its rightful owner. Juvenile proceedings, which are regarded as civil rather than criminal, are an interesting illustration of the difference between civil and criminal law. Assigning juveniles to the custody of reform schools is not intended as punishment but as an effort to correct their delinquency. Assigning an adult to the penitentiary, however, is considered punishment.*

Plaintiff
The party bringing a civil suit, usually a private person or institution.

Remedy
The means used to redress an injury, relief from ongoing injury or compensation for past damages.

CIVIL LAW

LO 10.1 Analyze civil law and the policy issues related to it.

The primary focus of civil law is defining and civilizing interpersonal relationships; it also enforces legitimate contracts between parties and assigns responsibilities for personal injuries. We will provide a sample of some civil laws, but you should remember that Texas civil law fills volumes of printed matter. Texas civil statutes are organized into 28 codes ranging from the Agriculture Code to *Vernon's Annotated Civil Statutes*. It is impossible to discuss the state's civil laws in detail—even the most competent attorneys tend to specialize in specific fields of law.

Types of Civil Law

Civil law in the states today is based in large part on centuries-old English *common law*. (We first discussed common law and statutory law in Chapter 3.) Common law is judge-made law; whether written or unwritten, it is based on **precedents**, previously decided cases used as a guiding principle for future cases. If the essential elements of a current case are like those of a case already decided, the judge makes the same decision as was made in the earlier case. These decisions made over the years have fallen into patterns that form the basis of common law. In contrast, *statutory law* is law that has been passed by legislative bodies and is written in codebooks. Legislatures have incorporated many common-law principles into civil statutes and thereby reduced the need to rely directly on common law.

Precedent
A previously decided legal case used as a guiding principle for future cases.

Family Law
The family is protected by civil law in Texas. For example, even if a man and a woman have not participated in a formal ceremony of marriage in the presence of authorized officers of religious organizations or judges, the law may nevertheless recognize the existence of a marriage. A man and a woman who live together, agree they are married, and publicly present themselves as husband and wife will have a common-law marriage, their children will be legitimate, and the marriage can be terminated through a legal divorce. However, divorce action must be taken within one year of separation, or the marriage will be treated as if it never existed.

Texas courts may require alimony between the filing and granting of a divorce or when one spouse is incapable of self-support and the marriage has existed at least ten years. As a *community property* state, Texas requires that a couple divide property acquired during marriage, and one spouse is not usually responsible for the other's support after divorce. Children, however, have the right to be supported by their parents even if the parents are divorced. Either parent might be given legal custody of the children, but the other parent may be responsible for part of their support. State licenses, including drivers' licenses, can now be revoked from parents who are delinquent in child support.

Real Estate Law   Titles to real property, like land and buildings, are registered in the office of the county clerk, and the legitimate use of any property by its owner is enforceable in the courts.

> **Did You Know?** An individual may gain ownership of another's property through "adverse possession" by fencing it and using it for 10 years without objection by the owner of record.

A person cannot lose title to a *homestead* in a civil suit except to satisfy tax liens, home-improvement loans, mortgage loans for initial purchase of the property, or home equity loans. The protected family homestead includes the home and 200 acres of land in rural areas or 10 acres in the city.

Probate Law   Even in death, property rights are protected because a person may control transfer of his or her estate through a will. If a will exists at the time of death, the function of the courts (usually the county courts) is to **probate** the will, which means to determine that it is the last and valid will of the deceased. If the deceased departed without leaving a will, civil law defines the right to inherit among various relatives; if there are no living relatives, the property passes to the state.

The right to inherit, bequeath, sell, lease, or transfer property is protected by law, but the rights of ownership do not include the privilege of misuse. The right to own a gun does not convey the right to use it as a weapon in murder; the privilege of opening an industrial plant does not include the right to pollute. The regulation of private property for public purposes is one of the oldest functions of law.

Probate
To determine that will is the last and valid will of the deceased.

Business Regulations   Texas law includes thousands of provisions regulating private property, and it establishes hundreds of courts and administrative agencies to elaborate, interpret, and enforce those regulations. State regulatory agencies include the Texas Railroad Commission, the Commissioner of Insurance, the Texas Finance Commission, the Public Utilities Commission, and occupational licensing boards. Their administrative regulations (administrative law) have the same binding effect as civil law, and they are enforced by civil rather than criminal courts.

Corporate Law   When corporations secure permission from the state to conduct business, the secretary of state issues them a **charter**, the organizing document that defines their structure, purposes, and activities. Civil law holds that when a new corporation is chartered, a new legal person is created—one who can sue, be sued, or be fined for criminal activity. The attorney general is responsible for bringing civil suits to seek **injunctions** (court orders compelling or prohibiting specific actions) to end violations of the Texas antitrust and consumer protection laws.

Charter
The organizing document for corporations or a municipalities, which defines their structure, purposes, and activities.

Injunctions
Court orders to compel or prohibit specific actions.

Labor Law   When two parties enter into a valid contract, the courts will enforce the terms of the contract. However, certain kinds of contracts are not enforceable in the courts—for example, contracts with minors. Texas **right-to-work laws** also forbid contracts between labor and management that establish a *closed shop* in which management agrees to hire only labor union members or a *union shop* in which management agrees to require all new employees to join the union as a condition for their continued employment. Because of these restrictions, Texas is considered inhospitable to unions.

Right-to-work laws
Laws that prohibit contracts between labor and management that establish a closed shop or a union shop.

Negligence

Failure to act with the prudence or care that an ordinary person would exercise.

Tort

A private or civil wrong or injury other than a breach of contract.

Torts Persons may be held liable when their negligence results in someone's bodily harm or other injury. **Negligence** is failure to act with the prudence or care that an ordinary person would exercise. If a personal injury suit results, it is a **tort** action (a case involving a private or civil wrong or injury other than a breach of contract).

Civil law also protects a person's reputation against false and malicious statements. *Slander* (spoken defamation) or *libel* (published defamation) may result in a lawsuit to recover monetary compensation for damage to one's reputation and earning potential. The law effectively extends the protection against libel to vegetables, and farmers may sue people who make unfounded allegations against their products.

Issues in Civil Law

These are only a few selected illustrations of civil law. More valuable to the average Texas citizen is an understanding of the major political issues surrounding civil suits. In fact, efforts to change civil law have been a major issue in Texas election campaigns and have occupied much of the legislature's time and energy.

Tort reform

Efforts to limit liability in civil cases.

Punitive damages

Judgments in excess of actual damages intended to punish a defendant in a civil suit.

Tort Reform Insurance companies, corporations, medical practitioners, and others have argued that society has become overly litigious—too inclined to go to court to settle differences. They asserted that "frivolous" lawsuits have overcrowded court dockets, and excessive damage awards have unnecessarily driven up insurance premiums and other business costs. As a result, former Governor Rick Perry and most Republican leaders joined with groups representing defendants in civil actions, the Texas Civil Justice League, Texans for Lawsuit Reform, insurance companies, and a wide range of business and medical interest groups to urge **tort reform** to limit liability in civil cases.

Because of the power of this political alliance, Texas has restricted lawsuits by prison inmates, has given judges the power to dismiss frivolous lawsuits, has limited liability in civil cases involving multiple defendants, and has capped jury awards for **punitive damages** (judgments in excess of actual damages that are intended to punish the defendant). Texans narrowly approved a constitutional amendment to allow the legislature to limit claims for pain and suffering and punitive damages.

Consumer and environmentalist groups, Public Citizen, Texas Watch, Texans for Public Justice, the Texas Trial Lawyers Association, and most Democratic Party leaders generally oppose sweeping tort reform of the type Texas enacted. They argue that isolated anecdotal instances of lawsuit abuse should not be used as a justification to restrict the fundamental right to trial by jury. They contend that only a jury hearing all evidence presented by both sides can make an appropriate judgment in cases of extreme negligence or abuse of an individual's rights.

Plaintiffs' attorneys view tort reform as a big business attack on the laws protecting consumers against defective products and deceptive trade practices; they argue that the threat of meaningful civil action is the only way to hold manufacturers and professionals responsible for their actions and to force companies to improve safety procedures. Tort reform makes lawyers reluctant to take the risk of bringing costly and time-consuming lawsuits against well-funded corporations. Under Texas's new "loser pays" system, if either party refuses an out-of-court settlement and if the jury awards damages significantly different from the settlement offer, the loser must pay all of the "winner's" legal expenses in the case.

Tort reform issues are becoming the primary driving force in judicial campaigns. Corporations, insurance companies, health professionals, and frequently sued business groups generally contribute money to Republican judicial candidates, who are inclined to interpret the law to limit damages in civil lawsuits. Consumer groups, environmentalists, plaintiffs' lawyers, patient-rights groups, and workers' organizations usually rally around Democratic judicial candidates, who tend to be friendlier to their causes. Our Texas Insiders feature puts a face on the political battle over tort reform.

Texas Insiders

Texans for Lawsuit Reform: Interest Groups and Justice

Dick Trabulsi, the owner of a chain of liquor stores, and Houston homebuilder Richard Weekley, organized Texans for Lawsuit Reform (TLR) to support tort reform. Whether or not one agrees with TLR, there is no doubt that the group has used political means to change Texas's concept of justice.

TLR first became a fund-raising juggernaut and a major force in Texas politics with the election of former Governor George W. Bush. Funded principally by around two dozen megadonors, TLR remains the largest and most prominent interest group to help bankroll Republican candidates for the legislature, the governorship, and the Texas Supreme Court.

Presenting itself as an opponent of frivolous lawsuits, TLR argued that excessive damage awards in civil cases drive up the costs of doing businesses and that those costs are passed on to consumers in the form of higher prices. The group persuaded the legislature and voters to amend the Texas Constitution to restrict jury awards of punitive damages. To further discourage civil suits, the legislature recently adopted a "loser pays" system for legal fees.

TLR's opponents, like plaintiffs' lawyers who represent consumers, injured workers, patients, and the insured, believe that tort reform dramatically altered the rights of injured parties to sue businesses, medical providers and insurance companies. They believe that tort reform "went far beyond limiting excessive jury awards and effectively barred the courtroom door to injured Texans with legitimate claims." Mark Kincaid of the Texas Trial Lawyers Association asked, "What else is left for them to do?"

Actually, the battle over tort reform extended into the 2014 gubernatorial election campaign. An ally of TLR, Republican Greg Abbott had made a number of decisions limiting defendants' liability during his time on the Texas Supreme Court and as attorney general. His Democratic opponent Wendy Davis charged Abbott with hypocrisy for receiving at least $6 million in damages after suing a homeowner and tree-care company over a tree limb snapping, disabling him, and putting him in a wheelchair.

Thinking about the role of elites in Texas politics Texas's political system tends to over-represent concentrated interests at the expense of diffused interests. Insurance companies, health-care providers, manufacturers, and retailers are often sued and have a strong interest in organizing to limit legal actions that raise their cost of doing business. Meanwhile, workers, patients, and consumers have little motivation to organize to protect their right to recover damages on the off chance that they will be injured by lax workplace safety standards, medical malpractice, or defective products.

 How do unorganized interests protect themselves in the political system?

Sources: Ross Ramsey, "What Comes with Tort Reform?" *Texas Tribune*, August 29, 2011 www.texastribune.org/texas-special-interest-groups/texans-for-lawsuit-reform/collateral-politics-what-comes-tort-reform and www.texastribune.org/texas-special-interest-groups/texans-for-lawsuit-reform/about; Nate Blakeslee, Paul Burka, and Patricia Kilday Hart, "Power Company: Who Are the Most Influential People Determining the Fate of Texas—and What Do They Want?" *Texas Monthly*, Volume 32, number 2, February 2011, pp. 92–93.

Liability Insurance Automobile insurance is one area for tort reform that the Texas legislature has not seriously considered. A *no-fault insurance* plan would allow an insured person to collect damages from the individual's own insurance company regardless of who is at fault in an accident. Under Texas's *liability insurance* plan, an expensive and time-consuming legal effort is often required to determine which of the individuals involved in an accident is to blame and thus legally responsible for damages. With no-fault insurance, insurance company costs for court trials could be substantially reduced, and the resulting savings could presumably be passed on to policy holders. Although some instances of fraud have been associated with no-fault insurance, at least a dozen states have successfully used limited no-fault insurance programs.

Eminent domain

When government takes private property for public use.

Eminent Domain The Texas Constitution, like the U.S. Constitution, requires that owners must be given "adequate" or "just" compensation in cases of **eminent domain**, when government takes their private property for public "use." "Just compensation" has long been interpreted to mean fair market value. Recently, however, the meaning of public use has become controversial. In *Kelo* v. *City of New London Connecticut*, 545 U.S. 469 (2005), the U.S. Supreme Court interpreted public use to include private commercial development as long as it benefits the community as a whole. In its ruling, the Court approved seizing private residences to make way for a resort hotel, office buildings, and posh apartments.

Although this is the interpretation of "use" that was used in Texas and many other states, property rights advocates were outraged. They hoped that the Court would ban taking, or condemning, private property for the benefit of other investors. Property rights activists argued that wealthy, politically well-connected buyers have the power to profit by influencing government to displace homeowners from property to use it for their own purposes.

In response, Texas joined several other states in limiting government's power of eminent domain. The legislature banned state and local governments from condemning private property for economic development projects except roads, parks, libraries, auditoriums, ports, and utilities. Voters confirmed these property rights with a state constitutional amendment and allowed property owners to sue state and local governments to invalidate certain policies that devalue their property by 25 percent or more.

However, these reforms disappointed some property rights advocates because they still allow local governments to transfer property from one owner to another for flood control and urban renewal projects.

THE ELEMENTS OF CRIME

LO 10.2 Analyze the elements and causes of crime.

Crime is a national issue, but despite the popularity of "law and order" as a campaign slogan in national elections, only 5 percent of crimes are prosecuted under federal law. The activities of the criminal justice system are primarily state, not federal, functions.

An act of Congress provides that federal offenses include crimes (1) committed on the high seas; (2) committed on federal property, territories, and reservations; (3) involving the crossing of state or national boundaries; (4) interfering with interstate commerce; or (5) committed against the national government or its employees while they are engaged in official duties. Otherwise, the vast majority of crimes are violations of state rather than federal law.

The Crime

As commonly used, the word *crime* refers to an act that violates whatever an authorized body (usually a state legislature) defines as the law. Many obey the law simply because it *is* law; others obey out of fear of punishment. Nevertheless, it is people's basic attitudes and values that are most important in determining whether they will respect or disobey a law. If a law reflects the values of most of society, as the law against murder does, it is usually obeyed. However, if a large element of society does not accept the values protected by law, as was the case with Prohibition in the 1920s, violation becomes widespread.

TABLE 10.1 Crime and Punishment under the Texas Penal Code

Offense	Terms*	Maximum Fine
Capital murder: including murder of a police officer, firefighter, prison guard, or child younger than the age of 6; murder for hire; murder committed with certain other felonies; mass murder	Execution or life sentence without parole	N\A
First-degree felony: including aggravated sexual assault, theft of money or property greater than $200,000, robbery, murder, sale of more than 4 grams of "hard" drugs such as heroin	5 to 99 years	$10,000
Second-degree felony: including theft of money or property greater than $100,000, burglary of a habitation	2 to 20 years	$10,000
Third-degree felony: including theft of money or property greater than $20,000, drive-by shootings, involuntary manslaughter	2 to 10 years	$10,000
State jail felony: including theft of money or property greater than $1,500, burglary of a building other than a habitation, sale of less than 1 gram of narcotics, auto theft, forgery	180 days to 2 years	$10,000
Class A misdemeanor: including theft of money or property greater than $500, driving while intoxicated, resisting arrest, stalking	Up to 1 year	$4,000
Class B misdemeanor: including theft of money or property greater than $50, possession of small amounts of marijuana, reckless conduct (such as pointing a gun at someone)	Up to 180 days	$2,000
Class C misdemeanor: including theft of money or property less than $50, smoking on a public elevator, disorderly conduct (such as indecent exposure)	—	$500

*Punishments may be reduced for murder committed in "sudden passion" or enhanced to the next level for crimes involving gang activity (three or more persons), the use of deadly weapons, previous convictions, or hate crimes (motivated by bias on the basis of ethnicity, religion, or sexual orientation).

© Cengage Learning®

Felonies Serious crimes punishable by state institutions are **felonies** (see Table 10.1). Murder is the illegal, willful killing of another human being. Robbery is attempting to take something from a person by force or threat of force. It is inaccurate to say that "a house was robbed"—this implies that a masked bandit stood at the front door with a pistol drawn on the doorbell and demanded that the building deliver up all its valuables. Buildings are burglarized—unlawfully entered to commit a felony or theft.

Theft (larceny) is simply taking property from the rightful possession of another. Grand larceny—taking something valued more than $1,500—is a felony. Regardless of value, livestock rustling is a felony. It is also a felony for an adult to have sexual relations with a child less than 17 years of age.

Misdemeanors In Texas, it is a crime to disturb game hunters or for a commercial fisherman to possess a flounder less than 12 inches in length. Possession of tobacco by minors is outlawed. Most traffic violations are crimes, and the resulting fine is a form of punishment. Such minor crimes are called **misdemeanors** and are punishable by a sentence in county jail or a fine.

Did You Know? Texas makes it illegal to wear a bulletproof vest while committing murder.

Felonies
Serious crimes punishable by state institutions.

Misdemeanors
Minor crimes punishable by a county jail sentence or fine.

Victimless Crimes Whether felonies or misdemeanors, some criminologists consider such crimes as prostitution, gambling, and illegal drug possession as being *victimless crimes* because their primary victims are the criminals themselves. However, the families of these criminals and society also pay a price for these activities, and they are often linked to more serious crimes. Now we will look at what causes people to commit crimes and what leads them to adopt values different from those reflected by the laws of society.

First-offense driving while intoxicated is a misdemeanor punishable in the county jail. Here a city police officer conducts a field sobriety test. Students can access alcohol-related regulations at www.tabc.state.tx.us.

 How much should the law regulate individual conduct when it endangers society at large? Consider personal consumption of tobacco, narcotics, and fossil fuels in your answer. Explain the trade-offs between personal freedoms and the public good.

The Criminal

What causes people to commit crimes? What leads them to adopt values different from those reflected in the laws? What are the factors in crime?

Failing to Accept Social Values Persons who become criminals vary across the broad spectrum of human personality and come from virtually any of the multitudes of social and economic classes. Yet persons who typically commit serious crimes are astonishingly similar. For one reason or another, they are unwilling to accept the **mores** (society's strong beliefs about "right" and "wrong") of the people who write the law. Lawbreakers are disproportionately young, poor, and members of racial or ethnic minority groups; many have acute emotional and social problems. They have little stake in the values that lawmakers hold dear.

Most crimes are committed by citizens who in one way or another are on the fringes of society. In many instances, these perpetrators simply live in an environment that promotes despair, low self-esteem, and weak emotional ties to the "legitimate" society. Some criminals consciously identify themselves as victims and rationalize their conduct based on their victim psychology.

Mores
Society's strong beliefs about right and wrong.

Age With the decline of traditional family life and the rise of single-parent households, many young people are inadequately socialized by adults and generally lack a useful and rewarding role in society. They lack the sense of responsibility that usually goes with a job or a family. The young person who has dropped out of school or who is unemployed has difficulty functioning in legitimate society.

In some neighborhoods, street gangs provide the sole opportunity for social life and capitalistic endeavor. Membership in a gang is a powerful source of approval and a sense of belonging—often a member's only source—and thus gangs become training grounds in crime for successive generations. Lessons not learned on the streets may be picked up from the thousands of demonstrations of crime seen in movies or on television and the Internet.

Whether as gangs or individuals, persons younger than the age of 25 commit a disproportionate share of crime. In Texas in 2012, those young people made up just 38 percent of the population but accounted for 52 percent of all arrests for theft, 61 percent for burglary, and 55 percent for arson.[1] Americans younger than age 25 accounted for 36 percent of all arrests nationwide for violent crimes (murder, non-negligent manslaughter, forcible rape, aggravated

---

[1]Calculated from data provided in Texas Department of Public Safety, *Texas Crime Report for 2012* (Austin: Department of Public Safety, 2013), pp. 75–82 and Census 2010 Summary File 1 (machine-readable data file), prepared by the U.S. Census Bureau, 2011 11AUG11 for *Texas Profile* prepared by the Texas State Data Center, at http://txsdc.utsa.edu, p. 2.

assault, and robbery) and 42 percent of property crimes (burglary, theft, motor vehicle theft, and arson).[2] Most of these make up **FBI index crimes**, which are used as a national barometer of the crime rate—murder and non-negligent manslaughter, forcible rape, robbery, aggravated assault, burglary, grand theft, and motor vehicle theft.

Many people refuse to recognize that the young are major perpetrators of crime, and others are convinced that they will "grow out of it." The truth is that disproportionate numbers of young people commit crimes and, rather than growing out of it, graduate into more serious crime; yet little is done to rehabilitate juveniles early in their criminal careers. Juvenile courts in Texas provide only limited social services for delinquents, and many have no access to vocational training, employment placement, emergency shelter, foster homes, or halfway houses. Severely limited in resources and facilities, Texas juvenile facilities not only fail to correct but also serve as breeding grounds for adult crime.

Gender Far more men than women are arrested for crimes. In 2012, men accounted for 90 percent of Texans arrested for murder, 86 percent for robbery, and 78 percent for aggravated assault.[3] Perhaps traditional masculine roles, social positions, and psychological attitudes make it difficult for some of them to accept certain mores of society. Aggression, violent sports, assertiveness, protectiveness, and earning money are often regarded as essentials of a boy's training for manhood. Apparently, many young men fail to learn the distinction between the kind of assertiveness that society approves and the kind it condemns.

Ethnicity Certain members of minority groups are arrested disproportionately for crime. Although African Americans consisted of only 12 percent of Texas's population in 2012, they accounted for 44 percent of Texans arrested for robbery, 32 percent of murder arrests, and 26 percent of arrests for rape. Meanwhile, 38 percent of Texans were Latinos, but they did not account for a disproportionate share of arrests—40 percent of arrests for murder, 40 percent for rape, and 33 percent for robbery.[4] Prejudice among law enforcement agencies may account for some of the disproportionate number of African Americans arrested, but it is likely that they actually commit a larger share of crime.

Income and Education Poverty is among the social injustices experienced disproportionately by ethnic minorities, but it is by no means unique to them. Poor education and substantial psychological problems are also a result of poverty. The poor, regardless of racial or ethnic background, are more likely to commit violent crimes than members of the middle and upper classes.

Urban Life Crime is more likely in large metropolitan areas. More than three-fourths of all Texans live in densely populated metropolitan areas of more than 50,000 people (called *metropolitan statistical areas*). The character of urban life may contribute to crime in that cities are more anonymous, and social sanctions seem less effective there than in rural areas and small towns. Not only is there greater freedom in the city to act criminally, but there are also gangs and other organizations that openly encourage criminal activity. A majority of inmates in Texas prisons are from the San Antonio, Dallas, and Houston areas.

FBI index crimes

Crimes used as a national barometer of the crime rate—murder and non-negligent manslaughter, forcible rape, robbery, aggravated assault, burglary, grand theft, and motor vehicle theft.

---

[2] Calculated using data from the Federal Bureau of Investigation, *Crime in the United States, 2012* (Washington, DC: Uniform Crime Reports, 2013), Table 38.

[3] *Texas Crime Report for 2012*, pp. 13–20.

[4] *Texas Crime Report for 2012*, pp. 13–18; *Texas Profile*, p. 2.

Drug Addiction Addiction contributes to crime in a variety of ways. In 2012, some 139,108 Texans were arrested for narcotics violations,[5] and it is impossible to estimate what percentage of robberies, burglaries, and thefts are committed to finance illegal habits. Narcotics and alcohol also reduce inhibitions, and at least one-third of all crimes are committed under their influence.

> **Did You Know?** A majority of narcotics arrests in Texas are for marijuana possession.[6]

White-Collar Crime In contrast to street criminals, few people think of a successful businessperson or a college professor as being a criminal, yet these people may stretch the meaning and intent of federal income tax laws, keep fraudulent business accounts, and pollute the environment. But because they seldom rob, rape, murder, or commit other violent acts, they are often punished less severely. Crimes such as bribery, tax fraud, business fraud, price-fixing, and embezzlement are **white-collar crimes**, usually committed by more prosperous people who have often benefited from the very best advantages that society has to offer.

White-collar crimes
Crimes such as bribery, tax fraud, business fraud, price-fixing, and embezzlement, which are usually committed by more prosperous people.

The American people have paid the costs of white-collar crime for centuries, but the recent near collapse of the economy has focused the public's attention, as never before, on white-collar crime. High-profile cases of fraud such as that committed by Bernie Madoff, R. Allen Sanford, and officials at Enron, and the resulting loss in confidence in the economy and stock values, cost victims many times more than all robberies, burglaries, and thefts in recent years.[7]

The Victim

Although more affluent areas of the state and nation are sometimes victimized by perpetrators of street crime, police reports continue to demonstrate that the greatest rates of victimization remain in the poor sections of our cities. Crime is largely a neighborhood affair and is often committed against friends and families of the criminal. Acquaintance rape, or date rape, has been well publicized, and at least 47 percent of Texas killers were acquainted with their victims. In fact, 15 percent of all murder victims were killed by members of their own family. Young people and African Americans were most likely to become murder victims—35 percent were African American.[8]

Victims have the right to be informed of investigations and court proceedings against the accused and to have their victim impact statements taken into account during sentencing and parole action. The Texas Crime Victims' Compensation Fund is administered by the attorney general and financed by small fees collected from criminals when they are convicted. These meager funds are available to victims with extreme personal hardships resulting from physical injury during a crime. However, most victims are not eligible; for example, the fund does not provide compensation for the billions of dollars of property stolen each year.

Violence-centered local news coverage and national reports of school shootings and gun crime have contributed to widespread fear of becoming a victim of crime. This fear has been used to promote several agendas, some advocates supporting harsher sentences for crimes with others supporting stricter gun control policies. Actually, Figure 10.1 shows that the crime rate has declined considerably—the crime rate has been cut in half since 1990.[9]

---

[5]*Texas Crime Report for 2012*, p. 30.
[6]Ibid.
[7]*Texas Crime Report for 2012*, p. 8.
[8]*Texas Crime Report for 2012*, p. 13.
[9]*Texas Crime Report for 2012*, p. 6.

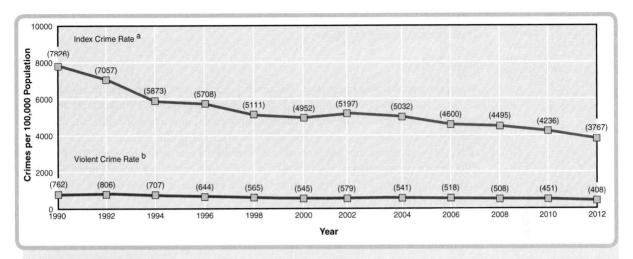

Figure 10-1

Texas Crime Rates since 1990

This figure shows that the violent crime rate and total index crime rate per 100,000 citizens in Texas have decreased for more than two decades.

[a]Total of violent and property crimes (burglary, theft, and motor vehicle theft) per 100,000 population.
[b]Murder, rape, robbery, and aggravated assault.

Source: Department of Public Safety, *Crime in Texas, 2012* (Austin: Department of Public Safety 2013), p. 6.

 Why do news media continue to focus on crime at a time when crime rates are declining?

THE DUE PROCESS OF LAW

LO 10.3 Analyze the concepts of due process.

It is in the courts that the most general concept of justice and the broadest norms of society are enforced against specific individuals. The courts must blend two conflicting goals of society: (1) to protect society according to the state's legal concepts of right and wrong and (2) to protect the rights of the individual charged with wrongdoing. As a result, elaborate traditions of court process and procedure have developed over the centuries; many of these traditional procedures came from the English experience, while others were developed more recently in the American states. Some court procedures have been written into state and national constitutions and statutes; others are included in written and unwritten traditional codes of court process. Following proper procedures is designed to promote justice and protect the individual from the government, and together they constitute

The quality of justice depends upon the values of the people who interpret and implement the law. In this chapter, you will learn the most important elements of due process and how they affect the basic rights and responsibilities of citizens.

what is called **due process**. Due process is essential to guaranteeing fairness before the government may deprive a person of life, liberty, or property, but these rights guaranteed to the accused are very nearly meaningless unless courts, prosecutors, and law enforcement agents

Due process

Proper procedures designed to promote justice and protect the individual from the government. Due process is essential to guaranteeing fairness before the government may deprive a person of life, liberty, or property.

are careful to protect them—in practice, due process depends on the values of those who administer and interpret the law.

Searches

At certain crucial points in the investigation and apprehension of suspected criminals, society has for centuries demanded various external checks and limits on law enforcement agencies to protect the innocent and the presumption of innocence. For example, the Texas Constitution and the Fourth Amendment to the U.S. Constitution prohibit "unreasonable" searches. However, warrants are not always required; warrantless searches of prisoners (to protect law enforcement personnel) and pedestrians (to protect the public safety) are permitted. Motor vehicles may be searched without warrants because it is simply impractical to require a warrant when evidence may be driven away.

Probable cause

Sufficient information to lead a "reasonable person" to believe that evidence is probably contained on the premises and thus a warrant for the invasion of privacy is justified.

Probable Cause For the most part, the reasonableness of a search is determined by supposedly neutral and independent courts, which supervise the law enforcement agencies that propose to intrude on private premises in search of evidence. In Texas, justices of the peace, municipal court judges, or other magistrates appointed by district courts usually determine **probable cause**—whether the facts and circumstances are sufficient to lead a "reasonable person" to believe that evidence is probably contained on the premises and thus a warrant for the invasion of privacy is justified.

Exclusionary rule

Evidence acquired in violation of the Fourth Amendment may not be admitted in federal courts.

The Exclusionary Rule To make the Fourth Amendment effective, the U.S. Supreme Court, in the 1914 case of *Weeks* v. *United States* (232 U.S. 383), established the **exclusionary rule**, under which evidence acquired in violation of the Fourth Amendment could not be admitted in federal courts. The decision discouraged law enforcement agents in federal cases from engaging in illegal invasions of privacy because the evidence obtained could not be used against the accused. In the 1961 case of *Mapp* v. *Ohio* (367 U.S. 643), the U.S. Supreme Court held the exclusionary rule also to be essential to the "due process of law" that the Fourteenth Amendment requires states to respect.

The U.S. Supreme Court has begun to modify the exclusionary rule. For example, under the "good faith" rule, evidence may be admitted when law enforcement agents acted on a search warrant they believed valid even though it was not (*United States* v. *Leon*, 468 U.S. 897, 1984); improperly obtained evidence may also be admitted under the "inevitable discovery" rule if agents otherwise would have discovered the evidence during their routine legal investigation (*Nix* v. *Williams*, 467 U.S. 431, 1984).

Arrests

Like privacy, an individual's liberty is a particularly valued right. The mere fact that a person has been arrested may damage his or her reputation in the community. In short, arrest is in itself a form of punishment. To prevent arrests for frivolous causes, the courts may authorize police to arrest suspects. In Texas, magistrates issue a warrant to take a person into custody when they are presented with probable cause that the person has committed a crime, when a prosecutor files for a *writ of information* (usually charging a person for a misdemeanor), or when a *grand jury* issues an *indictment* (usually for a felony).

Police officers may make arrests without a warrant when they have probable cause and when circumstances do not permit their obtaining one. They may make arrests for crimes they witness or those that are reported directly to them by a witness. Although an arrest resulting from investigation is technically illegal without a warrant, police have considerable flexibility. By contrast, *citizens' arrests* are legal only for felonies or other offenses against the public peace committed in the citizens' presence.

Detention

The time between a person's arrest and appearance before a magistrate is critical. Historically, this period was a time of much police abuse, during which law enforcement officers sometimes used physical violence or "third-degree" psychological tactics. Police would also delay taking a suspect before a magistrate, where probable cause for arrest would have to be shown and the suspect informed of certain constitutional rights. As a result, law enforcement agents were able to extract confessions or other evidence from the frightened and sometimes abused suspects. Confessions obtained in this manner are unreliable and violate the Fifth and Fourteenth Amendments of the U.S. Constitution guarantees against forced self-incrimination.

The Right to Remain Silent In Arizona, the Phoenix police unknowingly set the stage for a far-reaching U.S. Supreme Court decision when they extracted a confession from Ernesto Miranda, a young Latino. Having only an eighth-grade education, the suspect could not possibly have been expected to know his constitutional right to remain silent, and his interrogators did not inform him of his rights. The Court declared that confessions such as Miranda's could not be admitted as evidence. Its ruling established guidelines for informing a person of the following rights before a confession could be admitted as evidence:

1. The suspect has the right to remain silent.
2. Any statement made may be used against the suspect.
3. The suspect has the right to an attorney, whether or not he or she can afford one.

A suspect may knowingly waive these rights and agree to talk to police. The decision of the U.S. Supreme Court in *Miranda* v. *Arizona* (384 U.S. 436, 1966) was one of its most controversial, and many people claimed that the Court was "coddling criminals." Others argued that no system worth preserving should have to fear an accused person's being aware of basic constitutional rights.

Despite the outcry and controversy, there is little evidence that conviction rates have declined as a result of the *Miranda* decision. It is less sweeping than has been assumed—its purpose is to ensure that confessions are voluntary when they result *from interrogation*. An interrogation occurs when police focus questioning on a primary suspect, expecting to extract a confession. Information resulting from unsolicited confessions or general questioning is admissible. The courts have established several exceptions to the Miranda rule such as a public safety exception,[10] and using an improper confession at trial does not automatically result in reversal of conviction—if other evidence is sufficient to convict.[11]

Pretrial Court Activities

After arrest, the suspect is jailed while reports are completed and the district attorney's office decides whether or not to file charges and what bail to recommend. As soon as is practical, the accused is presented before a justice of the peace or other magistrate. This initial **arraignment** is a prisoner's initial appearance before a magistrate in which the charges and basic rights are explained. Its purpose is to:

Arraignment

A prisoner's initial appearance before a magistrate in which the charges and basic rights are explained.

1. Explain the charges against the accused.
2. Remind the suspect of the rights to remain silent and to be represented by counsel and to request a written acknowledgment that the Miranda warning was given and understood.
3. Set bail.
4. Inform the accused of the right to an examining trial.

---

[10]*New York* v. *Quarles,* 467 U. S. 649 (1984).

[11]*Arizona* v. *Fulminante,* 499 U.S. 279 (1991).

The Charges The suspect is usually told the charges multiple times—upon arrest, in the arraignment, and again in subsequent proceedings. Being told the nature of charges is one of the most fundamental aspects of due process. Because the states have governments of "laws and not men," a person should never be held in custody on a whim but only for *legal* cause. In other words, there must be sufficient justification—probable cause—for being held. If the law no longer justifies imprisonment, counsel may secure release through a *writ of habeas corpus* (see Chapter 3), a court order requiring that the prisoner be presented in person and legal cause shown for imprisonment.

The Right to an Attorney The right to counsel is vital to the accused—an attorney should clearly understand the constitutional rights of the accused and be familiar with the intricacies of the law and the courts. So important is the assistance of counsel that many suspects will contact an attorney even before they first appear in front of a magistrate.

Yet this right to counsel has never been absolute. Guaranteed in both the U.S. and Texas Constitutions, the right to counsel had traditionally been interpreted to mean that the accused has a right to counsel if he or she could afford one. In 1932, the U.S. Supreme Court ruled that the Sixth Amendment requires state courts to appoint counsel for the poor, but only in capital cases.[12] Later, the Court extended an indigent's right to counsel in other felony cases and in serious misdemeanor cases in which imprisonment might be involved, but it does not extend to petty offenses such as traffic violations.[13] However, the right to court-appointed counsel does not necessarily guarantee equal justice for the poor.

Some Texas counties still rely on an assigned counsel system in which private lawyers are selected and paid on a case-by-case basis or in which they work by contract to defend a group of indigent cases assigned to them. Paid by the county, some attorneys find that time spent defending poor people does not significantly advance either their practice or their income. Other attorneys have developed highly successful practices based on indigent defense, and some judges have been charged with cronyism for assigning cases to lawyers who have contributed to their political campaigns.

Did You Know? The federal Fifth Circuit Court of Appeals reversed one conviction because the defendant's attorney repeatedly fell asleep during the trial.

A number of Texas counties have established a system of salaried full-time public defenders to serve as advocates for indigents in serious criminal cases. Supporters of a public defender system have argued that it is more professional and less costly than the assigned counsel system. Despite the reforms adopted in some counties, the quality of indigent representation varies tremendously from county to county and from defendant to defendant.

Bail

The security deposit required for the release of a suspect awaiting trial.

Setting Bail The security deposit required for the release of a suspect awaiting trial is known as **bail**. Some persons released on bail fail to appear in court, and their security deposit is forfeited. Others commit still more crimes while out on bail. However, the legal system presumes that an individual is innocent unless convicted, and bail supports this assumption by permitting the accused to resume a normal professional and social life while preparing a defense.

Although bail may be reset or denied following indictment, the Texas Constitution guarantees the right to bail immediately after arrest, except where proof is "evident" in capital cases or when the defendant is being charged with a third felony after two previous felony convictions. The state constitution allows bail to be denied if the defendant is charged with committing a felony while released on bail or under indictment for another felony.

---

[12]*Powell* v. *Alabama*, 287 U.S. 45 (1932).

[13]*Gideon* v. *Wainwright*, 372 U.S. 335 (1963); *Argersinger* v. *Hamlin*, 407 U.S. 25 (1972).

In practice, the right to bail exists only for those who can afford it. Private, licensed bonding companies may be willing to post bond for a fee (usually 10 to 50 percent of the bail as set by the court), which, unlike bail, is not refunded. Many defendants cannot afford even this fee, and unless released on *personal recognizance* (the defendant's personal promise to appear), the prisoner will await trial in jail.

Bail was designed to free a person not yet found guilty of a crime, but some innocent people await trial in jail, unable to work, carry on their family life, or gather evidence for their own defense. In our criminal justice system, bail procedures, more than any other single practice, punish the poor for their poverty—a majority of Texas's jail inmates are simply awaiting trial and have not yet been convicted. Meanwhile, professional criminals released on bail often return to work. They may even commit more crimes to pay their attorneys' retainers and bonding fees.

Examining Trials Although few defendants request one, the accused has the right to an **examining trial** in felony cases. A magistrate reviews the facts to determine if there is sufficient evidence to send the case to a grand jury. Or, if the facts warrant, the charges may be dismissed or bail adjusted.

Formal Charges Although a grand jury sometimes issues an indictment before the accused is arrested, a felony case is usually bound over to a grand jury for indictment after arrest and arraignment. A grand jury should not be confused with a petit jury, which is the trial jury. Grand juries do not determine a person's guilt or innocence as trial juries do; the accused may not even be asked to appear before the grand jury. Instead of hearing the defense, the grand jury primarily weighs the evidence in the hands of the prosecutor to determine whether there is a *prima facie* case (sufficient evidence to convict when the case is taken to trial). If it determines the existence of such evidence, the grand jury issues an indictment (a *true bill*), which constitutes formal charges that enable the case to go to trial (a *no-bill* is a refusal to indict).

A *prima facie* case is necessary to bring formal charges because, if the prosecutor does not have enough evidence to convict, there is no point in bringing the case to trial. Trying a case on flimsy evidence not only costs the taxpayers money but also causes the accused to suffer needless expense, lost time, and a damaged reputation. The right to a grand jury indictment is guaranteed in both the Texas and federal courts to protect the rights of innocent citizens against harassment on unjustified charges.

In practice, grand juries are usually made up of ordinary citizens who have never been trained to critically evaluate cases and so usually act as a rubber stamp for the prosecutors. Some states have abolished the grand jury in favor of writs of information in which a judge evaluates the evidence to determine if there is sufficient evidence to go to trial. Texas guarantees the right to indictment in all felony cases but uses the writ of information to charge people with misdemeanors.

Pretrial Hearings After the indictment, the defendant has the right to yet another hearing, sometimes called the *second arraignment*. A district judge (rather than a justice of the peace) presides as the formal indictment is read, and the defendant enters a plea. If the plea is guilty, a later hearing is scheduled to set punishment. Most often the defendant pleads not guilty at this point, and the case is placed on the docket (schedule of court activity) for subsequent trial. A variety of motions may be presented, including a motion for delay (continuance) or for the suppression of certain evidence. Other subjects of pretrial hearings concern possible insanity or *change of venue* (change in the site of a trial).

A person cannot be held morally and criminally responsible for a crime if at the time of the offense, mental illness made it impossible for the person to recognize that it was wrong. There

Examining trial
An initial court hearing to determine if there is sufficient evidence to send a case to a grand jury.

is considerable controversy as to the effects of mental disorder, so professional testimony may be necessary to establish legal insanity, and psychiatric opinion is frequently divided. It is rare that the courts find a defendant not guilty by reason of insanity.

A change of venue may be necessary when the news media have so publicized a case that it becomes impossible to select an unbiased jury locally or when inflamed public opinion may prevent a fair trial. A real tension exists between the rights of the free press and the rights of the accused, and in a modern society, the rights of the accused can be protected only with great vigilance by our courts.

Plea Bargaining Ideally, the trial is the final step in society's elaborate guarantees of due process. Only through the deliberations in the courtroom can our system's genuine concern for justice emerge. Yet for most people who are accused of a crime, their final day in court never comes. In fact, the system is designed to discourage and even punish those who choose to exercise their right to trial. Most cases end in *plea bargaining*—a secret bargaining session with the prosecutor.

Facing overcrowded dockets and limited staff, prosecuting attorneys usually meet with the accused and offer a deal in exchange for a plea of guilty, which eliminates the need for a trial. The usual deal is to offer to drop some of the charges, to recommend probation or a lighter sentence, or to charge the accused with a lesser crime. The prosecutor may agree to delay prosecution (this is known as *deferred adjudication*) and later drop charges if the defendant agrees to meet conditions like those required under probation. Such plea agreements save tax money and court time and may be useful to law enforcement, such as when certain defendants are given a lighter sentence in exchange for testifying against fellow criminals who have committed more serious crimes.

On the other hand, the guilty obviously benefit from plea bargaining because they are not punished for the full measure of their crimes. Justice is thus exchanged for a cheaper system that benefits the guilty. Defense attorneys frequently encourage their clients to accept the bargain to save them the effort of a courtroom trial, and some become as much agents for the prosecution as advocates for the defense. The innocent and those who are unwilling to trade their rights for a secret backroom bargain take the chance of being punished more severely for demanding a trial.

The Trial

Unless the defense waives the right to a trial by jury, the first major step in a trial is the selection of a jury. The right to a trial by jury is often regarded as one of the most valuable rights available in the criminal justice system. In fact, every state provides for trial by jury in all but the most minor cases, and Texas goes even further, providing for the right to trial by jury in every criminal case.[14]

Nevertheless, the right to trial by jury in a criminal case is one of the most frequently waived rights, especially in cases where the defendant is an object of community prejudice (a member of an unpopular political group or ethnic minority) or if the alleged crime is particularly outrageous. If the right to a jury trial is waived, the presiding judge determines the verdict. Regardless of whether or not a person chooses to exercise it, the right to trial by jury remains a valuable alternative to decisions by possibly arbitrary judges.

Voir dire questioning
The initial questioning of jurors to determine possible biases.

Trial by Jury During initial questioning of prospective jurors (***voir dire*** questioning), they may be asked about possible biases, their previous knowledge of the case, or any opinions they may have formed. Either the prosecution or the defense may challenge a prospective juror

---

[14]The U.S. Supreme Court held in the case of *Duncan* v. *Louisiana,* 391 U.S. 145 (1968) that trial by jury is an essential part of due process when state criminal proceedings involve more than petty offenses.

for reason of prejudice, and the presiding judge will evaluate that challenge. Furthermore, both the prosecution and the defense may dismiss a number of jurors without cause by using a number of peremptory challenges, also called *strikes*, depending on the kind of case involved. Considering occupations, social status, and attitudes of possible jurors, experienced attorneys and prosecutors use peremptory challenges to select a friendly jury; some have been known to use psychologists to assist in the selection process, and lucrative consulting businesses have developed to assist attorneys in jury selection.

The Adversary System All English-speaking countries have developed an **adversary system** in which two parties to the case (the prosecution and the defense in criminal cases) arm themselves with whatever evidence they can muster and battle in court, under the rules of law, to final judgment. An adversary system cannot operate fairly unless both the defense and the prosecution have an equal opportunity to influence the decision of the court. Hence procedural guarantees are designed to ensure that both sides have equal access to an understanding of the laws and the evidence. So that equal knowledge of the laws is guaranteed, the legal knowledge of the prosecution is balanced by the right of the defendant to have legal counsel. Because the government (in the person of the prosecutor) has the power to seize evidence and to force witnesses to testify under oath, the defense must be given that same power (called **compulsory process**).

In the adversary system, each side can challenge the material evidence and cross-examine witnesses who have been presented by the opposition. Only evidence that is presented in court can be evaluated. Because both parties to a case have opposite biases and intentions, they have an interest in concealing evidence that could benefit the opposition.

Because it is the legal responsibility of the prosecutor to prove guilt beyond a reasonable doubt (the burden of proof lies with the state), the counsel for the defense has no responsibility to present evidence of the defendant's guilt, nor can the defendant be forced to take the stand to testify. On the other hand, because the responsibility of the prosecutor is to convict the guilty rather than the innocent, it is a violation of due process for the government to withhold evidence that could benefit the accused—but it happens. There is no way of knowing how many unjust verdicts have been decided because all the evidence was not presented.

The Jury Charge In jury trials, once the evidence has been presented, the judge reads the charge to the jury—the judge's instructions about how the law applies in the case. The judge will instruct the jurors to ignore such things as hearsay testimony and other illegal evidence to which they may have been exposed during the course of the trial. (Realistically, however, it is difficult for jurors to erase from their minds the impact of illegal testimony.) The judge is supposedly neutral and cannot comment on the weight of the evidence that has been presented.

The Verdict After the judge's charge to the jury, the prosecution and defense are each allowed to summarize the case. During their summary remarks, the prosecutor will comment that the evidence points toward guilt, and the defense will conclude that the evidence is insufficient to prove guilt beyond a reasonable doubt. The jury then retires to decide the verdict—guilty or not guilty. Texas law requires that all the jurors agree on the verdict in criminal cases. If the jury cannot agree, a *hung jury* exists, and the judge will declare a *mistrial*, but the defendant may be tried again.

The Sentence Regardless of whether the judge or the jury determines guilt, the judge may prescribe the sentence, unless the defendant requests that the jury do so. In considering the character of the defendant, any past criminal record, and the circumstances surrounding the crime, the judge may assess a penalty between the minimum and maximum provided

Adversary system
The legal system used in English-speaking countries in which two contesting parties present opposing views and evidence in a court of law.

Compulsory process
The power to seize evidence and to force witnesses to testify under oath.

Probation

A judge's sentence of an offender to serve outside a correctional institution but under specific restrictions, often under the supervision of a probation officer.

 Did You Know? A judge in Tarrant County sentenced a wealthy teenager to probation for killing four people while driving drunk. The judge was apparently convinced by the defense argument that the defendant suffered from "affluenza," an alleged mental disorder that afflicts the wealthy with a sense of entitlement and failure to learn responsibility for their conduct.[15]

by law. A judge may sentence an offender to **probation**, which allows the person to serve the sentence outside a correctional institution under specific restrictions, often under the supervision of a probation officer. Similarly, deferred adjudication allows judges to postpone final sentencing in criminal cases, and after a satisfactory probationary period, the charges are dismissed.

Judges have a great deal of latitude in assessing penalties, so the fate of a defendant will depend in large part on the attitudes of the presiding judge. Different judges sometimes assess vastly different penalties for the same crime committed under similar circumstances.

Upon sentencing, the prisoner will be sent to one of the state's penal institutions. Time served in jail before and during trial is usually deducted from the sentence of the guilty. For the innocent, however, the time served awaiting trial is a casualty of an imperfect system of justice that underlines the necessity for care in accusing and trying our citizens.

Post-Trial Proceedings

To protect the accused from double jeopardy, a person who is acquitted (found not guilty) cannot be tried again for the same offense. However, protection from double jeopardy is much more limited than many citizens believe. In the event of a mistrial or an error in procedure in which a person is not acquitted, another trial may be held for the same offense on the theory that the defendant was never put in jeopardy by the first trial. A person found not guilty of one crime may be tried for other related offenses. For example, a person who is accused of driving 75 miles per hour through a school zone, going the wrong way on a one-way street, striking down a child in the crosswalk, and then leaving the scene of the accident has committed four crimes. Being acquitted of one of them does not free the defendant of possible charges for each of the other offenses. Likewise, such acts as bank robbery and kidnapping may violate both federal and state law, and the accused may be tried by both jurisdictions.

The Appeals Process Although the state cannot appeal a not-guilty verdict, because doing so would constitute double jeopardy, prosecutors may appeal the *reversal* of a guilty verdict by a higher court, and the defendant may appeal a guilty verdict. Misdemeanor cases from justices of the peace and municipal courts may be either tried *de novo* (anew) or appealed in county courts. Appeals from county and district courts go to one of 14 courts of appeals and finally to the Texas Court of Criminal Appeals.

Appellate procedure is designed to review the law as applied by lower courts, not to evaluate evidence to determine guilt or innocence. Its major concern is procedure. Even if overruled, the antics of defense attorneys in raising frequent objections to court procedure may build a case for appeal. If serious procedural errors are found, the appellate courts may return the case to a lower court for retrial. Such a retrial does not constitute double jeopardy.

Having exhausted the rights of appeal in the Texas courts, a very few cases are appealed to the federal courts, which have jurisdiction in federal law. Thus, the grounds for appeal to federal courts would be the assertion that the state courts have violated the U.S. Constitution or other federal law.

[15]Ramit Plushnick-Masti, "Affluenza Defense in Criminal Case Criticized," *Ft. Worth Star-Telegram*, December 13, 2013, at www.star-telegram.com/2013/12/13/5416051/affluenza-defense-in-criminal.html?rh=1.

The Special Case of Juvenile Courts

As the result of a reform effort in the nineteenth century, most states began to provide special treatment for children. Texas followed their lead by replacing all adult criminal procedures in juvenile cases with special civil procedures. Under the legal fiction that juveniles were not being punished for crimes, lax procedures were used that would never have been permitted in adult criminal courts. Court proceedings were secret, the rights to counsel and to trial by jury were ignored, standards of evidence were relaxed, and frequently charges were not specific.

As a result of federal court rulings, much of due process has since been restored to juvenile proceedings—except the rights to bail, a grand jury indictment, and a public trial. Juvenile proceedings remain civil, and juvenile records may be sealed from the public with the approval of the juvenile judge, who is usually appointed by the county's judges or juvenile board to have exclusive jurisdiction in such cases. The law allows juvenile felony arrest warrants to be entered into statewide computers, and police can gather information such as juvenile fingerprints and photographs. Children as young as 14 years of age arrested for serious crimes may be certified to stand trial as adults, but a majority of those arrested for lesser crimes are counseled and released without further proceedings.

Children tried as adults seem to be more likely to commit future crimes than those who are dealt with in the juvenile system, according to the U.S. Centers for Disease Control and Prevention. (See www.cdc.gov/mmwr/PDF/rr/rr5609.pdf.) Texas allows children to be tried as adults at age 14.

 How should the legal rights and responsibilities of children differ from those of adults?

REHABILITATION AND PUNISHMENT

LO 10.4 Evaluate punishment and rehabilitation policies.

By providing public institutions that extract justice, society offers an alternative to private revenge and the resulting feuds that plagued the early stages of Western civilization. Until the eighteenth century, punishment meant imposing physical or financial pain. But ideas of human dignity led to the development of prisons to deny a person liberty as a more humane way of punishing. Today, although some prisoners brutalize each other, the death penalty is the only remnant of formal physical punishment left in the law.

Felony Punishment

The Texas Department of Criminal Justice (DCJ) supervises the state's adult correctional functions for convicted felons—probation, prison, and parole.

Probation Probation allows convicts to serve their sentences outside prisons but under varying degrees of supervision—probationers may be required to report to probation officers, submit to electronic monitoring, undergo treatment for chemical dependency, or live in community residence facilities or restitution centers. Although probation functions are largely the responsibilities of local community supervision and corrections departments, DCJ sets standards and provides funding, training, information, and technical assistance to local officers.

Prison The criminal justice department also operates correctional institutions for those offenders not granted probation. Texas has privatized some of its prisons and state jails, which now operate under contract with several prison management companies such as the

Parole

After an initial stay in prison, prisoners serving the remainder of their sentences under supervision in the community.

Corrections Corporation of America. Texas's prison population has tripled since the mid-1980s, and prison facilities, state jails, transfer facilities, and other confinement units now accommodate more than 150,000 inmates

Parole After an initial stay in prison, **parole** allows many inmates to serve the remainder of their sentences under supervision in the community. Whereas DCJ is responsible for their supervision after release, the Board of Pardons and Paroles decides which inmates will be granted early release under parole.

Inmates serving life sentences for capital crimes are not eligible for parole, and those convicted of other violent offenses must serve at least one-half of their sentences before being considered for parole. Those convicted of other offenses must serve only one-fourth of their sentences or 15 years, whichever is less. However, additional time against the sentence is allowed for making a positive effort toward rehabilitation, good behavior, and providing various services such as serving as a prison trusty (an inmate assigned to assist prison staff). As a result, an inmate may become eligible for parole in fewer calendar years than the original sentence indicated.

The Board of Pardons and Paroles does not grant parole to prisoners automatically when they become eligible. Instead, the board examines each inmate's record for positive evidence of rehabilitation. When granted parole, the freed prisoner must abide by strict codes of conduct under the general supervision of parole officers. Parole, as the concept has developed, should not be forgiveness but a continuation of the process of correction. Parole rehabilitation is based on the idea that the elimination of antisocial attitudes can be more effectively accomplished when the individual is not severed from society. Parole is far less expensive than incarceration—supervision of a prison inmate costs as much as 20 times that of a parolee. Seeking to cut prison costs, Texas has increased its efforts to reintegrate parolees back into society, and these efforts may gradually reduce parole revocations in future years.

Misdemeanor Punishment

State government assumes the responsibility for convicted felons, but those convicted of the misdemeanors for which confinement is prescribed will serve their terms in jails operated by local governments, usually counties. Jails fail to rehabilitate for three major reasons:

1. Jail staffs and physical facilities are designed to maintain custody rather than to rehabilitate. Many prisoners in county jails are either awaiting trial or being held for other agencies (federal or state)—our jails are designed as human warehouses.
2. Those who are actually serving their sentences in the county jail will be there for only a short period of time, usually less than one year. This is insufficient time to correct criminal attitudes that the prisoner may have been forming for a lifetime.
3. Many of the people who serve their sentence in local jails have been convicted of habitual vices such as gambling, prostitution, and drunkenness, which are not amenable to rehabilitation in a jail setting. Some courts, however, are now beginning to use diversionary programs that allow minor drug offenders to undergo rehabilitation as an alternative to jail sentences.

---

[16]Bureau of Justice Statistics, *Prisoners in 2012–Advance Counts*, July 2013, Appendix Table 8, p. 9, www.bjs.gov/content/pub/pdf/p12ac.pdf.

Juvenile Rehabilitation

Most juvenile offenders are handled by county authorities. They are usually detained in county facilities before a disposition of the case, and minor offenders are then released (on probation) to the custody of parents or placed in county facilities.

The 13-member Texas Juvenile Justice Board manages state juvenile probation policies and operates training schools, boot camps, and halfway houses for more serious offenders. The Texas Youth Commission once performed many of these functions until it was abolished after becoming notorious for child neglect and abuse, including widespread sexual assault by guards against children in their custody.

Clemency

Although it rarely does so, the Board of Pardons and Paroles may take the initiative to recommend executive clemency (leniency) to the governor. Three types of clemency are available: pardon, commutation of sentence, and reprieve. Because conviction for crime carries a legal condemnation as well as a possible sentence, a *full pardon* is designed to absolve a citizen from the legal consequences of his or her crime. A *commutation of sentence* is a reduction in punishment. A *reprieve* is temporary interruption of punishment. The governor may grant less, but not more, clemency than the board recommends. Without board approval, the governor may grant only one 30-day reprieve to delay execution in a capital case.

Evaluating Punishment and Rehabilitation Policies

Texas jails and penitentiaries are intended to have several functions:

1. *Justice* including punishment (or social vengeance) is society's way of settling accounts with those who have violated its norms. The concept of justice normally requires that punishment should fit the crime.
2. *Isolation* of criminals from the law-abiding population is designed to protect society from future crimes. Yet for most crimes, society is unwilling to prescribe the permanent imprisonment of convicted criminals.
3. **Deterrence** of criminals is society's effort at discouraging criminal behavior by threat of punishment; society uses punishment of convicted criminals as an example to discourage would-be lawbreakers.
4. **Rehabilitation** of convicted criminals is supposed to allow those who are ultimately released to take useful and noncriminal roles in society—the effort to correct criminals' antisocial attitudes and behavior.

The strongest critics of the criminal justice system argue that jails and prisons perform none of these functions in practice. Meanwhile its defenders contend that the state's criminal justice policies are at least partially responsible for reducing the state's crime rate.

Deterrence
Discouraging criminal behavior by threat of punishment.

Rehabilitation
The effort to correct criminals' antisocial attitudes and behavior.

Punishment and Isolation   Texans have increased legal penalties for crime. Despite plea bargaining, probation, and parole practices that cut short the punishment and isolation prescribed in the law, Texas still has one of the highest rates of imprisonment in the nation.

One might expect states, like Texas, with high rates of imprisonment would have a lower crime rate, yet ironically, Texas continues to have one of the highest crime rates in the United States. Table 10.2 shows that Texas has put a far larger percentage of its population in prison than most other states, yet Figure 10.2 shows that it still has one of the nation's highest crime rates. Texas has executed more people than any other state, yet it still has a murder rate far exceeding most other states.

HOW DOES TEXAS COMPARE?
Crime and Punishment

Texas's crime rate is greater than that of 38 other states—at least 50 percent higher than states like New York and New Jersey. Figure 10.2 shows that the highest crime rates are generally in southern and western states.

Ironically, states with the highest crime rates happen to be among those with the most severe criminal penalties. Among the 50 states, only four states have a larger number of prison inmates per 100,000 population than Texas. Table 10.2 also shows that Texas has a greater proportion of its population on parole and probation than most states. Perhaps, states with the highest crime rates are the ones most receptive to a "get tough" approach to crime.

FOR DEBATE

 Does Texas have a high rate of imprisonment because it has a high crime rate, or does the state's conservative political culture explain the high rate of imprisonment?

 From this evidence, is it possible to say whether the threat of punishment deters crime? Why or why not?

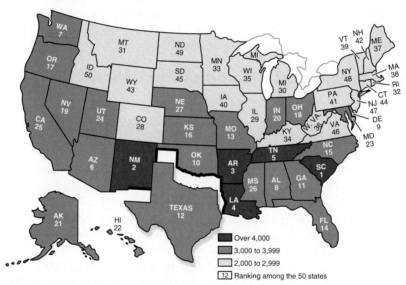

Figure 10-2
FBI Index Crime Rates per 100,000 Population, 2012

Source: Federal Bureau of Investigation, *Uniform Crime Reports: Crime in the United States,* 2012, Table 5, at www.fbi.gov/about-us/cjis/ucr/crime-in-the-u.s/2012/crime-in-the-u.s.-2012/tables/5tabledatadecpdf/table_5_crime_in_the_united_states_by_state_2012.xls

TABLE 10.2 Persons in Prison, on Probation, and on Parole per 100,000 Population*

	Federal	50 States	Texas	Texas Ranking among 50 States
Prisoners	62	418	601	5
On probation	9	1,624	2,107	10
On parole	46	307	583	5

*Prisoners reported per 100,000 residents; probationers and parolees reported per 100,000 adults on December 31, 2012.

Source: Bureau of Justice Statistics, *Prisoners in 2012–Advance Counts,* July 2013, Appendix Table 8, p. 9, www.bjs.gov/content/pub/pdf/p12ac.pdf; *Probation and Parole in the United States, 2012,* December 2013, Appendix Tables 2 and 4, www.bjs.gov/content/pub/pdf/ppus12.pdf.

Deterrence Criminologists usually argue that *severity* of punishment is less important in deterring crime than the *certainty* of punishment. Perpetrators rarely consider the severity of punishment when they commit their crimes because they expect to avoid punishment altogether. In fact, punishment is far from certain in Texas. Most crimes are never reported to police;[17] even among those index crimes known to law enforcement, only 20 percent are cleared with an arrest.[18] As a result, the vast majority of criminals are never punished for the crimes they commit.

Rehabilitation Some inmates may eventually become law-abiding citizens, but for many inmates, prisons are failures as institutions of rehabilitation—about half of those released from prison will again be arrested for crime within three years of their release.[19] As many as 80 percent of all felonies may be committed by **recidivists**—repeat offenders who have relapsed into crime. A major factor in crime remains the failure of our correctional systems to correct.

Recidivists
Repeat offenders who have relapsed into crime.

Sizing Up the Death Penalty Debate

While capital punishment is still being debated across the nation, many aspects of the death penalty can be analyzed by the same standards used to evaluate other forms of punishment. To what extent does capital punishment achieve justice? Is it an effective deterrent against crime?

The Case for the Death Penalty Proponents of the death penalty argue that some crimes such as mass murder and killing of children are so heinous that no punishment other than the death penalty can achieve justice. The Texas death-penalty statute is very specific as it limits capital punishment to murders committed against children, firefighters, and law enforcement officers or multiple murders or murders committed during other felonies such as rape and robbery.

Death penalty supporters contend that capital punishment is a deterrent to crime and that would-be murders and terrorists will avoid putting their own lives in jeopardy by committing these crimes. Proponents point out that inmates already serving life sentences would face no additional punishment for murdering prison guards unless they are subject to the death penalty. Death penalty supporters also argue that capital punishment is a useful tool in law enforcement; interrogators and prosecutors can use the threat of a death sentence as a way of persuading suspects to incriminate fellow criminals.

The Case against the Death Penalty Critics of the death penalty argue that capital punishment is not a deterrent to crime. Ironically, states with capital punishment have consistently had a *higher* murder rate than the states without it. For example, in 2011, the average murder rate was 4.9 per 100,000 in states with the death penalty, while the murder rate in states without it was only 4.1.[20] A historic pattern of such statistics has been interpreted to mean that death penalty laws do not act as a deterrent to murder.

Opponents believe that killing can never be just, even when it is punishment for a crime. They contend that justice cannot be served when innocent people may be executed. More than a dozen inmates on Texas's death row have been exonerated, and there is a real danger

[17]Bureau of Justice Statistics, *Criminal Victimization, 2012*, October 2013, Table 4, p. 4, at www.bjs.gov/content/pub/pdf/cv12.pdf.
[18]*Texas Crime Report for 2012*, p. 8.
[19]Legislative Budget Board, *Statewide Criminal Justice Recidivism and Revocation Rates*, January 2013, p. 5.
[20]Death Penalty Information Center at www.deathpenaltyinfo.org/deterrence-states-without-death-penalty-have-had-consistently-lower-murder-rates.

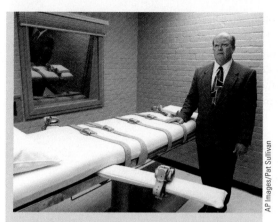

AP Images/Pat Sullivan

Lethal-injection gurney. Texas was the first state to use lethal injection in executions. Today, it is an option for execution in all states with the death penalty. Critics argue that the lethal drug cocktail can cause excruciating pain in still-conscious subjects, who show few signs of discomfort because of drug-induced paralysis. Despite these arguments, the U.S. Supreme Court ruled in 2008 that lethal injection does not violate the Eighth Amendment ban on cruel and unusual punishment[22].

PRQ **What are the ethical reasons to keep the death penalty? What ethical arguments can be made to abolish it?**

that innocent persons can be and have been executed. Pointing to examples like that of William Todd Cunningham,[21] opponents argue that once such a prisoner has been wrongfully executed, the mistake can never be corrected.

Instead, opponents argue that every state now allows adequate alternatives to the death penalty. Life sentences without the possibility of parole serve justice and are far less expensive than the death penalty process. Many states seem to agree with this logic. Eighteen states have now abolished the death penalty altogether; in those states that still include capital punishment in their penal codes, prosecutors are seeking the death penalty less often. Only nine mostly Southern states actually executed inmates in 2013, and a majority of those executions were in Texas and Florida.[23]

APPLYING WHAT YOU HAVE LEARNED ABOUT THE DUE PROCESS OF LAW

LO 10.5 Apply what you have learned about the due process of law.

In the following essay, you will explore the gap between the theory and practice of due process. You will see that the quality of justice depends on the values of those who interpret and implement the law. You will be presented with evidence of a local prosecutor abusing prosecutorial discretion and a pathologist providing incompetent testimony. You will see the importance of the right to counsel in ultimately dispensing justice.

After you have read the essay, you will be asked a series of questions that will require you to employ critical-thinking skills to apply what you have learned in this chapter to the new information in this essay. Your analysis will require you to identify critical elements in the due process of law and evaluate the quality of evidence the essay presents. You will be asked to reflect on the ethical issues presented in the many facets of this intriguing murder case.

A Historic Murder Case: Obstruction of Texas Justice

by Brian Farmer

Amarillo College

The criminal justice system in Texas is among the most decentralized segments of Texas Government where the most important actors are often found on local levels, including law enforcement and corrections officers, judges, and prosecutors. Many of these individuals are also provided with a great deal of discretion. When such discretion exists, unfortunately, there exists the opportunity for abuse. This is perhaps especially true in cases of violent crime

---

[21]The Innocence Project, *Cameron Todd Willingham: Wrongfully Convicted and Executed in Texas*, at www.innocenceproject.org/Content/Cameron_Todd_Willingham_Wrongfully_Convicted_and_Executed_in_Texas.php.
[22]*Baze et al.* v. *Rees et al.,* 553 U.S. 35 (2008).
[23]Death Penalty Information Center, *The Death Penalty in 2013: Year-End Report*, p. 2, at http://deathpenalty-info.org/documents/YearEnd2013.pdf.

due to public pressure on criminal justice officials to "get tough on crime" and the fact that District Attorneys are elected.

Since both arrests and convictions in Texas are higher among minorities with low levels of income and education, there can be pressure on prosecutors to avoid any leniency toward such individuals. When this is combined with the fact that these defendants cannot afford the best legal counsel, the chances that the defendant will actually find justice in the system are compromised. A review of the case of *Farmer* v. *Sherrod* (U.S. 2:93-CV-0017-J, 1993) illustrates the possible abuse of prosecutorial discretion and the importance of capable counsel for the defense.

In 1990, Douglas Palmer, an 18-year-old, low income, Hispanic male, together with five friends, was charged with capital murder for his role in the beating death of 72-year-old Hilton Merriman in Randall County, Texas. Palmer admitted his role in the beating, but argued that the entire affair had been unintentional. In order to prevent a friend, John Garcia, from losing property in a divorce, Palmer and his five friends agreed to burglarize Garcia's mobile home and remove his property so that he could file a false insurance claim. Palmer and his friends put their plan in motion the night of May 11, 1990; however, Palmer and his co-conspirators took a wrong turn in the mobile home park and broke into Merriman's home instead. Merriman surprised the intruders to his home and struck Palmer on the head with a flashlight. A struggle ensued, and the boys overwhelmed Merriman. Palmer later stated that they left a beaten Merriman alive and breathing when they departed. Merriman was found dead in his mobile home by his son two days later.[24]

Palmer and his accomplices were quickly arrested and indicted for capital murder. In January 1992, one defendant, Johnny Rey, was sentenced to death, and Palmer was facing the same fate. Palmer's court-appointed legal counsel, Bill Kolius, sought assistance in the case from well-known defense attorney and death penalty opponent Millard Farmer. Farmer agreed to help represent Palmer and did so without compensation.[25]

In his investigation of the case, Farmer discovered that in testimony in the Johnny Rey trial, the pathologist in the case, Ralph Erdmann, who had performed the Merriman autopsy, used tissue slides taken from a body of someone other than that of Mr. Merriman. Farmer also discovered that this information was known to Randall County Assistant District Attorney John Davis as well as by Randall County DA Randy Sherrod.[26]

Three other pathologists were called in to review the evidence and all three agreed that the evidence was not supportive of the conclusion that the cause of death was the direct result the beating. Instead, all three stated that it is possible that Merriman would have survived had it not been for a badly diseased heart. The exact cause of death was critical in this case because the state is required to show "deliberateness" in all capital cases.[27]

Other irregularities were discovered in Merriman's autopsy. Dr. Erdmann had not weighed the brain of Mr. Merriman, which is critical because Erdmann concluded that Merriman died of swelling of the brain. Erdmann also failed to take any notes during the autopsy and erased an audiotape made during the autopsy. Erdmann failed to report the approximate time of death, failed to record the body temperature, test the eye fluid, analyze the contents of the stomach, or dissect the heart, as well as record the degree of decomposition on microscopic slides. Erdmann had also failed to contact the radiologist about the results of the head X-rays. These findings led Palmer's counsel to do further investigation into the work of Erdmann, and a pattern of negligence and recklessness emerged.[28]

---

[24]Kyle Steinhauser, "Man Serving Life Sentence in Merriman Murder Testifies in Smith Trial," *Amarillo Globe News*, January 23, 1997; accessed online February 7, 2014.

[25]*Farmer v. Sherrod*, U.S. 2:93-CV0017-J (Plaintiff's Petition), pp. 2–3.

[26]Bill Hubbard, *Substantial Evidence: A Whistleblower's True Tale of Corruption, Death and Justice* (Far Hills, NJ: New Horizon Press, 1998), p. 77.

[27]*Farmer v. Sherrod*, U.S. 2:93-CV0017-J (Plaintiff's Petition), pp. 58–60.

[28]Ibid., pp. 21–37.

Erdmann's autopsies were usually incomplete, and Erdmann did not open the skulls or bodies, or remove and weigh organs. Erdmann took blood from the wrong parts of the body and did not take notes during the autopsies. In a case in Midland County, Texas, Erdmann phoned in autopsy results to a judge when the body had never been opened. When confronted with this fact, Erdmann claimed to have performed the autopsy by X-ray, but he could not produce the X-rays.[29] In Hale County, Texas, Erdmann once returned to Hale County officials a male skull with a headless female body.[30]

In another case, Erdmann concluded that a young woman had died choking on her own vomit while intoxicated. Erdmann failed to observe bruising and blood on the woman's face, however, and a second autopsy concluded that she had been smothered, the victim of a homicide. Shortly thereafter, a jury convicted a man for her murder.[31]

In still another case, Erdmann concluded that the cause of death was cocaine poisoning and again gave weights for internal organs. The man's relatives noticed that a weight for the spleen, which had been surgically removed some years earlier, was included. A second autopsy concluded that the cause of death was a heart attack.[32]

Finally, in a case where a man's body was badly burned, Erdmann first concluded the cause of death was smoke inhalation, but then changed his conclusion to pneumonia. Subsequently, police apprehended a suspect with the man's car and credit cards who stated that "he didn't know anything about the bullet hole in the head." Police requested that Erdmann re-examine the head, but Erdmann could not do so because the head had either been lost or thrown away.[33]

Palmer's counsel also discovered evidence that Erdmann tailored his testimony to match the prosecution's theories. Erdmann would simply ask the authorities what their theory was as to cause of death and then tailor his testimony to match the prosecution's case.[34] Erdmann eventually pleaded no contest to seven counts of criminal misconduct and surrendered his medical license. Erdmann was sentenced to 10 years of probation, ordered to pay $16,000 in restitution, and perform 680 hours of community service.[35]

Losing the pathologist that helped them get convictions, the DAs in Lubbock and Randall County retaliated. A Randall County grand jury put together by Assistant DA John Davis indicted Farmer for "tampering with a witness."[36] After obtaining the indictment, Randall County DA Randy Sherrod sought to have Millard Farmer disqualified from representing Palmer, but the court denied this motion.[37] Lubbock police officer William Hubbard, who had testified against Erdmann, was subsequently indicted by a Lubbock County grand jury on the charges that he had falsified a report to justify a search in 1990.[38] The incident for which Hubbard was indicted had been investigated by the Internal Affairs Division of the Lubbock Police Department in 1991, which concluded that there was no criminal conduct by William Hubbard in the incident.[39] Lubbock police detective Patrick Kelly was then

---

[29]Ibid., pp. 21–23.
[30]Ibid., p. 23.
[31]Ibid., pp. 29–30.
[32]Ibid., pp. 30–31.
[33]Ibid., p. 32.
[34]Hubbard, *Substantial Evidence*, pp. 61, 140.
[35]*Farmer* v. *Sherrod* (Plaintiff's Petition), p. 4.
[36]Ibid., p. 6.
[37]Ibid., p. 7.
[38]Ibid., pp. 8–9.
[39]Ibid., p. 9.

indicted by a Randall County grand jury through the efforts of Randall County DA Randy Sherrod on five counts of perjury stemming from his testimony against Erdmann in the Palmer case.[40]

In reaction to these indictments, Farmer, Hubbard, and Kelly filed a civil suit in federal district court naming Randall County DA Randy Sherrod, Lubbock County DA Travis Ware, and nine other public servants in Randall and Lubbock counties as defendants. Farmer, Hubbard, and Kelly argued that the indictments against them were made in bad faith and were attempts to defame their character. Farmer, Hubbard, and Kelly argued that their constitutional rights to free speech, and Douglas Palmer's constitutional rights to counsel, had been violated by the defendants. Farmer, Hubbard, and Kelly sought cessation of the prosecution against them, back pay for the police officers, and monetary damages for their rights violations.[41]

With overwhelming evidence in their favor, the U.S. district court in Amarillo did intervene and enter an injunction stopping the prosecution of Farmer, Hubbard, and Kelly. The parties eventually settled their civil suit outside of court, with Farmer, Hubbard, and Kelly receiving $300,000 in damages.[42] Travis Ware was voted out as district attorney in the next election in 1994. As a result of this political defeat, Ware filed suit against the local newspaper, the *Lubbock Avalanche Journal*, for defamation of his character. Ware was awarded no damages by the court and ordered to pay the legal fees of the *Lubbock Avalanche Journal*.[43] Douglas Palmer did not receive the death penalty for his role in the death of Hilton Merriman, and Johnny Rey eventually received a new trial where he also was sentenced to incarceration rather than execution.[44]

In the final analysis, it is possible that justice would not have been observed in this case if Douglas Palmer had not had the good fortune of securing an attorney of Millard Farmer's stature without compensation. Most indigent accused (Johnny Rey being a case in point) are not so fortunate. Without this type of legal representation, it is perhaps probable that Douglas Palmer and Johnny Rey would have been executed. Cases such as this one largely serve to fuel the arguments that discretion in the criminal justice system is biased against the poor and minorities. Although this West Texas case may be unique and extreme, the possibility that abuses of prosecutorial discretion exist elsewhere remain.

JOIN THE DEBATE

 Identify the constitutional rights that were jeopardized in this case and explain whether the judicial system was able to protect each of these rights.

 Show how the author presents actual evidence to justify his judgment about the incompetence of the pathologist. Explain why the evidence is or is not convincing to the reader.

 Explain why the prosecutor behaved in an unethical manner. Based on what you have learned in this essay, how well does the legal system correct for such ethical lapses?

---

[40]Ibid., pp. 9–10.
[41]Ibid., pp. 2–10.
[42]Hubbard, *Substantial Evidence*, p. 306.
[43]Ibid., p. 316.
[44]Steinhauser, "Man Serving Life Sentence in Merriman Murder Testifies in Smith Trial"; accessed online February 10, 2014.

CHAPTER SUMMARY

LO 10.1 Analyze civil law and the policy issues related to it. Within the American legal system, cases are classified as either civil or criminal. Civil cases primarily involve the rights of private parties or organizations. Resolution is based on the concept of responsibility rather than guilt.

Some examples of the broad categories of civil law include family law, real estate law, probate, corporate law, civil regulations, labor law, and torts. Recent political issues have developed around eminent domain, liability insurance, and tort claims. The Texas legislature has undertaken tort reform in an effort to lighten overcrowded court dockets and limit allegedly frivolous suits. At the urging of business, insurance companies, and medical professionals, the legislature has restricted lawsuits and limited awards for damages.

LO 10.2 Analyze the elements and causes of crime. In an attempt to impose their values on others, the dominant elements of society have turned to government with its power to define crime and punish it. Law reflects the values of the people who make and enforce it. Criminal cases deal with public concepts of proper behavior and morality as defined by law. Punishment for a violation of these concepts ranges from a fine to imprisonment to a combination of both. More serious crimes are called felonies, and minor crimes are called misdemeanors.

The cause of crime is the failure to accept society's mores, which is related to such factors as age, gender, ethnicity, income, education, urban life, and drug addiction. Overall crime rates have, in fact, declined in recent years in Texas and in most of the nation as well.

LO 10.3 Analyze the concepts of due process. The court procedures that constitute due process aim to promote justice and protect individuals from government abuse. These procedures are generally either written into state and national constitutions and statutes or included in traditional codes of court process. They govern every step in the criminal justice process from search and arrest to trial and final conviction. These procedures guarantee the rights against unreasonable search and arrest and against forced self-incrimination. Due process also includes the rights to an attorney, to reasonable bail, and to examining trials; the defendant has the right to be charged by a reliable process, to be able to present evidence, and to confront opposing witnesses at a trial by jury.

It is largely through due process that the courts aim to blend two conflicting goals of society: (1) to protect society according to the state's legal concepts of right and wrong, and (2) to protect the rights of the individual charged with wrongdoing. Unfortunately, the goal of due process is often an ideal rather than a reality. These careful guarantees of due process are often circumvented by the practice of plea bargaining.

LO 10.4 Evaluate punishment and rehabilitation policies. Correctional institutions such as prisons and jails are intended to punish, isolate, deter, and rehabilitate. Unfortunately, they perform these functions poorly—the low rates of arrest mean that most criminals will not be punished or isolated from society and, hence, they are not effectively deterred from committing crimes. Even among prisoners who have been arrested and punished, a majority of inmates return to crime after their release.

LO 10.5 Apply what you have learned about the due process of law. In the essay you learned how due process in practice depends on the values and competence of those who interpret and enforce the law. You utilized your critical-thinking skills to identify a defendant's constitutional rights and reflected on the ethical issues in a complex murder case. You learned how writers must present convincing evidence before evaluating social issues and drawing conclusions about them.

KEY TERMS

adversary system, *p. 273*
arraignment, *p. 269*
bail, *p. 270*
charter, *p. 259*
compulsory process, *p. 273*
deterrence, *p. 277*
due process, *p. 268*
eminent domain, *p. 262*

examining trial, *p. 271*
exclusionary rule, *p. 268*
FBI index crimes, *p. 265*
felonies, *p. 263*
injunctions, *p. 259*
misdemeanors, *p. 263*
mores, *p. 264*
negligence, *p. 260*

parole, *p. 276*
plaintiff, *p. 258*
precedent, *p. 258*
probable cause, *p. 268*
probate, *p. 259*
probation, *p. 274*
punitive damages, *p. 260*
recidivists, *p. 279*

rehabilitation, *p. 277*
remedy, *p. 258*
right-to-work laws, *p. 259*
tort, *p. 260*
tort reform, *p. 260*
voir dire questioning, *p. 272*
white-collar crime, *p.266*

REVIEW QUESTIONS

LO 10.1 Analyze civil law and the policy issues related to it.

- Differentiate between civil and criminal law. Give at least six broad categories of civil law and examples of each. Explain why each example is classified as civil rather than criminal law.

- Explain Texas policies regarding eminent domain, auto liability insurance, and tort reform. What are the political interests on each side of the tort-reform controversy?

LO 10.2 Analyze the elements and causes of crime.

- Define criminal law and how it develops from basic social mores. Distinguish felonies from misdemeanors and give examples of each.

- Discuss the root causes of crime. What are the social characteristics of the typical criminal?

LO 10.3 Analyze the concepts of due process.

- Define the due process of law and explain its origins in the state and national constitutions.

- Trace the criminal justice process step by step from search and arrest through final conviction. At each stage, show how the legal system is designed to guarantee a sense of fair play between the government and the accused.

- Identify gaps between the theory and practice of due process. Define plea bargaining and how it affects due process in practice.

LO 10.4 Evaluate punishment and rehabilitation policies.

- List the four major purposes of jails and penitentiaries and evaluate how effectively they achieve each of them. How does the death penalty measure up against these standards?

- Discuss whether certainty or severity of punishment is more effective at preventing recidivism and deterring crime. Why?

GET ACTIVE

- **Deal intelligently with your personal legal matters.** For tips on civil legal matters, browse **texaslawhelp.org** to get free legal advice, do-it-yourself, and low-cost legal strategies relating to bankruptcy, consumer complaints, divorce, identity theft, tenant rights, utility bills, and a wide range of other topics. Take control of legal issues in your life—learn about family law, tenants' rights, and how to sue in small claims court at **texasbar.com**. Click on "For the Public" and then on "Free Legal Information." Learn how to deal with identity theft and how to identify registered sex offenders in your neighborhood from the Texas Department of Public Safety at **www.txdps.state.tx.us**.

- **Link up with the group that reflects your position on civil lawsuits.** Fight frivolous lawsuits that drive up the costs of doing business and support limits on civil judgments with Texans for Lawsuit Reform at **www.tortreform.com**. Support workers', patients', and consumers' rights to compensation for negligence from businesses, medical providers, and insurance companies with Texas Watch at **www.texaswatch.org**.

- **CSQ** Develop a comparative analysis between Texas and national trends using Texas Department of Public Safety statistics at *www.txdps.state.tx.us/* *administration/crime_records/pages/crimestatistics.htm* and FBI data at *www.fbi.gov/about-us/cjis/ucr/ucr-publications#Crime*. Analyze trends in the rates of prosecution, prison, probation, and capital punishment using the data-rich Bureau of Justice Statistics website at *www.bjs.gov*. Use at least three visuals to show these changing trends in your presentation.

- **Join with those who share your views on crime and punishment.** Fight the death penalty by joining Texas Students Against the Death Penalty at **www.texasabolition.org** or the Texas Coalition to Abolish the Death Penalty at **www.tcadp.org**. Help The Innocence Project free the innocent at **ipoftexas.org**. Find a wealth of information about the death penalty at the Bureau of Justice Statistics and at the Death Penalty Information Center at **www.deathpenaltyinfo.org**. Support capital punishment with Pro-Death Penalty.com at **www.prodeathpenalty.com**. Fight for a vigorous criminal justice system and victims' rights with Justice for All at **www.jfa.net**. Search for studies that show capital punishment as a deterrent to murder.

- **PRQ** Identify the ethical issues on both sides in the death penalty debate.

CHAPTER 11

Local Government

John B. Mueller Photography/Moment/Getty Images

LEARNING OBJECTIVES

LO 11.1 Describe and evaluate the organization and structure of municipal governments.

LO 11.2 Describe and evaluate the organization and structure of county governments.

LO 11.3 Describe and evaluate the organization and structure of special-district governments.

LO 11.4 Evaluate the role of councils of governments as local government partners.

LO 11.5 Apply what you have learned about local government.

*L*ocal governments are primarily responsible for a variety of services that substantially affect the public on a daily basis, including law enforcement, mass transit, sewage treatment, flood control, and emergency services. Anyone who lives in a metropolitan area is likely to be governed by two **general-purpose governments**, municipal and county governments that provide a wide range of public services, in addition to numerous **special districts** such as school districts, hospital districts, metropolitan transit authorities, and municipal utility districts.

The sheer number of local governments across Texas and the rest of the nation can challenge even the most interested members of a community who want to contact local officials about the critical needs of one's own neighborhood, controversial social issues, or initiatives that can improve the community's quality of life. (See Table 11.1 for a comparison of local governments in Texas and in the United States as a whole.) To more effectively make our views known to those who are responsible for making and enforcing policies at the local level, it is vital that we learn about the inner workings of local government, that is, the various institutional features of cities, counties, and special districts. And because so many local problems affect entire regions, it's equally important to examine the role councils of governments (COGs) play in bringing the variety of local governments together for the purposes of planning and coordinating policies.

General-purpose government

A municipal or county government that provides a wide range of public services.

Special districts

Local governments that provide single or closely related services that are not provided by general-purpose county or municipal governments.

> **Did You Know?** Texas has more than 4,800 local governments, most of them governed by officials who are elected by voters.

MUNICIPALITIES

LO 11.1 Describe and evaluate the organization and structure of municipal governments.

How are municipalities relevant to our lives? Cities hire police and firefighters to protect the community. Cities enforce building and safety codes, pass anti-litter ordinances, issue garage sale permits, maintain recycling programs, launch anti-graffiti programs, impound stray animals for the safety of the community, and enforce curfews. These are just a few examples of how cities routinely affect our day-to-day lives.

Cities also become involved in high-profile, controversial issues. For example, in 2012, the Fifth Circuit Court of Appeals[1] struck down an ordinance passed in a Dallas suburb, Farmers Branch, that banned the rental of apartments to illegal immigrants. Farmers Branch appealed to the U.S. Supreme Court, but the Supreme Court refused to hear the appeal, and

	Total	County	Municipal	Town or Township	Special Districts	School Districts*
United States	90,056	3,031	19,519	16,364	38,266	12,880
Texas	5,147	254	1,214	0	2,600	1,079

TABLE 11.1 Local Governments and Public School Systems, United States and Texas, 2012

*Independent school districts and community college districts.

Source: U.S. Census Bureau, 2012 Census of Governments, *Local Governments by Type and State: 2012*, at http://factfinder2.census.gov/faces/tableservices/jsf/pages/productview.xhtml?src=bkmk.

This table shows the enormous numbers of local governments in the United States and in Texas.

 How is it possible for ordinary voters to keep track of the numerous elected officials that they elect to local offices? Think of ways to simplify the system of local governments to make them more accountable to the average citizen.

---

[1]*Villas at Parkside Partners* v. *City of Farmers Branch*, (Fifth Circuit 2013), No. 10-10751.

by doing so, let the Firth Circuit Court's ruling stand. In 2010, a controversial state law was passed in Arizona requiring police officers who stop individuals for lawful reasons to check their immigration status if they suspect those individuals are in the country illegally; the law was amended to ban racial profiling in its enforcement. In reaction to the Arizona law, the Austin City Council passed a resolution banning (with some exceptions) city employee trips to Arizona and official business dealings with the state.

All local governments are bound by federal and state laws as well as the U.S. and Texas Constitutions. The relationship between states and local governments follows from the fact that states, including Texas, have a *unitary system of government* (see Chapter 2). Municipalities—like counties, special districts, and school districts—are creatures of the state and have only as much power as the Texas Constitution and Texas legislature grant them. Texas has seen a marked increase in the number of municipalities in the state since the 1950s (see Table 11.2).

General-Law and Home-Rule Cities

General-law city

An incorporated community with a population of 5,000 or fewer that is limited in the subject matter upon which it may legislate.

Home-rule city

A city with a population of more than 5,000 that can adopt its own charter and structure its local government as it sees fit as long as charter provisions and local laws (also called ordinances) do not violate national and state constitutions and laws.

City charter

The organizing document for a municipality.

Texas cities are classified as either general-law or home-rule cities. A **general-law city** is an incorporated community with a population of 5,000 or fewer and is limited in the subject matter upon which it may legislate. A city with a population of more than 5,000 may, by majority vote, become a **home-rule city**. This means that it can adopt its own **city charter** (the organizing document for a municipality) and structure its local government as it sees fit as long as charter provisions and local laws (also called ordinances) do not violate national and state constitutions and laws.

The Texas Constitution allows a home-rule city whose population has dropped to 5,000 or fewer to retain its home-rule designation. According to the Texas Municipal League, the vast majority of Texas cities—about 75 percent—are general-law cities.

Direct Democracy at the Municipal Level Home rule permits local voters to impose their will directly on government through initiative, referendum, and recall, and most home-rule cities have all three provisions. With the initiative power, after the people obtain a designated percentage of signatures of registered voters, they can force a sometimes-reluctant city council to place a proposed ordinance on the ballot. If the proposal passes by a majority vote, it becomes law. Texas cities have used initiatives to resolve the following issues by popular vote:

★ Should a city allow stores within the city limits to sell beer and wine?
★ Should a city freeze the property tax exemption for senior citizens and people with disabilities?
★ Should a city increase the minimum wage?
★ Should a city impose a cap on the property tax rate?

TABLE 11.2 Municipal Governments in Texas, 1952–2012

1952	1962	1972	1982	1992	2002	2007	2012
738	866	981	1,121	1,171	1,196	1,209	1,214

Source: U.S. Census Bureau, 2012 Census of Governments, Municipal Governments, *General-Purpose Local Governments by State: Census Years 1942 to 2012*, at http://factfinder2.census.gov/faces/tableservices/jsf/pages/productview .xhtml?src=bkmk.

As general-purpose governments, municipal governments provide a variety of services that are critically important to the well-being of communities.

▲ As mayors and city councils attempt to prioritize the needs of their communities, what factors should they take into consideration?

Voters who want to repeal an existing ordinance can also petition the council to hold a referendum election to determine whether the law should remain in effect. For example, College Station and Houston voters approved referenda to remove red-light cameras. Smoking bans were put to a referendum vote in Lubbock and Baytown. In both cases, voters decided to retain the ban. A referendum election called by a city council can also permit voters to determine whether a law will go into effect. Finally, voters can, by petition, force the council to hold a **recall election** that would permit voters to remove the mayor or a member of the council before the official's term expires.

The Limits of Home Rule

Although home-rule cities have wider latitude than general-law cities in their day-to-day operations, they must still contend with state limitations on their authority. For example, state law determines the specific dates on which municipal elections can be held. Voters are free to amend city charters, but the Texas Constitution permits cities to hold charter elections only every two years. An election establishing a metropolitan transit authority can be held only in cities that meet a population requirement determined by the Texas legislature. Local governments in Texas are subject to "sunshine" laws such as the Public Information Act and the Open Meetings Act.

Forms of Municipal Government

The three common forms of municipal governments are council-manager, mayor-council, and commission.

Council-Manager System

In a **council-manager form of government** (see Figure 11.1), an elected city council makes laws and hires a professional administrator who is responsible for both executing council policies and managing the day-to-day operations of city government and who serves at the pleasure of the council.

The powers of the city manager come from the city charter and from the delegation of authority by the council through direct assignment and passage of ordinances. For example, the city manager is responsible for selecting key personnel and for submitting a proposed budget to the council for its approval. The city council will likely seek the manager's opinion on a wide variety of matters, including what tax rate the city should adopt, whether or not the city should call a bond election, and the feasibility of recommendations made by interest groups. But these issues are ultimately up to the council, and the city manager is expected to implement whatever decisions the council makes.

In a council-manager form of government, the mayor may be either selected by the council from among its members or independently elected by the voters. The mayor presides over council meetings, has limited or no veto power, and has for the most part only the same legislative authority as members of the council. The mayor also has important ceremonial powers, such as signing proclamations and issuing keys to the city to important dignitaries. Although the office is institutionally weak, a high-profile mayor can wield considerable political influence. Mayors of the two largest Texas cities using the council-manager system, former San Antonio mayor Henry Cisneros and former Dallas

Recall election
An election, called by petition, that permits voters to remove an elected official before the official's term expires.

Council-manager form of government
A form of government in which an elected city council makes laws and hires a professional administrator who is responsible for both executing council policies and managing the day-to-day operations of city government and who serves at the pleasure of the council.

STAN HONDA/AFP/Getty Images/Newscom

Former San Antonio Mayor Julian Castro headed a mayor-manager city, the most common type in Texas. Despite the relatively weak institutional powers of the mayor in such a system, Castro developed personal and political influence that made him a force to be reckoned with.

 Compare the mayor's powers in a weak-mayor system with those of a strong mayor. How are mayors in a weak-mayor system able to develop political power despite formal limits on the power of their office?

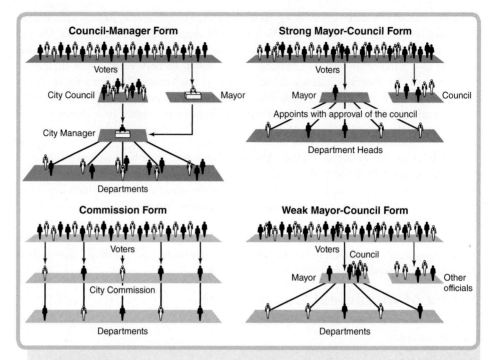

Figure 11.1
Common Forms of Municipal Government

This figure shows the four major forms of city government. Although voters are the ultimate authority in each type, scholars argue that some types are more efficient and responsive to residents' needs.

 What measures can the public take to make their views known to city officials in a way that makes city hall more accountable to the people?

mayor Ron Kirk, went on to be appointed as major federal officials. Former San Antonio Mayor Julian Castro first achieved national attention when he gave the keynote address at the 2012 Democratic National Convention. Castro's political stature continued to grow when President Barack Obama appointed him to the position of Secretary of Housing and Urban Development in 2014.

Council-manager government was initiated as part of a reform movement during the Progressive Era (1900–1917). Reformers were attempting to substitute "efficient and business-like management" for the then-prevalent system of boss rule, in which politics was the key consideration in city hall decisions. Although the council-manager system is seen as a means of separating politics from the administration of city government, critics charge that its principal shortcoming is that the voters do not directly elect the chief executive officer of the city.

Mayor-Council System
Although most Texas cities now use a council-manager system, a few, including Houston and Pasadena, still use a **mayor-council system** to govern their cities. While this system consists of a mayor and a city council, it includes both *strong-mayor* and *weak-mayor* variations.

In the **strong-mayor form of government** (see Figure 11.1), the mayor, who is chosen in a citywide election, is both the chief executive and the leader of the city council. The mayor makes appointments, prepares the budget, and is responsible for the management of city

---

Mayor-council system

A form of municipal government consisting of a mayor and a city council; this form includes both *strong-mayor* and *weak-mayor* variations.

Strong-mayor form of government

A form of municipal government in which the mayor, who is chosen in a citywide election, is both the chief executive and the leader of the city council.

government. The mayor also sets the council agenda, proposes policy, and in many cities may veto council actions.

Critics of the strong-mayor system fear that the office is too powerful and may become too politicized to distribute services fairly or efficiently. This system conjures up the image of nineteenth-century urban political party machines led by mayors who appointed political cronies as department heads, hired campaign workers as city employees, and awarded contracts to supporters.

Although the target of criticism of early twentieth-century reformers, the strong-mayor form of government did not die out but was often restructured to include an elected city comptroller (or controller) to separate the mayor from the city treasurer. (Houston, for example, elects a city controller who serves as the chief financial officer for the city.) Rules were also adopted to require that contracts be awarded to the lowest and best bidder. Other restrictions in place today that political bosses did not have to contend with include nonpartisan elections, ethics, and campaign finance laws.

The **weak-mayor form of government** (see Figure 11.1) lacks unified lines of authority because the mayor and council share administrative authority. Power is, in effect, decentralized. However, it is difficult for voters to know which officials to hold accountable when problems and mismanagement occur. This type of government is usually found in small cities and is not common in Texas.

AP images/David J. Phillip

Houston has a strong mayor-council form of government, which gives the mayor substantial authority when it comes to setting the council agenda and proposing the budget.

 How do the priorities of big-city mayors differ from those set by mayors of smaller communities? What challenges do all mayors face regardless of the size of their cities? What are key leadership traits that every mayor should have?

Commission System

The **commission form of government** (see Figure 11.1) is another approach to municipal government. Here, voters elect one set of officials who act as both executives and legislators. The commissioners, sitting together, are the municipal legislature, but individually each administers a city department. A manager or administrative assistant may be employed to assist the commissioners, but ultimate administrative authority still remains with the elected commissioners.

Commissioners may possess technical knowledge about city government because they supervise city departments. However, because power in the city bureaucracy is fragmented among separately elected commissioners, coordination is difficult, and the check-and-balance system is impaired because commissioners serve both legislative and executive functions— commissioners adopt the budget for the departments that they administer.

According to the International City/County Management Association, more than 90 percent of U.S. cities with a population of 2,500 or more use either the mayor-council or city-manager form of government. Also, between 1984 and 2012, the adoption of the city-manager system steadily increased, while use of the mayor-council form declined.

Municipal Election Systems

Mayors and city council members are usually elected for terms according to their city charter, usually two years. Scheduled at a different time from the state general election, municipal elections usually require that candidates receive a majority of the vote, and a runoff election may be required if no candidate receives more than 50 percent of the vote.

Nonpartisan Elections

In Texas, all city elections are *nonpartisan,* meaning that parties do not nominate candidates or officially campaign for them. Advocates of nonpartisan elections contend that municipal issues transcend traditional party divisions and that party labels are irrelevant. They argue that the two parties are overly polarized and that qualified candidates should not be excluded simply because they belong to the minority party.

Weak-mayor form of government

A form of municipal government in which the mayor and council share administrative authority.

Commission form of government

A municipal government in which voters elect one set of officials who act as both executives and legislators. The commissioners, sitting together, are the municipal legislature, but individually each administers a city department.

Several other states use partisan elections to select city officials. Supporters of partisan elections argue that party labels provide voters with useful cues as to how a candidate will govern; in nonpartisan elections, voters often take their cues from well-financed campaigns. Parties are useful because they help winnow the field of potential candidates; dozens of candidates sometimes clutter Texas municipal election ballots. Parties mobilize more voters and generate greater public interest than do nonpartisan campaigns. Critics of nonpartisan elections argue that they are dominated by low-visibility special interests with much to gain from city contracts and with enough money to hire campaign workers and to flood the airwaves with campaign ads.

Although all municipal elections are nonpartisan in Texas, cities have the choice to use at-large and single-member district systems—a choice that has generated considerable legal and political controversy.

Election System Options
Some cities use **at-large elections**, which are citywide elections in which some or all of the city council members are elected by voters of the entire municipality rather than from neighborhood districts. At-large systems are of two types.

Some cities use a **pure at-large system**, in which all candidates for city council run citywide and the top vote-getters are elected to fill the number of open seats. The voters simply choose from a common pool of all the candidates to fill the available council seats, with the winning candidates being those who receive the most votes. For example, if 20 candidates run for six seats, the six candidates getting the most votes are elected.

Some cities use an **at-large place system**—each candidate runs citywide for a specific seat on the council and voters cast one vote for each seat or place. For example, on a seven-member city council, the ballot would show perhaps several candidates running for place 1, different candidates running for place 2, and still others running for each place down through place 7. Voters would be able to cast one vote for each of the seven seats, and the candidate winning the majority of votes cast citywide would win each particular seat. Variations of either system may require a specific candidate to live in a particular district of the city, but the candidates are still elected by all the voters in the city. In contrast, in a system with **single-member council districts**, each council member is elected from a particular geographical district by only the voters who live in that district.

Supporters of at-large elections say that they promote the public interest because council members must take a citywide view of problems. They charge that council members elected from districts are focused on the needs of their district rather than the interests of the community as a whole. Opponents of single-member districts also claim that the election of individuals who have an outlook limited to their district makes it difficult for the council to build a consensus about the future of the city.

Critics of at-large elections maintain that the system allows a simple majority of voters to elect all council members and that, consequently, the interests of racial, ethnic, and ideological minorities in the community are not represented at city hall. Supporters of single-member districts argue that effective neighborhood representation reflects the diverse interests of the city; neighborhoods where political, cultural, and ethnic minorities live have a chance to elect at least some members to the city council when a district system is used.

Although major Texas cities usually resisted single-member districts, civil rights organizations such as the Mexican American Legal Defense and Educational Fund, the League of United Latin American Citizens, the American GI Forum, the National Association for the Advancement of Colored People, Texas Rural Legal Aid, and the Southwest Voter Registration Education Project brought successful legal action, and the federal courts forced several of them to abandon at-large elections. Several cities have instituted a mixed system in which a majority of the council members are elected from single-member districts, although the mayor and some of the council members are elected at large.

At-large elections
Citywide elections in which some or all of the city council members are elected by voters of the entire municipality rather than from neighborhood districts.

Pure at-large system
An election system in which candidates for city council run citywide and the top vote-getters are elected to fill the number of open seats.

At-large place system
An election system in which each candidate runs citywide for a specific seat on the council and voters cast one vote for each seat or place.

Single-member council districts
An electoral system in which each council member is elected from a particular geographical district by only the voters who live in that district.

Although the single-member district election system has served as the primary means of increasing minority representation on city councils, attention has also been drawn to other ways of achieving this goal. One alternative system is **cumulative voting.** Under this plan, members of city councils are elected in at-large elections, and the number of votes a voter can cast corresponds to the number of seats on the council. If, for example, the city council has five seats, a voter can cast all five votes for a single candidate. Or a voter can cast three votes for one candidate and the remaining two votes for another candidate. In other words, voters can distribute their votes among the candidates in whatever way they choose.

According to the organization FairVote, more than 50 local jurisdictions in Texas have adopted cumulative voting since the 1990s, most of them school districts. In approximately 20 percent of the communities in which cumulative voting is used, the method has been adopted by both the school board and the city council. Civil rights organizations such as the National Association for the Advancement of Colored People and the Mexican American Legal Defense and Educational Fund have backed cumulative voting in litigation, and the adoption of this election system is credited with leading to the election of minorities in two Texas independent school districts—Atlanta ISD and Amarillo ISD. The Amarillo Independent School District is the largest jurisdiction in the country to use this election system.

About 60 Texas cities joined the movement to impose *term limits*, that is, restrictions on the number of times that a politician can be reelected to an office or the number of years that a person may hold a particular office. Proponents of term limits believe that city hall is best governed by new blood and fresh ideas and that limiting the number of terms for council members is the best way to achieve that goal. Opponents, though, worry that cities stand to lose experienced, effective council members.

These term-limit laws are not uniform. Corpus Christi, for example, allows a person who has held a seat for four consecutive two-year terms to run again for the seat after sitting out three terms. In Austin, a council member is limited to two consecutive four-year terms, but that limit can be waived upon petition by 5 percent of the registered voters the council member represents. In Dallas, both city council members and the mayor are subject to term limits, but the mayor cannot serve as many terms as council members.

Attempts to weaken city term-limit laws by state law or by litigation have had mixed success. In 2000, voters in Austin rejected a proposition that would have repealed the city's term-limit law. However, in 2008, a proposal to extend the term limit to four two-year terms passed in San Antonio.

Revenue Sources and Limitations

The local political culture determines expectations about appropriate standards of services and tolerable levels of taxation. External forces—such as a downturn in the national economy, the closing of a military base, the downsizing of industries, federal and state mandates, and natural disasters—also influence the economic climate of a community.

The sources and amount of revenue used to meet a city's budgetary obligations vary greatly among Texas municipalities according to various factors, including the following:

★ The size of the city's population
★ The amount and type of taxes a city is allowed and willing to levy
★ The total assessed value of taxable property within the city limits
★ The needs of the residents

City revenues can also depend on how much aid money is available from the state and national governments. Our Texas Insiders feature shows that some cities, as well as some counties, use aggressive lobbying efforts to protect this intergovernmental revenue.

Cumulative voting
An election system in which members of city councils are elected in at-large elections, and the number of votes a voter can cast corresponds to the number of seats on the council.

Local Governments' Lobbyists: Promoting Local Interests

Local officials engage in intergovernmental lobbying using some of the same tactics that private interest groups employ to influence state and federal officials. Local officials, themselves, lobby when they make personal appeals to state and federal officials; they rely on local government associations like the Texas Municipal League to advocate for them, and they hire professional lobby outfits to represent their interests.

Mayors, city council members, and county officials appeal to the state legislature as well as state agencies for grants, special projects, revenues, and policies that benefit their communities. Individual cities and counties send local delegations consisting of elected officials and community leaders to Austin and Washington, D.C., to meet directly with state and federal representatives.

Local governments join together into umbrella organizations, such as the Texas Municipal League, the Texas Association of Counties, and the Texas Association of School Boards, that lobby Texas officials on behalf of their members. At the national level, the National Conference of Mayors and the National Association of Counties make their case to federal agencies and to Congress about the challenges facing local governments.

In recent years, cities and counties have also begun to rely on a newer, somewhat controversial type of intergovernmental lobbying. In an attempt to gain an inside track with state legislatures and Congress, some cities and counties hire outside lobby firms to promote their interests in funding dedicated for airports, roads, fire and police departments, or other special projects. For example, the city of Houston, the city of Austin, the Port of Houston Authority, Harris County, and the Tarrant Regional Water District together paid outside lobby firms at least $1.8 million for lobbying the Texas legislature in 2013.

Thinking about the role of elites in Texas politics Browse the website of either the Texas Municipal League or the Texas Association of Counties to find the organization's legislative agenda. Write a carefully constructed essay to explain the broad public policy goals that the organization attempts to achieve by lobbying the Texas legislature. To be complete, your essay should include at least six areas of public policy concern, many of which are also discussed in this chapter.

Sources: The Texas Municipal League at https://www.tml.org/legislative_faq; Texas Association of Counties at www.county.org/member-services/legislative-updates/Pages/Legislative-Briefs.aspx; Texans for Public Justice, *Major Report: Top Lobby Clients in the 2013 Legislative Session*, http://info.tpj.org/reports/Top%20Lobbyists%202013.pdf; Chuck Devore, "Let's Stop Cities from Using Tax Money to Seek More Tax Money," *Houston Chronicle*, May 25, 2012; Gary Halter, "Mandate Fears," *Houston Chronicle*, May 31, 2012.

Sales Taxes Figure 11.2 shows that Texas cities are heavily dependent on the sales tax. Although all taxes are affected by economic conditions, sales tax revenue is more sensitive to economic fluctuations than property taxes. And because budgetary problems make state and national government assistance unreliable, cities need to build into their budgets a reserve fund to compensate for these somewhat inconsistent sources of revenue.

Property Taxes Figure 11.2 shows that municipalities are also heavily dependent on ad valorem property taxes, in which the tax rate is a percentage of the assessed value of real estate. In a community with a low tax base, or total assessed value, the local government has a limited capacity to raise taxes from this source. Thus a "poor" city must set a very high tax rate to provide adequate services. Furthermore, any loss in property values causes a decline in the city's tax base.

Texas has established a countywide appraisal authority for property taxes, and all local governments must accept its property appraisals. However, Texas state law does not require

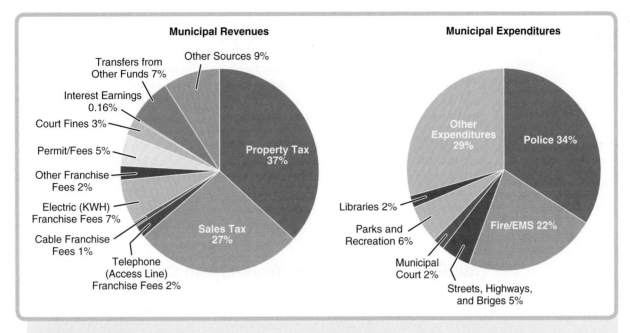

Figure 11.2
Texas Municipal Finances: General Revenue and Expenditures

These charts show where Texas municipalities get their revenues and how they spend them. The largest source of city revenue is the property tax, followed by sales taxes, and various fees. The majority of municipal expenditures are for protective services such as police, fire, and emergency medical services.

Source: Based on http://www.tml.org/HCW/WhereCitiesGetMoney.pdf

 What factors determine the budget priorities of municipal governments?

full disclosure of the sales price of residential and commercial property, making it difficult to accurately appraise property values.

The property tax rate of general-law cities depends on the size of the city, but the maximum property tax rate of a general-law city is $1.50 per $100 of the assessed value of a city's property. Home-rule municipalities can set property tax rates as high as $2.50 per $100 of assessed value.

Limits on Property Taxes Some Texas cities have taken measures to limit increases in property taxes. For example, Corpus Christi's city charter sets a property tax cap of $0.68 per $100 valuation except for taxes to finance voter-approved bonds. Texas cities, towns, counties, and junior college districts may freeze property taxes for the disabled and the elderly. Once the freeze is in place, the governing body cannot repeal it. Texas cities, as well as counties and hospital districts, may also call an election to lower property taxes by raising sales and use taxes.

Rollback Elections Voters in nonschool district jurisdictions (cities, counties, and special districts) may petition for a **rollback election** to limit an increase in the property tax rate to no more than 8 percent above that required for increased debt service. For school districts, an automatic rollback election is triggered if a school board raises taxes more than 6¢ per $100 valuation.

Rollback election
An election to limit an increase in the property tax rate to no more than 8 percent above that required for increased debt service.

User fees

Fees paid by the individuals who receive a particular government service.

Public debt

Money owed by government, ordinarily through the issuance of bonds. Local governments issue bonds to finance major projects with voter approval.

Mandate

A federal or state requirement that a lower level of government, like a city or county, provide a service or meet certain standards, often as a condition for receiving financial aid.

User Fees Fees paid by the individuals who receive a particular government service are called **user fees**. Such charges are increasingly popular because voters often oppose higher taxes and generally believe that people should pay for what they actually use. Cities may charge fees for city-provided electricity, water, sewage, and garbage collection as well as swimming pools, golf courses, and ambulance services. The Texas Municipal League has found that user fees bring in approximately 20 percent of municipal revenue. Permits, business licenses, and inspection fees round out the usual sources of city revenue.

Public Debt Local governments use **public debt**, which is money owed by government, ordinarily through the issuance of bonds. Local governments issue bonds to finance major projects with voter approval. Public debt funds infrastructure projects such as roads, buildings, and public facilities. Texas law explicitly limits the amount of long-term debt to a percentage of assessed valuation of property within the boundaries of the government. This restriction is intended to keep local governments from going bankrupt, as many did during the Great Depression of the 1930s.

Municipalities: Issues, Trends, and Controversies

Several trends and issues dominate city politics; understanding the dynamics of municipal policy making requires us to focus on population changes, economic development issues, federal and state mandates, and annexation issues.

Population Growth and Demographic Change
A community's size as well as its growth rate impact local officials' public policy choices. Growing cities must expand services ranging from sewage treatment, street building, and law enforcement to urban planning, parks and recreation, and building convention centers. Even a city with limited growth may see an internal shift in population, with one area of the city facing dramatic growth, while other areas contend with a loss of population and businesses, vacant buildings, and urban decay. Communities with stagnant or declining populations also face the challenge of funding services from a declining economic base. Cities with increasingly diverse, elderly, or youthful populations may face competing demands from the public, which will necessitate hard choices, especially if local revenue is limited.

Economic Development
The Development Corporation Act allows many Texas cities, with voter approval, to adopt additional sales taxes for economic development projects. Voters have approved such development sales taxes in more than 500 cities for property tax relief and to finance a wide range of projects, including professional and amateur sports facilities, public park improvements, and affordable housing.

Government Mandates
Texas cities—like most cities in the nation—have seen both federal and state governments cut funding even as they have increased the number of mandates imposed on local governments. A **mandate** is a federal or state requirement that a lower level of government, like a city or county, provide a service or meet certain standards, often as a condition for receiving financial aid. The federal government has imposed many such mandates as a condition for state or local governments to receive grants-in-aid. Some notable examples of federal mandates are the Americans with Disabilities Act, the National Voter Registration Act (Motor Voter Act), the Help America Vote Act, and the No Child Left Behind Act (see Chapter 2). Likewise, the state has imposed innumerable mandates on school districts, counties, and cities.

Supporters of mandates argue that they permit the federal and state governments to meet important needs in a uniform fashion. Critics charge that mandates—particularly those that are unfunded—impose a heavy financial burden on the governments that are required to fulfill the obligations they impose.

HOW DOES TEXAS COMPARE?
Population Changes in Large U.S. Cities

Texas population grew by 20.6 percent between the 2000 and 2010 censuses, adding more than 4 million persons. Although Texas added more people than any other state, most of this growth has been outside the city limits of the largest cities. Much of Texas's growth has been in suburban and exurban communities. Nevertheless, Table 11.3 shows that Texas still has three of the ten largest cities in the United States.

The city centers continue to serve as the economic and cultural hub of most metropolitan communities across the nation. Central city governments must therefore provide several services on which the smaller surrounding communities depend. In metropolitan areas, central city governments finance most economic development activities such as building sports stadiums and convention centers, financing airports, funding tourism bureaus, and providing incentives to lure business into the area.

FOR DEBATE

 How can slower-growing central cities finance the costs of economic development projects that benefit the faster-growing areas that surround them?

 What challenges do changing demographics present to large urban areas?

TABLE 11.3 The Ten Largest U.S. Cities

Rank	Place	State	2000 Census	2010 Census
1.	New York	New York	8,008,278	8,175,173
2.	Los Angeles	California	3,694,820	3,792,621
3.	Chicago	Illinois	2,896,016	2,695,598
4.	Houston	Texas	1,953,631	2,099,451
5.	Philadelphia	Pennsylvania	1,517,550	1,526,006
6.	Phoenix	Arizona	1,321,045	1,445,623
7.	San Antonio	Texas	1,144,646	1,327,407
8.	San Diego	California	1,223,400	1,307,402
9.	Dallas	Texas	1,188,580	1,197,816
10.	San Jose	California	894,943	945,942

Source: U.S. Census Bureau, *Population Change for the Ten Most Populous and Ten Fastest-Growing Metropolitan Statistical Areas: 2000 to 2010*, www.census.gov/prod/cen2010/briefs/c2010br-01.pdf.

The Unfunded Mandates Interagency Work Group, including the state auditor, comptroller, director of the Legislative Budget Board, a senator (selected by the lieutenant governor), and a representative (selected by the speaker), keeps a record of unfunded mandates the legislature passes. Mandates exempt from the list include those passed by voters and those adopted to comply with the Texas Constitution, federal law, or a court order.

Annexation   A policy that permits a city to bring unincorporated areas into the city's jurisdiction is **annexation**. According to the Texas Municipal League, "The inherent power to unilaterally annex adjoining areas is one of the most important home-rule prerogatives."[2] Big cities in Texas have suffered less than many other U.S. cities from white flight, urban decay, the evacuation of industry, and declining tax bases; one reason they have escaped

Annexation
A policy that permits a city to bring unincorporated areas into the city's jurisdiction.

---

[2]Texas Municipal League, *Local Government in Texas*, Chapter 1 at www.tml.org/MSWordTexts/HRChapter1.doc.

some of the worst of these problems is the state's broad annexation laws. The Municipal Annexation Act establishes an **extraterritorial jurisdiction (ETJ)**, which is a buffer area that extends beyond a city's limits. An ETJ extends one-half mile to five miles beyond the city's limits, depending on the city's population. The city may enforce zoning and building codes in the ETJ, and new cities may not be incorporated within the ETJ. The law also gives home-rule cities the power to annex as much as 10 percent of their existing area each year without the consent of the inhabitants of the area to be annexed.

With this protection and long-range planning, Texas cities can keep from being boxed in by suburban "bedroom" cities. Cities often use a strategy of spoke annexation to expand their ETJ into nearby areas and to prevent smaller communities from incorporating in those areas. They annex narrow "fingers" of land along highway right-of-ways outward from the existing city limits, thereby placing the area between the fingers into the ETJ. The unincorporated areas within the ETJ may then be annexed as they become sufficiently populated to warrant such action. Cities that plan ahead are therefore free to extend their boundaries and recapture both the tax base and the population that earlier fled the city center.

In recent years, some outlying areas have raised strong objections to the state's municipal annexation laws. Critics resent that their jurisdictions can be annexed without their permission. They fear higher taxes without comparable levels of services. In response to these criticisms, Texas's legislature passed a bill to require cities to give notice of annexation plans three years in advance, participate in arbitration with areas to be annexed, and deliver most city services within two and one-half years.

Usually cities have a powerful motivation to annex outlying areas to add to their tax base. However, they have resisted annexing **colonias**, severely impoverished unincorporated areas along the Texas–Mexico border with a multitude of problems, including substandard housing, unsanitary drinking water, and lack of proper sewage disposal, for which they may receive state assistance. The Texas Attorney General's Office has identified more than 1,800 colonias in 29 Texas counties, most of them along the U.S.–Mexico border. To encourage cities to assume responsibility for these areas, the state has given nearby cities incentives to annex them by allowing them to remain eligible for state aid for five years after they have been annexed.

City Hall and Social Issues In 2013 a hotly debated issue placed San Antonio in the national limelight. At issue was a proposed city ordinance that would expand non-discrimination protections beyond race, color, religion, national origin, sex, age, or handicap to also include sexual orientation and gender identity. The ordinance, which passed by an 8 to 3 vote, also includes veteran status as a protected classification, and replaces the term "handicap" with "disability." The ordinance "Provides protections in the areas of city employment, city contracts and subcontracts, appointments to Boards and Commissions, Discriminatory Housing Practices and Places of Public Accommodation."

At the same time, employment and public accommodations exemptions were placed in effect as follows:

★ The employment exemption allows a religious organization to show a preference in employment based upon religion and will apply to organizations whose "purpose and character are primarily religious."

★ The ordinance does not require a church or other non-profit to lease its accommodations to groups covered by the ordinance, provided the profits of such accommodations (above reasonable and necessary expense) are solely for the benefit of such organization.[3]

---

[3]City of San Antonio, "City of San Antonio Non-Discrimination Ordinance Facts," at http://www.sanantonio.gov/Portals/0/Files/NDO/ndo-fact-sheet.pdf.

COUNTIES

LO 11.2 Describe and evaluate the organization and structure of county governments.

County government provides a variety of services and makes public policies having widespread and direct impact on the public. The county commissioners court draws voting precinct boundaries and voting locations in each county. In most counties, the county clerk administers state elections, issues marriage licenses, and records birth and death certificates. The County Tax Office collects property taxes, issues license plates and stickers, and processes vehicle transfers. County Dispute Resolution Services help mediate conflicts between landlords and tenants. Sheriffs enforce state laws, and district or county attorneys prosecute most criminal violations. County and district courts try most civil and criminal cases.

The state constitution and the legislature established Texas counties to serve as a general-purpose government *and* as an administrative arm of the state, carrying out the state's laws and collecting certain state taxes. Although the county is an arm of the state, state supervision is minimal.

With 254 counties, Texas has more counties than any other state. County government is far less flexible than municipal government in its organization and functions. Texas counties do not have home rule and cannot pass ordinances unless the state legislature specifically authorizes them to do so. New statutes or constitutional amendments are often necessary to allow the county to deal with contemporary problems; many state laws apply to only one specific county's unique circumstances and do not grant flexibility to counties throughout the state. The needs of Harris County, for example, with a population of 4,092,459 in 2010, are significantly different from those of Loving County, which had only 82 inhabitants. Yet Texas law allows only modest variations to accommodate these differences.

For example, county property taxes are limited to a rate of 80 cents per $100 of assessed valuation unless voters approve additional taxes to cover long-term debt for infrastructure such as courthouses, criminal justice buildings, flood control, and county road or bridge maintenance.

Functions of Counties

County governments are general-purpose local governments that also serve as an administrative arm of the state. They administer county, state, and national elections but not those for municipalities, school, and other special districts. County governments act for the state in securing right-of-ways for highways; law enforcement; registering births, deaths, and marriages; housing state district courts; registering motor vehicles; recording land titles and deeds; and collecting some state taxes and fees.

County government also has optional powers specifically authorized by state law. For example, the Local Government Code authorizes counties to establish and maintain libraries, operate and maintain parks, establish recreational or cultural facilities such as auditoriums or convention centers, appoint a county historical commission, and regulate sexually oriented businesses. County governments may also enter into agreements with another local government to provide a service or program such as purchasing and maintaining parks, museums, and historical sites. Counties may contract with other local governments to carry out administrative functions such as assessing and collecting taxes or managing records or to provide public services such as police and fire protection, streets and roads, public health and welfare, and waste disposal. The Health and Safety Code gives county governments the authority to maintain a county hospital.

Structure and Organization of Counties
County government consists of several independent officials, elected for four-year terms in the partisan general election at the same time state officials are elected (see Figure 11.3). The county governing body, the

County governments

General-purpose local governments that also serve as administrative arms of the state.

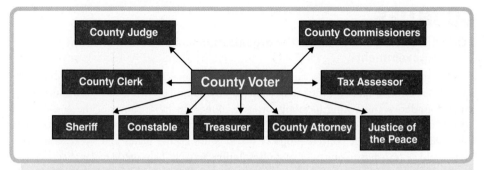

Figure 11.3

Texts County Officials Elected by Voters

Each of the 254 Texas counties has several officials, each of whom is independently elected in partisan elections.

 Should counties have fewer elected offices and nonpartisan elections, as is the case with Texas municipalities? Or do counties provide greater accountability with a divided executive structure in which voters elect numerous county administrators?

Commissioners court

The policy-making body of a county, consisting of a county judge (the presiding officer of the court), who is elected in a countywide election to a four-year term, and four commissioners, who are elected from individual precincts to four-year terms.

County judge

An official elected countywide for a four-year term to preside over the county commissioners court.

commissioners court, consists of the county judge and four county commissioners. It is not a judicial body; it is a legislature with limited authority to approve the budget for all county operations, set the tax rate, and pass ordinances on a narrow range of policies. The commissioners court does not have direct control over the many elected department heads in county government, but it wields considerable influence through its budgetary power. The sheriff, for example, is responsible to county voters for enforcing the law and maintaining order and security in the county jail, but the quality of law enforcement depends a great deal on county commissioners' decisions. The commissioners court must provide the funds to build the jail and approve its staff, authorize expenditures for each vehicle and its gas and repairs, and authorize deputies, clerks, and their salaries.

The **county judge** is an official elected countywide for a four-year term to preside over the commissioners court. In addition, the county judge has administrative functions that include preparing a budget proposal (a responsibility the county judge shares with the county clerk or auditor in counties with fewer than 225,000 population); supervising election-related activities (such as calling elections, posting election notices, and receiving and canvassing of election results); conducting hearings for beer and wine permits; performing marriage ceremonies; conducting hearings on state hospital admittance for people with mental illness; and serving as the head of civil defense and disaster relief for the county. In addition, a county judge may have judicial authority in many of the smaller counties.

Four county commissioners comprise the remaining membership of the court and are elected to four-year terms. Commissioners are elected in single-member districts (or precincts, as they are called in Texas). In 1968, the U.S. Supreme Court ruled that commissioner districts must be roughly equal in population based on the one-person, one-vote principle.[4]

Commissioners are sometimes called "road commissioners" because they are responsible for the county roads and bridges within their precincts (unless a county engineer has been hired to do that job). Each is given a certain amount of money and has almost total authority

---

[4]*Avery v. Midland County*, 390 U.S. (1968).

to determine how it will be spent on roads and bridges. Residents of rural areas often consider building and maintaining roads to be the commissioners' primary responsibility.

Law enforcement officers are the county sheriff and constables. The **sheriff** is the chief county law enforcement officer. Next to the county judge, the sheriff is usually the most powerful county officer because he or she has a relatively large budget and staff of deputies to assist in enforcing state law throughout the county. In the corporate limits of cities, the sheriff usually refrains from patrolling to better use scarce resources and avoid jurisdictional disputes with the city police. The sheriff's department also operates the county jail and delivers and executes court orders.

Constables are county law enforcement officials who are elected to serve as the process officer of justice of the peace courts and also have general law enforcement powers. Constables are elected from the same precincts as justices of the peace. They deliver summons and execute court orders. In some metropolitan counties, constables have added many deputies and have become important law enforcement agencies, but in others, the office is so unimportant that it has remained unfilled, and some county commissioners have abolished the office altogether.

Financial officers of the county include the tax assessor-collector, the treasurer, and the auditor. The responsibilities of the **tax assessor-collector** include collecting various county taxes and fees and registering voters. Additional responsibilities include collecting certain state taxes and fees, particularly motor vehicle registration fees (license plate fees) and the motor vehicle sales tax.

In many counties the **county treasurer** is responsible for receiving, depositing, and disbursing funds. However some counties have transferred this function to the county auditor. Although the treasurer holds a constitutional office, several counties have asked the legislature to propose statewide constitutional amendments to abolish this office in their counties. Because a general constitutional amendment to allow county voters to abolish the office is unlikely, elimination of this office is likely to proceed on a county-by-county basis.

The **county auditor** reviews all county financial records and ensures that expenditures are made in accordance with the law. Whereas other key county officials are elected, the county auditor is appointed to a two-year term by district judges.

Clerical officers in the county are the county and district clerks. The **county clerk** serves as the county's chief record keeper and election officer. In some ways, the office parallels that of the Texas secretary of state. The county clerk's duties include serving as clerk for the commissioners court; maintaining records for justices of the peace, county courts, and district courts in counties with a population of fewer than 8,000; recording deeds, mortgages, wills, and contracts; issuing marriage licenses and maintaining certain records of births and deaths; and serving on the county election

Sheriff
The chief county law enforcement officer.

Constables
County law enforcement officials who are elected to serve as the process officer of justice of the peace courts and also has general law enforcement powers.

Courtesy of Sheriff Greg Hamilton, Travis County Sheriff's Office.

The sheriff is usually the most powerful county officer, next to the county judge, because he or she has a relatively large budget and a staff of deputies to assist in enforcing state law throughout the county. But the sheriff's department budget must be approved by the commissioners court.

What should the commissioners court and the public study to determine if a sheriff's office is effectively meeting the county's law enforcement needs? How can voters hold county officials accountable when so many of them are elected to offices with divided and overlapping responsibilities?

Tax assessor-collector

A county financial officer whose responsibilities include collecting various county taxes and fees and registering voters.

County treasurer

In many counties, the official who is responsible for receiving, depositing, and disbursing funds.

County auditor

A financial officer whose duties include reviewing county financial records and ensuring that expenditures are made in accordance with the law.

County clerk

The officer who serves as the county's chief record keeper and election officer.

District clerk

The record keeper for the district court in counties with a population exceeding 8,000.

County attorney

A county legal officer whose responsibilities may include giving legal advice to the commissioners court, representing the county in litigation, and prosecuting crimes. In counties that also elect a district attorney, the county attorney specializes in civil matters.

District attorney

A county officer who prosecutes criminal cases and also handles civil matters in many counties.

Short ballot

The listing of only a few independently elected offices on an election ballot.

board, certifying candidates running for county office, and carrying out other housekeeping functions, such as preserving the results of state, county, and special-district elections.

The record keeper for the district court in counties with a population exceeding 8,000 is the **district clerk**. However, the county clerk continues to maintain records for the constitutional county court and any county courts-at-law.

The **county attorney** is a county legal officer whose responsibilities may include giving legal advice to the commissioners court, representing the county in litigation, and prosecuting crimes. A **district attorney** is a county officer who prosecutes criminal cases and also handles civil matters in many counties. Some counties have both a county attorney and a district attorney; in these counties, the county attorney deals primarily with civil matters and the district attorney prosecutes criminal matters. District attorneys are not subordinate to county government in Texas, nor are they considered county officials, but their office space and salaries are partly paid by the counties. County attorneys are wholly county officials.

Some counties have other executive officers, such as five or more members of the county board of school trustees, a county superintendent of schools, a county surveyor, and a county weigher. Counties may authorize such appointive officers as the county election administrator, county health officer, county medical examiner, county agricultural agent, and home demonstration agent.

Counties: Issues, Trends, and Controversies

The institutional features of Texas county government are largely a product of the nineteenth century, yet the demands of modern society are placing an increasingly heavy burden on this level of government. The following discussion focuses on some frequently cited criticisms of county government and the measures counties can take to deal with contemporary problems.

Constitutional Rigidity The great mass of detailed and restrictive material in the Texas Constitution creates problems of rigidity and inflexibility. Controls that are not embedded in the constitution are scattered throughout the Local Government Code and various other statutes. The result is a collection of legal requirements, many of which apply equally to the four largest counties in the state—Harris, Dallas, Tarrant, and Bexar—as well as the more than 100 counties that have populations of fewer than 20,000. The standardization of county structure and functions often fails to account for the great variation among the counties in their individual needs and problems. At present, deviations from the uniform structure and functions must be specifically authorized by the state legislature. Some reformers would entrust voters to restructure their own county governments using home-rule provisions similar to those now available to many Texas cities.

Long Ballot So many county officials are independently elected and the operations of county government are so decentralized that the voters may find it difficult to monitor the many positions involved. Reformers recommend a **short ballot**, that is, the listing of only a few independently elected offices on an election ballot. They argue that a simplified structure with a single county executive would allow voters to hold one high-profile officer accountable for administration of county programs. They contend that a chief county executive could coordinate county programs, engage in long-range planning, and eliminate duplication among various county offices.

Defenders of the *long ballot* (see Chapter 3) counter that the current system provides for the direct election of public officials to ensure that government remains responsive to the needs and demands of the voters. They fear that concentrating too much power in a single chief executive invites abuse and threatens personal liberty.

Unit Road System The *unit road system* is a system that concentrates the day-to-day responsibilities for roads in the hands of a professional engineer rather than individual county commissioners. The engineer is responsible to the commissioners court for efficient and economical construction and maintenance of county roads. The voters may petition for an election to establish the unit road system, or commissioners may initiate the change themselves.

Supporters of this system maintain that it brings greater coordination and professionalism to road building and maintenance in rural areas. Commissioners, however, are reluctant to give up the political influence that their individual control over road building brings; some voters like the idea of directly electing the officers who build their roads.

Spoils System versus Merit System Elected county officials hire county employees using a **spoils system**, a system that gives elected officials considerable discretion in employment and promotion decisions. This can make employee job security dependent on the continued election of and allegiance to their employer. Political loyalty rather than competence is often the main factor in the recruitment and retention of employees, and when a new official is elected, a large turnover of county employees may result.

The spoils system's defenders point out that the elected official is responsible for the employee's performance and therefore should have the authority to bring in more employees than just the personnel at the top echelon. They also argue that an elected official would be foolish to release competent employees simply because they had gained their experience under a predecessor. Finally, they argue that alternatives like the merit system provide so much job security that employees become complacent and indifferent to the public.

The spoils system's opponents propose a *merit system* that bases employment and promotion on specific qualifications and performance (see Chapter 8). Because it would also prohibit termination of employment except for proven cause, the merit system offers job security, which should attract qualified personnel. Supporters of the merit system maintain that it encourages professionalism, increases efficiency, and allows uniform application of equal-opportunity requirements.

Texas counties with a population of 200,000 or more may establish a *civil service* program for some county employees, and counties with populations of more than 500,000 may establish a civil service system for the sheriff's office. According to the Texas Association of Counties, half of the 20 counties that may establish a civil service system have done so, and all seven counties eligible to establish a civil service program in the sheriffs' department have one.

Consolidation Students of county government reform point to city–county consolidation as a means to reduce the number of local governments, to eliminate duplication of government services, and to increase greater government efficiency. **Consolidation** is the merging of county government with other local governments to form a single government.

The consolidation of governments faces many challenges. Consolidation requires legislative action, followed by local voter approval. Independently elected officials at the local level are likely to resist a move that would eliminate their offices and the power that goes with them. Although many cities and counties enter into partnership agreements to provide joint services, city–county consolidation bills have failed to win passage in the Texas legislature.

Spoils system
A system that gives elected officials considerable discretion in employment and promotion decisions.

Consolidation
The merging of county government with other local governments to form a single local government.

RODGER MALLISON/KRT/Newscom

Courthouses are the nerve center of county government, where courts conduct trials, the commissioners meet, taxes are collected, and vital records are kept. In Texas, county officials are elected in partisan elections on a long ballot.

 What are the advantages and disadvantages of commissioners, judges, and other major officials such as the sheriff running for office on party labels? Evaluate the use of a long ballot in terms of local government efficiency and responsiveness to public needs.

SPECIAL-DISTRICT GOVERNMENTS

LO 11.3 Describe and evaluate the organization and structure of special-district governments.

Special districts are local governments that provide single or closely related services that are not provided by general-purpose county or municipal governments. We will focus on the non-school special districts in this chapter, and in Chapter 12 we will discuss special-purpose governments related to education, such as school districts and community college districts.

These special districts do not always receive attention comparable with cities and counties, but they are no less important when it comes to serving the needs of the public. In a suburban area outside the city limits, for example, a special district may be established to provide water and sewer facilities for a housing development; such a special district has the authority to borrow to build the system and may assess taxes and user fees on property owners and residents.

Table 11.4 shows that the number of special districts has grown considerably. In fact, special districts are the most numerous of all local governments in Texas. Some examples are airport authorities, drainage districts, hospital authorities, municipal utility districts, library districts, navigation districts, metropolitan transit authorities (see Figure 11.4), river authorities, rural fire prevention districts, and noxious weed control districts. According to the U.S. Census Bureau, two-thirds of the special districts in Texas provide a single service. The rest are classified as "multiple-function districts," and most of those provide closely related functions like sewerage and water supply.

Multimember boards usually govern special districts. Voters elect members of some special-district boards either in partisan or nonpartisan elections; city councils and county commissioners appoint others; in some cases, city council members or county commissioners themselves serve ex officio as board members.

Dependent agency

A classification created by the U.S. Census Bureau for governmental entities that are closely tied to general-purpose governments but do not have as much independence as special-district governments.

Special districts should not be confused with dependent agencies. A **dependent agency** is a classification created by the U.S. Census Bureau for governmental entities that are closely tied to general-purpose governments but do not have as much independence as special-district governments. An example of a dependent agency is a crime control and prevention district, a temporary agency created with voter approval. Crime control districts have become increasingly popular since the 1990s, particularly in cities located in Tarrant County. Voters have authorized more than 60 crime control districts, and most of them collect either a one-half cent or one-fourth cent sales tax. In some communities, the establishment of crime control and prevention districts has substantially increased funding for law enforcement.

TABLE 11.4 Special Districts In Texas, 1952–2012

1952	1962	1972	1982	1992	2002	2007	2012
491	733	1,215	1,681	2,266	2,245	2,291	2,309

Source: U.S. Census Bureau, *List and Structure of Governments: Number of Special Districts*, www.census.gov/govs/go/number_of_special_districts_by_county.html.

Special districts have been on the rise since the mid-twentieth century. Some special districts have their own elected governing boards that have the authority to impose a property tax.

▲ **What are the benefits of having a specialized approach to providing government services? What are the drawbacks? What issues might encourage special districts to collaborate with cities and counties, and what challenges might make collaboration difficult?**

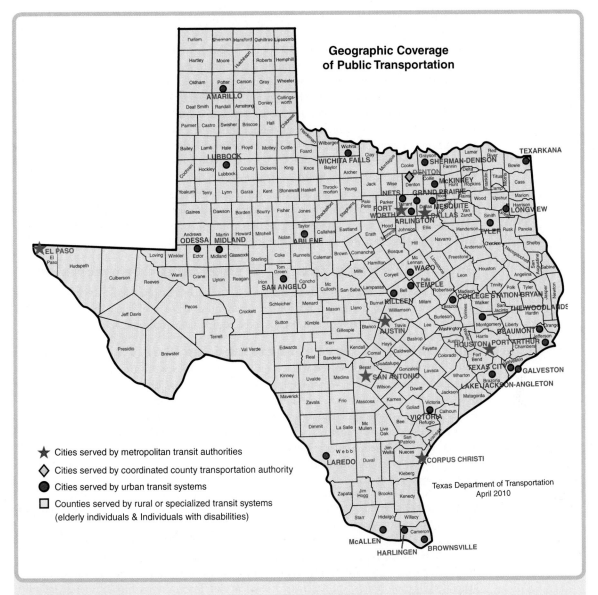

Figure 11.4
Cities and Counties Served by Public Transportation Systems

Texas Department of Transportation, http://ftp.dot.state.tx.us/pub/txdot-info/ptn/small_urban_map.pdf.

CTQ Should Texas cities invest more in public transportation? What factors are likely to encourage the public to use mass transit?

Reasons for Creating Special District Governments

Having a service provided by a special district rather than a general-purpose government is appealing to many residents for a variety of reasons. A city or county may have limited revenue because of a downturn in the economy, the loss of a major industry, new unfunded mandates, or fewer federal dollars. The general-purpose government may have reached its state-mandated sales tax ceiling of 2 percent. Popular or political sentiment may be that city and county property taxes are already too high, and a strong anti-tax organization in the community may be eager to make that point. Little or no support may exist for increasing taxes or cutting other services to accommodate another service responsibility.

Furthermore, only a small area within a city or county may need the service. Why tax the entire jurisdiction? A district may be created for the benefit of "underserved areas," as is the case with library districts in Texas that serve rural and suburban areas. The demand for a service may extend beyond a single jurisdiction, calling for a special district that is multicity or multicounty in scope. For example, a river authority with the power to govern the use of water throughout the river's watershed must transcend existing political boundaries; flood control districts similarly deal with a problem that crosses political boundaries. Municipal Utilities Districts (MUDs) are often created at the insistence of developers who want to provide water and sewerage for the subdivisions they establish outside city service areas. For a host of reasons, special districts serve as alternatives to general-purpose governments, and they are an attractive option as an alternative revenue source.

Special Districts: Issues, Trends, and Controversies

Although special districts provide valuable public services not provided by general-purpose governments, reformers charge that they are often too small to be efficient, too low-profile to be visible to the public, and too numerous to be readily held accountable to voters.

Multiplicity of Governments and Lack of Visibility Although special districts can be dissolved when a municipality annexes the area and provides it with services, the trend in Texas as across the rest of the nation has been toward the proliferation of special-district governments (see Table 11.4). The sheer number of special-district governments and their small size create serious challenges for special-district governments.

Special districts are sometimes called *hidden* governments because the actions of district officials and employees are less visible than if a county or city provided the services. When special-district elections are held at times or places other than those for general elections, voter turnout is quite low.

Cost and Inefficiency Because special districts are often small, they may purchase in limited quantities at higher prices than larger governments. In addition, if special districts have little or no authority to tax, they are forced to borrow money by issuing revenue bonds, which are paid from fees collected for the service provided, rather than *general-obligation bonds*, which are paid from tax revenue. Because revenue bonds are less secure than general-obligation bonds, special-district residents are forced to pay higher interest rates just to service the bonded indebtedness. Special districts may also have a lower bond rating than larger, general-function governments, which also increases their borrowing costs.

A study of special-purpose governments in more than 300 U.S. metropolitan areas concluded that the special-district approach to governing is more costly than the general-purpose approach. Moreover, social welfare functions (such as hospitals, housing, and welfare) tend to receive more revenue in metropolitan areas with fewer special districts. Housekeeping functions (including fire protection, natural resources, and police protection) and development functions (including airports, water, and highways) tend to receive more revenue in areas in which districts are more prevalent.

As an alternative to inefficient special districts, reformers advocate consolidation of small special districts. To deal with problems and fiscal challenges that transcend city and county boundaries, they urge general-purpose governments to negotiate interlocal agreements to meet the needs of their respective communities. They argue that the need for special districts can be reduced by transferring their functions to general-purpose governments.

COUNCILS OF GOVERNMENTS

LO 11.4 Evaluate the role of councils of governments as local government partners.

The multitude of local governments with different jurisdictions and missions can pose challenges when services are of a regional nature. These governments look for ways to coordinate activities and share information without compromising their respective legal responsibilities.

Councils of governments (COGs)

Advisory bodies consisting of representatives of various local governments brought together for the purposes of regional planning and cooperation are called **councils of governments**. COGs are not governments; instead, they are voluntary regional groupings of local governments.

Councils of governments emerged throughout the United States and in Texas beginning in the 1960s. According to the National Association of Regional Councils (http://narc.org) website, "By 1967, the more than 350 Regional Councils in the country were at the forefront of forging regional alliances for the purpose of addressing common, multi-jurisdictional challenges." Local governments are involved in the delivery of a variety of services that are the product of national, state, and local laws and policies, and many of the public needs and problems transcend governmental jurisdictions. Intergovernmental communication is essential and often makes the difference between successful or unsuccessful collaboration and delivery of services that are regional in nature.

The Texas Association of Regional Councils was established in 1973. Its membership consists of all COGs in the state. The association's website lists a wide range of services provided by Texas COGs including:

★ planning and implementing regional homeland security strategies;
★ operating law enforcement training academies;
★ promoting regional municipal solid waste and environmental quality planning;
★ providing cooperative purchasing options for governments;
★ managing region-wide services to the elderly;
★ maintaining and improving regional 9-1-1 systems;
★ promoting regional economic development;
★ operating specialized transit systems; and
★ providing management services for member governments.[5]

These services are commonly provided by COGs throughout the nation. COGs do not supersede the authority of the individual local governments that comprise their membership, but they do play an active role in helping local governments meet their service delivery responsibilities in their respective jurisdictions.

By bringing local officials together, COGs provide a base for the exchange of ideas and knowledge. Although COGs do not solve the problems that local governments face, they do encourage local officials to recognize the magnitude of these problems and cooperate to manage some of them.

Councils of governments (COGs)
Advisory bodies consisting of representatives of various local governments brought together for the purposes of regional planning and cooperation.

APPLYING WHAT YOU HAVE LEARNED ABOUT LOCAL GOVERNMENT

LO 11.5 Apply what you have learned about local government.

This chapter has presented you with a variety of issues that local governments must resolve as they make public policy. As you learned, local governments rely most heavily on property

[5]www.txregionalcouncilofgovernment.

taxes and sales taxes. The following article will focus on sales taxes (up to 2 percent) that cities, transit authorities, and certain special districts may collect on the sale of items subject to the state's general sales taxes. The article will challenge you to evaluate the fairness of local sales taxes because they depend on where you live, and where you travel. The sales taxes you pay are also determined by whether you shop online, across state lines, or across international boundaries.

After you have read the essay, you will be asked a series of questions that will require you to employ critical-thinking skills to apply what you have learned in this chapter to the new information in this essay. Your analysis will require you to consider local governments' strategies in developing tax policies and to evaluate the fairness of these policies as they impact on individual taxpayers.

Sales Tax Equitability

by Eric Miller

BLINN COLLEGE—BRYAN CAMPUS

Taxes—no one likes paying them. We keep looking for ways to pay less in taxes. Why not go to a place where the taxes are lower? Depending on where you live, you might just have that luxury.

Texas is a big state. Texas collects a statewide sales tax (6.25 percent) and then allows local government to add on to that tax up to 2 percent. The highest tax you'll pay is 8.25 percent of whatever it is you're buying. In some areas, the tax rate is actually less since the local governments choose to collect less tax. They may make do with their property tax revenues, or they may have a more efficient government.

Is this fair? I mean, what if you lived just down the street (in Texas terms, not quite literally) from an area where the sales tax was 7.25 percent. How would you feel? That's one whole cent per dollar less! Would you travel to make your purchases there? Before you answer that, would the stuff you want to buy even be sold there? It may be so small or so out of the way that the items you want aren't there. If they are available, is it worth the cost in gas and travel time to go get them? For a savings of a few cents?

You can do this if you have the ability to get there. Turn things around: What if you could NOT get to where the taxes were lower? How would it make you feel to know that you were always going to pay the most in sales taxes? And to further things along, what if the governing body who set those taxes was not yours? What if it was in the adjoining county and city? Those other elected officials set the taxes you have to pay because the businesses are located in their jurisdiction, and you live outside the boundaries.

Take DART for example. Those who live in the Dallas–Ft. Worth area probably know this as Dallas Area Rapid Transit. Those of you in other areas may know something different, or you may have no idea what public transportation means. In 2012, DART took in $432.5 million dollars in sales tax from its member cities.[6] Not all the cities in the DFW area are in DART; some face the maximum cap and can't divert the required 1 percent over to DART. That means when you shop in some of those cities, like Plano for example, your sales tax is funding DART, even if you aren't using it.[7] Is that fair? If you live your entire life in Plano and pay 1 percent of your purchases to DART and you never use it, what good is it doing you? And if you come from out of town, you pay the 1 percent sales tax on your purchases, AND you then have to pay the fare if you ride DART.

---

[6]*Dallas Area Rapid Transit Reference Book*, April, 2013, p. 4, at www.dart.org/about/dartreferencebookapr13.pdf.
[7]Ibid.

But that's the point of course. Visitors from out of town will come in and shop and do other activities that get charged the 1 percent sales tax. That 1 percent helps fund the locals who use DART and keeps the fares low so people can afford to ride. It is "public" transportation after all.

DFW is one area; what about those cities that border another state? How easy is it to cross into the other state to pay a lower sales tax? Going north from New Boston into Arkansas is an easy drive; you cross the Red River and the speed limit changes from 70 in Texas to 55 in Arkansas. And the sales tax changes too. But that requires a drive; what about something even closer? The city of Texarkana is in both states. That's even easier to move around.

Think about the folks that live in Texarkana. Depending on which side of the border they are on, the sales tax is either 8.25 percent for Texas or 9.75 percent for the Arkansas side. In the myriad of items for sale in the city, some have sales tax and some don't. Some items or services are taxed in one area and not the other. Is it enough to make one person drive a few extra miles and spend a few extra minutes in traffic to save what could amount to a few pennies on a purchase? Maybe. Is it enough to have a big retailer put their store in one state and not the other? Again, maybe. Local government has tools to influence those decisions, and the sales tax is normally not one of those considerations.

That was just two neighbor states; what about a whole different country all together? In January 2014, Mexico increased the federal sales tax to 16 percent along several border areas. The tax had been 11 percent and worked to keep sales in Mexico. However, the border areas competed not with Mexico, but with the United States. According to one source, some $4.5 billion is spent by Mexican shoppers in Texas.[8] That's a lot of sales tax. So think about that when you consider cross-border shopping—just try to avoid paying the sales tax without some paperwork to back it up.

Finally, it's obvious how much technology has changed just about everything on the planet. Many of you have probably shopped on the Internet at least a bit. Maybe you were just looking, or maybe that is your normal way to shop. States have laws regarding the rendition of sales tax, but that doesn't mean every business follows the laws. It's more complicated when different states have different laws regarding the same product or service. This is one area that some are trying to get leveled. There are bills in the U.S. Congress to address more sales tax fairness, such as the Market Place Fairness Act,[9] which would establish national standards for collecting state sales taxes for online purchases. Amazon.com, Walmart, and other retailers have joined the effort to regulate sales tax collections on Internet purchases. The International Council of Shopping Centers hopes to get shoppers' attention through signs in malls and on its website.[10] Another of its websites calls attention to the failure of the U.S. Supreme Court to weigh in on the issue.[11]

Even though most of us see the sales tax as a state and local tax, it has wider implications. It has been used as long as there have been sales, and will continue to be used to encourage and discourage actions of the general population, including those who work to find ways around the tax.

---

[8]Elliot Spagat, "Mexican Sales Tax Hike Could Drive Shoppers North of the Border," *The Huffington Post*, January 2, 2014, at www.huffingtonpost.com/2014/01/02/mexico-sales-tax-hike_n_4531042.html.
[9]Explained at www.marketplacefairness.org.
[10]www.icsc.org.
[11]21st Century Retail, "The Supreme Court Defers on Retail Fairness, Congress Must Act," *Press Room*, December 3, 2013, at www.21stcenturyretail.org/press-room/announcements/supreme-court-defers-retail.html.

JOIN THE DEBATE

 Do local governments intentionally develop taxing policies to generate revenues from out-of-town travelers who will not benefit from their services? Do sales taxes shift tax burdens to nonresidents more than property taxes? Why? Why not?

 Should local governments consider that sales taxes weigh more heavily on certain consumers more than others? Can you think of strategies that would fairly distribute the cost burden for public services among those who benefit from them?

 Do businesses consider sales tax burdens when they decide where to locate? Do consumers consider taxes in deciding where to shop? How do local governments balance the effect of taxation on economic activity with the need to finance vital public services?

CHAPTER SUMMARY

LO 11.1 Describe and evaluate the organization and structure of municipal governments. Municipalities with a population greater than 5,000 may adopt home rule, which allows them to write their own charters (comparable to a constitution) and ordinances, as long as they do not conflict with state or federal laws or constitutions. Cities that do not meet that population requirement must operate under a general-law charter established by the state.

The nonpartisan election is a key feature of Texas municipal government, and the council-manager form of government and at-large elections are also characteristics of many Texas cities. Some cities with large Latino and African-American populations have, under court order, replaced at-large elections with single-member districts, modified election systems, or instituted cumulative voting. Local voters may also influence their communities through initiative, referendum, and recall elections; rollback elections; term-limit elections; and economic development sales tax elections. Texas's broad annexation laws facilitate the jurisdictional expansion of home-rule cities, but are criticized by voters in unincorporated areas who object to being annexed against their will. State law has ushered in expectations of greater planning and quicker service delivery after annexation.

LO 11.2 Describe and evaluate the organization and structure of county governments. The structure and organization of county government are determined by the Texas Constitution and the state legislature. Texas counties range considerably in terms of population, yet they are quite similar when it comes to structural features, functions, and sources of funding. County governments have a plural executive system with many county departments being independently elected, including department heads such as law enforcement officers, financial officers, and clerical officers.

LO 11.3 Describe and evaluate the organization and structure of special-district governments. Special-district governments provide single or closely related services that are not provided by general-purpose county or municipal governments. Special districts are the most numerous of all local governments in Texas, and they have steadily increased in number since the mid-twentieth century. The type of service they provide, how their governing boards are selected, and their sources of revenue vary.

Having a service provided by a special district rather than a general-purpose government is appealing to many residents for a variety of reasons, including the lack of support among general-purpose governments for increasing taxes or cutting other services to accommodate another service responsibility. Critics charge that they are often too small to be efficient, too low-profile to be visible to the public, and too numerous to be readily held accountable to voters.

LO 11.4 Evaluate the role of councils of governments as local government partners. Government is largely fragmented at the local level. Although friction between governments is common, cooperation may also result when local governments agree to share responsibility for certain services. Nevertheless, any significant changes in the structural relationship between cities, counties, and special districts will likely continue to be more incremental than sweeping. But on a routine basis, local governments can cooperate with the assistance of councils of government (COGs), voluntary regional groupings of local governments that share information and coordinate government planning.

LO 11.5 Apply what you have learned about local government. You explored how municipalities and transit authorities rely heavily on sales taxes to finance their services. You evaluated the fairness of the sales tax in light of the fact that different taxpayers pay different sales taxes depending on where they live, what they buy, and how much they travel. You considered whether sales taxes should be applied to online purchases as they are to purchases from brick-and-mortar locations.

KEY TERMS

annexation, *p. 297*
at-large city elections, *p. 292*
at-large place system, *p. 292*
city charter, *p. 288*
colonias, *p. 298*
commission form of
  government, *p. 291*
commissioners court, *p. 300*
consolidation, *p. 303*
constables, *p. 301*
council-manager form of
  government, *p. 289*

councils of government
  (COGs), *p. 307*
county attorney, *p. 302*
county auditor, *p. 302*
county clerk, *p. 302*
county governments, *p. 299*
county judge, *p. 300*
county treasurer, *p. 302*
cumulative voting, *p. 293*
dependent agencies, *p. 304*
district attorney, *p. 302*
district clerk, *p. 302*

extraterritorial jurisdiction
  (ETJ), *p. 298*
general-law city, *p. 288*
general-purpose government,
  p. 287
home-rule city, *p. 288*
mandate, *p. 296*
mayor-council system, *p. 290*
public debt, *p. 296*
pure at-large system, *p. 292*
recall election, *p. 289*
rollback election, *p. 295*

sheriff, *p. 301*
short ballot, *p. 302*
single-member council
  districts, *p. 292*
special districts, *p. 287*
spoils system, *p. 303*
strong-mayor form of
  government, *p. 290*
tax assessor-collector, *p. 302*
user fees, *p. 296*
weak-mayor form of
  government, *p. 291*

REVIEW QUESTIONS

LO 11.1 Describe and evaluate the organization and structure of municipal governments.

- Why do cities adopt home rule? What are some examples of limitations that are imposed on home-rule cities?

- Explain the mayor's role and authority in the council-manager, weak-mayor, and strong-mayor forms of government.

- Compare and contrast at-large and single-member district election systems. Describe the cumulative-voting election system alternative.

LO 11.2 Describe and evaluate the organization and structure of county governments.

- In what ways are county governments restricted by state law?

- How are members of the commissioners court elected? What are the responsibilities of the commissioners court?

- Who are the county law enforcement officers and county financial officers? What are their responsibilities?

LO 11.3 Describe and evaluate the organization and structure of special-district governments.

- What is the primary purpose of special-district governments? What are some examples of special-district governments?

- What are some reasons for creating a special district to provide a service as opposed to giving a city or a county the responsibility for the service?

- What are some reasons for opposing the creation of special-district governments?

LO 11.4 Evaluate the role of councils of governments as local government partners.

- What factors contributed to the formation of councils of government?

- From the perspective of city councils, county commissioners courts, and special-district governments, what are the primary reasons for joining councils of government?

- What are particular examples of services provided by councils of government?

GET ACTIVE

Explore the structures of local governments in your area. You can find a list of Texas cities and counties at Texas.gov (**www.texas.gov**), which is the official website of the state of Texas. Click on "Discover," and then go to "State and Local Government." Click on the name of your city and county and visit their websites to learn about the organization and structure of each government.

Learn how local governments form interest groups. Visit the websites of the Texas Association of Counties (**www.county.org**) and the Texas Municipal League

(**www.tml.org**) to learn about the goals and responsibilities of these organizations.

 At the Texas Association of Counties and Texas Municipal League websites, you will find each organization's assessment of laws and court decisions that affect counties and cities, respectively. Drawing from this information, write a "local government priorities agenda" consisting of five major issues facing counties and cities that you think are particularly important and explain your perspective.

Go to the website of the Texas Border Coalition (www.texasbordercoalition.org) to see if you should include their priorities as part of your "local government agenda." Who are the members of this coalition? Explain challenges that border communities face and the measures they are taking to deal with these challenges.

Speak out at a city council meeting or a county commissioners court meeting. Sign up to speak during the time of the meeting set aside for public comments. Let city or county officials know what improvements you think could be made in your community.

Participate in a local political campaign. Candidates often need volunteers to help organize campaign rallies and get-out-the-vote drives, stuff envelopes with campaign literature for mail-outs, work phone banks, and pass out campaign literature. You will find the names of city council candidates listed on the election ballot at the official websites of Texas cities. For county elections, you will find the candidates listed on the ballot by going to the official websites of county governments.

 What kind of personal satisfaction can a political activist expect to get from being a part of a movement with shared goals that are larger than themselves?

CHAPTER 12

Public Policy in Texas

LEARNING OBJECTIVES

LO 12.1 Analyze and evaluate Texas tax policies.

LO 12.2 Describe the politics of state spending.

LO 12.3 Analyze Texas educational policies and the politics of education.

LO 12.4 Analyze Texas health and human service policies and the politics of income redistribution.

LO 12.5 Describe Texas transportation policies and evaluate the prospects for reform.

LO 12.6 Apply what you have learned about Texas public policy issues.

*T*he Texas legislature finally passed and sent to the governor a $200.4 billion budget for fiscal years 2014 and 2015. Counting one dollar every second without resting for weekends, holidays, and coffee breaks, it would take about 6,355 years to count these appropriations! Texas has the third-largest state budget, exceeded only by those of California and New York.

Until recently, state spending steadily rose as each successive budget was larger than the preceding one, resulting in a long succession of record expenditures. Figure 12.1 shows that inflation and population increases explained much of the historical growth in state spending.

Inflation alone explained some of the past increases in government spending; just as it drove up the costs of what citizens and families bought, it also drove up the costs of what government bought. However, inflation also drove up salaries and profits with which residents paid their taxes.

Texas's population grew more rapidly than that of most other states. Each new person had to be served, protected, and educated. Of course, the demands of a larger population for increased state services were offset by the fact that more people were also paying taxes to support them. Adjusted for population and inflation, state spending grew at an average annual rate of 0.9 percent over the last 20 years.

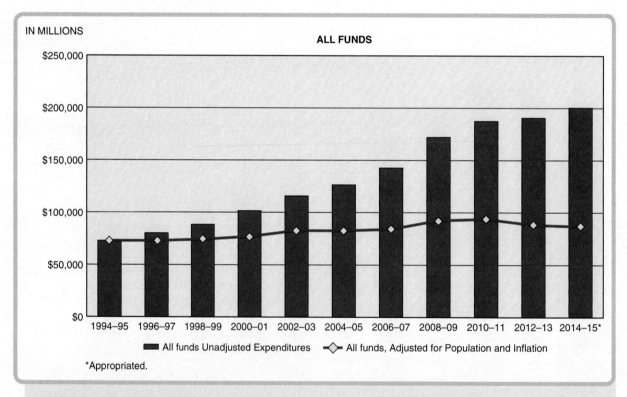

*Appropriated.

Figure 12.1

Trends in Texas State Expenditures—All Funds, by Biennial Budget Periods 1994–2015 (in millions of dollars)

The columns show that state expenditures have grown considerably, but the line shows only modest spending growth, controlling for inflation and population growth.

Based on Legislative Budget Board, Fiscal Size-Up, 20124–20135 (Austin: Legislative Budget Board, 20124), p.146. at http://www.lbb.state.tx.us/Documents/Publications/Fiscal_SizeUp/Fiscal_SizeUp.pdf.

 Why should measures of state spending be adjusted for inflation and population growth? Do unadjusted figures show anything meaningful about public policy?

REVENUES

LO 12.1 Analyze and evaluate Texas tax policies.

So, from where do the funds for this spending come? Surprisingly, much state revenue comes from sources other than state taxes. During the 2014–2015 fiscal years, 47 percent of estimated Texas revenues are from state taxes, whereas federal funding—mostly grants-in-aid—accounts for 36 percent. The remainder comes from interest on investments, revenues from public lands, and licenses, fees, and other minor non-tax sources such as the lottery. Figure 12.2 shows the major sources of Texas state revenues.

Taxation

Governments rely on a variety of tax sources, and each level of government—national, state, and local—tends to specialize in certain types of taxes.

National Taxes With the ratification of the Sixteenth Amendment to the U.S. Constitution in 1913, the income tax became available to the national government. Individual and corporate income taxes immediately became the national government's major source of funding and today constitute approximately 57 percent of federal tax revenues, with most of the remainder coming from payroll taxes for Social Security and Medicare.

State Taxes Property taxes were once the major source of state revenue, but property values collapsed during the Great Depression of the 1930s, and with them went the property tax revenues. At the same time, demands for economic assistance and other public services skyrocketed. Forced to seek other revenue sources, states came to rely on various sales taxes. Texas adopted a tax on cigarettes in 1931, on beer in 1933, and on distilled spirits in 1935. Additional selective sales taxes were adopted in the 1940s and 1950s, but it became apparent that a more general and more broadly based tax would be necessary to meet revenue needs. In 1961, Texas adopted a general sales tax on most items sold. At the same time, Texas, like most states, first drastically reduced its property taxes and then abandoned them for exclusive use by local governments. States have adopted several types of sales taxes:

1. **General sales taxes** are broadly based taxes collected on the retail price of most items.
2. **Selective sales taxes** are levied on the sale, manufacture, or use of specific items such as liquor, cigarettes, and gasoline; these are also sometimes known as excise taxes. Because these taxes are usually included in the item's purchase price, they are often **hidden taxes**.

General sales taxes
Broadly based taxes collected on the retail price of most items.

Selective sales taxes
Taxes levied on the sale, manufacture, or use of specific items such as liquor, cigarettes, and gasoline; these are also sometimes known as excise taxes.

Hidden taxes
Taxes included in an item's purchase price.

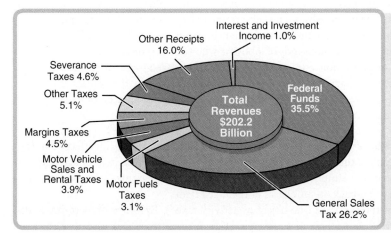

Figure 12.2

Sources of Estimated State Revenues, 2014–2015 Budget Period

This figure shows that Texas's largest single revenue source is federal funding, and the largest state tax is the general sales tax.

Based on Legislative Budget Board, Fiscal Size-Up, 20124–20135 (Austin: Legislative Budget Board, 20124), p. 299 at http://www.lbb.state.tx.us/Documents/Publications/Fiscal_SizeUp/Fiscal_SizeUp.pdf.

 Besides the general sales tax, which of Texas's other taxes should be considered sales taxes? What are the arguments for and against consumer taxes?

Gross-receipts tax

A tax on the gross revenues (sales) of certain enterprises

3. **Gross-receipts taxes** are taxes on the total gross revenue (sales) of certain enterprises. A broad-based margins tax (also known as the *franchise tax*) applies to the gross sales of most corporations and limited partnerships after taking a deduction for cost of goods or personnel. Small companies, sole proprietorships, and general partnerships are exempt.

Most state tax revenue in 2014–2015 came from various sales tax collections. The general sales tax (6.25 percent on retail sales of most items) yielded more of the state's revenues than any other tax, but Texas also has a margins tax, a motor fuels taxes, and a motor vehicle sales and rental tax. A growing source of state revenue, **severance taxes** (production taxes on raw materials such as oil and natural gas) now account for 4.6 percent. Texas also collects special taxes on a range of items and activities, such as tobacco, alcohol, registration of motor vehicles, hotel and motel occupancy, and insurance company operations.

severance taxes

Taxes on the production of raw materials such as oil and natural gas.

Local Taxes Many services financed by state governments in other states are left to local governments in Texas. State government has also imposed many mandates (required services) on local governments, especially school districts, without funding them. As a result, state taxes have remained low, but local taxes are higher than in many states.

Property taxes are the major source of revenue for virtually all local governments—cities, counties, and special districts. **Ad valorem taxes** may be applied according to the value of real property (land and buildings) and personal property (possessions such as furniture and automobiles). Most Texas local governments primarily tax real property. A central appraisal authority in each county determines property values for all taxing units in the county according to uniform state standards and procedures. The tax rate is set by local policy-making bodies—city councils, county commissioners courts, and boards of trustees for special districts.

Ad valorem taxes

Taxes assessed according to the value of real property (land and buildings) and personal property (possessions such as furniture and automobiles).

Local governments also impose other taxes. For operating expenses, most Texas cities have adopted a 1 percent city sales tax applied to items taxable under the state general sales tax. Cities in counties with populations of more than 500,000 may also collect an additional sales tax up to 1 percent for economic development projects. Mass transit authorities and other special districts also collect sales taxes, but total local sales taxes are capped at 2 percent. Other local revenue sources include miscellaneous taxes, user fees, and federal grants-in-aid.

The Politics of Taxation

Taxes cannot be evaluated objectively. As with all public policy, the state's tax policy is designed by elected politicians who make tax decisions on the basis of which groups will be most affected by different types of taxes. People tend to evaluate taxes according to their social and economic position. Although their arguments are usually about the "public interest," one must recognize that the millions of dollars in campaign funds, the millions of hours devoted to campaigning, the thousands of lobbyists who fill our state and national capitols—all the resources of persuasion our political system can muster—are called into play not simply to settle some abstract academic argument. Politics, especially the politics of taxation, affects the way people live in real and concrete ways. Any evaluation of taxes must be based on the way particular taxes affect various groups in society.

Tax rates

The amount per unit of taxable item or activity.

Tax base

The object or activity taxed.

The Tax Base: Who Should Pay? Not all taxes are equally effective in raising funds for the public till. **Tax rates** (the amount per unit on a given item or activity) may be raised or lowered, but simply raising the tax rate may not guarantee increased revenues because people may cut back on purchases of the taxed item.

Tax rates affect the **tax base** (the object or activity taxed). Excessive property taxes discourage construction and repair of buildings. High income taxes can discourage general economic activity and individual initiative, undermining the tax base. To raise necessary revenue, a tax must not discourage too much of the activity that produces the revenue.

Most governments tax a wide variety of items and activities because they have found that **broad-based taxes** (those paid by a large number of taxpayers), such as property taxes, general sales taxes, and income taxes, are most effective at raising revenue. High tax rates on a narrow base tend to destroy the base and thus make the tax ineffective as a source of revenue.

In the battle over taxation, one of the most intense issues is what should be taxed. The decision about *what* to tax is really a decision about *whom* to tax and how heavily. Those with influence on decision makers try to get special tax treatment for themselves and other taxpayers in their group. What seems to motivate almost every group is the principle that the best tax is the one somebody else pays. The three most common political rationalizations for taxing various social groups differently are (1) to regulate their behavior, (2) to tax them according to the benefits they receive, and (3) to tax them according to their ability to pay.

Regulatory Taxes Taxes do more than simply pay for the services of government; they often serve as a tool for social or economic control. Governments sometimes use **regulatory taxes** to reward approved behavior with lower taxation or punish socially undesirable action with a higher tax.

Most state regulatory taxes are designed to control isolated individual choices, especially those with moral overtones, and are sometimes called *sin taxes*. The most prominent example of such state regulatory taxation is the use tax to discourage the consumption of items such as alcohol or tobacco. Texas has an excise tax (selective sales tax) on alcoholic beverages, and its cigarette tax of $1.41 per pack is among the greatest in the nation.

Did You Know? Texas charges a tax on the admission to sexually oriented businesses that is sometimes called the *pole tax* in reference to a prominent stage prop in strip clubs.

Texans continue to drink, smoke, and frequent strip clubs, so such state use taxes do not entirely prevent sin, but they place a substantial share of the tax burden on the sinner. The regulatory intent of use taxes may be a rationalization to place the tax burden on others; the most vocal advocates of alcohol and tobacco taxes are those who abstain. Proponents argue that regulatory taxes have some effect on behavior without extensive enforcement. The small annual decline in cigarette sales in Texas may be partially attributed to cost, and young people may be deterred from smoking by the high price of cigarettes.

Benefits Received On the surface, nothing would seem fairer than taxation according to benefits received—let those who benefit from a public service pay for it. Americans have become accustomed to believing that this principle operates in the private sector of the economy and should be applied in the public sector as well.

A **benefits-received tax** is assessed according to the services received by the payers. Texas's 20-cent-per-gallon tax on gasoline is an example of a benefits received tax. Three-fourths of the income from gasoline and diesel fuel taxes is directed into the Texas highway trust fund, which also includes the state's share of license plate fees (much of which is retained by the counties). The amount of fuel used should represent the benefits from highway building and maintenance.

Although not strictly a tax, tuition paid by students in state colleges and universities is determined on the basis of the benefits-received principle. Although much of the cost of public college education in Texas is paid out of state and local tax revenues, an increasing share of the cost of higher education is paid by student tuitions on the presumption that students should pay a larger share of the cost of the service from which they so greatly benefit. Likewise, revenues from hunting and fishing permits are used for wildlife management.

Broad-based taxes
Taxes paid by a large number of taxpayers.

Regulatory taxes
Taxes that reward approved behavior with lower taxation or punish socially undesirable action with a higher tax.

Benefits-received tax
A tax assessed according to the services received by the payers.

The benefits-received principle seems reasonable, but few government services are truly special services that are provided only for special groups. Although the student is a major beneficiary of state-supported higher education, society also benefits from the skills that are added to the bank of human resources. Even the elderly widow who has never owned or driven a car benefits from highways when she buys fresh tomatoes from the supermarket or goes to the hospital in the event of illness. Most services of government, like highways, schools, or law enforcement, take on the character of a public or collective good because their beneficiaries cannot be accurately determined.

The benefits-received principle cannot be applied too extensively. Although private businesses efficiently provide services on a benefits-received basis, a major reason for government to provide a *public* service is to make that service available to all. Many could not afford to pay the full cost of vital public services. For example, few people could afford to attend Texas's public colleges and universities if they had to pay the full cost of higher education.

Ability to Pay   Most taxes are rationalized according to some measure of taxpayers' ability to pay them. The most common **ability-to-pay taxes** are apportioned according to some measure of the taxpayers' financial capacity such as property, sales, and income. Property taxes are rationalized on the premise that the more valuable people's property, the wealthier they are and hence the greater is their ability to pay taxes. Sales taxes are based on the premise that the more a person buys, the greater the individual's purchasing power. Income taxes are based on the assumption that the more a person earns, the greater is that person's ability to pay.

No base is completely adequate as a measure of a person's ability to pay. During Europe's feudal era, property reflected a person's wealth. With the coming of the commercial revolution, real wealth came to be measured in terms of money rather than land. Nevertheless, the taxes on real estate remained, while more modern forms of ownership, such as stocks, bonds, and other securities, are seldom taxed.

Taxes based on money (income or expenditure) also are an inadequate measure of true wealth. Income taxes reflect current taxable income and do not account for wealth accumulated in past years. Furthermore, exemptions allow the taxpayer to legally avoid taxes, even on current income. Taxes on consumption and spending (sales taxes) are an even less equitable measure of the ability to pay. Sales taxes measure wealth only as it is spent. Money saved or invested is not spent and, therefore, not taxed. Because it is a general rule of economic behavior that the wealthier a person is, the more the person saves or invests, sales taxes weigh disproportionately on the have-nots and have-littles, who must spend the largest portion of their income on the necessities of life.

Tax Rates: Progressive or Regressive Taxes?
Most people would like to pay as little in taxes as possible, but it turns out that they pay quite a bit. The average working American works almost one-third of the year (from the first day of January until about mid-April) to pay taxes to all levels of government—federal, state, and local.

However, these averages obscure the real effect of taxes on the individual taxpayer. The so-called loopholes in the federal income tax structure have been well publicized, but every tax—federal, state, and local—treats various taxpayers differently. What in the political world is used to justify the unequal burden of taxation?

Progressive Tax Rates   Federal income taxes illustrate **progressive tax rates** because the tax rates increase as income increases. Citizens at the very bottom of the financial totem pole have no taxable income and pay nothing, but as incomes increase, the rate increases stepwise from 10 percent to 35 percent. However, the greater rates apply only to *marginal* increments

---

Ability-to-pay taxes
Taxes apportioned according to taxpayers' financial capacity such as property, sales, and income.

Progressive tax rates
Tax rates that increase as income increases; for example, the federal income tax rates.

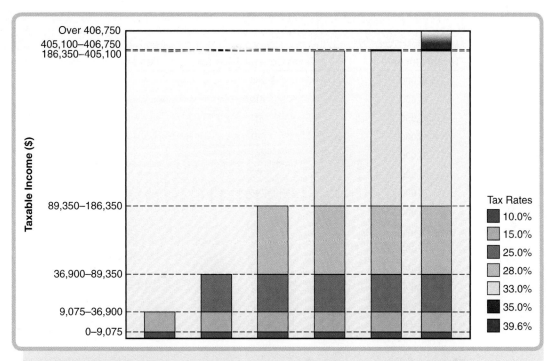

Figure 12.3
Federal Income Tax Rates for Single Individuals, 2014

Compare the five columns representing various levels of individual taxable income and the rates that apply. Notice that, regardless of total taxable income, the tax rate on the first $9,075 is 10 percent (blue), the 15 percent rate (green) applies only to the income between $9,075 and $36,900, and so on. Note that these rates apply only to taxable income after deductions, exemptions, and exclusions; more than 40 percent of Americans pay no income taxes at all. Also, capital gains tax rates are capped at a lower 20 percent rate.

Based on Internal Revenue Service, Individual

 What are the ethical arguments for and against taxing individuals with higher income at higher rates?

in income. For example, a single person with $400,000 in taxable income pays 10 percent on the first $9,075, just as lower-income taxpayers do; a rate of 15 percent applies only to taxable income above $9.075 and less than $36,900; and so forth, as shown in Figure 12.3. The highest rate, 39.5 percent, applies *only* to the amount greater than $306,750 and not to an individual's entire income.

Liberals and other supporters of progressive taxation argue that persons with larger incomes can better afford to pay higher tax rates and that lower-income persons should be left with enough of their incomes to maintain the necessities of life. Lower-income persons also spend a larger share of their incomes on consumption, which is the largest driving force in the economy.

Such arguments have not convinced Texans, who adopted a state constitutional amendment that forbids a state income tax unless voters approve. Even then, it can be used only for education and property tax relief.

Regressive Tax Rates   By contrast, Texas has **regressive tax rates**, whereby the effective tax rate declines as a person's income increases. For example, the state general sales

regressive tax rates
Tax rates that effectively decline as a person's income increases.

TABLE 12.1 Texas General Sales Tax Paid in Dollars and as a Percentage of Taxable Income, 2013*

Taxable Income	Texas General Sales Tax	Percentage of Taxable Income
$ 10,000	$ 246	2.46%
25,000	419	1.67
35,000	511	1.46
45,000	591	1.31
55,000	661	1.20
65,000	732	1.13
75,000	796	1.06
85,000	856	1.01
95,000	913	0.96
110,000	989	0.89
130,000	1,094	0.84
150,000	1,187	0.79
170,000	1,280	0.75
190,000	1,365	0.67
1,000,000	1,793	0.18

*For single individuals

Source: Internal Revenue Service, *Form 1040, 2013*, p. A-15.

Follow the income column down and notice that, as income increases, sales tax payments in dollars increase, but the rate declines as a percentage of income.

▲ **What are the arguments for this kind of regressive taxation?**

tax (6.25 percent, among the highest in the nation) is proportional to the value of sales, but because of patterns of consumption, the effective rate usually declines as a person's income increases. Table 12.1 shows that if a family's income increases, so does its general sales tax payment. That fact seems reasonable—one would expect the purchases of taxable items to increase as income increases. But note that as income increases, an ever-smaller *percentage* of that income is used for taxable purchases. Presumably, more money is saved, invested, or spent on tax-exempt items. Thus, despite exemptions for certain essential items, the effective rate of the Texas general sales tax declines as income increases; a working-class individual with an income of $25,000 pays an effective sales tax *rate* more than twice as high as an individual with an income of $190,000 annually. Similarly, taxpayers pay a smaller percentage of their incomes in property and excise taxes as their incomes increase.

There is a simple explanation for the regressive quality of most consumer taxes—the **declining marginal propensity to consume**. As income increases, a person saves and invests more, thus spending a smaller percentage of that income on consumer items. Compare two smokers. One earns $20,000 per year and the other $200,000 per year. Does the typical smoker who earns $200,000 per year smoke 10 times as much as the one who earns $20,000? Of course not! Let's assume that each smoker consumes one pack of cigarettes a day; each therefore pays $514.65 a year in Texas tobacco taxes. For the low-income individual, tobacco taxes represent almost 7 days of earnings, but the other smoker earned the money to pay tobacco taxes in only 5 hours and 21 minutes.

Declining marginal propensity to consume

The tendency, as income increases, for persons to save and invest more, thus spending a smaller percentage of their income on consumer items.

Consumption of most items follows a similar pattern. The mansion represents a smaller share of income for the millionaire than a shack does for a poor person. Proportionately, the Rolls Royce is less of a burden to its owner than the old Chevrolet to its less-affluent owner. Obviously, there are exceptions, but appetites do not increase proportionately with income. Consequently, almost any tax on consumption will not reflect ability to pay. Yet Texas's state and local taxes are based on some form of consumption—property taxes, general sales taxes, gross-receipts taxes, or selective sales taxes.

Even business taxes may be regressive for individuals because of **tax shifting**. Businesses regard their tax burden as part of their operating cost, and they pass much of that cost to customers in the form of higher prices. When property taxes increase, landlords raise rents. When business taxes are imposed, prices of consumer items usually increase as those taxes are passed on to customers as hidden taxes. Thus many business taxes become, in effect, *consumer* taxes and, like other consumer taxes, regressive relative to income.

Taking into account all state and local taxes and tax shifting, Texas has one of the most regressive tax structures among the 50 states. Table 12.2 shows the final incidence of major state and local taxes on Texas families. Those with the lowest fifth of household incomes paid over 7 percent of their income in general sales taxes—more than four times the percentage that upper-income households pay. Lower-income households paid an effective school property tax rate almost three times as high as upper-income households. And, for low-income households, the gasoline tax represents eight times the burden that it does for the upper-income households. Lower-income families even bear a disproportionate share of the state's franchise tax on business.

Some conservatives and high-income groups who support other regressive taxes argue that taxes on higher-income individuals should be kept low to allow them to save and invest to stimulate the economy—this is known as **supply-side economics**. They argue that applying higher rates to higher incomes is unfair and that sales and property taxes are easier to collect, harder to evade or

Tax shifting
Businesses passing taxes to consumers in the form of higher prices.

Supply-side economics
The theory that taxes on higher-income individuals should be kept low to allow them to save and invest to stimulate the economy.

Did You Know? Texans in the lowest-income households pay an effective sales tax more than four times higher than upper-income households.

TABLE 12.2	Texas Major State and Local Taxes as a Percentage of Household Income, Fiscal 2015*				
	Lower Income	Lower Middle	Middle Income	Upper Middle	Upper Income
General sales tax	7.3%	4.0%	3.5%	2.9%	1.7%
Franchise (margins) tax	1.0	0.6	0.5	0.4	0.3
Gasoline tax	0.8	0.5	0.4	0.3	0.1
Motor vehicle sales tax	0.8	0.5	0.5	0.5	0.3
School property tax	5.6	3.1	2.7	2.5	1.9

*Estimates based on an economic model that takes into account the effect of tax shifting. Household incomes are categorized by quintiles from the lowest one-fifth to the highest one-fifth, each representing 2,023,707 households.

Source: Texas Comptroller of Public Accounts, *Exemptions and Tax Incidence*, March 2013, pp. 45–62 at www.window.state.tx.us/taxinfo/incidence/incidence13/96-463_Tax_Incidence2013.pdf.

Look across each row in the table to see how major state and local taxes burden low- and middle-income taxpayers more.

▲ **Why do such consumer taxes burden high-income families least? How can a business tax like the margins tax weigh most heavily on low-income families?**

AP Images/Eric Gay

Texas Comptroller of Public Accounts Glenn Hegar is the state's chief tax collector and financial officer. His financial estimates are binding on the legislature during the appropriation process, meaning the state usually cannot spend more than the comptroller estimates it will receive in revenues.

CTQ How effective are Texas's balanced budget requirements? Should the national government also be required to balance its budget? Why? Why not?

General-obligation bonds
Bonds to be repaid from general revenues, such as those that voters have approved to finance prison construction.

avoid, and generally less burdensome than progressive income taxes. Some of them advocate a national sales tax, also known as the *fair tax*, to replace the progressive federal income tax.

Other Revenues

Much of the state's revenue comes from federal grants-in-aid, and a smaller amount is generated from non-tax revenues such as licenses, fees, and borrowing.

Federal Grants-in-Aid Much federal money is provided for Texas state and local government programs. For the 2014–2015 budget period, Texas will receive approximately $74 billion in federal funds, which represents 36 percent of state revenues. Much of what Texas spends for health and human services and for transportation originates as federal grants, which we discussed in depth in Chapter 2.

Borrowing and other Revenues At the beginning of each legislative session, the comptroller of public accounts reports to the legislature the total amount of revenues expected from current taxes and other sources, and the legislature can, in turn, appropriate no more than this amount unless it enacts new tax laws. The few exceptions to this general limit are (1) the legislature, by a nearly impossible four-fifths vote, may borrow in emergency situations, and (2) voters may amend the Texas Constitution to provide for the issuance of bonds for specific programs.

State bonds are classified as (1) **general-obligation bonds**, which are to be repaid from general revenues, such as those that voters have approved to finance prison construction, the veterans' real estate programs, water development, and higher education; and (2) **revenue bonds**, which are to be repaid with the revenues from the service they finance, such as higher education bonds financed by tuition revenue.

Other non-tax revenues account for a small share of the state's income from the lottery; various licenses, fines, and fees; dividends from investments; and the sale and leasing of public lands.

HOW DOES TEXAS COMPARE?
Tax and Spending Policies

- Consistent with Texas's conservative political culture, state and local taxes are lower and more regressive than in most other states. Figure 12.4 shows that Texans paid only 7.5 percent of personal income in all state and local taxes compared to the 50-state average of 9.8 percent—residents of only three states paid less than Texans.
- Most states rely heavily on sales and gross-receipts taxes, but few states are as dependent on them as Texas. Texas is one of seven states without a progressive personal income tax and one of only four states without a

corporate income tax. Because Texas relies so much on consumer taxes, it has one of the ten most regressive tax systems in the nation.
- Taxes ranked 46th among the 50 states in overall per capita spending (24 percent below the national average). Texas's per capita expenditures for education ranked 27th among the 50 states and for hospitals it ranked 25th. The state ranked toward the bottom in per capita spending for highways (45th) and for public welfare (41st).

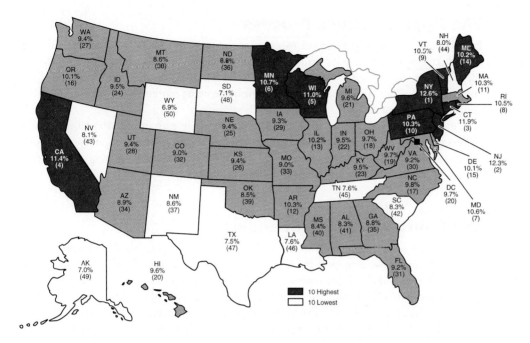

Figure 12.4
How State and Local Tax Burdens Rank among the 50 States

This figure shows the percentage of income residents paid to state and local governments in all 50 states and is based on a model that takes into account tax shifting. Note that Texans paid less than most other states.

National Tax Foundation, Annual State-Local Tax Burden Ranking Fy 2011, April 2, 2014 at http://taxfoundation.org/article/annual-state-local-tax-burden-ranking-fy-2011.

FOR DEBATE

 Do low tax rates attract business and promote economic growth in Texas? What is the effect of low state tax rates on the quality of state services?

 Should Texas follow the lead of many other states by adopting more progressive tax policies that are less dependent on consumer taxes? Why? Why not?

 Would higher rates of state spending in Texas drive up taxes and discourage economic growth in the state? Supporters argue state expenditures for education, health, and transportation are investments. If they are truly investments, how will the state realize economic gains from them?

Sources: Council of State Governments, *Book of the States*, 2013, pp. 390–391; Legislative Budget Board, *Fiscal Size-Up, 2014–2015*, p. 58, at www.lbb.state.tx.us/Documents/Publications/Fiscal_SizeUp/Fiscal_SizeUp.pdf; and Institute on Taxation and Economic Policy, *Who Pays? A Distributional Analysis of All 50 States*, January 2013, at www.itep.org/pdf/whopaysreport.pdf.

STATE SPENDING

LO 12.2   Describe the politics of state spending.

Having examined the revenue side of state policy, we now turn to the appropriations process and the politics of state spending.

Revenue bonds
Bonds to be repaid with revenues from the projects they finance, such as higher education bonds financed by tuition revenue.

The Appropriations Process

Appropriations

The process by which a legislative body legally authorizes a government to spend specific sums of money to provide various programs and services.

It is through the **appropriations** process that the legislature legally authorizes the state to spend money to provide its various programs and services. Appropriations bills follow the same steps (described in Chapter 7) as other legislation, through standing committee consideration, floor action, conference committee compromise, final voting, and then approval by the governor.

During most of the process, the legislature works closely with its presiding officers and it follows the recommendations of the Legislative Budget Board. The Texas governor has some influence on the appropriations process and may ultimately use the line-item veto to strike particular parts of the appropriations bill. Rarely does the governor veto a significant share of state spending.

The Politics of State Spending

A wide variety of political factors affect the level of state spending. Nowhere is the dynamic nature of politics so evident as in public finance; nowhere is the conflict between competing economic interests more visible than in the budgetary process. Behind the large figures that represent the state's final budget are vigorous conflict, compromise, and coalition building. Most of society's programs are evaluated not only according to their merit but also in light of the competing demands of other programs and other economic interests. Government programs and problems compete for a share of the public treasury—highways, education, urban decay, poverty, crime, the environment—in short, all the problems and challenges of a modern society.

Powerful political constituencies, interest groups, and their lobbyists join forces with state agencies to defend the programs that benefit them. This alliance between administrative agencies and interest groups brings great pressure to bear on the legislative process, especially targeting the powerful House Appropriations Committee, the Senate Finance Committee, and presiding officers. Individual legislators trade votes among themselves, a process called "logrolling," to fund local projects that benefit their constituents.

No single decision better typifies the political character of a state than the decisions made during the appropriations process. The whole pattern of spending is, in a sense, a shorthand description of which problems the state has decided to face and which challenges it has chosen to meet. The budget shows how much of which services the state will offer and to whom. Figure 12.5 shows how Texas spent its state revenues in the 2014–2015 biennium. The most costly service in Texas is education. Education accounted for 37 percent of the state budget; health and human services (including Medicaid and social services) were the second most expensive, accounting for 36.9 percent, and transportation, primarily highways, consumed 11.0 percent. These three services consume more than four-fifths of the state's budget, with a wide variety of miscellaneous services using up the remainder.

Both individuals and groups benefit from government services, and seeking these benefits, while denying them to others, is what motivates most political activity in the state. Political controversy develops because state services affect various groups differently and these groups evaluate state programs according to their competing self-interests and their conflicting views of the public interest. It is important to outline the state's most significant services and then explore some of the major political issues surrounding them.

EDUCATION

LO 12.3 Analyze Texas educational policies and the politics of education.

The educational system in Texas includes elementary and secondary schools (the public schools) and the college and university system (higher education).

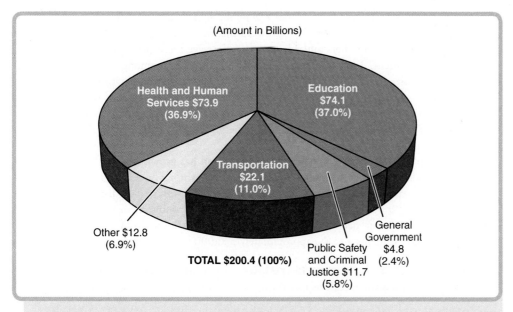

(Amount in Billions)

Health and Human Services $73.9 (36.9%)

Education $74.1 (37.0%)

Transportation $22.1 (11.0%)

Other $12.8 (6.9%)

TOTAL $200.4 (100%)

Public Safety and Criminal Justice $11.7 (5.8%)

General Government $4.8 (2.4%)

Figure 12.5

State Appropriations by Function, 2014–2015

The largest slice of Texas's budget pie goes to education, but the portion spent for health care is rapidly increasing.

Based on Legislative Budget Board, Fiscal Size-Up, 2014–2015 (Austin: Legislative Budget Board, 2014), p. 2 and p. 467 at http://www.lbb.state.tx.us/Documents/Publications/Fiscal_SizeUp/Fiscal_SizeUp.pdf.

 Explain why state spending decisions generate political controversy.

Elementary and Secondary Schools

The concept of public schools has changed dramatically over time. Although Texans now generally agree that the state should be responsible for providing elementary and secondary schools, they intensely disagree about issues related to school governance, funding, curriculum, and school accountability.

History Public schools were accepted institutions in the North by the early nineteenth century, but they did not take root in the South (including Texas) until after the Civil War. Not until the Constitution of 1876 provided that alternate sections of public land grants would be set aside to finance schools did the state begin to commit itself to locally administered, optional public schools.

Meaningful state support for public education started with a compulsory attendance law, enacted in 1915, and a constitutional amendment that provided for free textbooks in 1918. In 1949, the Gilmer-Aikin Act increased state funding and established the Texas Education Agency (TEA), which carries out the state's educational program.

Recent Trends Sweeping changes in education resulted when the 1984 legislature established statewide **school accountability** standards, using measurable standards to hold public schools responsible for their students' performance and their teachers' competence. Former President George W. Bush later took the use of high-stakes testing nationwide with his No Child Left Behind Act.

School accountability

Using measurable standards to hold public schools responsible for their students' performance and teachers' competence.

Although the standards used to measure public school performance are sometimes controversial, there has been a recent trend toward their use to bring market forces to the public school system. Some teachers and administrators receive merit pay—bonuses for improved student achievement. To introduce the element of competition among schools, the state legislature authorized the State Board of Education to establish schools with innovative special program charters that can recruit students from across existing school district boundaries. Many conservative state legislators now also favor adding even more school competition through *privatization* by providing vouchers to help students buy their education from private businesses and organizations.

Today, public elementary and secondary education has grown from a fledgling underfinanced local function into a major state–local partnership. The TEA administers approximately 26 percent of all state expenditures, helping local school districts educate the approximately 90 percent of Texas students who enroll in public elementary and secondary schools. Public policy decisions affect the knowledge, attitudes, and earning potential of these 5 million students and the approximately 320,000 teachers who teach them.

Public School Administration

As in other states, the Texas public school administration has three basic aspects:

1. Substantial local control in a joint state–local partnership
2. Emphasis on professional administration supervised by laypersons
3. Independence from the general structure of government

State Administration   The Texas Constitution, the legislature, and the State Board of Education (SBOE) have established the basic decision-making organizations and financial arrangements for public education in the state. The legislature approves the budget for the state's share of the cost of public education and sets statutory standards for public schools, but many policy decisions are left to the State Board of Education, the Texas Education Agency, and local school districts.

Members of the State Board of Education are elected to four-year overlapping terms in 15 single-member districts, and together they establish general rules and guidelines for the TEA. The SBOE approves organizational plans, recommends a budget to the governor and the Legislative Budget Board, and implements funding formulas established by the legislature. It sets curriculum standards, establishes guidelines for operating public schools, and requires management, cost accounting, and financial reports from local districts. The SBOE leaves most routine managerial decisions to the Commissioner of Education.

The commissioner is appointed by the governor with consent of the senate to serve as the state's principal executive officer for education. With a number of assistant and associate commissioners and professional staff, the commissioner carries out the regulations and policies established by the legislature and the SBOE concerning public school programs.

Independent School Districts   Texas has 1,025 independent school districts—more than any other state. These school districts are the basic structure for local control. Voters in independent school districts elect seven or nine members (depending on the district's population) for either three- or four-year terms. Board members may run at large or from single-member electoral districts. These trustees set the district's tax rate and determine school policies within the guidelines established by the TEA. They approve the budget, contract for instructional supplies and construction, and hire and fire personnel. Their most important decision is the hiring of a professional superintendent, who is responsible for the executive or administrative functions of the school district.

Elected state and local school boards usually follow the recommendations of professional administrators (the commissioner and the superintendents). Most educational decisions are made independently of general government. Nevertheless, one should not conclude that independence from general government, localization, or professionalism can keep education free of politics. On the contrary, elected boards, especially the State Board of Education, have become quite politically assertive in recent years. Whenever important policy decisions are made, political controversy and conflict arise.

Charter Schools Texas now has 552 charter school campuses and more have been authorized. **Charter schools** are publicly funded, privately managed schools that operate independently from the district system. The TEA gives them special charters with greater flexibility in the way they operate, including considerable latitude in developing their own academic goals and curricula, and in choosing their faculty and staff. Some charter schools have been able to use this flexibility to establish successful innovative programs that compare favorably to traditional public schools, while others have been closed because of poor academic performance or financial irregularities.

Charter schools

Publicly funded, privately managed schools that operate independently from the district system.

The Politics of Public Education

One of the most important decisions concerning public education is what education should be. Should it promote traditional views of society, reinforce the dominant political culture, and teach acceptable attitudes? Or, should it teach students to be independent thinkers, capable of evaluating ideas for themselves? Because the Texas state educational system determines the curriculum, selects textbooks, and hires and fires teachers, it must answer these fundamental questions.

Curriculum Most of the basic curriculum is determined by the SBOE. Some school districts supplement this basic curriculum with a variety of elective and specialized courses, but it is in the basic courses—history, civics, biology, and English—that students are most likely to be exposed to issues that may fundamentally affect their attitudes.

How should a student be exposed to the theory of evolution? Should sex education courses offer discussion of artificial birth control or present abstinence as the only reliable method of birth control? In the social sciences, should the political system be pictured in terms of its ideals or as it actually operates, with all its flaws and weaknesses? How should the roles of women and minorities be presented? How should elective Bible courses be taught and by whom? Should students who do not speak standard English be gradually taught English through bilingual education, or should they immediately be immersed in the core curriculum taught in English?

Aside from social and political content, the substance of education in Texas has other important practical consequences as well. Although a large proportion of public school students in Texas will never enroll in an institution of higher learning, much educational effort and testing have been directed toward college preparatory courses that provide graduates with few, if any, usable job skills.

Historically, vocational, agricultural, and home economics programs were viewed as burial grounds for pupils who had failed in the traditional academic programs. Today, almost one-half of high school students are enrolled in career and technology programs, and one in five are in family and consumer sciences. Although program titles have changed, much remains to be done to meet the need for highly skilled technical workers who possess other practical life skills.

The Curriculum and the Culture Wars After adopting controversial science and literature curriculum revisions in recent years, Texas's State Board of Education caused an even louder uproar in 2010 when it largely ignored the advice of professional educators and voted along party lines to establish social studies curriculum standards for the upcoming decade. Critics charged that the SBOE had hijacked the state's educational apparatus to impose a conservative, Christian fundamentalist political agenda on public school students.[1]

Critics focused on standards that require teaching the political beliefs of conservative icons like Phyllis Schlafly, Newt Gingrich, the now-disbanded Moral Majority, and the National Rifle Association. Meanwhile, students will be taught that Senator Joseph McCarthy's anticommunist crusade may have been justified. Confederate President Jefferson Davis's inaugural address will be taught alongside Abraham Lincoln's speeches, and the role of slavery as a cause of the Civil War is downplayed.

Requirements that students learn the concept of "responsibility for the common good" (which one board member described as "communistic") have been removed from the curriculum. Students will learn that the United States is a "constitutional republic" rather than a "democratic society" and that the "separation of church and state" is not in the Constitution. Students will evaluate how the United Nations undermines U.S. sovereignty and learn about the devaluation of the dollar, including the abandonment of the gold standard. The curriculum standards emphasize the biblical and Judeo-Christian influences on the Founding Fathers and the benefits of free enterprise, which is mentioned more than 80 times in the curriculum requirements.

Textbooks The SBOE selects a list of approved textbooks that the state may buy for public school courses, and like the curriculum, the textbook selection process generates intense political battles between conservative groups such as Texas Freedom Works and the Texas Public Policy Foundation (see the Texas Insiders feature) and liberal groups such as the Texas Freedom Network. The conservatives have dominated the battle, and some publishers have withdrawn their text offerings or changed the content of their texts to satisfy the SBOE.

Texas Insiders

Tapping into Texas Think Tanks and Their Influence on Public Policy: Information as Power

A successful Christian businessman, James R. Leininger founded the conservative Texas Public Policy Foundation (TPPF), modeled after the nationally famous Heritage Foundation. TPPF continues to be funded by important sympathetic powerbrokers like Charles G. Koch and has close ties to the conservative American Legislative Exchange Council. Results of recent TPPF policy studies have been critical of "Obamacare" and supportive of states' rights, school privatization, lower taxes, and the use of fossil fuels.

In contrast, a congregation of Benedictine sisters founded the Center for Public Policy Priorities (CPPP), which is now allied with the National Center on Budget and Policy Priorities, Kids Count, and other liberal groups. The organization focuses its research on poverty, health, education, and the needs of children. Although CPPP has been a vocal advocate for the needy and its studies have generated a great deal of press, CPPP has had only marginal success in advancing Texas's social service and health-care programs.

Thinking about the role of elites in Texas politics Policy makers, including legislators, elected executives, and appointed administrators, are usually generalists who depend upon specialists for specific information to make decisions about the details of public policy. They have long depended on industry lobbyists, state agency bureaucrats,

---

[1]The Texas Essential Knowledge and Skills (TEKS) curriculum standards are available on the TEA website at http://ritter.tea.state.tx.us/rules/tac/chapter113/index.html.

and their staffs to provide expert knowledge and advice in the policy-making process.

Lobbyists have long recognized that state officials' dependence upon their data is perhaps their greatest source of power—political power is the ability to persuade, and little is more persuasive than the facts. More recently, privately funded research organizations, known as "think tanks," have been established to harness the power of information by conducting broad-based policy research and presenting decision makers with integrated policy proposals reflecting the ideological leanings of their founders and funders. Although think tanks often bill themselves as nonprofit and nonpartisan, their work frequently represents viewpoint-driven research in guise of academic studies.

 How can information affect the policy-making process? Explain how information like that contained in "think tank" reports can be both accurate and biased at the same time.

Sources: Texas Public Policy Foundation at www.texaspolicy.com and www.texaspolicy.com/experts/brooke-rollins; Center for Public Policy Priorities at http://cppp.org; Nate Blakeslee, Paul Burka, and Patricia Kilday Hart, "Power Company: Who Are the Most Influential People Determining the Fate of Texas—and What Do They Want?" *Texas Monthly*, Volume 32, number 2, February 2011, p. 92; Sourcewatch at www.sourcewatch.org/index.php?title=Texas_Public_Policy_Foundation.

Legally, the SBOE can only determine the accuracy of textbooks, but it has used this power to pressure publishers to submit texts that reflect the political and religious values of its members. One publisher eliminated references to "fossil fuels formed millions of years ago" from a science text because it conflicts with some interpretations of the timeline in the Bible. Another eliminated sections that were too kind to Muslims by asserting that Osama bin Laden's actions were inconsistent with commonly accepted Islamic teachings (even though this is the official policy view of the U.S. government). An environmental science text was rejected because it favorably mentioned the Endangered Species Act and warned of the threat of global warming—one group argued that it was unpatriotic to refer to the fact that the United States represents 5 percent of the world's population but produces 25 percent of greenhouse gases. Under pressure from religious conservatives, publishers submitted health textbooks that presented an abstinence-only approach to sex education, excluding essential information about how to prevent unwanted pregnancies and sexually transmitted diseases.

Because Texas controls the second largest textbook market in the nation, the state's textbook decisions have historically determined the content of texts used in public schools in much of the nation. In the future, however, school systems in other states may have more alternatives to Texas-preferred texts. Electronic books, specialty publishing, and custom options are replacing market-dominant, fixed-content texts, and the national textbook market is becoming much more competitive.

Faculties Although the state board for educator certification establishes standards for qualification, conduct, and certification of public school teachers, actual hiring of teachers is a local matter. Most districts do not follow a publicly announced policy of hiring or dismissing teachers because of their political viewpoints, but in many districts, teachers are carefully screened for their attitudes.

Salary and working conditions are perpetual issues of dissatisfaction among teachers because they affect morale and recruitment. Increasing public demands for accountability have added reporting and other paperwork to teachers' workloads beyond the standard expectations for lesson planning, grading, and communicating with parents.

Expected income is certainly a factor when people choose their careers, and education simply does not compare favorably among the professions. Texas teachers earn even less than public school teachers in other states. The National Education Association estimates

Did You Know? The average annual earnings for Texas physicians is $190,490; lawyers, $129,510; pharmacists, $115,780; and elementary school teachers, $50,110.[3]

that Texas classroom teachers' average salary of $49,270 in 2013–2014 was 13 percent less than the national average.[2] The TEA reported that one-third of beginning teachers leave the profession by their fifth year.

Another issue for teachers has been the use of high-stakes testing such as the State of Texas Assessments of Academic Readiness (STAAR) test and the National Assessment of Education Progress ("The Nation's Report Card"). Teachers' groups have objected to the use of these test results in retention, promotion, and salary decisions on the grounds that they do not accurately measure the full range of teachers' contributions to student knowledge and that their use causes faculty to teach the test while ignoring other valuable skills and knowledge that are not included in standardized tests.

Students Public schools have changed considerably in recent years. The number of students attending Texas public schools has been increasing at a rate of approximately 2 percent per year, and that increase is expected to continue for the next decade. Texas students are also becoming more ethnically diverse and are increasingly from low-income backgrounds—50 percent of public school students are Latino and 13 percent are African American.

This changing student population seems to present a challenge to public schools because a significant achievement gap remains between the performance of Anglo students and that of African Americans and Latinos. Scores on the standard state performance tests like STAAR indicate that the achievement gap is closing, but Anglos' passing rate is still higher than African Americans or Latinos.

Public School Finance In 2014, Texas schools spent $8,998 per student—23 percent less than the national average. The actual distribution of these funds is governed according to extremely complex rules and mathematical formulas that occupy six chapters totaling more than 75,000 words in the Texas Education Code. Although public school accountants and financial officers must understand the nuances of these rules to maximize funding for

Did You Know? In 2014, Texas spent less per public school student than 45 other states.[5]

their respective districts, you need to understand only the system's most basic features to engage intelligently in the public debate that surrounds public school finance. Three elements make up public school funding—federal (11 percent), state (43 percent), and local (46 percent).[4]

Federal funding makes up a fairly small share of the cost of public education in Texas. Most federal funding pays for ongoing aid programs for child nutrition and special-needs, military, and low-income students.

State funding comes from a variety of sources. The Permanent School Fund was established in 1854 and invests receipts of rentals, sales, and mineral royalties from Texas's public lands. Only the interest and dividends from this permanent endowment may be spent.

---

[2]National Education Association, *NEA Rankings and Estimates*, March 2014, at www.nea.org/assets/docs/NEA-Rankings-and-Estimates-2013-2014.pdf.

[3]U.S. Department of Labor, Bureau of Labor Statistics, *May 2012 State Occupational Employment and Wage Estimates*, Texas table at www.bls.gov/oes/current/oes_tx.htm.

[4]Texas Taxpayers and Research Association, *An Introduction to School Finance in Texas*, January 2012, p. 4, available at www.ttara.org/files/document/file-4f1732f763446.pdf.

[5]National Education Association, *NEA Rankings and Estimates*, March 2014, at www.nea.org/assets/docs/NEA-Rankings-and-Estimates-2013-2014.pdf. www.nea.org/assets/img/content/NEA_Rankings_And_Estimates-2013_%282%29.pdf.

Earnings from the Permanent School Fund and one-fourth of the motor fuels tax make up the Available School Fund, some of which is used for instructional supplies such as textbooks, and the remainder is distributed to local school districts based on average daily student attendance. Basing distribution of state funds on attendance focuses a school district's attention on truancy.

The Foundation School Program (FSP) accounts for the largest portion of state and local funding by far. State funds from general revenues, a margins tax on business (the franchise tax), and a portion of tobacco taxes are distributed to districts according to formulas based on district and student characteristics. The FSP is structured as a state–local partnership to bring some financial equality to local districts despite vast differences in local tax resources.

Local funding comes primarily from ad valorem property taxes. The county appraisal authority determines the market value of property for all local governments within the county, and local district boards then set the property tax rate stated as an amount per $100 of property value. Local school district trustees may set the property tax rate for maintenance and operations up to $1.17 per $100 valuation.

These property taxes are used to pay about half of the FSP basic operating expenses, with the state paying for the remainder. The state supplements local funds to ensure that each district has a basic allotment per student of $4,765 and guarantees that each additional cent in local tax above the minimum must yield at least $31.95 per student.

The system of basic allotments and guaranteed yields is designed to provide some financial equity among local school districts. However, local revenues from property taxes vary so much among school districts that the state has also been forced to establish certain *recapture* requirements. Richer districts such as those with taxable property of more than $319,000 per student may be required to share their local revenue with poorer districts. They may choose one of several mechanisms to provide aid directly to poorer districts, but most send money to the state for redistribution to other districts.

Some local tax revenues are not subject to these recapture requirements. Without aiding poorer districts, wealthier districts may tax up to an additional 50¢ per $100 for construction, capital improvements, and debt service, and they may also collect a small amount (6¢ per $100) for educational enrichment.

The current finance system resulted from five decades of struggle and litigation in an effort to provide equitably funded public schools (see the end-of-chapter article for Chapter 3). But despite these efforts, some disparity still exists in revenues per student among school districts. A $1,300 per-student gap still exists in funding between Texas school districts in rich and poor areas.[6] And, as a result, legal challenges to the state's system of school finance seem destined to continue into the indefinite future.[7]

All of the legal action over equalization of school finances begs the question of whether spending more money on public schools actually enhances student achievement. Many factors in addition to public school spending seem to determine public students' success. For example, the Dallas Independent School District still spends $20,780 more on a class of 20 students than does the Huntsville Independent School District. Yet ironically, the poorer school district's students perform better on standard tests. And despite more equalized revenues, suburban school districts like Plano and Alamo Heights continue to have far more students passing standard achievement tests than urban school districts like Dallas and Houston, which include the largest share of minority students and those from economically

---

[6]John Reynolds, "The Brief: Next Chapter Begins in School Finance Challenge," *The Texas Tribune*, January 21, 2014, at www.texastribune.org/2014/01/21/brief.
[7]The Texas Association of School Boards provides a brief compendium of recent court challenges to the school finance system at www.tasb.org/legislative/resources/finance/lawsuit_news.aspx.

TABLE 12.3 Selected Texas School District Profiles

School District (1)	Enrollment (2)	Percent Minority (3)	Percent Economically Disadvantaged (4)	Percent Satisfying STAAR Standard (5)	Operational Spending per Student (6)
Houston I.S.D.	202,586	91.8%	79.9%	71%	$ 8,423
Dallas I.S.D.	158,680	92.5	89.0	69	8,725
Plano I.S.D.	54,921	58.7	27.5	90	8,038
Edgewood I.S.D.	11,931	99.5	95.7	59	9,887
Huntsville I.S.D.	6,321	58.2	64.1	70	7,686
Alamo Heights I.S.D.	4,805	45.1	22.1	87	8,607
West Orange-Cove I.S.D.	2,349	76.0	88.0	56	9,613
Wink-Loving I.S.D.	400	36.5	27.0	75	19,399

Source: Texas Education Agency, *Snapshot 2013: District Detail Search*, at http://ritter.tea.state.tx.us/perfreport/snapshot/2013/district.srch.html.

This sample of school district profiles is arranged by size of enrollment. The column on the far right shows that some financial inequity remains among school districts. Follow the Percent Satisfying STAAR Standard column (column 5) down and notice that there is little relationship with district revenues per student. Now look at ethnicity (Percent Minority, column 3) and Percent Economically Disadvantaged students (column 4) to see if these factors relate to the STAAR scores (column 5).

▲ **Which factors most affect student achievement? What public policy changes would best improve student performance?**

disadvantaged families. Table 12.3 shows that student test scores—and the factors sometimes thought to affect them—vary dramatically from district to district in Texas. Besides per-student revenues, ethnicity and family incomes are major variables that seem to determine public school outcomes.

School Privatization

Among recent proposals for school finance changes are various voucher plans to use public funds to enable students to attend private and parochial schools. Supporters, often including conservatives and particular religious groups, argue that voucher plans offer poorer parents the choice to transfer their children out of underperforming public schools, an alternative now available only to wealthier families. They believe that increasing competition between public and private schools should stimulate improvements in public education.

Opponents, including teachers' organizations and parents in prosperous suburban schools, charge that vouchers would damage public schools by draining their financial resources and some of their best students, leaving public schools to educate students with special problems and learning disabilities. Many rural legislators fear that vouchers would threaten local public schools that have traditionally been the center of small-town community life. Opponents can point to research indicating that similar students perform as well in public schools as they do in similar private schools.

Voucher opponents argue that public funds should not subsidize special private privileges; therefore, any fair voucher plan must include requirements that private schools adopt open-admissions, open-meetings, and open-records policies. Although the U.S. Supreme Court has upheld publicly funded voucher programs that subsidize students attending religious and private schools, opponents still contend that such programs invite state controls over parochial schools and compromise the separation of church and state.

Short of vouchers for students to attend private schools, several programs offer school choice and foster competitiveness within the public school system. Local

AP Images/LM Otero

Texas public opinion surveys indicate that Texans are divided about programs to divert money from public schools to private and parochial schools.

What are the arguments for and against school vouchers?

school districts have established magnet schools, and some supporters of school reform have now begun to focus their efforts on expanding the number of charter schools.

Higher Education

Like public schools, higher education is a major state service, accounting for 9 percent of state expenditure during the 2014–2015 budget period. Public institutions enroll 90 percent of all students in Texas higher education. Texas public institutions of higher education include 38 general academic institutions and universities, nine health-related institutions, and one technical college with four campuses. Fifty public community college districts operate more than 80 campuses.

Administration of Colleges and Universities The Texas Higher Education Coordinating Board (THECB) was established to coordinate the complex system of higher education. Its 18 members are appointed by the governor with the consent of the senate, and they serve for six-year terms. The Coordinating Board appoints the commissioner of higher education to supervise its staff. Together the board and staff outline the role of each public college and university and plan future needs for programs, curricula, and physical plants. Because Texas's colleges and universities were not established systematically, the Coordinating Board has difficulty imposing a rational, coherent system on their existing operations. Politically powerful boards of regents complicate the Coordinating Board's efforts as they compete to impose their views on higher education, as do other groups.

Boards of regents or trustees set basic policies for their institutions, within the limits of state law and the rules and guidelines established by the Coordinating Board. Governing boards provide for the selection of public university administrators, including system-wide administrators (chancellors), campus presidents, deans, and other officers. Certain boards govern institutions located on several campuses:

★ The University of Texas System includes The University of Texas at Austin (with the nation's largest student population on a single campus) and other campuses located at Arlington, Brownsville, Dallas, El Paso, Permian Basin, San Antonio, and Tyler as well as University of Texas–Pan American and several medical and health units.
★ The Texas A&M System has its main campus at College Station with additional campuses at Corpus Christi, Commerce, Texarkana, Galveston, Kingsville, Prairie View A&M, Tarleton State, West Texas A&M, Texas A&M International, and several smaller campuses.
★ The Texas State University System includes Sam Houston State, Texas State University, Sul Ross State, and Lamar University.
★ The University of Houston has its main campus in Houston as well as a downtown campus and campuses at Clear Lake and Victoria.
★ The Texas Tech System includes the main campus at Lubbock, several other western Texas campuses, health science centers, and Angelo State University.
★ The remaining boards each govern mainly single-campus institutions.

Authorized and financed largely by the state, community colleges are also generally supervised by the Coordinating Board. However, unlike four-year institutions, which are usually designed to attract students from larger regions of the state and nation as well as international students, voters establish community colleges in one or more school districts primarily to serve area residents. They are usually governed by independently elected boards.

The traditional role of the junior college has been to serve freshmen and sophomores by offering academic courses for credits transferable to senior colleges. Although most of their students are enrolled in these transferable academic courses, two-year colleges have responded

Community college approach

Higher education policy based on open admissions, maximizing accessibility, and incorporating technical, compensatory, and continuing education among the traditional academic course offerings.

to the demands resulting from economic diversification by adopting a **community college approach**, based on open admissions, maximizing accessibility, and incorporating technical, compensatory, and continuing education among the traditional academic course offerings. The curriculum, low cost, and geographic and financial accessibility of community colleges have resulted in increasing enrollments, especially in academic programs. Figure 12.6 shows that a majority of Texas students enroll in two-year institutions.

The Politics of Higher Education

It is difficult to measure objectively many of the benefits of higher education, such as personal satisfaction and contribution to society. Individual financial benefits, however, are very clear, contrary to critics' allegations that higher education is not worth increasing tuition costs. In 2012, high school graduates had a median annual income of $33,904 and an unemployment rate of 8.3 percent; those with an associate's degree earned $40,820 and had an unemployment rate of 6.2 percent; and those with a bachelor's degree had a median income of $55,432 and an unemployment rate of only 4.5 percent.[8] Those with college degrees earn substantially more and have a much lower risk of unemployment.

The economic benefits from investments in higher education seem quite impressive as well. According to a study funded by the Bill and Melinda Gates Foundation, every $1.00 invested in higher education yields $8.00 in enhanced productivity, greater ongoing capacity, reduced social costs, and stimulus to research and development.[9]

Despite its benefits, legislative bodies and boards of regents and trustees have often been critical in their evaluations of higher education and its results. Calls for faculty and student accountability have been frequent. Yet there are no generally agreed-upon answers to the

 What challenges do growing enrollments present to Texas institutions of higher learning? How successful are these institutions at retaining and graduating students who have enrolled in them?

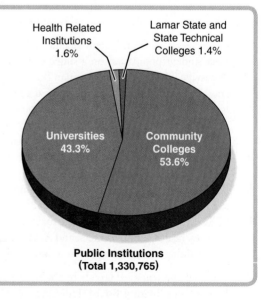

Figure 12.6
Texas Public Higher Education– Enrollments, Fall 2012

Nine out of ten students enrolled in higher education attend public institutions. Most students enroll in public community colleges.

Based on Texas Higher Education Coordinating Board and Legislative Budget Board, Fiscal Size-Up 2014–2015, p. 272 at http://www.lbb.state.tx.us/Documents/Publications/Fiscal_SizeUp/Fiscal_SizeUp.pdf.

Health Related Institutions 1.6%

Lamar State and State Technical Colleges 1.4%

Universities 43.3%

Community Colleges 53.6%

Public Institutions (Total 1,330,765)

---

[8]Bureau of Labor Statistics, *Earnings and Unemployment Rate by Educational Attainment*, December 19, 2013, at www.bls.gov/emp/ep_chart_001.htm.

[9]The Perryman Group, *A Tale of Two States—And One Million Jobs*, March 2007, published by the Texas Higher Education Coordinating Board at www.thecb.state.tx.us/reports/PDF/1345.PDF?CFID=8408072&CFTOKEN=72550084.

questions raised about higher education: What should its goals be? How should it measure success in achieving those goals? To whom should it be accountable? We examine some issues concerning higher education in the remainder of this section.

Faculty Issues Salaries are a perpetual issue when Texas institutions of higher education recruit new faculty. Average full-time public college and university faculty salaries, for example, are still significantly below the national average.

Rationalizing their attempts as an effort to promote faculty accountability, college and university administrators have long sought to dilute job-protection guarantees for professors. State law requires governing boards to adopt procedures for periodic reevaluation of all tenured faculty. Faculties generally fear that such policies can be a threat to academic freedom and a tool for political repression by administrators.

Financial Issues Financing higher education is a continuing issue. Like elementary and secondary schools, most colleges and universities in Texas must struggle with relatively small budgets. Meanwhile, increasing college enrollments and demands for specialized, high-cost programs are increasing at a time when unemployment compensation, social services, health care, and other services are also placing more demands on depressed state revenues. Reluctant to raise revenues to cover the increasing cost of higher education, Texas's legislature has shifted much of the cost burden to students.

Students advocate for more public spending on education. Policy making requires public officials to determine who gets what from government and who pays the costs.

SRQ Should students pay a greater share of public higher education costs because they are the primary beneficiaries of the program? Or should the public pay for most of the cost of higher education because society and the economy at large benefit from spending on higher education? Is your perspective on the answers to these questions affected by your current status as a student?

Student Accessibility Proposals to cope with financial pressures include closing institutions with smaller enrollments, reducing duplication, restricting student services, increasing tuition, and delaying construction plans or implementing new degree programs. Most of these policies have the effect of limiting student access to higher education, and increasing costs represent the greatest obstacle to a college education for most students.

Because the Texas legislature deregulated tuition, college and university boards have dealt with increasing costs by raising tuition, mandatory student fees, and residence costs. Between fall 2003 and 2013, average tuition and fees for full-time in-state students at Texas public universities doubled to $3,825 per semester. At community colleges, in-district tuition and fees increased to $1,184 for 15 credit hours.[10] Financial accessibility of higher education is a growing concern, especially because the size of Pell grants and other forms of financial aid are not keeping pace with increasing costs, and students are financing more of the increased cost of higher education by borrowing. Figure 12.7 shows the recent trends in costs of higher education for Texas students.

---

[10]Texas Higher Education Board, *College for All Texans*, "College Costs—2013-4—Public Universities" at www.collegeforalltexans.com/apps/collegecosts.cfm?Type=1&Level=1; Texas Higher Education Coordinating Board, *College for All Texans—2013–4—Public Community Colleges* at www.collegeforalltexans.com/apps/collegecosts.cfm?Type=1&Level=2.

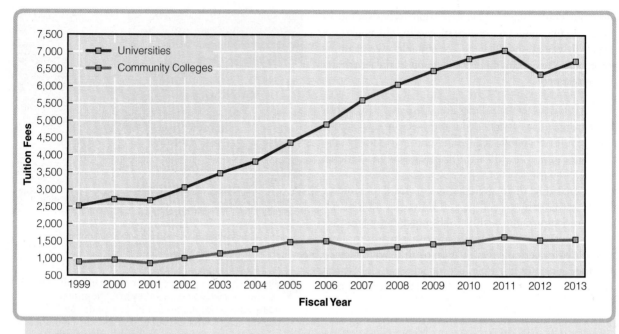

Figure 12.7
Full-Time Texas Resident Tuition and Fees per Year

This graph shows the dramatic rise of tuition resulting from state budget cuts and tuition deregulation.

Texas Higher Education Coordinating Board, *2013 Texas Public Higher Education Almanac: A Profile of State and Institutional Performance and Characteristics* (PDF), p. 7; *2012 Texas Public Higher Education Almanac: A Profile of State and Institutional Performance and Characteristics* (PDF), p. 7.

 Evaluate the alternatives to raising tuition in Texas institutions of higher learning. Should students or the public bear the greatest burden in financing higher education? Is higher education worth the cost?

Did You Know? Despite increases in tuition and fees, average tuition and fees at Texas public community colleges are the third least expensive in the nation, and at Texas public four-year institutions they rank 25th among the 50 states.

affirmative action

Positive efforts to recruit members of underserved populations such as ethnic minorities, women, and the economically disadvantaged. Sometimes these efforts are limited to recruitment drives among target groups, but such programs have sometimes included ethnicity or gender as part of the admissions criteria.

Student Diversity In addition to affordability, other cultural, structural, and historical factors have limited access to certain populations that have traditionally been underserved by Texas institutions of higher learning. Economically disadvantaged people, those who live in rural areas, women, and ethnic minorities are notably underrepresented in colleges and universities.

Institutions of higher education have struggled with minority student recruitment and have adopted positive efforts to increase diversity and offer more access to these underserved populations. Sometimes **affirmative action** efforts are limited to positive recruitment drives among target groups, but such programs have sometimes also included ethnicity or gender as part of the admissions criteria.

Supporters of affirmative action argue that ethnic, racial, and economic diversity encourages lively classroom discussions from multiple perspectives, fosters cross-racial harmony, and cultivates leaders among groups that have traditionally been at a disadvantage in society. Most opponents direct their arguments against those few affirmative action programs that use race-conscious criteria to select student applicants, contending that such policies can lead to reverse discrimination against Anglos as they are passed over in favor of less-qualified minority applicants.

Texas established a fairly non-controversial form of affirmative action after the federal Fifth Circuit Court of Appeals struck down admissions criteria at The University of Texas School of Law.[11] Texas responded with a state law that broadens student admissions without using gender or ethnicity directly in admissions criteria. General academic institutions must automatically admit students from the top 10 percent of their high school graduating class regardless of test scores.

Because various school districts serve very different populations as Table 12.3 demonstrates, granting automatic admission to the top 10 percent from each graduating class ensures that public universities draw from a diverse pool of applicants. The result has been that far more female, African-American, Latino, low-income, and rural students have been admitted to state universities under the "10 percent rule" than under traditional admission criteria.

Texas law was changed to allow The University of Texas at Austin to cap the number of entering freshmen admitted under the "10 percent" rule, and the university administrators began to admit additional students under criteria that included ethnicity among many other factors. Although U.S. Supreme Court decisions have allowed race to be considered directly in college admissions policies under very limited circumstances,[12] these race-conscious admissions policies at The University of Texas at Austin were quickly challenged in court.

In 2013, the U.S. Supreme Court ruled that the university's admission policies would be constitutional only if the university could meet strict legal standards by showing that its affirmative action policies were narrowly tailored to achieve a compelling public interest in an ethnically diverse student population.[13] The federal courts later held that the university's admissions policies met these strict constitutional standards. Thus, the courts have not altogether outlawed using race as a factor in admissions, but they have strictly limited its use.

Student Retention Of course, admission to institutions of higher learning is hardly the only measure of success. Although students may benefit from even a short experience in college and employers credit applicants for it, graduation or completion of occupational curriculum programs is society's respected measure of success.

Unfortunately, high costs, lack of course availability, inadequate academic preparation, and personal factors all contribute to the problem of student retention. Among full-time degree-seeking students at public universities, 28 percent graduate within four years, and 56 percent receive degrees within six years. In addition, community colleges have a much more difficult challenge to retain and graduate students—within three years, only 7 percent graduate and 27 percent transfer to a senior institution.[14]

Texas institutions of higher education are moving toward policies incentivizing timely degree completion, limiting the number of courses that students may drop, and counseling students to enroll primarily in courses that are part of their degree programs. Powerful political forces in the business community, including the Texas Association of Business and the Texas Public Policy Foundations (see the Texas Insiders feature), are pressing the legislature to change funding formulas to reward Texas colleges and universities that have higher graduation rates.

Quality However, even graduation rates do not fully measure the success of institutions of higher learning. Measuring the success of Texas colleges and universities must take into account their two major functions: (1) teaching—that is, imparting existing knowledge to students, and (2) research—that is, creating new knowledge.

---

[11]*Hopwood* v. *Texas*, 85 F.3d 720 (5th Cir., 1996).

[12]*Grutter* v. *Bollinger*, 539 U.S. 306 (2003); *Gratz* v. *Bollinger*, 539 U.S. 234 (2003).

[13]*Fisher* v. *University of Texas at Austin*, 570 U.S.__ (2013).

[14]Texas Higher Education Coordinating Board, *2013 Texas Public Higher Education Almanac: A Profile of State and Institutional Performance and Characteristics* (PDF), p 7.

> **Did You Know?** By one measure, Texas has only two public universities among the top 100 in the nation—The University of Texas at Austin ranks 52nd and Texas A&M University ranks 69th. Rice, a private university, ranks 18th.[15]

Various rankings show that the UT and Texas A&M flagship campuses are the two most recognized public institutions of higher learning in the state. Perhaps their rankings partly reflect the resources available to these institutions. General legislative appropriations have been relatively more generous for The University of Texas (UT) at Austin and Texas A&M University, and the state constitution earmarks revenues from more than two million acres of public land to the Permanent University Fund for the benefit of UT and Texas A&M.

A new National Research University Fund is designed to enable emerging research universities in Texas to achieve national prominence. Proposed Tier One research universities include the University of Houston, North Texas University, Texas Tech University, and University of Texas campuses at San Antonio, Dallas, Arlington, and El Paso. Of course, the results of these ambitious efforts cannot yet be fully foreseen or evaluated.

HEALTH AND HUMAN SERVICES

LO 12.4   Analyze Texas health and human service policies and the politics of income redistribution.

The second-most costly category of state spending can be broadly classified as health and human services, which encompass public assistance, Medicaid for the poor, and a variety of other programs. In the 2014–2015 budget period, these programs cost $73.9 billion (36.9 percent of the state's total budget). However, approximately 60 percent of this funding originates as grants-in-aid from the federal government.

Figure 12.8 shows that the Texas Health and Human Services Commission provides a variety of social services, including Temporary Assistance to Needy Families, Medicaid, and the Children's Health Insurance Program. The commission also coordinates planning, rule making, and budgeting among its four subsidiary social service agencies: the Department of Aging and Disability Services, the Department of Assistive and Rehabilitative Services, the Department of Family and Protective Services, and the Department of State Health Services.

Health Programs

Socialized medicine
Strictly defined, socialized medicine is a health-care system in which the government hires medical practitioners who work at government-owned facilities to directly provide health care, as in Great Britain and in U.S. veterans' and military hospitals. However, the term is often applied to health-care systems in which the government provides health-care insurance (such as Medicare or Medicaid) but benefit payments are made to private health-care providers.

Health has been a concern of public authorities since Moses imposed strict hygienic codes on the Jews during their biblical exodus from Egypt. In the United States, the federal government began to provide hospital care to the Merchant Marines in 1798. Today, health care has evolved into a growing public–private partnership and, after education, the second most expensive service that Texas provides.

Opponents of government's assuming responsibility for public health describe it as "socialized medicine." Strictly defined, **socialized medicine** is a health-care system in which the government hires medical practitioners who work at government-owned facilities to directly provide health care, as in Great Britain and in U.S. veterans' and military hospitals. However, the term is often applied to health-care systems in which the government provides health-care insurance (such as Medicare or Medicaid) but benefit payments are made to private health-care providers.

The state has three levels of involvement in health care: (1) In some instances, the state is the provider of direct health services, for example, it provides health care for certain special

---

[15]*U.S. News & World Report,* "National University Rankings," September 9, 2013, at http://colleges.usnews.rankingsandreviews.com/best-colleges/rankings/national-universities?int=a557e6. These imperfect rankings are based on reputation, exclusiveness in admissions, and financial resources.

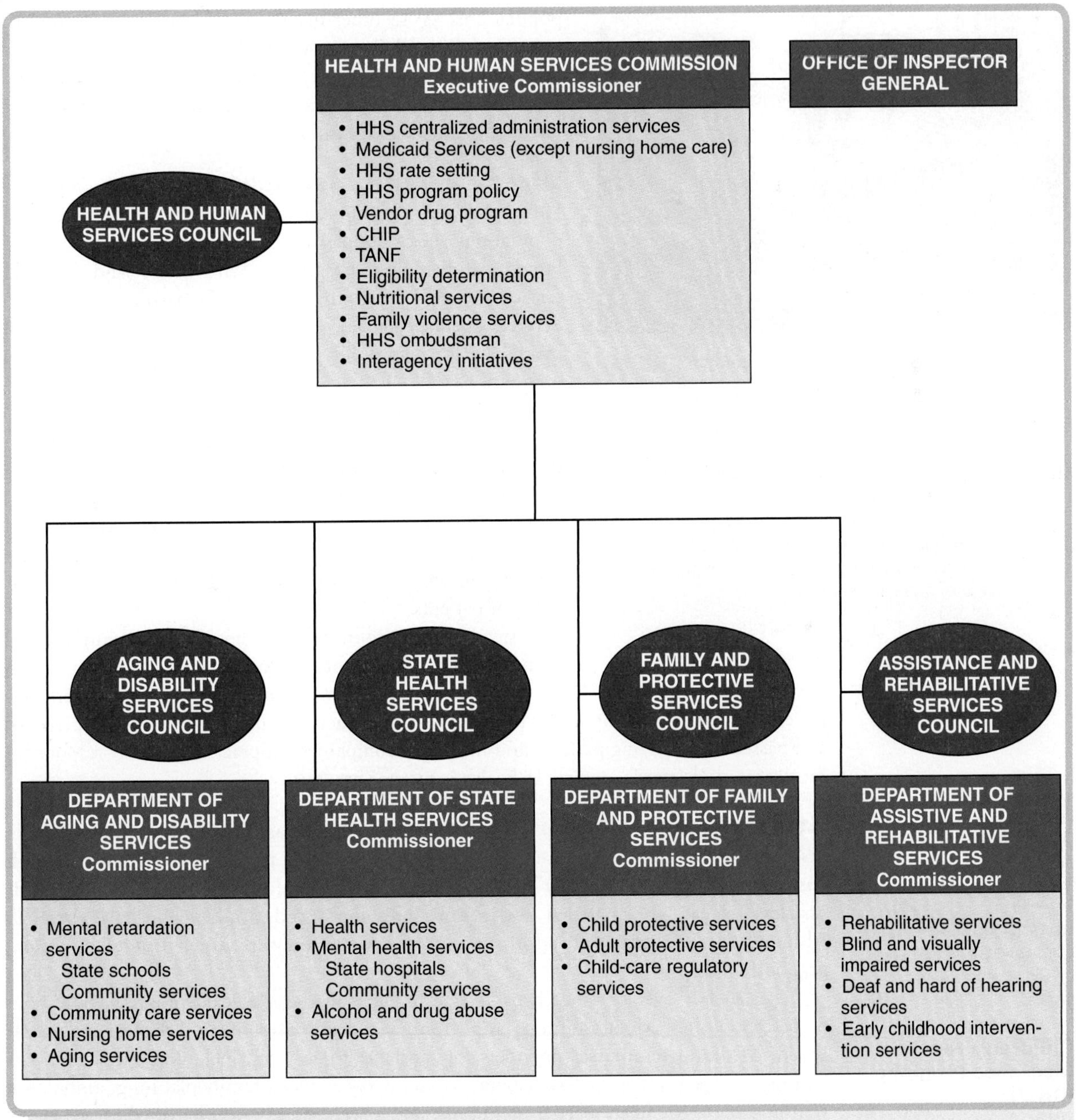

HEALTH AND HUMAN SERVICES COMMISSION
Executive Commissioner

OFFICE OF INSPECTOR GENERAL

HEALTH AND HUMAN SERVICES COUNCIL

- HHS centralized administration services
- Medicaid Services (except nursing home care)
- HHS rate setting
- HHS program policy
- Vendor drug program
- CHIP
- TANF
- Eligibility determination
- Nutritional services
- Family violence services
- HHS ombudsman
- Interagency initiatives

AGING AND DISABILITY SERVICES COUNCIL

STATE HEALTH SERVICES COUNCIL

FAMILY AND PROTECTIVE SERVICES COUNCIL

ASSISTANCE AND REHABILITATIVE SERVICES COUNCIL

DEPARTMENT OF AGING AND DISABILITY SERVICES
Commissioner

- Mental retardation services
  State schools
  Community services
- Community care services
- Nursing home services
- Aging services

DEPARTMENT OF STATE HEALTH SERVICES
Commissioner

- Health services
- Mental health services
  State hospitals
  Community services
- Alcohol and drug abuse services

DEPARTMENT OF FAMILY AND PROTECTIVE SERVICES
Commissioner

- Child protective services
- Adult protective services
- Child-care regulatory services

DEPARTMENT OF ASSISTIVE AND REHABILITATIVE SERVICES
Commissioner

- Rehabilitative services
- Blind and visually impaired services
- Deaf and hard of hearing services
- Early childhood intervention services

Figure 12.8
Texts Health and Human Service Agencies

This organizational chart illustrates the wide range of services provided by the Health and Human Services Commission.

Health and Human Services Commission.

 Identify the major social service programs shown in this chart. Why is it important for a single commission to coordinate so many of the state's human services?

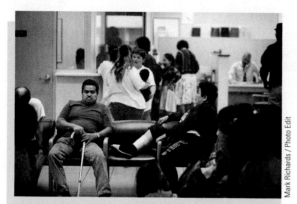

Mark Richards / Photo Edit

Many uninsured and indigent patients access medical services through hospital emergency rooms because federal and state laws require them to accept emergency patients regardless of their ability to pay.

 What are the alternatives to expensive emergency room treatment for the indigent? Should government assume responsibility to pay for indigent care, or is this a matter of personal responsibility beyond the proper purview of government?

populations. (2) In other instances, the state is the payer but not the provider. When it acts as a public health insurer as it does with Medicaid, it pays for the medical services offered by private practitioners. (3) The state also acts as a regulator and buyer of private health insurance.

Direct Health Services Texas's Department of Health Services provides personal health services for special populations. For example, the health department operates a lung and tuberculosis hospital in San Antonio and a general services hospital in Harlingen. The Department of Health Services operates general psychiatric hospitals and funds local mental health community centers and chemical dependency programs as well.

County hospitals and clinics are legally responsible for providing medical care for uninsured indigents, and therefore, they have become the health providers of last resort. County hospitals are usually operated by county hospital districts that have the authority to collect property taxes that partially fund their operations. Several government institutions also manage teaching hospitals that provide care to both indigent and non-indigent patients.

Instead of using county-funded hospitals and clinics, many uninsured and indigent patients access medical services through hospital emergency rooms because federal and state laws require them to accept emergency patients regardless of their ability to pay. The cost of such treatment is often uncompensated and passed on to paying patients and insurance companies—a practice partially responsible for the recent dramatic increase in health insurance premiums.

Medicaid

The program to provide medical care for qualified low-income individuals who have enrolled; although administered by the state, this program is largely funded by federal grants-in-aid.

Children's Health Insurance Program (CHIP)

The program that provides health insurance for qualified low-income children who have been enrolled by their parents; although administered by the state, this program is largely funded by federal grants-in-aid.

Medicare

The federal program to provide medical insurance for most persons older than 65 years of age.

State Health Insurance Programs Texas operates two major health insurance programs for those who qualify. **Medicaid** and the **Children's Health Insurance Program (CHIP)** are insurance programs designed to provide a minimal level of care for qualified low-income individuals and families who have enrolled. Although these programs are administered by the state, they are largely funded by federal grants-in-aid.

Texas spends over one-fourth of its state budget on the Medicaid program, but about 60 percent of these Medicaid funds come from the federal government in the form of grants-in-aid. Medicaid reimburses providers for most health services, including eyeglasses, prescription drugs, physicians' fees, laboratory and X-ray services, family planning, ambulance transportation, Medicare Part B premiums, and a wide variety of other medical expenses. Generally, these providers are in managed care (HMO-type) systems.

Medicaid should not be confused with **Medicare**, which is available to most persons older than 65 years of age regardless of income and is administered by the U.S. Department of Health and Human Services. In contrast, the Medicaid program is administered by the state and is available only to those who meet certain age and income requirements. These groups include (1) impoverished persons eligible for Temporary Assistance for Needy Families (TANF) or Supplemental Security Income (SSI), (2) individuals receiving medical assistance only (low-income persons residing in institutions who qualify for SSI except for certain income requirements), (3) children up to 19 years of age whose families would qualify for TANF, (4) children ages 6 through 18 who reside in families with income below the federal poverty level, (5) children younger than 6 whose family's income is at or less than 133 percent of the federal poverty level, and (6) pregnant women and infants younger than 1 year of age who reside in families with income less than 185 percent of the federal poverty level.[16] Of Texas's 3.7 million Medicaid recipients, 90 percent are elderly, disabled, or children.

CHIP helps insure children of parents with incomes less than 200 percent of the poverty level and who do not qualify for Medicaid. Even though more than 40 percent of Texas children are insured by either CHIP or Medicaid, one in six Texas children remains completely uninsured.[17]

Private Health Insurance Although approximately 25 percent of Texans have some sort of public insurance coverage such as Medicare, Medicaid, or CHIP, most others rely on private insurance companies to pay for their medical expenses. Table 12.4 shows employer-sponsored plans cover 45 percent of Texans and private individual policies cover 4 percent. The state itself pays private insurance companies for part of the premiums for its employees and teachers.

The Uninsured One in four Texans has no health insurance coverage. Among the states, Texas has the nation's highest percentage of uninsured residents. Texas employers are less likely to provide their workers health insurance, and fewer Texans have public health insurance than in other states. Texas has a large immigrant population ineligible for public insurance, and the state has resisted the health-care benefits available under the Affordable Care Act, also known as "Obamacare."

Health-Care Reform In 2010, Congress passed comprehensive health-care reforms known as the **Affordable Care Act (ACA)**, designed to expand Medicaid coverage, to limit objectionable insurance company practices, and to make subsidized health insurance available to businesses and individuals through competitive insurance exchanges. Ultimately, the ACA became the focus of an intense nationwide political controversy, especially among Texas conservatives who sought to limit its impact within the state.

The ACA provides federal funds to pay for at least 90 percent of the costs for states that expand Medicaid eligibility to all legal residents with incomes less than 133 percent of the federal poverty level. Before passage of the ACA, Medicaid was available for primarily for children, the disabled, and the elderly; adults earning more than 100 percent of poverty level were generally ineligible in many states, including Texas.

Affordable Care Act (ACA)

The comprehensive federal health-care reforms designed to expand Medicaid coverage, to limit objectionable insurance company practices, and to make subsidized health insurance available to businesses and individuals through competitive insurance exchanges.

TABLE 12.4 How People Get Health Insurance: Percent by Insurer

	Employer	Other Private	Medicaid	Medicare	Other Public	Uninsured
United States	48%	5%	16%	14%	1%	15%
Texas	45	4	15	10	1	24

Source: Kaiser Family Foundation, "Health Insurance Coverage of the Total Population," 2012, at http://kff.org/other/state-indicator/total-population.

This table shows how people get their primary insurance. It shows most Texans have employer-sponsored medical insurance, and despite public insurance, almost a quarter of Texans have no health insurance at all—a larger percentage than any other state.

▲ **Should health insurance be a public policy concern? Or is this a private matter beyond the proper purview of the government?**

---

[16]Health and Human Services Commision, "Texas Medicaid and CHIP in Perspective www.hhsc.state.tx.us/medicaid/reports/pb9/pinbook.pdf.

[17]U.S. Census Bureau, Current Population Survey, ASEC Supplement, *Health Insurance Table H105* at www.census.gov/hhes/www/cpstables/032013/health/toc.htm.

Texas Tea Party protesters attacked health-care reform as being too much big government.

CTQ **How does the ACA expand the role of the state and federal governments? Evaluate the need for the individual mandate and government regulation of the health-care industry.**

The ACA also ended some of the most unpopular insurance company practices. Health insurance companies can no longer arbitrarily drop beneficiaries when they get sick or because they have reached lifetime limits. Insurance companies must allow parents to keep their children covered under their family policies until age 26 and may not deny insurance to people with preexisting conditions.

To make it possible for insurance companies to meet these requirements, insurance companies must be able to spread risk among a larger pool of insured persons. As a result, the federal law establishes mandates requiring that individuals and larger businesses buy health insurance or pay a tax penalty. And to make insurance affordable, the federal government provides tax credits to subsidize premiums on a sliding scale based on income up to four times the federal poverty level ($95,400 in 2014). People may sign up for qualified insurance plans directly through insurance companies or through state-run or federally operated exchanges that provide side-by-side comparisons of private insurance offerings in their state.

Supporters of the ACA argued that, because Texas has the largest percentage of uninsured persons of any state in the nation, health-care reform would have had a more dramatic effect in Texas than in most states. Had Texas accepted federal funds, the ACA would have expanded Medicaid and CHIP eligibility by 2.1 million persons. Individual mandates, small business subsidies, affordability subsidies for middle-income families, and large business incentives could have further reduced the number of uninsured by as many as 4.3 million, depending on how many choose to ignore the individual mandate. The remaining uninsured would have been mostly illegal immigrants who are ineligible and eligible persons who choose to pay a tax rather than buy health insurance.

Opponents argued that Obamacare is a federal overreach and that it places government in the middle of health-care decisions that are better left to the market and to private individuals. Opponents charged that the ACA was an unconstitutional overreach by the federal government. Although states controlled by conservatives challenged the ACA in court, the U.S. Supreme Court upheld most of the health-care reform law,[18] but it did find that states could not be required to accept funds to expand Medicaid.

Despite the availability of federal funds for at least 90 percent of the cost of Medicaid expansion, Texas exercised its option to reject Medicaid expansion. Opponents argued that the federal government would renege on its commitment and that the state's share was too costly. Texas Health and Human Services Executive Commissioner Tom Suehs estimated the expansion of Medicaid and the Children's Health Insurance Program could cost the state $27 billion between 2014 and 2023.

Conservatives focused their political strategy on the most unpopular element of the ACA, the **individual mandate**, which is the requirement that individuals get health insurance or pay a tax penalty to the federal government. Adversaries also argued that the rollout of the ACA was very poorly managed and that the national exchange failed to function as planned for weeks. Critics charged that new employer health insurance requirements would discourage employers from hiring new or full-time employees.

Individual mandate

Requirement that individuals get health insurance or pay a tax penalty to the federal government.

---

[18]*National Federation of Independent Business* v. *Sebelius, Secretary of Health and Human Services,* 567 U.S.__(2012).

Resistance to health-care reform was highly successful in Texas. As we discussed in Chapter 2, Texas was among those conservative states that refused to accept Medicaid expansion. Texas also refused to establish a state-run exchange or marketplace for the uninsured to buy health insurance, and a federally operated exchange was set up instead. And, because opponents continue to bring both legal and political challenges to the ACA, the future of health-care reform remains uncertain.

Income Support Programs

Although health-care services are by far the most expensive of the social services the state provides, income-support programs are probably more controversial because they provide cash directly to beneficiaries. Although the amounts are relatively small, taxpayer funds are directly transferred or redistributed to recipients based on their need or lack of employment.

Temporary Assistance to Needy Families Among social service programs, Temporary Assistance to Needy Families (TANF) is designed for children whose parents are incapable of providing for their children's basic needs. More than two-thirds of TANF recipients are children who are deprived of support because of the absence, unemployment, or disability of one or both parents and whose family income is less than 12 percent of the poverty level. Adult care takers of such children are eligible for small grants, but unless they are disabled or needed at home to care for very young children, adult TANF and food stamp recipients are referred for employment counseling, assessment, and job placement.

Federal and state regulations now require recipients to cooperate in identifying an absent parent and, with few exceptions, limit TANF benefits to citizens; adult eligibility is usually limited to two years at a time, with a maximum five-year lifetime benefit. By making welfare less of an entitlement, these welfare reforms were intended to force able-bodied individuals out of dependency and into productive work. Some federal funds are now distributed as block grants to the states to allow them flexibility to develop support services, child care, job training and placement, and rehabilitation programs to help welfare recipients in finding work. These reforms have substantially reduced the number of TANF recipients in Texas.

In 2014–2015, the maximum monthly TANF grant for a family of three was $304, considerably below the national average. The Texas median TANF grant is about one-half the national median. Adjusting for inflation, TANF benefits have declined considerably over the years. Today, Texas spends about 0.1 percent of its budget for this income-assistance program for the poor.

Unemployment Insurance Whereas TANF is designed as an income supplement for the poor and is administered by the Health and Human Service Commission, **unemployment insurance** is designed to provide compensation as a partial income replacement for those who have lost their jobs. Unlike TANF, which is a welfare program determined by need, unemployment insurance is a social insurance program financed with taxes paid by employers, and eligibility is based on previous earnings rather than on need or family size.

The U.S. Congress established the system of unemployment insurance under the Social Security Act of 1935 as a partnership between the states and the federal government. This act imposed a tax on covered employers to establish a nationwide system of unemployment insurance administered by the federal government. However, the act provided that most of this tax would be set aside in all of the states that adopted an acceptable state program. Thus, every state was pressured to adopt state systems of unemployment insurance. Benefits are financed from state taxes on employers, but some administrative costs are paid with federal funds. These programs are actually administered by the states.

In Texas, unemployment insurance is administered by the Texas Workforce Commission (TWC), a three-member board appointed by the governor, with the consent of the senate,

Unemployment insurance

The insurance program designed to provide compensation as a partial income replacement for those who have lost their jobs; it is a social insurance program financed with taxes paid by employers.

for six-year overlapping terms. Outside the authority of the Health and Human Services Commission, the TWC administers benefit payments for a maximum of 26 weeks. In the past, Congress has usually extended the period of eligibility during periods of severe recessions when jobs were scarce, but it recently refused to approve further extended benefits.

Under Texas's rather restrictive laws, a worker must register for job placement with the TWC and is usually ineligible to receive benefits (at least for a time) if he or she voluntarily quit or was fired for cause. Because the rate at which employers are taxed is based on claims made by former employees, employers have an interest in contesting employee claims. For these reasons and others, only one-third of unemployed Texans receive benefits.

Until recently, handling unemployment insurance claims has not been a major priority among TWC's activities; its major functions have been providing a workforce for employers, gathering employment statistics, enforcing child-labor laws, and providing various special job-training and rehabilitation services. Able-bodied welfare recipients are referred to the TWC for training and child-care services. Regional workforce development boards plan one-stop career-development centers in 28 areas across the state.

The Politics of Welfare and Income Redistribution

Income redistribution

A public policy goal intended to shift income from one class of recipients to another, regardless of whether these programs are designed to benefit lower-, middle-, or upper-income groups.

Social service programs are among a wide range of public policies that employ mechanisms for **income redistribution**; these are public taxation, spending, and regulatory policies intended to shift income from one class of recipients to another. Some redistributive programs, like regressive taxation, business subsidies, and certain government contracting policies, shift income upward from lower- and middle-income families to high-income earners; others, like unemployment compensation, TANF, Medicaid, and food stamps, primarily benefit lower-income persons. Different views about these kinds of programs drive much of the ideological conflict between liberals and conservatives in Texas. (See Chapters 1 and 5 for a more complete discussion of these competing ideologies.)

Defining Welfare So many public policies redistribute income among various groups that the very concept of *welfare* has no uniformly recognized definition. The broadest view is that welfare is any unearned, government-provided benefit. Governments provide direct subsidies to businesses and corporations that far exceed TANF and food stamp costs combined. Such corporate welfare includes financial bailouts, most subsidies to agribusiness, and grants to weapons manufacturers to sell weapons to foreigners.

Did You Know? The top 20 percent of Texas households earned 51 percent of the income and the bottom 40 percent of households received only 12 percent of the income in the state. Only four states have more income inequality.[19]

Programs that primarily benefit the middle class, such as federal income tax deductions for mortgage interest, are also more costly than poverty programs. Because Social Security recipients now receive more benefits in the first three years of retirement than they paid in Social Security taxes during their working lifetimes, even Social Security is largely an unearned benefit and may be seen as a form of middle-class welfare. Because these programs are supported by powerful special interests or large numbers of middle-class voters, they are relatively secure from serious political threat.

Social insurance

Public insurance programs such as Social Security and unemployment compensation in which eligibility is based on tax premiums paid by the beneficiaries or their employers rather than need alone.

Means test

A standard of benefit eligibility based on need.

More often, the term *welfare* narrowly refers to controversial programs explicitly designed to assist the poor. Accordingly, old-age, survivors', and disability insurance (commonly referred to as Social Security), as well as unemployment insurance, are **social insurance** programs, not public welfare programs. Eligibility for social insurance programs is based not on need alone—that is, eligibility is not based on a **means test**—but on the tax paid by

---

[19]*Austin American-Statesman*, "Politifact Texas," January 18, 2010, www.politifact.com/texas/statements/2010/jan/28/ronnie-earle/ronnie-earle-says-income-gap-steadily-widening-tex.

beneficiaries and their employers. In this respect, they are like private insurance programs, differing primarily in that they are operated by the government and are compulsory for most employers and employees. Such programs are not aimed directly at the poor. In fact, many persons now receive public assistance for the very reason that they were ineligible to participate in adequate social insurance programs.

More myths and misunderstandings have developed about anti-poverty programs than probably any other public service.

Welfare Myths There is a mistaken impression that any poor person may be eligible for state public assistance benefits. Although more than 4.6 million Texans live in poverty, fewer than 3 percent of them receive monthly TANF aid, and the only able-bodied adults now receiving income assistance are parents with sole custody of young dependent children.

There is no general program of cash assistance for able-bodied adults without children, even though they may be unemployed or in need. However, the Supplemental Nutritional Assistance Program (popularly known as food stamps) and Medicaid are available to most who fall below the federally defined poverty level, and federal Supplemental Security Income (SSI) may be available to the aged, blind, and disabled.

Resentment can be expected when shoppers waiting in grocery checkout lines to part with hard-earned cash see the customer ahead paying with federally funded food stamps. Nevertheless, contrary to popular myth, few new Cadillac drivers are legally on Texas welfare rolls because benefits furnish less than the bare essentials of life.

Nor does it seem likely, as some critics suggest, that welfare mothers have more children just to increase their monthly TANF checks. The maximum monthly TANF grant is $304 per three-person family; even when these payments are combined with food stamps and Medicaid, the average TANF child still lives in a home with resources considerably below the poverty level. Children intensify the problems of the poor. Large family size probably results from carelessness, cultural attitudes, or lack of access to birth control rather than a deliberate effort to increase welfare payments.

Several reasons explain the myths that have grown around public welfare. Because welfare benefits people according to their needs rather than according to their efforts, it seems to violate the widespread American attitude that everyone ought to be paid according to the work one does. Consequently, even the lowest wage earner often feels superior to the welfare recipient. Most Texans prefer to identify themselves with the economically secure rather than with the poor. There is also prejudice against some groups that benefit from welfare because a disproportionate number of welfare recipients are mothers of children born out of wedlock or members of ethnic minority groups. Whatever the cause, these myths and prejudices remain major elements in the debate over public assistance.

Welfare Realities Public welfare faces serious substantive questions. Cheating and overpayment cost taxpayers money and dilute the limited resources that would otherwise be available for those in genuine need. It is difficult to estimate the amount of cheating. Although Texas's Lone Star Card was developed as a form of positive identification to reduce fraud, it is difficult to determine the amount of cheating that occurs during the application and qualification processes.

Probably the most serious problem for the welfare system today is that it alleviates rather than cures. Most public assistance programs are designed only to relieve the most severe pains of poverty, not to cure the disease. Welfare or other assistance programs may prevent starvation, but they offer no assurance that recipients will someday escape poverty and dependence. The vast majority of Texas welfare recipients are children, who are too young to do much about their problems. But for the able-bodied, chronic poverty is sometimes a symptom of a disease that affects both the individual and society at large.

The Causes of Poverty Those who support social service programs usually look at the problem of poverty as a systemic social problem largely beyond the control of individuals. They point to lack of job availability, poor neighborhood schools, racial or gender discrimination, and the concentration of wealth as causes of poverty. They argue that an environment of poverty disrupts family life, promotes emotional and physical disease, and denies young people role models to help them become productive members of society.

Critics of anti-poverty programs often view poverty as an individual rather than a social problem, arguing that the poor suffer their fate because of defects of character or problems of their own making. They point out that the long-term poor have typically dropped out of school at an early age and lack the education and skills necessary to earn a living wage. The poor may exhibit varying degrees of despair, alienation, hopelessness, emotional insecurity, or lethargy, and many have failed to form stable family relationships. The impoverished may lack a feeling that they can do much about their problem; others lack a sense of responsibility for their own fate.

TRANSPORTATION

LO 12.5 Describe Texas transportation policies and evaluate the prospects for reform.

Road building has been a government function since ancient times and, representing 11 percent of the state budget, it remains one of the three most expensive state functions in Texas today. A relatively small share of state funding is directed to mass public transportation, and the lion's share of Texas's transportation spending is for highway construction and maintenance.

Highway Programs

In Texas's early days, road construction was primarily the responsibility of the county. Most Texas counties still maintain a property tax dedicated to the construction and maintenance of roads, and in rural areas, road building remains a major function of county government. But their efforts are too small and too poorly financed to provide the expensive, coordinated statewide network of roads needed by highly mobile Texans in the modern world.

In 1916, the national government encouraged state governments to assume the major responsibility for highway construction and maintenance. The 1916 Federal Aid Road Act made available federal funds to cover one-half of the construction costs for state highways. To become eligible for those funds, a state was required to establish an agency to develop a coordinated plan for the state highway system and to administer construction and maintenance programs. Texas responded by establishing the Texas Highway Department, now known as the Texas Department of Transportation (TxDOT). The department is supervised by a five-member commission appointed by the governor, with the consent of the senate, for six-year overlapping terms. The commission appoints an executive director who oversees the department and supervises the work of regional district offices.

Newer federal aid programs and increased funding for existing ones have expanded TxDOT's responsibilities. The earliest highway-building program was designed to provide only major highways along primary routes. Federal funding later became available for secondary roads, and Texas established the farm-to-market program to assume state maintenance of many county roads as the rural road network was paved, extended, and improved. Finally, beginning in 1956, Congress made funds available for 90 percent of the cost of construction of express, limited-access highways to connect major cities in the United States. Today, the 80,000-mile state highway system carries about three-fourths of Texas's motor vehicle traffic (see Table 12.5).

TABLE 12.5 The Texas Highway System

Type of Roadway	Total Miles	Percentage of Traffic Accommodated
Interstate highways and frontage roads	10,517	26%
Farm-to-market roads	40,933	10
Federal and state highways	28,474	38

NOTE: Figures do not include almost a quarter-million miles of city streets and county roads, which accommodate approximately one-fourth of traffic.

Maintaining this extensive, aging highway system is becoming so costly that the state has diminishing funds available to finance new highway construction.

Source: Legislative Budget Board, *Fiscal Size-Up, 2014–2015*, p. 489.

▲ Does Texas have alternatives to the public highway system that would accommodate the transportation needs of its growing population? How would the state pay for these alternatives?

The Politics of Transportation

The Good Roads and Transportation Association, a private organization supported by highway contractors and other groups, lobbied for the establishment of the state highway fund and for increases in motor fuel taxes, and still attempts to guard the fund against those who would spend any part of it for other purposes. Despite the organization's efforts, per capita state highway funding is far below the national average.

Funding for the highway program is a joint federal–state responsibility. In 2014–2015, the federal government, mostly from the federal gasoline tax, provided 39 percent of the transportation department's revenues. This large federal contribution has allowed the national government to demand such restrictions as meeting clean air standards and setting a minimum drinking age of 18 as conditions for receiving federal aid.

State monies account for about 60 percent of TxDOT funding. The state highway fund is mostly supported by motor vehicle registration (license plate) fees and three-fourths of the 20-cent-per-gallon motor fuels tax, which has not been raised since 1991. Although the motor fuels tax is about average for the 50 states, Texas spends more money maintaining existing highways than it does constructing new ones.

As a result, the state has been forced to look to alternative revenue sources to pay for new highway construction to accommodate the population's transportation needs in one of the fastest-growing states in the nation. In a conservative state reluctant to raise motor fuels taxes or general revenue sources, such as the state general sales taxes, former Governor Perry and other state leaders turned to the idea of privatizing new highways.

Highway Privatization TxDOT planned to use comprehensive development agreements with private entities to develop a highly ambitious and controversial 50-year program to supplement existing highways. The $200 billion, 4,000-mile Trans-Texas Corridor would have included superhighways (with separate freight and commuter lanes), railways (with high-speed, commuter, and freight lines), and utility corridors (for water, electricity, natural gas, petroleum, fiber-optic telecommunications, and broadband lines). Funded by both state taxes and private investment, the project was to be operated largely by private enterprises such as toll companies.

Facing stiff opposition from property rights groups that objected to the use of eminent domain to enable such a massive state takeover of private land to benefit private investors, TxDOT abandoned the expansive Trans-Texas Corridor plan in favor of smaller, more localized projects, but it has not yet given up on the concept of highway privatization or the use of tolls to fund new highway construction. The future of highway funding remains a tough political problem for the Texas legislature and the state's political leadership.

Mass Transit   Texans, like most Americans, remain unreceptive to mass transit as an alternative to individual motor vehicles. **Mass transit** refers to transport systems that carry multiple passengers, such as train and bus systems; whether publicly or privately owned, mass transit systems are available to the general public and usually charge a fare. Only 4 to 6 percent of Texas residents regularly commute by urban mass transit. By contrast, mass transportation is a popular, viable alternative to personal vehicles in northeastern areas where one-third of all users of urban mass transit live in the New York City metropolitan area.

Automotive transportation is close to the hearts of Texans, and no other mode of transportation seems as convenient because no other is as individualized. Buses and trains cannot take individuals exactly where they want to go exactly when they want to go there. Automobiles have become a way of life, and their manufacture, maintenance, and fueling have become dominant elements of the economy.

TxDOT spends less than 1 percent of its budget on mass transit. Instead, most of the effort in mass transportation is sponsored by local metropolitan governments. As we mentioned in Chapter 11, municipalities may impose a city sales tax for economic development projects, and many of them have used such a tax to subsidize mass transit authorities (MTAs). Most MTAs have focused their resources on bus transportation, but several larger metro areas have begun to look at light rail. Houston, Dallas, Fort Worth, and Austin have serious rail projects in various stages of implementation, and plans are being developed for high-speed rail links between Houston, San Antonio, Austin, and the Dallas–Fort Worth Metroplex.

Proponents of mass transit point to the enormous social and personal costs of automotive transportation. Texas's annual highway death toll is close to 3,000, and thousands more are injured. The motor vehicle is also the single most important contributor to atmospheric pollution, a major factor in climate change, a cause of thousands of highway deaths and injuries, and a significant source of refuse that finds its way into junkyards and landfills. As the least efficient mode of transportation currently available, dependence on the individual motor vehicle is in direct conflict with the need to conserve energy and reduce our dependence on fossil fuels.

Urban mass transit was widely used before the end of World War II, and supporters of mass transit argue that adequate public funding could once again make railroads and buses rapid and comfortable alternatives to automotive transportation. When gasoline prices increase, more Texans seem to be receptive to the use of mass transit where it is available.

Critics argue that making mass transportation a viable alternative to motor vehicle transportation would require a massive investment of public funds. And, given Texans' love affair with the automobile and their strong cultural individualism, they are skeptical that the public will respond to a costly investment in mass transit with increased ridership without a catastrophic energy or environmental crisis. In Texas's conservative political environment, it is doubtful that Texas will readily increase public funding for local mass transit authorities, but high energy prices might drive the market for other fuel-efficient alternatives.

APPLYING WHAT YOU HAVE LEARNED ABOUT PUBLIC POLICY ISSUES

LO 12.6   Apply what you have learned about Texas public policy issues.

In this chapter you have learned that public policy making is the process of determining who gets what and who pays the price. You have learned that programs are evaluated not only according to their merit but also in light of the competing demands of other programs, conflicting group interests, and competing views of the public interest. Public policies like

Mass transit

Transport systems that carry multiple passengers, such as train and bus systems; whether publicly or privately owned, mass transit systems are available to the general public and usually charge a fare.

taxing, spending, and educational policy reflect the state's political character and represent a shorthand description of its priorities—which problems the state has decided to face and which challenges it has chosen to meet.

The following essay will give you the opportunity to examine the public's views on spending, education, and the size of government. After you have read the essay, you will be asked a series of questions that will require you to employ critical-thinking skills to apply what you have learned in this chapter to the new information in this essay. Your analysis will require you to explore how public opinion divides on spending and education policies, and you will be asked to reflect on the role that public opinion plays in public policy making in Texas.

Spending More to Improve Public Education? Texans Say Yes . . . and No

by James Henson

THE UNIVERSITY OF TEXAS AT AUSTIN
CO-DIRECTOR OF THE UNIVERSITY OF TEXAS/TEXAS TRIBUNE POLL

Public education is a perennial issue in both public discussion and the political process, from the heated political disputes over the public education during the writing of the present Texas Constitution right through each of the last several legislative sessions. Given this prominence, it's no surprise that elected officials and political observers pay attention to what public opinion polls tell them about voters' attitudes toward the education policy choices they face—especially how much money to spend on public education, and how to spend it.

Polling results, however, reveal that Texans' attitudes about spending on public education vary with the context in which they are asked questions about proposed spending on education. The variation in their responses illustrates the difficulties elected officials and political candidates can face in delivering policies that reflect public opinion.

Some polling results seem to confirm what many of us would expect: in general, voters think education should be an important priority of public policy, and is worthy of government funds. When asked whether they approve of various proposals to improve public education, that provided polling results suggest that that Texans approve of proposals that would inevitably involve spending more public money.

Among a battery of education proposals in the February 2014 University of Texas/Texas Tribune Poll, 74 percent of respondents said that increasing teacher pay would be an effective means of improving the education system. Figure 12.9 shows that 87 percent of Democrats and, perhaps surprisingly, 65 percent of Republicans agree that increasing teacher pay would be at least somewhat effective.

Presented with another proposal to improve public education that directly called for increasing overall public school funding, 68 percent of registered voters approved. When increasing spending was directly suggested in this item, the gap between Democrats and Republicans was larger: Figure 12.10 shows 89 percent of Democrats thought that increased funding would be effective, while only 51 percent of Republicans agreed. The decrease in Republican support notwithstanding, these proposals equaled or outpaced all the other options in terms of their perceived effectiveness, with the exception for a proposal that would create more incentives for individuals to choose teaching as a profession.

However, it is important to remember that the proposals in the education battery were just that—hypothetical proposals that did not convey any information about economic trade-offs like new sources of revenue, like tax increases or new taxes, or reduced spending in other areas.

If we look at public opinion over a longer duration, public opinion on education takes a different turn when it is put in the context of the kind of discussion of policy trade-off that

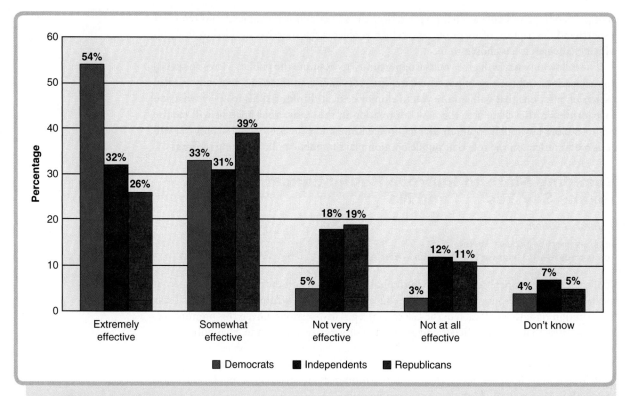

Figure 12.9

Support for Increasing Pay for Public School Teachers

This figure shows how Democrats, Republicans, and independents view the effectiveness of increasing pay for public school teachers at improving education.

Based on University of Texas/Texas Tribune Poll, February 2014 at http://laits.utexas.edu/txp_media/html/poll/features/201402_public_teacher_pay/slide2.html

are likely to take place in the legislative process. Public opinion becomes much more divided, showing much less support for spending on public education. This underlying dynamic, which isn't apparent in the seemingly broad support for spending in the February 2014 UT/TT poll (when the legislature was not in session), becomes clear in the responses to various education questions asked during previous legislative cycles.

Looking at the discussion of education over three successive legislative sessions starting in 2009, when the national recession created budget shortfalls in Texas and other states, the specific context shaping the public discussion of education funding potentially involved very significant trade-offs. The stage was set in 2009, when the legislature was saved from making major budget cuts by federal assistance from the Obama stimulus package passed by Congress. These federal funds significantly reduced pressure on the Texas legislature to confront potential spending cuts in public education. However, in the absence of another infusion of money from the federal government, the legislature was forced to make some difficult, deferred choices during the 2011 session. Amidst a very contentious debate, the legislature cut approximately $5 billion from the public education portion of the state budget.

Examining public opinion as these cuts were being debated and eventually passed during the 2011 session and during the subsequent discussion of restoring those cuts in 2013

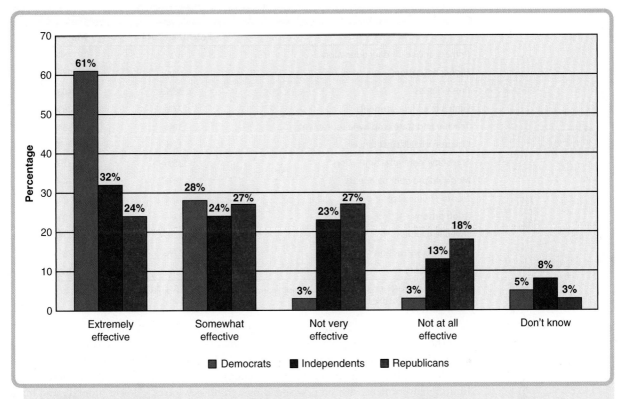

Figure 12.10

Support for Increasing Public School Funding

This figure shows how Democrats, Republicans, and independents view the effectiveness of increasing spending at improving education.

Based on University of Texas/Texas Tribune Poll, February 2014 at http://laits.utexas.edu/txp_media/html/poll/features/201402_public_school_funding/slide2.html

illustrates just how much public opinion changed when spending choices had to be made in the context of other priorities.

Public opinion during the 2011 cuts to public education confirms our initial suspicion that Texans support public education spending. Table 12.6 shows that support for those cuts wasn't overwhelming at the time. Over the course of that legislative session, only between 15 and 18 percent of Texans supported cuts to public education; roughly 40 percent supported cuts to pre-Kindergarten programs and approximately 34 percent supported cuts to teacher and state employee retirement programs. Republicans were slightly more willing than Democrats to make these cuts: 57 percent of Republicans expressed a willingness to cut pre-K funding, making that their most popular choice for cuts among the many non-public education choices.

The following legislative session in 2013 was presaged by renewed discussion of whether and how to spend on public education, especially after it came to light that the comptroller's budget projections had underestimated revenue by approximately $9 billion. This situation created circumstances in which lawmakers had the option of restoring the 2011 cuts to education—albeit in competition with other priorities.

TABLE 12.6 Support for Cuts in State Spending

	February 2011	May 2011
Primary and secondary education	n/a	15%
Higher education	n/a	27%
Pre-K classes	38%	40%
Grants to college students	27%	28%
Teacher and state employee retirement	32%	35%
Children's health insurance	13%	11%
State environmental regulation	35%	32%
Medicaid provider payments	14%	14%
Nursing home care	10%	7%
Adult prisons	33%	30%
Juvenile prisons	33%	31%
Highway construction	37%	28%
Border security	15%	16%

Source: The University of Texas/Texas Tribune poll, February 2011 and May 2011, at www.laits.utexas.edu/txp_media/html/poll/features/201105_budget/slide3.html.

At the outset of the legislative session, in February 2013, the UT/Texas Tribune Poll asked respondents what the legislature's priority should be and gave them a number of options. These choices including "restoring cuts to education and human services," in addition to "limiting government with no new spending and no new taxes," "lower property and business taxes" and "providing funds for infrastructure needs." In this instance, despite the deep cuts to education in the previous session and the seemingly available funds to restore those cuts, the plurality choice was to limit government with no new spending or taxes—the choice of 32 percent of registered voters. Figure 12.11 shows a slight majority of Democrats chose restoring the 2011 cuts, while 70 percent of Republicans chose to either limit government (51 percent) or lower property and business taxes (19 percent).

Overall, the polling reveals that Democrats and Republicans alike may see spending as an effective route to improving public education, but when it comes to making policy choices, limited government and tax cuts are a higher priority, especially among the more numerous Republican voters of Texas. So despite seeming overall support for spending on public education, political leaders can be expected to take into account partisan differences when it comes time to make hard choices among competing alternatives—and public education had lots of competition, particularly among the Republican majority in the state.

Partisan differences in opinions on funding and their impact on overall public opinion emerged in the 2014 gubernatorial campaigns. Both the Republican candidate, former Attorney General Greg Abbott, and the Democratic candidate, former Fort-Worth State Senator Wendy Davis, campaigned on positions that were designed to appeal primarily to voters in their respective parties. Greg Abbott adopted the fiscal priorities that have traditionally driven politics in the legislative process, advocating limited spending on pre-K programs and generally supporting the need for cuts in 2010. Davis sought to appeal to Democrats who seem to embrace an open-ended commitment to public education.

The discussion of education in the gubernatorial campaign illustrated the candidates' efforts to appeal to an electorate that seeks to meet competing priorities when it comes to their expectations in the area of public education policy. At the end of the day, public opinion embraces spending on education—so long as they aren't required to pay for it, either directly or even indirectly.

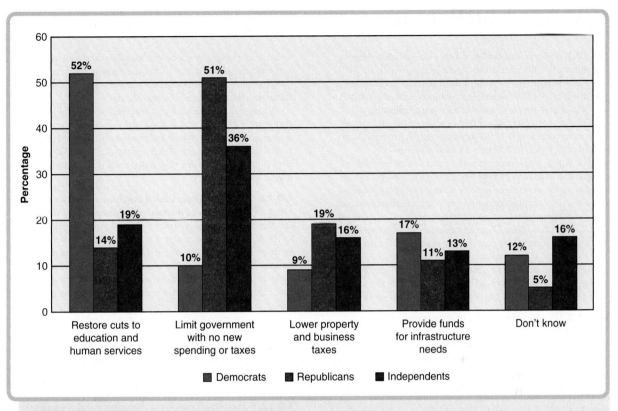

Figure 12.11

Support for 2013 Legislative Priorities

This figure shows what Democrats, Republicans, and independents thought should be the legislature's priorities in the 2013 session.

The University of Texas/Texas Tribune poll, February 2013, at http://laits.utexas.edu/txp_media/html/poll/features/201302_leg_priorites/slide2.html.

JOIN THE DEBATE

CTQ How do policy makers resolve the paradox that voters apparently favor increased spending for education and yet favor smaller government and lower taxes? Describe how voters would prioritize public spending.

SRQ Evaluate how well the Texas legislature has reflected public opinion as it has made budgetary decisions. Compare the actual budget priorities discussed in this chapter with the public's attitudes about spending discussed in this essay. Should elected decision makers always reflect the priorities of their constituents, or should they be willing to lead by making unpopular decisions?

PRQ Describe how you would change spending priorities in the state. Are there any compelling moral or ethical imperatives that the state is neglecting in its budget priorities? What are the ethical justifications for taxing one group of citizens to provide services to another?

CHAPTER SUMMARY

LO 12.1 Analyze and evaluate Texas tax policies. About half of state revenues are raised through taxes, which are low compared to other states. A substantial portion (more than one-third) comes from federal grants-in-aid, and miscellaneous sources account for the rest. State borrowing is limited.

Tax policy may be rationalized as serving some regulatory purpose or reflecting benefits received or ability to pay. Both narrow- and broad-based taxes are used in Texas.

The largest single state tax is the general sales tax, which is regressive relative to income because it falls most heavily on middle- and lower-income people. Most state taxes, including selective sales taxes and gross-receipts taxes, are also consumer taxes and regressive relative to income. Even business taxes are shifted onto consumers. Local ad valorem and sales taxes also burden those least able to pay. Among taxes that Texans pay, only the federal income tax is somewhat progressive.

Individuals and groups evaluate tax policies and virtually all public policies according to who benefits and who pays the cost. The process of allocating costs and benefits is the very essence of politics.

LO 12.2 Describe the politics of state spending. The Legislative Budget Board dominates the process of proposing Texas's state budget because the state legislature frequently follows its recommendations during the appropriations process. The governor's most effective tool in spending decisions is the item veto. The spending process is political. Perhaps no other type of decision evokes more consistent and passionate political efforts from interest groups, think tanks, and administrative agencies.

State spending as a percentage of personal income remains fairly steady and consistently lower than most other states. Education, health and human services, and transportation are the major services that state government offers, together constituting more than four-fifths of the total cost of Texas's state government. These services have a significant effect on the way Texans live and even on the way they think. It is nearly impossible to evaluate them objectively because they affect different groups so differently.

LO 12.3 Analyze Texas educational policies and the politics of education. The public educational system of Texas is generally decentralized and independent of the normal course of partisan politics. Its administrators and curricula are conservative, as is much of Texas politics. Public schools are financed by local school property taxes and a variety of state funds using funding formulas developed as a result of several lawsuits brought under state constitutional provisions guaranteeing a suitable and efficient school system. Today's efforts to privatize Texas public schools are less focused on vouchers and more directed at increasing the number of charter schools.

A majority of students in higher education attend public community colleges, which, together with state universities, face numerous challenges. Major political issues relate to funding, curriculum, student accessibility, quality, and diversity. Critics are beginning to challenge the nature and the very purpose of higher education itself.

LO 12.4 Analyze Texas health and human service policies and the politics of income redistribution. Health-care services are both publicly and privately financed in Texas, as in the rest of the nation, and they are plagued by a similar problem: the rising costs of providing better services to more people. A smaller proportion of residents are insured to cover these costs in Texas than in any other state, and national health-care reform is unlikely to dramatically expand either public or private health insurance in Texas.

Income support for the poor (such as Temporary Aid to Needy Families) is not a major state priority, and it is not designed to eliminate the root causes of poverty. However, the underlying goal of many social programs is income redistribution, and the politics of redistribution remains a central issue at all levels of government.

LO 12.5 Describe Texas transportation politics and evaluate the prospects for reform. Financed largely by motor fuels taxes and federal funds, the cost of maintaining the extensive highway system is growing faster than revenues. Construction of new highways to relieve traffic congestion has become problematic as the state seeks alternative funding sources such as the use of tolls. Facing budget limits, it is unlikely that TxDOT will substantially increase funding for local mass transportation authorities.

LO 12.6 Apply what you have learned about Texas public policy. You explored how policy makers must cope with a paradox in public opinion—Texans favor increased spending for education but also want to keep taxes low and keep government limited. You reflected on whether decision makers should follow public opinion or exercise leadership by being willing to take unpopular positions that they believe are right. Finally, you considered ethical dilemmas in the budget-making process.

KEY TERMS

ability-to-pay taxes, *p. 318*
ad valorem tax, *p. 316*
affirmative action, *p. 336*
affordable care act (ACA), *p. 341*
appropriations, *p. 324*
benefits-received tax, *p. 317*
broad-based tax, *p. 317*
charter schools, *p. 327*

children's health insurance program (CHIP), *p. 340*
community college approach, *p. 334*
declining marginal propensity to consume, *p. 320*
general-obligation bonds, *p. 322*
general sales tax, *p. 315*
gross-receipts tax, *p. 316*
hidden taxes, *p. 315*

income redistribution, *p. 344*
individual mandate, *p. 342*
mass transit, *p. 348*
means test, *p. 344*
medicaid, *p. 340*
medicare, *p. 340*
progressive tax rates, *p. 318*
regressive tax rates, *p. 319*
regulatory taxes, *p. 317*
revenue bonds, *p. 323*

school accountability, *p. 325*
selective sales (excise) tax, *p. 315*
severance tax, *p. 316*
social insurance, *p. 344*
socialized medicine, *p. 338*
supply-side economics, *p. 321*
tax base, *p. 316*
tax rate, *p. 316*
tax shifting, *p. 321*
unemployment insurance, *p. 343*

REVIEW QUESTIONS

LO 12.1 Analyze and evaluate Texas tax policies.

- Describe the major types of taxes imposed by state and local governments. How does Texas compare with other states?

- What are the advantages and disadvantages of regulatory taxes? Of taxes based on the benefits-received principle? Of taxes based on the ability-to-pay principle?

- Define *progressive* and *regressive* tax rates. What are the arguments for and against each type? Which social groups benefit from each type?

LO 12.2 Describe the politics of state spending.

- Describe the appropriations process from budgeting through legislative action and the item veto.

- Describe the state's budget priorities. How does spending on Texas public services compare with other states?

LO 12.3 Analyze Texas educational policies and the politics of education.

- Describe the functions of state and local institutions in governing Texas public elementary and secondary schools. What are the major issues that these institutions face?

- What are the major political issues that higher education faces in Texas?

LO 12.4 Analyze Texas health and human service policies and the politics of income redistribution.

- Explain why health care is the state's second-largest expenditure. How will national health-care reform affect Texas? Why are social service programs controversial?

- Describe the perspectives on income redistribution.

LO 12.5 Describe Texas transportation policies and evaluate the prospects for reform.

- Describe the state's role in providing transportation. What major political controversies have developed in planning for future transportation development?

- What is the future of highway privatization in Texas? What are the political prospects for mass transit?

GET ACTIVE

Compare conservative and liberal views on public policy. Check out the conservative view on taxes and other policies at the Texas Public Policy Foundation at **www.texaspolicy.com**. Connect with the Texas Taxpayers and Research Association representing the conservative and business perspective on taxation at **www.ttara.org**. Investigate the Private Enterprise Research Center at **http://perc.tamu.edu/perc/index.htm** and learn about its research on health care, welfare, and taxes. See the American Legislative Council (ALEC) at **www.alec.org**.

Tune into the liberal and labor position on taxes by browsing the Citizens for Tax Justice site at **www.ctj.org**. Select "State Tax Issues" and go to "Texas."

Engage Texas funding challenges with Texas's Center for Public Policy Priorities at **http://forabettertexas.org**. Probe budget and fiscal policies in the 50 states with the Center on Budget and Policy Priorities at **www.cbpp.org** and at Pew Charitable Trusts at **www.pewstates.org/projects/stateline**. Get the facts on health care in Texas and the rest of the nation at the Kaiser Family Foundation website at **www.statehealthfacts.org**.

 Develop a table describing how conservatives and liberals differ on the five major policy areas of taxing, spending, education, health care, and the environment.

Look into the causes of rising tuition costs. Investigate the conservative argument that an excess of demand for higher education in America is driving its costs higher than its actual value, and a bubble similar to the housing bubble is developing in higher education. See *The Economist* at **www.economist.com/blogs/schumpeter/2011/04/higher_education** and **http://techcrunch.com/2011/04/10/peter-thiel-were-in-a-bubble-and-its-not-the-internet-its-higher-education** and compare these arguments with those at *The Stanford Daily* at **www.stanforddaily.com/2011/05/16/editorial-higher-education-is-not-a-bubble**.

Evaluate affirmative action in higher education. Gather information about ethnic and gender group enrollment from the *2013 Texas Public Higher Education Almanac: A Profile of State and Institutional Performance and Characteristics* (PDF), p. 16, at **www.thecb .state.tx.us/index.cfm?objectId=26B0039A-944A-C4D9-C6092B25A2C7BA27&flushcache=1&show Draft=1**.

 Should Texas universities take gender and ethnicity into account in establishing their admissions criteria? Is it ethical for minorities who score lower on admissions tests to be given special consideration in an effort to educate underserved populations?

 Does affirmative action promote cross-cultural harmony and bring diverse perspectives into the classroom?

Ability-to-pay taxes Taxes apportioned according to taxpayers' financial capacity such as property, sales, and income.

Access The ability to "get in the door" to sit down and talk to public officials. Campaign contributions are often used to gain access.

Ad valorem taxes Taxes assessed according to the value of real property (land and buildings) and personal property (possessions such as furniture and automobiles).

Ad-hoc committee A committee designed to address one specific issue in the legislative process. Its function is temporary and is disbanded when the function is complete.

Administrative law The rules and regulations written by administrators to implement public policy.

Adversary system The legal system used in English-speaking countries in which two contesting parties present opposing views and evidence in a court of law.

Affirmative action Positive efforts to recruit members of underserved populations such as ethnic minorities, women, and the economically disadvantaged. Sometimes these efforts are limited to recruitment drives among target groups, but such programs have sometimes included ethnicity or gender as part of the admissions criteria.

Affordable Care Act (ACA) The comprehensive federal health-care reforms designed to expand Medicaid coverage, to limit objectionable insurance company practices, and to make subsidized health insurance available to businesses and individuals through competitive insurance exchanges.

Annexation A policy that permits a city to bring unincorporated areas into the city's jurisdiction.

Appellate jurisdiction The power vested in an appellate court to review and revise the judicial action of an inferior court.

Appropriations The process by which a legislative body legally authorizes a government to spend specific sums of money to provide various programs and services.

Arraignment A prisoner's initial appearance before a magistrate in which the charges and basic rights are explained.

Astroturf lobbying Special interest groups orchestrating demonstrations to give the impression of widespread and spontaneous public support.

At-large city elections Citywide elections in which some or all of the city council members are elected by voters of the entire municipality rather than from neighborhood districts.

At-large place system An election system in which each candidate runs citywide for a specific seat on the council and voters cast one vote for each seat or place.

Attorney general's opinion The attorney general's interpretation of the constitution, statutory laws, or administrative rules.

Australian ballot A ballot printed by the government (as opposed to the political parties) that allows people to vote in secret.

Bail The security required for release of a suspect awaiting trial.

Benefits-received tax A tax assessed according to the services received by the payers.

Beyond a reasonable doubt The standard used to determine the guilt or innocence of a person criminally charged. To prove a defendant guilty, the state must provide sufficient evidence of guilt such that jurors have no doubt that might cause a reasonable person to question whether the accused was guilty.

Bicameral Consisting of two houses or chambers; applied to a legislative body with two parts, such as a senate and a house of representatives (or state assembly).

Bicultural Encompassing two cultures.

Biennial regular session In Texas, regular legislative sessions are scheduled by the constitution. They are held once every two years, and hence referred to as biennial regular sessions.

Block grants Federal grants to state or local governments for more general purposes and with fewer restrictions than categorical grants.

Blocking bill The first bill placed on the senate calendar in each session, which is usually a bill that will never be considered by the full senate.

Brief A written argument prepared by the counsel arguing a case in court that summarizes the facts of the case, the pertinent laws, and the application of those laws to the facts supporting the counsel's position.

Broad-based taxes Taxes paid by a large number of taxpayers.

Budgetary power The power to recommend to the legislature how much it should appropriate for various executive agencies.

Burden of proof The duty and degree to which a party in a court case must prove its position.

Bureaucracy The part of the executive branch that actually administers government policies and programs.

Bureaucratic oversight The legislative function of reviewing state bureaucratic agencies and closing them down (called "sunsetting") if they are no longer viable for the state.

Cabinet system A system that allows the chief executive to appoint and remove top administrators.

Categorical grants Federal aid to state or local governments for specific purposes, granted under restrictive conditions and often requiring matching funds from the receiving government.

Chad The small pieces of paper produced when voting with punch-card ballots.

Challenge for cause A request to a judge that a certain prospective juror not be allowed to serve on the jury for a specific reason, such as bias or knowledge of the case.

Charter The organizing document for corporations or municipalities, which defines their structure, purposes, and activities.

Charter schools Publicly funded, privately managed schools that operate independently from the district system.

Checks and balances The concept that each branch of government is assigned power to limit abuses by the others.

Children's Health Insurance Program (CHIP) The program that provides health insurance for qualified low-income children who have been enrolled by their parents; although administered by the state, this program is largely funded by federal grants-in-aid.

Chubbing Includes debating earlier bills for the maximum allotted time, asking the bill's sponsor trivial questions, and proposing so many amendments and raising so many points of order that the house does not get around to the bill to which they ultimately object.

City charter The organizing document for a municipality.

Civil case Concerns private rights and remedies and usually involves private parties or organizations (*Garcia* v. *Smith*), although the government may on occasion be a party to a civil case.

Civil service (or merit) system An employment system using competitive examinations or objective measures of qualifications for hiring and promoting employees.

Clemency powers The governor's powers to pardon, parole, and grant reprieves to convicted criminals.

Clientele interest groups The groups most affected by a government agency's regulations and programs; frequently these interest groups form close alliances with the agency based on mutual support and accommodation.

Closed primary A type of primary where a voter is required to specify a party preference when registering to vote.

Coercive Federalism A relationship between the national government and states in which the former directs the states on policies they must undertake.

Colonias Severely impoverished unincorporated areas along the Texas–Mexico border with a multitude of problems, including substandard housing, unsanitary drinking water, and lack of proper sewage disposal.

Commerce clause An enumerated power in Article I, Section 8 of the U.S. Constitution that gives Congress the power to regulate commerce.

Commission form of government A municipal government in which voters elect one set of officials who act as both executives and legislators. The commissioners, sitting together, are the municipal legislature, but individually each administers a city department.

Commissioners court The policy-making body of a county, consisting of a county judge (the presiding officer of the court), who is elected in a countywide election to a four-year term, and four commissioners, who are elected from individual precincts to four-year terms.

Committee of the Whole The entire 31-member senate acting as a committee.

Common law The process under which law is developed based on judicial rulings and customs over time.

Community college approach Higher education policy based on open admissions, maximizing accessibility, and incorporating technical, compensatory, and continuing education among the traditional academic course offerings.

Community property Property acquired during marriage and owned equally by both spouses.

Compulsory process The power to seize evidence and to force witnesses to testify under oath.

Concurrent powers Those powers that are shared by the national government and the states.

Confederal system A system of government in which member state or regional governments have all authority and any central government has only the power that state governments choose to delegate to it; also known as a confederation.

Conference committee An ad-hoc committee that meets to resolve differences between senate and house versions of the same legislation; each piece of legislation has its own conference committee.

Conference committee report A compromise between the house and senate versions of a bill reached by a conference committee and then delivered to each house.

Conflict of interest A situation in which public officers stand to benefit personally from their official decisions.

Conservative A political ideology marked by the belief in a limited role for government in taxation, economic regulation, and providing social services; conservatives support traditional values and lifestyles and are cautious in response to social change.

Consolidation The merging of county government with other local governments to form a single local government.

Constables County law enforcement officials who are elected to serve as the process officers of justice of the peace courts and also have general law enforcement powers.

Constituency Those residents of the state who are directly affected by the law-making choices of a particular elected official; usually residents and businesses in the home district of the elected official.

Consulting fees Fees charged by legislators who may contract with business clients to consult on matters pending in the legislature, thereby helping clients to benefit from legislation currently active in the legislature.

Contract spoils or **contract patronage** A practice in which politicians award contracts to their political supporters and contributors in the business community.

Cooperative federalism A relationship where "the National Government and the States are mutually complementary parts of a *single* government mechanism all of whose powers are intended to realize the current purposes of government according to their applicability to the problem in hand."

Co-optation Such a close alliance that develops between state regulatory agencies and their clientele group that the regulated have, in effect, become the regulators; the interest group has captured such complete control of their regulatory agency that they are essentially self-regulated.

Council-manager form of government A form of government in which an elected city council makes laws and hires a professional administrator who is responsible for both executing council policies and managing the day-to-day operations of city government and who serves at the pleasure of the council.

Councils of government (COGs) Advisory bodies consisting of representatives of various local governments brought together for the purposes of regional planning and cooperation.

County attorney A county legal officer whose responsibilities may include giving legal advice to the commissioner's court, representing the county in litigation, and prosecuting crimes. In counties that also elect a district attorney, the county attorney specializes in civil matters.

County auditor A financial officer whose duties include reviewing county financial records and ensuring that expenditures are made in accordance with the law.

County clerk The officer who serves as the county's chief record keeper and election officer.

County governments General-purpose local governments that also serves as administrative arms of the state.

County judge An official elected countywide for a four-year term to preside over the county commissioners court.

County treasurer In many counties, the official who is responsible for receiving, depositing, and disbursing funds.

Cracking A gerrymandering technique in which concentrated political or ethnic minority groups are split into several districts so that their votes in any one district are negligible.

Creole A descendant of European–Spanish (or, in some regions, French) immigrants to the Americas.

Criminal case Involves a violation of penal law that is prosecuted by the state.

Crossover voting When members of one political party vote in the other party's primary to influence the nominee that is selected.

Cumulative voting An election system in which members of city councils are elected in at-large elections, and the number of votes a voter can cast corresponds to the number of seats on the council.

De novo Latin for "anew"; a *de novo* trial is a new trial conducted in a higher court (as opposed to an appeal). In *de novo* cases, higher courts completely retry cases. On appeal, higher courts simply review the law as decided by the lower courts.

Deadwood Inoperable constitutional provisions that either have been voided by a conflicting U.S. constitutional or statutory law or made irrelevant by changing circumstances and contexts.

Dealignment When increasing numbers of voters choose not to identify with either of the two parties and consider themselves to be independents.

Decentralization Exercise of power at the state and local levels of government in addition to the national level.

Declining marginal propensity to consume The tendency, as income increases, for persons to save and invest more, thus spending a smaller percentage of their income on consumer items.

Delegated powers Those powers that the constitution gives to the national government. These include those enumerated powers found in Article I, Section 8 of the U.S. Constitution as well as a few other powers that have evolved over time.

Demographics Population characteristics, such as age, gender, ethnicity, employment, and income, that social scientists use to describe groups in society.

Dependent agency A classification created by the U.S. Census Bureau for governmental entities that are closely tied to general-purpose governments but do not have as much independence as special-district governments.

Descriptive representation The idea that elected bodies should accurately represent not only constituents' political views but also the ethnic and social characteristics that affect their political perspectives.

Deterrence Discouraging criminal behavior by threat of punishment.

Devolution The attempt to enhance the power of state or local governments, especially by replacing relatively restrictive categorical grants-in-aid with more flexible block grants.

Direct primary A method of selecting party nominees in which party members participate directly in the selection of a candidate to represent them in the general election.

Directive authority The power to issue binding orders to state agencies.

Discharge process A rarely used legislative process for rescuing a bill pigeonholed in standing committee.

Discretion Wide latitude to make decisions within the broad requirements set out in the law.

District attorney A county officer who prosecutes criminal cases and also handles civil matters in many counties.

District clerk The record keeper for the district court in counties with a population exceeding 8,000.

Double jeopardy A second prosecution for the same offense after acquittal in the first trial.

Dual federalism The understanding that the federal government and state governments are both sovereign within their sphere of influence.

Due process Proper procedures designed to promote justice and protect the individual from the government. Due process is essential to guaranteeing fairness before the government may deprive a person of life, liberty, or property.

Early voting The practice of voting before election day at traditional voting locations, such as schools, and other locations, such as grocery and convenience stores.

Elective accountability Electing executive officers to make the bureaucracy directly accountable to the people through the democratic process.

Electronic voting Voting by using touch screens.

Elitist theory The view that the state is ruled by a small number of participants who exercise power to further their own self-interest.

Eminent domain When government takes private property for public use.

Evangelical (fundamentalist) Christians A bloc of conservative Christians who are concerned with such issues as family, religion, abortion, gay rights, and community morals, and often support the Republican Party.

Ex officio board members Persons who hold a position automatically because they also hold some other office.

Examining trial An initial court hearing to determine if there is sufficient evidence to send a case to a grand jury.

Exclusionary rule Evidence acquired in violation of the Fourth Amendment may not be admitted in court.

Expressed powers Those powers that are clearly listed in Article I, Section 8 of the U.S. Constitution.

Extraterritorial jurisdiction (ETJ) A buffer area that may extend beyond a city's limits.

FBI index crimes Crimes used as a national barometer of the crime rate—murder and non-negligent manslaughter, forcible rape, robbery, aggravated assault, burglary, grand theft, and motor vehicle theft.

Federal system A system of government in which governmental power is divided and shared between a national or central government and state or regional governments.

Felonies Serious crimes punishable by state institutions.

Filibuster A prolonged debate by a senator to delay passing of a bill.

Floor action Refers to action by the entire house or the entire senate to debate, amend, and vote on legislation.

Floor leaders The legislators who are responsible for getting legislation passed or defeated.

Formal (legal) powers Powers that are stated in the law or the constitution.

Fragmentation Division of power among separately elected executive officers. A plural executive is a fragmented executive.

General-law city An incorporated community with a population of 5,000 or fewer that is limited in the subject matter upon which it may legislate.

General-obligation bonds Bonds to be repaid from general revenues, such as those that voters have approved to finance prison construction.

General-purpose government A municipal or county government that provides a wide range of public services.

General sales taxes Broadly based taxes collected on the retail price of most items.

Gerrymander The practice of drawing district lines in such a way as to give candidates from a certain party, ethnic group, or faction an advantage.

Grand jury In Texas, consists of 12 people who sit in pretrial proceedings to determine whether sufficient evidence exists to try an individual and therefore return an indictment.

Gross-receipts tax A tax on the gross revenues (sales) of certain enterprises.

Hidden taxes Taxes included in an item's purchase price.

Hierarchies Structures in which several employees report to a higher administrator who reports to higher authorities until eventually all report to the single individual with ultimate authority over the entire organization.

Home-rule city A city with a population of more than 5,000 that can adopt its own charter and structure its local government as it sees fit as long as charter provisions and local laws (also called ordinances) do not violate national and state constitutions and laws.

Homestead An owner-occupied property protected from forced sale under most circumstances.

Hung jury A jury that is unable to agree on a verdict after a suitable period of deliberation; the result is a mistrial.

Impeachment Bringing formal charges against a public official and is the legislative equivalent of indictment for improper conduct in office.

Implementation Administrative agencies carrying out broad public policies, enforcing state laws, providing public services, and managing day-to-day government activities.

Implied powers Those delegated powers that are assumed to exist in order for the federal government to perform the functions that are expressly delegated. These powers are granted by the necessary and proper clause in Article I, Section 8 of the U.S. Constitution.

Income redistribution A public policy goal intended to shift income from one class of recipients to another, regardless of whether these programs are designed to benefit lower-, middle-, or upper-income groups.

Incumbent The currently elected official.

Independent expenditures Money individuals and organizations spend to promote a candidate without working or communicating directly with the candidate's campaign organization.

Indictment A formal written accusation issued by a grand jury against a party charged with a crime when it has determined that there is sufficient evidence to bring the accused to trial.

Indirect appointive powers Texas governor's authority to appoint supervisory boards but not the operational directors for most state agencies.

Individual mandate Requirement that individuals get health insurance or pay a tax penalty to the federal government.

Individualistic culture A political subculture that views government as a practical institution that should further private enterprise but intervene minimally in people's lives.

Informal (extralegal) powers Powers that are not stated in rules, law, or a constitution but are usually derived from formal or legal powers.

Information A written accusation made by the prosecutor against a party charged with a minor crime; it is an alternative to an indictment and does not involve a grand jury.

Inherent powers Those delegated powers that come with an office or position—generally the executive branch. Although the U.S. Constitution does not clearly specify powers granted to the executive branch, over time, inherent powers have evolved as part of the powers needed to perform the functions of the executive branch.

Initiative An election method that empowers citizens to place a proposal on the ballot for voter approval. If the measure passes, it becomes law (permitted in some Texas cities but not at the state level).

Injunctions Court orders to compel or restrain a particular action.

Interest group A voluntary organization that strives to influence public policy; sometimes known as a pressure group.

Interim committees Committees that meet between legislative sessions.

Iron triangles Long-standing alliances among interest groups, legislators, and bureaucrats held together by mutual self-interest that they act as a subsystem in the legislative and administrative decision-making process.

Issue networks Dynamic alliances among a wide range of individuals and groups activated by broad public policy questions.

Jim Crow laws State and local laws that mandated racial segregation in almost every aspect of life.

Joint committees Committees that include members of both houses.

Ku Klux Klan (KKK) A white supremacist organization.

Late-train contributions Campaign funds given to the winning candidate after the election up to 30 days before the legislature comes into session. Such contributions are designed to curry favor with winning candidates.

Legislative Audit Committee Appoints and supervises the state auditor, who, with the consent of the senate, heads the state auditor's office.

Legislative Budget Board (LBB) A ten-member board responsible for creating the state's initial budget and providing planning, analysis, and impact of the budgeting process.

Legislative Council The body that provides research support, information, and bill-drafting assistance to legislators.

Legitimacy General public acceptance of government's right to govern; also, the legality of a government's existence conferred by a constitution.

Liberal A political ideology marked by the advocacy of positive government action to improve the welfare of individuals, government regulation of the economy, support for civil rights, and tolerance for political and social change.

Line-item veto The power to strike out sections of a bill without vetoing the entire bill.

Little legislatures Another way of referring to committees—refers to the amount of work and decision-making power of the committees.

Lobbying Directly contacting public officials to advocate for a public policy.

Long ballot A ballot that results from the independent election of a large number of executive and judicial officers; giving the chief executive the power to appoint most executive and judicial officers results in a short ballot.

Malapportionment The process of the unequal distribution of population during the districting process that would make one district substantially larger or smaller than another.

Mandate A federal or state requirement that a lower level of government, like a city or county government, provide a service or meet certain standards, often as a condition for receiving financial aid.

Maquiladora Mexican factories where U.S. corporations employ inexpensive Mexican labor for assembly and piecework.

Marking up Rewriting or changing a bill by adding or deleting portions of it before it is considered for passage.

Mass transit Transport systems that carry multiple passengers, such as train and bus systems; whether publicly or privately owned, mass transit systems are available to the general public and usually charge a fare.

Mayor-council system A form of municipal government consisting of a mayor and a city council; this form includes both *strong-mayor* and *weak-mayor* variations.

Means test A standard of benefit eligibility based on need.

Medicaid The program to provide medical care for qualified low-income individuals who have enrolled; although administered by the state, this program is largely funded by federal grants-in-aid.

Medicare The federal program to provide medical insurance for most persons older than 65 years of age.

Merit plan or **Missouri plan** A method of selecting judges on the basis of the merit or quality of the candidates and not on political considerations. Under this system, the governor fills court vacancies from a list of nominees submitted by a judicial commission, and these appointees later face retention elections.

Merit system An employment and promotion system based on specific qualifications and performance rather than party affiliation or political support.

Message power The constitutional power to deliver the state of the state message and special messages to the legislature.

Mestizo A person of both Spanish and Native-American lineage.

Metroplex The greater Dallas–Fort Worth metropolitan area.

Misdemeanors Minor crimes punishable by a county jail sentence or fine.

Moralistic culture A political subculture that views government as a positive force, one that values the individual but functions to benefit the general public.

Mores Society's strong beliefs about right and wrong.

Necessary and proper clause The last clause in Article I, Section 8 of the U.S. Constitution, also known as the elastic clause, which was given a very expansive meaning early in the nation's history.

Negative campaigning A strategy used in political campaigns in which candidates attack opponents' issue positions or character.

Negligence Failure to act with the prudence or care that an ordinary person would exercise.

No bill A grand jury's refusal to return an indictment filed by the prosecutor.

North American Free Trade Agreement (NAFTA) A treaty among Canada, Mexico, and the United States that has helped remove trade barriers.

Office-block ballot A type of ballot used in a general election where the names of the parties' candidates are randomly listed under each office.

Ombudsman An official who takes, investigates, and mediates complaints about government bureaucrats or policy.

Open primary A type of party primary where a voter can choose on election day in which primary they will participate.

Open-meetings laws Laws requiring that meetings of government bodies at all levels of government be open to the general public with some exceptions.

Open-records laws Laws that require most records kept by government to be open to the public.

Original jurisdiction The power to try a case being heard for the first time.

Packing Gerrymandering technique in which members of partisan or minority groups are concentrated into one district, thereby ensuring that the group will influence only one election rather than several.

Pairing Placing two incumbent officeholders and parts of their political bases in the same elective district through redistricting.

Parole After an initial say in prison, prisoners serving the remainder of their sentences under supervision in the community.

Participation paradox The fact that citizens vote even though a single vote rarely determines an election.

Partisan elections General elections where the candidates are nominated by the political parties and their respective party labels appear on the ballot.

Partisan identification A person's attachment to one political party or the other.

Party platform The formal issue positions of a political party; specifics are often referred to as planks in the party's platform.

Party realignment The transition from one dominant party system to another.

Party–column ballot A type of ballot used in a general election where all of the candidates from each party are listed in parallel columns under the party label.

Per diem The amount paid each day that a legislator is working, both in regular and special sessions, and when committees meet during the interim between sessions.

Peremptory challenge A challenge made to a prospective juror without being required to give a reason for removal; the number of such challenges allotted to the prosecution and defense is limited.

Petit jury A jury for a civil or criminal trial.

Pigeonhole To set a bill aside and not take any action on it throughout the entire legislative session; most bills are pigeonholed.

Plaintiff The party bringing a civil suit, usually a private person or institution.

Plea bargaining Negotiations between the prosecution and the defense to obtain a lighter sentence or other benefits in exchange for a guilty plea (commonly to a less serious crime) by the accused.

Plural executive An executive branch where power is divided among several independently elected officials, thereby weakening the power of the chief executive, which in Texas is the governor.

Pluralist theory The view that, in a free society, public policy should be made by a multitude of competing interest groups, assuring that policies will not benefit a single elite at the expense of the many.

Plurality vote An election rule in which the candidate with the most votes wins regardless of whether it is a majority.

Pocket veto The power to kill legislation by simply ignoring it after the end of the legislative session; this power is not available to Texas's governor.

Point of order A formal objection that rules of procedure are not being followed on the house floor.

Political action committees (PACs) Organizations that raise and then contribute money to political candidates.

Political culture The dominant political values and beliefs in a people.

Political movement A mass alliance of like-minded groups and individuals seeking broad changes in the direction of government policies.

Popular recall A special election to remove an official before the end of his or her term, initiated by citizen petition (permitted in some Texas cities but not at the state level).

Position issues Issues on which the public is divided.

Pragmatism The philosophy that ideas should be judged on the basis of their practical results rather than on the purity of their principles.

Precedent A previously decided legal case used as a guiding principle for future cases.

Precinct convention A gathering of party members who voted in the party's primary for the purpose of electing delegates to the county or district convention.

Pre-clearance Any administrative or legislative change to the rules governing elections in covered states must be submitted for preapproval to either the U.S. Department of Justice or the U.S. District Court for the District of Columbia.

Preponderance of the evidence The party having more evidence or proof on its side should win the case, no matter how slight the differential is.

Presidential preference primary A primary election that allows voters in the party to vote directly for candidates seeking their party's presidential nomination.

Primary An election held by a political party to nominate its candidates. Texas party primary elections are usually held in the spring.

Privatization The hiring of private contractors to perform government services and functions.

Probable cause Sufficient to lead a "reasonable person" to believe that evidence is probably contained on the premises and thus a warrant for the invasion of privacy is justified.

Probate To determine that a will is the last and valid will of the deceased.

Probation A judge's sentence of an offender to serve outside a correctional institution but under specific restrictions, often under the supervision of a probation officer.

Progressive tax rates Tax rates that increase as income increases; for example, the federal income tax rates.

Proposal of constitutional amendments In Texas, the proposal of a constitutional amendment must be approved by two-thirds of the total membership of each house of the Texas legislature (at least 21 senators and 100 representatives).

Public debt Money owed by government, ordinarily through the issuance of bonds. Local governments issue bonds to finance major projects with voter approval.

Punitive damages Judgments in excess of actual damages intended to punish a defendant in a civil suit.

Pure at-large system An election system in which candidates for city council run citywide, and the top vote-getters are elected to fill the number of open seats.

Quorum To take official action, both houses require two-thirds of the total membership to be present.

Ranchero culture A quasi-feudal system whereby a property's owner, or patrón, gives workers protection and employment in return for their loyalty and service. The rancher and workers all live on the *ranchero*, or ranch.

Ratification Approval by a majority of those persons voting on the amendment in either a general or a special election.

Reapportionment Redistricting or redrawing district lines after every census to reflect the population changes.

Recall election An election, called by citizen petition, that permits voters to remove an elected official before the official's term expires.

Recidivists Repeat offenders who relapsed into crime.

Recorded vote On final bill passage, votes and the names of those who cast the vote are recorded in each house's journal.

Reduction veto The power to reduce amounts in an appropriations bill without striking them out altogether; this power is not available to Texas's governor.

Referendum An election that permits voters to determine if an ordinance or statute will go into effect (permitted in some Texas cities but not at the state level).

Regressive tax rates Tax rates that effectively decline as a person's income increases.

Regulatory taxes Taxes that reward approved behavior with lower taxation or punish socially undesirable action with a higher tax.

Rehabilitation The effort to correct criminals' antisocial attitudes and behavior.

Remedy The means used to redress an injury, relief from ongoing injury, or compensation for past damages.

Removal powers The authority to fire appointed officials.

Reserved powers Those powers that belong to the states. The legitimacy of these powers comes from the Tenth Amendment.

Resolution A formal recognition by the state legislature to provide support or non-support of events, people, or law changes; or, a way for the legislative body to make an agreement to support or not support upcoming changes in federal law or laws adopted by other states.

Retainer fees Fees charged by lawyer–legislators for services to clients, including those who have business with state agencies or may have lawsuits against state agencies.

Revenue bonds Bonds to be repaid with revenues from the projects they finance, such as higher education bonds financed by tuition revenue.

Revolving door The interchange of employees between government agencies and the private businesses with which they have dealings.

Right-to-work laws Laws that prohibit contracts between labor and management that establish a closed shop or a union shop.

Rollback election An election to limit an increase in the property tax rate to no more than 8 percent above that required for increased debt service.

Runoff primary A second primary election that pits the two top vote-getters from the first primary where the winner in that primary did not receive a majority. The runoff primary is used in states such as Texas that have a majority election rule in party primaries.

School accountability Using measurable standards to hold public schools responsible for their students' performance and teachers' competence.

Select committee A committee designed to address one specific issue in the legislative process. Its function is temporary and is disbanded when the function is complete.

Selective sales taxes Taxes levied on the sale, manufacture, or use of specific items such as liquor, cigarettes, and gasoline; these are also sometimes known as excise taxes.

Senatorial courtesy The tradition of allowing a senator to reject the governor's appointment of a political enemy from the senator's district.

Separate-but-equal doctrine Doctrine that resulted from the Supreme Court ruling in *Plessy* v. *Ferguson* that legalized segregation.

Separation of powers The principle behind the concept of a government where power is distributed among at least three different branches—legislative, executive, and judicial.

Severance taxes Taxes on the production of raw materials such as oil and natural gas.

Sheriff The chief county law enforcement officer.

Short ballot The listing of only a few independently elected offices on an election ballot.

Single-member council districts An electoral system in which each council member is elected from a particular geographical district by only the voters who live in that district.

Single-member districts Districts that are represented by one representative; districts should be equal in population.

Social insurance Public insurance programs such as Social Security and unemployment compensation in which eligibility is based on tax premiums paid by the beneficiaries or their employers rather than need alone.

Socialized medicine Strictly defined, socialized medicine is a health-care system in which the government hires medical practitioners who work at government-owned facilities to directly provide health care, as in Great Britain and in U.S. veterans' and military hospitals. However, the term is often applied to health-care systems in which the government provides health-care insurance (such as Medicare or Medicaid) but benefit payments are made to private health-care providers.

Soft money Money spent by political parties on behalf of political candidates, especially for the purposes of increasing voter registration and turnout.

Special districts Local governments that provide single or closely related services that are not provided by general-purpose county or municipal governments.

Special session A 30-day session of the legislature that can only be called by the governor, which takes place after a regular session to complete work or to consider the agenda set by the governor.

Split-ticket voting A voter selecting candidates from one party for some offices and candidates from the other party for other offices.

Spoils system A system in which elected officials hire campaign workers as public employees.

Standing committees Permanent committees that function throughout the legislative session; there are two types: substantive and procedural.

Statute-like detail Detailed state constitutional policies of narrow scope, usually handled by statutes passed by legislative bodies.

Statutory law Law passed by legislatures and written into books of code.

Straight-ticket voting Selecting all of the candidates of one particular party.

Strong-mayor form of government A form of municipal government in which the mayor, who is chosen in a city-wide election, is both the chief executive and the leader of the city council.

Subcommittees Subdivisions of standing committees that consider specialized areas and categories of proposed legislation.

Suffrage The legal right to vote.

Sunset Advisory Commission Recommends keeping, abolishing, reorganizing, or giving a new scope and authority to an agency.

Supply-side economics The theory that taxes on higher-income individuals should be kept low to allow them to save and invest to stimulate the economy.

Supremacy clause States that the U.S. Constitution, as well as laws and treaties created in accordance with the U.S. Constitution, supersede state and local laws.

Suspension of the rule The setting aside of the rule of chronologically ordering bills so that other bills can be considered.

Swing voters Voters who are not bound by party identification and who support candidates of different parties in different election years.

Tagging A senate rule that allows a senator to demand a 48-hour advance notification before a standing committee holds hearings on a particular bill.

Tax assessor-collector A county financial officer whose responsibilities include collecting various county taxes and fees and registering voters.

Tax base The object or activity taxed.

Tax rate The amount per unit of taxable item or activity.

Tax shifting Businesses passing taxes on to consumers in the form of higher prices.

Tea party A faction or groups of very conservative Republicans generally resistant to compromise of its principles.

Tenth Amendment Section of the U.S. Constitution that reserves powers to the states. It reads as follows: "The powers not delegated to the United States by the Constitution, nor prohibited by it to the States, are reserved to the States respectively, or to the people."

Term limits Legally mandated restrictions on the number of times that a politician can be reelected to an office or the number of years that a person may hold a particular office.

Texas Register The official publication of the state that gives the public notice of proposed actions and adopted policies of executive branch agencies.

The Valley An area along the Texas side of the Rio Grande known for its production of citrus fruits.

Tipping A phenomenon that occurs when a group that is becoming more numerous over time grows large enough to change the political balance in a district, state, or county.

Tort A private or civil injury or wrong other than a breach of contract.

Tort reform Efforts to limit liability in civil cases.

Traditionalistic culture A political subculture that views government as an institution to maintain the dominant social and religious values.

True bill An indictment returned by a grand jury.

Two-party system A political system characterized by two dominant parties competing for political offices. In such systems, minor or third parties have little chance of winning.

Umbrella organizations Associations formed by smaller interests joining together to promote common policy goals by making campaign contributions and hiring lobbyists to represent their interests.

Unemployment insurance The program to provide compensation as a partial income replacement for those who have lost their jobs; it is a social insurance program financed with taxes paid by employers.

Unfunded mandates Obligations that the federal government imposes on state governments with little or no funding to help support the program.

Unit road system A system that concentrates the day-to-day responsibilities for roads in the hands of a professional engineer rather than individual county commissioners.

Unitary system A system of government in which constitutional authority rests with a national or central government; any regional or local governments are subordinate to the central government.

User fees Fees paid by the individuals who receive a particular government service.

Valence issues Issues on which virtually all of the public agree, for instance, such as peace and prosperity.

Veto A power that allows the governor to stop a bill from becoming law.

Voice vote To cast an oral vote that is not recorded in the official record.

Voir dire questioning The initial questioning of jurors to determine possible biases.

Voter turnout The proportion of eligible Americans who actually vote.

Voting-age population The total number of persons in the United States who are 18 years of age or older.

Weak-mayor form of government A form of municipal government in which the mayor and council share administrative authority.

Whistle-blowers Government employees who expose bureaucratic excesses, blunders, corruption, or favoritism.

White primary The practice of excluding African Americans from primary elections in the Texas Democratic Party.

White-collar crime Crimes such as bribery, tax fraud, price-fixing, business fraud, and embezzlement usually committed by more prosperous people.

Writ of habeas corpus A court order requiring that an individual be presented in person and that legal cause be shown for confinement; it may result in release from unlawful detention.

In this index f indicates figure, n indicates note, p indicates photo, and t indicates table

A

A. T. Massey Coal Company, 249
Abbott, Greg, 42, 86p, 125p, 200p, 211, 261, 352
Ability-to-pay taxes, 318
Abortion, 15, 45–46, 159
Abraham, Henry J., 243n
Abramson, Paul R., 83n
ACA. *See* Patient Protection and Affordable Care Act
Access, 147
Ad-hoc committees, 183
Adjutant general, 213
Administration
  of colleges/universities, 333–334
  of primary elections, 91–92
  of public schools, 326–327
Administration, Texas, 210–219
  appointed executives, 213–214
  attorney general, 211–212
  boards and commissions, 214–216
  bureaucracy in, 216–219. *See also* Bureaucracy *entries*
  commissioner of agriculture, 213
  commissioner of General Land Office, 212
  comptroller of public accounts, 212
  governor, 221–222
  lieutenant governor, 210
Administrative law, 224
Ad valorem taxes, 315
Adversary system, 273
Advertising, campaign, 104–105
Advisory board, 215–216
Affirmative action, 336–337
Affordable Care Act (ACA). *See* Patient Protection and Affordable Care Act
AFL-CIO, 18–19, 120, 140t
African Americans
  diversity, equality and, 15–17
  segregation and, 16–17
  slavery and, 16

See also Discrimination; Diversity; Ethnicity; Minorities; Race
Age
  of criminals, 264–265
  of Texas executive branch, 201
  voting and, 80, 83
Agency-clientele alliance, 220–221
Agriculture
  in Far West Texas, 10
  lobbyists and, 150
  in South Texas, 10
  in West Texas, 12
Aldrich, John H., 83n
Alinsky, Saul, 159
Allsup, V. Carl, 18n, 19n
Ambulatory surgical centers (ASC), 45
Amending/revising, Texas Constitution, 70–72
Amendment procedures, 70
American Civil Liberties Union of Texas, 140t
American federalism, 49–50
American Federation of Labor-Congress of Industrial Organizations (AFL-CIO), 18–19, 120, 140t
American Federation of State and County Municipal Employees, 140t
American GI Forum, Corpus Christi, 18, 23, 120
American Legion, 140t
American Legislative Exchange Council (ALEC), 153, 328
American National Election Studies, 80n
American Recovery and Reinvestment Act, 151
Americans for Prosperity, 159
Americans for Tax Reform, 159
Americans with Disabilities Act, 296
Amicus brief, 42
Annexation, 297–298
Annual registration, for voting, 87
Appeals courts, 240–242
Appeals process, 274
Appellate jurisdiction, 234–235
Appointed boards, 215
Appointed executives, 213–214

adjutant general, 213
health and human services commissioner, 213–214
insurance commissioner, 214
secretary of state, 213
Appointees, evaluating, 202
Appointive powers, of governor, bureaucracy and, 204
Appointment process, lobbyist and, 144
Appropriation process, 324
Appropriations Committee, 184
AQUAPAC (Water Quality Association), 104
Argersinger v. Hamlin, 270n
Arizona v. Fulminante, 269n
Arlington National Cemetery, 18
Armey, Dick, 159
Arraignment, 269
Arrests, due process and, 268
Article I, Section 8, U.S. Constitution, 31, 32, 33t, 42
Articles of Confederation, 29, 30
Astroturf lobbying, 148
At-large city elections, 292
At-large place system, 292
AT&T, 148, 157
Attorney, right to, 270
Attorney general, 211–212
Austin, Texas, 13
Australian ballot, 98
Automated teller machines (ATMs), 101
Available school fund, 331
Avery v. Midland County, 300n

B

Bachmann, Michele, 155, 156n
Bail, setting, 270–271
Ballot(s)
  fees for listing on party primary, 91f
  long, 57, 302
  party-column, 95
  sample, 79
  sample multilingual, 99f
  short, 302
  typical Texan, 96f
  See also Election *entries*

Ballots, construction of, 95–100
  early voting, 100
  getting on the ballot, 97
  multilingualism, 98–100
  politics of, 95–97
  secret ballot, 98
  write in candidates, 97–98
Barak, Aharon, 252n
Barnes, Ben, 19
Barrow, Charles W., 97
Baze et. al. v. Rees et al., 280n
Beare v. Smith, 87
Beck, Glenn, 159
BEEF-PAC (Texas Cattle Feeders Association), 104
Benefits-received taxes, 317–318
Berger, Raoul, 252n
Bernstein, Robert, 172n
Beyond a reasonable doubt, 234
Bicameral, 63
Bicultural, 10
Biden, Joe, 45
Biennial regular sessions, 63
Biennial sessions, 166
Big government, 216
Bill of Rights, Texas Constitution, 60–62
Bills
  become law, 187–190
  in conference committees, 187
  floor action/quorum, 185–186
  house floor action and, 186–187
  senate floor action and, 186
Birth control, 15
Blakeslee, Nate, 261n
Blind voting, 130
Block grants, 35
Blocking bill, 185
Board of Criminal Justice, 215
Board of elections, 95
Board of Pardons and Paroles, 205, 276
Board of Transportation, 215
Boards, 183
Boards and commissions, Texas, 204f, 214–216
  advisory boards, 215–216
  appointed boards, 215
  elective boards, 214
  ex-officio boards, 215
Bond elections, property ownership and, 87
Bonneau, Chris W., 253n
Border, Texas, as cultural region, 10–11
Boston Harbor, 50
Boyle, Thad, 210n
Brace, Paul, 102n
Brennan, William (Justice), 73
Brief (lawyer's), 234

Broad-based taxes, 317
Brown v. Board of Education, 17, 20t, 22n, 36
Budgetary power, 66
Budget powers, of executive branch, 207
Budget preparation, executive branch and, 202
Burden of proof, 233
Bureaucracy, characteristics, 216–219
  expertise and, 218
  hierarchy, 218
  neutrality, 216–217
  privatization, 217–218
  public support, 218
  size, 216
Bureaucracy, politics/public policy and, 220–224
  administration of the law, 224
  clientele groups, 220–221
  governor, 221–222
  information, control of, 224
  Iron Texas star and, 222–223
  legislature, 223–225
Bureaucracy and the Welfare State in Texas (Hogan), 228–229
Bureaucratic accountability
  to chief executive, 225–226
  to people, 224–225
  responsibility and, 226–227
Bureaucratic oversight, 166
Bureau of Justice Statistics, 276n
Burka, Paul, 261n
Bush, George P., 213
Bush, George W., 40, 100, 116, 121, 123, 261, 325
Business
  interest group classification and, 140t
  spending for lobbyists, 150
Business regulation, 259
Bustamante, Jorge, 11n
Butt, Charles C., 143

C

Cabinet system, 225–226
Cadena, Carlos, 19
Caldeira, Gregory A., 247n
Calendars, legislative scheduling and, 184–185
California, marijuana legalization and, 46
Campaign funding
  judicial elections, 247–250
  supreme court elections, 249–250
  for Texas executive branch, 201
  for Texas legislature, 170–172
Campaign Reform Act, 107
Campaigns, election, in Texas, 101–108

general, 102–104. See also General election campaigns
  lobbyists and, 147
  money in, 104–107. See also Money, in election campaigns
  who gets elected?, 107–108
Campaign trail, 103
Campbell, Angus, 122n
Campbell, Donna, 160
Candidates for office, elections and, 108
Cann, Damon M., 253n
Caperton v. A. T. Massey Coal Co. Inc., 249, 254n
Carmines, Edward, 123n
Carr, Waggoner, 19
Carrington v. Rash, 87
Carter, Jimmy, 123
Carville, James, 116
Cases of imperative public necessity, 186
Casey, Linda, 252n
Casey case, 46
Casino gambling, federalism and, 47–48
Casinos, proximate to Texas border, neighboring states, 47f
Castro, Julian, 289p
Categorical grants, 35
Cato Institute, 159
Center for Public Integrity, 156, 157, 157n
Center for Public Policy Priorities, 328
Central America, illegal immigration and, 11–12
Central Texas, cultural region, 13
Central Texas Constitution Alliance, 160
Ceremonial role, of governor, 206
Chad (ballot feature), 100–101
Challenge for cause, 244
Champagne, Anthony, 252n, 253n, 254n
Chande, Roberto Ham, 11n
Change of venue, 271
Charges, pretrial process and, 270, 271
Charters, 69, 259
Charter schools, administration of, 327
Checks and balances, Texas Constitution, 62
Cheek, Kyle, 252n, 253n, 254n
Chief executive
  bureaucratic accountability and, 225–226
  governor as, 203–206
Chief trial courts, 239–240
Children's Health Insurance Program (CHIP), 229, 338, 339f, 340–341

Chronicles of Higher Education, 173
Chubbing, 187
Cipriano v. City of Houma, 87
Cisneros, Henry, 289–290
Cities, ten largest U.S., 297*t*
Citizen initiatives, 68*f*
Citizens, bureaucratic accountability and, 224–225
Citizens' arrests, 268
Citizen's Councils, 24
Citizenship, Latinos and, 18
Citizens United v. Federal Election Commission, 107, 107*n*
City charter, 288
City hall, social issues and, 298
City manager, 289
Civil cases, jurisdiction and, 233–234
 criminal cases *v.*, 234*t*
 in district courts, 240*f*
Civil law, 258–260
 business regulation, 259
 corporate law, 259
 eminent domain, 262
 family law, 258–259
 issues in, 260–262
 labor law, 259
 liability insurance, 261–262
 probate, 259
 real estate, 259
 tort reform, 260–261
 torts, 260
Civil rights
 African Texans and, 15–17
 Big Four shapers of, 17
 Latinos and, 17–19
 quest for, politicians, vigilantes and, 22–24
 segregation and civil rights and, 36
 states rights *v.*, 35–37
Civil Rights Act of 1964, 36
Civil service, 303
Civil service system, 217
Clemency, rehabilitation/punishment and, 277
Clemency powers, of executive branch, 205
Clements, Bill, 66, 74, 117, 120
Clientele groups, 145
 agency-clientele alliance, 220–221
Clinton, Bill, 93, 116
Clinton, Hillary, 110
Closed primary election, 92
Closed shop, 259
Coahuila y Texas, 30
Coalition functions, 223
Coates, Neal, 48–51
Coercive federalism, 38–39
COGs (councils of governments), 307
Coke, Richard, 58
Cole, Richard L., 49

Colleges/Universities, 333–338. *See also* Higher education
Collier, Kiah, 247*n*
Colonias, 298
Colorado, marijuana legalization and, 46
Commerce, ACA and, 42
Commerce clause, 32
Commissioner of agriculture, 213
Commissioner of Education, 326
Commissioner of General Land Office, 212
Commissioners, election of county, 300–301
Commissioners court, 300
Commission form of government, 291
Committee of the Whole, 186
Common Cause, 140, 140*t*
Common Law (English), 56
Communities Organized for Public Service, 159
Community college approach, 334
Community property, 56, 258–259
Commutation of sentence, 277
Compare, Texas to other states. *See* How Does Texas Compare
Comptroller of public accounts, 212
Compulsory process, 273
Concurrent powers, 31, 32*t*
Confederal systems, 29
Conference committee report, 188
Conference committees, 183, 187
Confessions, Miranda and, 269
Conflicts of interest, 7, 154
Congratulatory and Memorial Resolutions Calendar, 184
Congress, powers granted to under Article I, Section 8, 33*t*, 42
Congress of Racial Equality, 17
Connally, John, 19
Conservative caucus, 127
Conservatives, 2
 abortion in Texas and, 15
 ideology of, 2–3, 118–119
 liberals, Texas Democrats and, 119–120
 moderates, Texas Republicans and, 125–126
 partisanship, 3
 public policy, 5
 ranking score, 195*f*
 tea party and, 125
Conservative Texas PAC, 159, 160
Consolidation, 303
Constables, county, 301
Constituency, 166
Constitution, of Texas
 Article I, Section 27, 151–158
 charter elections and, 289
 convention of 1875, 58–60

 delegates to convention of 1875, 59
 of 1845, 57
 of 1861, 57
 of 1866, 57
 of 1869, 57–58
 executive powers and, 202–206
 justices in, 238
 legislative officers' role and, 180–181
 public school funding and, 72–75
 reconstruction constitutions, 57–60
 Republic of Texas, 56–57
 rigidity/inflexibility in, 302
 school administration and, 326
Constitution, of Texas, amending/revising, 70–72
 amendment procedures, 70
 criticisms of, 71–72
 in off-year elections, 71*t*
 1995–2014, amendments, 70–71
 revision attempts, 72
Constitution, of Texas, current, 60–70
 basic rights in, 61*t*
 Bill of Rights, fundamental liberty, 60–62
 checks and balances, 62*t*
 direct democracy, 67, 69
 Executive Branch, 62*f*, 65–67
 Judicial Branch, 62*f*, 67
 Legislative Branch, 62*f*, 63–65
 local government, 69–70
 public education, 69
 separation of powers, 62
 suffrage, 67
Constitutional Amendment Calendar, 184
Constitutional county court, 238–239
Constitutional county judge, 238–239
Constitutional republic, 328
Consulting fees, 167
Consumer taxes, 321
Continental Congress, 29
Contract patronage, 217
Contract spoils, 217
Converse, Philip E., 122*n*
Cooperative federalism, 34–35
Co-optation, 145
CORE protests, 17
Cornyn, John, 121
Corona, John, 154
Corporate law, 259
Corporation for Enterprise Development, 229
Corrections Corporation of America, 276
Corriher, Billy, 146
Corruption
 lobbying and, 155–157
 in Texas, comparing, 156
Corruption Risk Report Card, 156

Cortez, Ernesto, 159
Corwin, Edward S., 33*n*, 34
Council-manager form of government, 289–290
Councils of governments (COGs), 307
Counties, 299–303
  consolidation, 303
  constitutional rigidity, 302
  elected officials in, 300*f*
  governments, 299
  law enforcement, 301
  long ballot, 302
  spoils *v.* merit system, 303
  structure/organization of counties, 299–302
  unit road system, 303
Counting ballots, 100–101
County attorney, 302
County auditor, 301
County clerk, 301
County conventions, 128
County courts, 238–239
County Education Districts (CEDs), 74
County Elections Commission, 95
County governments, 299
County judge, 300
County-level election administration, 95
County-level organization, 129–130
County treasurer, 301
County websites, 79
Courthouse, county, 303*p*
Court of criminal appeals, 240–242
Courts, lobbyists and, 145–146
  filing suit, in court, 146
  judicial selection, influencing, 145–146
Courts, organization of
  appeals court districts, 241*f*
  county courts, 238–239
  court of criminal appeals, 240–242
  courts of appeals, 240
  district courts, 239–240
  judicial qualifications/selection in Texas, 237*f*
  justices of the peace, 238
  municipal courts, 235–237
  structure of, in Texas, 236*f*
  supreme court, 242–243
Courts of appeals, 240
Courts of record, 235
Cracking (gerrymandering), 178
Craddick, Tom, 63, 143, 192–194
Crain, Ernest, 91*n*
Creoles, 10
Crime
  defining, 262
  felonies, 263
  misdemeanors, 263
  punishment for, 263*t*, 278

rates, Texas, 267*f*
  victimless, 264
  victims, 266–267
Criminal
  age of, 264–265
  drug addiction and, 266
  education of, 265
  ethnicity of, 265
  gender of, 265
  income of, 265
  social values and, 264
  urban life and, 265
  white-collar crime and, 266
Criminal cases, jurisdiction and, 233–234
  civil cases *v.*, 234*t*
  in district courts, 240*f*
Cross, Malcolm L., 132–135
Crossover voting, 93
Cruz, Ted, 50–51, 160
Crystal City, 10
Cultural diversity, politics and, 14–21
  Latinos, 17–19
  modern, 21
  sexual orientation, discrimination and, 19–20
  women, equal rights, 14–15
Cultural regions, Texas, 8–13
  Central Texas, 13
  East Texas, 8
  Far West Texas, 10
  German Hill Country, 12
  Houston, 9–10
  immigration/national security and, 11–12
  North Texas, 13
  Panhandle, 12–13
  South Texas, 10
  Texas Border, 10–11
  West Texas, 12
Culture
  political, voting and, 88–89
  school curriculum and, 327–329
Cumulative voting, 293
Cunningham, Minnie Fisher, 14–15, 14*p*
Cunningham, William Todd, 280
Curriculum (school)
  culture wars and, 327–329
  school, politics and, 327

D

Dallas-Fort Worth metropolitan area, 13
DART (Dallas Area Rapid Transit), 308–309
Davis, E. J., 58, 117, 121
Davis, Jefferson, 328
Davis, John, 282

Davis, Wendy, 45–46, 64–65, 86*p*, 151, 154, 186, 261, 352
Deadwood, 65
Dealignment, 122
DeAnda, James, 19
Death penalty, 242, 279–280
Debate
  in house, 186–187
  in senate, 186
Decentralization, political parties and, 116–117
Declining marginal propensity to consume, 320
Decriminalization, of marijuana, 46
Defense of Marriage Act (DOMA), 20
DeLay, Tom, 97
Delegated powers, 31, 32*t*
Delgado, Minerva, 19
Delgado v. Bastrop ISD, 19
Delisi, Diedre, 155
Democrats
  African Texans and, 15, 90
  one-party tradition in Texas and, 117–118
  percentage in Texas, 3
  Texas, 119–120. *See also* Texas Democrats
  win rates in Texas, 193*f*
Demographics
  ethnic populations, 21*f*
  in municipalities, 296
  racial diversity in government, 172–173
  of school students, 330
  shifts in, voter participation and, 109–110
  in voting, 88
  who votes?, 80–81
Demonstrations, interest groups organize, 148
De novo trial, 235
Department of Aging and Disability Services, 338
Department of Agriculture, 213
Department of Assistive and Rehabilitative Services, 338
Department of Banking, 220
Department of Family and Protective Services, 338
Department of Health, 340
Department of State Health Services, 338
Dependent agency, 304
Descriptive representation, 172–173
Desegregation, 17, 22–24, 36
Deterrence, punishment and, 277, 279
Development Corporation Act, 296
Devers, Lindsey, 239*n*
Devolution, 35
Dewhurst, David, 119*p*, 143, 160

Dietz, John, 75
Direct democracy, 67–69, 288–289
Direct health services, 340
Directive authority, 66
Direct primary, 90
Discretion, 144
Discrimination
 history of, in Texas, 174
 Latinos and, 19
 redistricting and, 37
 sexual orientation and, 19–20
 See also Diversity; Ethnicity;
  Minorities; Race
Discriminatory Housing Practices and
  Places of Public Accommodation,
  298
District attorney, 302
District clerk, 302
District courts, 239–240
Diversity
 cultural, 14–21
 in judicial elections, 250–251
 in North Texas, 13
 student, higher education and,
  336–337
 See also Cultural diversity, politics
  and; Discrimination; Diversity;
  Ethnicity; Minorities; Race
Divorce laws, 14
Doggett, Lloyd, 121
DOMA. *See* Defense of Marriage Act
Domestic violence, 14
Double jeopardy, 235
Douglas, Davison M., 23*n*
Douglass, William O. (Justice), 73
Drinking age, 38
Drug(s)
 addiction, criminals and, 266
 trafficking in border region, 11–12
Dual federalism, 33–34
Du Bois, Philip L., 247*n*
Ducat, Craig, 253*n*
Due process, 19–20, 267–275
 arrests, 268
 detention, right to remain silent
  and, 269
 pretrial court activities, 269–272.
  See also Pretrial court, processes
 searches, probable cause,
  exclusionary rule, 268
Duncan v. Louisiana, 272*n*
Dunn v. Blumstein, 87
Duverger, Maurice, 115*n*
Duverger's Law, 115*n*
Duzak, Alexander, 106*n*
Dworkin, Richard, 252*n*

E

Early registration, voting and, 87
Early voting, 100

East Texas, cultural region, 8
Economic development, of
  municipalities, 296
Economic interest groups, 139, 140*f*
Economics
 in Central Texas, 13
 in East Texas, 8
 in Far West Texas, 10
 Gulf Coast region, 8
 Houston boom, 9–10
 Panhandle, 12–13
 South Texas, 10
 in West Texas, 12
*Edgewood Independent School
  District v. Kirby,* 69, 74
Education, 324–338
 civil rights and, 16–17
 of criminal, 265
 elementary/secondary schools,
  325–327. *See also* Elementary/
  secondary schools
 funding for public, 72–75
 Hazelwood acts and, 41
 higher, 333–338. *See also* Higher
  education
 interest group classification and,
  140*t*
 level of, representatives, 173
 local governments and public
  school systems (U.S. and Texas),
  287*f*
 politics of public, 327–333. *See also*
  Politics, of public education
 public, in Texas Constitution, 69
 segregation and, 16–17, 19
 See also Higher education;
  Schools
Efficiency clause, 74
Eisenhower, Dwight D., 17, 120
EJT (extraterritorial jurisdiction), 298
Elazar, Daniel J., 7, 8, 9*f,* 89*n*
Elected officials, of Texas, 203*f,* 261
 attorney general, 211–212
 lieutenant governor, 210
Electioneering
 lobbying and, 146–147
 Tea Party and, 160
Elections
 at-large, 292
 campaigns, 101–108. *See also*
  Campaigns, election in Texas
 judicial, 245–250
 municipal election systems,
  291–293
 nonpartisan, 291–292
 presidential, voter turnout
  1932–2012, 83*f*
 primary. *See* Primary elections
 pure-at-large system, 292
 representation and, 109–110

 results of 2012 presidential, in
  Texas, 124*f*
 system options, 292–293
 of Texas county officials, 300*f*
 websites, 79
Elections, conduct and
  administration of
 ballot construction, 95–100
 counting/recounting ballots,
  100–101
 county-level administration, 95
 electronic voting, 101
Elections, for Texas legislature,
  169–180
 campaign funding, 170–172
 demographic identity, 172–173
 economic statues of
  representatives, 173
 education of representatives, 173
 geographic redistricting, 173–180.
  See also Redistricting
 gerrymandering, 178–180
 occupation of representatives, 173
 party affiliation and, 169–170
Elections, types of, 90–94
 general, 93–95
 primary elections, 90–93. *See also*
  Primary elections
 special, 94
Elective accountability, 224–225
Elective boards, 214–215
Electorate, political party in the, 130
Electronic voting, 101
Elementary/secondary schools
 administration of, 326–327. *See also*
  Administration, of public schools
 history, 325
 recent trends, 325–326
Elites, role in state politics, 106,
  221–222, 249, 294, 328–329
Elitism, culture of nonparticipation,
  interest groups and, 153
Elitist theory, 153
Elkins, Gary, 154
Emergency calendar, 184
Eminent domain, 262
Emmert, Craig, 246*n*
Endangered Species Act, 329
Endorsements, electioneering and,
  160
English Common Law, 56
Enstam, Elizabeth York, 14*n*
Environment, interest group
  classification and, 140*t*
Environmental Protection Agency
  (EPA), 39, 161
Equality Texas, 140*t*
Equal protection, 19
Equal rights
 court cases, 20*t*

Equal rights (*Continued*)
for women, 14–15
Equal Rights Amendment of 1972, 15, 61
Erdmann, Ralph, 281–283
Erikson, Robert S., 102*n*, 103*n*
Ethics Commission, 63
Ethnicity
of criminals, 265
demographics of Texas office holders, 172–173
income, poverty and, in Texas, 22*f*
in judicial elections, 250–251
multilingual ballots, 98–100
school students and, 330
student diversity. higher education, 336–337
of Texas executive branch, 200
voter participation and, 109–110
See also Discrimination; Diversity; Ethnicity; Minorities; Race
Ethnic populations, 21*f*
European migration, to Texas, 12
European Union (EU), 29
Evangelical, 125
Evangelical Christians, 125
Evans, Larry, 188
Examining trial, 271
Exclusionary rule, 268
Executive branch, 200
age/occupation of, 201
appointive powers, 204
attorney general, 211
board and commission system and, 204*f*
campaign funding for, 201
ceremonial role, chief of state, 206
clemency powers, 205
compensation, 201
ethnicity of, 200
federal-state relations, 206
governor's power, 209–210
interest groups and, 204
international functions, 206
judicial powers, 206
law enforcement powers, 205
legislative tools of, 207–209. *See also* Legislative tools, executive branch
lieutenant governor, 210
military powers of, 205
national issues, position on, 207
national party leader, 207
nomination to, 201
as party chief, 206–207
party of, 201
plural executive system and, 210–213
qualifications, elections and, 200–201

removal powers, 205
senate influence, on appointive powers, 204
staff of, 202
Executive branch, lobbyists and, 144–145
Executive Branch (Texas), 62*t*, 65–67
Ex officio, 174
Ex-officio boards, 215
Expertise, bureaucracy and, 218
Expressed powers, 31, 32*t*
Extralegal powers, 202
Extraterritorial jurisdiction (ETJ), 298

F

Fact-check, politicians, website, 79
Fact-finding commissions, executive branch and, 209
Faculty, politics of
higher education and, 335
public education and, 329–330
FairVote, 293
Family law, 258–259
Family Research Council, 159
Farmer, Brian, 280–283
Farmer, James, 17
Farmer, Millard, 281–283, 282
Farmer v. Sherrod, 281
FBI index crimes, 265
Federal Aid Road Act, 346
Federal Election Commission, 105, 107*n*
Federal Elections Campaign Act, 105, 107
Federal funding (education), 330
Federal grants-in-aid, 34–35, 39–40, 322
Federalism
cooperative, 34–35
debates over, 54
defining, 29–30. *See also* Government, systems of
history of, in America, 49–50
overreach, states and, 51
Federalist 10 (Madison), 30
Federalist Papers, 51
Federal system of government, 30
cooperative federalism, 34–35
dual federalism and Tenth Amendment, 33–34
Texas and, 37–48. *See also* Texas, federal government and
types of power in, 31, 32*t*
Felonies, 263
Felony punishment, 275–276
parole, 276
prison, 275–276
probation, 275
Ferguson, Jim, 14, 167, 200
Ferguson, Miriam A. (Ma), 108, 200

Field sobriety test, 264*p*
Fifteenth Amendment, 20*t*
Filibuster, 64–65, 151, 186
Filing suit, in court, lobbyists and, 146
Final passage vote (FPV), 192
Financial aid, government, 296–297
Financing
higher education, 335–336
highways, 347
Medicaid, 340
primary elections, 91
public schools, 330–332, 349–353
First Amendment, 151
Fisher v. University of Texas at Austin, 337*n*
Flango, Victor, 253*n*
Floor action, 185
Floor leaders, 186
Formal powers, 202
Foundation School Program (FSP), 331
Founding Fathers, 30
Fourteenth Amendment, 19–20, 20*t*, 31, 60, 161, 178
FOX News, 159
Franchise tax, 316
Franklin, Mark N., 83*n*
FreedomWorks, 159
Friedman, Kinky, 115
Fuchs, Edward P., 102*n*
Full pardon, 277
Fundamentalist Christians, 125
Funding, campaign, 170–172

G

Galanes-Rosenbaum, Eva, 100*n*
Gamkhar, Shama, 51*n*
Gandhi, Mahatma, 17
Garcia, Gustavo C., 19, 19*p*
Garcia, Hector, 18
Garcia, John, 281
Garcia-Monet, Patricia A., 100*n*
Gardasil, HPV vaccine, 156
Garza, Alicia A., 18*n*
Gay rights, in Texas, 19–20
Gender
candidates for office and, 108
of criminals, 265
interest group classifications and, 140*t*
in judicial elections, 250–251
jury duty and, 15
of Texas executive branch, 200
women, jury duty and, 15
women's suffrage, 87
General elections, in Texas, 93–95
campaign, 102–104
campaign trail, 103
issues, choosing, 103
timing, 103–104
See also Election *entries*

General Land Office, 203, 212
General-law charters, 69
General-law city, 288–289
General-obligation bonds, 322
General-purpose governments, 287
General trial courts, 239–240
Geographic redistricting, 173–180. *See also* Redistricting
German Hill Country, 12
Gerry, Elbridge, 178
Gerrymandering, techniques/ alternatives for, 178–180
Gibbons, James, 155*n*
Gibson, James L., 247*n*
Gideon v. Wainwright, 270*n*
Gilbreath, Robert, 253*n*
Gilmer-Aikin Act, 325
Gingrich, Newt, 328
Glick, Henry, 246*n*
Gold standard, 328
Gonzalez, Raul, 108, 253
Government
 county, 299
 hidden, 306
 political parties in, 131
 special district, 304–306. *See also* Special district
 structure of, 152
Government, systems of
 Confederal, 29
 federal, 30
 unitary, 29
Government mandates, as revenue source, 296–297
Governor
 administrative agencies and, 221–222
 as chief executive, 203–206
 powers of office, 66–67, 209–210, 209–210
 revolving door lobbying and, 221–222
 See also Executive branch
Gramm, Phil, 120, 121
Grandfather clause, voting, 87
Grand jury, 243–244, 268
Grangers, 58
Grant, Ulysses S., 58
Grants-in-aid (federal), 34–35
Grassroots Texans Network, 160
Great Debaters, The (movie), 17
Great Depression, 35, 315
Great Plains, 12
Great Recession, 39
Green, George B., 17*n*
Green, George N., 23*n*
Green Party, 115
Griffin, Ernest, 150*n*
Grissom, Brandi, 155*n*, 169*n*

Griswold v. Connecticut, 15
Gross-receipt taxes, 316
Grovey v. Townsend, 16, 90*n*
Grutter v. Bellinger, 337*n*
Guerra, Carlos, 101*n*
Gulf Coast, cultural region, Texas, 8
Gur-Arie, Mira, 252*n*

H

Hall, Charles, 252*n*
Hall, Robert E., 19*n*
Hart, Patricia Kilday, 261*n*
Hazelwood Act of 1929, 41
Hazelwood Legacy Act of 2009, 41
HB2, Texas, 45
Health and human services, 338–346
 agencies, 339*f*
 health programs. *See* Health programs
 income support programs, 343–344
 insurance, how people get health, 341*f*
 politics of welfare, income redistribution, 344–346
Health and Human Services Commissioner, 213–215, 343–344
Health-care reform, 341–343
Health insurance, how people get, 341*f*
Health programs, 338–343
 direct health services, 340
 private health insurance, 341
 state health insurance programs, 340–341
 uninsured, 341
Heath and Safety Code, 299
Hecht, Nathan (Justice), 75
Heclo, Hugh, 151*n*
Hegar, Glenn, 212*p*, 322*p*
Help America Vote Act, 296
Henry, O., 124*f*
Henson, James, 349–353
Herminica Hernandez et al. v. Driscoll Consolidated ISD, State of Texas, 19, 20*t*
Hernandez, Pete, 19
Herrera, John, 19
Hershey, Marjorie Randon, 115*n*, 117*n*
Hidden taxes, 315
Hierarchy, bureaucracy and, 218
Higher education
 accessibility of, 335–336
 administration of colleges/ universities, 333–334
 politics of, 334–338. *See also* Politics, of higher education
 rankings, school, 337–338
 tuition fees, Texas resident, 336*f*
Higher Education Coordinating Board, 215

High Plains, 12
High-tech industries, 13
Hightower, Jim, 105*n*
Highway privatization, 347–348
Highway programs, 346–347
Highway system, 347*t*
Hill, John, 121
HillCo, Texas lobby group, 143
Hill Country, 12
Hillsdale College, 159
Hill v. Stone, 87
Hispanics, in South Texas, 10
Historic Murder Case: Obstruction of Texas Justice (Farmer), 280–283
Hobby, William P., 15
Hogan, Alexander, 228–229
Home-rule charters, 69
Home-rule city, 288–289
Homestead, 56, 259
Hoover, Herbert, 118
Hopwood v. Texas, 337*n*
House Appropriations Committee, 324
House committee membership, 184
House Committee on Calendars, 184–185
House Committee on Local and Consent Calendars, 184–185
House of Representatives, districts, 175*f*
Houston, cultural region, boom in, 9–10
Houston, Sam, 57, 117
How Does Texas Compare features
 corruption risk, 156
 crime and punishment, 278
 direct democracy, methods of, 68*f*
 governor's power, 209–210
 legislature, limits on terms, salaries, sessions, 168
 Medicaid expansion, 44
 party control of government in the fifty states, 131–132
 population changes in large U.S. cities, 297
 quality of life/public policy, 6*f*
 selecting judges, 246
 tax and spending policies, 322–323
 voter turnout, 85
Hoye, Timothy, 73–75
HPV vaccines, 155
Hubbard, Bill, 281–283
Human trafficking, 11–12
Hung jury, 245, 273
Hutchinson, Kay Bailey, 108, 121

I

Identification, voting and, 82. *See also* Voter ID laws
Ideological factions, 118–119

Ideological factions (*Continued*)
  conservatives, 2–3, 4*f*, 118–119
  liberals, 119
Immigration
  European, 12
  illegal, 11–12
Impartiality, ideals of, 252
Impeachment, 201
Impeachment session, 167
Implementation, 144
Implied powers, 31, 32*t*
Income
  of criminal, 265
  ethnicity, poverty and, 22*f*
  redistribution, politics of, 344–346
Income redistribution, 344–346
Income support programs, 343–344
  Temporary Assistance to Needy
    Families (TANF), 343
  unemployment insurance, 343–344
Income tax rates, federal, 319*f*
Incumbents, 180
Independence, ideals of impartiality
    and, 252
Independent expenditures, 107
Independent voters, 83
Independent school districts,
    administration of, 326–327
Indian Gaming Regulatory Act, 47
Indictment, 243, 268
Indirect appointive powers, 66
Individualistic culture, 7, 23, 89
Individual mandate, 342–343
Industrial Areas Foundation, 159
Industry, in North Texas, 13
Influence peddling, lobbying and,
    155–157
Informal powers, 202
Information
  control of, 224
  grand jury and, 243
Inherent powers, 31, 32*t*
Initiatives, 67–69
Injunctions, 259
Insurance commissioner, 214
Integration, in schools, 16–17, 22–24
Interest group alliances, 150–151
Interest groups
  classifications and examples, 140*t*
  defined, 139
  economic, 139
  executive appointive powers ad, 204
  government structure and, 152
  lawsuit reform and, 261
  mixed, 140
  noneconomic, 139–140
  powerful, in Texas, 148–150
  representation/mobilization,
    152–153
Interest groups, criticism and
    reforms, 153–158

revolving door, 154–155
  state institutions, exploitation of,
    153–154
  suspect practices, 155–157
Interest groups, influence of, 151–158
  criticism and reforms, 153–158. *See
    also* Interest groups, criticism and
    reforms
  lobbying, regulation of, 157–158
  pluralism, benefits of, 152–153
  positive role, 152–153
Interest groups, targets/tactics,
    140–148
  courts, targeting, 145–146
  executive branch, 144–145
  lobbying the legislature, 141–143
  political environment, shaping,
    146–148
Interim committees, 183
Internal Revenue Service (IRS), 42,
    319*f*
International City/council
    Management Association, 291
Invisible trade, 11–12
Iron Texas Star, 222–223
Iron triangles, 150
Isolation, as punishment, 277–278
Issue networks, 151
Issues, choosing for election, 103
Item veto, 208

J

Jackson, Andrew, 93
Jails, functions of, 277
  deterrence, 277. 279
  isolation, 277
  justice, 277
  rehabilitation, 277, 279
Jim Crow laws, 35–36
Johnson, Andrew, 57
Johnson, Jake, 186
Johnson, Lyndon B., 18, 36, 121, 123
Joint committees, 183
Jones, Mark P., 192–196
Jones, Neal (Buddy), 143
Jones, Sam Houston, 97
Jordan, Barbara, 139
Judges
  in municipal courts, 235
  racial/ethnic/gender composition
    of, 251*t*
  selection of, 245–251
Judges, selection of
  comparing Texas, 246
  politics of, 247–250
Judicial Branch (Texas), 62*t*, 67
*Judicial Impartiality and
  Independence in Texas:
  Democratic Ideals vs. Electoral
  Realities* (Saenz-Rivera), 251–254

ideals of impartiality/independence,
    252
Judicial powers, of executive branch,
    206
Judicial qualifications/selection in
    Texas, 237*f*
Judicial selection, lobbyists and,
    145–146
Juries
  grand jury, 243–244
  petit/trial, 244–245
  women, minorities and, 15
Jurisdiction
  appellate, 234–235
  civil/criminal cases, 233–234
  of district courts, 239
  original, 234–235
Jury, trial by, 272–273
Jury charge, 273
Jury duty, voting and, 87
Justice, William Wayne (Federal
    District Judge), 17
Justice of the peace, 238
Juvenile courts, 275

K

Kansas City, 12
Kauffman, Albert H., 74*n*
Keffer, Jim, 187*p*
Kelly, Patrick, 282–283
*Kelo v. City of New London
    Connecticut,* 262
Key, V. O., 130
Kibbe, Matt, 159*n*
Kickapoo Casino, Eagle Pass, 47
Kids Count, 328
Killer Bees, 185
Killer D's, 185
Kincaid, John, 49
Kincaid, Mark, 261
King, Anthony, 151*n*
King, Martin Luther, Jr. (Dr.), 17
"King Caucus," 90
Kingwood Tea Party, 159
Kinkaid, John, 38
Kirby, William N., 74
Kirk, Ron, 290
Koch, Charles G., 328
Kolius, Bill, 281
Konrad, Rachel, 101*n*
Kraemer, Richard H., 91*n*
Kramer v. Union Free District No. 15, 87
Krause, Matt, 160
Ku Klux Klan (KKK), 15–16, 24

L

Labor
  interest group classifications and, 140*t*
  Latino civil activism and, 18–19
  peonage and, 17–18

Labor law, 259
Lancaster, Thomas B., 103*n*
Languages, on ballots, 98–100
La Raza Unida Party, 90*n*
La Réunion, French socialist colony, 13
Late-train contributions, 156
Latinos
　citizenship and, 18
　cultural, civil rights, labor issues, 17–19
　equal protection and, 19
　segregation and, 15–16
　in South Texas, 10
　in Texas Border region, 11
　veterans, 18
　See also Discrimination; Diversity; Ethnicity; Minorities; Race
Law, administration of, 224
Law enforcement
　county, 301
　powers of executive branch, 205
Lawrence v. Texas, 19–20, 20*t*
Lawsuit reform, 261
Lax, Jeffrey R., 168*n*
Leadership, institutional tools of, 190–191
　Legislative Audit Committee, 191
　legislative budget board, 190
　Legislative Council, 190–191
　Sunset Advisory Commission, 191
League of United Latin American Citizens (LULAC), 16, 23, 120, 140*t*, 178
Legal constraints, voter turnout and, 86–88
　annual registration, 87
　early registration, 87
　jury duty, 87
　long residence requirement, 87
　military vote, 87
　poll tax, 87
　property ownership, bond elections and, 87
　white primary, 87
　women's suffrage, 87
Legal powers, 202
Legislative agenda, Tea Party, 161
Legislative Audit Board, 210
Legislative Audit Committee, 191
Legislative Branch, Texas, 62*t*, 63–65
Legislative Budget Board (LBB), 183, 190, 210, 225, 297
Legislative Council, 190–191, 210
Legislative Criminal Justice Board, 210
Legislative Education Board (LEB), 183
Legislative liaisons, 202
Legislative organization

ad-hoc/select, 183
conference committees, 183
interim committees, 183
joint committees, 183
lieutenant governor, 180–181
speaker of the house, 181
standing committees, 182
subcommittees, 183
Legislative process, 183–190
　bill becoming law, 187–190
　conference committees, 187
　scheduling, 184–187. *See also* Scheduling, as legislative process
　senate calendar, 185
　two-thirds rule, 185–186
Legislative Redistricting Board, 174
Legislative tools, executive branch, 207–209
　budget powers, 207
　fact-finding commissions, 209
　item veto, 208
　message power, 207
　pocket veto, no, 208
　special sessions, 209
　veto, 207–208
　veto threat, 208
Legislature (Texas), 62*t*, 141–143
　bureaucratic accountability to, 225
　electing, 169-180. *See also* Elections, for Texas legislature
　leadership, tools of, 190–191
　limited, 165–169
　partisanship in, 170*f*
　salaries/compensation, 167
　staff of, 169
　terms, 165–167
　See also Lobbying, the legislature
Legitimacy, 56
Lesbian rights, in Texas, 19–20
Let's Party (Cross), 132–135
Levendusky, Matthew, 122*n*
Levin, Mark, 50–51
Levinthal, Dave, 106*n*
Lewis, George, 24*n*
Liability insurance, 261–262
Liberals, 3, 13
　ideological faction, 119
　ranking score, 195*f*
Libertarian Party, 115, 118–119, 125
Liberty Amendments, The: Restoring the American Republic (Levin), 51
Lieutenant governor, office of, 180–181, 210
Lincoln, Abraham, 328
Line-item veto, 66, 208
Little legislature, 190
Livestock culture
　Panhandle, 13
　of South Texas, 10

Lobbying
　revolving door, 221–222
　Texas Supreme Court election contributors, 250*t*
Lobbying, regulation of, 157–158
　evaluating reporting requirements, 157–158
　lobbyist reports, 157
Lobbying, the legislature, 141–143
　key legislature, targeting key, 142–143
　persuasion, using tools of, 142
　preparing to lobby, 141
　socializing, 142
　spending, 147
Lobbyist(s)
　reports, 157
　vetoes and, 208
Local and Consent Calendar, 184
Local funding, schools, 331
Local government
　promoting local interests, 294
　public school systems and, U.S. and Texas, 287*f*
　in Texas Constitution, 69–70
Local Government Code, 299, 302
Local taxes, 316
Lone Star Card, 345
Lone Star Community College, 159
Long, Christopher, 16*n*
Long ballot, 57, 302
Longoria, Felix, 18
Lubbock Avalanche Journal, 283
LULAC. *See* League of United Latin American Citizens
Lutz, Donald S., 102*n*
Lynching, 16

M

MacLaggan, Corrie, 228*n*
Madison, James
　Federalist 10, 30
　limiting government powers, 34
Madoff, Bernie, 266
Majority rule, primary election and, 92
Major State Calendar, 184
Malapportionment, 174
Mandate, 296
Manges, Clinton, 253
Manges v. Guerra, 253
Mansfield school desegregation, 17, 22–23
Mapp v. Ohio, 268
Maquiladoras, 11
Marginal increments, 319–320
Marijuana legalization, 46
Marital Property Act, 15
Mark Levin Show, The, 50–51
Mark up, 182
Marriage
　same-sex, 20
　women's rights and, 14–15

Marshall, John (Chief Justice), 32, 34
Marshall, Thurgood (Justice), 73
Mass transit, 348
Mauzy, Oscar (Justice), 74
Maxwell, William E., 91n
Mayor-council form of government, 290–291
McArthur, Denese, 22–24
McCarthy, Joseph, 328
McCorvey, Norma, 45–46
McCulloch v. Maryland, 32, 50
McDonald, Craig, 158n
McKool, Mike, 186
McNeely, Dave, 103n
McWilliams, Andrea, 155
Means test, 344–345
Media
  campaign spending, 104–105
  effect of mass, 8
  in election campaigns, 103–104
  lobbyist spending and, 150
Medicaid, 338, 339f, 340
  ACA expansion of, 42–43, 161
  fraud, 211
  Texas, compare expansion, 44
Medicare, 340
Medicare Part B, 340
Meese, Edwin, 50
Megadonors, to Texas election campaigns, 106
Meier, Bill, 186
Meinig, D. W., 8, 9f
Merck, 155–156
Merit plan, 245
Merit system, 217, 303
Merriman, Hilton, 281
Message power, of executive branch, 207
Mestizos, 10
Metroplex, 13
Metropolitan statistical areas, 265
Mexican American Democrats (MAD), 120
Mexican American Legal Defense and Education Fund MALDEF 74, 120, 146, 293
Mexico
  illegal immigration and, 11–12
  sales tax in, 309
  Texas Border region and, 11
Meyers, Lawrence, 247
Migration
  German Hill Country and, 12
  Houston and, 9–10
  North Texas and, 13
Military powers, of executive branch, 205
Military vote, 87
Miller, Arthur H., 103n
Miller, Bill, 143

Miller, Eric, 308–309
Miller, Peter A., 100n
Miller, Warrant E., 122n
Miller v. Johnson, 178
Mino, Wolfgang P. Hirczy De, 83n
Minorities
  jury duty and, 15
  Republican Party and, 125
  women's rights and, 14
  See also Discrimination; Diversity; Ethnicity, Race
Miranda, Ernesto, 269
Miranda v. Arizona, 269
Misdemeanors, 263, 276
Missouri plan, 245
Mistrial, 273
Mitchell, Glenn, II, 86n
Mixed interest groups, 140, 140t
Mobilization, interest groups and, 152–153
Moderate-progressive caucus, 127
Money, in election campaigns, 104–107
  control over, 105, 107
  following, campaign spending, 171–172
  how spent?, 104–105
  lobbyists, 149t
  megadonors, 108
Montesquieu, Charles-Louis de Secondat Baron de, 252n
Morales, Don, 108
Moralistic culture, 7, 89
Moral Majority, 328
Mores, 264
Motor Voter Act, 296
Motor voter legislation, 81
Multilingualism, on ballots, 98–100
Municipal Annexation Act, 298
Municipal courts, 235–237
Municipal election systems, 291–293
Municipalities, 287–296
  annexation, 297–298
  city hall, social issues and, 298
  commission system, 291
  common forms of government of, 290f
  council-manager system, 289–290
  demographic change, 296
  direct democracy and, 288–289
  economic development of, 296
  election system options, 292–293
  general-law/home-rule cities, 288–289
  government mandates, 296–297
  home rule, limits of, 289
  mayor-council system, 290–291
  municipal election systems, 291–293
  municipal finances, Texas, 295f

nonpartisan elections, 291–292
  population growth, 296
  revenue sources, 293–296
Municipal Utilities Districts (MUDs), 306
Murphy, Ryan, 173n
Murray, Richard, 102n

N

NAACP. *See* National Association for the Advancement of Colored People
NAFTA. *See* North American Free Trade Agreement
National Assessment of Education Process, 330
National Association for the Advancement of Colored People (NAACP), 16, 23, 120, 140t, 293
National Association of Regional Councils, 307
National Beer Wholesalers Association, 104
National Center for Constitutional Studies, 159
National Center on Budget and Policy Priorities, 328
National Education Association, 329–330
National Federation of Independent Business v. Sebelius, 42, 342n
National Institute on Money in State Politics, 157n, 170–172
National Minimum Drinking Age Act of 1984, 38
National Rifle Association, 140t, 146, 328
National security, Texas Border region and, 11–12
National taxes, 315
National Voter Registration Act, 296
Native Americans
  casinos, 47–48
  tribal governments, 50
  See also Discrimination; Discrimination; Diversity, Ethnicity; Minorities; Race
Natural Resources Defense Council, 140t
Necessary and proper clause, 32, 50
Negative campaigning, 103
Negligence, 260
Nelson, Colleen McCain, 201n
NE Tarrant Tea Party, 160
Neutrality, of bureaucracy, 216–217
New Deal, 35, 51, 120
New England, moralistic culture in, 7
New Revolutions Now, 159
New York v. Quarles, 269n
Nie, Norman H., 80n

Nineteenth Amendment, 87
Nixon, L. H., 16
Nixon, Richard, 120
Nixon v. Herndon, 16
Nix v. Williams, 268
No bill, 243, 244, 271
No Child Left Behind Act, 40, 296, 325
Nomination, to executive branch, 201
Noneconomic interest group, 139–140*t*
Nonparticipation, elitism and culture of, 153
Nonpartisan elections, 291–292
Norris, Mark, 51*n*
North American Free Trade Agreement (NAFTA), 10, 11
Northern West Texas, 12
North Texas, cultural region, 13

O

Obama, Barack, 37*p,* 42, 45, 93, 110
Obamacare, 32, 41–44, 341–343.
    See also Patient Protection and Affordable Care Act
Occupation
    of state representatives, 173
    of Texas executive branch, 201
Office-block ballot, 95
Office of State-Federal Relations (OSFR), 206
Officers, of legislature
    lieutenant governor, 180–181
    speaker of the house, 181
Ogallala Aquifer, 12, 13, 145
Oil, in Gulf Coast region, 8
Ombudspersons, 227
One-party state, 90
    tradition of, in Texas, 117–118
Open-meeting Act, 289
Open-meeting laws, 227
Open primary election, 92
Open-record laws, 227
Organization, political party as, 130–131
Original jurisdiction, 234–235
Overstreet, Morris, 108

P

Packing (gerrymandering), 178
Pairing (gerrymandering), 179
Palmer, Douglas, 281, 282–283
Panhandle, cultural region, 12–13
Parole, as felony punishment, 276
Participation paradox, 80
Partisan balance, in Texas, 122
Partisan elections, 67
Partisan identification, 122
Partisanship, 3, 4*f*
    judicial elections and, 247

in Texas House of Representatives, 170*f*
Party affiliation, selections, for Texas legislature and, 169–170
Party chief, governor as, 206–207
Party-column ballot, 95
Party competition, voting and, 88
Party identification, in Texas, 122*t*
Party platform, 125
    excerpt from 2012 Texas Democratic/Republican party, 129*t*
Party realignment, 122
Party switching, 123
Party system, of Texas, development of, 117–126
    changes in number of Republican/Democratic officeholders in Texas, 121*f*
    conservatives/liberals, TX democrats and, 119–120
    conservatives/moderates, republicans ad, 125–126
    ideological factions, in America and Texas, 118–119
    one-party tradition in, 117–118
    republican party, rise of, 120–124
    results of 2012 presidential election, 124*f*
Patient Protection and Affordable Care Act, 32, 38–39, 42, 151, 161, 341–343
    abortion and, 46
    Texas and, 41–44
    See also Obamacare
Patrick, Don, 119*p,* 161
Patronage system, 217–218
Patterson, Thomas, 50*n*
Paxton, Ken, 211*p*
Pell grants, 335
Peonage, 17–18
Per diem, 167
Peremptory challenge, 245
Permanent-party organization, 128–130
    county-level, 129–130
    precinct-level, 129
    state-level, 130
Permanent school fund, 330–331
Perot, Ross, 97
Perry, Bob, 143, 155, 161
Perry, Rick
    on abortion, 45
    as governor, 37*p,* 38–39, 40, 65, 66, 75, 104, 159, 221
    on marijuana legalization, 46
Personal recognizance, 271
Personal Responsibility Agreement, 228
Persons in prison, on probation, and on parole, 278*t*

Peterson, Liz Austin, 155*n*
Petitions, signing as political participation, 89*p*
Petit jury, 244–245
Pew Research Center, 158, 160*n*
Philips, Tom, 235
Philips Justin H., 168*n*
Pickerill, Mitchell, 51*n*
Pierpont Communications, 105*n*
Pigeonholed, 182
Plaintiff, 258
Planning
    executive branch and, 202
    municipalities, annexation and, 298
Plea bargaining, 239, 272
Plessy v. Ferguson, 17, 35
Plural executive, 65, 210–213
Pluralism, interest groups and, 152–153
Pluralist theory, 152–153
Plurality vote, 93
Plurality voting rule, 115
Plushnick-Masti, Ramit, 274*n*
Pocket veto, 67, 208
Point of order, 186–187
Polarization, political parties and, 116
Pole tax, 317
Political action committees (PACs), 104–107
Political corruption, 7
Political culture, 2
    conservative, 2
    liberal, 3
    political participation and, 7
    state. *See* State political cultures
    Texas, 9*f*
    voting and, 88–89
Political environment, lobbyists and, 146–148
    campaign contributions, 147
    educating the public, 147
    electioneering, 146–147
    public demonstrations, organizing, 148
Political movements, 151
Political participation, 79–89
    low voter turnout, reasons for, 86–89. *See also* Voter turnout, reason for low
    political culture and, 7
    practice of voting, 81–82
    in U.S. and Texas, 82–86
    who votes, 80–81
    why people vote, 79–80
Political parties
    control of government in 50 states, 131–132
    functions of, 130–132
    government in, 131
    identification with, voting and, 83

Political parties (*Continued*)
  membership percentages, in Texas, 3
  national party organizations,
    decentralization, 117*f*
  as organization, 130–131
  polarization, 116
  redistricting and, 37
  organization of, in Texas, 126–130.
    See also Texas political parties,
    organization of
  in West Texas, 12
  White Primary Law and, 16
Political parties, characteristics of
    American, 114–117, 115*n*
  decentralization, 116–117
  pragmatism and, 115–116
  two-party system, 114–115
Political power, interest groups and,
    148–151
Politicians
  fact check website for, 79
  representation and, 109–110
*Politicians, Vigilantes, and the Quest
    for Civil Rights* (McArthur), 22–24
*Politicians Don't Represent Most
    Texans* (Ramsey), 109–110
Politics
  of ballot construction, 95–97
  civil rights, desegregation and,
    22–24
  cultural diversity and, 14–21
  school funding and, 349–353
  of state spending, 324
  of taxation, 316–323. *See also*
    Taxation, politics of
  voter turnout and, 88
Politics, of higher education, 334–338
  diversity, student, 336–337
  faculty issues, 335
  financial issues, 335
  quality, graduation rates and,
    337–338
  retention, student, 337
  student accessibility, 335–336
Politics, of public education, 327–333
  culture, curriculum ad, 327–329
  curriculum, 327
  faculties, 329–330
  financing public schools, 330–332
  privatization, 332–333
  students, 330
  textbooks, 328–329
Politics, of selecting judges, 247–250
  campaign contributions, 247–250
  ethnic/racial/gender diversity,
    250–251
  partisanship and, 247
  voter knowledge, 247
Politics, of transportation, mass
    transit and, 347–348

Politics, of welfare/income
    redistribution, 344–346
  defining welfare, 344–345
  poverty, causes of, 346
  realities of welfare, 345
  welfare myths, 345
Poll tax, 87
Popular recalls, 67–69
Populations
  changes in large U.S. cities, 297
  ethnic, 21*f*
  in municipalities, 296
Populist Party, 115, 117–118
Position issues, 116
Poverty
  causes of, 346
  income, ethnicity, in Texas, 22*f*
Poverty level, 42–43
Powell, G. Bingham, Jr., 84*n*
Powell, Lewis (Justice), 73
Powell v. Alabama, 270*n*
Power(s)
  granted to Congress (Article I,
    Section 8), 33*t*
  dual federalism, Tenth Amendment
    and, 33–34
  in federal system, 31, 32*t*, 49
  necessary and proper clause and,
    32
Pragmatism, 115–116
Precedents, 258
Precinct convention, 126–128
Precinct party organization, 129
Pre-clearance, 36
Preponderance of the evidence, 234
Presidential preference primary, 128
Pretrial court, processes, 269–272
  bail setting, 270–271
  charges, 270
  examining trials, 271
  formal charges, 271
  plea bargaining, 272
  pretrial hearings, 271–272
  right to attorney, 270
Pretrial hearings, 271–272
Prima facie, 271
Primary elections, 90–93
  administering, 91–92
  closed, 92
  crossover voting, 93
  financing, 91
  majority rule, 92
  who must hold?, 90–91
Primozich, Blayne, 158–161
Prison, as punishment, 275–276
Privacy, court cases on, 20*t*
Private health insurance, 341
Privatization, 217–218, 326, 332–333
Probable cause, 268
Probate law, 259

Probation, 274
Probation, as punishment, 275
Progressive Era, 290
Progressive tax rates, 318–319
Prohibition, 11–12
Property ownership, voting and, 87
Property taxes
  municipalities, and limits on,
    294–295
  schools and, 331
Proposal of constitutional
    amendments, 70
Proposition 2 (2013), 70
Proposition 6 (2013), 70
Protests, interest groups and, 148
Public, educating, lobbying and, 147
Public Citizen, 260
Public debt, 296
Public defenders, 270
Public education, in Constitution, 69
Public Information Act, 289
Public interest, interest group
    classification and, 140*t*
Public opinion, 3–5, 5*p*
  financing education and, 349–353
  ideology/partisanship, 4*f*
  public policy and, 4*f*–5*f*
Public policy, 5
  compare Texas, 6*f*
  Iron Texas Star and, 222–223
Public Safety Commission, 205
Public service, 318
Public support, bureaucracy and, 218
Public transportation systems, city,
    county, 305*f*
Public Utilities Commission, 150, 154
Punch-card ballots, 100
Punishment
  death penalty, pros/cons, 279–280
  evaluating, rehabilitation policies
    and, 277–279
  felony, 275–276. *See also* Felony
    punishment
  isolation and, 277
  juvenile rehabilitation, 277
  misdemeanor, 276
  persons in prison, probation, and
    on parole, 278*t*
Punitive damage, 260–261
Purple legislation, 194–196

Q

Quality of life, compare Texas, 6*f*
Quorum, 185

R

Race
  African Texans, 15–17
  candidates for office and, 108

crime victims and, 266
demographic factors in voting and, 88
demographics of Texas office holders, 172–173
desegregation and, 22–24. *See also* Desegregation
in East Texas, 8
in German Hill Country, 12
gerrymandering and, 178
interest group classifications and, 140*t*
in judicial elections, 250–251
minority voters, Republicans and, 125
multicultural Houston, 10
multilingual ballots and, 98–100
participation in primary elections and, 90
school students and, 330
South Texas and, 10
states' rights and, 35–36
student diversity, higher education, 336–337
in Texas Border region, 11
voting and, 80–81
in West Texas, 12
white primary and, 87
See also Discrimination; Diversity; Ethnicity; Minorities
Racism, in Texas, 15–17. *See also* Discrimination; Diversity; Ethnicity; Minorities; Race
Radical Republicans, 57
Railroad Commission, 147, 203
Railroads, 12, 13
Ramsey, Ross, 109–110, 261*n*
Ramshaw, Emily, 154*n*
Ranchero culture, 10
Rangel, Enrique, 178*n*
Ratification, 70
Raymondville Peonage, 17–18
Reagan, Ronald, 120
Real estate law, 259
Reapportionment, 174
Recall election, 289
Recidivists, 279
Reconstruction
constitutions of, 57–60
post Civil War, 15, 16*n*
Reconstruction Act of 1867, 57
Recorded vote, 187
Recount, ballot, 98, 100–101
Redistricting, 37, 109, 173–180
Reduction veto, 67
Reed, Douglas S., 73
Referendums, 67–69
Reform
lawsuit, 261
lobbying and, 153–154

Registration, voting, 81–82
Regressive tax rates, 319–323
Regulatory taxes, 317
Rehabilitation
clemency, 277
juvenile, 277
Religion
conservative, 3
conservatives/moderates, Texas Republicans and, 125
in East Texas, 8
in Far West Texas, 10
in German Hill Country, 12
interest group classification and, 140*t*
racism and, 16
school curriculum and, 327–328
in Texas Border region, 11
in West Texas, 12
Remedy, 258
Remerer, Frank R., 17*n*
Reporting requirements, lobbyists, 157–158
Representation, interest groups and, 152–153
Reprieve, 277
Republicans
minority voters and, 125
one-party system in Texas and, 117–118
percentages in Texas, 3
tea party and, 50–51, 125
Texas, 120–124. *See also* Texas Republican Party
win rates in Texas, 193*f*
Republic of Texas Constitution, 56–57
Reserved powers, 31, 32*t*
Residence requirement, voting, 87
Resolution, 167
Resolutions Calendar, 184
Retainer fees, 167
Retention, student, higher education and, 337
Revenue
borrowing and other, 322
from federal government, 40*f*
federal grants-in-aid, 322
sources of estimated state, 2014–2015, 315*f*
tax and spend policies, comparing state, 322–323
taxation and politics of, 315–322. *See also* Taxation *entries*
Texas, by source, 39*t*
Revenue, municipalities, 293–296
government mandates, 296–297
public debt, 296
rollback elections, 295
user fees, 296
Revenue bonds, 322, 323

Revision attempts, of Texas Constitution, 72
Revolving door, interest groups and, 154–155
Rey, Johnny, 281–283
Reynolds, John, 331*n*
Reynolds v. Sims, 174
Richards, Ann, 108, 121, 200
Right to attorney, 270
Right to remain silent, detention, due process and, 269
Right-to-work laws, 259
RINOs (Republicans in name only), 160
Roberts, John (Chief Justice), 42
Robin Hood Plan, 74
Roe v. Wade, 15, 20*t*, 45–46
Rollback elections, 295
Romero, David W., 103*n*
Roosevelt, Franklin D., 51, 120
Root, Jay, 154*n*
Rosenstone, Steven, 80*n*
Rules for Radicals (Alinsky), 159
Runaway grand juries, 244
Runoff primary, 92

S

Saenz-Rivera, Sergio, 251–254
Saffel, David C., 89*n*
Saitas, Jeff, 145
Sales Tax Equity (Eric Miller), 308–309
Sales tax(es)
municipality revenue source, 294
Texas general, paid in dollars, 320*t*
Same-sex relationships, 19–20
San Antonio, nondiscrimination ordinance, 298
San Antonio v. Rodriguez, 73–74
Sanford, R. Allen, 266
Santa Anna, Antonio López de, 30, 56
Schalfly, Phyllis, 328
Scheduling, as legislative process, 184–187
house calendar committees, 184–185
house floor action, 186–187
senate floor action, 186
two-thirds rule, 185–186
Schlueter, Stan, 155
School accountability, 325
School Land boards, 212
Schools
elementary/secondary, 325–327. *See also* Elementary/secondary schools
funding for public, 72–75
higher education rankings, 337–338
integration, 16–17, 22–24
segregation in, 36. *See also* Segregation

Schools (*Continued*)
  select Texas district profiles, 332*t*
  See also Education; Higher
    education
Second arraignment, 271
Secretary of state, 213
Secret ballot, election integrity and,
  98
Segal, Jeffrey, 252*n*, 253*n*
Segregation, 15–16, 35–36
  African Americans and, 16–17
  civil rights and, 36
Select committees, 183
Selective taxes, 315
Senate calendar, 185
Senate committee membership, 184
Senate Finance Committee, 324
Senate floor action, 186
Senate influence, on appointive
  powers, 204
Senatorial courtesy, 204
Senatorial district convention, 128
Senators, number of, districts, term
  limits, 63
Separate-but-equal, 17, 35
Separation of church and state, 328
Separation of powers (Texas
  Constitution), 62
Sessions, in Texas legislature,
  165–167, 168
Seventeenth Amendment, 51, 161
Severance taxes, 316
Sex education, 329
Sexual orientation, discrimination
  and, 19–20
Shankle, Glenn, 145, 154
Shannon, Kelly, 158*n*
Shaw v. Reno, 178
Shelby County v. Holder, 36–37
Sheriff, county, 301
Sherrod, Randy, 281–283
Shivers, Allan, 17, 22–23, 66, 120
Short ballot, 302
Shortland, Roy, 246*n*
Sierra Club, 120, 140*t*
Silva, Maria da, 252*n*
Simmons, Harold, 145
Sims, Nancy, 105*n*
Single-member council districts, 292
Single-member district, 173–174
Sit-in, 18*p*
SIX-PAC (National Beer Wholesalers
  Association), 104
Sixteenth Amendment, 51, 161, 315
Sixth Amendment, 270
Size, of bureaucracy, 216
Skaggs, Adam, 252*n*
Slater, Wayne, 144*n*
Slavery, African Texans and, 16
Smith, D. Todd, 253*n*

Smith v. Allwright, 16, 20*t*, 87, 90*n*
Social insurance, 344–345
Socializing, lobbying and, 142
Social media, electioneering and, 160
Social Security, 118–119, 344–345
Social values, crime an, 264
Sodomy laws, 19–20
Soft money, 107
Sorauf, Frank J., 104*n*
Spaeth, Harold, 252*n*, 253*n*
Spagat, Elliot, 309*n*
Sparks, Sam, 97
Special districts, 287, 304–306
  cost and inefficiency, 306
  as hidden governments, 306
  in Texas, 304*t*
  why create?, 305–306
Special elections, 94
Special interest groups, donations to
  Texas political campaigns, 106*t*
Special sessions, 64, 74, 75, 166, 209
Spending
  campaign distribution, 104–105
  influence peddling and, 155–157
  on lobbyists, in Texas, 149*t*
  public schools, financing, 330–332,
    349–353
  state, 323–324
  trends in Texas state, all funds, by
    biennial budget, 314*f*
*Spending More to Improve Public
  Education? Texans say Yes...and
  No* (Henson), 349–353
Split-ticket voting, 95
Spoils system, 217, 303
STAARs testing, 159
Staff
  executive, 202
  legislature, 169
Standing committees, 182
  house committee membership, 184
  senate committee membership, 184
State administration, of schools, 326
State Affairs Committee, 184
State agencies, lobbying process and,
  145
State appropriations, by function,
  325*f*
State Board of Education, 326
State conventions, 128
State Department of Health, 220
State funding (education), 330
State health insurance programs,
  340–341
Statehood, of Texas, 30
State institutions, lobbyist
  exploitation of, 153–154
State-level organization, 130
State of Federalism, The (Coates),
  48–51

State of Texas Assessments of
  Academic Readiness (STAAR), 330
State of Texas v. Smith, 233
State political cultures, 7
  individualistic, 7
  moralistic, 7
  traditionalistic, 7
States
  constitutions, citizens initiatives,
    popular referendums, 68*f*
  cooperative federalism and, 34–35
  corruption risk, compare 156
  crime and punishment in, 278
  direct democracy methods and, 68*f*
  federal overreach and, 51
  governor's power, compare
    209–210
  legislature, limits on terms,
    salaries, sessions, 168
  rights *v.* civil, 35–37
  Medicaid expansion, compare 44
  party control of government in the
    50 states, 131–132
  population changes in large U.S.
    cities, 297
  quality of life/public policy,
    compare, 6*f*
  selecting judges, compare, 246
  tax and spending policies, 322–323
  voter turnout, 85
State spending, 323–324
  appropriation process, 324
  politics of, 324
State taxes, 315–316
  general sales, 315
  gross-receipt, 316
  hidden, 315
  selective sales, 315
  severance, 316
Statutory law, 61, 258
Steinhauser, Kyle, 281*n*, 283*n*
Stephenville Educational Advisory
  Committee, 134
Stevens, Gary, 51*n*
Stiles, Matt, 155*n*
Stimson, James, 123*n*
Stokes, Donald E., 122*n*
Straight-ticket voting, 95
Strauss, Joe, 181, 192–194
Strayhorn, Carole Keeton, 115
Strike list (voting), 81
Strikes, 273
Strong-mayor form of government,
  290–291
Subcommittees, 183
Suffrage
  national, 15
  in Texas, 14
  Texas Constitution and, 67
  women's, 87

Sunset Advisory Commission, 191, 210

Sunshine laws, 289

Supplemental Nutritional Assistance Program (SNAP), 345

Supplemental Security Income (SSI), 340

Supply-side economics, 321

Supremacy Clause, 31

Supreme Court, of Texas. *See* Texas Supreme Court

Suspension of the rule, 185

Sweatt, Heman, 16–17, 17*p*, 36

Sweat v. Painter, 17*p,* 20*t,* 36

Swing voters, 126

T

Tale of Two Speakers and the Purple Legislation of 2013 (Jones), 192–196
  purple legislation, 194–196
  Tom Craddick/Joe Strauss, 192–194

Taney, Roger (Chief Justice), 34

TANF. *See* Temporary Assistance for Needy Families

Tarr, G. Alan, 243*n*

Tax assessor-collector, 301

Taxation, 315–323
  local taxes, 316
  national taxes, 315
  Social Security, 344–345
  state/local burden, rank among states, 323*f*
  state and local, as percentage of household income, 321*t*
  state taxes, 315–316

Taxation, politics of, 316–322
  ability-to-pay, 318
  benefits-received, 317–318
  regulatory taxes, 317
  who should pay?, 316–317

Tax base, 316–317

Tax elections, property ownership and, 87

Taxes, as revenue source
  ACA and, 342
  property, 294–295
  sales, 294, 308–309
  school funding and, 331
  Texas general sales, paid in dollars, 320*t*

Tax rates, 316
  progressive, 318–319
  regressive, 319–323

Tax shifting, 321

TEA (Texas Education Agency), 214–215, 325–326

Tea party
  health-care reform and, 342
  Republican Party and, 125

of Texas, 38*p,* 50–51

Tea Party, The: Civic Activism and Grassroots Change (Primozich), 158–161
  democracy views, 161
  electioneering, 160
  legislative agenda, 161
  message of, 159
  no squishy republicans, 160

Tea Party Caucus, 161

Tea Party Express, 159

Tea Party Nation, 159

Tea Party Patriots, 159

Tedin, Kent, 102*n*

Temporary Assistance to Needy Families (TANF), 228, 338, 339*f,* 340, 343

Temporary-party organization, 126–128
  county/senatorial district conventions, 128
  precinct convention, 126–128
  state conventions, 128

Tenth Amendment, 31, 36, 38, 42
  dual federalism and, 33–34

Term limits, 166, 168, 293

Terms, in Texas legislature, 165–167

Terrell Election Law, 90

Texan Association of Business and Chambers of Commerce, 140*t*

Texans for Education Reform, 149

Texans for Lawsuit Reform, 149, 260, 261

Texans for Public Justice, 140, 140*t,* 141*n,* 155*n,* 157*n*

Texas, federal government and, 37–48
  ACA (Obamacare), 41–44. *See also* Patient Protection and Affordable Care Act
  casino gambling, 47–48
  coercive federalism, 38–39
  federal grants-in-aid, 39–40
  marijuana legalization, 46
  unfunded mandates, 40–41

Texas Abortion Rights Action League, 120

Texas Agricultural Finance Authority, 213

Texas Appraiser Licensing and Certification Board, 215

Texas Association of Business, 149, 153, 221

Texas Association of Counties, 41, 303

Texas Association of Realtors, 140*t,* 149

Texas Bond Review, 215

Texas border, cultural region, 10–11

Texas Cable Association, 149

Texas Cattle Feeders Association, 104

Texas Choices program, 229

Texas Christian Life Commission, 140*t*

Texas Civil Justice League, 260

Texas Commission on Environmental Quality (TCEQ), 39, 145, 154, 161, 215

Texas Conservative Coalition, 161

Texas Constitution, 41. *See also* Constitution, of Texas

Texas Constitution and Public School Funding (Hoye), 73–75

Texas Court of Criminal Appeals, 242*p*

Texas Crime Victims' Compensation Fund, 266

Texas Democrats
  conservatives/liberals and, 119–120
  platform of, 2012, 129*t*
  Texas Democratic Party, 15, 16
  Texas Republicans *v.,* 126

Texas Department of Criminal Justice, 218, 275

Texas Department of Transportation, 150, 218, 219*f,* 346

Texas Education Agency (TEA), 214–215, 325–326

Texas Education Code, 330

Texas Eleven, 185

Texas Ethics Commission, 106*n,* 143, 156, 157–158, 167

Texas Ethics Commission Rules, 157*n*

Texas Farm Bureau, 140*t*

Texas Farmers Union, 120

Texas Farm Workers Union (TFWU), 18–19

Texas Freedom Works, 328

Texas Good Reads, 223

Texas Grange, 58

Texas Health and Human Services Commission (THHSC), 228, 338, 339*f*

Texas Higher Education Coordinating Board (THECB), 333

Texas Highway Department, 346

Texas Insiders feature
  campaign contributors, following the money, 171–172, 249–250
  HillCo, Texas lobby group, 143
  lawsuit reform, interest groups, justice and, 261
  profiles of Texas campaign megadonors, 106
  revolving door lobbying, Mike Toomey and, 221–222
  think tank influences on public policy, 328–329

Texas Judicial Council, 238

Texas Lone Star Card, 345

Texas Medical Association (TMA), 43, 140*t,* 149, 153, 220

Texas Municipal League, 288, 294

Texas National Guard, 205, 213

Texas Oil and Gas Association, 149

Texas party system, development of, 117–126. *See also* Party system, development of Texas

Texas Patriots PAC, 159, 160

Texas political parties, 126–130
permanent-party, 128–130. *See also* Permanent-party organization
temporary-party organization, 126–128. *See also* Temporary-party organization
temporary/permanent, 127f

Texas Public Policy Foundation, 328

Texas Racing Commission, 215

Texas Railroad Commission, 150, 154, 214

Texas Rangers, 185, 218
civil rights and, 18–19, 22–23
segregation and, 16

Texas Register, 144

Texas Republican Party, 120–124
competitiveness of, 121
conservative/moderates and, 125–126
Democrats *v.*, 126
dominant era of, 122–123
party platform, 2012, 129t
strengths/weaknesses, sources of, 123–124

Texas revenue by source, 39t

Texas Right to Life, 146

Texas Senate districts, 176f

Texas Southern University (TSU), 36

Texas State Board of Education, 214–215

Texas State Guard, 205, 213

Texas State Teachers' Association, 140t, 223

Texas Sunset Act, 191

Texas Supreme Court, 242–243, 243p

Texas Supreme Court cases
Edgewood Independent School District v. Kirby, 69, 74
West Orange-Cove, 75

Texas Trial Lawyers Association, 140t, 149, 260

Texas Tribune, 109–110

Texas Two-Step, 128

Texas Watch, 260

Texas White Primary Law, 16

Texas Workforce Commission, 229, 343–344

Textbooks, Texas politics and, 328–329

TFWU. *See* Texas Farm Workers Union

Thevenot, Brian, 155n

Third parties, political, 115

Thompson, John D., 74n

Thurgood Marshall School of Law (of TSU), 36

Timing, in election campaign, 103–104

Tipping, 126

Tomlinson, Chris, 178n

Tompkins, Mark E., 102n

Toomey, Mike, 221–222

Tort reform, 260–261

Torts, 260

Tower, John, 120, 121

Traditionalistic culture, 7, 23, 89

Transgendered rights, in Texas, 19–20

Trans-Pecos region, 10

Transportation systems, public, 305f, 346–348
highway programs, 346–347
highway systems, 347t
politics of, 347–348

Trans-Texas Corridor, 347–348

Treasurer, county, 301

Trial jury, 244–245

Trial process, 272–275
adversary system, 273
appeals process, 274
by jury, 272–273
jury charge, 273
juvenile, 275
post-trial proceedings, 274
sentencing, 273–274
verdict, 273

Tribal Class II gaming facility (Kickapoo, Eagle Pass), 47

Trinity River, 13

True bill, 243, 244, 271

Truman, Harry, 120

Tucker, Harvey J., 102n

Tucker Tudor, 34

Tuition fees, Texas resident, full time student, 336f

Turner, Sylvester, 155p

Twenty-fourth Amendment, 87

Twenty-sixth Amendment, 83

Two-party system, 114–115

Two-thirds rule, 185–186

U

UFW. *See* United Farm Workers

Umbrella organizations, 149

Unemployment insurance, 343–344

Unfunded mandates, 40–41

Unfunded Mandates Interagency Work Group, 297

Unfunded Mandates Reform Act of 1995, 40

Uninsured Texans, 341

Union shop, 259

Unitary systems, or government, 29, 288

United Farm Workers (UFW), 18–19

United Mexican States, 30

United Nations, 328

United States v. Leon, 268

United States v. Texas, 87

Unit road system, 303

Universities and colleges
administration of, 333–338.
See also Higher education

University of Texas Law School, 16–17, 36

Urban life, criminals and, 265

U.S. Advisory Commission on Intergovernmental Relations, 38

U.S. Census Bureau, 88n, 228n, 304

U.S. Centers for Disease Control and Prevention, 275p

U.S. Congressional Districts, 177f

U.S. Constitution
Article I, Section 8, 31, 32, 42
Article VI, Section 2, 31
basic rights in, 61t
Bill of Rights, 60–61
federalism and, 30–37. *See also* Federal system of government
Fifteenth Amendment, 20t
First Amendment, 151
Fourteenth Amendment, 19, 31, 60, 161, 178
Nineteenth Amendment, 87
Seventeenth Amendment, 51, 161
Sixteenth Amendment, 51, 161, 315
Sixth Amendment, 270
Tenth Amendment, 31, 33–34, 36, 38, 42
Texas violations of, 20t
Twenty-fourth Amendment, 87
Twenty-sixth Amendment, 83

U.S. Constitutional Convention, 30

U.S. Department of Agriculture, 213

U.S. Department of Health and Human Services, 340

U.S. Department of Justice, 36, 81, 174

U.S. District Courts, 36

U.S. Fifth Circuit Court of Appeals, 17

U.S. Judiciary Department, 174

U.S. News & World Report, 338n

U.S. Supreme Court (cases)
Argersinger v. Hamlin, 270n
Arizona v. Fulminante, 269n
Avery v. Midland County, 300n
Baze et al. v. Rees et al., 280n
Beare v. Smith, 87
Brown v. Board of Education, 17, 20t, 22n, 36
Caperton v. A. T. Massey Coal Co. Inc., 249, 254n
Carrington v. Rash, 87
Casey case, 46
Cipriano v. City of Houma, 87
Citizens United v. Federal Election Commission, 107, 107n
Delgado v Bastrop ISD, 19

Duncan v. Louisiana, 272n
Dunn v. Blumstein, 87
Farmer v. Sherrod, 281
Fisher v. University of Texas at
    Austin, 337n
Gideon v. Wainwright, 270n
Griswold v. Connecticut, 15
Grovey v. Townsend, 16, 90n
Grutter v. Bellinger, 337n
Herminica Hernandez et al. v.
    Driscoll Consolidated ISD, State
    of Texas, 19, 20t
Hill v. Stone, 87
Kelo v. City of New London
    Connecticut, 262
key court decisions, privacy/
    equality, 20t
Kramer v. Union Free District No.
    15, 87
Lawrence v. Texas, 19–20, 20t
Mapp v. Ohio, 268
McCulloch v. Maryland, 32, 50
Miller v. Johnson, 178
Miranda v. Arizona, 269
National Federation of Independent
    Business v. Sebelius, 42, 342n
New York v. Quarles, 269n
Nixon v. Herndon, 16
Nix v. Williams, 268
Plessy v. Ferguson, 17, 35
Powell v. Alabama, 270n
Reynolds v. Sims, 174
Roe v. Wade, 15, 20t, 45–46
San Antonio v. Rodriguez, 73–74
Shaw v. Reno, 178
Shelby County v. Holder, 36–37
Smith v. Allwright, 16, 20t, 87, 90n
Sweatt v. Painter, 17p, 20t, 36
United States v. Leon, 268
United States v. Texas, 87
on voting, 81
Weeks v. United States, 268
Windsor v. United States, 20
User fees, 296

V

Valence issues, 115
Valley, The (Rio Grande), 10
Verba, Sydney, 80n
Verdict, 273
Vernon's Annotated Civil Statutes, 258
Veterans, Latino-Texan, 18
Veterans Administration, 18
Veterans Land Board, 212
Veterans' Land Program, 65

Veto, 207–208
Veto, threat of, 208
Victimless crimes, 264
Victim of crime, 266–267
Vietnam War, 83
Villas at Parkside Partners v. City of
    Farmers Branch, 287n
Voice vote, 187
Voir dire questioning, 272–273
Voter ID laws, 24n, 37, 82
Voter knowledge, judicial selection
    and, 247
Voter turnout
    comparing Texas, 85
    reason for low, 86–89
    in Texas, 7, 82–86
    in U.S., 82–86
Voting
    African American, 17
    citizen initiatives/popular
        referendums, 68f
    in counties, 300f
    county long/short ballot, 302
    cumulative, 293
    in house/senate, 187
    judicial election and, 247–250
    percentage of population, 70–71t
    political participation, 79–89
    practice of, 81–82
    registration, 81–82
    turnout around the world, 84f
    who votes, 80–81
    why people vote, 79–80
    women and, in Texas, 14–15
    See also Election entries
Voting-age population (VAP), 82–86
Voting Rights Act of 1965, 36,
    98, 174
Vouchers, school, 332

W

Wade, Henry, 45–46
Waffle House, Inc., 104
WAFFLEPAC (Waffle House, Inc.), 104
Walker, Billy D., 74n
Walkouts, 128
Washington, Denzel, 17
Washington-on-the-Brazos, historic
    site, 57
Washington state, marijuana legaliza-
    tion and, 46
Waste Control Specialists, 145, 154
Water, in West Texas, 12
Water Quality Association, 104
Ways and Means Committee, 184

Weak-mayor form of government,
    290–291
Weber, Paul J., 178n
Weber, Ronald E., 102n
Websites
    CDC, 275p
    www.localvoter.com, 79
    www.politifact.com/texas, 79
    www.state.tx.us, 79
Weekley, Richard, 261
Weeks, John R., 11n
Weeks v. United States, 268
Welfare
    defining, 344–345
    myths, 345
    politics of, 344–346
    programs, 343–344
    realities, 345
Welfare state, Texas as, 228–229
West, Royce, 154
West Orange-Cove case, 75
West Texas, 12
Whataburger Corporation of Texas,
    104
WHATAPAC (Whataburger
    Corporation of Texas), 104
Wheeler, Russell, 252n
Whistleblowers, 227
White, Bill, 93, 104
White, Byron (Justice), 73
White, William, 144
White-collar crime, criminals and, 266
White primary, 15, 87
Wilkings, Roy, 17
Windsor v. United States, 20
Winter Garden, 10
Wlezien, Christopher, 86n, 102n, 103n
Wolfinger, Raymond E., 80n
Women
    jury duty and, 15
    suffrage, 87
    See also Gender entries
Women's Health and Family Planning
    Association of Texas, 140t
Women's suffrage, 14–15, 87
World War II, Latino veterans and, 18
Write-in candidates, 97–98
Writ of habeas corpus, 61, 270
Writ of information, 268

Y

Yarborough, Don, 97
Yarborough, Ralph, 94
Young, Whitney, 17
Young Conservatives of Texas, 160